Wisden on Bradman

Wisden on Bradman

Edited by Graeme Wright

Hardie Grant Books

First published in 1998 by
Hardie Grant Books
Level 3, 44 Caroline Street
South Yarra Victoria 3141

Reprinted in 1999

National Library of Australia cataloguing-in-publication data:

Wright, Graeme.
Wisden on Bradman

ISBN 1 86498 080 X
1. Bradman, Donald, Sir, 1908–. 2. Cricket players – Australia – Biography. 3. Cricket – Australia – History.
I. Title.

796.358092

Text design: David Rosemeyer
Cover design: Polar Design
Typesetting: Melbourne Media Services
Cover photo: Courtesy of the Bradman Foundation
Printed in Australia by Griffin Press

About the Author

Graeme Wright was editor of *Wisden Cricketers' Almanack* from 1986 to 1992. A New Zealander, he was the first non-Englishman to hold this position. He was also one of *Wisden's* youngest editors, and one of its hardest hitting. His final 'Notes by the Editor' were described in *The Times* as 'in parts resembling a valedictory v-sign to all within cricket that he resents'. He continues to write on cricket regularly for the *Independent on Sunday* and is the author of the acclaimed and controversial *Betrayal: The Struggle for Cricket's Soul.*

CONTENTS

The publisher thanks the Bradman Foundation for providing photographic material for use in this book.

The Bradman Foundation is a non-profit charitable trust, which operates the Bradman Museum, located adjacent to Bradman Oval in Bowral, NSW, the ground where Don Bradman began his cricketing career in the 1920s. The Foundation has also purchased Sir Donald's former home in Glebe Street, opposite the Museum and the Oval.

The Bradman Foundation established the Museum and Library to document the history of the game of cricket. The Foundation also conducts regular cricket coaching clinics and promotes matches on Bradman Oval. In developing the Bradman Museum the Foundation has created a living centre of cricket which not only pays tribute to past cricketers but also provides inspiration for the future of the game.

For further information about the Bradman Foundation or Museum phone 02 4862 1247.

Plates

Introduction

When nineteen-year-old Don Bradman hit a hundred on his first-class debut, for New South Wales against South Australia in December 1927, *Wisden Cricketers' Almanack* was well established as cricket's book of record. By the time he retired from first-class cricket in 1949, Sir Donald Bradman, as he now was, had rewritten many of the game's records and his name was indelibly inked in *Wisden* for all time. Almost fifty years later he still headed the career averages for Test Matches (99.94) and first-class cricket (95.14). In Tests he headed the qualifiers by 38.97; in *Wisden*'s first-class list there was no-one within 23 points of him.

Of the twenty-three batsmen in the 1998 *Wisden* with 100 or more hundreds to their name, Bradman is the only one not to have played county cricket in England and he took half as many innings to reach his 100th hundred as the next fastest. It almost goes without saying that he was the first non-English cricketer to attain this milestone. He has more double-hundreds (37) and triple-hundreds (6) than anyone else. For almost thirty years his unbeaten 452 for New South Wales against Queensland was the world record individual score. Only two men have passed it since. And so the list goes on. Most double-hundreds in a season (6 in 1930), most hundreds on a tour of England (13 in 1938). The pages that follow proclaim landmarks passed as regularly as the passing of time. For unlike Napoleon, an earlier conqueror of fields at home and abroad, Bradman never did have to confront his 'burnt-out hour'.

This is what *Wisden* does so well. It encapsulates cricket's past. The match reports capture the essence of Bradman's playing days; the essays give substance to the figures by offering a more rounded portrait of the cricketer who dominated his game for two decades as few men have dominated any sport at any time. They tell us something of the character and temperament of the batsman to whom scoring centuries was not a pastime but a career. His hundreds came at an average of one for every three times he batted, and newspapers, not surprisingly, labelled him 'the century-maker' and 'the run-machine'. 'Bradmanesque' entered the language to describe values of high proportions.

Crowds flocked to see him bat. To borrow from Neville Cardus, they came to see him 'knock solemnity to smithereens', and many left the ground as soon as he was out. When he toured England, as he did four times, county secretaries would seek an assurance that Bradman would play, such was the effect his presence had on gate receipts.

When Glamorgan played the Australians in 1930, Dai Davies, the county's off-break bowler, could not believe his ears when his captain, Maurice Turnbull, took him off just after he'd almost bowled Bradman late on the opening day, Saturday. He pleaded in vain for another chance, promising Turnbull that he'd get Bradman out in his next over. 'That's what we don't want,' replied Turnbull, only too aware of the crowds who would come to watch Bradman bat on the Bank Holiday Monday. And indeed, Glamorgan's small profit at the end of the season owed everything to the receipts from that game.

While past *Wisdens* recount the crowds and the runs and the records, what they do not do is take the readers beyond the cricketer. We see nothing of the family man or the successful businessman. Bradman was a sharebroker and later held directorships in many Australian companies. Nor do we see what it was, beyond the run-scoring, that made him both a hero of his time and a legendary figure in Australian life.

R. L. (Bob) Arrowsmith, who was *Wisden*'s principal obituary writer from 1975 to 1987, held the view that what a man does off the field had nothing to do with *Wisden*. 'A man may be a horrible piece of work,' he said, 'but at the same time get on all right in the cricket world.' *Autres temps, autres moeurs.*

Not that Don Bradman was a horrible piece of work. Far from it. But the Arrowsmith way of thinking does give an indication of why *Wisden* concerned itself only with the cricketer, rather than putting him within the context of his times. When Don Bradman returned from England in 1930, Australia having regained the Ashes thanks in major measure to his 131 at Trent Bridge, 254 at Lord's, 334 at Headingley and 232 at the Oval, he was greeted with unparalleled adulation. And it was more than those scores that counted. His youth and genius caught the mood of an age that was looking to its young men and women to build a new way for Australia. At the same time his modest manner and his strict moral upbringing were in tune with a society not yet ready to abandon the established codes of conduct. Even so, as some well-publicised conflicts with the Australian cricket establishment illustrated, he was always prepared to fight his corner. No respecter of position for position's sake, Don Bradman was an Australian's Australian.

That was why England's body-line tactics in 1932-33 struck so deeply at the core of Australia. Devised and implemented to stop Bradman from making his match-winning centuries, it was a negative philosophy born of defeatism. It was alien to the tenets of sportsmanship, and it cut Australians as surely as 'the bloodsuckers of the Bank of England', with their policy of calling in British loans just when Australia was struggling through the Depression years. Its employment by the patrician Jardine was interpreted as a symbol of Britain's determination to keep Australia under her dominion. In that series Don Bradman transcended the cricket field and entered the consciousness of the young nation. He became Australia.

In compiling this anthology, I was mildly amused at the way *Wisden* gave 'England' or the 'MCC Team' pride of place in the heading of the match reports of games in Australia. The convention these days is to name the home side first, and indeed when the Australians toured England, the home team did come first. So it would be, for example, Worcestershire v Australians, but in Australia it was always MCC Team v New South Wales and England v Australia. From this distance in time it seems a small point, but it reflects the mindset of empire, whether it was conscious or subconscious.

Sir Donald Bradman's Knighthood in the 1949 New Year Honours recognised his services to cricket; his investiture in 1979 as a Companion of the Order of Australia honoured a life dedicated to the game. Among the many appointments he held, he was from 1960 to 1963 and again from 1969 to 1972 the Chairman of the Australian Cricket Board – the first Test cricketer to hold this post. He endeavoured, he said, to encourage all that was best for the development of cricket.

Yet for all the endless intrusions that accompany fame and public office, Sir Donald remained a humble and private man. He was extremely fortunate in his marriage to Jessie Menzies, a childhood friend, describing their life together as 'the greatest partnership of my life'. Even so, their happiness did not pass untainted by sadness, as one line in *Wisden* does record. In 1936 Bradman withdrew from South Australia's first match against the MCC touring team following the death of their first child, a son, within two days of his birth. How this affected him we are not told. *Wisden* tells us simply that 'After a disappointing start [to the Test series], he had an aggregate of 810 runs ...' *Autres temps, autres moeurs.*

Graeme Wright

Editor's Note

The essays and match reports that make up this anthology come from editions of *Wisden Cricketers' Almanack* ranging from 1929 to 1986. Over those years, styles and fashions have changed as *Wisden* passed across the desk of seven editors and through several publishing houses. For the purpose of this book, I have tried to be typographically consistent with such things as capital letters, hyphens and numbers, even though it meant changing a style used in a particular year or years of *Wisden*. For clarity's sake, I have also added some commas in years when it seemed there had been a moratorium on them, and I have inserted asterisks and daggers to indicate the captains and wicket-keepers respectively. *Wisden* did not include these until 1961.

Where I have allowed inconsistency to remain, and so, I suppose, leave myself open to charges of inconsistency, is in the contentious area of players' initials. After much head-scratching, if not soul-searching, I have left them as they appeared in *Wisden* at the time, so that D. Bradman needed a year before his upgrading to D. G. Bradman. Others weren't so fortunate. Stan McCabe had to go through a tour of England before his 'J' was recognised. Only when an incorrect initial could lead to the wrong conclusion that there were two players of a certain surname, rather than one, or the wrong initials suggested a different player altogether, have I altered the original version. I have amended the date of some games, invariably because they finished earlier than *Wisden* allowed, but I have not corrected scores. This anthology is not intended as an addition to the game's impressive statistical library. It is simply a celebration of a great cricketer and his career.

Once the decision was taken to include each of Sir Donald Bradman's 234 first-class games, the restrictions of space precluded providing complete scorecards. Therefore, only the innings of Bradman's teams are given in full, complemented by the players and summarised scores of the opposing teams. Similarly, match reports have been abridged to concentrate on Bradman without, I trust, losing the flavour of *Wisden*. Where *Wisden* did not publish a match report and scorecard, but gave only a 'potted' score, the teams and fuller summarised scores are given. In the few instances when one of Bradman's first-class games did not appear in *Wisden*, a similar method is used, with square brackets placed around the heading to show it was not taken from *Wisden.* I have also used square brackets to provide what I hope is useful in addition information to that which appeared in *Wisden* at the time.

The numbers to the right of each first-class match denote the number of the match and innings played by Bradman. For example, the numbers 6(11, 12) denote that this was the sixth game and the eleventh and twelfth innings of his first-class career. His Test Matches have been numbered similarly on a separate line.

Finally, I would like to pay tribute to Ray Webster's two magisterial volumes, *First-Class Cricket in Australia*, which have been an invaluable reference work, not just in compiling this anthology but, with regard to Volume 1, in the years when I was Editor of *Wisden.* A useful ready-reckoner has been *D. G. Bradman*, compiled by the late Derek Lodge for the Famous Cricketers Series published by the Association of Cricket Statisticians and Historians.

Five Cricketers of the Year – Donald George Bradman

By Sydney J. Southerton

Following his success on his first tour of England, in 1930, Don Bradman was chosen as one of Wisden*'s Five Cricketers of the Year in the 1931 Almanack. The other four were his fellow Australian, Clarrie Grimmett, Bev Lyon (Gloucestershire), Ian Peebles (Oxford University, Middlesex and England) and Maurice Turnbull (Glamorgan). S. J. Southerton was a partner in the Cricket Reporting Agency, which for many years was responsible for compiling the Almanack, and he was editor of the 1934 and 1935 editions of* Wisden.

DONALD GEORGE BRADMAN, who, coming to England for the first time met with greater success as a batsman than any other Australian cricketer who has visited this country, was born at Cootamundra, a small up-country township in New South Wales on August 27, 1908. While still a child he accompanied his parents when they moved to Bowral, some fifty miles from Sydney. Although not his birthplace, therefore, Bowral enjoys the distinction of giving the first insight into the game to a young man who, at the present moment, is one of the most remarkable personalities in cricket. When it is considered that Bradman made his first appearance in a big match only just over three years ago – to be exact it was at Adelaide in December, 1927 – his rise to the very top of the tree has been phenomenal. Yet in that particular encounter, his first for New South Wales in the Sheffield Shield series of engagements, he showed clearly he was someone out of the common by scoring 118 and 33. Later on in that season in Australia he put together 73 against South Australia and not out 134 against Victoria and those performances stamped him as a future representative batsman. Sure enough, he got his place in the Australian team a year afterwards when the MCC side, under A. P. F. Chapman, were in that country. He did not justify expectations in a Trial match in October but in the same month he scored 131 and not out 133 against Queensland. Subsequent scores for his State included 71 not out against Victoria, 340 not out in the return with Victoria and 175 against South Australia. Meanwhile, he had secured a place in the Australia eleven at Brisbane but, dismissed for scores of 18 and 1, was passed over for the next Test. It was obvious a bad mistake had been made in leaving him out and, chosen for the third match at Melbourne, he put together 79 and 112. At Adelaide in the Fourth Test, in which England were successful by 12 runs, he scored 40 and 58, being run out in the second innings when he and Oldfield looked like winning the match for Australia, while in the concluding Test Match – the only one in which Australia was successful during that tour – he obtained 123 and not out 37, being in with Ryder at the finish.

By this time he had, of course, firmly established himself, and it did not need another even more successful season in 1929-30 to make his inclusion in the team for England a certainty. He put together many fine scores in Sheffield Shield matches and at Sydney in the first week in January eclipsed everything else by an astonishing innings of 452 not out for New South Wales against Queensland. This score – the highest individual ever hit in first-class cricket – occupied him only 415 minutes and included forty-nine 4's. A month before this, playing in the Trial match prior to the team for England being selected, he put together for Woodfull's Eleven against Ryder's Eleven 124 and 225, while on the journey to England he hit up 139 against Tasmania. In Sheffield Shield matches that season he averaged over 111, or more than twice as many as any other cricketer in the tournament, with an aggregate of 894 runs.

Already, therefore, he had in a very short space of time accomplished wonders, but his triumphs were far from being at an end, for in England he left further records behind. In the second innings of his first Test Match in this country, at Trent Bridge, he made 131, following that with 254 at Lord's, 334 at Leeds and, after failing at Manchester, putting together 232 at the Oval. With his big innings at Leeds he beat the record individual score in Test Matches between England and Australia which had stood since 1903-04 to the credit of R. E. Foster, with 287 at Sydney. Without a not out to help him, an aggregate of 974 runs in seven innings gave him an average of over 139 for the five Test Matches, and in the course of the summer he altogether played eleven three-figure innings for his side, six of these being over 200.

Just as they did during the last tour of the Englishmen in Australia, so, at the present time, opinions differ as to the merit of Bradman's abilities, judged purely from the standpoint of the highest batsmanship. Certain good judges aver that his footwork is correct; others contend the reverse is the case. Both are right. For a fast, true wicket his footwork, if not on quite such a high plane as that of Charles Macartney, is wonderfully good. When the ball is turning, however, there are limitations to Bradman's skill. As was observed by those who saw him on a turning wicket at Brisbane and on one nothing like so vicious at Old Trafford last summer, this young batsman still has something to learn in the matter of playing a correct offensive or defensive stroke with the conditions in favour of the bowler. Still, as a run-getter, he stands alone. He does not favour the forward method of defence, much preferring to go halfway or entirely back. His scoring strokes are many and varied. He can turn to leg and cut with delightful accuracy, but above all he is a superb driver. One very pronounced feature of his batting is that he rarely lifts the ball, and as he showed English spectators so frequently last season, and particularly against England at Lord's, he will send two consecutive and similar deliveries in different directions. In grace of style he may not be a Trumper or a Macartney but his performances speak for themselves. Over and above his batting he is a magnificent field and, like all Australians, a beautiful thrower. Occasionally he has met with success as a bowler, but while his powers as a run-getter remain with him there is no need for him to cultivate the other side of the game.

Bradman first learned his cricket in pick-up matches at the Bowral Intermediate High School, and when he went to Sydney in 1926 at the invitation of the State Selectors for a practice at the nets he was a somewhat uncouth, uncultured batsman. Still, he made 37 in a Trial match and then played in the Southern Districts country team. He reached first-grade cricket in Sydney for the St George Club in 1926 and, as has already been told, proceeded thence into the New South Wales eleven. After he left school, where he was entirely self-taught in batting, he played for the Bowral club and, with scores of 234 and 300, had an aggregate of 1,318 and an average of 109. In the one match he played for them in 1926-27 he scored 320 not out. Not yet twenty-three, Bradman should have years of cricket in front of him and, judging by what he has already accomplished, there would seem to be no limit to his possibilities.

D. G. Bradman 1927–37

An Australian View

By The Hon. Mr Justice Herbert V. Evatt

This article appeared in the 1938 edition of Wisden. *It included a number of statistical tables which have been omitted, as much of the data they contained appears in the career figures that supplement R. C. Robertson-Glasgow's article, 'Sir Donald Bradman'.*

IN 1937 D. G. BRADMAN completed ten years of first-class cricket. During that period many of his batting performances have been unprecedented. He has broken one record after another and already, in actual achievement, he has far surpassed the performances of all other batsmen of Australia. There is an easy-going tendency to discount the significance of cricket records and averages, and in some circumstances they may be misleading. But, in the long run, the records may lead irresistibly to certain conclusions, and in Bradman's case they prove beyond doubt that he is one of the very greatest batsmen of all time, possessing the faculty of doing his best on the most important occasions.

Owing to the limited quantity of first-class cricket, the feat of scoring 1,000 runs in an Australian season is rarely performed. Very few Australian cricketers have done it at all and, with the exception of Bradman, not one of them more than twice. Bradman has scored 1,000 runs in every season he has played except his first, ie, on eight separate and consecutive occasions [1928-29 to 1936-37] ...

Bradman, in first-class cricket, has made sixty-one centuries, which is a record number for any Australian cricketer .... [He] has scored eighteen centuries in Test Matches, having equalled Hobbs's record in obtaining twelve centuries in England v Australia Tests. Bradman obtained four Test centuries against South Africa and two against the West Indies. Of his eighteen Test centuries, ten have exceeded 200, seven of the ten having been made against England. He has taken part in five series of Tests for Australia v England, his amazing figures being:

Season	*Innings*	*Times not out*	*Highest Score*	*Total Runs*	*Average*
1928-29	8	1	123	468	66.85
1930	7	0	334	974†	139.14
1932-33	8	1	103*	396	56.57
1934	8	0	304	758	94.75
1936-37	9	0	270	810	90.00
Total	40	2	334	3,406	89.63

** Signifies not out. † A record aggregate for any Test series.*

In no fewer than twenty-seven of his sixty-one three-figure innings, Bradman has scored 200 runs or more. It follows that, provided Bradman has reached 100, it is almost an even chance that he will reach 200. Averaging his century scores, the result is 194 runs per innings, or 242 per completed innings.

His performances in minor cricket may be briefly mentioned. In Australian grade or pennant cricket, he has scored 4,304 runs at an average of 86 per innings. In all second-class matches he has scored 19,131 runs, also at an average of 86 per innings. During the tour of the Australian team to America in 1932, he scored 3,779 runs at an average of 102, obtaining eighteen centuries. In first- and second-class cricket, he has aggregated 141 centuries.

Bradman's figures are necessarily silent as to important aspects of his batting. At times the speed of his scoring has been phenomenal. For instance, his world's record score of 452 was made in 406 [415] minutes. Typical of his brilliant hitting in Sheffield Shield cricket was the 238 in 195 minutes obtained for New South Wales against Victoria in 1932. His record Test score of 334 at Leeds in 1930 was made in 381 minutes. In 1934 at Folkestone he hit Freeman for 30 runs in an over. At Scarborough in the same season he scored 132 in ninety minutes. In 1931-32, in a second-class fixture at Blackheath, New South Wales, Bradman and Wendell Bill scored 102 runs in three eight-ball overs, Bradman obtaining 100 out of the 102. He hit ten 6's and nine 4's including 40 from one over. His total for the innings was 256, including fourteen 6's and twenty-nine 4's.

Whatever the original limitations of his stroke repertoire, Bradman has become the master of every stroke in the game. But the outstanding quality of his batting skill is that he employs it functionally, ever adjusting it to the task in hand. In England in 1934, when he was fighting against the onset of illness, some of the critics declared that he had degenerated into a mere slogger. But he rose to the great occasions of the Fourth and Fifth Tests. Undoubtedly his big partnerships with Ponsford in those two games accentuated his illness, and the operation he subsequently underwent prevented his playing cricket again until 1935-36. He then captained South Australia to its first Sheffield Shield championship since 1926-27. Most recently, what I have called the functional character of his batting has been shown during his three great Test centuries against the last England side. Characteristic of Bradman's in-cricket is his perfect running between wickets and his shepherding of younger players during critical periods of an innings. Moreover, the team value of his performances is also evidenced by the fact that they have frequently synchronised with partnerships during which Bradman's partner has also batted with remarkable success.

Indeed, the team value of his mammoth scores has been immense. His innings have ensured not only practical freedom from the risk of defeat, but very often actual victory. Thus, in games without time limit, he has exceeded 200 on seven occasions (all of them Tests), and each time his side has won. Upon the other twenty occasions when he has scored 200 or more, his side has lost only once – a Testimonial match where the result was of no significance. Bradman's powers include, but are not limited to, magnificent batting skill, backed by patience, concentration and determination. In addition he has the extremely rare quality of cricket imagination and employs it scientifically. Throughout his Sheffield Shield cricket career, the four-and-a-third-day or the four-day time limit has been in force. Bradman it was who first appreciated the increased importance of the time factor in such matches. He also perceived that, even in limitless Test Matches, and certainly in Tests subject to a time limit, quick scoring must usually be of enormous advantage to his side. Thus, both in Australia and England, Bradman has always endeavoured to accelerate the rate of scoring during the course of the day's cricket, a practice which few batsmen of modern times have adopted.

During the period of Bradman's career, the treatment of international cricket by the 'popular' Press has often added to the responsibilities of the players; and in Bradman's case, praise and blame have sometimes succeeded each other with bewildering rapidity. Fortunately his character has enabled him to concentrate all his attentions upon the game itself. Further he has vindicated the opinions of many that he would be a great success as captain, and it now seems certain that he will captain Australia for some time to come.

I cannot part with the subject of this sketch without expressing gratitude for the infinite pleasure which Bradman's batting has given to all cricket lovers. Unique as his record is, it cannot adequately describe his cricketing genius. Despite all his honours, Donald Bradman is still as modest and unassuming as the young country lad who came to Sydney in 1927 intent upon success in the greatest of all games.

Cricket at the Cross Roads

By D. G. Bradman

'This year,' Wilfrid H. Brookes wrote in his Editor's Preface to the 1939 Wisden, *'I have been favoured with articles by several well-known cricket personalities. Mr Don Bradman readily agreed to help and his views on important points of present-day cricket are sure to prove of widespread interest.' The previous year, 1938, Bradman had captained the Australians on their tour of England and, with his century in Australia's victory at Leeds, had helped ensure that they retained the Ashes.*

THE EDITOR OF *WISDEN* has honoured me by asking for a contribution from my pen. He has left the subject of the article to me, but in doing so has helpfully made suggestions regarding various phases of cricket which are today the cause of much discussion. As I looked through those suggestions, I conceived the title of this article. It is intended to convey a meaning but not to be misunderstood.

No matter how much we love cricket and desire to regard it as a friendly pastime we cannot possibly disassociate its future, at least in the first-class category, from the cold, hard facts of finance. Nor can we blind ourselves to the fact that at this very moment public support for cricket (possibly excepting Test cricket, around which there is special glamour) suggests either that cricket is becoming less attractive or other forms of entertainment are gaining ground. It is a state of affairs calling for very serious consideration from player and legislator alike.

I am all in favour of 'hastening slowly' and have admired the peaceful but purposeful way in which cricket has for so long been administered in England. Nevertheless, I cannot help feeling that with the quickening of modern tempo, the more Americanised trend which is demanding speed, action and entertainment value, it behoves all of us to realise we are the custodians of the welfare of cricket and must guard its future even more zealously than its present.

No matter what we may desire individually, we cannot arrest nor impede the tenor of everyday life whether it be in business or sport. With such thoughts uppermost in my mind, my reflections are intended to convey the impressions gleaned by an Australian who will naturally view things from a slightly different angle to the average Englishman. Also my opinions are based upon experience in the middle allied to contact with administrative officers and the public.

DURATION OF TEST MATCHES

One of the most debated subjects at the moment is whether Test Matches should be limited or played out. Considerable colour has been lent to this particular aspect of cricket because of the remarkable happenings at the Oval last August. I have always held the opinion that it is futile to expect Australian teams to travel many thousands of miles to compete in a series of matches for the Ashes, and yet play under conditions which allow quite a big possibility of one match deciding the rubber, especially when that result may depend entirely on the weather and be inconsistent with the degree of skill otherwise displayed. But I rather doubt whether the big issue is limited or played-out Tests. I think the first consideration is the mental outlook of the individual who can, if he chooses, spoil any game by his interpretation of its character. And secondly, would it not be a better game if, by virtue of rules and conditions, the possibility of a match extending beyond three or four days became extremely improbable?

If these problems were attended to, maybe the other one would disappear. At least, I think it very largely would. There can be no doubt that in recent years changes have taken place in the methods adopted for preparing certain English wickets. The popular term used for the latest and questionable method is 'doping the wicket'. From my experience on this tour and discussions with people who are in a position to know, I am satisfied that some groundsmen can, and do 'dope' their wickets. The effect is to produce an absolutely dead and lifeless wicket, useless to any type of bowler and not conducive to stroke-play by the batsman.

It is imperative that we should have wickets which are true and not dangerous (fiery wickets produce a crop of accidents, rob batsmen of confidence and drive them into less dangerous sports), but let them be reasonably natural and amenable to some fair degree of wear, not the sort upon which the world's best spin bowlers can't turn the ball an inch until the pitch is three days' old. This difficulty with wickets mainly applies to Test Matches. County matches are usually played on wickets offering some degree of equality, whilst practice wickets on most English grounds receive so little consideration that one has virtually no chance of getting real practice except in the middle. The scales are not evenly balanced, and the question of wickets needs serious consideration.

A prominent English International, writing in the daily Press, declared: 'Give me another half hour of Leeds and let me forget the Oval'. He probably conveys in that statement the innermost thoughts of the majority of the players and the public. I agree with him, if I may add 1934 and 1938 after 'the Oval'. I do that to ensure that my concurrence will not be misconstrued. At the Oval in 1934 we Australians accomplished approximately what England did in 1938, so that I have experienced both winning and losing under those conditions. People left the Oval tired of watching the unequal fight. They did it when Ponsford and I were batting in 1934. They did it when Hutton and Hardstaff were batting in 1938. Not so at Leeds. The match was one succession of thrills. People fought to get into the ground, not out of it. Their hearts beat frantically with excitement, mine along with the rest of them. Did anyone think of that curse of modern cricket – batting averages? No! It was the game which mattered. Australia won. She nearly lost and if she had it would have been a greater game still. It was stirring, exhilarating cricket. There wasn't time to think of timeless Tests at Leeds.

VIEWS ON LBW

I believe the time is imminent when another change in the LBW law should be made. When our forefathers devised this beautiful game, I have no doubt they intended it to remain a contest between bat and ball. But evidently, to use the words of an eminent politician, 'they didn't make it clear', and the practice of pad obstruction eventually reached such proportions that it became necessary to legislate against the use of pads.

Irrespective of where the batsman's pads or feet are, I believe that if a ball is pitched in a line between wicket and wicket or on the off side of the wicket and would have hit the stumps but is prevented from doing so by part of the batsman's person (providing the ball has not first touched his bat or hand) the bowler is entitled to be rewarded. Under the existing law, that part of the batsman's person which is struck by the ball *must be between wicket and wicket.* Those last six words afford the batsman too much latitude.

An experiment could be tried with my suggestion similar to the experiment tried before the last alteration. I am confident that it would result in further reducing huge scores, increasing off-side shots, brightening the play and reducing the effectiveness of the purely defensive 'rabbit'. The leg side may have to be considered in later years, but it would possibly be too drastic a step to alter both sides at once. Just prior to the introduction of the last alteration in the LBW rule, there was a great deal of adverse comment about it. I then stated that these hypothetical ills would be found to disappear in practice. They did – and they would do so again.

Even if we assume a reasonably severe result and found county matches ending in two days, and the leading batting average dropping from 70 to 50, what would it matter? All figures would alter correspondingly and the gates for two days would exceed what they now are for three.

AN EXPERIMENT is going to be made with the eight-ball over. It has been used in Australia for years, has proved a great success and saved a tremendous amount of time. The only people who can reasonably object to it are the fast bowlers. Whilst their claims may be reasonable, we must consider the welfare of the game itself before any of its component parts. And in any event, if the authorities consider that fast bowlers are going to be unjustly handicapped, there may be other ways of assisting them, such as by allowing a new ball earlier than after the scoring of 200 runs as at present.

We very frequently hear a suggestion that the old method of tossing should be dispensed with. If any person has grounds for objection, surely it is I, after my 1938 experiences, but, on the contrary, I favour retention of the present method. To enable one captain to know in advance which team would have the choice of batting would pave the way to so many undesirable possibilities that I do not think it worth while discussing.

A PLEA FOR MODERN SCORE BOARDS

I do, however, counsel very urgently the need of up-to-date scoring-boards of the Australian type at your principal grounds. I have just been reading an article in a leading English cricket publication by a very well-known writer. He was describing the happenings in an important match at Lord's. After telling of a glorious innings by a young player, he wrote: 'I had no idea of his identity – there were no score-cards about at the time.' Subsequently, he told how he discovered the player's name.

Such a state of affairs to an Australian enthusiast is hard to comprehend. I am well aware of the forceful argument regarding the revenue produced from selling score-cards, but I submit that 10,000 spectators who do not need score-cards to tell them what is happening are going to be a happier and more virile advertisement for the game than 8,000 who do. Cricket needs to retain its present followers and to gain new ones. Modern scoring-boards would be a big help, and any temporary loss would be recouped eventually through the turnstiles.

THERE ARE MANY other factors upon which I could enlarge, such as playing hours, the number of matches, and so on. They are sure to form a basis for future debate and argument, but their importance is, for the present at any rate, subservient to other problems.

Whether my suggestions prove practicable or otherwise, time alone will tell. They are at least submitted in an honest endeavour to assist in ensuring that the game we all cherish so much will be enjoyed by future generations no less than our own.

I doubt if a happier series of Test Matches than the 1938 series has been played and I am quite sure the administrators of England and Australia are more closely united now than ever before. To me, therefore, it seems an appropriate time to try to achieve a greater measure of uniformity of opinion upon current cricket problems.

Sir Donald Bradman

By R. C. Robertson-Glasgow

Affectionately known as 'Crusoe', Robertson-Glasgow played against Bradman in 1930 for An England XI at Folkestone. Principally a bowler, although a useful batsman as well, he played for Oxford University and Somerset before going on to write widely and entertainingly about cricket. He became Cricket Correspondent of the Morning Post *in 1933 and during the Second World War wrote the 'Notes on the Season' for* Wisden. *This article appeared in the 1949 edition of the Almanack.*

DON BRADMAN will bat no more against England, and two contrary feelings dispute within us: relief, that our bowlers will no longer be oppressed by this phenomenon; regret, that a miracle has been removed from among us. So must ancient Italy have felt when she heard of the death of Hannibal.

For sheer fame, Dr W. G. Grace and Don Bradman stand apart from all other cricketers – apart, indeed, from all other games-players. The villagers used to crowd to their doors when 'W.G.' and his beard drove through their little main street. Bradman, on his visits to England, could never live the life of a private citizen. He couldn't stroll from his hotel to post a letter or buy a collar-stud. The mob wouldn't let him. There had to be a car waiting with engine running, and he would plunge into it, like a cork from a bottle. When cricket was on, Bradman had no private life. He paid for his greatness, and the payment left some mark. The informal occasion, the casual conversation, the chance and happy acquaintance, these were very rarely for him, and his life was that of something between an Emperor and an Ambassador. Yet, for all that, there remained something of that boy who, thirty years before, had knocked a ball or ball-like object about in the backyard of a small house in New South Wales. He never lost a certain primitive and elemental 'cheekiness', and mingled, as it were, with his exact and scientific calculations, there was the immortal impudence of the *gamin.*

But, above all, Bradman was a business-cricketer. About his batting there was to be no style for style's sake. If there was to be any charm, that was for the spectator to find or miss. It was not Bradman's concern. His aim was the making of runs, and he made them in staggering and ceaseless profusion. He seemed to have eliminated error, to have perfected the mechanism of stroke. Others before him had come near to doing this; but Bradman did it without abating the temperature of his attack.

No other batsman, surely, has ever been able to score so fast while at the same time avoiding risk. He was, as near as a man batting may be, the flawless engine. There were critics who found surfeit in watching him. Man, by his nature, cannot bear perfection in his fellow. The very fact that something is being done which had been believed to be impossible goads and irritates. It is but a short step from annoyance to envy, and Bradman has never been free from envy's attacks. So, when, first in 1930, he reeled off the centuries, single, double and treble, there were not wanting those who compared him unfavourably with other great ones – Trumper, Ranjitsinhji, Hobbs, Macartney. And Bradman's answer was more runs. Others, perhaps, *could* have made them, but they didn't. No one before had ever been quite so fit, quite so ruthless.

It was a coolly considered policy. Cricket was not to be his hobby, his off-hours delight. It was to be his life and his living. A few hundreds here and there for Australia and State – what use in that? Others had done it, would do it again. He did not mean to be just one of the stars, but the sun itself. Never was such ambition achieved and sustained. Never was the limelight directed so unwaveringly on one man in one game. To set such a standard was unique. To keep it was a miracle.

But the sun itself has degrees of splendour; and, whatever the numbers may say, Bradman was never again quite so incredible as in England in the summer of 1930. Like all great artists, he knew how to begin. So he made 236 at Worcester and 185 not out at Leicester. Then, with a mere trifle of 78 against Yorkshire he relented into rest. At Nottingham, in the First Test, he was set fair to win the match for Australia when R. W. V. Robins bowled him with a googly. It is a freak of chance that in both his first and last Test Matches in England he should have fatally mistaken a googly for a leg-break. It is also reassuring to mere mortality. In that First Test he scored 131. This was a *hors d'oeuvre* of the feast to follow. At Lord's, in the Second Test, he made 254, and the innings only ended with one of those catches that set A. P. F. Chapman apart from the other England fieldsmen. Then, at Leeds, he scored 334.

George Duckworth, who was keeping wicket for England, rates this innings as the greatest he ever saw. Archie Jackson, that glorious and ill-fated batsman, had opened the Australian innings with W. M. Woodfull. Off the fifth ball of the second over from Maurice Tate, Jackson was caught at short-leg. Bradman joined his captain. The first ball that he received from Tate whizzed just over his off stump, and Duckworth, believing that Bradman must be bowled, let it go for byes. Then the show began. Bradman never hit in the air. Boundaries sprang from his bat with murderous precision and calculated profusion. Larwood, Tate and Geary – no mean trio – were helpless. A new machine was at work. A new standard of ambition had been set. At Manchester, Ian Peebles induced Bradman into error to the leg-break. But Bradman returned to himself with 232 at the Oval in the Fifth Test. In the five Tests he had scored 974 runs at an average of 139. Statistics cannot record the number of runs he carried with him to each innings. But, in a country of great fieldsmen, he stood out pre-eminent. His gathering and throwing approached perfection. Only in catching, probably owing to the smallness of his hands, he was no better than the next man.

Then, after he had taken his pleasure of the South African bowling in Australia, came the first eclipse. A new style of attack, popularly known as 'body-line', with the great fast bowler Larwood as its spearhead, was launched on the Australians in Australia by D. R. Jardine. This is no place for discussing the ethics of the matter. Technically, Bradman found no satisfactory answer. He met it, certainly, with a virtuosity of footwork possible to him alone. But his average in eight Test innings sank to a mere trifle of 57, including a score of 103 not out.

When Bradman next came to England, in 1934, there was no Larwood against him, and no Voce. He resumed his mastery. In the Leeds Test he scored 304; at the Oval 244. But, whereas in 1930 he had annihilated doubt, there were now certain qualifications. He was found to be incomplete against the great left-hand bowler, Hedley Verity, on a sticky wicket. At Lord's, in the Second Test, he lost his head, if one may use such a phrase of such a master of calculation and coolness. Perhaps it was attributable to his uncertain health. But too much emphasis has been laid on this failure. Verity himself did not agree with the popular generalisation that Bradman 'couldn't play on the bad ones'. And he knew. But it should be said that, with the exception of Larwood in Australia during the 1932-33 tour, Verity was the one bowler who battled with Bradman on something like level terms, even on the truest of pitches. Besides this failure at Lord's in 1934, another man, one of his own team, contributed to some dimming of the Bradman glory. That was W. H. Ponsford, of Victoria. He was playing in his last Test series against

England. Most of his records, once seemingly unassailable, had been stolen by Bradman; but now Ponsford, one of the greatest players of spin bowling that ever batted, ran level with his rival, and actually beat him in the matter of Test average by a decimal point.

Already Bradman had proved his power to live on a pinnacle of success. Now, against G. O. Allen's team in Australia, 1936-37, he was to show that he could return from failure. He started downright badly, and the vultures that await the fall of the great hovered expectantly. But he disappointed them, and, by the end of the tour, he was once more the authentic Bradman. In 1938, his third visit to England, he came as captain. Henceforward, in Tests, except for one innings of 234 at Sydney, he was to deal in single centuries only. It was a concession to old man Time.

Where does Bradman stand as a captain? Such a question opens the way to opinions which, even when gathered from those who played with him from day to day, cannot be reduced to any certain conclusion. On the field he was superb. He had seen and weighed it all. Shrewd and tough, he was not likely to waste anything in dreams or mercy. No one ever saw Bradman not attending. Cricket to one who made and kept his way from hard beginnings, was a business, not a pastime.

He made mistakes. He took only three regular bowlers on to the field for the last Test at the Oval in 1938. For him, as for Australia, the match was a disaster. Bradman, when bowling, fell and injured his leg. England scored 903 for seven wickets; Hutton 364. Both these totals are Test records. Bradman was unable to bat, and Australia lost by the record margin of an innings and 579. How different from the scene of ten years later, when Lindwall went through the England batting like a steam drill. But, all in all, Bradman was the supreme tactician.

On the personal side, his success was more doubtful. Great captaincy begins off the field. True leadership springs from affection even more than from respect. Bradman certainly earned the respect. But, by his very nature, he was bound to have admirers rather than friends. Stripped to the truth, he was a solitary man with a solitary aim. It was what the man did rather than what he was that invited obedience. There are humorously affectionate stories about most great cricketers; intimate, if somewhat apocryphal tales about them; of what Dr Grace said when Ernest Jones bowled a ball through his beard; of Patsy Hendren's reply to a criticism from the Sydney 'Hill'; of what Johnny Douglas uttered when second slip floored a catch. But there are no funny stories about the Don. No one ever laughed about Bradman. He was no laughing matter.

During the War, disturbing rumours reached England about his health; and, whatever truth there may have been in them, certainly the England team under W. R. Hammond found Bradman uncommonly near to being a sick man. But, happily, he recovered. So did his batting. Not without luck, surely earned, he first groped, then rushed, his way back to normal. Enough of the old skill returned for him to score 187 at Brisbane and 234 at Sydney.

There followed his last visit as a Test cricketer to England. As a batsman he no longer flamed high above his fellows. He was now no more than a very fine player, and it was arguable that both S. G. Barnes and A. R. Morris were stronger factors in the quelling of bowlers. But Bradman's fame, if possible, increased. Next to Mr Winston Churchill, he was the most celebrated man in England during the summer of 1948. His appearances throughout the country were like one continuous farewell matinée. At last his batting showed human fallibility. Often, especially at the start of the innings, he played where the ball wasn't, and spectators rubbed their eyes. But such a treasury of skill could spare some gold and still be rich. He scored 138 against England at Nottingham, and, when it much mattered, 173 not out at Leeds.

Most important of all, he steered Australia through some troubled waters and never grounded on the rocks. Returning home, he received the first Knighthood ever given to a playing cricketer.

Bradman's place as a batsman is among the few who have been blessed with genius. He was the most wonderful run-scorer that the game has yet known, and no batsman in our own time has so highly excited expectation and so rarely disappointed it.

D. G. BRADMAN, 1927–49

CAREER AT A GLANCE

** Signifies not out.*

Season	*Innings*	*Not Outs*	*Runs*	*Highest Innings*	*Average*
1927-28	10	1	416	134*	46.22
1928-29	24	6	1,690	340*	93.88
1929-30	16	2	1,586	452*	113.28
1930	36	6	2,960	334	98.66
1930-31	18	0	1,422	258	79.00
1931-32	13	1	1,403	299*	116.91
1932-33	21	2	1,171	238	61.63
1933-34	11	2	1,192	253	132.44
1934	27	3	2,020	304	84.16
1934-35	(Did not play)				
1935-36	9	0	1,173	369	130.33
1936-37	19	1	1,552	270	86.22
1937-38	18	2	1,437	246	89.91
1938	26	5	2,429	278	115.66
1938-39	7	1	919	225	153.16
1939-40	15	3	1,475	267	122.91
1940-41	4	0	18	12	4.50
1945-46	3	1	232	112	116.00
1946-47	14	1	1,032	234	79.38
1947-48	12	2	1,296	201	129.60
1948	31	4	2,428	187	89.92
1948-49	4	0	216	123	54.00
Totals	338	43	28,067	452*	95.14

AGGREGATES

	Innings	*Not Outs*	*Runs*	*Highest Innings*	*Average*
In Australia	216	25	18,147	452*	95.01
In England	122	18	9,920	334	95.38
Totals	338	43	28,067	452*	95.14

IN TEST MATCHES

	Innings	*Not Outs*	*Runs*	*Highest Innings*	*Average*
v England	63	7	5,028	334	89.78
v India	6	2	715	201	178.75
v South Africa	5	1	806	299*	201.50
v West Indies	6	0	447	223	74.50
Totals	80	10	6,996	334	99.94

AGAINST ENGLAND IN ENGLAND

	Innings	*Not Outs*	*Runs*	*Highest Innings*	*Average*
1930	7	0	974	334	139.14
1934	8	0	758	304	94.75
1938	6	2	434	144*	108.50
1948	9	2	508	173*	72.57
Totals	30	4	2,674	334	102.84

AGAINST ENGLAND IN AUSTRALIA

	Innings	*Not Outs*	*Runs*	*Highest Innings*	*Average*
1928-29	8	2	468	123	66.85
1932-33	8	1	396	103*	56.57
1936-37	9	0	810	270	90.00
1946-47	8	1	680	234	97.14
Totals	33	3	2,354	270	78.46

FOR AUSTRALIANS AGAINST TEAMS IN ENGLAND

	Innings	*Not Outs*	*Runs*	*Highest Innings*	*Average*
Derbyshire	4	1	183	71	61.00
Essex	2	0	206	187	103.00
Glamorgan	3	1	94	58	47.00
Gloucestershire	2	0	56	42	28.00
Hampshire	3	1	336	191	168.00
Kent	4	1	355	205*	118.33
Lancashire	10	4	446	133*	74.33
Leicestershire	3	1	331	185	165.50
Middlesex	6	1	254	160	50.80
Northamptonshire	5	0	149	65	29.80
Nottinghamshire	3	0	286	144	95.33
Somerset	3	0	336	202	112.00
Surrey	8	2	839	252*	139.83
Sussex	1	0	109	109	109.00
Warwickshire	3	1	179	135	89.50
Worcestershire	4	0	807	258	201.75
Yorkshire	7	0	460	140	65.71
MCC	5	0	451	278	90.20
Oxford University	3	0	127	58	42.33
Cambridge University	3	0	169	137	56.33
An England XI	2	1	212	149*	212.00
H. D. G. Leveson Gower's XI	3	0	381	153	127.00
Gentlemen of England	2	0	254	150	127.00
South of England	1	0	143	143	143.00
Totals	90	14	7,163	278	94.25

FOR NEW SOUTH WALES

	Innings	*Not Outs*	*Runs*	*Highest Innings*	*Average*
v MCC	8	1	504	157	72.00
v Queensland	11	2	1,299	452*	144.33
v Rest	2	0	114	92	57.00
v South Africa	3	0	384	219	128.00
v South Australia	20	0	1,269	258	63.45
v Victoria	21	7	2,065	340*	147.50
v West Indies	4	0	178	73	44.50
Totals	69	10	5,813	452*	98.52

For South Australia

	Innings	*Not Outs*	*Runs*	*Highest Innings*	*Average*
v India	2	0	168	156	84.00
v MCC	6	0	187	76	31.14
v New South Wales	14	5	1,178	251*	130.88
v New Zealand	1	0	11	11	11.00
v Queensland	14	2	1,658	246	138.16
v Services XI	1	0	112	112	112.00
v Tasmania	1	0	369	369	369.00
v Victoria	20	0	1,583	357	79.15
v Western Australia	4	1	487	209*	162.33
Totals	63	8	5,753	369	104.60

For Australian XI

	Innings	*Not Outs*	*Runs*	*Highest Innings*	*Average*
v India	2	0	198	172	99.00
v MCC	6	1	294	106	58.80
v Tasmania	5	0	409	144	81.80
v Western Australia	2	0	217	115	108.50
Totals	15	1	1,118	172	79.85

For Other Teams

	Innings	*Not Outs*	*Runs*	*Highest Innings*	*Average*
Combined XI v MCC	2	0	13	13	6.50
MCC Centenary Match	1	0	118	118	118.00
Patriotic Match	2	0	12	12	6.00
Rest v Australia	2	0	19	14	9.50
Rest v New South Wales	2	0	27	25	13.50
Testimonial Matches	8	0	584	212	73.00
Trial Match	2	0	349	225	174.50
W. M. Woodfull's XI v J. Ryder's XI	2	0	102	73	51.00
Totals	21	0	1,224	225	58.28

SUMMARY

	Innings	*Not Outs*	*Runs*	*Highest Innings*	*Average*
Test Matches	80	10	6,996	334	99.94
For Australians in England	90	14	7,163	278	94.25
For New South Wales	69	10	5,813	452*	98.52
For South Australia	63	8	5,753	369	104.60
For Australian XI	15	1	1,118	172	79.85
For Other Teams	21	0	1,224	225	58.28
Totals	338	43	28,067	452*	95.14

HIGHEST INDIVIDUAL SCORES

452* New South Wales v Queensland, at Sydney 1929-30

369 South Australia v Tasmania, at Adelaide 1935-36

357 South Australia v Victoria, at Melbourne 1935-36

340* New South Wales v Victoria, at Sydney 1928-29

334 Australia v England, at Leeds 1930

304 Australia v England, at Leeds 1934

RECORDS BY BRADMAN

The only player who has scored over 300 runs in an innings six times, he holds the record for scores over 200 – 37.

The only Australian to score more than 100 hundreds – 117 in all; 76 in Australia and 41 in England.

He scored a hundred on his first appearance in first-class cricket and in his own Testimonial match after announcing retirement.

Two separate hundreds in a match four times. This is exceeded only by C. B. Fry, W. R. Hammond and J. B. Hobbs.

He shares with C. B. Fry the record number of hundreds in succession – six.

Most hundreds in a season by an Australian in England – thirteen in 1938.

Most hundreds in an Australian season – eight in 1947-48.

He twice scored over 1,000 runs before the end of May. No other Australian has accomplished this, and no Englishman more than once.

Highest aggregate by an Australian in an English season – 2,960 runs in 1930.

Highest aggregate in Australia – 1,690 in 1928-29.

Over 1,000 runs in sixteen seasons, twelve of them in Australia. No other Australian has accomplished this feat more than three times.

The only Australian to exceed 2,000 runs on four English tours.

Most hundreds in Test Matches – twenty-nine: nineteen v England, four v India, four v South Africa, two v West Indies.

Most double-hundreds in Australia v England Test Matches – eight.

Highest score in Test Matches in Australia – 299* v South Africa at Adelaide in 1931-32.

Highest aggregate for one series of Tests – 974 in England in 1930.

Second-wicket world record – 451 with W. H. Ponsford against England at [Kennington] Oval in 1934.

Fifth-wicket world record – 405 with S. G. Barnes against England at Sydney in 1946-47.

HUNDREDS – 117

**Signifies not out.*

1927-28

118 New South Wales v South Australia, at Adelaide.

134* New South Wales v Victoria, at Sydney.

1928-29

132* New South Wales v MCC, at Sydney.

112 Australia v England, at Melbourne.

123 Australia v England, at Melbourne.

131 }
133* } New South Wales v Queensland, at Brisbane.

340* New South Wales v Victoria, at Sydney.

175 New South Wales v South Australia, at Sydney.

1929-30

157 New South Wales v MCC, at Sydney.

124 }
225 } Trial Match, at Sydney.

452* New South Wales v Queensland, at Sydney.

139 1930 Australian XI v Tasmania, at Hobart.

1930

236 Australians v Worcestershire, at Worcester.

185* Australians v Leicestershire, at Leicester.

252* Australians v Surrey, at [Kennington] Oval.

191 Australians v Hampshire, at Southampton.

131 Australia v England, at Nottingham.

254 Australia v England, at Lord's.

334 Australia v England, at Leeds.

117 Australians v Somerset, at Taunton.

232 Australia v England, at [Kennington] Oval.

205* Australians v Kent, at Canterbury.

1930-31

223 Australia v West Indies, at Brisbane.

152 Australia v West Indies, at Melbourne.

121 New South Wales v South Australia, at Sydney.

258 New South Wales v South Australia, at Adelaide.

220 New South Wales v Victoria, at Sydney.

1931-32

135 New South Wales v South Africans, at Sydney.

219 New South Wales v South Africans, at Sydney.

167 New South Wales v Victoria, at Sydney.

226 Australia v South Africa, at Brisbane.

112 Australia v South Africa, at Sydney.

167 Australia v South Africa, at Melbourne.

299* Australia v South Africa, at Adelaide.

1932-33

103* Australia v England, at Melbourne.

237 New South Wales v Victoria, at Sydney.

157 New South Wales v Victoria, at Melbourne.

1933-34

200 New South Wales v Queensland, at Brisbane.

187* New South Wales v Victoria, at Melbourne.

253 New South Wales v Queensland, at Sydney.

128 New South Wales v Victoria, at Sydney.

101 Testimonial Match, at Melbourne.

1934

206 Australians v Worcestershire, at Worcester.

160 Australians v Middlesex, at Lord's.

140 Australians v Yorkshire, at Sheffield.

304 Australia v England, at Leeds.

244 Australia v England, at [Kennington] Oval.

149* Australians v An England XI, at Folkestone.

132 Australians v H. D. G. Leveson Gower's XI, at Scarborough.

1935-36

117 South Australia v New South Wales, at Adelaide.

233 South Australia v Queensland, at Adelaide.

357 South Australia v Victoria, at Melbourne.

369 South Australia v Tasmania, at Adelaide.

1936-37

270 Australia v England, at Melbourne.

212 Australia v England, at Adelaide.

169 Australia v England, at Melbourne.

192 South Australia v Victoria, at Melbourne.

123 South Australia v Queensland, at Brisbane.

212 Testimonial Match, at Sydney.

1937-38

245 South Australia v Queensland, at Adelaide.

107 }
113 } South Australia v Queensland, at Brisbane.

104* South Australia v New South Wales, at Sydney.

101 South Australia v Western Australia, at Adelaide.

144 1938 Australian XI v Tasmania, at Hobart.

102 1938 Australian XI v Western Australia, at Perth.

1938

258 Australians v Worcestershire, at Worcester.

137 Australians v Cambridge University, at Cambridge.

278 Australians v MCC, at Lord's.

143 Australians v Surrey, at [Kennington] Oval.

145* Australians v Hampshire, at Southampton.

144* Australia v England, at Nottingham.

104 Australians v Gentlemen of England, at Lord's.

101* Australians v Lancashire, at Manchester.

102* Australia v England, at Lord's.

135 Australians v Warwickshire, at Birmingham.

144 Australians v Nottinghamshire, at Nottingham.

103 Australia v England, at Leeds.

202 Australians v Somerset, at Taunton.

1938-39

118 Melbourne Club Centenary Match, at Melbourne.

143 South Australia v New South Wales, at Adelaide.

225 South Australia v Queensland, at Adelaide.

107 South Australia v Victoria, at Melbourne.

186 South Australia v Queensland, at Brisbane.

135* South Australia v New South Wales, at Sydney.

1939-40

251* South Australia v New South Wales, at Adelaide.

138 South Australia v Queensland, at Adelaide.

267 South Australia v Victoria, at Melbourne.

209* South Australia v Western Australia, at Perth.

135 South Australia v Western Australia, at Perth.

1945-46

112 South Australia v A Services XI, at Adelaide.

1946-47

106 An Australian XI v MCC, at Melbourne.

119 South Australia v Victoria, at Adelaide.

187 Australia v England, at Brisbane.

234 Australia v England, at Sydney.

1947-48

156 South Australia v India, at Adelaide.

100 South Australia v Victoria, at Adelaide.

172 An Australian XI v India, at Sydney.

185 Australia v India, at Brisbane.

132 }
127* } Australia v India, at Melbourne.

201 Australia v India, at Adelaide.

114 1948 Australian XI v Western Australia, at Perth.

1948

107 Australians v Worcestershire, at Worcester.

146 Australians v Surrey, at [Kennington] Oval.

187 Australians v Essex, at Southend.

109 Australians v Sussex, at Hove.

138 Australia v England, at Nottingham.

128 Australians v Surrey, at [Kennington] Oval.

173* Australia v England, at Leeds.

133* Australians v Lancashire, at Manchester.

150 Australians v Gentlemen of England, at Lord's.

143 Australians v South of England, at Hastings.

153 Australians v H. D. G. Leveson Gower's XI, at Scarborough.

December 1948

121 Bradman Testimonial Match, at Melbourne.

HONOURS FOR BRADMAN

During the match with Gentlemen of England at Lord's, Don Bradman was presented with a special birthday cake and a copy of Sir Pelham Warner's *Lord's 1787-1945* inscribed, 'Presented to Don Bradman on his 40th birthday by the President, committee and members of the Marylebone Cricket Club in memory of the great pleasure he has given at Lord's since 1930 to countless lovers of cricket.'

Bradman said: 'To bid farewell to cricket on this great ground is for me a very sad occasion. I hope, however, to come to England again, though not as a player, and watch many Tests.'

At Scarborough Don Bradman received the honorary life membership of the Yorkshire County Club. He was presented by Mr T. L. Taylor, President of the club, with a 1948 Yorkshire handbook and a silver salver inscribed with his scores made in the four Test Matches in which he played at Headingley. Apart from Yorkshire players, Bradman was the first recipient of this distinction.

As the outcome of a Testimonial match at Melbourne in December, Sir Donald Bradman received in January a cheque for £9,342 18*s.* 8*d.*

Six Giants of the Wisden Century – Sir Donald Bradman

By Neville Cardus

The 1963 Wisden *was the 100th annual edition of the Cricketers' Almanack, and among the special features commissioned to commemorate this landmark was 'Six Giants of the Wisden Century'. In response to the Editor's request, Neville Cardus, to cricket writing perhaps what Herodotus was to the writing of history, delivered 'appreciations' of the six he considered to be great cricketers of the past 100 years. His selections were S. F. Barnes, Sir Donald Bradman, W. G. Grace, Sir Jack Hobbs, Tom Richardson and Victor Trumper.*

SIR DONALD BRADMAN (hereinafter to be named Bradman or 'The Don') must be called the most masterful and prolific maker of runs the game has so far known. He was, in short, a great batsman. Critics have argued that he was mechanical. So is a majestically flying aeroplane. The difference between Bradman and, say, Victor Trumper as batsmen, was in fact the difference between an aeroplane and a swallow in flight. But it is nonsense to say that Bradman's batsmanship was without personality or character, or nature, or that it was in the slightest anonymous. He had a terrifically dynamic style. It was thrilling to see him gathering together his energy at the last second to hook, a stroke somehow reminding me of a boxer's swinging stunning 'right'.

Like all great players, he made his strokes very late. He didn't move at all until the ball was on him; then the brilliant technique shot forth concentrated energy – and the axe fell. All the strokes were at his command. After he had appeared almost for the first time in an Australian State match, J. V. Ryder, Australian captain, was asked, 'How does this young Bradman bat?' And Ryder, a man of few but eloquent words, replied: 'He belts the hell out of everything he can reach.'

Bradman's achievements stagger the imagination. No writer of boys' fiction would dare to invent a 'hero' who performed with Bradman's continual consistency. Nobody would even suspend disbelief as he read such fiction. Between 1927 and 1948 he scored 28,067 runs. (The war interrupted his genius at its high noon.) In his career as cricketer he scored these 28,067 runs with an average of 95.14, an average 'for life' twice as high as that of most other master batsmen. He made 117 centuries in 338 innings, forty-three times not out – a century every third time he walked to the wicket. He scored 6,996 runs in Test Matches, average 99.94. He scored 1,000 runs between April 30 and May 31 in an English season. He scored 1,000 runs in a season sixteen times. He scored 974 runs in one and the same rubber v England. He scored a triple Test Match century – 309 – in a day. He scored thirteen centuries in the English season of 1938. He scored six centuries in consecutive innings. He hit 30 runs in one over. He scored two centuries in the same Test Match, v India.

Moreover, I think he knew at the time that he was about to do these extraordinary things; for he planned everything. No cricketer has had a quicker, shrewder brain than Bradman's. At Leeds in 1934, Australia bowled England out on a beautiful turf for 200. Then, at the afternoon's fall, Australia lost three wickets for 39. That evening Bradman cancelled dinner with me, saying he was going to bed early as, next day, it would be necessary for him to score 200 'at least!' I reminded him that on his previous Test appearance at Leeds, in 1930, he had scored 334. 'The law of averages is against you pulling off another big score here tomorrow in a Test,' I said. He replied: 'I don't believe in the law of averages.' Next day he set about scoring 304.

The extraordinary point of this innings is that, until his Leeds Test, Bradman had battled in the rubber with a certain lack of concentration, as though the effects of the Jardine–Larwood 'body-line' assaults on him of 1932-33 were still shaking him. At Nottingham and Lord's, he played fast bowling with a rhetorical slash, a quite wild impetuosity. Now, at Leeds, in a serious hour for Australia, he could summon back at one call the old cool, premeditated craft and foresight.

I asked him once, in Melbourne, to give me some idea of how he did it all. 'Every ball for me is the first ball,' then, he added, taking away my breath, 'and I never think there's a possibility of anybody getting me out.'

The critics say he couldn't bat on a turning pitch. Hedley Verity held the opposite opinion – from experience. It is a fact, though, that 'The Don' seemed occasionally not to face up to a 'sticky' pitch, *on principle.* He argued that wickets should be covered from rain, especially in his own country. It wasn't fair that a side should bat in perfect run-getting conditions one day. Then next day the other side could be trapped on a spitting pitch.

Bradman had all the attributes needed to cope with the spinning, kicking ball – swift feet, and an eye rapid and comprehensive. Against Larwood's devastating 'body-line' attack, dangerous to breastbone and skull, Bradman in the Tests scored 396 runs, average 56.57. Jardine reduced his powers temporarily by half; but no other mortal batsman could have coped with Larwood as Bradman coped with him. In spite of Larwood's velocity and menace – seven fieldsmen on the leg or on side – Bradman was driving or punching, to the vacant off side, bowling coming like lightning from a spot on or outside the leg stump, often rising shoulder high.

He first came to England in 1930, twenty-one years old. He began at Worcester with 236 in four and a half hours, twenty-eight boundaries. To Leicester he proceeded, to score 185 not out. Then, on the soft wicket v Yorkshire, he scored 78. And a newspaper placard announced, 'Bradman fails'. It was in 1930 that he exhibited, I think, the most wonderful batsmanship of his life, when during the Lord's Test Match he came to the wicket after Ponsford had got out. In two hours and forty minutes before half-past six, he cut, drove and hooked the England attack, to the tune of 155. J. C. White, the untouchable, was brought on immediately to keep 'The Don' quiet. White's first ball, a good length, was slapped to the on-boundary, near the clock at the Nursery. Bradman leapt yards out of his crease; and the crack of his bat sent the Lord's pigeons flying in affrighted circles.

It was at Lord's, in 1938, during the MCC v Australians match that the effervescent J. W. A. Stephenson, a splendid opening bowler, appealed for lbw against Bradman, and Bradman had not yet got into double figures. Stephenson leapt skywards as he appealed. The 'near thing' was negatived. If the reply had been in the affirmative, I imagine Stephenson would have been the first into and beyond the 'barrier'. Bradman went on to amass 278. He was ruthless. None the less, he didn't ever fail to respond to a bowler's challenge.

Nobody ever saw Bradman show mercy to a loose ball. If he went on the defensive, there was good reason. At Trent Bridge, in 1938, Australia followed on after they had scored 411 in response to England's 658 for eight (declared). McCabe made history with a marvellous and gallant 232. But the pitch grew dusty and the closing day had a severe ordeal waiting for Bradman. Early that day Bradman wrote home to the young lady he was later to marry [actually the Bradmans had married some six years earlier, in 1932], telling her that a job of work had to be done, but, he guessed, all would have turned out well for Australia long before his letter reached her. Bradman then set forth to Trent Bridge and saved the day by batting nearly six hours.

Never, as I say, did he play with sterile negation. He was a Test cricketer of our contemporary temper, realistic and without cant. He reacted to the environment in which he found himself. He hadn't to play, as Trumper was obliged to play, in this country, in games limited to three days. If he didn't throw his wicket away, as Trumper frequently did on reaching his hundred, the reason was that he played in a different economy of the game than Trumper ever knew. If and when Bradman stayed at the wicket all day he not only put his team in a position pretty secure from defeat but into a position from which the Australian bowlers could attack, with time to bring in victory; also he was holding the crowd in thrall.

He was a born batsman, out of a remote part of his beloved Australia, never coached academically; consequently he was free to give rein to his innate and rare gifts. He was born, too, with a good brain. Nobody has excelled Bradman's 'cricket sense', his intuitions and understanding. He must be counted among Australia's cleverest, most closely calculating cricket captains.

After he had scored a triple-century on a warm day at Leeds in 1930, he came from the field apparently cool, no sign of perspiration, not a buckle out of place, flannels immaculate, and, as the crowd roared him home, he seemed withdrawn and impersonal. People said that he lacked emotion. Maybe he was content to be the cause of 'emotion' in others – in bowlers, for example. 'Stripped to the truth,' wrote Robertson-Glasgow, in a brilliant appreciation of Bradman in *Wisden*, 'he was a solitary man with a solitary aim.' Personally I have found in Sir Donald plenty of friendliness and humour. But, then, I was never called on to bowl or play cricket against him! Discussing him entirely from the point of view of a writer on the game, I am happy to say that he was for me a constant spur to ideas. A newspaper column couldn't contain him. He was, as far as a cricketer can be, a genius.

Sir Donald Bradman – Selector

By Irving Rosenwater

Irving Rosenwater's Sir Donald Bradman: A Biography *won the Cricket Society Literary Award in 1978. His other works include co-authorship of* England v Australia, *and he was the scorer for BBC TV in England and Channel 9 in Australia. This article appeared in the 1972* Wisden.

'Selectorship – a fascinating job really, despite its complexities.'
Sir Donald Bradman in 1958.

ONE ASPECT OF the career of Sir Donald Bradman that seems to have escaped the myriad of writers who have penned their multitude of words on him is his role as a Selector. As both a State Selector and a Test Selector, Sir Donald gave a span of service which, in terms of years, far exceeded his playing career. Although Australians generally tend to retain their positions as Selectors longer than Englishmen, Sir Donald's period of service was uncommonly lengthy by any standards. More than half his life has been spent as a South Australian and Test Selector, and though he had shed both roles by the start of the recent Australian season, at the age of 63 he is by no means old as Selectors go. Jack Ryder was still selecting Sheffield Shield sides for Victoria and Test sides for Australia as an octogenarian.

But Sir Donald is, and will be, far from idle. As Chairman of the Australian Board of Control (he is in his second term, with his final year to serve under the normal rotation system), President of the South Australian Cricket Association, one of South Australia's three representatives on the Board of Control and at the Interstate Conference of Sheffield Shield States, member of several committees with South Australia, director of some sixteen Australian companies – to all of which he gives his time and attention – there is plenty to exercise his agile mind. For sporting recreation he turns, as he has now done for many years, to golf.

Sir Donald announced his retirement from Test selectorship on February 9, 1971, shortly after the side for the final Test against England had been chosen. He had been chairman of the panel for the 1970-71 series, as well as for many series before that. His announcement gave family and business pressures, as well as 'health problems', as the reason for his retirement. Richie Benaud, who made his Test debut in 1951-52 when Sir Donald was a Selector, declared in the Melbourne *Herald*: 'Sir Donald was easily the best Selector I came across in the game anywhere in the world, not just in Australia.' The shrewd judgment of Sir Donald, backed by an unparalleled career as a player, was undoubtedly a potent factor in the general success of Australian sides over the last thirty-five years.

The appointment of D. G. Bradman as a Test Selector, just a few days after his twenty-eighth birthday in 1936, was to some extent fortuitous, for although he was generally expected to be made captain by the Australian Board for the Tests against G. O. Allen's side, the vacant position on the selection committee, to which Bradman was appointed, arose only through the death on June 11, 1936, of Dr C. E. Dolling, who happened to be the South Australian representative. Dr Dolling had been both a State and Test Selector and a good enough batsman to have scored 140 for South Australia in his first innings against an English side, in 1907-08. A prominent member of the medical profession, he suffered a sudden seizure in his surgery in Adelaide and died about an hour later, aged only forty-nine. He was a man of sound judgment and very straight in his methods, and Bradman's own tribute to him at the time said that he was 'a wise and tactful administrator, and that, as a Selector, he enjoyed the confidence of everybody'. Those same qualities Bradman himself sought to display on behalf of Australian cricket.

The three Australian Selectors for the 1936-37 series against England were appointed by the Australian Board of Control at their meeting in Adelaide on September 10, 1936. Bradman was the only newcomer, to join E. A. Dwyer (NSW) and W. J. Johnson (Victoria), and he accepted the position, as he later said, 'with some reservations'. There had never been – and still has not been – a younger Selector appointed by the Australian Board. Clem Hill and H. L. Collins had both been appointed at the age of thirty-one, and Darling, McAlister, Ryder and Woodfull had all been in their middle or late thirties. In pre-Board days, however, both Joe Darling and S. E. Gregory had also been aged twenty-eight when they were two of the Selectors of the 1899 side for England, and W. Bruce was the same age when he helped to select the 1893 team.

At the time of his appointment Bradman had already had one season's experience as a State Selector for South Australia, having commenced those duties when he transferred to Adelaide from New South Wales and assumed the State captaincy for the 1935-36 season. He was to remain a South Australian and Test Selector until he temporarily retired from both positions (due to the illness of his son, John) before the 1952-53 season. He took no part in selecting Australia's sides that summer against the visiting South Africans or in choosing South Australia's Shield teams, his place in both roles being taken by the experienced Phil Ridings, who had succeeded Bradman as captain of South Australia four years before. Likewise, Sir Donald had no hand in the selection of the 1953 Australian team in England (whose tour he covered as a special writer), but in the autumn of 1953 he was restored to the South Australian selection committee, and before the arrival of MCC in 1954-55 he was also back as a Test Selector. Before the start of the 1970-71 season Sir Donald retired as a State Selector for health reasons, but continued for the season at national level. Before the season was over he decided not to stand for election in either capacity in the future.

For South Australia in Sheffield Shield matches, Sir Donald Bradman was a Selector in twenty-eight seasons in all, twenty-three of them after the war. In that period his State won the Shield only four times (including twice when he was captain), though it is strange that for the two seasons that he stood down, 1952-53 and 1970-71, South Australia emerged winners. The full record of South Australia in the Sheffield Shield for matches in which Sir Donald Bradman was one of the Selectors is as follows:

Played	*Won*	*Lost*	*Drawn*	*Points*	*Possible Points*	*Average Position in Shield Table*
201	55	76	70	560	1,525	3rd

In the twenty-eight seasons involved, South Australia finished first four times; second five times; third (or joint-third) seven times; fourth three times; and fifth nine times. The only seasons they were undefeated were in 1935-36 and 1938-39, both under Bradman's captaincy.

It is at Test level, of course, that a Selector's record is always more interesting, though a Selector, naturally, is always one of a team. The normal method in Australia, ever since the formation of the Board of Control, has always been to appoint three Selectors, both for home series of Tests and for choosing overseas sides. The only exception to this was in the 1928-29 series, when there were four Selectors. Unlike the situation in England, the Australian Board never appoints a formal chairman. There has in fact never been any official record of such a position, and when, before the 1928-29 selection panel was appointed, opinion was obtained by the Board whether it had constitutional power to appoint a

Chairman of Selectors, it was advised that the Board had no such power. The Selectors have in fact always arranged the chairman among themselves – and it seems that they have never even been required to report to the Board who has been so appointed. Sir Donald Bradman acted in the capacity of chairman on all occasions that he served since the Second World War, though the position was an unofficial one.

It is astonishing to consider that Sir Donald has been involved in the selection of very nearly half of all the Test sides that have ever taken the field for Australia, from 1877 to date. Add to those the matches in which he played before becoming a Selector, and his personal involvement in his country's Tests extends to 55 per cent of all matches – a prodigious record, considering that Test cricket was already half a century old before Bradman made his first-class (let alone his Test) debut.

The full record of Australia in Test cricket for the matches in which Sir Donald was one of the Selectors is as follows:

Played	*Won by Australia*	*Lost by Australia*	*Drawn*	*Tied*
151	68	32	50	1

Thus, in these games, Australia lost an average of one in five Tests, though immediately after the war she had a wonderful (and at that time a record) run of twenty-five matches without defeat. Four successive losses to South Africa in 1969-70 somewhat spoiled the average. The measure of success against each country is:

	Played	*Won by Australia*	*Lost by Australia*	*Drawn*	*Tied*
v England	70	27	15	28	0
v South Africa	24	9	8	7	0
v West Indies	25	13	5	6	1
v New Zealand	1	1	0	0	0
v India	25	16	3	6	0
v Pakistan	6	2	1	3	0
	151	68	32	50	1

In terms of Test sides that have left Australia, Sir Donald was jointly responsible for fourteen such touring sides – every side in fact from the 1938 team to England to the 1969-70 team to India and South Africa, with the sole exception of Lindsay Hassett's side to England in 1953.

These fourteen teams played altogether in twenty series away from Australia (including on three occasions a solitary Test) and, of their eighty Tests against all countries, lost less than a quarter – virtually the same record that home Australian teams experienced in the same period. The playing record of Australia in Tests, at home and away, during Sir Donald Bradman's selectorship is as follows:

	Played	*Won*	*Lost*	*Drawn*	*Tied*
In Australia	71	35	14	21	1
Away from Australia	80	33	18	29	0
	151	68	32	50	1

In addition, Sir Donald was one of the Selectors for the five Australian sides that visited New Zealand, without playing Tests, under W. A. Brown in 1949-50, I. D. Craig in 1956-57 and 1959-60, L. E. Favell in 1966-67, and S. C. Trimble in 1969-70. On all these selection committees, Sir Donald served with the regular Test Selectors of the time, except that in 1949-50 E. A. Dwyer (NSW) acted as manager of the Australian team to South Africa and his place as Selector for the New Zealand tour was taken by A. Vincent (NSW).

Altogether, the selection committees on which Sir Donald served were responsible for sending into the field 114 Australian Test players, ranging from R. N. Harvey, W. M. Lawry and G. D. McKenzie, all of whom made sixty or more appearances, to twenty players who were chosen for but a solitary Test. Charges of State rivalry and favouritism have often been levelled against Australian administrators (and Selectors in particular), but in fact the strongest States have had the strongest representation in Australian sides, and Sir Donald's own State of South Australia can hardly be said to be favoured in the distribution. South Australia has had a Test Selector now ever since the Australian Board Selectors first functioned, in the 1907-08 season (and continues to have one with the appointment of P. L. Ridings to fill the vacancy left by Sir Donald's retirement), though in exactly the same way that, on figures, South Australia emerges as the third strongest of the Sheffield Shield sides, so she comes third in the table of Test representation. The 114 players have been chosen from the five Sheffield Shield States as follows: Victoria 38, New South Wales 31, South Australia 21, Queensland 13 and Western

Australia 11. In cases of dual affiliation, the State recorded is that for which the player was playing when first chosen for a Test during the relevant period.

It is often said that Australia introduces fewer players into the Test arena than England, and that it is more difficult to get out of an Australian side than into it. In the course of the seventy Tests played between England and Australia during Sir Donald's tenure as a Test Selector, ninety-nine Australian players (including Sir Donald himself) took the field, while the number who appeared for England was 111 – so the difference was not all that great. Sir Donald of course was merely one of a team as a Selector, and he did not always have the decisive voice, despite the aura that has evolved over the years that his influence was such that the last word was automatically – and emphatically – his. Through a dozen years of his term, from 1954-55, he was one of a triumvirate together with Jack Ryder (Victoria) and Dudley Seddon (NSW) – though he also served for lesser periods with E. A. Dwyer (NSW), W. J. Johnson (Victoria), R. N. Harvey (NSW) and S. J. E. Loxton (Victoria) – and we may never know to what extent Sir Donald himself instigated, concurred or was overruled in such talking-points as the omission of Grimmett and Tallon in 1938, Miller and O'Neill to South Africa in 1949 and 1957 respectively, Simpson to Pakistan and India in 1959, and Walters to the West Indies in 1965. Perhaps the shroud of history is best left undisturbed in such instances.

From now on, for better or for worse, Australian Test selection will proceed without the thoughts of Sir Donald Bradman. His involvement with the game outside the Selectors' room will doubtless remain as intense, profound and invaluable as hitherto – it would be a pity, and a major loss, if it were otherwise. In recent years the time involved in selectorial duties, coupled with the necessary absences from home and business, have made things for him increasingly difficult to manage. And there are occasional health problems as well. Sir Donald himself has estimated that he spent 'about eight years' away from home during his period as a Test Selector – a voluntary act of adherence to cricket that sometimes gets submerged in the charisma of brilliance of the Bradman career. 'Selectors,' said Sir Donald once, 'are very conscientious people who are in the unenviable position of not being able to make public their views or policy.' In a moment of candour on another occasion he said:

'When I was Australian XI captain and Selector, I was castigated more than once for the omission of a certain man when in fact I fought for his inclusion. But those details can't be published. I simply mention them in the hope that the difficulties of selection committees may be more fully understood.' Such restraining factors do not inhibit the scribes of cricket. We may salute, in public, a Selector and man whose selectorial energies in the cause of Australian cricket were, in their special way, as notable as his distinguished achievements on the field. Mr S. C. Griffith, Secretary of MCC, expressed the view in 1971 that 'Sir Donald must be one of the most able and highly respected Test Selectors in the history of the game.' Few will cavil at that. Sir Donald Bradman, Selector, will assuredly hold a place of high significance in the history of Australian cricket.

Whither Cricket Now?

By Sir Donald Bradman

'I am especially pleased that Sir Donald Bradman is among the contributors,' the Editor, John Woodcock, wrote in his preface to the 1986 edition of Wisden. *'His only previous article for the Almanack, in 1939, was headed Cricket at the Cross Roads. He chose that title himself (as he did this), saying that it was "intended to convey a meaning but not to be misunderstood". It was written after what he felt had been a singularly happy series of Test Matches between England and Australia. Last summer's, also between England and Australia, was the same; but it is now another world we live in, as the great batsman observes.'*

AT THE REQUEST of the Editor I wrote a short piece for the 1939 *Wisden.* My main theme then was a plea for cricket to adapt itself to the quickening tempo of modern life, for administrators to consider ways of speeding up the game, to provide more modern scoreboards (especially in England), to face up to financial problems, and so on. Little did I appreciate at the time what a revolution would engulf cricket before another fifty years had passed.

The great stadiums of Sydney and Melbourne now display huge electronic scoreboards costing millions of dollars and giving a wealth of information to the spectators. The enormous electric light towers turn night into day at the flick of a switch. That, in turn, demands the use of a white ball, and to satisfy the television and marketing moguls the players turn out in a variety of coloured outfits.

The whole scene stirs up human emotions ranging from those of a largely new and young audience (more liberally sprinkled with females than of yore), who yell and scream their support, to those of the dyed-in-the-wool lovers of Test cricket, who yearn for more peaceful, bygone days. As with so many things, it becomes well-nigh impossible to bring about a reconciliation between the opposing attitudes.

But where does the truth lie and what about the future?

Despite my deep feeling for the traditional game, and my conviction that a vast majority of players and the public still regard Test cricket as the supreme contest, we must accept that we live in a new era. If Sir Neville Cardus were alive today, I can well imagine how eloquently he would bemoan the huge attendances at pop concerts compared with the lack of support for opera or a Beethoven evening. But I am sure he would also admit that, irrespective of the quality of the music or the musicians, the public are primarily interested in entertainment. Perhaps he would throw in his well-known reference to an eagle, no matter how beautiful in flight, being no match for the Concorde. I am satisfied that one-day cricket, especially day/night cricket, is here to stay. If there is a threat to the survival of the game of cricket, that threat lies in the first-class arena, and it behoves the administrators to understand the challenge and face up to it.

I confess to a love for both types of game. Nothing can match the continuous cut and thrust of a Test Match, where the advantage see-saws and the result is unpredictable to the last ball. I can't imagine any sporting event being more exciting than the tied Test between West Indies and Australia. It wasn't only the finish. Here you had two teams of great players, led by imaginative and intelligent captains determined from the first ball to pursue victory by adhering to the principles upon which the game was founded. The match had spin and speed, superb batting and fielding; every facet of the game was manifested as both sides strove for victory.

It starkly revealed the Achilles' heel of the limited-overs match, namely the premium placed on defensive bowling and negative and defensive field-placing. One can get bored to death watching countless singles being taken when even the world's fastest bowler may be operating with no slips and five men on the boundary.

But let me turn to the good things about one-day cricket.

It rids the game of the unutterable bore who thinks occupancy of the crease and his own personal aggrandisement are all that matter. It demands fieldsmen of great speed and agility with good throwing arms. The standard of fielding at all levels of cricket has undoubtedly been lifted. Running between the wickets, too, has taken on a new dimension. Risks must be taken to maintain the essential run-rate. Umpires are put under enormous pressure, having to adjudicate frequently on split-second issues: to their credit, I believe they have responded in a very positive manner and improved their standards.

Inevitably one sees the odd umpiring mistake, graphically portrayed by the modern marvel of the instant replay on television. With this new aid available, I should see no loss of face or pride if umpires were to agree, when in doubt about a decision, to seek arbitration from 'the box'. This could never apply to LBW, but for run-outs, and, on odd occasions, for stumpings or a disputed catch, it would seem logical.

My first-class playing career began in 1927, and I remain a Trustee of the Adelaide Oval and a member of the main South Australian Cricket Association committee. Having watched first-class cricket in 1921, I have seen as observer, player or administrator, all the great players of the last sixty-five years. Indeed, I can probably claim to span seventy-five years because many of the 1920-21 players also played before the Great War. It is still absolutely fascinating to me to watch and compare players of different generations.

How often I was asked in 1985 whether Clive Lloyd's West Indians were the best team of all time! Unhesitatingly I replied that they were the best fielding combination I have seen. But no matter how competent their batting, bowling and fielding, they were so reliant on fast bowlers that they became out of balance on a slow, turning pitch. In addition, the batting became vulnerable, which was proved in Sydney when Australia's two spinners, Bennett and Holland, tore the heart out of the West Indian batting to win a convincing victory for Australia. And without detracting from the skill of Bennett and Holland, it was clear to any knowledgeable observer that they were not of the quality of O'Reilly and Grimmett. To me these facts are indisputable and tend to place matters in their proper perspective. Australia's victory confirmed my view that my 1948 side was the best I ever saw, with Lloyd's 1984-85 team and Armstrong's 1920-21 Australian side not far behind. And my reading of history causes me to think Joe Darling's 1902 Australians were perhaps equal to any.

How lovely to be able to speculate without having to prove the answer!

Many cricket enthusiasts claim that the one-day game has brought in its wake a decline in batting technique. This may have some validity, but it is not necessarily true. People get confused between a normal mode of play and the essential improvisation needed to circumvent defensive fields. Vivian Richards and Clive Lloyd are marvellous examples of batsmen capable of coping quite adequately in both types of cricket without sacrificing any basic soundness of technique. The main difference in their one-day attitude has been a willingness to take the risk of lofting the ball over fieldsmen's heads. I doubt if modern players in general cut or pull quite as well as some of their forebears did, but I attribute this largely to the ultra-heavy bats they use. These hinder shots other than those of the perpendicular kind, such as the drive.

Undeniably the limited-overs game caters for a plethora of fast and medium-pace bowlers who tend to bowl just short of a length. In general it discourages, in fact it almost tolls the knell of, the slow leg-spinner. But here again one must acclaim the marvellous leg-spin bowling of the young Indian, Sivaramakrishnan, who proved against the best batting in the world in Sydney and Melbourne early in 1985 that he could bowl his ten-overs stint, get wickets, and still be economical. I don't doubt that O'Reilly, Grimmett, Benaud, Verity and others would have done the same. So perhaps, after all, the game is highlighting the fact that *top-quality* spinners can and will survive any challenge.

An interesting facet of the limited-overs game is the general rule governing bouncers. It unquestionably controls them in a sensible and practical way, and is a rule which I believe should be adopted in all grades of cricket without delay. It clearly reveals the way experimental laws could be used in one-day games to ascertain their effectiveness and/or desirability in first-class matches.

I also believe we have now reached the stage when some limitation in the length of a bowler's run-up is warranted. It would be the first and most logical step towards speeding up the over-rate. In Australia that magnificent player, Malcolm Marshall (excluding Frank Tyson, the fastest bowler I have seen since Larwood), has repeatedly shown us that a short run-up is sufficient to generate maximum speed.

The money now being paid to players has spawned professionalism beyond anything dreamed of fifty years ago. With so much money at stake I doubt if the modern professionals enjoy their cricket as much as did the players who were financially independent of the game and played purely for the love of it. Perhaps, too, monetary reward is responsible for some of the theatrical performances and even bad manners occasionally portrayed in recent years on the field. Happily I feel this unhealthy phase is on the wane, as players understand that good sportsmanship and keen competitiveness are not incompatible.

Most people agree that too much cricket was played during the Australian summer of 1984-85, owing to the Melbourne anniversary tournament being added to the schedule. It highlighted the need to strike a proper balance between one-day games and normal first-class matches. The attendances at Sheffield Shield matches were adversely affected. Indeed, the mounting losses on Shield games, now amounting to hundreds of thousands of dollars annually, constitute the most seemingly intractable problem confronting Australian cricket today. We need the

Shield to produce Test cricketers, but can receipts from sponsorship, television rights etc, continue to make up the losses? The current threat to the legality of certain sponsorships compounds the problem.

Looking on the bright side, 1984-85 produced the best Indian and Pakistan teams of my lifetime, and that is a great gain for the future of cricket in the international sphere. The advance of these two coincided with some lacklustre efforts from England and Australia.

Lovers of cricket will find in the pages of *Wisden* plenty of evidence that cricket has had its problems for a century past. Things have not changed much. Problems are still there – they are just different. It remains for players and administrators to accept the challenge to keep cricket alive and vibrant, and not to shrink from the decisions needed to ensure that end.

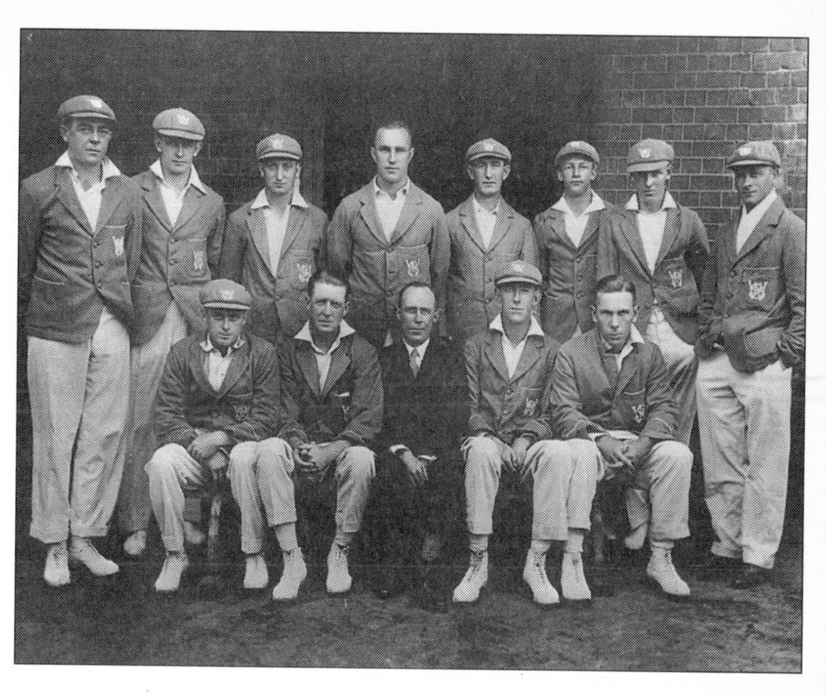

Match Records

1927-28

1927-28

Important alterations in the rules of the Sheffield Shield competition were in operation during the season of 1927-28. It was made clear during Queensland's first year in the tournament that, to enable the programme to be adhered to, a time limit was necessary, and the rules were altered to provide that matches should be restricted to four full days and a portion of the fifth day. Moreover, a system of scoring by points was adopted and instead of Queensland and South Australia, as previously, meeting once each year, all the States had to play each other twice. So far as can be judged as the result of one season, the innovations have been beneficial to the game. ...

From 'Cricket in Australia: The Inter-State Matches'

SOUTH AUSTRALIA v NEW SOUTH WALES 1 (1, 2)

Played at Adelaide, December 16, 17, 19, 20, [21, 1927]. A keenly fought match ended in exciting fashion, South Australia, despite some splendid bowling by McNamee, getting home by one wicket. Bradman joined the select band of cricketers who have made a century in their first Sheffield Shield match ...

[The nineteen-year-old Bradman came into the New South Wales team for his first-class debut when Archie Jackson, suffering from a boil on his knee, was named as twelfth man.]

New South Wales

N. E. Phillips b Whitfield	112	–	lbw b Grimmett	11
G. Morgan b Scott	11	–	b Grimmett	34
T. J. E. Andrews c Williams b Grimmett	58	–	b Scott	20
*A. F. Kippax c Alexander b Williams	143	–	c and b Grimmett	0
A. Scanes c Williams b Schneider	44	–	c Whitfield b Grimmett	26
† W. A. Oldfield c Hack b Grimmett	12	–	c Richardson b Grimmett	4
D. Bradman c Williams b Scott	118	–	b Grimmett	33
F. Jordon lbw b Scott	1	–	lbw b Grimmett	0
S. C. Everett st Hack b Grimmett	5	–	c Harris b Scott	8
A. A. Mailey b Scott	0	–	c Schneider b Grimmett	5
R. L. A. McNamee not out	1	–	not out	1
B 2, l-b 5, w 1, n-b 6	14		B 1, l-b 1, w 1, n-b 5	8
	519			**150**

South Australia bowling: *First innings*—Scott 19.6–1–99–4; Whitfield 17–3–43–1; Grimmett 31–1–160–3; Williams 11–0–70–1; Lee 17–1–76–0; Schneider 6–0–39–1; Alexander 3–0–14–0; Johnson 1–0–4–0. *Second innings*—Scott 17–3–46–2; Whitfield 7–1–26–0; Grimmett 21.7–5–57–8; Williams 2–0–13–0.

South Australia

K.J. Schneider, G.W. Harris, *V.Y. Richardson, W.C. Alexander, E. A. Johnson, H.E.P. Whitfield, †A. Hack, P.K. Lee, C.V. Grimmett, J.D. Scott and N.L. Williams.

First innings: 481 (Schneider 108, Harris 77, Richardson 80, Alexander 42, Hack 45, Grimmett 43 not out; Everett three for 92, Mailey three for 143). *Second innings:* Nine for 189 (Alexander 49, Grimmett 32; McNamee five for 53).

Umpires: G.A. Hele and J.J. Quinn

VICTORIA v NEW SOUTH WALES 2 (3, 4)

Played at Melbourne, December 23, 24, 26, 27 [1927]. Victoria won by 222 runs, largely owing to Ponsford and Woodfull, their first-wicket batsmen, but the great performance of the match was that of McNamee of New South Wales, who, tall and of medium pace, took seven wickets for 77 – the finest achievement in bowling during the season. ... Woodfull ... was prompted to close the second Victoria innings – an action in a second innings taken for the first time in the history of the competition.

[By following his 437 against Queensland a week earlier with 202 in Victoria's first innings, Ponsford became the first batsman to score successive double-centuries in Australia.]

Victoria

W.H. Ponsford, *W.M. Woodfull, H.L. Hendry, A.E.V. Hartkopf, J. Scaife, A.E. Liddicut, C. Sindrey, †J.L. Ellis, D.D. Blackie, F.L. Morton and H. Ironmonger.

First innings: 355 (Ponsford 202, Woodfull 99; McNamee seven for 77, Mailey three for 117). *Second innings:* Seven for 386 dec (Ponsford 38, Woodfull 191 not out, Hendry 59, Scaife 54; Everett three for 66).

New South Wales

N. E. Phillips b Ironmonger	26	–	b Morton	4
G. Morgan lbw b Ironmonger	93	–	lbw b Morton	4
T. J. E. Andrews b Ironmonger	110	–	c Hartkopf b Morton	53
*A. F. Kippax lbw b Morton	26	–	lbw b Blackie	35
A. Jackson c Woodfull b Blackie	6	–	lbw b Blackie	16
D. Bradman lbw b Hartkopf	31	–	b Blackie	5
A. Scanes b Ironmonger	3	–	lbw b Blackie	1
†W. A. Oldfield not out	30	–	not out	11
S. C. Everett lbw b Blackie	10	–	c Hendry b Ironmonger	13
A. A. Mailey c Woodfull b Ironmonger	8	–	c and b Blackie	0
R. L. A. McNamee b Blackie	1	–	c Hendry b Blackie	0
B 11, l-b 7, w 1, n-b 4	23		B 4, l-b 4, n-b 2	10
	367			**152**

Victoria bowling: *First innings*—Morton 13–1–41–1; Liddicut 8–1–23–0; Blackie 26.2–3–103–3; Hendry 3–0–17–0; Ironmonger 34–5–108–5; Hartkopf 10–0–52–1. *Second innings*—Morton 10–0–52–3; Blackie 11.6–3–32–6; Ironmonger 12–0–58–1.

Umpires: J. Richards and D. Elder

NEW SOUTH WALES v QUEENSLAND 3 (5, 6)

Played at Sydney, December 31 [1927], January 2, 3, 4, 5 [1928]. Recovering splendidly after following on 417 in arrear, Queensland went very near to victory, New South Wales, with eight second innings wickets down, being 127 behind at the finish. Kippax played his highest innings in first-class cricket ... When New South Wales had to bat again on a pitch damaged by rain, Nothling made a great effort to force a win against time ...

[Queenslanders Rowe and Higgins followed first-ball dismissals in the first innings with centuries in the second innings.]

New South Wales

N. E. Phillips c Hurwood b Bensted	17	–	lbw b Nothling	29
J. M. Gregory c and b Nothling	63	–	run out	0
T. J. E. Andrews b Hurwood	41	–	b Nothling	11
*A. F. Kippax not out	315	–	c O'Connor b Nothling	9
A. Ratcliffe c O'Connor b Nothling	25	–	b Nothling	0
A. Jackson c O'Connor b Bensted	19	–	c O'Connor b Hurwood	9
G. Morgan c O'Connor b Bensted	121	–	c Gough b Thompson	12
D. Bradman b Gough	0	–	c O'Connor b Nothling	13
†H. S. Love b Rowe	26	–	not out	13
E. O'Brien b Gough	6	–	not out	0
R. L. A. McNamee st O'Connor b Gough	1			
B 2, w 1, n-b 2	5		B 2, l-b 1, n-b 1	4
	639		(eight wkts)	**100**

Queensland bowling: *First innings*—Bensted 27–1–126–3; Hurwood 27–4–118–1; Nothling 28–3–109–2; Gill 8–0–57–0; Thompson 17–1–68–0; Gough 16.5–0–100–3; Rowe 13–1–56–1. *Second innings*—Bensted 2–0–4–0; Hurwood 18–4–40–1; Nothling 21–7–39–5; Gill 1–0–1–0; Thompson 4–1–5–1; Gough 2–1–3–0; Rowe 2–0–4–0.

Queensland

L. L. Gill, L. E. Oxenham, W. Rowe, F. C. Thompson, L. Litster, O. E. Nothling, *†L. P. D. O'Connor, F. J. Gough, R. L. Higgins, E. Bensted and A. C. Hurwood.

First innings: 276 (Litster 82, Nothling 74, O'Connor 37; Phillips four for 26). *Second innings:* 590 (Higgins 179, Bensted 38, Thompson 68, Rowe 147, O'Connor 32, Oxenham 50, Gough 42; Bradman two for 41).

Umpires: A. Williams and S. Parsons

NEW SOUTH WALES v SOUTH AUSTRALIA 4 (7, 8)

Played at Sydney, January 6, 7, 9, 10 [1928]. In this match, Jackson of New South Wales enjoyed the distinction of making two separate hundreds. ... Another important factor in a New South Wales victory by 118 runs was the fast bowling of Nicholls.

New South Wales

H. C. Steele b Scott	14	–	b Scott	5
A. Jackson c McKay b Wall	131	–	b Grimmett	122
T. J. E. Andrews b Wall	44	–	lbw b Scott	2
*A. F. Kippax c Wall b Lee	17	–	lbw b McKay	58
A. Ratcliffe c Richardson b Grimmett	10	–	c Hack b Scott	30
D. Bradman c and b McKay	2	–	st Hack b Grimmett	73
F. Jordan c Alexander b Wall	12	–	b Grimmett	31
C. O. Nicholls b Scott	18	–	st Hack b Grimmett	5
A. A. Mailey st Hack b Grimmett	1	–	b Scott	7
†H. Davidson c Hack b Wall	10	–	b Scott	2
R. L. A. McNamee not out	0	–	not out	4
B 14, l-b 8, w 7, n-b 3	32		B 15, l-b 8, w 3, n-b 3	29
	291			**368**

South Australia bowling: *First innings*—Scott 13–2–57–2; Wall 17–3–51–4; Lee 2–0–15–1; Grimmett 24–1–106–2; McKay 7–0–30–1. *Second innings*—Scott 22.2–2–108–5; Wall 11–2–51–0; Lee 2–0–18–0; Grimmett 26–0–137–4; McKay 1–0–4–0.

South Australia

K.J. Schneider, G.W. Harris, *V.Y. Richardson, A.J. Ryan, †A. Hack, C.V. Grimmett, W. C. Alexander, D.G. McKay, P.K. Lee, J.D. Scott and T. Wall.

First innings: 248 (Ryan 41, Hack 50, Grimmett 54, Alexander 58; Nicholls five for 115, Bradman none for 11). *Second innings:* 293 (Schneider 54, Richardson 86, McKay 40, Lee 30; Nicholls four for 84, Mailey three for 113).

Umpires: G. Borwick and W. Bowes

NEW SOUTH WALES v VICTORIA 5 (9, 10)

Played at Sydney, January 26, 27, 28, 30, 31 [1928]. The return match between these States furnished a new Shield [and Australian] record in the making of eight individual hundreds, and so great was the mastery of the batting that during four and a half days 1,513 runs were scored and only twenty-nine wickets fell.

[The match, which was drawn, 'drew a record attendance of 67,615 people and produced a "gate" of over £4,606'.]

New South Wales

J. M. Gregory lbw b Morton	12	–	c Ryder b a'Beckett	4
A. Jackson c Hendry b a'Beckett	11	–	b Blackie	44
T. J. E. Andrews c and b Morton	4	–	b Blackie	32
*A. F. Kippax b a'Beckett	134	–	b Blackie	42
G. Morgan b Blackie	110	–	c and b Blackie	0
D. Bradman st Ellis b Blackie	7	–	not out	134
N. E. Phillips lbw b a'Beckett	0	–	b Morton	2
†W. A. Oldfield c sub b a'Beckett	101	–	b Blackie	49
C. O. Nicholls b a'Beckett	110	–	c Rigg b Blackie	18
A. A. Mailey b a'Beckett	12	–	not out	11
R. L. A. McNamee not out	8			
B 16, l-b 1, w 1, n-b 6	24		B 9, l-b 4, w 2, n-b 2	17
	533		(eight wkts dec)	**353**

Victoria bowling: *First innings*—Morton 26–0–175–2; a'Beckett 32.6–3–119–6; Blackie 41–10–128–2; Ironmonger 19–4–67–0; Hendry 5–0–20–0. *Second innings*—Morton 12–1–55–1; a'Beckett 17–2–63–1; Blackie 29–2–101–6; Ironmonger 21–2–80–0; Hendry 5–1–12–0; Ponsford 3–0–25–0.

Victoria

*W. M. Woodfull, W. H. Ponsford, H. L. Hendry, J. Ryder, K. L. Rigg, J. Scaife, E. L. a'Beckett, †J. L. Ellis, D. D. Blackie, F. L. Morton and H. Ironmonger.

First innings: 422 (Woodfull 94, Hendry 138, Ryder 106, Scaife 35 not out; Gregory four for 81, Mailey three for 128). *Second innings:* One for 205 (Woodfull 81 not out, Rigg 110 not out; Bradman none for 14).

Umpires: W.G. French and A. C. Jones

1928-29

1928-29

New South Wales, going through the season without defeat, carried off the Sheffield Shield; they won three games outright and gained first innings points in the three other matches. Naturally, the competition was overshadowed by the tour of the MCC team, and interest in the contests suffered to some extent through States having to take the field without some of their leading players. This state of things, however, had one good result, as it gave opportunity for younger players to be tried out in the best company, and New South Wales, in wresting the trophy from Victoria, owed much to the success of their colts, notably Bradman, Jackson and Fairfax.

Bradman during the season scored 1,690 runs [24 innings – 13 games] in first-class cricket, thereby setting up a new record [previously 1,534 in 27 innings – 14 games by G. A. Faulkner on South Africa's tour of Australia in 1910-11], and in Sheffield Shield matches averaged 148.33. His 340, not out, against Victoria was the highest individual score ever made on the Sydney ground. Moreover, Bradman, making 131 and 133 not out against Queensland at Brisbane, joined the distinguished band of cricketers who have put together two separate centuries in a match. . . .

From 'Cricket in Australia: The Inter-State Matches'

[*Note:* On MCC's tour of Australia, W. R. Hammond also passed Faulkner's mark, scoring 1,553 in 18 innings – 13 games.]

AUSTRALIA v THE REST OF AUSTRALIA 6 (11, 12)

(TEST TRIAL MATCH)

Played at Melbourne, October 19, 20, 22 [1928]. The Trial match gave little help to the Australian Selectors in their task of strengthening the batting for a Test eleven, The Rest failing lamentably at their first attempt and suffering defeat on the third day by an innings and 43 runs. . . .

Rest of Australia

G. W. Harris c Oxenham b Gregory	6	–	st Oldfield b Grimmett	51
†L. P. O'Connor b Oxenham	31	–	b Oxenham	0
A. Jackson c Oldfield b Oxenham	18	–	c and b Grimmett	27
C. Kelleway run out	15	–	lbw b Oxenham	26
*V. Y. Richardson c Hendry b Gregory	5	–	b Oxenham	0
D. G. Bradman c Oldfield b Grimmett	14	–	b Oxenham	5
F. C. Thompson st Oldfield b Grimmett	5	–	c Oldfield b Grimmett	20
Dr O. E. Nothling lbw b Grimmett	8	–	not out	62
C. O. Nicholls lbw b Oxenham	0	–	st Oldfield b Grimmett	47
J. D. Scott b Oxenham	0	–	b Oxenham	1
H. Ironmonger not out	2	–	b Oxenham	4
B 1, l-b 5, n-b 1	7		L-b	1
	111			**244**

Australia bowling: *First innings*—Gregory 11–2–26–2; Blackie 17–8–21–0; Oxenham 17.2–9–28–4; Grimmett 11–3–29–3. *Second innings*—Gregory 9–1–34–0; Blackie 9–0–22–0; Oxenham 19.2–2–62–6; Grimmett 19–1–125–4.

Australia

W. H. Ponsford, H. L. Hendry, T. J. E. Andrews, A. Kippax, R. K. Oxenham, J. Scaife, *W. M. Woodfull, J. M. Gregory, C. V. Grimmett, †W. A. Oldfield and D. D. Blackie.

First innings: 398 (Ponsford 79, Hendry 45, Andrews 44, Kippax 34, Gregory 38, Grimmett 43, Oldfield 58; Kelleway three for 72, Bradman one for 36).

Umpires: J. Richards and P. E. Smith

QUEENSLAND v NEW SOUTH WALES 7 (13, 14)

Played at [Exhibition Ground] Brisbane, October 27, 29, 30, 31, November 1 [1928]. If failing to justify expectations in the Test Trial, Bradman batted so brilliantly in the first of the Sheffield Shield matches that he scored a hundred in each innings. In winning by six wickets, after being 76 behind on the first innings, New South Wales owed nearly everything to Bradman and Hooker, the former making 264 for once out and the latter taking ten wickets for less than 12 runs each. . . . [In their first innings, New South Wales lost their last six wickets for two runs; in their second, needing 399 to win, an] opening partnership of 121 by Jackson and Loder and a third-wicket stand of 185 by Bradman and Kippax brought victory with plenty of time to spare.

Queensland

R. K. Oxenham, *†L. P. O'Connor, F. J. Gough, W. Rowe, F. C. Thompson, R. Higgins, Dr O. E. Nothling, E. Knowles, E. C. Bensted, P. M. Hornibrook and H. M. Thurlow.

First innings: 324 (O'Connor 72, Gough 67, Higgins 58, Bensted 36 not out; Hooker six for 46, Morgan three for 36). *Second innings:* 322 (Gough 39, Thompson 158 not out, Knowles 30, Higgins 33; Hooker four for 72).

New South Wales

A. Jackson c Hornibrook b Nothling	50	–	c Nothling b Rowe	71
R. Loder b Thurlow	1	–	run out	49
D. G. Bradman c O'Connor b Thurlow	131	–	not out	133
*A. F. Kippax b Thurlow	47	–	c Hornibrook b Rowe	96
G. Morgan lbw b Thurlow	4	–	b Thurlow	6
†H. S. B. Love c O'Connor b Thurlow	5	–	not out	31
C. O. Nicholls b Thurlow	2			
H. Hooker b Oxenham	0			
J. Carter lbw b Oxenham	0			
N. Campbell b Oxenham	0			
R. McNamee not out	0			
L-b 4, n-b 4	8		B 11, l-b 3, n-b 1	15
	248		(four wkts)	**401**

Queensland bowling: *First innings*—Hornibrook 12–2–52–0; Thurlow 15–3–59–6; Oxenham 18.2–3–56–3; Nothling 8–1–22–1; Rowe 5–0–15–0; Bensted 6–0–30–0; Thompson 1–0–6–0. *Second innings*—Hornibrook 20.4–3–62–0; Thurlow 21–2–94–1; Oxenham 29–2–77–0; Nothling 13–0–52–0; Rowe 11–3–45–2; Bensted 9–0–35–0; Thompson 8–3–21–0.

Umpires: J. P. Orr and J. A. Scott

MCC TEAM v NEW SOUTH WALES 8 (15, 16)

Played at Sydney, Friday, Saturday, Monday, Tuesday, November 9, 10, 12, 13 [1928]. The match with New South Wales was ... drawn, 1,447 runs being scored while only twenty wickets went down. MCC put together the great total of 734 ... [their highest score in first-class matches at the time. The fourth-wicket stand of 333 between Hammond and Hendren] was the highest stand ever made for any wicket against New South Wales. Hendren, having twice driven Bradman over the sight-screen for 6, was caught in the long field off the next ball. ... New South Wales lost three wickets for 52 [by stumps on Saturday: the third wicket fell at 38] but on the Monday, Kippax, Bradman and Kelleway played uncommonly well. The first two added 90 for the fourth wicket, while Bradman and Kelleway put on 68. Bradman, who hit to leg and drove very hard, survived two or three appeals for leg-before before Freeman, with whom he was never comfortable, bowled him round his legs. ... Following on 385 behind, New South Wales had three men out for 115 soon after lunch on the last day, but no further success fell to the English bowlers, Kippax and Bradman each making a hundred and adding 249 in rather more than two and a half hours. The batting during this time was extremely good, Kippax showing his finest form in cutting and driving and Bradman playing much better than in the first innings.

MCC Team

H. Sutcliffe, Mr D. R. Jardine, E. Tyldesley, W. R. Hammond, E. Hendren, M. Leyland, †L. Ames, *Mr A. P. F. Chapman, M. W. Tate, H. Larwood and A. P. Freeman.

First innings: Seven for 734 dec (Sutcliffe 67, Jardine 140, Hammond 225, Hendren 167, Leyland 47 not out; Bradman one for 55 off five overs).

New South Wales

G. Morgan b Hammond	1	–	c Ames b Larwood	18
A. Jackson b Tate	4	–	run out	40
T. J. E. Andrews c Chapman b Tate	14	–	b Tate	19
*A. F. Kippax lbw b Hammond	64	–	not out	136
D. G. Bradman b Freeman	87	–	not out	132
C. E. Kelleway not out	93			
J. M. Gregory st Ames b Tate	7			
†W. A. Oldfield c Ames b Freeman	33			
C. O. Nicholls c Jardine b Freeman	26			
H. Hooker c Hammond b Freeman	14			
N. Campbell c Chapman b Freeman	0			
B 3, l-b 3	6		B 14, l-b 5	19
	349		(three wkts)	**364**

MCC Team bowling: *First innings*—Tate 28–3–98–3; Hammond 17–3–64–2; Freeman 37.2–3–136–5; Larwood 4–1–10–0; Leyland 12–1–35–0; *Second innings*—Tate 15–2–36–1; Hammond 15–0–73–0; Freeman 25–3–81–0; Larwood 16–5–33–1; Leyland 12–1–61–0; Jardine 3–0–22–0; Hendren 5–0–21–0; Sutcliffe 4–1–18–0.

Umpires: W. Bowes and A. C. Jones

MCC TEAM v AN AUSTRALIAN XI 9 (17, 18)

Played at Sydney, Friday, Saturday, Monday, Tuesday, November 16, 17, 19, 20 [1928]. In a match of comparatively modest scoring, the MCC gained by eight wickets their first victory of the tour – over an Australian Eleven drawn, with the exception of Nothling of Queensland, entirely from New South Wales and South Australia. [Victoria felt that the expenses of £1 per day were not sufficient.] Larwood, Tate and White all bowled admirably in dismissing the Australian Eleven in less than four hours and a half for 231. Andrews gave promise of doing well ... but until Bradman went in, no real resistance was offered to the attack. Bettington, who after some years in England had returned to Australia by the same vessel as that on which the English cricketers travelled, made some good cuts in a useful innings, and in the end Bradman took out his bat after a stay of three hours and twenty minutes. ...

Australian XI

*V. Y. Richardson b White	24	–	c Geary b Larwood	21
G. W. Harris b Larwood	19	–	b White	56
T. J. E. Andrews b White	39	–	c Hobbs b Geary	25
A. Jackson c Geary b Larwood	14	–	c Duckworth b Tate	61
D. G. Bradman not out	58	–	lbw b Tate	18
G. Morgan c Duckworth b Tate	15	–	b Geary	9
Dr O. E. Nothling c Sutcliffe b White	11	–	not out	29
Dr R. H. Bettington c Hendren b Geary	34	–	b Larwood	8
†W. A. Oldfield c Hendren b Tate	0	–	run out	7
J. D. Scott c Hendren b Larwood	5	–	b Tate	0
H. Hooker c Larwood b Tate	2	–	c Hendren b Geary	1
W	1		B 3, l-b 4, w 1	8
	231			**243**

MCC Team bowling: *First innings*—Larwood 18–1–80–3; Tate 16.7–4–38–3; Geary 13–1–65–1; White 28–8–47–3. *Second innings*—Larwood 19–0–81–2; Tate 22–2–65–3; Geary 14.1–4–42–3; White 19–5–47–1.

MCC Team

J.B. Hobbs, H. Sutcliffe, Mr D.R. Jardine, C.P. Mead, E. Tyldesley, E. Hendren, H. Larwood, M.W. Tate, *Mr J.C. White, G. Geary and †G. Duckworth.

First innings: 357 (Hobbs 58, Sutcliffe 42, Mead 58, Tyldesley 69, Tate 59, Geary 33; Nothling three for 61, Bettington three for 98). *Second innings:* Two for 118 (Hobbs 67 not out, Sutcliffe 31).

Umpires: W.G. French and S. Parsons

ENGLAND v AUSTRALIA 10 (19, 20)

(FIRST TEST MATCH) 1 (1, 2)

Played at [Exhibition Ground] Brisbane, Friday, Saturday, Monday, Tuesday, Wednesday, November 30, December 1, 3, 4, 5 [1928]. Having by now run into first-rate all-round form, England entered upon the opening Test Match with feelings of confidence, but not even the most sanguine member of the team could have anticipated that they would gain a victory by such an astounding margin as that of 675 runs – easily the most pronounced success by runs in the history of Test Matches. ... Australia relied largely upon tried men, Bradman being the one youngster to secure inclusion. On paper, their eleven appeared quite formidable ... All ideas on this point were upset by the damage to Gregory [knee injury] and Kelleway's indisposition [food poisoning]. ...

[In their second innings] Australia's wretched position was made hopeless by heavy rain during the night followed in the morning by bright sunshine. ... The last six wickets – the two invalids being still unable to bat – went down in fifty minutes, Australia being all out for 66. Woodfull, batting splendidly, received no support at all, nearly everyone who joined him hitting out wildly immediately on going in. ...

England

J.B. Hobbs, H. Sutcliffe, C.P. Mead, W.R. Hammond, Mr D.R. Jardine, E. Hendren, *Mr A.P.F. Chapman, M.W. Tate, H. Larwood, Mr J.C. White and †G. Duckworth.

First innings: 521 (Hobbs 49, Sutcliffe 38, Hammond 44, Jardine 35, Hendren 169, Chapman 50, Larwood 70; Gregory three for 142, Grimmett three for 167). *Second innings:* Eight for 342 dec (Sutcliffe 32, Mead 73, Jardine 65 not out, Hendren 45, Larwood 37; Grimmett six for 131).

Australia

W. M. Woodfull c Chapman b Larwood	0	–	not out	30
W. H. Ponsford b Larwood	2	–	c Duckworth b Larwood	6
A. F. Kippax c and b Tate	16	–	c and b Larwood	15
H. L. Hendry lbw b Larwood	30	–	c Larwood b White	6
C. E. Kelleway b Larwood	8	–	absent ill	0
*J. Ryder c Jardine b Larwood	33	–	c Larwood b Tate	1
D. G. Bradman lbw b Tate	18	–	c Chapman b White	1
†W. A. Oldfield lbw b Tate	2	–	c Larwood b Tate	5
C. V. Grimmett not out	7	–	c Chapman b White	1
H. Ironmonger b Larwood	4	–	c Chapman b White	0
J. M. Gregory absent hurt	0	–	absent hurt	0
B 1, l-b 1	2		N-b	1
	122			**66**

England bowling: *First innings*—Larwood 14.4–4–32–6; Tate 21–6–50–3; Hammond 15–5–38–0. *Second innings*—Larwood 7–0–30–2; Tate 11–3–26–2; Hammond 1–0–2–0; White 6.3–2–7–4.

Umpires: D. Elder and G. A. Hele

VICTORIA v NEW SOUTH WALES 11 (21, 22)

Played at Melbourne, December 22, 24, 25, 26, 27 [1928]. Putting on 307 for the last wicket – a world's record – Kippax and Hooker resisted the Victoria attack for more than five hours and were clearly responsible for New South Wales gaining a first innings lead. ... Hooker played fine, defensive cricket while Kippax – at the wickets from late Monday afternoon until after midday on Wednesday – batted with such delightful ease and effect that the whole aspect of the game was altered. ...

Victoria

H. L. Hendry, F. Baring, *J. Ryder, K. Rigg, R. Ellis, J. Scaife, E. a'Beckett, †J. L. Ellis, H. I. Ebeling, W. J. Rayson and H. Ironmonger.

First innings: 376 (Ryder 175, a'Beckett 113; Hooker three for 100). *Second innings:* Six for 251 dec (Baring 30, a'Beckett 95, Hendry 69 not out; Fairfax three for 45).

New South Wales

A. Jackson c J. Ellis b Ironmonger	19			
A. Fairfax c Ironmonger b a'Beckett	2	–	b R. Ellis	30
T. J. E. Andrews b Hendry	33			
*A. F. Kippax not out	260			
D. G. Bradman b Hendry	1	–	not out	71
C. Kelleway b Hendry	0	–	c a'Beckett b Ironmonger	13
D. Seddon lbw b Ironmonger	0	–	not out	38
†H. S. B. Love lbw b Ebeling	0			
C. O. Nicholls b Ebeling	10			
S. Everett lbw b Ironmonger	20			
H. Hooker c Ryder b a'Beckett	62			
B 5, l-b 6, n-b 2	13		L-b 3, w 1	4
	420		(two wkts)	**156**

Victoria bowling: *First innings*—a'Beckett 29.1–2–92–2; Ebeling 25–1–81–2; Ironmonger 33–4–95–3; Hendry 18–5–58–3; Rayson 7–0–42–0; R. Ellis 10–1–31–0; Baring 5–1–8–0. *Second innings*—a'Beckett 10–3–19–0; Ebeling 4–1–10–0; Ironmonger 8–2–12–1; Rayson 5–0–41–0; R. Ellis 6–1–29–1; Baring 5–0–22–0; Rigg 2–0–19–0.

Umpires: J. Richards and P. E. Smith

ENGLAND v AUSTRALIA 12 (23, 24)
(THIRD TEST MATCH) 2 (3, 4)

Played at Melbourne, Saturday, Monday, Tuesday, Wednesday, Thursday, Friday, Saturday, December 29, 31 [1928], January 1, 2, 3, 4, 5 [1929]. England, having proved successful in the two previous Test games, naturally approached the third with a certain amount of confidence. In the end they won by three wickets, this victory giving them the rubber and the retention of the Ashes. There were many changes of fortune in the course of the great struggle, but scarcely anything in the whole tour approached the long, drawn-out tension of the last innings before the winning hit was made. In ordinary circumstances, little might have been thought of the task of getting 332, but these runs had to be made on a rain-ruined wicket and anybody who knows the Melbourne ground will appreciate the stupendous effort required. ...

England had the same eleven as Sydney, but Australia made further changes, bringing in Bradman, a'Beckett and Oxenham for Ponsford, Nothling and Ironmonger. These alterations undoubtedly made Australia a better combination ... Bradman, with two fine displays of batting, showed what a mistake had been made in leaving him out of the second match. ... [He] helped Ryder to put on 64 in less than an hour [after which he] and a'Beckett added 86 ... Bowled by a yorker at 373, Bradman scored well in front of the wicket, hitting nine 4's during his stay of over three hours. ... On the second day 62,259 people witnessed the play, this being a record attendance for one afternoon. ...

When Australia went in a second time, Richardson again failed, and although Woodfull batted uncommonly well and Kippax helped to add 78, there were four wickets down for 143. England then stood in a good position, but Bradman – nearly bowled by White when seven – assisted Woodfull to put on a valuable 58, and subsequently proceeded to make his first hundred in a Test Match. ... There were seven men out for 252, but Oxenham helped to add 93 at a rate of a run a minute before Bradman's innings closed at 345. Bradman batted over four hours, hit eleven 4's and brought off many splendid drives. ...

The total attendance at the match reached 262,467, the receipts being £22,561 18*s*. The attendance was easily a record.

Australia

W. M. Woodfull c Jardine b Tate	7	–	c Duckworth b Tate	107
V. Y. Richardson c Duckworth b Larwood	3	–	b Larwood	5
H. L. Hendry c Jardine b Larwood	23	–	st Duckworth b White	12
A. F. Kippax c Jardine b Larwood	100	–	b Tate	41
*J. Ryder c Hendren b Tate	112	–	b Geary	5
D. G. Bradman b Hammond	79	–	c Duckworth b Geary	112
†W. A. Oldfield b Geary	3	–	b White	7
E. L. a'Beckett c Duckworth b White	41	–	b White	6
R. K. Oxenham b Geary	15	–	b White	39
C. V. Grimmett c Duckworth b Geary	5	–	not out	4
D. D. Blackie not out	2	–	b White	0
B 4, l-b 3	7		B 6, l-b 7	13
	397			**351**

England bowling: *First innnings*—Larwood 37–3–127–3; Tate 46–17–87–2; Geary 31.5–4–83–3; Hammond 8–4–19–1; White 57–30–64–1; Jardine 1–0–10–0. *Second innings*—Larwood 16–3–37–1; Tate 47–15–70–2; Geary 30–4–94–2; Hammond 16–6–30–0; White 56.5–20–107–5.

England

J. B. Hobbs, H. Sutcliffe, W. R. Hammond, *Mr A. P. F. Chapman, E. Hendren, Mr D. R. Jardine, H. Larwood, G. Geary, M. W. Tate, †G. Duckworth and Mr J. C. White.

First innings: 417 (Sutcliffe 58, Hammond 200, Jardine 62; Blackie six for 94). *Second innings:* Seven for 332 (Hobbs 49, Sutcliffe 135, Jardine 33, Hammond 32, Hendren 45).

Umpires: D. Elder and G. A. Hele

SOUTH AUSTRALIA v NEW SOUTH WALES 13 (25, 26)

Played at Adelaide, January 11, 12, 14, 15, 16 [1929]. Narrowly missing the triumph of two separate hundreds, Jackson particularly distinguished himself in a match which New South Wales won by 60 runs.

New South Wales

D. G. Bradman c Grimmett b Wall	5	–	b Wall	2
T. J. E. Andrews b Wall	32	–	c Richardson b Wall	7
*A. F. Kippax lbw b McKay	107	–	b Wall	7
A. Jackson b Grimmett	162	–	c Grimmett b Carlton	90
A. Fairfax c Hone b Grimmett	36	–	c and b Grimmett	20
D. Seddon c Alexander b Carlton	8	–	b Grimmett	0
C. Andrews lbw b Grimmett	1	–	c Pellew b Wall	87
†W. A. Oldfield c Pellew b Carlton	26	–	c and b Grimmett	48
C. O. Nicholls b Carlton	5	–	c Wall b Williams	29
B. A. Cooper b Carlton	9	–	c Wall b Williams	12
N. Morris not out	2	–	not out	0
B 4, l-b 3, n-b 2	9		B 5, l-b 6	11
	402			**313**

South Australia bowling: *First innings*—Wall 22–2–92–2; Carlton 34–6–95–4; Grimmett 37–4–128–3; Williams 8–0–43–0; Pellew 3–1–15–0; McKay 5–0–20–1. *Second innings*—Wall 24-1–78–4; Carlton 21–3–51–1; Grimmett 32–2–105–3; Williams 11.2–0–52–2; McKay 4–0–16–0.

South Australia

G. W. Harris, *V. Y. Richardson, C. E. Pellew, W. C. Alexander, †A. Hack, B. W. Hone, D.G. McKay, N. L. Williams, C. V. Grimmett, T. W. Wall and T. A. Carlton.

First innings: 304 (Hack 34, Hone 35, Grimmett 71 not out, Wall 43; Nicholls three for 63, Fairfax four for 54). *Second innings:* 351 (Harris 42, Alexander 79, McKay 74, sundries 34; Fairfax three for 82, Bradman none for 22).

Umpires: G. A. Hele and A.G. Jenkins

NEW SOUTH WALES v VICTORIA 14 (27)

Played at Sydney, January 24, 25, 26, 28, 29 [1929]. This proved to be the key match of the competition and New South Wales, taking first innings points, made sure of the Sheffield Shield. Of absorbing interest, the cricket was especially notable for the feat of Bradman, who made 340 not out – the highest score by a New South Wales player in Sheffield Shield games and the highest in a first-class match on the Sydney ground. Bradman batted for roughly eight hours and did not give a chance. ... Hooker and Bettington ... bowled with such success that Victoria had to follow on 448 behind. Hooker actually took four wickets with four balls, his victims being Ebeling, Gamble and Ironmonger in one over, and Austen with his next ball – his first in the second innings. ...

New South Wales

A. Jackson b Ironmonger	41	A. Marks c Lansdown b Darling	56
A. Fairfax b Gamble	104	R. H. Bettington c Austen b Darling	40
D. G. Bradman not out	340	J. Fingleton not out	25
*T. J. E. Andrews lbw b Ironmonger	19	B 11, l-b 15, n-b 2	28
S. McCabe b Gamble	60	(six wkts dec)	**713**

†H. L. Davidson, C. O. Nicholls and H. Hooker did not bat.

Victoria bowling: Gamble 29–1–193–2; Ebeling 39–3–142–0; Ironmonger 56–7–220–2; Darling 18–1–77–2; Scaife 2–0–14–0; Austen 1–0–17–0; Onyons 1–0–22–0.

Victoria

B.A. Onyons, E.T. Austen, J. Scaife, L. Darling, W. Reddrop, H.C. Lansdown, T. Bird, *†J. L. Ellis, H.I. Ebeling, H.S. Gamble and H. Ironmonger.

First innings: 265 (Onyons 61, Scaife 42, Darling 37, Reddrop 33; Hooker six for 42, Bettington three for 92). *Second innings:* Seven for 510 (Onyons 131, Scaife 91, Darling 96, Lansdown 48 not out, Bird 63, sundries 41).

Umpires: A. C. Jones and W. H. Bayfield

ENGLAND v AUSTRALIA — 15 (28, 29)
(FOURTH TEST MATCH) — 3 (5, 6)

Played at Adelaide, Friday, Saturday, Monday, Tuesday, Wednesday, Thursday, Friday, February 1, 2, 4, 5, 6, 7, 8 [1929]. The rubber having been won, the English team had no cause for anxiety beyond the desire to preserve their unbeaten record. Still, they did not exhibit any lack of keenness in the Fourth Test Match which, characterised by very even scoring throughout, had a most exciting finish, England gaining a victory by 12 runs. This success atoned for the defeat on the same ground in the previous tour, when Australia won by 11 runs. England had no reason for changing their eleven, but Australia brought in Jackson for Richardson, the young New South Wales batsman enjoying the distinction of playing a three-figure innings in his first Test Match. Before going further, it is only right to pay a great tribute to his performance. Accomplished, as will be told later, in circumstances calculated to daunt a player of mature experience, it was, in point of style and beauty of execution and stroke-play, the best innings played against the Englishmen during the whole tour. Other achievements made the match memorable. Hammond followed his innings of 251 and 200 at Sydney and Melbourne respectively by making two separate hundreds … and, above all, White, sending down over 124 overs, obtained thirteen wickets for 256 runs, eight of them in the second innings. …

Going in on the second day just before half-past three, Australia made a deplorable start, three wickets falling for 19 runs. … It was then that Jackson revealed his great powers. … Ryder helped him to add 126, Bradman stayed while 82 were put on, and then 60 more came in fifty minutes before his superb innings ended at 287. …

[Needing 349 to win, Australia began their second innings on Wednesday evening, scoring 24 without loss] and on Thursday and Friday there came a fight which will long be remembered by those who saw it. … [When play ended on Thursday] Australia, with six men out for 260, required 89 to win. When, next morning, Bradman and Oxenham carried the score to 308, victory for Australia appeared more than likely. These two had added 50 in 65 minutes. At 320, with Bradman run out [for the only time in his Test career], fortunes changed again. Oldfield hit a ball to cover-point, both batsmen dashing for the run, but Hobbs returned like lightning for Duckworth to put the wicket down. Grimmett stayed for half an hour, but left at 336, Tate at short-leg knocking up the ball from a hard hit and bringing off a great catch. Blackie went in amidst tense excitement and carefully played four balls from White. Then came one pitched just a little shorter; Blackie hooked it high into the long field in front of square-leg where Larwood, running a few yards, brought off a fine catch and finished a wonderful struggle.

England

J.B. Hobbs, H. Sutcliffe, W.R. Hammond, Mr D.R. Jardine, E. Hendren, *Mr A.P.F. Chapman, †G. Duckworth, H. Larwood, G. Geary, M.W. Tate and Mr J.C. White.

First innings: 334 (Hobbs 74, Sutcliffe 64, Hammond 119 not out, Chapman 39; Grimmett five for 102). *Second innings:* 383 (Hammond 177, Jardine 98, Tate 47; Oxenham four for 67).

Australia

W. M. Woodfull c Duckworth b Tate	1	–	c Geary b White	30
A. Jackson lbw b White	164	–	c Duckworth b Geary	36
H. L. Hendry c Duckworth b Larwood	2	–	c Tate b White	5
A. F. Kippax b White	3	–	c Hendren b White	51
†J. Ryder lbw b White	63	–	c and b White	87
D. G. Bradman c Larwood b Tate	40	–	run out	58
E. L. a'Beckett b White	36	–	c Hammond b White	21
R. K. Oxenham c Chapman b White	15	–	c Chapman b White	12
*W. A. Oldfield b Tate	32	–	not out	15
C. V. Grimmett b Tate	4	–	c Tate b White	9
D. D. Blackie not out	3	–	c Larward b White	0
L-b 5, w 1	6		B 9, l-b 3	12
	369			**336**

England bowling: *First innings*—Larwood 37–6–92–1; Tate 42–10–77–4; White 60–16–130–5; Geary 12–3–32–0; Hammond 9–1–32–0. *Second innings*—Larwood 20–4–60–0; Tate 37–9–75–0; White 64.5–21–126–8; Geary 16–2–42–1; Hammond 14–3–21–0.

Umpires: D. Elder and G. A. Hele

MCC TEAM v NEW SOUTH WALES 16 (30)

Played at Sydney, Friday, Saturday, Monday, Tuesday, February 15, 16, 18, 19 [1929]. The return match with New South Wales – like the first, left drawn – was quite spoiled by rain. A very heavy downpour prevented cricket on Friday and the match did not start until three o'clock on Saturday afternoon. Few people, indeed, expected cricket to be possible even then, but the ground made a good recovery. Some of the English team had become scattered, but fortunately they were got together in time. ... More rain came on the Tuesday and, cricket being impossible, the game was at once given up.

New South Wales

A. Jackson lbw b Tate	5	†W. A. Oldfield not out	3
A. Fairfax c Tyldesley b Tate	40	H. Hooker lbw b White	3
T. J. E. Andrews c and b White	2	C. Morris c sub b White	4
*A. F. Kippax c Tate b Geary	17	R. L. McNamee c Mead b White	0
D. G. Bradman c Tyldesley b White	15	B 9, l-b 2	11
A. Marks b Freeman	17		**128**
S. McCabe b Freeman	11		

MCC Team bowling: Tate 10–2–21–2; White 23.5–8–48–5; Geary 9–3–16–1; Freeman 13–3–32–2.

MCC team

J. B. Hobbs, M. Leyland, E. Tyldesley, C. P. Mead, *Mr A. P. F. Chapman, †L. Ames, M. W. Tate, G. Geary, Mr J. C. White, A. P. Freeman and H. Sutcliffe.

First innings: Four for 144 (Hobbs 39, Tyldesley 68 not out; Fairfax three for 36).

Umpires: W. H. Bayfield and A. C. Jones

NEW SOUTH WALES v SOUTH AUSTRALIA 17 (31, 32)

Played at Sydney, March 1, 2, 4, 5, 6 [1929]. This match had a most exciting finish, South Australia – set 446 to get – losing by only 60 runs. ... Bradman was seen at his best when New South Wales went in for the second time. ... Davidson and Walker both 'kept' admirably. Davidson caught six and stumped three and Walker [making his first-class debut] caught three and stumped five, so that between them they had a hand in taking seventeen wickets.

New South Wales

A. Fairfax lbw b Grimmett	17	–	st Walker b Grimmett	41
A. Jackson c Walker b Scott	6	–	st Walker b Grimmett	38
D. G. Bradman c Walker b Grimmett	35	–	c Walker b Carlton	175
*T. J. E. Andrews c Carlton b Whitfield	0	–	b Wall	23
S. McCabe c Grimmett b Wall	5	–	c Scott b Alexander	27
A. Marks run out	92	–	lbw b Grimmett	26
†H. Davidson run out	16	–	b Grimmett	13
F. Jordon st Walker b Grimmett	65	–	not out	19
H. Hooker st Walker b Grimmett	62	–	st Walker b Grimmett	6
W. Lampe c Richardson b Whitfield	3	–	run out	17
N. Morris not out	8			
B 7, l-b 7, w 1, n-b 2	17		B 5, l-b 3, w 1, n-b 5	14
	326		(nine wkts dec)	**399**

South Australia bowling: *First innings*—Wall 17–1–64–1; Scott 10–1–62–1; Whitfield 16–3–47–2; Grimmett 27–1–112–4; Carlton 6–0–24–0. *Second innings*—Wall 17–0–59–1; Scott 11–2–61–0; Whitfield 13–2–69–0; Grimmett 26.4–1–116–5; Carlton 18–2–47–1; Hack 4–0–23–0; Alexander 1–0–10–1.

South Australia

*V. Y. Richardson, G. W. Harris, A. Hack, H. E. P. Whitfield, †C. W. Walker, W. C. Alexander, P. M. Hutton, C. V. Grimmett, T. W. Wall, J. D. Scott and T. A. Carlton.

First innings: 280 (Harris 107, Grimmett 43; Hooker three for 73, Andrews four for 34). *Second innings:* 385 (Harris 94, Hack 79, Richardson 56, Whitfield 91; Fairfax four for 55, Bradman one for 26).

Umpires: A. C. Jones and A. H. Farrow

ENGLAND v AUSTRALIA 18 (33, 34)
(FIFTH TEST MATCH) 4 (7, 8)

Played at Melbourne, Friday, Saturday, Monday, Tuesday, Wednesday, Thursday, Friday, Saturday, March 8, 9, 11, 12, 13, 14, 15, 16 [1929]. Lasting eight days – the greatest duration of any Test Match [at that time] – the concluding representative engagement saw Australia successful by five wickets. ... Judged from the English standpoint, the cricket all through proved dreadfully slow, but such keenness characterised the spectators – every ball being closely followed – that the rate of scoring was not noticed. ...

Australia did well to reply [to England's first innings of 519] with a total of 491. Their batting was very sound throughout, the honours being carried off by Woodfull and Bradman. ... Fourth out at 203, Woodfull, with three 4's as his chief strokes, batted nearly five hours and a half. Then followed the stand which put Australia almost on terms, Bradman and Fairfax scoring 183 together for the fifth wicket in three hours and a half. Bradman put together a delightful innings of three hours and a half's duration, his stroke-play being remarkable, and his driving very powerful, well kept down and nicely placed. He hit eight 4's. ... Geary, bowling 81 overs – [at the time] a record for a Test Match – had a fine record, and on the fifth day actually obtained his five wickets for 51 runs. When the Australian innings ceased, play had lasted eighteen hours and twenty-seven minutes for 1,010 runs....

[On the second Saturday of the match, Australia having set out late on Thursday to attain a target of 286] two incidences occurred which probably affected the result. In the first case, Bradman, when five, gave a chance of stumping while Ryder, at 27, had his wicket thrown down by Leyland, who had run behind the bowler from mid-off. It was the general opinion that Ryder was at least a yard out, but to the obvious surprise and chagrin of the Englishmen, Jones, the umpire, gave the batsman in. The score at lunch was 248 and, in about twenty minutes afterwards, the remaining runs were hit off without further loss. Both Bradman and Ryder batted very well.

England

J.B. Hobbs, Mr D.R. Jardine, W.R. Hammond, E. Tyldesley, †G. Duckworth, E. Hendren, M. Leyland, H. Larwood, G. Geary, M.W. Tate and *Mr J.C. White.

First innings: 519 (Hobbs 142, Hammond 38, Tyldesley 31, Hendren 95, Leyland 137; Wall three for 123, Hornibrook three for 142). *Second innings:* 257 (Hobbs 65, Leyland 53 not out, Tate 54; Wall five for 66).

Australia

W. M. Woodfull c Geary b Larwood	102	–	b Hammond	35
A. Jackson run out	30	–	b Geary	46
A. F. Kippax c Duckworth b White	38	–	run out	28
J. Ryder c Tate b Hammond	30	–	not out	57
D. G. Bradman c Tate b Geary	123	–	not out	37
A. Fairfax lbw b Geary	65			
R. K. Oxenham c Duckworth b Geary	7			
W. A. Oldfield c and b Geary	6	–	b Hammond	48
C. V. Grimmett not out	38			
T. W. Wall c Duckworth b Geary	9			
P. M. Hornibrook lbw b White	26	–	b Hammond	18
B 6, l-b 9, w 2	17		B 12, l-b 6	18
	491		(five wkts)	**287**

England bowling: *First innings*—Larwood 34–7–83–1; Tate 62–26–108–0; Geary 81–36–105–5; White 75.3–22–136–2; Hammond 16–3–31–1; Leyland 3–0–11–0. *Second innings*—Larwood 32.1–5–85–0; Tate 38–13–72–0; Geary 20–5–31–1; White 18–8–28–0; Hammond 26–8–53–3.

Umpires: G.A. Hele and A.C. Jones

1929-30

1929-30

A lack of good bowlers to support A. Fairfax largely accounted for the inability of New South Wales to retain the Shield, but a wealth of batting talent was available and, in D.G. Bradman, the outstanding batsman of Australia. For all first-class matches, Bradman had an aggregate of 1,586 runs and an average of 113.28. He made cricket history with a wonderful score of 452 not out – the highest individual innings ever played – against Queensland at Sydney. . . .

Partly as a result of wet weather the receipts from the Sheffield Shield games generally showed a decided falling-off, but the New South Wales v Queensland match at Sydney brought in £1,088 as compared with £141 in 1928-29.

From 'Cricket in Australia: The Inter-State Matches'

QUEENSLAND v NEW SOUTH WALES 19 (35, 36)

Played at [Exhibition Ground] Brisbane, November 8, 9, 11, 12 [1929]. Despite fine all-round play by Oxenham, who in the course of the match scored 166 and took six wickets for 113, New South Wales won the first of the Sheffield Shield games by 23 runs. . . . New South Wales in their second innings did not repeat their previous batting success. Indeed, against skilful bowling by Hornibrook and Brew, half the side were out for 73. Bradman and Marks alone played with real skill. . . .

New South Wales

A. Fairfax lbw b Oxenham	49	–	lbw b Oxenham	21
A. Jackson c O'Connor b Oxenham	80	–	c Amos b Hornibrook	7
D. G. Bradman run out	48	–	c O'Connor b Brew	66
C. Andrews lbw b Amos	40	–	lbw b Amos	12
S. McCabe c Brew b Oxenham	77	–	b Hornibrook	3
Dr R. H. Bettington c O'Connor b Oxenham	9	–	c Nothling b Hornibrook	8
A. Marks c Brew b Amos	46	–	c O'Connor b Hornibrook	51
*†W. A. Oldfield run out	3	–	lbw b Brew	7
H. Hooker c O'Connor b Amos	2	–	not out	6
A. A. Mailey not out	4	–	c and b Brew	0
F. H. Dupain c Levy b Oxenham	10	–	b Brew	6
B 2, l-b 3	5		B 4, l-b 7	11
	373			**198**

Queensland bowling: *First innings*—Hornibrook 17–4–51–0; Amos 20–2–98–3; Brew 13–0–88–0; Oxenham 25–3–72–5; Bensted 5–0–17–0; Nothling 16–4–42–0. *Second innings*—Hornibrook 19–6–43–4; Amos 11–1–45–1; Brew 14–2–31–4; Oxenham 28–12–41–1; Nothling 9–1–27–0.

Queensland

R.M. Levy, †L.P. O'Connor, R.J. Higgins, R.K. Oxenham, V. Goodwin, *Dr O.E. Nothling, F.J. Gough, F.M. Brew, E.C. Bensted, G. Amos and P.M. Hornibrook.

First innings: 273 (O'Connor 35, Oxenham 49, Gough 69; Fairfax three for 47, Hooker three for 38, Mailey three for 103). *Second innings:* 275 (Oxenham 117; Fairfax three for 47, McCabe three for 41).

Umpires: J.P. Orr and J.A. Scott

MCC TEAM v NEW SOUTH WALES 20 (37)

Played at Sydney, November 22, 23, 25, 26 [1929]. To such an extent did the bat beat the ball in this match that 1,607 runs were scored for the loss of twenty-two wickets. Kippax twice declared but did not allow sufficient time for his bowlers to have much chance of winning the game and, with a draw inevitable, the last part of the cricket was not taken seriously. ... Handicapped [by illness and injury] the MCC attack underwent heavy punishment for seven hours. Jackson and Bradman added 117, Bradman and Kippax put on 149, and on the second day Allsopp and McCabe raised a partnership to 185. Bradman made 157 out of 266 obtained during his stay of less than three hours. Allsopp started his first-class career with almost equal freedom in scoring the third century of the innings. ...

New South Wales

A. Fairfax lbw b Allom	14	–	lbw b Worthington	19
A. Jackson c Benson b Allom	49	–	not out	168
D. G. Bradman b Worthington	157			
*A. F. Kippax c Dawson b Bowley	108			
A. Marks c and b Bowley	38	–	lbw b Woolley	26
A. Allsopp c Turnbull b Allom	117	–	not out	63
S. McCabe b Worthington	90			
C. Andrews not out	11	–	c and b Woolley	17
†W. A. Oldfield c Duleepsinhji b Worthington	3			
J. E. H. Hooker not out	6			
Byes, etc	36		Byes, etc.	12
(eight wkts dec)	**629**		(three wkts dec)	**305**

F. H. Dupain did not bat.

MCC Team bowling: *First innings*—Barratt 30–1–130–0; Allom 27–1–127–3; Worthington 24–1–151–3; Bowley 13.3–0–80–2; Woolley 16–0–77–0; Duleepsinhji 4–0–28–0. *Second innings*—Allom 19–0–92–0; Worthington 13–1–63–1; Woolley 12–0–84–2; Duleepsinhji 4–0–24–0; Dawson 3–0–30–0.

MCC Team

Mr E.W. Dawson, *Mr A.H.H. Gilligan, K.S. Duleepsinhji, F.E. Woolley, Mr M.J. Turnbull, S. Worthington, Mr G.B. Legge, †Mr E.T. Benson, F. Barratt, Mr M.J.C. Allom and E.H. Bowley.

First innings: 469 (Gilligan 45, Duleepsinhji 34, Woolley 219, Turnbull 100, Legge 42; Fairfax four for 102, Bradman one for 83). *Second innings:* Two for 204 (Dawson 83 not out, Duleepsinhji 47, Legge 47 not out; Bradman none for 34).

Umpires: W.H. Bayfield and M. Carney

TEST TRIAL MATCH 21 (38, 39)

Played at Sydney, December 6, 7, 9, 10, 11 [1929]. The performance of Bradman in scoring two centuries in a match – the second time he had achieved the distinction – constituted the chief feature of some remarkable cricket in the trial arranged by the Australian Selectors with a view to choosing the team to tour England in 1930. Ryder's XI had so much the best of the game to begin with that the follow-on was enforced with Woodfull's side 354 in arrear. That policy, however, nearly brought about the defeat of Ryder's XI, who, left to get 188 to win, experienced such difficulty in playing Hornibrook and Blackie on a rain-damaged pitch that ultimately they only struggled home by one wicket. Jackson and Ponsford with a partnership of 278 laid the foundation of a huge score by Ryder's team. ... Bradman, however, overshadowed these successes by scoring 349 in his two innings. [He scored 275 of these on the third day, having opened the batting when Woodfull's XI followed on.] Rigg in the first innings and Kippax, who in the second made a splendid three-figure score, shared with Bradman in important stands and the three players between them were responsible for 592 of the 850 runs scored for Woodfull's XI. ... Eleven of the players taking part in the match afterwards made the trip to England.

J. Ryder's XI

A. Jackson, W.H. Ponsford, A. Marks, *J. Ryder, S. McCabe, W. Horrocks, H.E.P. Whitfield, R.K. Oxenham, †C.W. Walker, C.V. Grimmett and H.H. Alexander.

First innings: 663 (Jackson 182, Ponsford 131, Marks 83, McCabe 35, Whitfield 68, Oxenham 84 not out; Hornibrook three for 102, Blackie three for 163, Bradman one for 56). *Second innings:* Nine for 191 (McCabe 46; Hornibrook four for 67, Blackie three for 65).

W.M. Woodfull's XI

A. Fairfax c and b Alexander	27	–	st Walker b Grimmett	26
*W. M. Woodfull st Walker b Oxenham	36	–	c and b Grimmett	43
A. F. Kippax st Walker b Grimmett	17	–	c Walker b Oxenham	170
D. G. Bradman c Jackson b Oxenham	124	–	lbw b Grimmett	225
A. Allsopp b Oxenham	4	–	c McCabe b Grimmett	5
K. Rigg b Whitfield	73	–	c Ponsford b McCabe	9
A. O. Burrows b Oxenham	7	–	c and b Grimmett	0
†J. L. Ellis lbw b Oxenham	4	–	b Oxenham	24
D. D. Blackie c McCabe b Grimmett	0	–	b Grimmett	11
P. M. Hornibrook st Walker b Grimmett	2	–	c Alexander b Grimmett	1
T. W. Wall not out	0	–	not out	2
B 2, l-b 9, w 3, n-b 1	15		B 14, l-b 7, w 3, n-b 1	25
	309			**541**

J. Ryder's XI bowling: *First innings*—Alexander 11–1–73–1; Whitfield 12–2–46–1; Oxenham 14.6–3–42–5; Grimmett 15–2–68–3; McCabe 3–0–26–0; Marks 5–0–39–0. *Second innings*—Alexander 11–0–73–0; Whitfield 14–0–71–0; Oxenham 30.5–7–97–2; Grimmett 33–3–173–7; McCabe 7–1–42–1; Marks 6–0–45–0; Ryder 5–0–15–0.

Umpires: A. C. Jones and M. Carney

SOUTH AUSTRALIA v NEW SOUTH WALES 22 (40, 41)

Played at Adelaide, December 19, 20, 21, 23, 24 [1929]. New South Wales, after the failure of some of their leading run-getters, effected a good recovery but South Australia established a big lead on the first innings and won by five wickets. ... [In their second innings] thanks to Jackson and Bradman, New South Wales reduced their arrears of 194 to 22 before losing a wicket, and Allsopp and McCabe repeated their batting success of the opening day, but South Australia, set 241 to make, experienced no difficulty in completing their task.

[Following this match, Jackson, who had been diagnosed as suffering from TB, was admitted to hospital in Adelaide.]

New South Wales

A. Fairfax c Wall b Whitfield	39	–	c Hone b Grimmett	46
A. Jackson c Walker b Grimmett	19	–	c Pritchard b Grimmett	82
D. G. Bradman run out	2	–	lbw b Grimmett	84
*A. F. Kippax c Palmer b Wall	26	–	b Palmer	6
A. Marks c and b Wall	1	–	c Pritchard b Whitfield	23
S. McCabe b Wall	69	–	lbw b Grimmett	70
A. Allsopp c Walker b Grimmett	77	–	c and b Grimmett	73
S. C. Everett lbw b Whitfield	1	–	b Whitfield	10
H. Hooker not out	13	–	c Pritchard b Grimmett	9
†H. L. Davidson c Richardson b Grimmett	52	–	c and b Grimmett	7
J. N. Campbell c Pritchard b Whitfield	7	–	not out	4
L-b 3, n-b 5	8		B 13, l-b 5, n-b 2	20
	314			**434**

South Australia bowling: *First innings*—Wall 17–1–74–3; Whitfield 15.1–1–67–3; Grimmett 31–9–91–3; Palmer 13–2–74–0. *Second innings*—Wall 5–0–25–0; Whitfield 25–2–104–2; Grimmett 44.1–5–136–7; Palmer 26–3–121–1; Richardson 7–0–28–0.

South Australia

G. W. Harris, B. W. Hone, D. E. Pritchard, *V. Y. Richardson, H. C. Nitschke, A. R. Lonergan, C. V. Grimmett, H. E. P. Whitfield, †C. W. Walker, T. W. Wall and G. S. Palmer.

First innings: 508 (Harris 46, Hone 126, Pritchard 148, Richardson 64, Grimmett 35, Whitfield 45; Fairfax three for 80, Bradman two for 93). *Second innings:* Five for 244 (Hone 61, Pritchard 75, Richardson 44; Bradman none for 8).

Umpires: G. A. Hele and T. W. Cook

VICTORIA v NEW SOUTH WALES 23 (42, 43)

Played at Melbourne, December 26, 27, 28, 30, 31 [1929]. Victoria appeared a well-beaten side when, going in a second time, they lost five wickets and still required 47 to avert an innings reverse. By a wonderful recovery, as the outcome of which another 215 runs were added, however, they saved the game. Still, at the close New South Wales, with eight wickets to fall, needed only 26 to win. ... New South Wales, after having two men out for 24, batted very consistently. Bradman, Kippax and McCabe were especially sound and attractive in their methods and the visitors, gaining the lead with six wickets in hand, finished the innings 173 ahead. Hendry hitting up a hundred and a'Beckett and Scaife showing much skill at a critical time, Victoria just managed to destroy New South Wales' hopes of winning.

Victoria

*J. Ryder, W.H. Ponsford, R.N. Ellis, H.L. Hendry, K. Rigg, E.L. a'Beckett, †J.L. Ellis, J. A. Scaife, D.D. Blackie, H.H. Alexander and H. Ironmonger.

First innings: 229 (Ponsford 65, Hendry 43, Rigg 44; Everett five for 57, Hooker three for 48). *Second innings:* 343 (Hendry 103, a'Beckett 50, J.L. Ellis 40, Scaife 60 not out, Blackie 37; Fairfax five for 104).

New South Wales

N. E. Phillips c Blackie b Alexander	10	–	st J. Ellis b Ryder	45
A. Fairfax c Blackie b a'Beckett	2	–	c and b Blackie	15
D. G. Bradman b Alexander	89	–	not out	26
*A. F. Kippax lbw b Blackie	80			
A. Marks b Alexander	68			
S. McCabe c J. Ellis b Ironmonger	70	–	not out	50
A. Allsopp c Ironmonger b a'Beckett	26			
†H. L. Davidson c J. Ellis b Blackie	24			
S. C. Everett lbw b Blackie	17			
H. Hooker c Ponsford b Ironmonger	3			
H. Chilvers not out	0			
B 6, l-b 6, n-b 1	13		B 8, n-b 1	9
	402		(two wkts)	**145**

Victoria bowling: *First innings*—Alexander 16–1–115–3; Blackie 20–4–71–3; Ironmonger 28.7–3–89–2; a'Beckett 19–2–48–2; R. Ellis 4–0–33–0; Hendry 4–0–27–0; Ryder 1–0–6–0. *Second innings*—Alexander 4–1–8–0; Blackie 6–0–31–1; Ironmonger 8–0–33–0; a'Beckett 7–2–12–0; R. Ellis 4–0–27–0; Hendry 1–0–2–0; Ryder 4–0–23–0.

Umpires: J. Richards and W. J. Moore

NEW SOUTH WALES v QUEENSLAND 24 (44, 45)

Played at Sydney, January 3, 4, 6, 7 [1930]. Everything else in this game paled before the phenomenal performance of Bradman who, in scoring 452 not out – a feat that occupied him 415 minutes – played the highest individual innings recorded in first-class cricket. That splendid exhibition led the way to a victory for New South Wales by 685 runs [the largest victory on record by a runs margin]. Displaying a wider range of strokes than usual, Bradman batted without a trace of error during his long stay and hit no fewer than forty-nine 4's. His prolific scoring followed upon comparatively low totals in the first innings of each side. ... New South Wales, going in again eight runs ahead, gained a complete mastery over the bowling. Bradman, batting with such brilliancy, made matters easy for his colleagues. ... Faced with the appalling task of getting 770 runs, Queensland offered scarcely any resistance. Half the wickets actually fell for 23, and on the last morning Everett finished off the innings. In the two spells of bowling he disposed of six batsmen at a cost of less than four runs each.

New South Wales

C. Andrews st Leeson b Hurwood	56	–	c Levy b Hurwood	16
D. G. Bradman c Leeson b Hurwood	3	–	not out	452
A. Marks c Hurwood b Thurlow	40	–	c Bensted b Hurwood	5
*A. F. Kippax lbw b Thurlow	15	–	lbw b Rowe	115
S. McCabe c Leeson b Thurlow	15	–	c Leeson b Hurwood	60
A. Allsopp c and b Hurwood	9	–	b Hurwood	66
A. Fairfax b Brew	20	–	st Leeson b Hurwood	10
S. C. Everett c Bensted b Brew	41	–	c Goodwin b Hurwood	4
†H. L. Davidson lbw b Hurwood	14	–	c and b Goodwin	22
S. Burt b Thurlow	10			
H. Chilvers not out	6			
B 3, l-b 3	6		B 6, l-b 1, w 2, n-b 2	11
	235		(eight wkts dec)	**761**

Queensland bowling: *First innings*—Thurlow 18.1–0–83–4; Hurwood 22–6–57–4; Bensted 6–0–39–0; Brew 8–0–50–2. *Second innings*—Thurlow 25–0–147–0; Hurwood 34–1–179–6; Bensted 12–0–70–0; Brew 6–0–61–0; Rowe 19–0–143–1; Thompson 15–0–90–0; Gough 4–0–40–0; Levy 2–0–20–0; Goodwin 0.1–0–0–1.

Queensland

R. M. Levy, *L. P. O'Connor, F. C. Thompson, W. Rowe, F. J. Gough, E. C. Bensted, V. Goodwin, A. Hurwood, F. M. Brew, †H. Leeson and H. M. Thurlow.

First innings: 227 (Bensted 51, Goodwin 67; Fairfax three for 53, McCabe five for 36). *Second innings:* 84 (Everett six for 23).

Umpires: G. Borwick and E. J. Shaw

NEW SOUTH WALES v SOUTH AUSTRALIA 25 (46)

Played at Sydney, January 9, 10, 11, 13 [1930]. Displaying all-round superiority, New South Wales won after three days' actual play by an innings and 220 runs. South Australia had very much the worst of the wicket which, following the completion of their opponents' innings of 535, was much damaged by rain. Still their batting, making every allowance for the conditions, was unusually weak. ... In the course of his innings on the opening day, Bradman [before scoring] received a blow on the head from the ball [thrown in from cover by Grimmett, forcing him to retire hurt until the fall of the fifth wicket] and did not afterwards field.

New South Wales

C. Andrews b Wall	9	A. Allsopp c Richardson b Grimmett	136
†H. S. Love st Walker b Whitfield	38	S. C. Everett b Whitfield	62
D. G. Bradman c Richardson b Whitfield	47	H. Hooker not out	39
*A. F. Kippax b Whitfield	14	H. Chilvers c Harris b Grimmett	52
A. Marks lbw b Grimmett	11	B 6, l-b 6, n-b 5	17
S. McCabe c Nitschke b Grimmett	81		**535**
A. Fairfax lbw b Whitfield	29		

South Australia bowling: Wall 26–2–145–1; Whitfield 26–2–106–5; Grimmett 33.7–3–163–4; Carlton 18–2–99–0; Richardson 2–1–5–0.

South Australia

G. W. Harris, B. W. Hone, D. E. Pritchard, *V. Y. Richardson, H. C. Nitschke, H. E. P. Whitfield, A. Hack, †C. W. Walker, C. V. Grimmett, T. A. Carlton and T. W. Wall.

First innings: 215 (Hone 42, Grimmett 42, Wall 33 not out; Fairfax three for 43, Chilvers four for 57). *Second innings:* 100 (Fairfax four for 19, Chilvers four for 38).

Umpires: A. C. Jones and G. Borwick

NEW SOUTH WALES v VICTORIA 26 (47)

Played at Sydney, January 24, 25, 27, 28, 29 [1930]. The return encounter between New South Wales and Victoria, one of the most important fixtures of the series, was almost completely spoiled by rain which prevented play on any of the first three days and so compelled a draw. Originally additional interest attached to the contest from the fact that during the struggle the team to tour England was to be announced, but in the adverse circumstances the Selectors naturally gained little or no assistance from such play as took place. Sent in to bat on a drying pitch New South Wales had five wickets down for 149, but some cautious, skilful work by Bradman, and successful efforts on the part of Allsopp and Fairfax, resulted in the addition of 181 more runs before the innings ended. . . .

New South Wales

A. Jackson b a'Beckett	5
C. Andrews b Alexander	12
D. G. Bradman c R. Ellis b Ironmonger	77
*A. F. Kippax b Ironmonger	9
S. McCabe c Blackie b a'Beckett	29
A. Allsopp lbw b Blackie	65
A. Fairfax c J. Ellis b Hendry	64
H. Chilvers c J. Ellis b Ironmonger	0
†H. L. Davidson b Hendry	22
H. Hooker c Hendry b Ryder	30
H. Theak not out	2
B 6, l-b 7, n-b 2	15
	330

Victoria bowling: Alexander 14–0–79–1; a'Beckett 21–2–57–2; Ironmonger 20–0–100–3; Blackie 11–0–69–1; Hendry 2.1–0–4–2; Ryder 1–0–6–1.

Victoria

W. H. Ponsford, R. N. Ellis, H. L. Hendry, *J. Ryder, E. L. a'Beckett, K. Rigg, J. A. Scaife, †J. L. Ellis, H. Ironmonger, D. D. Blackie and H. H. Alexander.

First innings: Three for 222 (Hendry 95, Ryder 100 not out).

Umpires: A. C. Jones and G. Borwick

AUSTRALIAN XI MATCHES

At the end of the season, an Australian XI comprising the players selected to tour England in 1930 played two matches against Tasmania and one against Western Australia. These matches do not appear in *Wisden*.

[TASMANIA v AUSTRALIAN XI] 27 (48)

Played at Launceston, March 8, 10, 11 [1930]. The Australian XI won by ten wickets.

Tasmania: *J. A. Atkinson, D. C. Green, N. W. Davis, G. W. Martin, L. J. Nash, A. C. Newton, C. L. Badcock, G. T. H. James, V. L. Hooper, R. C. Townley and †E. A. Pickett.

First innings: 157 (Atkinson 50, Nash 31; Fairfax four for 36, Hornibrook three for 38). *Second innings:* 158 (Nash 49; Fairfax four for 43, Hornibrook three for 51).

Australian XI: W. H. Ponsford, S. J. McCabe, A. F. Kippax, V. Y. Richardson, D. G. Bradman, A. G. Fairfax, *W. M. Woodfull, †W. A. Oldfield, A. Hurwood, P. M. Hornibrook and T. W. Wall.

First innings: 311 (Ponsford 36, McCabe 103, Richardson 33, Bradman lbw b Nash 20, Woodfull 50 not out; James five for 97). *Second innings:* None for 6.

Umpires: P. T. Henty and G. S. Pennfather

[TASMANIA v AUSTRALIAN XI] 28 (49)

Played at Hobart, March 13, 14, 15 [1930]. After the first day had been lost to the weather, the match ended as a draw.

Tasmania: *J. A. Atkinson, A. W. Rushforth, L. J. Nash, D. C. Green, A. O. Burrows, G. W. Martin, A. C. Newton, C. L. Badcock, †D. M. Vautin, G. T. H. James and R. C. Townley.

First innings: 131 (Green 47; Hornibrook three for 42, Grimmett five for 30). *Second innings:* Five for 174 (Nash 93; Bradman none for 21).

Australian XI: W. H. Ponsford, S. J. McCabe, D. G. Bradman, A. F. Kippax, A. G. Fairfax, V. Y. Richardson, *W. M. Woodfull, C. V. Grimmett, †C. W. Walker, A. Hurwood and P. M. Hornibrook.

First innings: Four for 419 dec (Ponsford 166, Bradman c Rushforth b Atkinson 139, Kippax 53 not out, Fairfax 33).

Umpires: M. Leonard and W. T. Lonergan

[WESTERN AUSTRALIA v AUSTRALIAN XI] 29 (50)

Played at Perth, March 21, 22, 24, [1930]. The Australian XI won by an innings and 25 runs.

Western Australia: F. J. Bryant, H. K. Lang, W. J. Horrocks, R. J. Wilberforce, E. H. Bromley, *R. J. Bryant, M. Inverarity, W. A. Evans, H. E. Fidock, †W. J. Truscott and R. A. Halcombe.

First innings: 167 (Fidock 35; Grimmett six for 75). *Second innings:* 132 (Inverarity 30; a'Beckett four for 26, Bradman none for 5).

Australian XI: S. J. McCabe, A. Jackson, D. G. Bradman, A. F. Kippax, *V. Y. Richardson, A. G. Fairfax, E. L. a'Beckett, C. V. Grimmett, A. Hurwood, †C. W. Walker and P. M. Hornibrook.

First innings: 324 (Bradman c R. J. Bryant b Evans 27, Kippax 114, Richardson 45, Grimmett 40; Evans three for 71).

Umpires: W. L. Menkens and F. R. Buttsworth

1930

1930

Even after the Australians had been here some time and had shown, only too clearly, that they would always be a difficult lot to beat, I don't think many people regarded them as likely to win the rubber. Admittedly in Woodfull, Ponsford, Bradman and Kippax, the tourists commanded the services of four exceptionally able batsmen, and in Grimmett those of a bowler puzzling even to players of the highest class, but in other respects the team, for a body of representative cricketers, appeared to be nothing out of the ordinary. Unhappily for England, the crack batsmen, except on that drying pitch on the Saturday afternoon at Trent Bridge, nearly always accomplished great things in the Test Matches, and on the big occasions Grimmett's only failure as a bowler was at Old Trafford where, incidentally, he rendered invaluable service as a batsman. That extraordinary young cricketer, Bradman, meeting with truly phenomenal success, put together scores of 334, 254, 232 and 131 in the course of the five Tests and the Australians' totals, after the first innings at Nottingham, were 335, 729 for six wickets, 566, 345 and 695. Those figures speak only too eloquently for the run-getting powers of our visitors. Against such performances practically no side could have prevailed. …

From 'Notes by the Editor' (C. Stewart Caine), *Wisden 1931*

Coming to England while the experience of four consecutive defeats in Test Matches in their own land was still fresh in their memories, the seventeenth Australian team to visit this country accomplished a very fine performance. They not only achieved the great object of the tour by winning the rubber and so regaining possession of the Ashes but, in the course of thirty-one engagements against first-class sides, they were beaten but once – in the opening Test Match at Nottingham.

It is true that in the general results of the tour their record was unimpressive, for of the thirty-one important games they won only eleven, lost one and drew eighteen, while the encounter with Gloucestershire towards the latter part of August ended in a tie. … The large proportion of drawn games was due to the fact that in most of them bad weather interfered. Indeed, the weather placed the Australians at a considerable disadvantage. In a number of their early matches they had to contend against not only a lot of wet but [also] a decidedly low temperature, feeling the cold so much that heavy underclothing under flannel shirts, and a couple of sweaters in addition, failed to keep them reasonably warm in the field. As no fewer than eleven of the fifteen who made the trip had not visited England before, the handicap under which they laboured may be imagined. Still, they triumphed in a remarkable fashion over the discomforts of a wet and cheerless English summer, and a chosen few of the newcomers adapted themselves, in a manner of which few people thought them capable, to the varying paces of the different wickets on which they had to play. . . .

This particular tour will always be remembered by reason of the amazing batting successes which attended the efforts of Bradman. It is not too much to say that he took both England and the whole cricket world by storm. Those who, like myself, had seen him play in Australia against the team captained by A. P. F. Chapman were fully prepared for something out of the common but little did we dream that his progress would be of such a triumphal nature. Nothing like his series of colossal innings in the Test Matches had ever before been witnessed. He put the coping-stone on a – so far – very brief career when, in the Third Test Match at Leeds, following innings of 131 at Nottingham and 254 at Lord's, he made 334 which eclipsed the previous highest score ever obtained in Test Matches between England and Australia – 287 by the late R. E. Foster at Sydney during the MCC tour of 1903-04. As if that were not sufficient, Bradman, although failing at Manchester, wound up with 232 in the final Test Match at Kennington Oval.

He lost no time in demonstrating to the English public that he was a most remarkable young cricketer, for, leading off with 236 in the opening fixture against Worcestershire, he hit up, in addition to his four hundreds in representative engagements, seven other three-figure innings – one of them in a minor match. For Test Matches alone, without a not-out to help him, he had an average of rather more than 139 with an aggregate of 974 runs in seven innings. Easily top – far away ahead of everyone else in this table of figures – he was also first in batting in first-class matches [27] with an aggregate of 2,960 and an average of over 98, while in all games [29] he scored 3,170 runs and averaged over 99.

Bradman had established himself before he reached this country, but it has been given to no Australian on his first experience of English wickets to enhance an already big reputation in so striking a manner, the performance, moreover, being all the more remarkable in view of the wet nature of the summer. In the course of the tour he demonstrated that he could play two entirely different games and that while, as at Lord's and at periods in his other Test Match innings, he could be brilliant to a degree, he could also, as in the second innings at Nottingham and in the last Test Match at the Oval, bat with a patience and restraint second only to that of Woodfull himself. There were several features about his batting with which one could not fail to be struck. To an eye almost uncanny in its power to gauge the length of a ball was allied really beautiful footwork. Bradman seldom played forward as a means of defence; he nearly always stepped back to meet the ball with a vertical bat. And this is where he had his limitations, for the tour proved that when he met a bowler either left-hand or right who could make the ball just go away, he never seemed quite such a master as against off-break or straight fast bowling. A glorious driver, he hit the ball very hard, while his placing was almost invariably perfect. He scored most of his runs by driving but he could cut, hook, or turn the ball to leg with nearly the same certainty. And only on rare occasions did he lift it. Without any disparagement to a batsman of abilities so pronounced, it is only fair to say that on more than one occasion his task was rendered the easier by the skilful manner in which Woodfull and Ponsford, by batting of different description, had taken the sting out of the England bowling.

Over and above his batting, Bradman showed himself to be a brilliant and dashing field. In match after match his work at deep mid-off and in the long field was a joy to watch. The number of potential 4's he turned into singles in the Test Match at the Oval was extraordinary. Possessed of a fine turn of speed, he picked up most cleanly and with deadly accuracy had the ball back to the wicket-keeper in a flash. Nothing during the whole tour could have been more dazzling than the manner in which at Leeds he threw Hobbs out from deep mid-off.

From 'The Australians in England', by S.J. Southerton

WORCESTERSHIRE v AUSTRALIANS 30 (51)

Played at Worcester, Wednesday, Thursday, Friday, April 30, May 1, 2 [1930]. The Australians opened their tour in most successful fashion, outplaying Worcestershire so completely that they won early on the third day by an innings and 165 runs. To no particularly high standard did the fielding attain, and the bowling, apart from that of Grimmett, was not impressive, but rather chilly weather handicapped the tourists who, moreover, had enjoyed little practice. Still, on the opening day the visitors, after disposing of Worcestershire for 131, put on 199 for the loss of one wicket. This was essentially the work of Woodfull and Bradman. Altogether the second-wicket partnership lasted two hours and ten minutes and produced 208 runs. ... Bradman put together the first of the many big scores he obtained during the summer. Batting for just over four hours and a half, he drove, hit to leg and hooked with wonderful power and certainty and, apart from a hard return when 215, gave no chance. Altogether he made 236 out of 423, among his strokes being twenty-eight 4's. The Australians registered their 492 runs in five hours and forty minutes. ...

Worcestershire

*Mr M. F. S. Jewell, L. Wright, M. Nichol, H. H. Gibbons, W. V. Fox, Mr C. F. Walters, F. Root, G. Brook, †S. W. Styler, Mr H. A. Gilbert and P. Jackson.

First innings: 131 (Gibbons 31 not out; Grimmett four for 38, Fairfax four for 36). *Second innings:* 196 (Walters 44, Root 48; Grimmett five for 46, Hornibrook three for 30).

Australians

*W. M. Woodfull b Brook	133	E. L. a'Beckett c Gilbert b Root	24
A. Jackson c Walters b Brook	24	†W. A. Oldfield c Jackson b Root	4
D. G. Bradman c Walters b Brook	236	C. V. Grimmett not out	15
S. McCabe c Root b Brook	15	T. W. Wall not out	9
V. Y. Richardson run out	24	B 4, l-b 2, w 1, n-b 1	8
A. Fairfax c Root b Jackson	0	(eight wkts dec)	**492**

P. M. Hornibrook did not bat.

Worcestershire bowling: Root 43–0–112–2; Jackson 25–1–105–1; Gilbert 4–0–30–0; Brook 36–1–148–4; Wright 18–1–68–0; Gibbons 2–0–21–0.

Umpires: J. Hardstaff and T. Oates

LEICESTERSHIRE v AUSTRALIANS 31 (52)

Played at [Aylestone Road] Leicester, Saturday, Monday, Tuesday, May 3, 5, 6 [1930]. Leaving off on Monday with only five men out and possessed of a lead of 217, the Australians might well have gained another single innings victory, but to such a condition had rain reduced the pitch on Tuesday that at eleven o'clock the captains decided to abandon the game. Bradman followed up his triumph at Worcester with another masterly display. Against bowling appreciably more formidable than that of Worcestershire, he found run-getting so difficult to begin with that his first 50 occupied him more than two hours. Afterwards he was not often seriously troubled, and when the second day's play came to an end he had brought his score to 185 in five hours and a quarter. Except for a difficult return chance when 44 he made no mistake and he hit sixteen 4's. Quite as notable as the batting of Bradman was the bowling of Grimmett, who on Saturday in one spell sent down seventeen overs for 29 runs and seven wickets. ... The Australians on Monday had four men out for 80, but Richardson rendered Bradman such excellent assistance that a partnership of two hours and a half produced 179 runs. Richardson drove in powerful fashion and hit cleanly to leg.

Leicestershire

A. Shipman, L.G. Berry, N. F. Armstrong, J. C. Bradshaw, H. Riley, Mr A. T. Sharp, W. E. Astill, G. Geary, *Mr J. A. de Lisle, †T. E. Sidwell and H. C. Snary.

First innings: 148 (Shipman 63, Berry 50; Wall three for 37, Grimmett seven for 46).

Australians

W. H. Ponsford lbw b Geary	25	*V. Y. Richardson c Armstrong b Geary	100
A. Jackson b Geary	4	A. Fairfax not out	21
D. G. Bradman not out	185	B 2, l-b 4	6
A. F. Kippax c Sidwell b Snary	22	(five wkts)	**365**
S. McCabe b Geary	2		

C. V. Grimmett, †C. W. Walker, A. Hurwood and T. W. Wall did not bat.

Leicestershire bowling: Shipman 22–2–59–0; Snary 29–6–89–1; Geary 35–9–85–4; Astill 30–2–99–0; Armstrong 9–2–27–0.

Umpires: W. Bestwick and W. A. Buswell

YORKSHIRE v AUSTRALIANS 32 (53)

Played at Sheffield, Saturday, Monday, Tuesday, May 10, 12, 13 [1930]. A splendid bowling performance on the part of Grimmett, who took all ten Yorkshire wickets for 37 runs, was the outstanding feature of a match in which rain, after interfering considerably with play on the first two days, ruined the pitch so completely that on the Tuesday no cricket could be attempted.... From the time he went on at 46, Grimmett bowled with wonderful accuracy and varied his break and flight with delightful ingenuity. He received excellent assistance from Walker who caught one batsman and stumped three. On two previous occasions all ten wickets in an innings had been taken in England by an Australian, Howell performing the feat in 1899 and Mailey in 1921. When the tourists went in, rain and bad light prevented much progress being made but 69 runs were scored for one wicket. So much rain fell on Sunday that on Monday the game could not be resumed until after two o'clock. Woodfull and Bradman, who had come together at 35, then played so well on the soft pitch that they raised the total to 142, Bradman by brilliant cricket making 78 out of 107 in a hundred minutes....

Yorkshire

P. Holmes, H. Sutcliffe, E. Oldroyd, M. Leyland, *Mr A. T. Barber, A. Mitchell, E. Robinson, †A. Wood, G.G. Macaulay, W. Rhodes and W. E. Bowes.

First innings: 155 (Holmes 31, Sutcliffe 69; Grimmett ten for 37).

Australians

*W. M. Woodfull c Barber b Macaulay	121	C. V. Grimmett not out	23
W. H. Ponsford lbw b Robinson	6	†C. W. Walker c Macaulay b Leyland	3
D. G. Bradman c and b Macaulay	78	T. W. Wall c Robinson b Leyland	1
A. F. Kippax lbw b Leyland	3	P. M. Hornibrook st Wood b Rhodes	6
S. McCabe c Oldroyd b Robinson	16	L-b 4	
V. Y. Richardson c Wood b Rhodes	45		**320**
E. L. a'Beckett st Wood b Rhodes	14		

Yorkshire bowling: Robinson 28–8–60–2; Bowes 26–7–63–0; Macaulay 28–2–80–2; Rhodes 31.5–5–95–3; Leyland 8–3–18–3.

Umpires: T. Oates and G. Beet

LANCASHIRE v AUSTRALIANS 33 (54, 55)

Played at Liverpool, Wednesday, Thursday, Friday, May 14, 15, 16 [1930]. Although 61 runs in arrear on the first innings, the Australians had the best of the game when stumps were pulled up soon after four o'clock on Friday, wanting only 90 runs and having eight wickets to fall. ... [In their first innings] the Australians, on a drying pitch, lost half their wickets for 63 and the next day, when play was delayed until nearly two o'clock, the last four wickets – despite a fine effort by Kippax – fell for 10 runs, the last three going down in one over from Hopwood.

Lancashire

F. Watson, C. Hallows, E. Tyldesley, J. Iddon, C. Hopwood, E. Paynter, *Mr P. T. Eckersley, F. M. Sibbles, †G. Duckworth, R. Tyldesley and E. A. McDonald.

First innings: 176 (Watson 37, Eckersley 54; Grimmett six for 57, Hornibrook three for 45, Bradman none for 5). *Second innings:* 165 (Eckersley 38; Hornibrook five for 38).

Australians

*W. M. Woodfull b R. Tyldesley	21			
A. Jackson lbw b McDonald	19	–	lbw b Sibbles	40
D. G. Bradman b McDonald	9	–	not out	48
A. F. Kippax not out	40	–	not out	6
V. Y. Richardson c Hopwood b McDonald	0	–	lbw b R. Tyldesley	39
†C. W. Walker lbw b R. Tyldesley	4			
A. Fairfax st Duckworth b Hopwood	18			
E. L. a'Beckett lbw b R. Tyldesley	3			
C. V. Grimmett c R. Tyldesley b Hopwood	0			
A. Hurwood c R. Tyldesley b Hopwood	0			
P. M. Hornibrook b Hopwood	0			
L-b	1		B 1, l-b 1, w 2	4
	115		(two wkts)	**137**

Lancashire bowling: *First innings*—McDonald 20–3–51–3; Sibbles 14–4–33–0; R. Tyldesley 14–7–17–3; Hopwood 10–4–13–4. *Second innings*—McDonald 11–1–36–0; Sibbles 15–6–18–1; R. Tyldesley 12–3–19–1; Hopwood 13–1–29–0; Iddon 4–0–16–0; Watson 4–0–7–0; E. Tyldesley 1–0–8–0.

Umpires: W. A. Buswell and A. Dolphin

MCC v AUSTRALIANS 34 (56, 57)

Played at Lord's, Saturday, Monday, Tuesday, May 17, 19, 20 [1930]. To meet the Australians, Marylebone placed in the field a distinctly strong side. At no time, however, did a definite issue appear likely to be reached and the end came with the Club having an innings to play and wanting 241 runs for victory. The Australians occupied the wickets for the whole of Saturday, the best batting being that of Bradman and Woodfull who stayed together for a hundred minutes and put on 119 runs. ... [In their second innings] the tourists lost Woodfull and Bradman for 23 runs, but any cause for anxiety disappeared when next morning, after rain had delayed the game for eighty minutes, Hornibrook stayed with Jackson for an hour and a quarter. Jackson at length showed some approach to his Australian form.

Australians

*W. M. Woodfull c Lee b Kennedy	52	–	b Allom	7
A. Jackson c Lyon b Allom	0	–	c Hendren b Stevens	64
D. G. Bradman b Allom	66	–	lbw b Stevens	4
A. F. Kippax b Peebles	18	–	c Lyon b Allen	24
W. H. Ponsford not out	82	–	c Duleepsinhji b Allen	15
V. Y. Richardson c Hendren b Kennedy	34	–	c Duleepsinjhi b Kennedy	5
A. Fairfax lbw b Allom	1	–	st Lyon b Stevens	26
C. V. Grimmett b Allom	4	–	b Allen	15
†C. W. Walker c Lyon b Allom	0	–	not out	10
T. W. Wall lbw b Kennedy	5	–	b Allen	2
P. M. Hornibrook lbw b Peebles	6	–	b Peebles	11
B 11, l-b 6	17		B 18, l-b 9, w 1, n-b 2	30
	285			**213**

MCC bowling: *First innings*—Allen 16–5–38–0; Allom 32–11–67–5; Peebles 25.3–1–87–2; Kennedy 34–13–60–3; Stevens 9–2–16–0. *Second innings*—Allen 14–6–28–4; Allom 12–3–27–1; Peebles 19–4–48–1; Kennedy 10–3–16–1; Stevens 24.3–5–64–3.

MCC

H. W. Lee, †Mr M. D. Lyon, K. S. Duleepsinhji, E. Hendren, Mr D. R. Jardine, *Mr A. P. F. Chapman, Mr G. T. S. Stevens, Mr G. O. Allen, A. Kennedy, Mr M. J. C. Allom and Mr I. A. R. Peebles.

First innings: 258 (Duleepsinhji 92, Hendren 31, Stevens 48; Fairfax six for 54).

Umpires: J. Hardstaff and H. Young

DERBYSHIRE v AUSTRALIANS 35 (58)

Played at Chesterfield, Wednesday, Thursday, Friday, May 21, 22, 23 [1930]. Hornibrook, bowling in great form, obtained twelve wickets for 143 runs and the Australians gained a ten-wickets victory. ... Ponsford put together his first hundred of the tour, raising the score to 127 in company with Jackson and afterwards sharing in a partnership of 106 with Bradman. ... After [Ponsford] left, the Derbyshire bowlers, on a pitch which, from being extremely easy, turned rather difficult, secured eight wickets for 115 runs.

Derbyshire

G. M. Lee, H. Storer, A. E. Alderman, A.G. Slater, Mr N. M. Ford, S. Worthington, L. Townsend, *Mr G. R. Jackson, J. M. Hutchinson, †H. Elliott and T. B. Mitchell.

First innings: 215 (Storer 65, Ford 33, Worthington 79; Wall three for 48, Hornibrook six for 61, Bradman one for 24). *Second innings:* 181 (Alderman 38, Ford 48, Townsend 38; Hornibrook six for 82).

Australians

W. H. Ponsford c Hutchinson b Worthington	131	–	not out	30
A. Jackson c Elliott b Worthington	63	–	not out	18
D. G. Bradman c Elliott b Worthington	44			
A. F. Kippax c Elliott b Mitchell	25			
*V. Y. Richardson b Townsend	10			
S. McCabe c Hutchinson b Townsend	5			
A. Fairfax b Mitchell	20			
†W. A. Oldfield c and b Worthington	14			
A. Hurwood b Mitchell	15			
P. M. Hornibrook not out	2			
T. W. Wall lbw b Mitchell	0			
B 6, l-b 5, w 2, n-b 6	19		L-b 3, n-b 1	4
	348		(no wkt)	**52**

Derbyshire bowling: *First innings*—Slater 21–9–34–0; Worthington 38–6–103–4; Townsend 37–13–68–2; Mitchell 34.5–10–78–4; Lee 4–0–22–0; Storer 7–1–24–0. *Second innings*—Worthington 5–2–9–0; Townsend 6–1–11–0; Mitchell 6–3–3–0; Ford 2–0–9–0; Jackson 1.1–0–16–0.

Umpires: L. C. Braund and J. Hardstaff

SURREY v AUSTRALIANS 36 (59)

Played at Kennington Oval, Saturday, Monday, Tuesday, May 24, 26, 27 [1930]. To a single day's cricket was the first of the Australians' two matches with Surrey restricted, the ground, owing to rain, being reduced to such a muddy condition that not a ball could be bowled on either Monday or Tuesday, but the one day's play produced some wonderful batting on the part of Bradman. The remarkable young Australian had previously put together huge scores at Worcester and at Leicester so this further success occasioned no great surprise. Still, the performance reached an exceptionally high standard of excellence. Going in first wicket down at 11, Bradman – at great pains to play himself in – took an hour and a half to reach 50, but doubled that score in less than an hour and then travelled so fast that he went from 100 to 200 in eighty minutes. Altogether, in five hours and thirty-five minutes, he made 252 out of 368 and was still unbeaten when rain caused stumps to be drawn five minutes before the usual hour. Scoring at first chiefly on the leg side, he afterwards employed the late cut to fine purpose and in the course of the day brought almost every stroke into play. Not until his figures stood at 207 did he make a real mistake – at that point he gave a chance to short-leg – and among his hits were twenty-one 4's, ten 3's and twenty-six 2's. Woodfull played sound cricket for two hours and a quarter, using the drive as his chief scoring stroke and helping Bradman to put on 116. In another good stand Richardson and Bradman added 113 in seventy minutes but, although at tea there were 234 runs on the board and only two wickets had fallen, half the side were out for 250. There Surrey's measure of success ended, Fairfax, who took fifty minutes to reach double figures, rendering Bradman such stubborn help that subsequently 129 more runs were obtained without further loss. . . .

Australians

*W. M. Woodfull c Shepherd b Fender	50	S. McCabe c Fender b Allom	2
A. Jackson c Brooks b Allom	9	A. Fairfax not out	28
D. G. Bradman not out	252	B 3, l-b 1, w 1	5
V. Y. Richardson c Stroud b Allom	32	(five wkts)	**379**
W. H. Ponsford lbw b Fender	1		

†W. A. Oldfield, P. M. Hornibrook, T. W. Wall and C. V. Grimmett did not bat.

Surrey bowling: Allom 34–8–74–3; Lock 22–5–73–0; Stroud 16–1–66–0; Fender 21–1–75–2; Shepherd 20–5–46–0; Gregory 10.4–1–40–0.

Surrey

*Mr P.G.H. Fender, Mr M.J.C. Allom, Mr D.R. Jardine, Mr E.G. Stroud, J.B. Hobbs, A. Sandham, A. Ducat, T. Shepherd, R.J. Gregory, †E. W. Brooks and H. Lock.

Umpires: J. H. King and W. A. Buswell

OXFORD UNIVERSITY v AUSTRALIANS 37 (60)

Played at [the Christ Church ground] Oxford, Wednesday, Thursday, May 28, 29 [1930]. Such a sorry figure did the University team cut that the Australians hit up 406 runs for the loss of only two wickets and, having declared at that score, proceeded to gain the easiest of victories by an innings and 158 runs. ... Bradman, after batting nearly an hour, was bowled in playing back to a well-pitched-up ball. ... Oxford's batting on an easy-paced pitch was truly pitiful.

Australians

S. McCabe b Garland-Wells	91	A. F. Kippax not out	56
W. H. Ponsford not out	220	B 3, l-b 2, w 1, n-b 1	7
D. G. Bradman b Garland-Wells	32	(two wkts dec)	**406**

*W. M. Woodfull, V. Y. Richardson, A. Fairfax, C. V. Grimmett, †C. W. Walker, T. W. Wall and A. Hurwood did not bat.

Oxford University bowling: Hill-Wood 25–2–75–0; Nevinson 23–3–72–0; Peebles 22–3–71–0; Garland-Wells 25–4–99–2; Melville 6–1–45–0; Moore 3–0–12–0; Kingsley 5–1–25–0.

Oxford University

*Mr P.G.T. Kingsley, Mr D.N. Moore, Nawab of Pataudi, Mr A. Melville, Mr N.M. Ford, Mr I. Akers-Douglas, Mr H.M. Garland-Wells, Mr C.K. Hill-Wood, Mr I.A.R. Peebles, †Mr J. F. N. Mayhew and Mr J. H. Nevinson.

First innings: 124 (Moore 34; Grimmett five for 48). *Second innings:* 124 (Ford 31; Wall four for 29, Bradman two for 19).

Umpires: W. Reeves and J. W. Day

HAMPSHIRE v AUSTRALIANS 38 (61)

Played at Southampton, Saturday, Monday, May 31, June 2 [1930]. Thanks mainly to Grimmett, who secured fourteen wickets for seven runs apiece, the Australians defeated Hampshire by an innings and eight runs. Of more general interest than the particular issue of the contest was the achievement of Bradman in completing his 1,000 runs by the end of May. In so doing Bradman accomplished a feat which no Australian had to his credit. Incidentally the circumstances attending Bradman's triumph were quite dramatic. The batsman required 46 runs to reach four figures and those had to be registered on the opening day. Hampshire batting first, there existed no small likelihood that Bradman would lack the chance of making the necessary runs. As it was, Grimmett's bowling provided the opportunity, but Bradman had only brought his aggregate to 1,001 when rain set in and stopped play for the day. Last man out, Bradman played exceptionally brilliant cricket, making his runs in four hours and giving no real chance. He off-drove splendidly and all through placed the ball with wonderful skill. Among his hits were one 6 and twenty-six 4's. McCabe on Monday played delightful cricket, hitting twelve 4's and helping Bradman to put on 141 in sixty-five minutes. ...

Hampshire

†G. Brown, Mr A. L. Hosie, Mr W.G. Lowndes, C. P. Mead, J. Newman, A. Kennedy, Capt. T. O. Jameson, *Lord Tennyson, W. L. Creese, G. S. Boyes and O. W. Herman.

First innings: 151 (Brown 56; Grimmett seven for 39). *Second innings:* 175 (Brown 47; Hornibrook three for 51, Grimmett seven for 56).

Australians

D. G. Bradman c Mead b Boyes	191	†W. A. Oldfield lbw b Kennedy	1
A. Jackson c Boyes b Herman	0	C. V. Grimmett c Brown b Boyes	1
W. H. Ponsford b Newman	29	T. W. Wall lbw b Boyes	0
A. F. Kippax c Kennedy b Boyes	20	P. M. Hornibrook not out	0
*W. M. Woodfull st Brown b Boyes	4	B 4, l-b 2, w 1, n-b 2	9
S. McCabe b Lowndes	65		**334**
A. Fairfax c Hosie b Boyes	14		

Hampshire bowling: Kennedy 30–5–89–1; Herman 9–1–47–1; Newman 18–3–80–1; Boyes 26–4–90–6; Creese 2–0–13–0; Lowndes 3–0–6–1.

Umpires: F. Chester and W. R. Parry

MIDDLESEX v AUSTRALIANS 39 (62, 63)

Played at Lord's, Wednesday, Thursday, Friday, June 4, 5, 6 [1930]. Middlesex could not regain the ground lost by a poor batting performance on Wednesday and suffered defeat by five wickets. So badly did the side collapse before Hornibrook that after lunch eight wickets fell for 46 runs. The Australians also began badly, but when four batsmen had been dismissed for 72, Kippax and McCabe added 65. . . .

Middlesex

Mr G. T. S. Stevens, H. W. Lee, J. W. Hearne, E. Hendren, Mr G. O. Allen, *Mr N. Haig, Mr H. J. Enthoven, Mr G. C. Newman, E.G. Canning, T. J. Durston and †W. F. Price.

First innings: 103 (Hornibrook seven for 42, Grimmett three for 36). *Second innings:* 287 (Hendren 138, Enthoven 38; Hornibrook four for 60, Grimmett three for 81).

Australians

W. H. Ponsford lbw b Allen	5	–	b Haig	10
A. Jackson c Canning b Stevens	14	–	lbw b Hearne	26
D. G. Bradman b Hearne	35	–	b Stevens	18
A. F. Kippax lbw b Allen	102	–	not out	17
*V. Y. Richardson lbw b Hearne	1	–	c Newman b Stevens	11
S. McCabe c Lee b Allen	31	–	c Allen b Stevens	18
A. Fairfax b Lee	34	–	not out	13
C. V. Grimmett b Allen	21			
A. Hurwood b Allen	1			
†C. W. Walker not out	5			
P. M. Hornibrook lbw b Allen	4			
B 9, l-b 6, n-b 2	17		B 2, l-b 4, w 2	8
	270		(five wkts)	**121**

Middlesex bowling: *First innings*—Allen 37.1–8–77–6; Haig 13–3–24–0; Durston 15–3–27–0; Stevens 23–2–70–1; Hearne 25–10–34–2; Lee 3–2–1–1; Enthoven 7–3–20–0. *Second innings*—Allen 7.4–3–19–0; Haig 11–3–18–1; Stevens 17–1–47–3; Hearne 13–3–27–1; Newman 1–0–2–0.

Umpires: P. Toone and A. Nash

CAMBRIDGE UNIVERSITY v AUSTRALIANS 40 (64)

Played at Cambridge, Saturday, Monday, Tuesday, June 7, 9, 10 [1930]. Beating Cambridge by an innings and 134 runs, the Australians, immediately prior to the First Test Match, registered their fourth consecutive victory. Killick put together two good scores in skilful fashion and, with the issue a foregone conclusion, the last three University wickets produced 126 runs, but otherwise the Light Blues gave almost as poor an exhibition as that of Oxford ten days earlier. Indeed, seeing that the Cambridge batsmen allowed themselves to be mastered by McCabe and Bradman, it might be contended that their failure was the more pronounced. . . .

Cambridge University

Mr G. D. Kemp-Welch, Mr A. T. Ratcliffe, Mr E. T. Killick, Mr G. C. Grant, *†Mr J. T. Morgan, Mr T. W. T. Baines, Mr H. R. W. Butterworth, Mr R. H. C. Human, Mr F. R. Brown, Mr W. H. Webster and Mr A. H. Fabian.

First innings: 145 (Killick 48; McCabe four for 25, Bradman three for 35). *Second innings:* 225 (Killick 44, Human 47, Brown 52; McCabe four for 60, Bradman three for 68).

Australians

*W. M. Woodfull c Fabian b Webster	216	†W. A. Oldfield c Human b Webster	28
W. H. Ponsford b Kemp-Welch	7	P. M. Hornibrook b Human	6
D. G. Bradman c Baines b Human	32	T. W. Wall not out	9
S. McCabe run out	96	A. Hurwood not out	8
V. Y. Richardson c Kemp-Welch b Human	34	B 24, l-b 8, w 7, n-b 4	43
A. Jackson run out	25	(eight wkts dec)	**504**

C. W. Walker did not bat.

Cambridge University bowling: Kemp-Welch 30–3–100–1; Human 35–3–106–3; Fabian 26–4–104–0; Brown 31–5–72–0; Webster 21–8–45–2; Grant 1–0–13–0; Butterworth 2–0–21–0.

Umpires: G. Watts and J. W. Day

ENGLAND v AUSTRALIA 41 (65, 66)
(FIRST TEST MATCH) 5 (9, 10)

Played at Nottingham, Friday, Saturday, Monday, Tuesday, June 13, 14, 16, 17 [1930]. England won the first of the series of Test Matches shortly after half-past five on the fourth day by 93 runs. This was a satisfactory start but in gaining the initial success the England team were helped to no inconsiderable extent by the weather, Australia, on the second afternoon, having to bat on a pitch made difficult by hot sunshine following heavy rain during the night and early morning. As an offset to this, however, the Englishmen were greatly handicapped in Australia's last innings by being without Larwood for the whole of the concluding day. The Notts fast bowler, owing to an attack of gastritis, had to keep to his bed. Australia, who were set to get 429 runs to win, had scored 60 runs for the loss of Woodfull's wicket overnight, and with the England attack thus weakened made, thanks to Bradman, a very fine fight of it. Indeed, when shortly before three o'clock they had 229 runs on the board and only three men out, they possessed, with the wicket probably in better condition than at any previous time during the game, a reasonable chance of winning.

Bradman was well set and McCabe playing a bold and successful innings, but at that point McCabe fell to a splendid catch very low down at mid-on by Copley, a member of the ground staff at Trent Bridge fielding as substitute for Larwood. Copley made a lot of ground, took the ball at full length and, although rolling over, retained possession.

This catch, as it happened, turned the game in England's favour, for although Fairfax stayed some time and Richardson made a few hits, nobody, after Bradman's dismissal at 267, offered any real resistance. ...

[In England's first innings] play ceased with the score at 241 for eight wickets and the turf was so wet next day that not a ball could be bowled until a quarter past two. There were many who held that Chapman should have declared but, thanks to some fine hitting by Robins, 29 useful runs were added in twenty-five minutes. ...

By the time the Australians went in, the sun had come out and in less than an hour they lost Ponsford, Woodfull and Bradman for only 16 runs. Woodfull was out to a brilliant catch in the gully and Bradman completely beaten by a break-back. ...

[After England had batted a second time] fifty minutes remained for play when Australia entered upon their task of getting 429 runs to win. Duleepsinhji fielded as substitute for Sutcliffe who had split his thumb. With only 12 scored, Woodfull was again caught in the gully but Ponsford and Bradman played out time, carrying the score to 60. The next morning Ponsford, playing back to a half-volley, was bowled at 93, but England without Larwood had to work tremendously hard for the rest of the day. Bradman, who had been quite brilliant overnight, played such an entirely different game that not until quarter to three did he hit another 4. ... Bradman and McCabe soon played themselves in after lunch and it was quickly obvious that they might rob England of victory, but then at 229 came the catch by the substitute Copley to which reference has been made.

The partnership realised 77 runs in seventy minutes. Bradman's fine innings ended at 267, Robins bowling him with a googly which the batsman made no attempt to play. At the wickets four hours and twenty minutes, Bradman hit ten 4's in scoring his hundred in his first Test Match in England. Off the first ball he received he made a lucky snick over slip's head, and when 60 he again snicked a ball which went off Duckworth's glove to Hammond's left hand and then on to the ground, while at 75 he was nearly bowled by a leg-break. Thus his display, if in the circumstances very remarkable, was not free from fault. ...

England

J. B. Hobbs, H. Sutcliffe, W. R. Hammond, F. E. Woolley, E. Hendren, *Mr A. P. F. Chapman, H. Larwood, Mr R. W. V. Robins, M. W. Tate, R. Tyldesley and †G. Duckworth.

First innings: 270 (Hobbs 78, Chapman 52, Robins 50 not out; Grimmett five for 107). *Second innings:* 302 (Hobbs 74, Sutcliffe 58 retired hurt, Hendren 72; Wall three for 67, Grimmett five for 94).

Australia

*W. M. Woodfull c Chapman b Tate	2	–	c Chapman b Larwood	4
W. H. Ponsford b Tate	3	–	b Tate	39
A. Fairfax c Hobbs b Robins	14	–	c Robins b Tate	14
D. G. Bradman b Tate	8	–	b Robins	131
A. F. Kippax not out	64	–	c Hammond b Robins	23
S. McCabe c Hammond b Robins	4	–	c sub b Tate	49
V. Y. Richardson b Tyldesley	37	–	lbw b Tyldesley	29
†W. A. Oldfield c Duckworth b Robins	4	–	c Hammond b Tyldesley	11
C. V. Grimmett st Duckworth b Robins	0	–	c Hammond b Tyldesley	0
P. M. Hornibrook lbw b Larwood	0	–	c Duckworth b Robins	5
T. W. Wall b Tyldesley	0	–	not out	8
B 4, l-b 4	8		B 17, l-b 5	22
	144			**335**

England bowling: *First innings*—Larwood 15–8–12–1; Tate 19–8–20–3; Tyldesley 21–8–53–2; Robins 17–4–51–4. *Second innings*—Larwood 5–1–9–1; Tate 50–20–69–3; Tyldesley 35–10–77–3; Robins 17.2–1–81–3; Hammond 29–5–74–0; Woolley 3–1–3–0.

Umpires: W. R. Parry and J. Hardstaff

SURREY v AUSTRALIANS 42 (67)

Played at Kennington Oval, Wednesday, Thursday, Friday, June 18, 19, 20 [1930]. To such a pronounced extent did the Australians, up to a point, outplay Surrey that, having established a lead of 226, they were able to declare with five men out. Hobbs, however, came to the rescue, putting together what was at once the second hundred recorded against the tourists and the 173rd of his career, with the result that in the end Surrey were 23 ahead and had eight wickets to fall. [On the first day] play had lasted less than three hours, Surrey meanwhile losing five batsmen for 140, when rain flooded the ground....

Surrey

J. B. Hobbs, A. Sandham, T. H. Barling, T. Shepherd, E. F. Wilson, R. J. Gregory, *Mr P. G. H. Fender, H. G. Baldwin, H. A. Peach, Mr M. J. C. Allom and †E. W. Brooks.

First innings: 162 (Shepherd 56; Grimmett six for 24). *Second innings:* Two for 249 (Hobbs 146 not out, Shepherd 65 not out; Bradman none for 31).

Australians

*W. M. Woodfull c Wilson b Shepherd	141
A. Fairfax lbw b Shepherd	36
D. G. Bradman c Allom b Shepherd	5
A. F. Kippax c and b Peach	36
S. McCabe b Shepherd	42
A. Jackson not out	37
E. L. a'Beckett not out	67
B 18, l-b 6	24
(five wkts dec)	**388**

†C. W. Walker, A. Hurwood, C. V. Grimmett and T. W. Wall did not bat.

Surrey bowling: Allom 27–2–66–0; Peach 32–16–66–1; Fender 29–6–93–0; Gregory 28–6–74–0; Shepherd 27–6–65–4.

Umpires: F. Chester and W. Phillips

LANCASHIRE v AUSTRALIANS 43 (68, 69)

Played at Manchester, Saturday, Monday, Tuesday, June 21, 23, 24 [1930]. Rain caused several interruptions and the play generally being marked by rather pronounced restraint, there never existed much likelihood of a definite issue being reached. On the opening day, although the county attack was greatly weakened through the inability of McDonald to turn out, the Australians occupied four hours and forty minutes in making 231 for five wickets ... and in the end, batting more than eight hours, [they] registered the largest total obtained against Lancashire during the season....

Australians

*W. M. Woodfull st Duckworth b Sibbles	27			
A. Jackson b Hodgson	52			
D. G. Bradman c Duckworth b Sibbles	38	–	not out	23
A. F. Kippax st Duckworth b Hopwood	120			
S. McCabe c Duckworth b Hodgson	34	–	not out	36
V. Y. Richardson c R. Tyldesley b Hodgson	13	–	c Eckersley b Hodgson	12
A. Fairfax st Duckworth b R. Tyldesley	63			
†W. A. Oldfield not out	34			
A. Hurwood c Taylor b Hopwood	9			
T. W. Wall lbw b R. Tyldesley	0			
P. M. Hornibrook b Sibbles	20			
B 4, l-b 13	17		B	8
	427		(one wkt)	**79**

Lancashire bowling: *First innings*—Hodgson 37–7–97–3; Sibbles 50–6–89–3; R. Tyldesley 38–8–87–2; Hopwood 43–11–92–2; Watson 4–1–10–0; Iddon 16–4–35–0. *Second innings*—Hodgson 3–1–6–1; Sibbles 2–0–13–0; Watson 1–0–3–0; Eckersley 2–0–12–0; Duckworth 2–0–13–0; Hallows 2–0–15–0; E. Tyldesley 1–0–9–0.

Lancashire

F. Watson, C. Hallows, E. Tyldesley, J. Iddon, C. Hopwood, M. L. Taylor, *Mr P. T. Eckersley, F. M. Sibbles, †G. Duckworth, R. Tyldesley and G. Hodgson.

First innings: 259 (Watson 74, Hallows 42, Tyldesley 48, Hopwood 40; Wall four for 92, Fairfax four for 29, Bradman none for 24).

Umpires: W. Bestwick and W. R. Parry

ENGLAND v AUSTRALIA (SECOND TEST MATCH)

44 (70, 71)
6 (11, 12)

Played at Lord's, Friday, Saturday, Monday, Tuesday, June 27, 28, 30, July 1 [1930]. Beating England, after a memorable struggle, by seven wickets Australia took ample revenge for their overthrow a fortnight previously at Trent Bridge. The batting of the Australians and particularly that of Bradman will assuredly live long in the minds of those who saw it but, while giving the visitors the fullest praise for winning so handsomely after having to face a first innings total of 425, it is only proper to observe that to a large extent England played right into the hands of their opponents. Briefly, the Englishmen lost a match, which, with a little discretion on the last day, they could probably have saved. ... It can with truth be said, however, that the England bowling in no other game [of the series] not only looked but actually was so entirely lacking in sting and effect.

Records went by the board. Australia, in putting together a total of 729 before declaring with only six wickets down, broke four – the highest score by Australia in England, 551 at Kennington Oval in 1884; the highest score in this country, 576 by England at the Oval in 1899; the highest score by Australia, 600 at Melbourne in 1924; and the highest score in the whole series of Test Matches, 636 by England at Sydney in December, 1928. Bradman himself, with a score of 254, played the second-highest individual innings in the whole series of Test Matches between England and Australia, while Duleepsinhji not only made a hundred on the occasion of his first appearance in a Test Match against Australia but scored the highest number of runs ever obtained by an England player in these matches at Lord's. There was one other notable point, A. P. F. Chapman, after leading England to victory six times, captaining the losing side. As some set-off against that, he enjoyed, for the first time in his career, the distinction of making a hundred in a Test Match. ...

[Commencing their reply on Saturday morning] Australia, by skilful and judicious batting, remained in for the rest of the day and scoring 404 for the loss of only two batsmen left off no more than 21 runs behind – a very great performance. ... The Australians batted to a set plan, Woodfull and Ponsford steadily wearing down the bowling for Bradman later on to flog it. Nearly three hours were occupied over the first 162 runs, but in another two hours and three-quarters no fewer than 242 came. While in the end Bradman made most runs, very great credit was due to Woodfull and Ponsford who, when England's bowling was fresh, put on 162 for the first wicket. Curiously enough the partnership terminated almost directly after a break in play while the members of both teams were presented to the King in front of the pavilion, Ponsford, who had batted very soundly, being caught at slip. ... Just before the King arrived, Woodfull, with his score at 52 playing forward to Robins, dragged his foot over the crease. Duckworth gathered the ball and swept it back to the stumps but omitted to remove the bails. That little error cost England dear. Bradman, who went in when Ponsford was out and the bowling had been mastered, seized his opportunity in rare style and, hitting all round the wicket with power and accuracy, scored in two hours and forty minutes 155 runs and was not out at the close. ...

On the Monday, Australia kept England in the field for another four hours and a half and added 325 runs for the loss of four more batsmen before declaring their innings closed at the tea interval. The partnership between Bradman and Kippax, which did not end until ten minutes to three when Bradman was caught right-hand at extra mid-off, produced 192 runs in less than three hours. In obtaining his 254, the famous Australian gave nothing approaching a chance. He nearly played on at 111 and, at 191, in trying to turn the ball to leg, he edged it deep into the slips but, apart from those trifling errors, no real fault could be found with his display. Like Woodfull he scarcely ever lifted the ball and, while his defence generally was perfect, he hit very hard in front of the wicket. Altogether he batted five and a half hours, his chief strokes being twenty-five 4's, three 3's, and twenty-six 2's. ... For their huge total Australia batted ten hours and ten minutes.

England thus found themselves requiring 304 runs to escape an innings defeat. [Although they accomplished this, the Australians then] had to make only 72 to win, but in twenty minutes there was much excitement. Ponsford was bowled at 16, Bradman caught low down at backward-point at 17, and Kippax taken at the wicket at 22. Visions of a remarkable collapse arose but Woodfull, exercising sound generalship by taking most of Robins' bowling himself, tided over an anxious period and by five o'clock he and McCabe had obtained the remaining runs.

In the course of the four days, 110,000 people watched the cricket, the takings being roughly £14,500.

England

J. B. Hobbs, F. E. Woolley, W. R. Hammond, K. S. Duleepsinhji, E. Hendren, *Mr A. P. F. Chapman, Mr G. O. Allen, M. W. Tate, Mr R. W. V. Robins, Mr J. C. White and †G. Duckworth.

First innings: 425 (Woolley 41, Hammond 38, Duleepsinhji 173, Hendren 48, Tate 54; Wall three for 118, Fairfax four for 101). *Second innings:* 375 (Hammond 32, Duleepsinhji 48, Chapman 121, Allen 57, sundries 30; Grimmett six for 167, Bradman none for 1).

Australia

*W. M. Woodfull st Duckworth b Robins	155	–	not out	26
W. H. Ponsford c Hammond b White	81	–	b Robins	14
D. G. Bradman c Chapman b White	254	–	c Chapman b Tate	1
A. F. Kippax b White	83	–	c Duckworth b Robins	3
S. McCabe c Woolley b Hammond	44	–	not out	25
V. Y. Richardson c Hobbs b Tate	30			
†W. A. Oldfield not out	43			
A. Fairfax not out	20			
B 6, l-b 8, w 5	19		B 1, l-b 2	3
(six wkts dec)	**729**		(three wkts)	**72**

C. V. Grimmett, P. M. Hornibrook and T. W. Wall did not bat.

England bowling: *First innings*—Allen 34–7–115–0; Tate 64–16–148–1; White 51–7–158–3; Robins 42–1–172–1; Hammond 35–8–82–1; Woolley 6–0–35–0. *Second innings*—Tate 13–6–21–1; White 2–0–8–0; Robins 9–1–34–2; Hammond 4.2–1–6–0.

Umpires: F. Chester and T. Oates

YORKSHIRE v AUSTRALIANS 45 (72)

Played at Bradford, Wednesday, Thursday, Friday, July 2, 3, 4 [1930]. Lacking the services of Sutcliffe, Yorkshire batted so poorly that a little play on the third day saw them beaten by ten wickets. Once again the big factor in the Australians' success was the bowling of Grimmett, who took eleven wickets for just over 12 runs apiece. In the course of the match Grimmett secured his 100th wicket [of the tour]. ... Yorkshire, although Bradman let off W. Barber, had four men out for 42 and ... could not retrieve the early disasters. ...

Australians

*W. M. Woodfull c Wood b Dennis	3			
W. H. Ponsford c and b Hall	143			
D. G. Bradman lbw b Robinson	1			
S. McCabe c Macaulay b Hall	40			
A. Jackson lbw b Macaulay	46			
V. Y. Richardson c Dennis b Robinson	3			
E. L. a'Beckett not out	30	–	not out	6
C. V. Grimmett c and b Hall	1			
A. Hurwood c A. T. Barber b Rhodes	4			
P. M. Hornibrook c Mitchell b Rhodes	10			
†C. W. Walker st Wood b Rhodes	6	–	not out	1
B 4, l-b 7, w 1, n-b 3	15			
	302		(no wkt)	**7**

Yorkshire bowling: *First innings*—Robinson 21–5–69–2; Dennis 13–6–25–1; Macaulay 32–10–58–1; Hall 24–6–61–3; Rhodes 25.3–8–49–3; Leyland 10–1–25–0. *Second innings*—Robinson 0.1–0–2–0; Hall 1–0–5–0.

Yorkshire

P. Holmes, A. Mitchell, *Mr A.T. Barber, M. Leyland, W. Barber, E. Robinson, W. Rhodes, F. Dennis, †A. Wood, G.G. Macaulay and C. Hall.

First innings: 146 (Rhodes 35; a'Beckett three for 42, Grimmett six for 75). *Second innings:* 161 (W. Barber 42; Hurwood four for 35, Grimmett five for 58).

Umpires: G. Beet and A. Nash

ENGLAND v AUSTRALIA 46 (73)
(THIRD TEST MATCH) 7 (13)

Played at Leeds, Friday, Saturday, Monday, Tuesday, July 11, 12, 14, 15 [1930]. The Third Test Match, while it afforded that remarkable young batsman, Bradman, the opportunity of leaving all individual batting records in representative matches far behind, was in many respects an unsatisfactory affair. England had the worst of it from start to finish but escaped with a draw, a heavy storm on Sunday night, followed by further rain on the Monday, restricting the third day's play to forty-five minutes while, on the Tuesday, further delay occurred owing to defective light.

The game will go down to history on account of the wonderful batting performance accomplished by Bradman who, with an innings of 334, beat the previous highest – 287 by R. E. Foster for England at Sydney – which had stood since December, 1903. In the course of this, Bradman achieved fame in other directions. Like C.G. Macartney on the same ground four years previously, he reached three figures before lunch-time on the first day. Not out 309 at the close he had then exceeded a total of 1,000 runs in Test cricket and reached an aggregate of exactly 2,000 runs for the season. In playing two consecutive innings of over 200 in Test Matches he equalled the performance of Hammond during the previous tour in Australia. He also equalled Macartney's performance of 1926 in scoring three separate hundreds in successive Test Matches. Truly could it be called 'Bradman's Match'. Bigger though it was and characterised by splendid stroke-play, Bradman's innings did not quite approach his 254 at Lord's in freedom from fault, but as to its extraordinary merit there could be no two opinions. As usual, he rarely lifted the ball and when making two or more consecutive scoring strokes seldom sent it in the same direction. His footwork was admirable as was the manner in which he played his defensive strokes to balls just short of a length. . . .

This time, Woodfull won the toss and Australia led off so brilliantly that, when the first day's play ended, they had 458 runs on the board with only three wickets down. The pitch, like those at Nottingham and Leeds, was, on the first day at any rate, lacking in life and pace and all in favour of batsmen. Opening the innings with Woodfull [because Ponsford was suffering from gastritis], Jackson off the fifth ball of the second over was caught at forward short-leg, but England had to wait until five minutes past three before they took another wicket, Woodfull and Bradman, in the meantime, putting on 192 runs in two hours and thirty-five minutes. This was very largely the work of Bradman who, quick to settle down, completed 102 out of the first 127 in ninety-five minutes. All the same, Woodfull, by another great display of defensive cricket, rendered his side invaluable assistance. After Woodfull left, bowled in trying to hook a shortish ball, Bradman found another admirable partner in Kippax who, if overshadowed by his colleague, played uncommonly well in helping to add 229 in rather less than two and three-quarter hours. The next day McCabe, who had batted twenty minutes overnight, stayed until 63 runs had been put on but nothing of any consequence was accomplished by the rest, the last seven wickets falling in a hundred minutes for 108 runs. Bradman, sixth out at 508, obtained his 334 in six hours and a quarter, his score being made up of forty-six 4's, six 3's, twenty-six 2's, and eighty singles. When he had made 141 he put up a ball towards mid-wicket and at 202 he skied a ball over Tate's head at mid-on. Indeed, a man a little quicker on his feet than Tate might have made a catch of it. Actually, Bradman gave only one chance, being missed at the wicket off Geary at 273 when the total was 385. He hit very hard in front of the wicket, scored splendidly on the leg side and very often cut in dazzling fashion. Nobody could have had a better reception than that accorded to Bradman on his return to the pavilion. . . .

[Bowled out for 391 in their first innings] England followed on 179 behind and, as over three hours remained for cricket, there was always the possibility of them losing. Hobbs and Sutcliffe opened the innings in a very poor light. After a quarter of an hour, they appealed against it and the players went in. For some extraordinary reason the crowd took this in very bad part, booing the batsmen and cheering the Australians, while on the game being resumed there was a continuance of this unseemly behaviour. With 24 scored, Hobbs was brilliantly thrown out by Bradman from deep mid-off but Sutcliffe and Hammond stayed nearly an hour to add 50. After Duleepsinhji had been caught at point off a ball which he afterwards confessed he did not see, another appeal against the light was made at ten minutes to six and no further cricket took place.

Australia

*W. M. Woodfull b Hammond	50	†W. A. Oldfield c Hobbs b Tate	2
A. Jackson c Larwood b Tate	1	C. V. Grimmett c Duckworth b Tyldesley	24
D. G. Bradman c Duckworth b Tate	334	T. W. Wall b Tyldesley	3
A. F. Kippax c Chapman b Tate	77	P. M. Hornibrook not out	1
S. McCabe b Larwood	30	B 5, l-b 8, w 1	14
V. Y. Richardson c Larwood b Tate	1		**566**
E. L. a'Beckett c Chapman b Geary	29		

England bowling: Larwood 33–3–139–1; Tate 39–9–124–5; Geary 35–10–95–1; Tyldesley 33–5–104–2; Hammond 17–3–46–1; Leyland 11–0–44–0.

England

J. B. Hobbs, H. Sutcliffe, W. R. Hammond, K. S. Duleepsinhji, M. Leyland, G. Geary, †G. Duckworth, *Mr A. P. F. Chapman, M. W. Tate, H. Larwood and R. Tyldesley.

First innings: 391 (Sutcliffe 32, Hammond 113, Duleepsinhji 35, Leyland 44, Duckworth 33, Chapman 45; Grimmett five for 135). *Second innings:* Three for 95 (Hammond 35).

Umpires: W. Bestwick and T. Oates

SCOTLAND v AUSTRALIANS 47

Played at Edinburgh, Wednesday, Thursday, Friday, July 16, 17, 18 [1930]. While a three-day fixture had been arranged for the meeting of Scotland with the Australians, the weather proved so unkind that progress with the game was restricted to something less than three hours on Wednesday. Play proceeded without interruptions up to lunch-time and was resumed at the usual hour, but after half an hour's more cricket rain caused a considerable delay and a further endeavour to continue the contest was, within a few minutes, checked by a downpour of so pronounced a description that nothing further could be done that day. Unhappily the rain continued through the night and next morning with the consequence that on Thursday play was out of the question, while on Friday when, with the weather clearing somewhat, it had been agreed to make a start after two o'clock, there came more rain which compelled the abandonment of the match. …

Scotland

Mr J. Kerr, *Mr G. W. A. Alexander, †Mr A. K. McTavish, Mr B. R. Tod, Mr W. Nicholson, Mr W. Anderson, Mr A. D. Baxter, Mr J. F. Jones, Mr R. W. Sievwright, Mr A. R. Simpson and Mr T. Watson.

First innings: Three for 129 (Alexander 51, McTavish 35; Bradman none for 4).

Australians

*W. M. Woodfull, V. Y. Richardson, W. H. Ponsford, A. Jackson, D. G. Bradman, A. F. Kippax, E. L. a'Beckett, C. V. Grimmett, P. M. Hornibrook, A. Hurwood and †C. W. Walker.

Umpires: R. A. Haywood and G. Deyes

A SCOTTISH XI v AUSTRALIANS

Played at Glasgow, Saturday, Monday, July 19, 21 [1930]. If not so deplorable as on the occasion of the match at Edinburgh, the weather associated with a two-day contest at Glasgow still left much to be desired. Indeed, on Saturday, when the Scotsmen batted with a measure of caution which neither the conditions nor the quality of the Australians' bowling justified, rain held up the game for seventy minutes in the course of the afternoon and bad light afterwards brought play to a close. On Monday the Scottish captain at once declared and the Australians put on 337 runs for the loss of nine wickets. Bradman, seizing upon the occasion to register his eighth hundred, gave a brilliant display, making 140 out of 210 in two hours and a half. He offered no chance and among his hits were a drive for 6 and nineteen 4's. Woodfull, also batting freely, helped to add 198 for the second wicket.

A Scottish XI

Mr J. Kerr, Mr B. W.G. Atkinson, Mr A. K. McTavish, *Mr G. W. A. Alexander, Mr W. Nicholson, Mr B. R. Tod, Ackroyd, Mr A. D. Baxter, †Mr D. A. Bompas, H. J. Preston and Mr T. Watson.

First innings: Six for 140 dec (Tod 34; Hornibrook three for 40).

Australians

*W. M. Woodfull c Kerr b Preston	65	A. Hurwood lbw b Watson	3
W. H. Ponsford b Baxter	6	P. M. Hornibrook b Preston	8
D. G. Bradman b Baxter	140	†C. W. Walker c Kerr b Baxter	0
A. F. Kippax lbw b Watson	0	T. W. Wall not out	2
S. McCabe b Baxter	1	B 8, l-b 8, n-b 1	17
A. Jackson not out	52	(nine wkts)	**337**
E. L. a'Beckett st Bompas b Tod	43		

A Scottish XI bowling: Baxter 35–8–89–4; Preston 40–7–94–2; Ackroyd 16–4–45–0; Watson 20–3–47–2; Tod 8–0–45–1.

Umpires: Guy and Joyce

[Although Bradman was not selected to play in the two-day match against Durham at Sunderland on July 23 and 24, readers may be interested to know that rain followed the Australians south from Scotland and prevented any play.]

ENGLAND v AUSTRALIA
(FOURTH TEST MATCH)

48 (74)
8 (14)

Played at Manchester, Friday, Saturday, Monday, Tuesday, July 25, 26, 28, 29 [1930]. Interfered with by rain to a much greater extent than was the case in the game at Leeds, the Fourth Test Match had also to be left drawn. Cricket went on without interruption on the first two days, but play lasted only forty-five minutes on the third afternoon – as at Leeds – and not a ball was bowled on the last day.

Under conditions which were expected to confer an advantage on the home team, England again had the worst of matters. For the fourth time the batting of the side proved inconsistent, a promising start being discounted by certain failures which were only partially retrieved, while the bowling, apart from that of Peebles, did not really inspire confidence or achieve the success anticipated when Australia, on winning the toss, batted on a soft wicket. ... So soft was the turf that the start had to be delayed for half an hour and the foothold proved so uncertain that Chapman, fielding at silly-mid-off, had to put down a lot of sawdust to prevent himself slipping.

Woodfull and Ponsford gave their side another fine start, staying in until a quarter to three and putting on 106 for the first wicket. Ponsford batted admirably ... Woodfull, until Peebles went on, also played extremely well, but for a long time before lunch he was definitely uncomfortable and uncertain in dealing with that bowler. The Middlesex amateur caused Ponsford little trouble; he constantly made Woodfull play false strokes. …

Bradman had a most unhappy experience. He was nearly bowled first ball by Peebles and, when 10, gave a chance low down in the slips. He hit one 4 off a full-toss and then, trying to cut a leg-spinner, was nicely caught at second slip at 138. Just about this time, Peebles was bowling extremely well. …

[When England batted, Hobbs and Sutcliffe put on 108 in two hours for the first wicket.] Sutcliffe … gave a brilliant display of driving, pulling and hooking. … He was out to a remarkable catch at long-leg off a big hit, Bradman taking the ball high up and then falling among the spectators. …

Australia

*W. M. Woodfull c Duckworth b Tate	54
W. H. Ponsford b Hammond	83
D. G. Bradman c Duleepsinhji b Peebles	14
A. F. Kippax c Chapman b Nichols	51
S. McCabe lbw b Peebles	4
V. Y. Richardson b Hammond	1
A. Fairfax lbw b Goddard	49
†W. A. Oldfield b Nichols	2
C. V. Grimmett c Sutcliffe b Peebles	50
P. M. Hornibrook c Duleepsinhji b Goddard	3
T. W. Wall not out	1
B 23, l-b 3, n-b 7	33
	345

England bowling: Nichols 21–5–33–2; Tate 30–11–39–1; Goddard 32.1–14–49–2; Peebles 55–9–150–3; Leyland 8–2–17–0; Hammond 21–6–24–2.

England

J. B. Hobbs, H. Sutcliffe, W. R. Hammond, K. S. Duleepsinhji, M. Leyland, *Mr A. P. F. Chapman, M. W. Tate, M. S. Nichols, Mr I. A. R. Peebles, †G. Duckworth and T. W. Goddard.

First innings: Eight for 251 (Hobbs 31, Sutcliffe 74, Duleepsinhji 54, Leyland 35; Wall three for 70, McCabe four for 41).

Umpires: F. Chester and J. Hardstaff

SOMERSET v AUSTRALIANS 49 (75)

Played at Taunton, Wednesday, Thursday, July 30, 31 [1930]. So completely did the Australians outplay Somerset that in the course of two days' cricket they defeated the western county by an innings and 158 runs. Batting first on a pitch of varying pace, the home side lost half their wickets for 30 and from that wretched start there was, as it happened, no recovery. For a blunder early in the Australians' innings a tremendously heavy price had to be paid. Ponsford was bowled at 13 and one run later Jackson, with his score at six, was missed by Wellard in the slips. To such an extent did Jackson profit by this escape that he remained to add, in company with Bradman, 231 runs for the second wicket, the partnership lasting just over three hours and a half. … Following upon a very cautious start, Bradman batted with his customary skill and confidence, and hit thirteen 4's. After Bradman's dismissal, the last eight wickets fell for 116 runs. . .. The match proved so large an attraction that on the opening day the holding capacity of the ground was taxed to its limit.

Somerset

A. Young, Mr E. F. Longrigg, Mr R. A. Ingle, F. S. Lee, *Mr J. C. White, Mr C. C. Case, Mr L. Hawkins, A. W. Wellard, J. W. Lee, G. Hunt and †Mr A.G. Marshall.

First innings: 121 (White 38, Wellard 38; Grimmett three for 38). *Second innings:* 81 (Grimmett seven for 33).

Australians

W. H. Ponsford b Hunt	8	C. V. Grimmett c Young b White	16
A. Jackson c J. W. Lee b Young	118	A. Hurwood hit wkt b Young	10
D. G. Bradman c and b Young	117	P. M. Hornibrook not out	4
S. McCabe c and b Young	1	†C. W. Walker c Wellard b White	0
*V. Y. Richardson c Hulme b Young	27	B 1, l-b 4	5
W. M. Woodfull c and b White	30		**360**
E. L. a'Beckett c Young b White	24		

Somerset bowling: Wellard 22–3–66–0; Hunt 38–13–91–1; J.W. Lee 19–8–37–0; White 30.4–8–91–4; Young 34–12–70–5.

Umpires: A. Morton and A. Nash

GLAMORGAN v AUSTRALIANS 50 (76, 77)

Played at Swansea, Saturday, Monday, Tuesday, August 2, 4, 5 [1930]. Although much interfered with by rain, which on Saturday prevented a start being made until after four o'clock and on Tuesday delayed play until a quarter to one, the match yielded a most interesting finish. The tourists, declaring with one man out in their second innings, set Glamorgan 218 to get in two hours and three-quarters and in the end there were 21 runs wanted and three wickets to fall. On Saturday the visitors scored 149 for the loss of Ponsford and Jackson, and on Monday, Bradman and McCabe raised the total to 196, but the last seven wickets produced only 49 runs. The Australians could not make their opponents follow on but on Tuesday they declared at lunch-time. Playing at first merely to avert defeat, Glamorgan scored 59 for two wickets but then Bates and Turnbull hit out so finely that 93 runs were obtained in sixty-five minutes. The attempt by other batsmen to force the runs, however, did not meet with success.

Australians

W. H. Ponsford b D. Davies	53	–	not out	35
A. Jackson c Hills b Mercer	39	–	c Clay b D. Davies	11
D. G. Bradman b Ryan	58	–	not out	19
S. McCabe c D. Davies b Ryan	53			
*V. Y. Richardson st Every b Ryan	3			
A. Fairfax c D. Davies b Ryan	8			
E. L. a'Beckett not out	18			
C. V. Grimmett c D. Davies b Ryan	0			
T. W. Wall c Turnbull b Ryan	2			
A. Hurwood lbw b Mercer	0			
†C. W. Walker b Mercer	1			
B 1, l-b 6, n-b 3	10		B 4, l-b 2	6
	245		(one wkt dec)	**71**

Glamorgan bowling: *First innings*—Mercer 32.3–7–70–3; E. Davies 6–0–31–0; Clay 16–3–35–0; Ryan 34–3–76–6; D. Davies 11–3–23–1. *Second innings*—Mercer 3–0–15–0; Clay 10–2–28–0; Ryan 4–1–13–0; D. Davies 4–1–9–1.

Glamorgan

W. Bates, A. H. Dyson, *Mr M.J. Turnbull, D. Davies, J. T. Bell, J. Hills, E. Davies, Mr J. C. Clay, J. Mercer, †G. Every and F. Ryan.

First innings: 99 (Grimmett four for 34). *Second innings:* Seven for 197 (Bates 73, Turnbull 52; Grimmett four for 69).

Umpires: J. H. King and A. Morton

NORTHAMPTONSHIRE v AUSTRALIANS 51 (78, 79)

Played at Northampton, Saturday, Monday, Tuesday, August 9, 11, 12 [1930]. Northamptonshire enjoyed the distinction of dismissing the Australians for the smallest score registered by the tourists during the tour. Still, the visitors drew the game in handsome style, leaving off 249 ahead with two wickets to fall. The county team occupied the wickets for the whole of Saturday . . . Following upon a lot of rain on Sunday, the weather turned very bright. Jupp and Thomas bowled in deadly form, the former disposing of six batsmen for 32 runs. Bradman helped Woodfull to take the score from 15 to 51 but the last eight wickets fell for 42 runs. Made to follow on, the Australians, thanks to Woodfull and Jackson, cleared off 91 of their arrears before they lost a wicket. . . .

Northamptonshire

C. N. Woolley, A. H. Bakewell, Mr A. P. R. Hawtin, J. E. Timms, *Mr V. W. C. Jupp, A.G. Liddell, A. L. Cox, A. D. Matthews, †B. Bellamy, Mr E. F. Towell and A. E. Thomas.

First innings: 249 (Bakewell 84, Timms 78; Hornibrook four for 45, Bradman none for 31).

Australians

*W. M. Woodfull b Jupp	15	–	c Bellamy b Towell	116
A. Jackson c and b Thomas	9	–	c and b Cox	52
D. G. Bradman b Jupp	22	–	c Hawtin b Cox	35
A. Fairfax b Jupp	1	–	c Bellamy b Timms	1
A. F. Kippax b Thomas	10	–	c Cox b Jupp	20
V. Y. Richardson c Bellamy b Thomas	7	–	c Jupp b Towell	116
E. L. a'Beckett c Bakewell b Matthews	13	–	c and b Matthews	22
A. Hurwood st Bellamy b Jupp	2	–	b Jupp	12
P. M. Hornibrook b Jupp	2	–	not out	16
T. W. Wall lbw b Jupp	3			
†C. W. Walker not out	0			
B 7, l-b 2	9		B 10, l-b 2, w 1, n-b 2	15
	93		(eight wkts)	**405**

Northamptonshire bowling: *First innings*—Thomas 29–14–29–3; Matthews 10–3–18–1; Jupp 23.4–10–32–6; Towell 3–0–5–0. *Second innings*—Thomas 25–12–32–0; Matthews 35.5–5–83–1; Jupp 21–5–47–2; Towell 24–4–84–2; Cox 28–2–87–2; Liddell 12–3–36–0; Timms 5–1–21–1.

Umpires: F. Chester and W. R. Parry

ENGLAND v AUSTRALIA 52 (80)
(FIFTH TEST MATCH) 9 (15)

Played at Kennington Oval, Saturday, Monday, Tuesday, Wednesday, Thursday, Friday, August 16, 18, 19, 20, 21, 22 [1930]. Beating England in an innings with 39 runs to spare, Australia won the rubber and so regained possession of the Ashes they had lost four years previously on the same ground. Each side having proved successful once and the other two games being drawn, the concluding Test Match had to be played to a finish irrespective of the number of days involved. Including the Thursday when, owing to rain, not a ball could be bowled, the encounter was spread over six days – a longer time than had ever before been occupied by a Test Match in England.

Australia won the match fairly and squarely . . . but just as rain had assisted England in the First Test Match at Nottingham, so it operated against them at the Oval. England had to play their second innings on a pitch so entirely suited to bowlers that in the circumstances they actually accomplished a good performance in scoring as many runs as they did on the last day. . . . Admitting the weather bore hardly upon the losers, it is but proper to observe that England contributed to their undoing by faulty work in the field. To stress the mistakes of any particular individual is never a congenial task, but as a matter of history it must be set down that Duckworth, who, usually so dependable a wicket-keeper, had gone through the previous Australian tour in brilliant fashion, failed badly. At the very outset of the Australian innings he missed Woodfull, let off Ponsford twice before that batsman had made 50 and, on the Tuesday, failed to catch Bradman at the wicket. Between them these three Australian cricketers made 396 runs …

Once more Australia owed a great deal to Bradman, who followed up his previous batting successes at Nottingham, Lord's and Leeds with an innings of 232. As usual he scored well in front of the wicket but he obtained a large number of runs on the leg side, while from start to finish his defence was altogether remarkable. All the same he did not play in anything like the attractive style he had shown at Lord's; indeed, there were periods when he became monotonous. Scoring so heavily as he did, Bradman again overshadowed everyone else, but his task was made the easier by the good work accomplished, before he went in, by Ponsford and Woodfull, who once more wore the bowling down by their workmanlike and steady cricket. …

… Before Bradman reached the wicket there was a delay through defective light and a little while afterwards came a further break from the same cause. With the score up to 190, Woodfull was out … [and when] play ceased, Australia, with two men out for 215, were only 190 runs behind. In all, Bradman and Kippax added 73 for the third wicket. Then came the big stand of the innings, Bradman and Jackson not being separated until Wednesday at one o'clock, by which time they had put on 243 runs in four and a half hours. Jackson was nearly run out before he had scored and almost bowled when five, while Bradman, at 82, gave a chance at the wicket. Rain came on during lunch-time on the Tuesday, the score then standing at 371 for three wickets, and, play being resumed soon after three o'clock, a further break through rain and bad light just about four o'clock occurred with the score at 402. It looked as though there would be no more cricket that day but the players went out at twenty-five minutes past six and in the five minutes one more run was obtained. On the Wednesday morning the ball flew about a good deal, both batsmen frequently being hit on the body. The partnership might have ended at 458 had Leyland returned the ball to the right end, and on more than one occasion each player cocked the ball up dangerously but always, as it happened, just wide of the fieldsmen. Caught at length, at extra cover-point, Jackson played nothing like as well as those who saw him in Australia knew he could. For the most part he was very restrained and, except that it helped in a record Australia stand for the fourth wicket, his innings was hardly worthy of his reputation. Bradman all this time had gone steadily on but when joined by McCabe was overshadowed, the latter driving brilliantly. Another 64 runs were added and then Bradman, at 570, was caught by Duckworth standing back. In seven hours he made 232 out of 411 with sixteen 4's, ten 3's and twenty-eight 2's as his chief hits. …

England, 290 behind, went in again at a quarter to six. When Hobbs and Sutcliffe reached the wickets, the Australians gathered round Hobbs and gave three cheers as a tribute to the great batsman playing presumably his last innings for England. …

No play took place on the Thursday owing to rain. On Friday the sun shone and everyone realised that only a miracle could save England. … With [Leyland's] dismissal England's hope of saving the innings defeat disappeared. Hammond went on hitting but received no support. With the last man in Hammond was missed at long-off by Bradman, but three runs later he fell to a catch in the slips and at ten minutes to four the match was all over. …

Except towards the end of the first day, the Australian fielding in both innings was uncommonly good. Nobody did better than Bradman who, whether at fine-leg or long-off, covered so much ground, picked up and returned so swiftly that many a possible four was turned into a single. …

In the course of the match, more than 110,000 people witnessed the cricket, the sum taken at the gates amounting to over £13,000. Very appropriately, the day on which Australia regained the Ashes with this victory coincided with the birthday of Woodfull, their captain, who was then 33.

England

J. B. Hobbs, H. Sutcliffe, W. Whysall, K. S. Duleepsinhji, W. R. Hammond, M. Leyland, *Mr R. E. S. Wyatt, M. W. Tate, H. Larwood, †G. Duckworth and Mr I. A. R. Peebles.

First innings: 405 (Hobbs 47, Sutcliffe 161, Duleepsinhji 50, Wyatt 64; Fairfax three for 52, Grimmett four for 135). *Second innings:* 251 (Sutcliffe 54, Duleepsinhji 46, Hammond 60; Hornibrook seven for 92).

Australia

*W. M. Woodfull c Duckworth b Peebles	54
W. H. Ponsford b Peebles	110
D. G. Bradman c Duckworth b Larwood	232
A. F. Kippax c Wyatt b Peebles	28
A. Jackson c Sutcliffe b Wyatt	73
S. McCabe c Duckworth b Hammond	54
A. Fairfax not out	53
†W. A. Oldfield c Larwood b Peebles	34
C. V. Grimmett lbw b Peebles	6
T. W. Wall lbw b Peebles	0
P. M. Hornibrook c Duckworth b Tate	7
B 22, l-b 18, n-b 4	44
	695

England bowling: Larwood 48–6–132–1; Tate 65.1–12–153–1; Peebles 71–8–204–6; Wyatt 14–1–58–1; Hammond 42–12–70–1; Leyland 16–7–34–0.

Umpires: J. Hardstaff and W. R. Parry

GLOUCESTERSHIRE v AUSTRALIANS 53 (81, 82)

Played at Bristol, Saturday, Monday, Tuesday, August 23, 25, 26 [1930]. There was a memorable finish to this match, the Australians, who had been set 118 to make to win, being all dismissed for 117 and the contest thus ending in a tie. Never before in England had a first-class match, in which an Australian team figured, terminated in this way. For a long time after the Australians entered upon their second innings the contest held out no promise of excitement. Indeed, of the 118 runs needed for victory no fewer than 59 – exactly half the number – were put on by Jackson and McCabe for the opening partnership. The pitch was obviously in a condition to assist the bowlers but to begin with Parker proved so erratic that the score reached 50 in forty minutes. Gradually, however, Parker not only found his length but a worn spot and thenceforward he was deadly in the extreme. … [T]here were three men out for 67 at the luncheon interval.

… On play being resumed the game took a most dramatic turn. Six runs were added and then, with the total at 73, not only did Parker get Kippax leg before but Sinfield, picking up smartly and getting in a splendid return, threw out Ponsford from mid-on. Bradman still remained but neither he nor a'Beckett, against skilful bowling and most brilliant fielding, could get the ball away. Roused to tremendous excitement, the spectators cheered everything and their enthusiasm knew no bounds when at 81 Parker bowled Bradman. They had still further occasion for joy five runs later when a catch in the slips disposed of a'Beckett. [This left Australia needing 32 runs with three wickets in hand.] …

Unhappily for the home side, there came just afterwards a blemish on what up to that point had been a superb display of fielding, Lyon, when Grimmett had made seven, getting his hand to a ball put up by that batsman but failing to effect the catch. … Grimmett and Hurwood offered such a determined resistance to Parker and Goddard that they added 22 for the eighth wicket before Hurwood was leg before. Thus only 10 runs were wanted when Hornibrook joined Grimmett. The newcomer surviving two appeals for lbw, the score had been advanced to 115 – three to win – when Parker dismissed Grimmett, who had withstood the attack for an hour. Walker followed in and two singles brought the total to 117. With the scores level, there came three maidens in succession and then on a further appeal against Hornibrook being answered in the bowler's favour, the Australians were all out and the match ended in a tie. …

On Monday [when Australia batted for the first time] the pitch, while still on the soft side, was, in the absence of sunshine, too slow to be really difficult. [Saturday's play had not begun until four o'clock because the ground was saturated.] Ponsford, second out at 78, batted in attractive fashion for an hour and a half but Bradman, although staying for an hour and three-quarters, never mastered the attack. Subsequent to lunch, seven wickets fell for 64 runs. …

Gloucestershire

R.A. Sinfield, A.E. Dipper, W.R. Hammond, *Mr B.H. Lyon, †H. Smith, C.C. Dacre, Mr F.J. Seabrook, W.L. Neale, C.J. Barnett, C. Parker and T.W. Goddard.

First innings: 72 (Hurwood three for 13, Grimmett three for 28, Hornibrook four for 20). *Second innings:* 202 (Hammond 89; Hornibrook five for 49).

Australians

W. H. Ponsford b Sinfield	51	–	run out	0
A. Jackson b Goddard	8	–	lbw b Goddard	25
D. G. Bradman c Sinfield b Parker	42	–	b Parker	14
A. F. Kippax lbw b Sinfield	3	–	lbw b Parker	0
S. McCabe c Smith b Parker	5	–	b Parker	34
*V. Y. Richardson lbw b Goddard	12	–	st Smith b Parker	3
E. L. a'Beckett c Sinfield b Goddard	1	–	c Lyon b Parker	2
A. Hurwood b goddard	0	–	lbw b Parker	14
C. V. Grimmett not out	7	–	c Seabrook b Parker	12
P. M. Hornibrook b Goddard	9	–	lbw b Goddard	4
†C. W. Walker c Seabrook b Parker	7	–	not out	0
B 5, l-b 7	12		B 2, l-b 7	9
	157			**117**

Gloucestershire bowling: *First innings*—Sinfield 14–5–18–2; Barnett 4–3–3–0; Goddard 26–7–52–5; Parker 30.5–9–72–3. *Second innings*—Goddard 34.1–10–54–2; Parker 35–14–54–7.

Umpires: W. A. Buswell and W. Huddleston

KENT v AUSTRALIANS 54 (83, 84)

Played at Canterbury, Wednesday, Thursday, Friday, August 27, 28, 29 [1930]. Yet another great display of batting on the part of Bradman was the outstanding feature of this drawn match, the famous young Australian in the second innings withstanding the Kent bowling for four hours and three-quarters and being still unbeaten with 205 runs to his credit when Woodfull made a belated declaration. In putting together his fifth score of more than 200 [six including his triple-century in the Third Test] Bradman did not give a single chance. … [In Kent's first innings] Todd carried restraint to extreme limits, being at the wickets seventy-five minutes before he registered his second run and in all batting nearly three hours and a half for 42.

Australians

*W. M. Woodfull run out	16	–	lbw b Freeman	45
W. H. Ponsford c Ashdown b Freeman	21	–	b Ashdown	11
D. G. Bradman lbw b Freeman	18	–	not out	205
A. Jackson lbw b Freeman	11	–	not out	50
V. Y. Richardson c Ames b Ashdown	45			
A. Fairfax b Freeman	4			
E. L. a'Beckett run out	4			
C. V. Grimmett c Chapman b Ashdown	0			
A. Hurwood c Ames b Hardinge	45	–	run out	
T. W. Wall not out	12			
†C. W. Walker lbw b Freeman	1			
B 1, l-b 1, n-b 2	4		B 7, l-b 2	9
	181		(three wkts dec)	**320**

Kent bowling: *First innings*—Wright 7–2–18–0; Ashdown 18–4–38–2; Freeman 39.2–8–78–5; Hardinge 21–10–43–1. *Second innings*—Wright 16–4–40–0; Ashdown 21–4–68–1; Freeman 33–12–68–1; Hardinge 31–6–86–0; Woolley 16–7–21–0; Knott 2–0–28–0.

Kent

H. T. W. Hardinge, Mr J. L. Bryan, F. E. Woolley, †L. Ames, L. Todd, W. Ashdown, Mr A. P. F. Chapman, Mr C. H. Knott, *Mr G. B. Legge, C. Wright and A. P. Freeman.

First innings: 227 (Hardinge 39, Bryan 31, Todd 42 not out, Ashdown 48; Wall five for 60, Grimmett four for 80). *Second innings:* Two for 83 (Woolley 60 not out).

Umpires: J. Hardstaff and H. Young

AN ENGLAND XI v AUSTRALIANS 55 (85)

Played at Folkestone, Wednesday, Thursday, Friday, September 3, 4, 5 [1930]. Batting in strangely restrained fashion under conditions quite favourable for run-getting, the English team, although Grimmett owing to an injury could bowl very little, scored only 249 for five on the opening day and thenceforward a draw was always practically certain. … Woodfull and Ponsford gave the Australians a capital start, staying together for an hour and three-quarters and raising the score to 117. … Bradman and Jackson put on 103 in seventy minutes. …

An England XI

Mr R. E. S. Wyatt, J. W. Hearne, W. R. Hammond, Jas. Langridge, †L. Ames, *Mr A. P. F. Chapman, Mr R. C. Robertson-Glasgow, M. W. Tate, Hon. F. S. G. Calthorpe, Mr M. J. C. Allom and A. P. Freeman.

First innings: Eight for 403 dec (Wyatt 51, Hearne 33, Hammond 54, Ames 121, Chapman 40, Tate 50; Wall three for 104, a'Beckett three for 81, Bradman none for 7). *Second innings:* One for 46.

Australians

*W. M. Woodfull run out	34
W. H. Ponsford c Calthorpe b Allom	76
D. G. Bradman lbw b Allom	63
A. F. Kippax lbw b Allom	0
A. Jackson b Langridge	78
S. McCabe b Allom	14
E. L. a'Beckett c Hammond b Freeman	53
†W. A. Oldfield lbw b Freeman	10
C. V. Grimmett c Langridge b Freeman	1
P. M. Hornibrook c Hearne b Freeman	43
T. W. Wall not out	40
B 9, l-b 11	20
	432

An England XI bowling: Tate 14–5–31–0; Allom 32–5–94–4; Freeman 41.5–3–131–4; Robertson-Glasgow 11–2–12–0; Langridge 16–1–54–1; Hammond 5–1–10–0; Wyatt 5–0–32–0; Calthorpe 5–2–12–0; Chapman 1–0–5–0; Hearne 8–2–31–0.

Umpires: F. Chester and A. E. Street

CLUB CRICKET CONFERENCE v AUSTRALIANS

Played at Lord's, Saturday, Monday, September 6, 8 [1930]. The two days set apart for the decision of this match proved sufficient for that purpose, the Australians winning by an innings and 41 runs. ... For the first and only time during the tour the wider and higher wicket was used [see page 110]. Bradman, despite some capital fast bowling by Smith and Brindley, batted so brilliantly that he scored 70 in seventy-five minutes and incidentally completed his 3,000 runs. ...

Australians

W. H. Ponsford c Summers b Brindley	0
A. Fairfax b Brindley	25
D. G. Bradman c Whitehead b Nazeer Ali	70
A. F. Kippax b Smith	63
S. McCabe b Brindley	0
E. L. a'Beckett b Smith	14
*W. M. Woodfull c Summers b Brindley	69
†W. A. Oldfield b Smith	0
A. Hurwood b Smith	0
P. M. Hornibrook lbw b Brindley	1
C. W. Walker not out	7
B 18, l-b 11	29
	278

Club Cricket Conference bowling: Smith 23–3–70–4; Brindley 30.1–4–71–5; Nazeer Ali 25–5–52–1; Taylor 14–1–45–0; Jarvis 4–0–11–0.

Club Cricket Conference

Mr T.G. Grinter, Mr L.W. Newman, Mr T.N. Pearce, Mr G.F. Summers, Mr W.T. Brindley, Mr S. Nazeer Ali, Mr H. Taylor, *Mr F.E. Whitehead, Mr V.E. Jarvis, Mr H.T.O. Smith and †Mr H.E.L. Piercy.

First innings: 133 (Summers 53, Brindley 34; Fairfax four for 41, Hurwood five for 14). *Second innings:* 104 (Pearce 30; a'Beckett three for 1, Hornibrook four for 37).

Umpires: Marshall and Dray

MR H.D.G. LEVESON GOWER'S XI v AUSTRALIANS 56 (86)

Played at Scarborough, Wednesday, Thursday, Friday, September 10, 11, 12 [1930]. In the concluding fixture of the tour rain caused a considerable loss of play and consequently there existed no chance of bringing the game to a definite issue. Richardson winning the toss sent the Englishmen in to bat ... Next day, when cricket proved impossible until a quarter to three, the Australians lost two wickets for 53 but Bradman and Kippax added 110 before bad light brought play to a close. Bradman should have been caught at mid-off first ball and just after reaching 60 was twice missed, all three chances being off Rhodes. Next day he ought, when 74, to have been easily run out. In the end he was bowled off his pads. The cricket when the Englishmen entered upon their second innings was taken in a very light-hearted spirit. ... Despite the weather the match attracted a large crowd each day.

Mr H.D.G. Leveson Gower's XI

J.B. Hobbs, H. Sutcliffe, K.S. Duleepsinhji, A. Sandham, M. Leyland, *Mr R.E.S. Wyatt, M. W. Tate, H. Larwood, W. Rhodes, †G. Duckworth and C. Parker.

First innings: Nine for 218 dec (Sutcliffe 45, Sandham 59; Hornibrook five for 69). *Second innings:* 247 (Hobbs 59, Duleepsinhji 41, Leyland 50; Hornibrook three for 100, Bradman three for 52).

Australians

A. Jackson b Rhodes	24	C. V. Grimmett c Wyatt b Rhodes	3
A. Fairfax st Duckworth b Rhodes	8	P. M. Hornibrook lbw b Parker	0
D. G. Bradman b Parker	96	T. W. Wall c Wyatt b Rhodes	6
A. F. Kippax b Larwood	59	†W. A. Oldfield absent hurt	0
S. McCabe c Larwood b Parker	24	B 6, l-b 3	9
*V. Y. Richardson not out	8		**238**
A. Hurwood b Rhodes	1		

Mr Leveson Gower's XI bowling: Larwood 14–4–34–1; Tate 10–3–14–0; Parker 31–7–81–3; Rhodes 30.5–5–95–5; Wyatt 2–0–5–0.

Umpires: D. Denton and A. Morton

1930-31

1930-31

The larger wicket* was used in all Sheffield Shield games during the 1930-31 season, which proved of particular interest by reason of the close rivalry between Victoria (holders) and New South Wales. In the end Victoria, for the thirteenth time, won the trophy, but New South Wales finished up no more than one point behind. ... Bradman, playing six innings for New South Wales [in the Sheffield Shield], scored 695 runs and returned an average of 115. In the game with South Australia at Adelaide, he and Jackson, by putting on 334 for the second wicket, set up a new record for Shield cricket. ...

Attendances at the games during the season were greatly affected by the bad weather often experienced. ... Sheffield Shield matches in 1930-31, however, were limited to four days, with no option of continuing play on the fifth day, and this arrangement, of course, caused some decline in aggregate attendances at some matches. ...

From 'Cricket in Australia: The Inter-State Matches'

*In the first change to the size of the wicket for 108 years, the height (ie, stumps and bails) was increased by 1½ inches (3.81 cm) to 28½ inches (72.39 cm) and the width by 1 inch (2.54 cm) to 9 inches (22.86 cm). These have remained the dimensions of the wicket.

NEW SOUTH WALES v SOUTH AUSTRALIA 57 (87, 88)

Played at Sydney, November 7, 8, 10, 11 [1930]. The absence of Grimmett and Wall greatly weakened the bowling of South Australia, and although on the last day Nitschke ... played a strong defensive innings, New South Wales, with plenty of time to spare, won by 213 runs. Bradman, Fairfax and Hooker between them scored all but 51 of the New South Wales first innings total and Hooker, when South Australia went in, bowled with much skill, taking five wickets for 28. Left with a lead of 104, New South Wales, thanks to a hundred apiece from Bradman and Kippax, placed themselves in a very strong position, finishing up on the second day 421 ahead with half their wickets left. South Australia ultimately was set the tremendous task of scoring 501 to win. ...

New South Wales

C. Andrews b Deverson	6	–	c Parry b Carlton	0
O. W. Bill c Parry b Carlton	2	–	run out	5
D. G. Bradman c Pritchard b Deverson	61	–	c Waite b Deverson	121
*A. F. Kippax lbw b Tobin	19	–	b Deverson	104
A. Allsopp b Tobin	9	–	b Carlton	93
A. G. Fairfax b Carlton	62	–	b Deverson	6
†H. L. Davidson c Walsh b Deverson	2	–	c Tobin b Deverson	19
H. Hooker b Deverson	54	–	absent hurt	0
H. C. Chilvers b Carlton	3	–	c Lonergan b Lee	29
W. A. Hunt st Parry b Carlton	2	–	not out	7
G. L. Stewart not out	4	–	run out	2
W 1, n-b 3	4		B 4, l-b 1, w 1, n-b 4	10
	228			**396**

South Australia bowling: *First innings*—Deverson 15–1–60–4; Carlton 9.1–1–28–4; Lee 5–0–21–0; Tobin 9–0–75–2; Waite 9–0–40–0. *Second innings*—Deverson 19–1–86–4; Carlton 15.3–1–61–2; Lee 15–0–107–1; Tobin 3–0–25–0; Waite 16–1–107–0.

South Australia

G. W. Harris, H. C. Nitschke, *D. E. Pritchard, A. R. Lonergan, B. J. Tobin, L. S. Walsh, P. K. Lee, M.G. Waite, †C. N. Parry, T. A. Carlton and C. S. Deverson.

First innings: 124 (Nitschke 31, Lee 40; Stewart three for 25, Hooker five for 28). *Second innings:* 287 (Nitschke 141, Pritchard 30, Lee 36; Fairfax four for 54, Hunt three for 37, Bradman none for 41).

Umpires: W. H. Bayfield and M. Carney

AUSTRALIA v REST OF AUSTRALIA 58 (89, 90)

Played at Melbourne, November 14, 15, 17, 18 [1930]. A game arranged as a Testimonial to J. Ryder, Australia's former captain, also served to welcome the return of the victorious seventeenth Australian team in England. Unfortunately it was much interfered with by bad weather, the third day being entirely blank. On the Saturday, however, over 44,000 people attended and altogether Ryder received about £3,000. ... Bradman, Kippax and Woodfull batted skilfully, if with some lack of freedom, for Australia ... Set to get 118 in an hour and a half, Australia made a determined effort to win against the clock but lost half their wickets and failed by 22 runs.

Rest of Australia

G.W. Harris, H.L. Hendry, K.E. Rigg, *J. Ryder, A. Allsopp, T.J.E. Andrews, †J.L. Ellis, D.D. Blackie, H. Alexander, A.A. Mailey and H. Ironmonger.

First innings: 293 (Harris 108, Hendry 45, Ryder 38; Grimmett five for 89). *Second innings:* Three for 191 dec (Rigg 74, Ryder 65 not out; Bradman none for 27).

Australia

W. H. Ponsford lbw b Alexander	14	–	lbw b Ironmonger	0
A. A. Jackson c Ellis b Alexander	4	–	b Alexander	5
D. G. Bradman b Mailey	73	–	c and b Mailey	29
A. F. Kippax lbw b Blackie	70	–	b Blackie	17
S. J. McCabe c Alexander b Ironmonger	27	–	b Blackie	20
*W. M. Woodfull b Ironmonger	53	–	not out	13
A. G. Fairfax c Alexander b Ironmonger	39			
E. L. a'Beckett c Andrews b Mailey	30			
†W. A. Oldfield run out	18			
C. V. Grimmett b Mailey	28			
T. W. Wall not out	2			
B 4, l-b 5	9		B 8, l-b 2, w 1, n-b 1	12
	367		(five wkts)	**96**

Rest of Australia bowling: *First innings*—Alexander 15–1–64–2; Hendry 7–0–27–0; Blackie 17–2–45–1; Ironmonger 28–3–76–3; Mailey 23.3–2–126–3; Ryder 2–0–11–0; Andrews 2–0–9–0. *Second innings*—Alexander 5–1–24–1; Blackie 5.5–0–15–2; Ironmonger 6–0–17–1; Mailey 4–0–28–1.

Umpires: A. N. Barlow and D. Elder

WEST INDIES v NEW SOUTH WALES 59 (91, 92)

Played at Sydney, November 21, 22, 24, 25 [1930]. Defeat by four wickets from a powerful New South Wales Eleven was by no means an unsatisfactory start for the West Indies [in their first-ever first-class match in Australia. When in their second innings New South Wales were chasing 224 to win]. The total reached 97 before a wicket fell, but Headley caught Bradman brilliantly in the long field and half the side were out for 131. ... On the second day nearly 20,000 people watched the cricket, and for the first two days the gate receipts amounted to £2,900.

West Indies

F. R. Martin, C. A. Roach, E. L. Bartlett, G. Headley, L. S. Birkett, *G. C. Grant, L. N. Constantine, G. N. Francis, †I. Barrow, E. St Hill and O. C. Scott.

First innings: 188 (Roach 43, Birkett 31, Grant 30; Chilvers four for 84, Fairfax three for 42, McCabe three for 23). *Second innings:* 241 (Headley 82, Grant 44, Constantine 59; Chilvers five for 73).

New South Wales

A. G. Fairfax b Constantine	9	–	not out	32
O. W. Bill c Constantine b St Hill	13	–	lbw b Martin	34
D. G. Bradman c Barrow b Francis	73	–	c Headley b Martin	22
*A. F. Kippax b Constantine	6			
S. J. McCabe b Constantine	18	–	not out	37
A. A. Jackson lbw b Constantine	13	–	b Martin	62
A. Allsopp run out	32	–	b Constantine	3
†W. A. Oldfield st Barrow b Scott	21	–	lbw b Constantine	0
W. A. Hunt b Francis	5			
H. C. Chilvers b Francis	8			
G. L. Stewart not out	1	–	c Roach b St Hill	20
L-b 1, n-b 6	7		B 3, l-b 4, n-b 7	14
	206		(six wkts)	**224**

West Indies bowling: *First innings*—Constantine 11–1–43–4; Francis 11–2–38–3; St Hill 10–2–46–1; Martin 3–0–22–0; Scott 8–0–50–1. *Second innings*—Constantine 11.1–2–53–2; Francis 8–0–37–0; St Hill 14–1–57–1; Martin 8–0–35–3; Scott 4–0–28–0.

Umpires: G. Borwick and W.G. French

AUSTRALIA v WEST INDIES 60 (93)
(FIRST TEST MATCH) 10 (16)

Played at Adelaide, December 12, 13, 15, 16 [1930]. Australia, with Hurwood for Hornibrook the only change from the Eleven that beat England at the Oval during the previous [northern] summer, gained a decisive victory by ten wickets. Up to the point that Australia had lost their first three batsmen for 64, West Indies made a capital fight, but Kippax and McCabe added 182 by admirable cricket. Scott on the third morning took the last four wickets without conceding a run but West Indies were outplayed for the rest of the match. . . .

West Indies

C. A. Roach, L. S. Birkett, G. Headley, F. R. Martin, L. N. Constantine, *G. C. Grant, E. L. Bartlett, †I. Barrow, G. N. Francis, O. C. Scott and H. C. Griffith.

First innings: 296 (Roach 56, Martin 39, Grant 53 not out, Bartlett 84; Grimmett seven for 87, Hurwood three for 55, Bradman none for 7). *Second innings:* 249 (Birkett 64, Grant 71 not out; Grimmett four for 96, Hurwood four for 86, Bradman one for 8).

Australia

W. H. Ponsford c Birkett b Francis	24	–	not out	92
A. A. Jackson c Barrow b Francis	31	–	not out	70
D. G. Bradman c Grant b Griffith	4			
A. F. Kippax c Barrow b Griffith	146			
S. J. McCabe c and b Constantine	90			
*W. M. Woodfull run out	6			
A. G. Fairfax not out	41			
†W. A. Oldfield c Francis b Scott	15			
C. V. Grimmett c Barrow b Scott	0			
A. Hurwood c Martin b Scott	0			
T. W. Wall lbw b Scott	0			
B 2, l-b 10, n-b 7	19		B 8, w 1, n-b 1	10
	376		(no wkt)	**172**

West Indies bowling: *First innings*—Francis 18–7–43–2; Constantine 22–0–89–1; Griffith 28–4–69–2; Martin 29–3–73–0; Scott 20.5–2–83–4. *Second innings*—Francis 10–1–30–0; Constantine 9.3–3–27–0; Griffith 10–1–20–0; Martin 11–0–28–0; Scott 13–0–55–0; Birkett 2–0–2–0.

Umpires: G. A. Hele and A.G. Jenkins

SOUTH AUSTRALIA v NEW SOUTH WALES 61 (94)

Played at Adelaide, December 18, 19, 20, 22 [1930]. Brilliant batting by Bradman and Jackson largely determined the result of this return fixture, New South Wales winning by an innings and 134 runs. The South Australian bowlers, including Grimmett, went through a heart-breaking experience on the first day when Bradman hit up 258 in four hours and three-quarters and with Jackson, who played his usual stylish game, shared in a second-wicket stand which, extending over three hours and three-quarters, produced 334 runs. This was a record for the competition. At first uncomfortable against Grimmett, Bradman afterwards was completely master of the situation and hit so freely that 148 of his runs came in 4's. Next day the play went overwhelmingly in favour of bowlers. . . .

New South Wales

J. H. Fingleton st Walker b Grimmett	6	†H. S. Love lbw b Grimmett	4
A. A. Jackson c Richardson b Waite	166	H. Hooker b Carlton	45
D. G. Bradman b Richardson	258	W. A. Hunt not out	15
*A. F. Kippax b Grimmett	42	H. C. Chilvers run out	23
S. J. McCabe lbw b Carlton	7	B 4, l-b 2	6
A. G. Fairfax b Grimmett	38		**610**
O. W. Bill lbw b Grimmett	0		

South Australia bowling: Wall 23–0–89–0; Carlton 20.2–0–99–2; Lee 38–4–144–0; Grimmett 48–5–180–5; Waite 7–0–54–1; Richardson 8–0–38–1.

South Australia

G. W. Harris, H. C. Nitschke, D. E. Pritchard, *V. Y. Richardson, A. Hack, P. K. Lee, M.G. Waite, T. A. Carlton, C. V. Grimmett, T. W. Wall and †C. W. Walker.

First innings: 166 (Nitschke 69; Hunt five for 36, Chilvers five for 68). *Second innings:* 310 (Nitschke 102, Wall 45 not out; Hunt four for 105, Bradman three for 54).

Umpires: G. A. Hele and A.G. Jenkins

VICTORIA v NEW SOUTH WALES 62 (95)

Played at Melbourne, December 24, 26, 27, 29 [1930]. Scoring 30 for the loss of three wickets on the opening day, Victoria, owing to rain, were unable to continue their batting until the last morning and not even a first-innings decision could be reached. . . .

Victoria

*W. M. Woodfull, W. H. Ponsford, H. L. Hendry, J. Ryder, K. E. Rigg, E. L. a'Beckett, L. Darling, †B. A. Barnett, D. D. Blackie, H. Alexander and H. Ironmonger.

First innings: 185 (Ponsford 109 not out; Fairfax four for 41).

New South Wales

J. H. Fingleton run out	9	A. G. Fairfax st Barnett b Ironmonger	3
A. A. Jackson not out	52	†W. A. Oldfield c Rigg b Ironmonger	8
D. G. Bradman c Hendry b a'Beckett	2	H. Hooker not out	2
S. J. McCabe b Blackie	10	L-b 3, n-b 4	7
*A. F. Kippax hit wkt b Blackie	4	(six wkts)	**97**

H. C. Chilvers, W. A. Hunt and G. L. Stewart did not bat.

Victoria bowling: Alexander 6–1–21–0; a'Beckett 10–2–26–1; Ironmonger 15–5–26–2; Blackie 7–2–16–2; Darling 1–0–1–0.

Umpires: A. N. Barlow and J. Richards

AUSTRALIA v WEST INDIES 63 (96)

(SECOND TEST MATCH) 11 (17)

Played at Sydney, January 1, 2, 3, 5 [1931]. Unfortunately for West Indies, rain that prevented any play on the second day completely altered the conditions which had obtained at the start and Australia won very easily by an innings and 172 runs. To add to their bad luck, West Indies had to bat a man short, Bartlett in catching Kippax from a powerful hit at mid-on having a finger crushed against his boot and being unable to take any further part in the match. Ponsford playing in his most resolute and skilful style, Australia scored 323 for four wickets on a perfect Sydney pitch, but after the rain the character of the cricket changed so completely that on the third day twenty wickets fell for 220 runs. …

Australia

W. H. Ponsford b Scott	183
A. A. Jackson c Francis b Griffith	8
D. G. Bradman c Barrow b Francis	25
A. F. Kippax c Bartlett b Griffith	10
S. J. McCabe lbw b Scott	31
*W. M. Woodfull c Barrow b Constantine	58
A. G. Fairfax c Constantine b Francis	15
†W. A. Oldfield run out	0
C. V. Grimmett b Scott	12
A. Hurwood c Martin b Scott	5
H. Ironmonger not out	3
B 6, l-b 5, w 5, n-b 3	19
	369

West Indies bowling: Griffith 28–4–57–2; Constantine 18–2–56–1; Francis 27–3–70–2; Scott 15.4–0–66–4; Martin 18–1–60–0; Birkett 10–1–41–0.

West Indies

C. A. Roach, L. S. Birkett, G. Headley, F. R. Martin, L. N. Constantine, *G. C. Grant, G. N. Francis, †I. Barrow, H. C. Griffith, O. C. Scott and E. L. Bartlett.

First innings: 107 (Fairfax three for 19, Grimmett four for 54). *Second innings:* 90 (Hurwood four for 22, Ironmonger three for 13).

Umpires: G. Borwick and W.G. French

AUSTRALIA v WEST INDIES 64 (97)

(THIRD TEST MATCH) 12 (18)

Played at [Exhibition Ground] Brisbane, January 16, 17, 19, 20 [1931]. Early on the fourth morning, Australia were successful by an innings and 217 runs, so winning the rubber with three consecutive victories. … West Indies had an early encouragement in the fall of Jackson without scoring, but stands of 229 and 193 followed and, naturally, Australia never lost their hold on the game. Apart from a chance just before getting out, Ponsford batted faultlessly but Kippax was unsteady and Bradman, when four, was missed in the slips. Apart from this chance Bradman, in putting together the highest innings played for Australia in any Test Match in that country, showed that exceptional combination of skill and judgment that has produced for him so many triumphs. Next morning, on a pitch drying under the influence of strong sunshine, Bradman did not add to his overnight score. Batting for five hours, he hit twenty-four 4's. …

Australia

W. H. Ponsford c Birkett b Francis	109
A. A. Jackson lbw b Francis	0
D. G. Bradman c Grant b Constantine	223
A. F. Kippax b Birkett	84
S. J. McCabe c Constantine b Griffith	17
*W. M. Woodfull c Barrow b Griffith	8
A. G. Fairfax c Sealy b Scott	9
R. K. Oxenham lbw b Griffith	48
C. V. Grimmett c Constantine b Francis	4
H. Ironmonger c Roach b Griffith	2
†W. A. Oldfield not out	38
B 2, l-b 7, n-b 7	16
	558

West Indies bowling: Francis 26–4–76–3; Griffith 33–4–133–4; Scott 24–0–125–1; Constantine 26–2–74–1; Martin 27–3–85–0; Sealy 3–0–32–0; Birkett 7–0–16–1; Grant 1–0–1–0.

West Indies

C. A. Roach, F. R. Martin, G. Headley, J. E. D. Sealy, *G. C. Grant, L. N. Constantine, L. S. Birkett, †I. Barrow, O. C. Scott, G. N. Francis and H. G. Griffith.

First innings: 193 (Headley 102 not out; Oxenham four for 39, Grimmett four for 95). *Second innings:* 148 (Grimmett five for 49).

Umpires: J. P. Orr and A. E. Wyeth

NEW SOUTH WALES v VICTORIA 65 (98, 99)

Played at Sydney, January 24, 26, 27, 28 [1931]. Victoria took first innings points from a drawn game marked by several good individual performances. Fairfax, batting doggedly for two hours, alone met Victoria's attack with resolution on the first day. ... Bradman, however, came out in brilliant form when New South Wales batted again. He played his third innings of over 200 during the season and with Bill added 234 in two hours and a quarter for the fifth wicket. Declaring, New South Wales left Victoria ten minutes under five hours in which to score 296 to win. Defensive batting was general. Rigg stayed over four hours for 98.

New South Wales

A. G. Fairfax c a'Beckett b Blackie	46	–	c O'Brien b Blackie	12
J. H. Fingleton b Alexander	6	–	st Barnett b Blackie	4
D. G. Bradman c Barnett b Alexander	33	–	c Rigg b Ironmonger	220
*A. F. Kippax b Alexander	6	–	c and b Blackie	26
S. J. McCabe c Barnett b Ironmonger	29	–	b Alexander	20
A. E. Marks b Blackie	9	–	b Ironmonger	9
O. W. Bill c a'Beckett b Blackie	39	–	b Blackie	100
†W. A. Oldfield c Barnett b a'Beckett	9	–	c Darling b Ironmonger	1
H. Hooker c Barnett b a'Beckett	0	–	not out	0
W. A. Hunt st Barnett b Blackie	15	–	c Rigg b Blackie	16
H. C. Chilvers not out	1			
B 1, l-b 1, w 1	3		B 3, l-b 4, w 2	9
	196		(nine wkts dec)	**417**

Victoria bowling: *First innings*—Alexander 13–0–43–3; a'Beckett 14–2–41–2; Ironmonger 16–5–56–1; Hendry 2–0–8–0; Blackie 12.3–0–45–4. *Second innings*—Alexander 15–1–89–1; a'Beckett 13–0–58–0; Ironmonger 22.4–0–91–3; Hendry 3–0–20–0; Blackie 23–2–101–5; Ryder 4–0–39–0; Darling 2–0–10–0.

Victoria

H. L. Hendry, L. P. O'Brien, K. E. Rigg, *J. Ryder, H. H. Oakley, L. Darling, E. L. a'Beckett, D. D. Blackie, †B. A. Barnett, H. Alexander and H. Ironmonger.

First innings: 318 (Hendry 39, O'Brien 119, Ryder 31; McCabe four for 46, Bradman none for 31). *Second innings:* Six for 202 (Rigg 98, Ryder 36; Hunt three for 38, Bradman none for 16).

Umpires: H. Armstrong and W.G. French

AUSTRALIA v WEST INDIES 66 (100)
(FOURTH TEST MATCH) 13 (19)

Played at Melbourne, February 13, 14 [1931]. Beaten in two days by an innings and 122 runs in the Fourth Test Match, West Indies gave their most disappointing batting display of the whole tour. On a pitch that seemed in perfectly good order they made a fair start, but Ironmonger brought about an astonishing collapse and in the second innings also bowled with considerable success. Altogether Ironmonger took eleven wickets for 79 and fairly shared with Bradman the chief honours of Australia's easy victory. Thanks to Woodfull and Bradman, Australia led by 98 at the end of the first day for the loss of Ponsford – dismissed at 50. Following upon rain in the night, Australia continued batting until three o'clock, when the closure was applied with eight wickets down for 328. Woodfull lost his wicket over an ill-judged run when the second partnership had realised 212, but Bradman – 92 overnight – went on batting brilliantly. Altogether at the wickets for four hours and three-quarters, Bradman hit fifteen 4's. West Indies ... never looked like taking the match into the third day.

West Indies

C.A. Roach, F.R. Martin, L.S. Birkett, G. Headley, E.L. Bartlett, *G.C. Grant, †I. Barrow, L. N. Constantine, O.C. Scott, H.C. Griffith and G.N. Francis.

First innings: 99 (Headley 33; Ironmonger seven for 23). *Second innings:* 107 (Fairfax four for 31, Ironmonger four for 56).

Australia

*W. M. Woodfull run out	83
W. H. Ponsford st Barrow b Constantine	24
D. G. Bradman c Roach b Martin	152
A. A. Jackson c Birkett b Constantine	15
S. J. McCabe run out	2
A. F. Kippax b Martin	24
A. G. Fairfax c Birkett b Martin	16
R. K. Oxenham c Constantine b Griffith	0
†W. A. Oldfield not out	1
B 7, l-b 3, n-b 1	11
(eight wkts dec)	**328**

H. Ironmonger and C. V. Grimmett did not bat.

West Indies bowling: Francis 13–0–51–0; Griffith 8–1–33–1; Scott 11–0–47–0; Constantine 25–4–83–2; Martin 30.2–3–91–3; Birkett 3–0–12–0.

Umpires: A. N. Barlow and J. Richards

WEST INDIES v NEW SOUTH WALES 67 (101, 102)

Played at Sydney, February 21, 23, 24, 25 [1931]. Although New South Wales were much below full strength, West Indies in winning by 86 runs accomplished an admirable performance. Consistent batting followed by very good work in the field earned a first innings lead of 149 ... Further rapid scoring enabled Grant to declare with nine men out and there remained scarcely time for New South Wales to get 553 runs required for victory. Still, Kippax and McCabe batted so well that at tea-time the home team had made 373 with only four men out, but a collapse ensued. ...

West Indies

F.R. Martin, C.A. Roach, G. Headley, *G.C. Grant, J.E.D. Sealy, L.N. Constantine, O.S. Wight, †I. Barrow, O.C. Scott, G.N. Francis and H.C. Griffith.

First innings: 339 (Roach 55, Headley 70, Grant 36, Sealy 58, Constantine 41; Chilvers three for 56). *Second innings:* Nine for 403 dec (Martin 56, Sealy 92, Constantine 93, Barrow 45, Scott 67 not out; Chilvers three for 53).

New South Wales

†H. L. Davidson b Constantine	16	–	b Francis	32
O. W. Bill run out	41	–	lbw b Francis	11
D. G. Bradman b Constantine	10	–	lbw b Griffith	73
*A. F. Kippax lbw b Griffith	32	–	c Sealy b Griffith	141
S. J. McCabe b Constantine	26	–	c Barrow b Martin	100
A. Bennett b Griffith	0	–	c Barrow b Scott	16
W. A. Hunt b Constantine	2	–	c Sealy b Scott	6
H. Theak b Constantine	0	–	b Francis	2
J. H. Fingleton not out	32	–	lbw b Constantine	26
H. C. Chilvers c Headley b Scott	6	–	not out	43
L. McGuirk b Constantine	15	–	b Francis	2
B 6, l-b 3, n-b 1	10		B 9, l-b 5	14
	190			**466**

West Indies bowling: *First innings*—Constantine 10.3–0–45–6; Francis 8–0–25–0; Griffith 9–2–36–2; Scott 19–0–74–1. *Second innings*—Constantine 8–0–39–1; Francis 20.6–4–76–4; Griffith 19–0–115–2; Scott 19–0–107–2; Martin 19–2–68–1; Sealy 11–0–47–0.

Umpires: A. C. Jones and E. J. Shaw

AUSTRALIA v WEST INDIES (FIFTH TEST MATCH)

68 (103, 104)
14 (20, 21)

Played at Sydney, February 27, 28, March 2, 3, 4 [1931]. Favoured by the conditions – rain over the weekend and subsequently [the] state of the pitch – West Indies gained a notable triumph by 30 runs. Apart from the result, the match was memorable for the fact that Grant twice applied the closure. Each time the wet wicket, becoming difficult under a hot sun, influenced the West Indies captain to adopt this course and on both occasions his judgment proved correct. Headley followed his success at Brisbane by scoring his second Test Match century. Martin, enjoying that distinction for the first time, carried out his bat when Grant declared on the second day. … With the pitch again affected by sunshine after continuous rain, which prevented any cricket on Tuesday, Grant took the risk of leaving Australia to get 247 runs in unlimited time, it having been arranged to play the match to a finish. Half the wickets falling for 74 runs before lunch, the match seemed as good as over, but McCabe hit finely while Fairfax showed admirable defence until a catch by Grant broke up the partnership. …

[Bradman's duck in the second innings was his first in Test cricket.]

West Indies

F. R. Martin, C. A. Roach, G. Headley, *G. C. Grant, J. E. D. Sealy, L. N. Constantine, E. L. Bartlett, †I. Barrow, O. C. Scott, G. N. Francis and H. C. Griffith.

First innings: Six for 350 dec (Martin 123 not out, Roach 31, Headley 105, Grant 62; Grimmett three for 100). *Second innings:* Five for 124 dec (Roach 34, Headley 30).

Australia

*W. M. Woodfull c Constantine b Martin	22	–	c Constantine b Griffith	18
W. H. Ponsford c Bartlett b Francis	7	–	c Constantine b Martin	28
D. G. Bradman c Francis b Martin	43	–	b Griffith	0
A. F. Kippax c Sealy b Constantine	3	–	c Roach b Constantine	10
K. E. Rigg c Barrow b Francis	14	–	c Barrow b Constantine	16
A. G. Fairfax st Barrow b Scott	54	–	not out	60
S. J. McCabe c Headley b Francis	21	–	c Grant b Martin	44
R. K. Oxenham c Barrow b Francis	0	–	lbw b Scott	14
†W. A. Oldfield run out	36	–	lbw b Griffith	0
H. Ironmonger b Griffith	1	–	run out	4
C. V. Grimmett not out	15	–	c Constantine b Griffith	12
B 1, l-b 7	8		B 3, l-b 7, w 2, n-b 2	14
	224			**220**

West Indies bowling: *First innings*—Francis 19–6–48–4; Griffith 13.2–3–31–1; Martin 27–3–67–2; Constantine 10–2–28–1; Scott 10–1–42–1. *Second innings*—Francis 16–2–32–0; Griffith 13.3–3–50–4; Martin 18–4–44–2; Constantine 17–2–50–2; Scott 11–0–30–1.

Umpires: H. Armstrong and W.G. French

1931-32

1931-32

If the visit of the South Africans tended to lessen interest in Sheffield Shield cricket during 1931-32 and to deprive the States of the services of leading players when the Test Matches were in progress, the struggle for the Shield again proved remarkably close. South Australia, last on the list the previous year, developed much greater bowling strength and, by beating New South Wales at Sydney in the final game of the series, finished level on points with that State. New South Wales, however, had the better percentage on average and so carried off the trophy – their nineteenth success since the institution of the competition.

For the first time since a time limit was placed on Sheffield Shield fixtures, every one of the matches was played to a finish. To what extent this was due to the larger wicket – tried originally the preceding season – can only be conjectured. ...

S.J. McCabe (New South Wales) had a phenomenal batting record [his average from his three Shield innings was 438] ... D.G. Bradman also assisted New South Wales in three matches and hit up 167 against Victoria, but his average for five innings came out at no more than 42 as against 115 the previous year when he batted in six innings. Against South Africa, however, he showed brilliant form, and accomplished a feat unparalleled in Australian cricket by making seven centuries in successive matches.

From 'Cricket in Australia: The Inter-State Matches'

These particular ... matches served to emphasise the wonderful ability of Bradman as a batsman, for this marvellous young cricketer scored a hundred in every Test Match except the last, when he was injured. His name appeared in the list of those playing but he took no part in the game. Leading off with 226 in the First Test Match at Brisbane, he followed with 112 in the next at Sydney, 167 in the Third at Melbourne, and 299 not out at Adelaide in the Fourth. In addition to these huge scores he also made 219 and 135 for New South Wales. As the outcome of all this he headed the batting figures against the tourists with the extraordinary average of 201.50.

From 'The South African Team in Australia and New Zealand',
by S.J. Southerton

[With an aggregate of 1,190 runs against the South Africans, Bradman was the first, and until I. M. Chappell (1,062) v the West Indians in 1968-69 the only, batsman to score 1,000 runs against a touring team in Australia.]

QUEENSLAND v NEW SOUTH WALES 69 (105)

Played at Brisbane, November 6, 7, 9, 10 [1931]. Queensland, after being dismissed for 109, secured the wickets of Bill and Bradman [in Gilbert's first over] before their opponents scored a run, but afterwards their bowling was mastered and New South Wales won by an innings and 238 runs. Amos, with five wickets for 22, figured prominently in the early rout of Queensland, and a magnificent innings by McCabe went far towards deciding the issue. . . .

Queensland

R. Higgins, *F.J. Gough, F.W. Sides, R.K. Oxenham, D. Hansen, K. Mossop, A. Hurwood, †L. Waterman, V.B. Suche, H.M. Thurlow and E. Gilbert.

First innings: 109 (Mossop 44 not out; Amos five for 22). *Second innings:* 85 (Hunt four for 25, Campbell three for 13).

New South Wales

O. W. Bill c Waterman b Gilbert	0
J. H. Fingleton b Oxenham	93
D. G. Bradman c Waterman b Gilbert	0
*A. F. Kippax retired hurt	16
A. Fairfax b Gilbert	5
S. J. McCabe not out	229
S. F. Hird lbw b Oxenham	3
†W. A. Oldfield b Hurwood	46
J. N. Campbell c Oxenham b Hurwood	4
G. S. Amos lbw b Gilbert	2
W. A. Hunt run out	3
B 17, l-b 9, n-b 5	31
	432

Queensland bowling: Thurlow 22–4–69–0; Gilbert 20.7–2–74–4; Hurwood 25–5–95–2; Oxenham 27–7–79–2; Suche 14–1–50–0; Gough 5–0–34–0.

Umpires: J. Bartlett and J. A. Scott

NEW SOUTH WALES v SOUTH AFRICANS 70 (106, 107)

Played at Sydney, November 13, 14, 16, 17 [1931]. A lot of runs were made in the first match in which the South Africans met New South Wales and in the end the game had to be left drawn. . .. On the third day . . . when rain stopped play at five o'clock the South Africans, with three men out for 190 [in their second innings], were 447 runs ahead. The innings was declared closed next morning, but so far from losing the match New South Wales went very close to winning it. Fingleton, who made a hundred, and McCabe played fine cricket but they were both overshadowed by Bradman, who hit up 135 in his most brilliant style. When at length stumps were pulled up and the match left drawn, New South Wales, with seven wickets to fall, were within 18 of victory. This was a great day's cricket on the part of the New South Wales team.

South Africans

J.A.J. Christy, S.H. Curnow, B. Mitchell, *†H.B. Cameron, H.W. Taylor, E.L. Dalton, D.P.B. Morkel, X. Balaskas, Q. McMillan, C.L. Vincent and A.J. Bell.

First innings: 425 (Curnow 39, Cameron 74, Taylor 124, Dalton 87, Morkel 30; McCabe three for 89, Hunt four for 84, Bradman none for 35). *Second innings:* Three for 190 dec (Curnow 79 not out, Mitchell 42, Cameron 49; Hunt three for 62).

New South Wales

J. H. Fingleton b Bell	30	–	c McMillan b Morkel	117
O. W. Bill b Bell	0	–	b Morkel	47
D. G. Bradman c and b McMillan	30	–	c Bell b Morkel	135
S. J. McCabe st Cameron b McMillan	37	–	not out	79
A. A. Marks b Vincent	16	–	not out	36
A. G. Fairfax c Dalton b Vincent	3			
S. F. Hird c Mitchell b McMillan	18			
*†W. A. Oldfield c Vincent b McMillan	10			
R. H. Bettington b Bell	7			
W. A. Hunt st Cameron b Bell	3			
G. S. Amos not out	3			
Byes, etc.	11		Byes, etc.	16
	168		(three wkts)	**430**

South Africans bowling: *First innings*—Bell 14.6–2–36–4; Morkel 5–0–23–0; Vincent 20–7–46–2; McMillan 13–1–52–4. *Second innings*—Bell 27–2–100–0; Morkel 18–1–80–3; Vincent 27–4–125–0; McMillan 8–0–72–0; Balaskas 4–1–27–0.

Umpires: G. Borwick and W.G. French

AUSTRALIA v SOUTH AFRICA (FIRST TEST MATCH)

71 (108)
15 (22)

Played at Brisbane, November 27, 28, 30, December 1, 2, 3 [1931]. Entering upon the first of their five Test Matches against Australia with a very moderate record behind them, South Africa cut a poor figure and ... they suffered a heavy defeat, Australia winning in an innings with 163 runs to spare. Still, South Africa were served a very bad turn by the weather. They had to field out while Australia were putting together their total on a firm, true pitch, and in reply had made 126 for three wickets on the Saturday. Then rain came to prevent any cricket at all on the Monday and Tuesday, and for the rest of the match the conditions were all against the visitors. The outstanding feature of the game was the splendid innings of 226 put together by Bradman. He and Woodfull added 163 for the second wicket, and later on Oldfield played well, but nobody else on the side accomplished anything of note. Bradman enjoyed a good deal of luck, being missed off Quinn when 11 and again at 15. After those escapes he completely mastered the bowling and, before being leg-before in trying to force Vincent to the on, he hit twenty-two 4's....

Australia

*W. M. Woodfull lbw b Vincent	76	†W. A. Oldfield not out	56
W. H. Ponsford c Mitchell b Bell	19	C. V. Grimmett b Bell	14
D. G. Bradman lbw b Vincent	226	T. W. Wall lbw b Quinn	14
A. F. Kippax c Cameron b Vincent	1	H. Ironmonger b Quinn	2
S. J. McCabe c Vincent b Morkel	27	B 5, l-b 1, w 1, n-b 1	8
H. C. Nitschke c Cameron b Bell	6		**450**
R. K. Oxenham b Bell	1		

South Africa bowling: Bell 42–5–120–4; Morkel 13–1–57–1; Quinn 38.3–6–113–2; Vincent 34–0–100–3; McMillan 10–0–52–0.

South Africa

J.A.J. Christy, S.H. Curnow, B. Mitchell, *†H.B. Cameron, H.W. Taylor, E.L. Dalton, Q. McMillan, D.P.B. Morkel, C.L. Vincent, N.A. Quinn and A.J. Bell.

First innings: 170 (Mitchell 58, Taylor 41; Ironmonger five for 42). *Second innings:* 117 (Taylor 47; Wall five for 14, Ironmonger four for 44).

Umpires: G. A. Hele and G. Borwick

NEW SOUTH WALES v SOUTH AFRICANS 72 (109)

Played at Sydney, December 5, 7, 8, 9 [1931]. Restricted to two days owing to rain on the first and last afternoons, the return match of the South Africans with New South Wales was left drawn. However, it afforded Bradman the opportunity of making another big innings against the tourists. New South Wales lost their first two wickets for 12 runs but Bradman, playing in brilliant fashion, hit up 219 in rather less than four hours. He was caught at mid-off, this being the first chance he had offered. Among his hits were fifteen 4's. ...

New South Wales

J. H. Fingleton lbw b Morkel	2
O. W. Bill c Morkel b Bell	10
D. G. Bradman c Curnow b McMillan	219
S. J. McCabe c Christy b Bell	28
A. A. Marks c Cameron b Bell	6
C. Solomon st Cameron b McMillan	11
*†W. A. Oldfield c Mitchell b McMillan	29
W. A. Hunt c Curnow b McMillan	45
S. Hird c Cameron b McMillan	101
G. S. Amos st Cameron b McMillan	24
H. Theak not out	10
Byes, etc.	15
	500

South Africans bowling: Bell 26–2–107–3; Morkel 8–0–33–1; Vincent 11–0–51–0; Quinn 20–1–105–0; McMillan 23.4–0–189–6.

South Africans

J.A.J. Christy, S.H. Curnow, D.P.B. Morkel, B. Mitchell, *†H.B. Cameron, K.F. Viljoen, X. Balaskas, Q. McMillan, C.L. Vincent, A.J. Bell and N.A. Quinn.

First innings: One for 185 (Curnow 81 not out, Morkel 70 not out).

Umpires: G. Borwick and W.G. French

AUSTRALIA v SOUTH AFRICA (SECOND TEST MATCH) 73 (110) 16 (23)

Played at Sydney, December 18, 19, 21 [1931]. Although the conditions did not operate against them as they had at Brisbane, South Africa fared no better in the Second Test Match and suffered defeat at the end of three days' cricket, Australia winning in an innings with 155 runs to spare. On the opening day the visitors could do little with the bowling of Grimmett. Indeed, before lunch that player kept batsmen in such subjection that of the sixty-six balls he delivered only four were scored off. ...

South Africa were all out for 153, after which Australia made 78 for one wicket, and on the next afternoon the home side ran their score to 444 for seven wickets. ... Rigg ... enjoyed the distinction of making a hundred in his first Test Match. He and Bradman added 111 runs before Rigg was out, and then Bradman and McCabe put on 93, Bradman being out to a glorious catch in the long field. Fourth to leave at 347, Bradman, although suffering from a slightly strained leg, batted in brilliant fashion for about two hours and three-quarters, being very severe on the South African slow bowlers. ...

South Africa

J.A.J. Christy, B. Mitchell, D.P.B. Morkel, *†H.B. Cameron, H.W. Taylor, K.F. Viljoen, E.L. Dalton, C.L. Vincent, L.S. Brown, N.A. Quinn and A.J. Bell.

First innings: 153 (Viljoen 37, Vincent 31 not out; McCabe four for 13, Grimmett four for 28). *Second innings:* 161 (Christy 41, Vincent 35; Grimmett four for 44, Ironmonger three for 22).

Australia

*W. M. Woodfull c Mitchell b Vincent	58	†W. A. Oldfield c Cameron b Bell	8
W. H. Ponsford b Quinn	5	C. V. Grimmett not out	9
K. E. Rigg b Bell	127	T. W. Wall c Morkel b Bell	6
D. G. Bradman c Viljoen b Morkel	112	H. Ironmonger c Cameron b Bell	0
S. J. McCabe c Christy b Vincent	79	B 5, l-b 12, w 1	18
H. C. Nitschke b Bell	47		**469**
P. K. Lee c Cameron b Brown	0		

South Africa bowling: Bell 46.5–6–140–5; Quinn 42–10–95–1; Brown 29–3–100–1; Vincent 24–5–75–2; Morkel 12–2–33–1; Mitchell 1–0–8–0.

Umpires: G. A. Hele and G. Borwick

AUSTRALIA v SOUTH AFRICA (THIRD TEST MATCH)

74 (111, 112)
17 (24, 25)

Played at Melbourne, December 31 [1931], January 1, 2, 4, 5, 6 [1932]. South Africa made a much better fight of it with their opponents in the Third Test Match, but in the end had to admit defeat by 169 runs. This result gave Australia the rubber. Australia did not start in a manner which suggested their ultimate victory for, losing Ponsford, Woodfull and Bradman for 25 runs, they were all out for a total of 198 ... and altogether the innings lasted just over three hours and a half. ...

[The South Africans scored 358 and] Australia thus had to go in a second time 160 runs behind, but any anxiety they may have had was soon dispelled, Ponsford and Woodfull putting on 54 for the first wicket and Woodfull and Bradman then carrying the score to 206 without being separated. Thus the situation had been retrieved and on the Monday the Australian score stood, at the close of play, at 554 for nine wickets. Woodfull and Bradman were not separated until the total reached 328, their partnership for the second wicket having realised 274 runs. This beat the previous highest for the second wicket in Test Matches of 235 made by Macartney and Woodfull against England at Leeds in 1926. The South Africans bowled and fielded well, but Bradman scored with much freedom during the three hours he was at the wicket. In his 167 he hit eighteen 4's, his batting generally being of high order. The only bowler to trouble him was Vincent. ...

Australia

*W. M. Woodfull c Cameron b Bell	7	–	c Mitchell b McMillan	161
W. H. Ponsford b Bell	7	–	c Mitchell b Bell	34
D. G. Bradman c Cameron b Quinn	2	–	lbw b Vincent	167
A. F. Kippax c Bell b Quinn	52	–	c Curnow b McMillan	67
S. J. McCabe c Morkel b Bell	22	–	c Mitchell b McMillan	71
E. L. a'Beckett c Mitchell b Quinn	6	–	b Vincent	4
†W. A. Oldfield c Vincent b Quinn	0	–	lbw b McMillan	0
K. E. Rigg c Mitchell b Bell	68	–	c Mitchell b Vincent	1
C. V. Grimmett c Morkel b Bell	9	–	not out	16
T. W. Wall not out	6	–	b Vincent	12
H. Ironmonger run out	12	–	b Quinn	0
B 1, l-b 4, w 1, n-b 1	7		B 17, l-b 3, n-b 1	21
	198			**554**

South Africa bowling: *First innings*—Bell 26.1–9–69–5; Quinn 31–13–42–4; Morkel 3–0–12–0; Vincent 12–1–32–0; McMillan 2–0–22–0; Christy 3–0–14–0. *Second innings*—Bell 36–0–101–1; Quinn 36.4–6–113–1; Morkel 4–0–15–0; Vincent 55–16–154–4; McMillan 33–3–150–4.

South Africa

S.H. Curnow, B. Mitchell, J.A.J. Christy, H.W. Taylor, D.P.B. Morkel, *†H.B. Cameron, C.L. Vincent, K.F. Viljoen, Q. McMillan, N.A. Quinn and A.J. Bell.

First innings: 358 (Curnow 47, Morkel 33, Cameron 39, Viljoen 111; Wall three for 98, Ironmonger three for 72). *Second innings:* 225 (Mitchell 46, Christy 63, Taylor 38, Vincent 34; Ironmonger four for 54, Grimmett six for 92, Bradman none for 2).

Umpires: G.A. Hele and G. Borwick

NEW SOUTH WALES v VICTORIA 75 (113, 114)

Played at Sydney, January 22, 23, 25, 26 [1932]. Two brilliant hundreds by McCabe, a big second innings by Bradman, and a plucky effort for Victoria by Oakley were the features of this match which New South Wales won by 239 runs. McCabe proved the mainstay of New South Wales in their first innings, and on the third day he and Bradman placed their State in such a strong position that a declaration was made possible with only four wickets down. Bradman completed his 1,000 runs in first-class cricket for the season for the fourth successive year. …

New South Wales

O. W. Bill c Barnett b McCormick	27	–	lbw b McCormick	15
J. H. Fingleton c a'Beckett b Nagel	40	–	lbw b Smith	40
D. G. Bradman c Smith b Ironmonger	23	–	b Nagel	167
S. J. McCabe c Barnett b Ironmonger	106	–	not out	103
R. N. Nutt c Darling b a'Beckett	15	–	not out	8
S. F. Hird c Barnett b McCormick	23			
*A. F. Kippax c and b Darling	36	–	c Barnett b McCormick	44
†W. A. Oldfield c Oakley b Darling	2			
W. A. Hunt c Darling b Ironmonger	0			
W. J. O'Reilly not out	26			
H. J. Theak run out	17			
B 16, l-b 11, w 5, n-b 1	33		B 3, l-b 3, w 4, n-b 2	12
	348		(four wkts dec)	**389**

Victoria bowling: *First innings*—McCormick 15.4–4–42–2; a'Beckett 15–3–44–1; Ironmonger 20–2–94–3; Nagel 14–1–63–1; Smith 5–0–33–0; Darling 8–0–39–2. *Second innings*—McCormick 13–0–54–2; a'Beckett 13.3–0–68–0; Ironmonger 17–4–52–0; Nagel 12–1–57–1; Smith 14–1–100–1; Darling 3–0–34–0; Ryder 4–0–12–0.

Victoria

J. Thomas, L.P. O'Brien, L. Darling, *J. Ryder, E.L. a'Beckett, †B.A. Barnett, H.H. Oakley, L.E. Nagel, E.L. McCormick, S.A. Smith and H. Ironmonger.

First innings: 204 (O'Brien 38, Oakley 48, Nagel 30; McCabe three for 57, O'Reilly three for 52, Bradman none for 6). *Second innings:* 294 (Thomas 70, O'Brien 34, Oakley 93 not out; Bradman one for 4).

Umpires: H. Armstrong and W.G. French

AUSTRALIA v SOUTH AFRICA
(FOURTH TEST MATCH)

76 (115)
18 (26)

Played at Adelaide, January 29, 30, February 1, 2 [1932]. Up to a point South Africa rendered a fairly good account of themselves but, as in previous matches, the combination of Bradman and Grimmett as batsman and bowler proved too much for them and Australia won the Fourth Test Match by ten wickets. Bradman played a great innings of 299 not out, while Grimmett took fourteen wickets – seven in each innings – for 199 runs. Rarely in a Test Match can two men have contributed so materially to the defeat of the opposing side. . . .

. . . In reply to [South Africa's first innings of 308] Australia made 302 for four wickets [by stumps on the second day]. This was almost entirely the work of Woodfull and Bradman, who added 176 for the second wicket. Rigg, later, gave Bradman useful assistance, the latter at the close being 170 not out.

On Monday the Australian total amounted to 513, Bradman remaining undefeated until the end. In his attempt to reach his 300th run, however, he ran Thurlow out [on his Test debut]. Bradman's score of 299 was the highest ever made by one man in a Test Match in Australia, but it fell short by 35 of his record made against England at Leeds in 1930. He dominated the proceedings on this day after he and Rigg had increased their overnight partnership to 114. There were times, however, when he was not at all comfortable. During one particular hour he scored only 25 runs and survived several appeals for leg-before and catches at the wicket. Oldfield and Grimmett gave valuable help, and with O'Reilly [another playing in his first Test] 78 runs were added. The innings closed just before tea, South Africa being left to get 205 to save the innings defeat. . . .

South Africa

S. H. Curnow, B. Mitchell, J. A. J. Christy, H. W. Taylor, *†H. B. Cameron, D. P. B. Morkel, K. F. Viljoen, C. L. Vincent, Q. McMillan, N. A. Quinn and A. J. Bell.

First innings: 308 (Mitchell 75, Taylor 78, Cameron 52, Vincent 48; Grimmett seven for 116). *Second innings:* 274 (Mitchell 95, Christy 51, Taylor 84; Grimmett seven for 83).

Australia

*W. M. Woodfull c Morkel b Bell	82	–	not out	37
W. H. Ponsford b Quinn	5	–	not out	27
D. G. Bradman not out	299			
A. F. Kippax run out	0			
S. J. McCabe c Vincent b Bell	2			
K. E. Rigg c Taylor b Bell	35			
†W. A. Oldfield lbw b Vincent	23			
C. V. Grimmett b Bell	21			
W. A. Hunt c Vincent b Quinn	0			
W. J. O'Reilly b Bell	23			
H. M. Thurlow run out	0			
B 18, l-b 3, w 1, n-b 1	23		B 4, l-b 5	9
	513		(no wkt)	**73**

South Africa bowling: *First innings*—Bell 40–2–142–5; Quinn 37–5–114–2; Vincent 34–5–110–1; McMillan 9–0–53–0; Morkel 18–1–71–0. *Second innings*—Quinn 3–0–5–0; Vincent 7–0–31–0; McMillan 7.2–0–23–0; Morkel 2–0–5–0.

Umpires: G. A. Hele and G. Borwick

AUSTRALIA v SOUTH AFRICA 77
(FIFTH TEST MATCH) 19

Played at Melbourne, February 12, 13, 15 [1932]. Before proceeding to New Zealand, South Africa engaged in their concluding Test Match with Australia and for the fifth time were defeated, Australia, although scoring only 153, winning in an innings with 72 runs to spare. For this game Australia brought in L. Nash, a Tasmanian fast bowler ... Short, but of powerful build, Nash made the ball rise in very awkward fashion, several of them getting head high. He and Ironmonger proved so effective on a pitch slightly on the soft side that in a little more than ninety minutes South Africa were dismissed for the sorry total of 36. This was not their lowest total in Test cricket for they had twice been got rid of previously by England for 30 – at Port Elizabeth in 1895-96 and at Birmingham in 1924. Their lowest score before this in Test Matches against Australia was 80 at Melbourne in 1910-11. Cameron alone reached double figures [11] ...

Before the day was over there were further surprises, Australia being got rid of for 153. ... Woodfull was out first ball ... [and] Australia's total was their smallest against South Africa, the previous lowest being 175 at Johannesburg in 1902-03. [Bradman took no part in the first day's play, having twisted his ankle when his sprigs caught in the dressing-room matting as he was going out to field.] South Africa, 117 behind, lost one wicket for five runs before play ceased for the day, and on the Saturday no cricket took place, heavy rain during the night and a further downpour soon after two o'clock preventing any chance of a resumption. On the Monday, however, there came more sensational play.

The game was not proceeded with until quarter past two, and then in less than an hour and a half the last nine South African wickets went down for another 40 runs. Thus South Africa were twice dismissed for an aggregate of 81, the lowest total for two innings ever recorded in the history of Test Match cricket [as indeed is the match aggregate]. The wicket was very difficult and Ironmonger once more proved practically unplayable. ... Five batsmen failed to score and only Curnow [16] reached double figures ...

South Africa

B. Mitchell, S. H. Curnow, J. A. J. Christy, H. W. Taylor, K. F. Viljoen, *†H. B. Cameron, D. P. B. Morkel, C. L. Vincent, Q. McMillan, N. A. Quinn and A. J. Bell.

First innings: 36 (Nash four for 18, Ironmonger five for 6). *Second innings:* 45 (Ironmonger six for 18, O'Reilly three for 19).

Australia

*W. M. Woodfull b Bell	0	C. V. Grimmett c Cameron b Quinn	9
J. H. Fingleton c Vincent b Bell	40	W. J. O'Reilly c Curnow b McMillan	13
K. E. Rigg c Vincent b Quinn	22	H. Ironmonger not out	0
A. F. Kippax c Curnow b McMillan	42	D. G. Bradman absent hurt	0
S. J. McCabe c Cameron b Bell	0	L-b 3	3
L. J. Nash b Quinn	13		**153**
†W. A. Oldfield c Curnow b McMillan	11		

South Africa bowling: Bell 16–0–52–3; Quinn 19.3–4–29–3; Vincent 11–2–40–0; McMillan 8–0–29–3.

Umpires: G. A. Hele and G. Borwick

NEW SOUTH WALES v SOUTH AUSTRALIA 78 (116, 117)

Played at Sydney, March 19, 21, 22 [1932]. Winning a thoroughly interesting struggle by 132 runs, South Australia finished level with New South Wales in the matter of points, but the latter

State won the Shield by virtue of their better averages. ... [In the New South Wales second innings] with McCabe still unfit to bat, Bradman dismissed without scoring and Grimmett's skilful bowling too much for all their batsmen except Fingleton and Bill, New South Wales were easily overcome.

South Australia

*V.Y. Richardson, H.C. Nitschke, A.R. Lonergan, W.E. Catchlove, H.E.P. Whitfield, M.G. Waite, P.K. Lee, C.V. Grimmett, †C.W. Walker, T.W. Wall and T.A. Carlton.

First innings: 272 (Nitschke 45, Lonergan 68, Whitfield 51; Theak three for 68, O'Reilly five for 68). *Second innings:* 225 (Nitschke 119; O'Reilly five for 59).

New South Wales

J. H. Fingleton b Wall	0	–	b Grimmett	24
W. A. Hunt b Wall	0	–	c Richardson b Lee	1
R. N. Nutt b Lee	33	–	b Whitfield	6
S. J. Hird lbw b Carlton	2	–	lbw b Grimmett	5
D. G. Bradman b Carlton	23	–	b Wall	0
J. Donnelly c Walker b Wall	57	–	c Carlton b Grimmett	18
O. W. Bill not out	76	–	st Walker b Grimmett	46
*†W. A. Oldfield lbw b Grimmett	31	–	c Richardson b Lee	6
W. J. O'Reilly c Richardson b Lee	5	–	run out	0
H. J. Theak st Walker b Lee	1	–	not out	4
S. J. McCabe absent hurt	0	–	absent hurt	0
B 8, l-b 7, w 1, n-b 3	19		B 3, l-b 5	8
	247			**118**

South Australia bowling: *First innings*—Wall 16–1–63–3; Whitfield 8–0–31–0; Carlton 8–1–30–2; Grimmett 16–1–75–1; Lee 7.1–2–29–3. *Second innings*—Wall 5–0–24–1; Whitfield 4–1–8–1; Carlton 4–1–12–0; Grimmett 19–9–32–4; Lee 14.2–1–34–2.

Umpires: G. Borwick and W.G. French

1932

AUSTRALIAN TOUR IN AMERICA

During the summer months of 1932 a strong team of Australian cricketers under the captaincy of V. Y. Richardson visited Canada and the United States. They played no fewer than fifty-one matches – the majority of minor interest, though Canada and British Columbia were met – and of these forty-four were won, six drawn, and one lost – to Vancouver.

D.G. Bradman secured remarkable batting figures, scoring 3,782 runs in fifty-one innings (fourteen times not out), giving an average of 102.21 with a highest of 260 against Western Ontario on July 4, which constitutes a Canadian record. He followed this with 200 (not out) against Montreal and in all played eighteen three-figure innings. ... Against a Victoria XV, [he] captured six wickets in an eight-ball over ...

1932-33

1932-33

Owing to the presence in Australia of the English cricketers, several of the Sheffield Shield matches were contested with teams which did not include leading players, and consequently interest in the competition temporarily diminished. ... New South Wales won the Shield fairly easily. ... Outstanding performances in the competition were the splendid batting of Bradman and the bowling of O'Reilly and Grimmett. Bradman, again the predominating Australian batsman, played in only three Shield matches, but scored 600 runs with a highest innings of 238 and an average of 150. In addition to his double-century against Victoria, he scored 157 against the same State in the return match. ...

From 'Cricket in Australia: The Inter-State Matches'

At the moment of writing these notes the Third Test Match has just ended in a handsome victory for England, but while followers of cricket in this country rejoice exceedingly over that success the public in Australia appear to be getting very excited about the fast bowling of some of the Englishmen and what is variously known as the 'leg theory', 'shock tactics' and 'body-line methods'. Leg theory, as we have understood that kind of bowling, ... consisted in the delivery ... of a slow ball, with an off-break, pitched on the leg stump or well outside it, with three or four men fielding close in at leg and to the on. ...

The ball to which such strong exception is being taken in Australia is not slow or slow-medium but fast. It is dropped short and is alleged in certain quarters to be aimed at the batsman rather than at the wicket. It may at once be said that, if the intention is to hit the batsman and so demoralise him, the practice is altogether wrong – calculated, as it must be, to introduce an element of pronounced danger and altogether against the spirit of the game of cricket. Upon this point practically everybody will agree. No one wants such an element introduced. That English bowlers, to dispose of their opponents, would of themselves pursue such methods or that Jardine would acquiesce in such a course is inconceivable. ...

... In suggesting, as has the Australian Board of Control, that bowling such as that of the Englishmen has become a menace to the best interests of the game, is causing intensely bitter feelings between players and, unless stopped at once, is likely to upset the friendly relations between England and Australia, the Commonwealth cricket authorities seem to have lost their sense of proportion. . . .

From 'Notes by the Editor' (C. Stewart Caine), *Wisden 1933*

. . . I have purposely omitted to use the expression 'body-line bowling'. It may have conveyed to those to whom it was presented at the outset the meaning the inventor of it wished to infer, but to my mind it was an objectionable term, utterly foreign to cricket, and calculated to stir up strife when the obvious aim of everybody should have been directed towards the prevention of any breach. . . .

Happily the controversy is now at an end, and little reason exists, therefore, to flog what we can regard as a 'dead horse'. But, obviously from the historical point of view, something on the subject must be said. I hope and believe that the ventilation of their grievances by the Australians, and the placatory replies of the MCC, will have done much towards imparting a better spirit to Test Matches which of recent years have become battles rather than pleasurable struggles. A false atmosphere has pervaded them. During the last few tours of MCC teams in Australia, and the visits of the Australians to this country, one could not fail to detect a subtle change taking place in the conduct of Test Matches – reflected unfortunately in the style of the cricketers themselves. The result of the contests was given a prominence out of keeping with the importance of Test Matches, and the true sense of perspective stood in danger of disappearing altogether. . . .

And now, what of this fast leg-theory method of bowling to which not only the Australian players themselves, but a vast majority of the people of Australia took such grave exception? With the dictum of the MCC that any form of bowling which constitutes a direct attack by the bowler on the batsman is contrary to the spirit of the game, everyone must unquestionably concur. D. R. Jardine, on his return to England, stated definitely in his book that the bowling against which the Australians demurred was not of this description, and Larwood, the chief exponent of it, said with equal directness that he had never intentionally bowled at a man. On the other hand, there are numerous statements by responsible Australians to the effect that the type of bowling adopted was calculated to intimidate batsmen, pitched as the ball was so short as to cause it to fly shoulder and head high and make batsmen, with the leg-side studded with fieldsmen, use the bat as a protection for their bodies or their heads rather than in defence of the wicket or to make a scoring stroke. Victor Richardson, the South Australian batsman, has said that when he took his ordinary stance at the wicket he found the ball coming on to his body; when he took guard slightly more to the leg side he still had the ball coming at him; and with a still wider guard the ball continued to follow him. I hold no brief either for Jardine or Larwood or for Richardson, Woodfull or Bradman; but while some of the Australians may have exaggerated the supposed danger of this form of bowling, I cling to the opinion that they cannot all be wrong. When the first mutterings of the storm were heard, many people in this country were inclined to the belief that the Australians, seeing themselves in danger of losing the rubber, were not taking defeat in the proper spirit always expected from honourable opponents. I will confess that I thought they did not relish what seemed to me at that stage to be a continuous good-length bombardment by our fast bowlers on to their leg stump. This idea I afterwards found was not quite correct. …

From 'The Bowling Controversy', by the Editor (S.J. Southerton), *Wisden 1934*

MCC TEAM v A COMBINED AUSTRALIAN XI 79 (118, 119)

Played at Perth, October 27, 28, 29 [1932]. Despite deadly bowling by Verity, MCC, though they carried off all the honours, could not win. Sutcliffe and the Nawab of Pataudi [shared] in a second-wicket stand of 283 – a record for the ground … The Australians replied with 59 without loss on the second day but, the pitch becoming sticky, Verity sent back the first six batsmen up to tea-time for 23 runs and altogether took seven wickets for just over five runs apiece. …

MCC Team

H. Sutcliffe, M. Leyland, Nawab of Pataudi, W.R. Hammond, L.E.G. Ames, *Mr D.R. Jardine, Mr G.O. Allen, E. Paynter, H. Verity, T.B. Mitchell and †G. Duckworth.

First innings: Seven for 583 dec (Sutcliffe 169, Pataudi 129, Hammond 77, Jardine 98, Paynter 32 not out; Bradman two for 106).

Combined XI

J. H. Fingleton c Duckworth b Verity	29	–	not out	53
V. Y. Richardson c Sutcliffe b Verity	27	–	b Allen	0
D. G. Bradman c Hammond b Verity	3	–	c Pataudi b Allen	10
A. R. Lonergan c Duckworth b Verity	10	–	b Paynter	23
S. J. McCabe b Paynter	43			
W. Hill-Smith c Jardine b Verity	17	–	c Duckworth b Ames	32
*R. Bryant c Mitchell b Verity	0	–	not out	12
†O. Lovelock c Hammond b Mitchell	11			
A. Evans c Allen b Verity	0			
E. Martin st Duckworth b Mitchell	1			
R. Halcombe not out	1			
B 11, l-b 5, n-b 1	17		L-b 7, w 1, n-b 1	9
	159		(four wkts)	**139**

MCC Team bowling: *First innings*—Allen 4–0–24–0; Hammond 9–1–29–0; Mitchell 13–2–37–2; Verity 18–7–37–7; Leyland 2–0–15–0; Paynter 0.2–0–0–1. *Second innings*—Allen 7–2–16–2; Hammond 3–1–7–0; Verity 1–0–2–0; Leyland 8–1–23–0; Paynter 12–1–31–1; Ames 6–0–25–1; Sutcliffe 3–0–18–0; Jardine 2–1–8–0.

Umpires: F. Buttsworth and J. Hart

NEW SOUTH WALES v VICTORIA 80 (120, 121)

Played at Sydney, November 4, 5, 7, 8 [1932]. Great individual performances marked this game, which New South Wales won by nine wickets. Ponsford, who could not bat a second time as he twisted an ankle while fielding, and Woodfull scored 138 for Victoria's first wicket, Ponsford playing a fine innings which lasted four and a half hours. Bradman's display for New South Wales was, however, one of the most brilliant exhibitions ever seen on the Sydney ground. During a stay of three and a quarter hours [in which he hit the fastest double-hundred in a Shield match] he hit thirty-two 4's. ...

Victoria

*W. M. Woodfull, W. H. Ponsford, L. P. O'Brien, K. E. Rigg, L. S. Darling, J. Thomas, †B. A. Barnett, D. D. Blackie, L. O'B. Fleetwood-Smith, H. H. Alexander and H. Ironmonger.

First innings: 404 (Woodfull 74, Ponsford 200, Barnett 36, Fleetwood-Smith 38; O'Reilly five for 81, Hird three for 115, Bradman one for 8). *Second innings:* 150 (Woodfull 83; Hird six for 56).

New South Wales

J. H. Fingleton lbw b Alexander	6	–	not out	20
O. W. Bill b Fleetwood-Smith	19	–	b Alexander	8
D. G. Bradman c O'Brien b Fleetwood-Smith	238	–	not out	52
*A. F. Kippax c Barnett b Alexander	52			
S. J. McCabe c Fleetwood-Smith b Alexander	56			
S. F. Hird c Barnett b Alexander	6			
F. S. Cummins b Alexander	13			
W. J. O'Reilly c Barnett b Alexander	0			
†W. A. Oldfield not out	22			
C. Hill b Ironmonger	10			
H. J. Theak b Alexander	39			
B 8, l-b 6	14		B 1, l-b 1	2
	475		(one wkt)	**82**

Victoria bowling: *First innings*—Alexander 22–1–95–7; Darling 7–0–40–0; Fleetwood-Smith 19–0–145–2; Ironmonger 26.1–3–96–1; Blackie 19–1–85–0. *Second innings*—Alexander 3–0–23–1; Darling 1–0–7–0; Fleetwood-Smith 5–0–27–0; Ironmonger 5–2–17–0; Blackie 1.2–0–6–0.

Umpires: G. Borwick and W.G. French

MCC TEAM v AN AUSTRALIAN XI 81 (122, 123)

Played at Melbourne, November 18, 19, 21, 22 [1932]. Rain interfering when play had become very exciting – the Australian eleven wanted 106 to win with eight wickets in hand – this match was left drawn. The Englishmen, with the exception of Sutcliffe, Allen and Leyland, gave a most disappointing batting display on an easy pitch. ... The Australians, too, fared only moderately. During one period after tea on the second day six wickets went down for 58 runs ... On the last day Larwood brought some consolation [to MCC] by sending back Bradman and Woodfull at small cost before the rain came on.

[The total attendance of 109,501 was a record for a first-class match in Australia, other than a Test Match, as was the attendance of 53,916 on the second day, which saw the introduction of body-line tactics in the Australian XI's first innings.]

MCC Team

*Mr R. E. S. Wyatt, H. Sutcliffe, Nawab of Pataudi, M. Leyland, Mr G. O. Allen, E. Paynter, H. Larwood, Mr F. R. Brown, W. Voce, †G. Duckworth and W. E. Bowes.

First innings: 282 (Sutcliffe 87, Leyland 38, Allen 48; Nash three for 39, Oxenham five for 53). *Second innings:* 60 (Nagel eight for 32).

An Australian XI

*W. M. Woodfull lbw b Bowes	18	–	c Duckworth b Larwood	0
L. P. O'Brien b Larwood	46	–	not out	5
D. G. Bradman lbw b Larwood	36	–	b Larwood	13
K. E. Rigg c Brown b Bowes	13	–	not out	0
L. S. Darling b Bowes	4			
R. K. Oxenham c Larwood b Voce	12			
L. J. Nash b Larwood	0			
P. K. Lee c Paynter b Brown	28			
†B. Barnett b Voce	20			
L. E. Nagel lbw b Larwood	15			
H. Ironmonger not out	5			
B 11, l-b 2, n-b 8	21		B	1
	218		(two wkts)	**19**

MCC Team bowling: *First innings*—Larwood 14–0–54–4; Bowes 15–2–63–3; Voce 15.5–2–55–2; Brown 7–0–25–1. *Second innings*—Larwood 3.7–1–5–2; Allen 3–1–13–0.

Umpires: A. N. Barlow and J. Richards

MCC TEAM v NEW SOUTH WALES 82 (124, 125)

Played at Sydney, November 25, 26, 28, 29 [1932]. Bradman [who was unwell] failing twice, New South Wales proved no real match for the tourists, who won deservedly by an innings and 44 runs. ... Jardine allowed [H. S.] Love, not even twelfth man, to act as wicket-keeper in the absence of Oldfield, ill. [In addition to catching Jardine, Love also effected the first stumpings by a substitute in Australian first-class cricket.]

New South Wales

O. W. Bill c Jardine b Tate	22	–	b Voce	1
J. H. Fingleton not out	119	–	b Brown	18
D. G. Bradman lbw b Tate	18	–	b Voce	23
*A. F. Kippax c Voce b Tate	3	–	c Sutcliffe b Voce	24
S. J. McCabe c Allen b Tate	67	–	c Brown b Voce	29
S. J. Hird c Ames b Allen	9	–	c Tate b Voce	15
F. S. Cummins lbw b Voce	0	–	c Jardine b Brown	71
†W. A. Oldfield c Sutcliffe b Allen	5	–	absent ill	0
W. J. O'Reilly b Allen	0	–	b Allen	11
H. J. Theak b Allen	9	–	b Allen	4
W. Howell b Allen	7	–	not out	0
L-b 8, n-b 6	14		B 2, l-b 6, w 1, n-b 8	17
	273			**213**

MCC Team bowling: *First innings*—Allen 16.2–2–69–5; Voce 19–3–53–1; Tate 17–2–53–4; Brown 5–0–28–0; Hammond 5–0–26–0; Verity 6–1–30–0. *Second innings*—Allen 10–1–52–2; Voce 15–1–85–5; Tate 6–1–21–0; Brown 5.5–0–19–2; Hammond 4–0–12–0; Verity 4–1–7–0.

MCC Team

Mr R.E.S. Wyatt, H. Sutcliffe, W.R. Hammond, Nawab of Pataudi, Mr F.R. Brown, †L.E.G. Ames, *Mr D.R. Jardine, Mr G.O. Allen, W. Voce, H. Verity and M.W. Tate.

First innings: 530 (Wyatt 72, Sutcliffe 182, Pataudi 61, Ames 90, Voce 46, sundries 30; O'Reilly four for 86, Hird six for 135, Bradman none for 24).

Umpires: G. Borwick and W.G. French

ENGLAND v AUSTRALIA
(FIRST TEST MATCH)

Played at Sydney, December 2, 3, 5, 6, 7 [1932]. Leading off in fine style in the series of Test Matches, England won this, the first, early on the fifth day by ten wickets. ...

Reference to the fact that Bradman, owing to illness, was unable to play in the match must not be omitted, although in view of subsequent events it is, to say the least, questionable if his presence would have staved off disaster.

VICTORIA v NEW SOUTH WALES 83 (126)

Played at Melbourne, December 23, 24, 26, 27 [1932]. This game could not be started until the third of the four days set apart for it, but when play commenced the sun shone and the good crowd [21,187] was provided with some bright cricket. New South Wales, put in by Woodfull, were given a useful start with an opening partnership of 145 by Fingleton and Brown, who retired injured, but returned, and Bradman played a fine innings. After completing his hundred in two and three-quarter hours, he took his score to 157 in another thirty minutes [becoming with his 130th run the youngest player (24 years and 121 days) to score 10,000 runs in first-class cricket] ...

New South Wales

J. H. Fingleton lbw b Nagel	85			
W. Brown not out	35			
D. G. Bradman c Bromley b Ironmonger	157			
S. J. McCabe lbw b Alexander	48			
*A. F. Kippax c King b Ironmonger	17			
S. F. Hird c Barnett b Ironmonger	3			
F. S. Cummins c Bromley b Ironmonger	15			
†H. S. Love lbw b Alexander	1			
W. J. O'Reilly c and b Alexander	2	–	not out	7
W. Howell b Alexander	5			
G. L. Stewart c Darling b Ironmonger	7	–	not out	1
B 6, l-b 7	13			
	388		(no wkt)	**8**

Victoria bowling: *First innings*—Alexander 26–3–107–4; L. E. Nagel 24–1–90–1; Ironmonger 30.2–6–87–5; Fleetwood-Smith 14–0–73–0; Darling 4–0–18–0. *Second innings*—Bromley 1–0–8–0.

Victoria

*W. M. Woodfull, W. H. Ponsford, L. P. O'Brien, L. S. Darling, S. P. King, E. H. Bromley, †B. A. Barnett, L. E. Nagel, L. O'B. Fleetwood-Smith, H. H. Alexander and H. Ironmonger.

First innings: 258 (O'Brien 53, King 30, Bromley 84, Barnett 39; Howell four for 69, O'Reilly four for 52, Bradman none for 8).

Umpires: A. N. Barlow and W. J. Moore

ENGLAND v AUSTRALIA (SECOND TEST MATCH)

84 (127, 128)
20 (27, 28)

Played at Melbourne, December 30, 31 [1932], January 2, 3 [1933]. ... Jardine again lost the toss, but England started even better than they had done at Sydney and, at the end of the first day, Australia had seven men out for 194. This splendid work was not followed up at all well when it came England's turn to bat and the match – over in four days – resulted in a victory for Australia by 111 runs. ... Having recovered from his indisposition, Bradman was able to play for Australia ... [and] dismissed for nought on the opening day [he] afterwards scored a brilliant 103 not out ...

For a Test Match in Australia, this was a game of small scores ... and it can be said at once that the pitch proved quite different from any experienced in former tours by England cricketers. For some reason or other it lacked the usual firmness of bounce associated with wickets at the Victorian capital and Jardine, playing all his pace bowlers by including Bowes for Verity, was completely misled in his assumption that fast bowling would be likely to win the match. ... Australia had their worst shock when Bradman was out first ball to Bowes. He tried to hook it, but edged it down on to the stumps. Previously Woodfull had also been dismissed cheaply. At times the ball bounced a good deal, Woodfull on one occasion being struck over the heart. ...

On the third day there was a record crowd of nearly 70,000 people [68,238] present. The England innings was finished off for 169, which gave Australia a lead of 59 runs. At their second attempt Australia, thanks almost entirely to Bradman, made 191, and towards the end of the day England, left to get 251 in the last innings, had forty-five minutes' batting. ... The day's cricket really was dominated by Bradman who, after a succession of failures, simply took his courage in both hands and played a wonderful innings. In a way his batting was masterly. He went in when two wickets had fallen for 27 runs; resisted a lot of good bowling for over three hours and a half to complete his hundred when Ironmonger, the last man, was in with him. While Wall and O'Reilly were his partners he sacrificed many runs in order to keep the bowling. To few other Australian batsmen could such an innings as Bradman played have been possible. The England bowling was very good all the time, Hammond doing excellent work.

So, on the last day, England, with all their wickets in hand, required 208 runs, but O'Reilly and Ironmonger proved too much for them on a pitch which by this time took the spin of the ball to a pronounced degree and England were all out for 139. ... The fact that in fine weather forty wickets went down in four days for an aggregate of 727 runs clearly suggested that at no time was the pitch all that it should have been.

Australia

J. H. Fingleton b Allen	83	–	c Ames b Allen	1
*W. M. Woodfull b Allen	10	–	c Allen b Larwood	26
L. P. O'Brien run out	10	–	b Larwood	11
D. G. Bradman b Bowes	0	–	not out	103
S. J. McCabe c Jardine b Voce	32	–	b Allen	0
V. Y. Richardson c Hammond b Voce	34	–	lbw b Hammond	32
†W. A. Oldfield not out	27	–	b Voce	6
C. V. Grimmett c Sutcliffe b Voce	2	–	b Voce	0
T. W. Wall run out	1	–	lbw b Hammond	3
W. J. O'Reilly b Larwood	15	–	c Ames b Hammond	0
H. Ironmonger b Larwood	4	–	run out	0
B 5, l-b 1, w 2, n-b 2	10		B 3, l-b 1, w 4, n-b 1	9
	228			**191**

England bowling: *First innings*—Larwood 20.3–2–52–2; Voce 20–3–54–3; Allen 17–3–41–2; Hammond 10–3–21–0; Bowes 19–2–50–1. *Second innings*—Larwood 15–2–50–2; Voce 15–2–47–2; Allen 12–1–44–2; Hammond 10.5–2–21–3; Bowes 4–0–20–0.

England

H. Sutcliffe, Mr R. E. S. Wyatt, W. R. Hammond, Nawab of Pataudi, M. Leyland, *Mr D. R. Jardine, †L. E.G. Ames, Mr G. O. Allen, H. Larwood, W. Voce and W. E. Bowes.

First innings: 169 (Sutcliffe 52, Allen 30; Wall four for 52, O'Reilly five for 63). *Second innings:* 139 (Sutcliffe 33; O'Reilly five for 66, Ironmonger four for 26).

Umpires: G. A. Hele and G. Borwick

ENGLAND v AUSTRALIA (THIRD TEST MATCH)

85 (129, 130)
21 (29, 30)

Played at Adelaide, January 13, 14, 16, 17, 18, 19 [1933]. The Third Test Match of the tour, in which England – well on top when an innings had been completed on each side – were victorious by no fewer than 338 runs, will go down to history as probably the most unpleasant ever played. So hostile was the feeling of the Australian public against Jardine that, on the days before the game started, people were excluded from the ground when the Englishmen were practising. As Jardine won the toss and England batted first, nothing out of the common occurred to begin with, but later on, when Australia went in and Woodfull was hit over the heart again while Oldfield had to retire owing to a blow he received on the head, the majority of the spectators completely lost all hold on their feelings. Insulting remarks were hurled at Jardine, and when Larwood started to bowl his leg theory he came in for his share of the storm of abuse. Not to put too fine a point on it, pandemonium reigned. A passage of words between P. F. Warner [the MCC team's co-manager] and Woodfull in the dressing-room increased the bitter feeling prevalent in the crowd, and the dispatch of the cablegram protesting against 'body-line' bowling served no purpose in whatever endeavours were made to appease tempers already badly frayed by the various happenings.

[In their second innings Australia's target was 532 to win, on a wicket showing 'definite signs of wear'.] Before the fifth day's play ended, [they] lost four of their best batsmen for 120 runs and to all intents and purposes the game was as good as over. ... Fingleton and Ponsford [were] out with only 12 runs on the board, but then came an excellent stand by Woodfull and Bradman, 88 being put on in an hour and a quarter. Bradman was in first-rate form, hitting a 6 and ten 4's, but just when he was becoming dangerous Verity caught him from a hard return. . . . The greatest praise is due to Woodfull, who for the second time in his career in a Test Match carried his bat through the innings. He was in for nearly four hours, making most of his runs from strokes on the leg side. ...

England

H. Sutcliffe, *Mr D. R. Jardine, W. R. Hammond, †L. E.G. Ames, M. Leyland, Mr R. E. S. Wyatt, E. Paynter, Mr G. O. Allen, H. Verity, W. Voce and H. Larwood.

First innings: 341 (Leyland 83, Wyatt 78, Paynter 77, Verity 45; Wall five for 72). *Second innings:* 412 (Jardine 56, Hammond 85, Ames 69, Leyland 42, Wyatt 49, Verity 40, sundries 32; O'Reilly four for 79, Ironmonger three for 87, Bradman one for 23).

Australia

J. H. Fingleton c Ames b Allen	0	–	b Larwood	0
*W. M. Woodfull b Allen	22	–	not out	73
D. G. Bradman c Allen b Larwood	8	–	c and b Verity	66
S. J. McCabe c Jardine b Larwood	8	–	c Leyland b Allen	7
W. H. Ponsford b Voce	85	–	c Jardine b Larwood	3
V. Y. Richardson b Allen	28	–	c Allen b Larwood	21
†W. A. Oldfield retired hurt	21	–	absent hurt	0
C. V. Grimmett c Voce b Allen	10	–	b Allen	6
T. W. Wall b Hammond	6	–	b Allen	0
W. J. O'Reilly b Larwood	0	–	b Larwood	5
H. Ironmonger not out	0	–	b Allen	0
B 2, l-b 11, n-b 1	14		B 4, l-b 2, w 1, n-b 5	12
	222			**193**

England bowling: *First innings*—Larwood 25–6–55–3; Allen 23–4–71–4; Hammond 17.4–4–30–1; Voce 14–5–21–1; Verity 16–7–31–0. *Second innings*—Larwood 19–3–71–4; Allen 17.2–5–50–4; Hammond 9–3–27–0; Voce 4–1–7–0; Verity 20–12–26–1.

Umpires: G. A. Hele and G. Borwick

MCC TEAM v NEW SOUTH WALES 86 (131, 132)

Played at Sydney, January 26, 27, 28 [1933]. MCC won a game of low scoring by four wickets. New South Wales on the first day lost four batsmen for 68, but Brown and Rowe brought about an improvement in a stand of 101. A rain-damaged pitch next day gave bowlers everything their own way, sixteen wickets going down for 246 runs. The last five New South Wales wickets fell for 11, and MCC had to fight hard for a lead of 19 runs. ... In [a second] innings marked by a curious mixture of good and bad strokes, Bradman on the last day saved New South Wales from collapse, but MCC needed only 110 to win. ...

New South Wales

J. H. Fingleton b Mitchell	19	–	lbw b Tate	7
W. Brown c Ames b Bowes	69	–	c Duckworth b Hammond	25
D. G. Bradman b Mitchell	1	–	c Ames b Hammond	71
*A. F. Kippax c Mitchell b Bowes	3	–	c Verity b Hammond	1
F. Cummins b Mitchell	0	–	c Verity b Hammond	3
R. Rowe c Mitchell b Verity	70	–	c Bowes b Hammond	11
†H. S. Love c Ames b Hammond	4	–	b Verity	2
C. Hill c Verity b Hammond	0	–	c Mitchell b Hammond	0
H. Chilvers lbw b Hammond	4	–	run out	0
W. Howell c Brown b Verity	0	–	b Verity	6
G. L. Stewart not out	0	–	not out	0
B 7, l-b 2, n-b 1	10		B 1, l-b 1	2
	180			**128**

MCC Team bowling: *First innings*—Bowes 15–2–48–2; Tate 10–1–42–0; Mitchell 10–1–32–3; Hammond 8.5–1–22–3; Verity 5–1–9–2; Brown 3–0–17–0. *Second innings*—Bowes 7–1–19–0; Tate 4–0–10–1; Mitchell 5–0–28–0; Hammond 13–1–43–6; Verity 9.1–3–26–2.

MCC Team

*Mr R. E. S. Wyatt, Nawab of Pataudi, W. R. Hammond, H. Verity, L. E.G. Ames, M. Leyland, Mr F. R. Brown, M. W. Tate, †G. Duckworth, W. E. Bowes and T. B. Mitchell.

First innings: 199 (Wyatt 63, Verity 33; Hill three for 39, Chilvers five for 73). *Second innings:* Six for 110 (Leyland 33; Chilvers three for 29).

Umpires: G. Borwick and W.G. French

NEW SOUTH WALES v SOUTH AUSTRALIA 87 (133, 134)

Played at Sydney, February 3, 4, 6 [1933]. Despite a great bowling feat by Wall, South Australia lost this return match by 98 runs. On the opening day New South Wales had 87 on the board for two wickets, but after lunch Wall's fast bowling was almost unplayable. Fingleton, McCabe, Rowe and Cummins were sent back in one over without a run being scored, and Wall took all ten wickets for 36 runs – nine for five runs after the interval and six clean-bowled. [This was the first instance of a bowler taking all ten wickets in the Sheffield Shield, and the second of a bowler doing so in a first-class match in Australia.] The pitch gave him little assistance, but a stiff breeze helped him swing the ball. … When New South Wales went in again, Brown, Bradman and McCabe batted freely, and South Australia were set 356 for victory. … [Bradman brought both South Australian innings to an end when he had Shepherd caught in the first and Wall stumped in the second.] The win of New South Wales enabled them to retain the Shield.

New South Wales

J. H. Fingleton b Wall	43	–	c Tobin b Wall	0
W. Brown c Whitington b Wall	0	–	c Walker b Wall	79
D. G. Bradman c Ryan b Wall	56	–	b Lee	97
S. J. McCabe c Walker b Wall	0	–	lbw b Grimmett	67
R. Rowe b Wall	0	–	c Tobin b Lee	19
F. S. Cummins c Walker b Wall	0	–	b Grimmett	36
*†H. S. Love b Wall	1	–	lbw b Ryan	31
C. Hill b Wall	0	–	not out	9
W. Howell b Wall	0	–	b Ryan	8
W. J. O'Reilly b Wall	4	–	c Walker b Lee	5
G. L. Stewart not out	2	–	b Lee	0
L-b 1, w 1, n-b 5	7		B 1, l-b 2, n-b 2	5
	113			**356**

South Australia bowling: *First innings*—Wall 12.4–2–36–10; Tobin 5–0–23–0; Grimmett 11–0–47–0. *Second innings*—Wall 22–1–91–2; Tobin 12–0–69–0; Grimmett 20–2–84–2; Ryan 17–3–38–2; Lee 16.5–2–69–4.

South Australia

*V. Y. Richardson, H. C. Nitschke, A. R. Lonergan, A. J. Ryan, R. S. Whitington, B. J. Tobin, A.G. Shepherd, P. K. Lee, C. V. Grimmett, T. W. Wall and †C. W. Walker.

First innings: 114 (Shepherd 32; Howell five for 31, Bradman one for 4). *Second innings:* 257 (Richardson 35, Nitschke 105, Ryan 33; O'Reilly five for 56, Hill four for 61, Bradman one for 36).

Umpires: G. Borwick and W.G. French

ENGLAND v AUSTRALIA (FOURTH TEST MATCH)

88 (135, 136)
22 (31, 32)

Played at Brisbane, February 10, 11, 13, 14, 15, 16 [1933]. England won the Fourth Test Match by six wickets, so being successful in the rubber and regaining the Ashes. ... their cricket in this game proved from first to last better than that of the Australians. Once more Jardine captained his side with remarkable skill, his management of his bowlers and his placing of the field being worthy of great praise. In this respect he certainly outshone Woodfull, who had under his command three new men ... Bromley and Darling were brought into the Australian eleven as left-handers likely to counteract the effect of Larwood's leg-theory bowling, and Love kept wicket as Oldfield was not well enough to take his usual place behind the stumps [the blow to his head by a ball from Larwood in the Third Test had fractured his skull].

The Australians at times seemed to have more than a reasonable chance, but they failed to drive home a temporary advantage, and generally speaking they did not appear to be a well-balanced side, while there is no doubt that nearly all of them were overawed by Larwood. The match will always be memorable for the great part played in the victory of England by Paynter. Suffering from an affection of the throat, he left a sick-bed to bat, and put together a splendid innings of 83, while he enjoyed the additional satisfaction later on of making the winning hit with a 6.

Woodfull again won the toss, and this time took in with him to open the Australian innings Victor Richardson. This move proved highly successful ... and thanks to their opening partnership of 133 Australia on the first day stayed in all afternoon to make 251 for the loss of three wickets ... Richardson after lunch made some splendid hits and Bradman carried on the good work, being not out 71 when stumps were pulled up. ... In getting rid of Australia for less than 400 runs, the Englishmen could congratulate themselves. Larwood did great work in taking four wickets, bowling Bradman at 264 and Ponsford at 267. The quick dismissal of these two renowned batsmen meant a great deal to the visiting team. Bradman did not play at all well in the closing stages of his innings, drawing away more than once from Larwood's bowling. After that there was little of note in the batting.... The third day did not go quite so well for England, for at the close England had eight men out for 271 and thus were still 69 runs behind.... [The] negative kind of batting following the opening partnership of 114 runs was disappointing.... Paynter, ill and weak, obviously could not force matters, but he was 24 not out at the close of the day, and on the next morning he gave a superb exhibition.... He was in for nearly four hours... As near as possible England were batting ten hours for their total of 356, which on the face of it seemed absurd.

In the last two and a half hours of the day, however, they atoned for this by some splendid bowling and fielding so that Australia lost four wickets in their second innings for 108 and wound up only 92 runs in front. Richardson led off in rare style, and Bradman batted brightly before falling once more to Larwood at 79.... Once more, the Australians showed what a long tail they had to their team, the last five men scoring between them only 16 runs.

England were thus left with only 160 runs to get ... and play ceased [for the day] with the score at 107 for two wickets. On the last day the flags all round the ground were at half-mast owing to the death that morning of Archie Jackson [at the age of twenty-three].... soon after the match was won rain came on and poured steadily for twelve hours....

Australia

*W. M. Woodfull b Mitchell	67	–	c Hammond b Mitchell	19
V. Y. Richardson st Ames b Hammond	83	–	c Jardine b Verity	32
D. G. Bradman b Larwood	76	–	c Mitchell b Larwood	24
S. J. McCabe c Jardine b Allen	20	–	b Verity	22
W. H. Ponsford b Larwood	19	–	c Larwood b Allen	0
L. Darling c Ames b Allen	17	–	run out	39
E. H. Bromley c Verity b Larwood	26	–	c Hammond b Allen	7
†H. S. Love lbw b Mitchell	5	–	lbw b Larwood	3
T. Wall not out	6	–	c Jardine b Allen	2
W. J. O'Reilly c Hammond b Larwood	6	–	b Larwood	4
H. Ironmonger st Ames b Hammond	8	–	not out	0
B 5, l-b 1, n-b 1	7		B 13, l-b 9, n-b 1	23
	340			**175**

England bowling: *First innings:* Larwood 31–7–101–4; Allen 24–4–83–2; Hammond 23–5–61–2; Mitchell 16–5–49–2; Verity 27–12–39–0. *Second innings*—Larwood 17.3–3–49–3; Allen 17–3–44–3; Hammond 10–4–18–0; Mitchell 5–0–11–1; Verity 19–6–30–2.

England

*Mr D. R. Jardine, H. Sutcliffe, W. R. Hammond, Mr R. E. S. Wyatt, M. Leyland, †L. E.G. Ames, Mr G. O. Allen, E. Paynter, H. Larwood, H. Verity and T. B. Mitchell.

First innings: 356 (Jardine 46, Sutcliffe 86, Paynter 83; O'Reilly four for 120, Ironmonger three for 69, Bradman none for 17). *Second innings:* Four for 162 (Leyland 86).

Umpires: G. A. Hele and G. Borwick

ENGLAND v AUSTRALIA (FIFTH TEST MATCH)

89 (137, 138)
23 (33, 34)

Played at Sydney, February 23, 24, 25, 27, 28 [1933]. The rubber having been won by England, the batting of both sides in their first innings in the last Test Match was generally much brighter than that which previously had been seen. The strain was lifted from both sides, but Australia gave a poor display in the second innings and England demonstrated their superiority over their opponents in no uncertain fashion in winning by eight wickets. Unfortunately the match was marred by bad catching, each side being at fault [in Australia's first innings 'it was ... estimated that England missed no fewer than fourteen catches'], and to Victor Richardson in particular it must have proved a dismal memory, for going in first again with Woodfull he was dismissed without scoring in each innings. ... Larwood, although damaging his foot when bowling [in the second innings; he suffered a broken toe], came out as a batsman with a splendid innings of 98. What a pity he could not have capped his great bowling successes by obtaining a hundred in a Test Match! ... For the fourth time Jardine lost the toss, and in the first over Richardson was out. Woodfull and Bradman carried the score to 59, but then Woodfull played on and in the next over Bradman left at 64. Thenceforward, matters went well for Australia. ... On the Saturday, England batted all day and finished up only 17 runs behind with two wickets to fall. Continuing his innings, Hammond did not play in quite the same brilliant style, and most of the applause was earned by Larwood [who had joined Hammond on Friday evening as night-watchman] who drove in glorious fashion and treated the spectators to a great display ... [until], trying to place the ball to the on for a two to reach three figures, [he] did not time his stroke properly and was caught by Ironmonger, a notoriously bad fieldsman. Larwood treated the bowling as no other of the Englishmen had previously done. He made his runs in two hours and a quarter, hitting a 6, a 5 and nine 4's, and ... was loudly cheered. ...

Monday was full of sensation. England increasing their score to 454 gained a lead of 19 runs ... When Australia went in again the first wicket once more fell before a run had been scored, but then Woodfull and Bradman put on 115. Bradman was in his most daring mood, often stepping back to the leg-theory bowling of Voce and Larwood and forcing the ball to the off. Verity, however, bowled Bradman when the batsman misjudged the flight of the ball, and with his dismissal a breakdown occurred. ... [Later] Verity dismissed O'Reilly and Alexander with consecutive balls, and as Ironmonger was next in the Yorkshireman had a good chance of doing the 'hat-trick'. This he did not accomplish. ...

[When England batted again, requiring 164 to win] Jardine, who took Wyatt in with him, complained about Alexander running down the pitch after his delivery [as the Englishmen had in the first innings], and the crowd booed and hooted. Alexander then bumped several balls down to Jardine, and when the England captain was struck on the thigh, sections of the crowd cheered. A disgraceful exhibition. ... [When Jardine and Leyland were out] Hammond surprised everyone by on-driving O'Reilly for 6 – one of the biggest hits ever seen on the Sydney ground. Hammond, after that, played in brilliant fashion and finished the match in dramatic style with another big 6 [off the bowling of Lee].

Australia

V. Y. Richardson c Jardine b Larwood	0	–	c Allen b Larwood	0
*W. M. Woodfull b Larwood	14	–	b Allen	67
D. G. Bradman b Larwood	48	–	b Verity	71
L. P. O'Brien c Larwood b Voce	61	–	c Verity b Voce	5
S. J. McCabe c Hammond b Verity	73	–	c Jardine b Voce	4
L. S. Darling b Verity	85	–	c Wyatt b Verity	7
†W. A. Oldfield run out	52	–	c Wyatt b Verity	5
P. K. Lee c Jardine b Verity	42	–	b Allen	15
W. J. O'Reilly b Allen	19	–	b Verity	1
H. H. Alexander not out	17	–	lbw b Verity	0
H. Ironmonger b Larwood	1	–	not out	0
B 13, l-b 9, w 1	23		B 4, n-b 3	7
	435			**182**

England bowling: *First innings*—Larwood 32.2–10–98–4; Voce 24–3–80–1; Allen 25–1–128–1; Hammond 8–0–32–0; Verity 17–3–62–3; Wyatt 2–0–12–0. *Second innings*—Larwood 11–0–44–1; Voce 10–0–34–2; Allen 11.4–2–54–2; Hammond 3–0–10–0; Verity 19–9–33–5.

England

H. Sutcliffe, *Mr D. R. Jardine, W. R. Hammond, H. Larwood, M. Leyland, Mr R. E. S. Wyatt, †L. E.G. Ames, E. Paynter, Mr G. O. Allen, H. Verity and W. Voce.

First innings: 454 (Sutcliffe 56, Hammond 101, Larwood 98, Leyland 42, Wyatt 51, Allen 48; O'Reilly three for 100, Lee four for 111). *Second innings:* Two for 168 (Wyatt 61 not out, Hammond 75 not out).

Umpires: G. A. Hele and G. Borwick

1933-34

1933-34

For the third time in five seasons Victoria carried off the Sheffield Shield. The result of the competition was not decided until the final match – that between New South Wales and Victoria at Sydney. New South Wales had to win outright to retain the trophy, but as they could only lead on the first innings their opponents finished one point in front. ...

Bradman again proved the outstanding batsman for New South Wales ... and of the season. Scoring 922 runs in Shield matches he had the remarkable figures of 184.40 per innings, and put together two double-centuries, both against Queensland, and two hundreds against Victoria. He and Kippax created a new Sheffield Shield third-wicket record, the pair putting on 363 against Queensland at Sydney. [This remained the highest third-wicket partnership in Australia until 1981-82.] In all first-class games, Bradman exceeded a thousand runs for the sixth successive season, a performance unequalled by any player in Australia. ...

Before the commencement of the 1933-34 season the Inter-state conference decided to adopt the Australian Board of Control's 'anti-body-line' law, for the Sheffield Shield competition. The law reads: 'Any ball delivered which, in the opinion of the umpire at the bowler's end, is bowled at the batsman with intent to intimidate or injure him, shall be considered unfair and "no-ball" shall be called and the bowler notified of the reason. If the offence be repeated by the same bowler in the same innings, he shall be immediately instructed by the umpire to cease bowling and the over shall be regarded as completed. Such bowler shall not again be permitted to bowl during the course of the innings then in progress.'

From 'Cricket in Australia: Inter-State Matches 1933-34'

QUEENSLAND v NEW SOUTH WALES 90 (139)

Played at Brisbane, November 3, 4, 6, 7 [1933]. Splendid bowling by O'Reilly ... followed by brilliant batting from Bradman were outstanding features of a one-sided match that New South Wales won by an innings and 171 runs. ... When New South Wales went in, Bradman scored 200 runs, including twenty-six 4's, in 184 minutes. He and Brown put on 294 in less than three hours and made a record second-wicket stand for their State against Queensland. Heavy rain caused a blank Monday, but Queensland's batsmen again failing before O'Reilly on a bowler's wicket, New South Wales won easily.

Queensland

*R. M. Levy, T. Allen, C. W. Andrews, F. C. Thompson, E. C. Bensted, R. K. Oxenham, R. C. Raymond, †H. Leeson, H. S. Gamble, F. Yeates and E. R. H. Wyeth.

First innings: 183 (Andrews 59, Bensted 70; O'Reilly six for 58). *Second innings:* 140 (Levy 37, Andrews 31; O'Reilly seven for 53, Mair three for 30).

New South Wales

J. H. Fingleton c Leeson b Yeates	53	S. J. McCabe c Thompson b Oxenham	20
W. A. Brown st Leeson b Yeates	154	R. Rowe not out	13
D. G. Bradman c Andrews b Levy	200	B 2, l-b 1, n-b 5	8
*A. F. Kippax not out	46	(four wkts dec)	**494**

†W. A. Oldfield, F. Mair, C. J. Hill, W. J. O'Reilly and W. Howell did not bat.

Queensland bowling: Gamble 24–6–89–0; Bensted 8–3–33–0; Oxenham 30–8–81–1; Raymond 12–0–57–0; Wyeth 10–3–54–0; Yeates 22–1–155–2; Thompson 1–0–11–0; Levy 1–0–6–1.

Umpires: J. A. Scott and J. Bartlett

W. M. WOODFULL'S XI v V. Y. RICHARDSON'S XI 91 (140, 141)

Played at Melbourne, November 17, 18, 20, 21, 22 [1933]. This [Test Trial] match ... primarily intended as a Benefit to Blackie and Ironmonger, was left drawn. Rain prevented a start on Friday, and after lunch on Saturday the weather stopped further proceedings until Monday. ... Unfortunately for Woodfull, Ironmonger, owing to an injured knee, could do little bowling [nor was he able to bat]. ... [After the teams had batted once] Bradman dominated the remaining cricket. Of the 169 runs scored in Richardson's XI second innings before the game was given up, he obtained 101 by hard and well-timed strokes all round the wicket.

V. Y. Richardson's XI

*V. Y. Richardson run out	28			
J. H. Fingleton lbw b McCabe	105	–	b Wall	0
D. G. Bradman c Woodfull b Wall	55	–	c Darling b Blackie	101
K. E. Rigg b Blackie	94	–	b McCabe	2
L. P. O'Brien c Ponsford b Fleetwood-Smith	90	–	run out	42
P. K. Lee lbw b Fleetwood-Smith	17			
†B. A. Barnett st Oldfield b Blackie	60			
H. I. Ebeling c Wall b Blackie	4			
C. V. Grimmett not out	16			
L. E. Nagel not out	8			
W. J. O'Reilly (did not bat)		–	not out	20
B 6, l-b 7, n-b 1	14		L-b 3, n-b 1	4
(eight wkts dec)	**491**		(four wkts)	**169**

W.M. Woodfull's XI bowling: *First innings*—Wall 25–2–104–1; McCabe 14–1–51–1; Fleetwood-Smith 36–3–140–2; Ironmonger 20–5–88–0; Darling 5–0–25–0; Blackie 25–5–69–3. *Second innings*—Wall 10–5–20–1; McCabe 11–3–25–1; Fleetwood-Smith 9–0–49–0; Darling 2–0–16–0; Blackie 11.7–2–36–1; Kippax 2–0–19–0.

W. M. Woodfull's XI

*W.M. Woodfull, W.H. Ponsford, H.C. Nitschke, S.J. McCabe, A.F. Kippax, L.S. Darling, †W. A. Oldfield, D.D. Blackie, T.W. Wall, L. O'B. Fleetwood-Smith and H. Ironmonger.

First innings: 350 (Woodfull 118, Ponsford 42, McCabe 82, Kippax 34, Darling 30; Ebeling five for 72, Bradman none for 18).

Umpires: G.A. Hele and A.N. Barlow

NEW SOUTH WALES v REST OF AUSTRALIA 92 (142, 143)

Played at Sydney, November 24, 25, 27, 28 [1933]. The second Benefit Trial Match – played as a Testimonial for Collins, Andrews and Kelleway – which the Rest won by two wickets, yielded several good performances. ... [When] New South Wales batted again Fingleton, Bradman, Kippax and Rowe all made good scores. ... Declaring with a lead of 408, New South Wales found their opponents in great batting form. Woodfull's soundness, and dashing innings by Darling and Nitschke, saw the Rest secure a rather unexpected but well-deserved victory in the last over of the day.

New South Wales

J. H. Fingleton b Ebeling	33	–	c Walker b Ebeling	78
W. A. Brown b Nash	8	–	b Chilvers	29
D. G. Bradman c Walker b Chilvers	22	–	b Ebeling	92
*A. F. Kippax c Walker b Chilvers	15	–	not out	111
S. J. McCabe c Walker b Darling	110	–	st Walker b Chilvers	8
R. Rowe c Walker b Ebeling	66	–	not out	66
F. Mair b Ebeling	2			
†W. A. Oldfield c Bromley b Ebeling	4			
C. J. Hill c Walker b Darling	2			
W. J. O'Reilly c Darling b Ebeling	4			
W. Howell not out	1			
B 3, l-b 2, w 1	6		B 5, l-b 1	6
	273		(four wkts dec)	**390**

Rest of Australia bowling: *First innings*—Nash 10–0–48–1; Ebeling 22.1–3–66–5; Lee 14–2–39–0; Chilvers 19–2–69–2; Bromley 7–1–31–0; Darling 6–1–14–2. *Second innings*—Nash 11–0–57–0; Ebeling 28–4–87–2; Lee 23–2–67–0; Chilvers 26–2–95–2; Bromley 7–0–33–0; Darling 8–0–45–0.

Rest of Australia

*W.M. Woodfull, W.H. Ponsford, L.P. O'Brien, L.S. Darling, H.C. Nitschke, E.H. Bromley, P.K. Lee, L.J. Nash, H.I. Ebeling, H.C. Chilvers and †C.W. Walker.

First innings: 255 (Ponsford 70, Lee 69; O'Reilly three for 59, Mair three for 81). *Second innings:* Eight for 409 (Woodfull 129, O'Brien 44, Darling 77, Nitschke 76, Bromley 42; Bradman one for 30, Kippax three for 10).

Umpires: G. Borwick and W.G. French

SOUTH AUSTRALIA v NEW SOUTH WALES 93 (144, 145)

Played at Adelaide, December 15, 16, 18 [1933]. South Australia, in the Ernest Jones Benefit game, accomplished an excellent performance in beating the [Shield] holders by ten wickets. . .. [In their first innings] New South Wales generally [showed] to very poor advantage. ... In [their] second innings, Bradman and Kippax got runs readily without ever appearing quite comfortable against Grimmett, who took advantage of a worn patch, and Lee. ...

New South Wales

J. H. Fingleton c Walker b Tobin	27	–	c Walker b Grimmett	30
W. A. Brown c Ryan b Wall	4	–	c Walker b Collins	38
D. G. Bradman b Collins	1	–	c Wall b Grimmett	76
*A. F. Kippax b Tobin	9	–	st Walker b Grimmett	90
R. Rowe c Wall b Tobin	1	–	b Wall	6
†W. A. Oldfield run out	0	–	c Richardson b Grimmett	20
H. C. Chilvers not out	16	–	b Grimmett	0
F. Mair b Grimmett	14	–	lbw b Lee	2
W. J. O'Reilly c Richardson b Grimmett	6	–	not out	2
C. J. Hill run out	24	–	b Lee	1
W. Howell b Lee	1	–	b Lee	0
B 1, l-b 1, n-b 3	5		L-b 6	6
	108			**271**

South Australia bowling: *First innings*—Wall 10–3–24–1; Collins 9–1–30–1; Tobin 8–1–20–3; Lee 4.1–0–12–1; Grimmett 6–2–17–2. *Second innings*—Wall 18–1–66–1; Collins 13–0–43–1; Tobin 10–0–49–0; Lee 5–2–4–3; Grimmett 33–3–103–5.

South Australia

*V. Y. Richardson, H. C. Nitschke, A. R. Lonergan, A. J. Ryan, A. G. Shepherd, B. J. Tobin, F. H. Collins, P. K. Lee, †C. W. Walker, C. V. Grimmett and T. W. Wall.

First innings: 316 (Nitschke 82, Lonergan 50, Ryan 94 not out, Shepherd 43; Chilvers three for 48, Mair four for 69). *Second innings:* None for 65 (Nitschke 44 not out).

Umpires: J. D. Scott and E. H. Kitson

VICTORIA v NEW SOUTH WALES 94 (146, 147)

Played at Melbourne, December 22, 23, 26, 27 [1933]. Victoria gained innings points after much splendid cricket. ... Despite good defence by Fingleton and splendidly accurate batting on the part of Bradman, New South Wales lost six men for 259. Then Bradman scored all but 16 of the 96 runs realised by the remaining wickets, the visitors finishing 27 behind. O'Reilly, spinning and flighting the ball skilfully, followed by dismissing nine Victorian batsmen ... Only Ponsford and Darling dealt effectively with him. New South Wales, set 228 to get, finished in the better position, Bradman again carrying his bat.

Victoria

*W. M. Woodfull, W. H. Ponsford, L. P. O'Brien, K. E. Rigg, L. S. Darling, E. H. Bromley, †B. A. Barnett, L. E. Nagel, H. I. Ebeling, L. O'B. Fleetwood-Smith and H. Ironmonger.

First innings: 382 (Woodfull 60, Ponsford 30, O'Brien 86, Darling 91, Ebeling 32; Howell five for 97, O'Reilly three for 92). *Second innings:* 200 (Ponsford 40, Darling 53; O'Reilly nine for 50).

New South Wales

J. H. Fingleton lbw b Ebeling	76			
W. A. Brown lbw b Fleetwood-Smith	23			
D. G. Bradman not out	187	–	not out	77
*A. F. Kippax b Fleetwood-Smith	23	–	c Barnett b Ebeling	28
A. McGilvray b Fleetwood-Smith	11			
R. Rowe c Barnett b Fleetwood-Smith	5	–	not out	39
†W. A. Oldfield c Darling b Fleetwood-Smith	2			
H. C. Chilvers b Ironmonger	5			
W. J. O'Reilly lbw b Fleetwood-Smith	6			
F. Mair c Barnett b Ironmonger	3			
W. Howell b Fleetwood-Smith	2			
B 8, l-b 2, n-b 2	12			
	355		(one wkt)	**144**

Victoria bowling: *First innings*—Ebeling 29–7–53–1; Nagel 20–3–70–0; Ironmonger 30–10–51–2; Fleetwood-Smith 32–3–138–7; Bromley 7–0–31–0. *Second innings*—Ebeling 10–0–56–1; Nagel 3–0–28–0; Ironmonger 9–0–26–0; Bromley 3–0–26–0; Darling 2–0–8–0.

Umpires: A. N. Barlow and G. A. Hele

NEW SOUTH WALES v QUEENSLAND 95 (148)

Played at Sydney, December 30 [1933], January 1, 2, 3 [1934]. Another great double-century by Bradman against Queensland featured [in] the victory of New South Wales by an innings and 84 runs. … Bradman surpassed everyone. Exploiting all the strokes, he dealt unmercifully with the bowling, actually scoring his 253 in less than three and a half hours. His execution of the cut, drive, pull and leg-glance was perfect. Kippax was by no means overshadowed. Batting with his usual grace he reached his hundred in two hours. His record third-wicket stand of 363 with Bradman occupied only two and a quarter hours. …

Queensland

G.G. Cook, F.M. Brew, C.W. Andrews, F.C. Thompson, *R.M. Levy, E.C. Bensted, T. Allen, R.K. Oxenham, A. Tait, †H. Leeson and H.S. Gamble.

First innings: 372 (Andrews 38, Thompson 92, Levy 45, Allen 86, Oxenham 51; Hill three for 51, Bradman none for 2). *Second innings:* 158 (Tait 35; Chilvers six for 62).

New South Wales

J. H. Fingleton c Bensted b Brew	42	A. G. Chipperfield c Leeson b Andrews	84
W. A. Brown c Levy b Oxenham	50	A. McGilvray not out	34
D. G. Bradman b Brew	253	C. J. Hill not out	2
*A. F. Kippax c sub b Oxenham	125	B 8, l-b 2, w 5, n-b 2	17
R. Rowe c Leeson b Oxenham	7	(six wkts dec)	**614**

†A. Easton, H. C. Chilvers and W. Howell did not bat.

Queensland bowling: Gamble 6–0–17–0; Bensted 19–2–97–0; Brew 25–1–176–2; Oxenham 42–0–116–3; Tait 10–1–77–0; Cook 4–0–32–0; Andrews 3–0–19–1; Levy 5–0–63–0.

Umpires: G. Borwick and H. Armstrong

NEW SOUTH WALES v VICTORIA 96 (149)

Played at Sydney, January 26, 27, 29, 30 [1934]. A draw won Victoria the Sheffield Shield by a single point. For New South Wales, Bradman [in what was to be his last game for his home State] hit four 6's and seventeen 4's in an hour and a half; Brown combined caution with aggression in a sound 205, and Fingleton made 145 after being given out when 86 only to be recalled following a talk between Woodfull and Borwick, the umpire. [Having been dropped at slip, Fingleton left his ground to tap down the pitch and was adjudged run out by Borwick, standing at square-leg, when wicket-keeper Barnett removed the bails.] ...

New South Wales

J. H. Fingleton c Bromley b Ironmonger	145
W. A. Brown lbw b Fleetwood-Smith	205
D. G. Bradman c Darling b Fleetwood-Smith	128
*A. F. Kippax c Barnett b McCormick	44
R. Rowe run out	42
A. G. Chipperfield c Barnett b Ebeling	9
H. C. Chilvers run out	42
†W. A. Oldfield run out	2
C. J. Hill not out	32
W. J. O'Reilly not out	11
B 4, l-b 8	12
(eight wkts dec)	**672**

H. Theak did not bat.

Victoria bowling: McCormick 35–1–148–1; Ebeling 29–1–154–1; Fleetwood-Smith 31–0–178–2; Ironmonger 22–3–86–1; Bromley 6–0–42–0; Darling 9–0–52–0.

Victoria

*W. M. Woodfull, L. P. O'Brien, K. E. Rigg, J. Scaife, L. S. Darling, E. H. Bromley, †B. A. Barnett, H. I. Ebeling, E. L. McCormick, L. O'B. Fleetwood-Smith and H. Ironmonger.

First innings: 407 (Woodfull 83, Scaife 120, Bromley 92; Hill three for 40). *Second innings:* Five for 274 (Rigg 35, Scaife 80, Darling 93, Bromley 33 not out; Bradman none for 19).

Umpires: G. Borwick and H. Armstrong

1934

1934

The Australian team of 1934 arrived in [the United Kingdom] with the knowledge that during the previous series of Test Matches in Australia they had been beaten four times and successful only once, and to the majority of people at home the idea of England losing the rubber was as remote as it had been in 1930. Australia, however, won two Test Matches to England's one – the struggles at Manchester and Leeds being left drawn – and, by a remarkable coincidence, Woodfull, again as in 1930, led his side at the Oval to the victory which regained the Ashes, on the anniversary of his birthday – August 22. ...

There is no need here to go deeply into those occurrences which, marring the enjoyment of the tour of the MCC team in 1932, so nearly ended in a breach of the cricketing relations between this country and Australia. Yet it is necessary to refer to the upheaval which the so-called 'body-line' bowling, as practised during that tour, caused. Matters were smoothed over sufficiently to ensure the visit of the Australians ... but the echoes of the controversy continually arose and the Australian team themselves were just a trifle doubtful as to the kind of welcome they would receive. Happily for everyone concerned, any fears our visitors may have entertained on this point were quickly removed by the enthusiasm expressed about their cricket during the early matches and the genuine feeling of goodwill shown towards them at public receptions and at most places they went to play. ...

The advent of fine, sunny weather, after very miserable conditions prior to their opening match, enabled them to jump almost at once into form, and with the exception of the débacle in the Test Match at Lord's they remained at their very best until the end. Still, they had their troubles in the way of illness and accident. Quite early ... they had to contend with an epidemic of influenza. ... After the First Test Bradman hurt his leg, catching it in a rope when running off the field, at Nottingham ... illness kept Ponsford out of the Second Test, at Lord's ... another epidemic, this time described as 'Wimbledon throat', swept through the team during the Manchester Test Match so that Chipperfield and Kippax were detained in an isolation hospital ... and then at Leeds Bradman had to leave the field with a strained thigh. ... Finally Bromley, on the eve of the last Test Match, developed appendicitis and underwent an operation while, when the tour had been completed, Bradman was also operated on for appendicitis and prevented from leaving England with the rest of his colleagues. Few, if any, teams visiting this country, therefore, can have experienced such an anxious time ... as did the Australians last summer. ...

The batting of the team was tremendously strong. In all first-class matches six men scored over 1,000 runs each, Bradman heading the list with an average of over 84 and an aggregate of 2,020. [The other five were McCabe (2,078), Ponsford (1,784), Brown (1,308), Woodfull (1,268) and Darling (1,022).] ... For purposes of comparison Bradman obtained 940 fewer runs than in 1930 ... In Test Matches ... despite innings of 304 at Leeds and 244 at the Oval, [he] totalled, in eight appearances as against five, 216 fewer runs, his average dropping from 139 to 94. ...

Bradman [who was vice-captain of the touring team] had a curious season. He reached three figures seven times ... As in 1930 he led off in the opening match with an innings of over 200 against Worcestershire but then for a time he was, for Bradman, less than normal. Indeed, after his 206 at Worcester his only three-figure innings until the middle of July at Sheffield was 160 against Middlesex at Lord's. Yet that 160 was, in all probability, the most dazzling exhibition he gave throughout the tour. On the first afternoon he reached his hundred off the last ball of the day, having obtained these runs out of 135 in seventy-five minutes. Although going at such a tremendous pace his timing and placing were so certain and his execution so powerful that he did not make a single mistake. Old habitués of Lord's were almost unanimous afterwards in saying that they had never before seen such a brilliant and perfect display. Bradman finished the season in great style, his 140 against Yorkshire being the prelude to a succession of big scores, of which 304 in the Leeds Test was most noteworthy. He was out of the team for five first-class matches after this; then came his 244 at the Oval and he ended with 149 not out at Folkestone and 132 at Scarborough. It was noticeable that in many innings Bradman lifted the ball to a far greater extent than when he came here first, and there were many occasions on which he was out to wild strokes. Indeed at one period he created the impression that, to some extent, he had lost control of himself and went in to bat with an almost complete disregard for anything in the shape of a defensive stroke. To those, however, who watched him closely in his big innings, it was obvious that in the course of four years he had improved his technique almost out of knowledge. He was much more interesting to look at because of the wider range of his scoring strokes. At his best he was probably harder to get out than ever, and at times so marvellous was his footwork and power of execution that all bowlers were at a complete loss as to where they should pitch the ball. An amazingly brilliant batsman, he retained that faculty, given to most really great players, of delaying his stroke until the last possible moment. …

… [A]s in 1930, the team went through their programme of matches with only one defeat – in the Second Test Match at Lord's. Including minor engagements they won fifteen of the thirty-four fixtures arranged and drew eighteen. Actually, apart from the match they lost, they never really looked to be in danger.

From 'The Australians in England', by S.J. Southerton

WORCESTERSHIRE v AUSTRALIANS 97 (150)

Played at Worcester, Wednesday, Thursday, May 2, 3 [1934]. A great innings by Bradman and the skilful bowling of Grimmett had most to do with the overwhelming victory by an innings and 297 runs gained by the Australians in the opening engagement of the tour. … Bradman immediately settled down to his finest form, driving, pulling and hooking with perfect timing and strength. He and Woodfull added 114 for the second wicket, and McCabe and Bromley joined with Bradman in partnerships that yielded 70 and 111 respectively. Sixth out at 359, Bradman, except for one chance of stumping, made no mistake during nearly three and a half hours at the crease. He punished fully any deliveries of imperfect length, twice scoring 14 runs in an over, and he hit twenty-seven 4's. …

Worcestershire

*Mr C.F. Walters, H.H. Gibbons, Nawab of Pataudi, M. Nichol, S.H. Martin, C.H. Bull, †Mr B.W. Quaife, R. Howorth, G.W. Brook, P.F. Jackson and R.T.D. Perks.

First innings: 112 (Walters 32; Grimmett five for 53). *Second innings:* 95 (Grimmett five for 27, O'Reilly four for 25).

Australians

*W. M. Woodfull c Perks b Martin	48	C. V. Grimmett c Brook b Howorth	7
W. H. Ponsford c Nichol b Jackson	13	H. I. Ebeling b Perks	13
D. G. Bradman b Howorth	206	T. W. Wall lbw b Brook	24
A. F. Kippax b Jackson	0	W. J. O'Reilly not out	25
S. J. McCabe c Brook b Perks	20	B 26, l-b 5, n-b 5	36
E. H. Bromley c Brook b Howorth	45		**504**
†W. A. Oldfield c Martin b Howorth	67		

Worcestershire bowling: Perks 26–2–83–2; Jackson 30–4–95–2; Martin 14–4–41–1; Brook 22–2–114–1; Howorth 23–0–135–4.

Umpires: T. Oates and A. Dolphin

LEICESTERSHIRE v AUSTRALIANS 98 (151)

Played at [Aylestone Road] Leicester, Saturday, Monday, Tuesday, May 5, 7, 8 [1934]. Though leading by 216 on the first innings, the Australians could not force a win. Their bowlers laboured under the handicap of a wet ball on the last day ... The pitch on Saturday helped O'Reilly to take seven wickets ... but the turf rolled out well on Monday when, aided by fielding errors, the Australians played themselves into an impregnable position. Brown and Bradman made 65 together. ... Bradman declaring with five men out, Leicestershire faced a heavy task, but Dawson and Berry, in a third stand of 116, pulled the game round. [After a collapse] Astill and Geary came to the rescue.

Leicestershire

Mr E.W. Dawson, A. Shipman, N.F. Armstrong, L.G. Berry, *Mr A.G. Hazlerigg, Mr A.G. Weston, A. Riddington, G. Geary, W.E. Astill, H.A. Smith and †P. Corrall.

First innings: 152 (Shipman 30; O'Reilly seven for 39). *Second innings:* Nine for 263 (Dawson 91, Berry 48, Astill 50 not out; O'Reilly four for 40, Fleetwood-Smith four for 83).

Australians

W. H. Ponsford lbw b Geary	9	S. J. McCabe not out	108
W. A. Brown b Smith	28	†B. A. Barnett not out	30
*D. G. Bradman b Geary	65	B 1, l-b 2, n-b 1	4
A. F. Kippax c Armstrong b Shipman	89	(five wkts dec)	**368**
L. S. Darling c Corrall b Shipman	35		

W. J. O'Reilly, L. O'B. Fleetwood-Smith, E. H. Bromley and H. I. Ebeling did not bat.

Leicestershire bowling: Shipman 25–1–88–2; Smith 34–7–81–1; Geary 31–8–48–2; Riddington 14–1–37–0; Astill 24–4–69–0; Armstrong 7–0–17–0; Hazlerigg 5–0–24–0.

Umpires: F. Chester and J. Stone

CAMBRIDGE UNIVERSITY v AUSTRALIANS 99 (152)

Played at Cambridge, Wednesday, Thursday, Friday, May 9, 10, 11 [1934]. The Australian bowling meeting with little resistance, the tourists won easily by an innings and 163 runs. On Wednesday the Australians lost three wickets for 71 – Bradman failed to score for the first time in England – but subsequently the University attack, lacking a bowler of real pace, was mastered. Batting throughout an innings lasting six and a quarter hours, Ponsford put together, up to then, his highest score in England. ... Brown, in a stylish innings, registered his first century of the tour in the course of a partnership of 262 – a record fifth stand for an Australian team in England. ...

Australians

*W. M. Woodfull c Cox b Davies	21	W. A. Brown c Barlett b Grimshaw	105
W. H. Ponsford not out	229	†B. A. Barnett not out	1
D. G. Bradman b Davies	0	B 5, l-b 5, w 1, n-b 1	12
S. J. McCabe c Human b Grimshaw	15	(five wkts dec)	**481**
L. S. Darling c Human b Cox	98		

T. W. Wall, L. O'B. Fleetwood-Smith, H. I. Ebeling and C. V. Grimmett did not bat.

Cambridge University bowling: Jahangir Khan 41–5–127–0; Cox 42–8–115–1; Davies 39–11–89–2; Grimshaw 43–5–102–2; Human 6–0–36–0.

Cambridge University

Mr A.W. Allen, Mr A.F. Skinner, Mr R. de W.K. Winlaw, Mr H.P. Dinwiddy, Mr H.T. Bartlett, *Mr J.H. Human, Mr J.G.W. Davies, M. Jahangir Khan, Mr H.R. Cox, †Mr A.G. Powell and Mr J.W.T. Grimshaw.

First innings: 158 (Jahangir Khan 33; Grimmett nine for 74). *Second innings:* 160 (Cox 51 not out; Fleetwood-Smith three for 31).

Umpires: A. Morton and L.C. Braund

MCC v AUSTRALIANS 100 (153)

Played at Lord's, Saturday, Monday, Tuesday, May 12, 14, 15 [1934]. To two members of the MCC team, Wyatt and Hendren, belonged chief credit for a draw. Between them, this pair scored 326 of the runs obtained by their side, and each completed a hundred. ... The Australian innings was practically a one-partnership affair, Ponsford and McCabe, against an attack containing no pace bowler, establishing a third-wicket record by adding 389 in four and a half hours. Ponsford made his highest score in England ...

MCC

Mr R.E.S. Wyatt, Rev. E.T. Killick, Mr M.J. Turnbull, E. Hendren, Mr B.H. Valentine, *Mr A.P.F. Chapman, Mr F.R. Brown, Mr J.C. White, Mr I.A.R. Peebles, †Mr P.C. Oldfield and Mr C.S. Marriott.

First innings: 362 (Wyatt 72, Turnbull 33, Hendren 135, Valentine 40, Chapman 46 not out; Wall six for 74). *Second innings:* Eight for 182 (Wyatt 102 not out; O'Reilly three for 29, Grimmett four for 90).

Australians

*W. M. Woodfull c White b Brown	20	W. A. Brown c Oldfield b Brown	2
W. H. Ponsford not out	281	†W. A. Oldfield b Brown	7
D. G. Bradman c and b Brown	5	C. V. Grimmett not out	26
S. J. McCabe b Peebles	192	B 9, l-b 6	15
L. S. Darling c Hendren b White	11	(six wkts dec)	**559**

T. W. Wall, W. J. O'Reilly and L. O'B. Fleetwood-Smith did not bat.

MCC bowling: Wyatt 9–1–38–0; Valentine 6–0–28–0; Peebles 40–5–141–1; Marriott 41–9–126–0; Brown 37–2–134–4; White 28–4–77–1.

Umpires: A. Morton and J. Hardstaff

OXFORD UNIVERSITY v AUSTRALIANS 101 (154)

Played at [the Christ Church ground] Oxford, Saturday, Monday, May 19, 21 [1934]. On a pitch that generally proved helpful to bowlers, the Australians overwhelmed the University by an innings and 33 runs. Darling and Ponsford, for the tourists, and de Saram, for Oxford, were the only batsmen really to overcome the conditions. ... Bradman played a subdued innings. ...

Australians

W. H. Ponsford c Singleton b Dyson	75	†W. A. Oldfield b Tindall	8
W. A. Brown lbw b Townsend	20	C. V. Grimmett b Tindall	0
*D. G. Bradman lbw b Dyson	37	H. I. Ebeling c Walker b Tindall	0
L. S. Darling lbw b Tindall	100	L. O'B. Fleetwood-Smith not out	2
S. J. McCabe b Tindall	15	B 13, l-b 4, n-b 2	19
E. H. Bromley b Barlow	3		**319**
A. G. Chipperfield c Stainton b Barlow	40		

Oxford University bowling: Tindall 24–3–94–5; Barlow 32.4–2–102–2; Townsend 9–3–18–1; Singleton 7–0–38–0; Dyson 17–4–48–2.

Oxford University

Mr D.F. Walker, Mr D.C.H. Townsend, Mr F.C. de Saram, Mr N.S. Mitchell-Innes, *Mr F.G.H. Chalk, Mr R.G. Stainton, Mr R.G. Tindall, Mr E.A. Barlow, †Mr M.H. Matthews, Mr A.P. Singleton and Mr J.H. Dyson.

First innings: 70 (Ebeling four for 34, Fleetwood-Smith five for 30). *Second innings:* 216 (de Saram 128; Grimmett seven for 109).

Umpires: A. Stoner and J. H. King

HAMPSHIRE v AUSTRALIANS 102 (155)

Played at Southampton, Wednesday, Thursday, Friday, May 23, 24, 25 [1934]. Bad light caused a match full of variety and changing fortune to end tamely in a draw, though a definite result appeared unlikely some time before the finish. Arnold saved Hampshire from a second-innings collapse that might have meant defeat, despite the highest total to date from the Australian bowling and the best partnership against the tourists by Mead and Lowndes [who] put on 247 in less than three hours for the fourth wicket …

Hampshire

J. Arnold, Mr R.H. Moore, A.E. Pothecary, C.P. Mead, *Mr W.G. Lowndes, Lord Tennyson, W. L. Creese, A. Kennedy, G.S. Boyes, †N. McCorkell and Mr A.E.G. Baring.

First innings: 420 (Mead 139, Lowndes 140, Tennyson 56; McCabe four for 79, O'Reilly three for 123). *Second innings:* Seven for 169 dec (Arnold 109 not out; Fleetwood-Smith three for 86, O'Reilly four for 34).

Australians

*W. M. Woodfull c and b Baring	2			
W. A. Brown c McCorkell b Baring	0			
D. G. Bradman c Mead b Baring	0			
S. J. McCabe c McCorkell b Baring	79	–	not out	0
L. S. Darling lbw b Kennedy	96	–	c McCorkell b Lowndes	1
A. F. Kippax c Tennyson b Boyes	38			
E. H. Bromley lbw b Boyes	37			
A. G. Chipperfield not out	116	–	not out	5
†W. A. Oldfield b Lowndes	22			
W. J. O'Reilly lbw b Baring	23			
L. O'B. Fleetwood-Smith c sub b Kennedy	4			
B 9, l-b 7	16		B	4
	433		(one wkt)	**10**

Hampshire bowling: *First innings*—Baring 26–1–121–5; Kennedy 23.5–3–81–2; Creese 7–0–34–0; Lowndes 21–3–95–1; Boyes 23–6–86–2. *Second innings*—Kennedy 1–1–0–0; Creese 2–0–6–0; Lowndes 1.1–1–0–1.

Umpires: W. Reeves and D. Hendren

MIDDLESEX v AUSTRALIANS 103 (156)

Played at Lord's, Saturday, Monday, May 26, 28 [1934]. Until the second day, Middlesex fought hard, but then they broke down badly and the Australians won easily by ten wickets. … An amazing innings by Bradman overshadowed everything else in the Australian reply. After the quick fall of two wickets, he hit the bowling all over the field. He and Darling put on 132 and he and Kippax 84, while altogether Bradman obtained 160 out of 225 in just over two hours. For all his freedom, Bradman gave no chance. Enthoven accomplished the 'hat-trick' after lunch on Monday, but the Australians led by 87 and, Middlesex losing eight wickets in clearing the arrears, the result was soon beyond doubt. …

Middlesex

†W. F. Price, G. E. Hart, J. Hulme, E. Hendren, Mr R. W. V. Robins, Mr G. C. Newman, Mr G. O. Allen, *Mr H. J. Enthoven, J. Smith, Mr P. F. Judge and Mr I. A. R. Peebles.

First innings: 258 (Hendren 115, Robins 65; Wall three for 41, Grimmett three for 80). *Second innings:* 114 (Hendren 35; O'Reilly three for 34, Grimmett five for 27).

Australians

*W. M. Woodfull lbw b Smith	0			
W. H. Ponsford lbw b Smith	0			
D. G. Bradman c Hulme b Peebles	160			
L. S. Darling c Price b Smith	37	–	not out	9
A. F. Kippax lbw b Robins	56			
A. G. Chipperfield c and b Enthoven	35			
†B. A. Barnett b Smith	40	–	not out	14
C. V. Grimmett c Price b Enthoven	8			
H. I. Ebeling st Price b Enthoven	0			
T. W. Wall b Enthoven	0			
W. J. O'Reilly not out	7			
B 1, l-b 1	2		B 4, l-b 1, w 1	6
	345		(no wkt)	**29**

Middlesex bowling: *First innings*—Smith 20.2–2–99–4; Judge 6–0–41–0; Enthoven 16–2–59–4; Robins 12–1–61–1; Peebles 16–0–83–1. *Second innings*—Hulme 2–0–8–0; Allen 1.4–0–15–0.

Umpires: A. Skelding and W. A. Buswell

SURREY v AUSTRALIANS 104 (157)

Played at Kennington Oval, Wednesday, Thursday, Friday, May 30, 31, June 1 [1934]. As many as 1,266 runs being scored for the loss of nineteen wickets, the game never looked like providing a definite result. … [The] Australians gained the lead without much difficulty. McCabe, let off time and again, shared with Ponsford in the first opening stand of three figures during the tour … Bradman helped add 130 for the second wicket, and the tourists finished 154 ahead …

Surrey

J. B. Hobbs, A. Sandham, R.J. Gregory, H.S. Squires, †E.W. Brooks, T.H. Barling, *Mr E.R. T. Holmes, Mr H.M. Garland-Wells, Mr F.R. Brown, Mr P.G.H. Fender and A.R. Gover.

First innings: Seven for 475 dec (Sandham 219, Gregory 116, Barling 44). *Second innings:* Two for 162 (Gregory 59 not out, Brown 54 not out).

Australians

W. H. Ponsford c Brooks b Holmes	125	†W. A. Oldfield not out	33
S. J. McCabe c Fender b Garland-Wells	240	C. V. Grimmett b Gover	25
D. G. Bradman c Squires b Gover	77	W. J. O'Reilley c Brooks b Gover	8
A. F. Kippax b Gover	5	T. W. Wall c Fender b Holmes	10
A. G. Chipperfield b Gover	34	B 3, l-b 3, w 1, n-b 8	15
*W. M. Woodfull c Fender b Holmes	1		**629**
E. H. Bromley c Gregory b Fender	56		

Surrey bowling: Gover 34–4–147–5; Holmes 25.2–5–136–3; Fender 24–2–114–1; Brown 20–0–108–0; Garland-Wells 19–1–76–1; Gregory 4–0–15–0; Squires 2–0–18–0.

Umpires: F. Chester and F. Walden

ENGLAND v AUSTRALIA (FIRST TEST MATCH)

105 (158, 159)
24 (35, 36)

Played at Nottingham, Friday, Saturday, Monday, Tuesday, June 8, 9, 11, 12 [1934]. Australia began the series of Test Matches with a splendid victory by 238 runs. On the first three days, at any rate, the fortunes of the game changed sufficiently to keep interest at its highest pitch, while on the last afternoon everyone was on the tip-toe of excitement in watching England's desperate but unavailing effort to stave off defeat. Thus it came about that the decision of the contest was not determined until only ten more minutes remained for play. ...

As a matter of fact, England up to a point fared quite satisfactorily, for, after Woodfull and Ponsford had made 77 together in ninety-five minutes, two wickets fell before lunch, and shortly before quarter to four Australia had five men out for 153. Ponsford made his runs by varied strokes and hit eight 4's; Woodfull was very solid for nearly two hours; Bradman hit six 4's in half an hour; and Brown stayed for eighty minutes, but the fact remained that Australia, up to then, had scarcely made sufficient use of their opportunity of batting first on a nice easy wicket. ... On Saturday McCabe was out at 234, but unexpected assistance was given to Chipperfield by Oldfield and Grimmett ... Chipperfield, in his first Test Match, just missed the distinction of making a hundred. He was 99 at lunch-time, and out third ball afterwards. ...

... England fared well for a time ... [but] were all out by three o'clock [on Monday], and they found themselves 106 runs behind. Still, Australia at their second attempt lost their first three wickets for 69 before the game turned once more with a partnership between McCabe and Brown ... All the other batsmen on the Tuesday morning went out for runs in order to give Woodfull the chance of declaring at the earliest possible moment. He did not do this until half-past twelve ... [by which time] the wicket was showing signs of wear ... O'Reilly bowled superbly. Clever variation in flight and pace combined with spin off the worn turf made him very difficult, and he deserved all the congratulations showered upon him at the close by his delighted colleagues.

Australia

*W. M. Woodfull c Verity b Farnes	26	–	b Farnes	2
W. H. Ponsford c Ames b Farnes	53	–	b Hammond	5
W. A. Brown lbw b Geary	22	–	c Ames b Verity	73
D. G. Bradman c Hammond b Geary	29	–	c Ames b Farnes	25
S. J. McCabe c Leyland b Farnes	65	–	c Hammond b Farnes	88
L. S. Darling b Verity	4	–	c Hammond b Farnes	14
A. G. Chipperfield c Ames b Farnes	99	–	c Hammond b Farnes	4
†W. A. Oldfield c Hammond b Mitchell	20	–	not out	10
C. V. Grimmett b Geary	39	–	not out	3
W. J. O'Reilly b Farnes	7	–	c Verity b Geary	18
T. W. Wall not out	0			
B 4, l-b 5, n-b 1	10		B 22, l-b 9	31
	374		(eight wkts dec)	**273**

England bowling: *First innings*—Farnes 40.2–10–102–5; Geary 43–8–101–3; Hammond 13–4–29–0; Verity 34–9–65–1; Mitchell 21–4–62–1; Leyland 1–0–5–0. *Second innings*—Farnes 25–3–77–5; Geary 23–5–46–1; Hammond 12–5–25–1; Verity 17–8–48–1; Mitchell 13–2–46–0.

England

*Mr C. F. Walters, H. Sutcliffe, W. R. Hammond, Nawab of Pataudi, M. Leyland, E. Hendren, †L.E.G. Ames, G. Geary, H. Verity, Mr K. Farnes and T. B. Mitchell.

First innings: 268 (Sutcliffe 62, Hendren 79, Geary 53; Grimmett five for 81, O'Reilly four for 75). *Second innings:* 141 (Walters 46; Grimmett three for 39, O'Reilly seven for 54).

Umpires: A. Dolphin and F. Chester

NORTHAMPTONSHIRE v AUSTRALIANS 106 (160, 161)

Played at Northampton, Wednesday, Thursday, Friday, June 13, 14, 15 [1934]. After dismissing the Australians for the two lowest totals of the tour to date, Northamptonshire, needing 332 to win, collapsed badly on Friday and narrowly avoided defeat. The finish was most exciting, nine minutes remaining when the last county batsman went in. Although Ponsford and Brown scored 93 for the opening wicket, half the Australian side were out for 116 on Wednesday, and only a stand of 127 by Chipperfield and Bradman saved the tourists. ... [In Northamptonshire's first innings] Snowden, putting together his first hundred in big cricket, went in first and was last out. ... Brown, opening the innings and being last to leave, averted a second innings breakdown by the tourists.

Australians

W. H. Ponsford lbw b Pitt	56	–	c Bellamy b Matthews	11
W. A. Brown b Partridge	30	–	c Bellamy b Matthews	113
L. S. Darling b Bakewell	3	–	c Bellamy b Pitt	17
A. F. Kippax lbw b Matthews	12	–	c and b Partridge	9
E. H. Bromley c Bakewell b Partridge	5	–	c and b Partridge	3
*D. G. Bradman c Bakewell b Matthews	65	–	b Matthews	25
A. G. Chipperfield c Pitt b Partridge	71	–	run out	0
†B. A. Barnett c Partridge b Matthews	7	–	b Matthews	44
W. J. O'Reilly not out	13	–	c Timms b Matthews	4
H. I. Ebeling b Matthews	14	–	c Matthews b Pitt	1
L. O'B. Fleetwood-Smith run out	0	–	not out	1
B 1, l-b 7	8		B 3, l-b 3	6
	284			**234**

Northamptonshire bowling: *First innings*—Matthews 23–0–71–4; Pitt 12–1–53–1; Partridge 24.1–2–67–3; Towell 11–1–27–0; Bakewell 11–1–38–1; Cox 7–1–20–0. *Second innings*—Matthews 26.5–3–87–5; Pitt 14–2–42–2; Partridge 27–8–57–2; Towell 8–0–20–0; Bakewell 3–0–22–0.

Northamptonshire

Mr A.W. Snowden, A.H. Bakewell, N. Grimshaw, J.E. Timms, †B. Bellamy, A.L. Cox, Mr E.F. Towell, A.D. Matthews, *Mr W.C. Brown, R.J. Partridge and Mr T.A. Pitt.

First innings: 187 (Snowden 105; Fleetwood-Smith five for 63, O'Reilly three for 46). *Second innings:* Nine for 133 (Bakewell 53, Timms 50; Ebeling three for 26, Fleetwood-Smith five for 29).

Umpires: J. Stone and W. Reeves

ENGLAND v AUSTRALIA (SECOND TEST MATCH)

107 (162, 163)
25 (37, 38)

Played at Lord's, Friday, Saturday, Monday, June 22, 23, 25 [1934]. For their defeat at Trent Bridge, England took an ample revenge at Lord's, winning the match in three days in an innings with 38 runs to spare. This was England's first success in a Test Match against Australia at Lord's since 1896 when Lohmann and Tom Richardson, in a memorable struggle, swept the Australians off their feet. While everyone in England naturally was jubilant over the triumph of the Englishmen, it could not be denied that they were helped in a pronounced degree by the weather.

Winning the toss, England stayed in until nearly three o'clock on the Saturday ... but before the end of the day Australia had 192 runs on the board with only two men out. In view of this splendid start by the visitors there existed no sound reason why they should not have closely approached if not even passed the England total, but they suffered the cruellest luck, rain falling during the weekend and rendering their chances almost hopeless. Fortunately England had in the team a bowler capable of taking full advantage of the conditions that prevailed, and Verity, obtaining seven wickets in the first innings for 61 runs, followed this up with eight in the second for 43, to be the chief factor in giving England such a pronounced success. ... Verity had taken one of the Australian wickets which fell on Saturday [that of Bradman], and on the Monday he dismissed fourteen men for 80 runs, six of them after tea at a cost of 15. ... Verity's length was impeccable and he made the ball come back and lift so abruptly that most of the Australians were helpless. The majority of them had had no experience in England of such a pitch ['it could scarcely be described as genuinely "sticky" except for one period after lunch'], and they showed no ability or skill in dealing with bowling like that of Verity under these conditions. Those who tried to play forward did not get far enough, and their efforts at playing back were, to say the least, immature. ...

[In Australia's first innings] Bradman, with seven 4's, hit up 36 [of 73 runs scored while he was at the wicket] but actually he never looked like staying very long, making many of his strokes without restraint. ... [In their second innings, following on] Verity, coming on at 17, quickly got to work again, dismissing McCabe and Bradman at 43 and 57, while after tea Woodfull, who had defended stubbornly for two hours, was fourth to leave at 94. The rest of the innings was a mere procession ...

England

Mr C.F. Walters, H. Sutcliffe, W.R. Hammond, E. Hendren, *Mr R.E.S. Wyatt, M. Leyland, †L.E.G. Ames, G. Geary, H. Verity, Mr K. Farnes and W.E. Bowes.

First innings: 440 (Walters 82, Wyatt 33, Leyland 109, Ames 120; Wall four for 108, Chipperfield three for 91).

Australia

*W. M. Woodfull b Bowes	22	–	c Hammond b Verity	43
W. A. Brown c Ames b Bowes	105	–	c Walters b Bowes	2
D. G. Bradman c and b Verity	36	–	c Ames b Verity	13
S. J. McCabe c Hammond b Verity	34	–	c Hendren b Verity	19
L. S. Darling c Sutcliffe b Verity	0	–	b Hammond	10
A. G. Chipperfield not out	37	–	c Geary b Verity	14
E. H. Bromley c Geary b Verity	4	–	c and b Verity	1
†W. A. Oldfield c Sutcliffe b Verity	23	–	lbw b Verity	0
C. V. Grimmett b Bowes	9	–	c Hammond b Verity	0
W. J. O'Reilly b Verity	4	–	not out	8
T. W. Wall lbw b Verity	0	–	c Hendren b Verity	1
B 1, l-b 9	10		B 6, n-b 1	7
	284			**118**

England bowling: *First innings*—Farnes 12–3–43–0; Bowes 31–5–98–3; Geary 22–4–56–0; Verity 36–15–61–7; Hammond 4–1–6–0; Leyland 4–1–10–0. *Second innings*—Farnes 4–2–6–0; Bowes 14–4–24–1; Verity 22.3–8–43–8; Hammond 13–0–38–1.

Umpires: F. Chester and J. Hardstaff

SOMERSET v AUSTRALIANS 108 (164)

Played at Taunton, Wednesday, Thursday, June 27, 28 [1934]. Somerset proved no match for the Australians, who won in an innings with 77 runs to spare. The county were unfortunate in getting the worst of the wicket on the opening day, for Ingle, who won the toss, could not be blamed for taking first innings. Heavy rain preceded the match and the wicket, though covered, gave bowlers considerable assistance. O'Reilly seized his opportunity ... Keeping a perfect length and concentrating on the leg stump, he caused trouble to everybody, nine wickets falling to him after lunch for 75 runs. Frank Lee, who carried his bat through the innings, alone offered much resistance. By the time the tourists went in, the turf had recovered ... Going in again 193 behind, Somerset soon experienced trouble with Fleetwood-Smith, losing three men for 14 runs. ...

Somerset

J.W. Lee, F.S. Lee, Mr G.M. Bennett, Mr J.C. White, Mr C.C. Case, *Mr R.A. Ingle, Mr H.D. Burrough, A. W. Wellard, Mr J. H. Cameron, Mr P.J. Davey and †W. T. Luckes.

First innings: 116 (F.S. Lee 59 not out; O'Reilly nine for 38). *Second innings:* 116 (Ebeling three for 24, Fleetwood-Smith six for 56).

Australians

*W. M. Woodfull run out	84	†B. A. Barnett b Wellard	51
W. H. Ponsford st Luckes b White	17	H. I. Ebeling c sub b Wellard	21
D. G. Bradman c Luckes b White	17	W. J. O'Reilly not out	22
L. S. Darling c Davey b Wellard	79	L. O'B. Fleetwood-Smith b Wellard	0
A. F. Kippax c Luckes b Wellard	1	L-b	4
A. G. Chipperfield hit wkt b Wellard	12		**309**
E. H. Bromley lbw b J. W. Lee	1		

Somerset bowling: Wellard 36.4–6–111–6; J.W. Lee 30–9–70–1; White 27–4–92–2; Cameron 3–0–18–0; Davey 8–1–14–0.

Umpires: W. Reeves and E.J. Smith

SURREY v AUSTRALIANS 109 (165, 166)

Played at Kennington Oval, Saturday, Monday, Tuesday, June 30, July 2, 3 [1934]. Surrey did so well in their first game with the Australians that they were expected to put up a good fight in their second meeting. Although their bowlers performed satisfactorily, however, the county batting failed and the tourists won by six wickets. ... Surrey gave a disappointing display in their first innings. The Australians, too, found run-getting no easy matter on an excellent pitch ... [but in their second innings, needing 109 to win] Bradman, batting in his best form, destroyed any possibility of a surprise result, he and Darling, after three wickets fell cheaply, adding 73 together.

Surrey

A. Sandham, R.J. Gregory, H.S. Squires, T.H. Barling, *Mr E.R.T. Holmes, Mr F.R. Brown, E. A. Watts, Mr P.G.H. Fender, A.R. Gover, Mr M.J.C. Allom and †E.W. Brooks.

First innings: 175 (Gregory 48, Brooks 32; McCabe four for 24, Grimmett four for 64). *Second innings:* 184 (Gregory 48, Brown 46; Grimmett five for 33, Fleetwood-Smith three for 48).

Australians

W. H. Ponsford c Holmes b Allom	85	–	c Allom b Gover	10
W. A. Brown lbw b Allom	34	–	c Fender b Gover	0
L. S. Darling c Watts b Fender	20	–	lbw b Holmes	31
*D. G. Bradman c Brooks b Holmes	27	–	not out	61
†B. A. Barnett c Holmes b Gover	1			
S. J. McCabe b Fender	0	–	not out	0
A. F. Kippax b Gover	50			
E. H. Bromley c Holmes b Allom	0	–	c Gover b Allom	3
C. V. Grimmett c Brooks b Watts	7			
H. I. Ebeling b Allom	12			
L. O'B. Fleetwood-Smith not out	2			
B 1, l-b 5, w 1, n-b 6	13		B 1, l-b 3, n-b 2	6
	251		(four wkts)	**111**

Surrey bowling: *First innings*—Gover 22–3–73–2; Allom 17.4–2–60–4; Brown 6–0–14–0; Fender 18–4–58–2; Watts 5–0–18–1; Holmes 5–1–15–1. *Second innings*—Gover 6–0–36–2; Allom 6–0–23–1; Fender 3.2–0–28–0; Watts 2–0–14–0; Holmes 2–1–4–1.

Umpires: D. Hendren and J. Hardstaff

ENGLAND v AUSTRALIA 110 (167)
(THIRD TEST MATCH) 26 (39)

Played at Manchester, Friday, Saturday, Monday, Tuesday, July 6, 7, 9, 10 [1934]. The Third Test Match had to be left drawn, the scoring being so heavy that in the course of the four days 1,307 runs were obtained and only twenty wickets fell. For more than one reason, however, the game will always be remembered by those who saw it. Changed at the request of Lancashire from its usual order in the rota of Tests – Old Trafford for some years had been the scene of the fourth encounter in the series of Test Matches in this country – the alteration from the point of view of weather was more than justified. Seldom, indeed, can an International engagement in this country have been played throughout the whole of four days under such wonderful conditions. From first to last the sun blazed down, the heat being at times almost unbearable.

Another point of remembrance was the fact that the Australians played through the greater part of the game under a very serious handicap, an affection of the throat seizing Bradman, Chipperfield and Kippax in particular and others in a lesser degree, so that at one period it was feared that an attack of diphtheria had overtaken the visitors. ... In these circumstances, therefore, the Australians – kept in the field until nearly four o'clock on the Saturday while

England were scoring, in nine and a half hours, a total of 627 for nine wickets – naturally played in rather a depressed spirit, but they did not allow this to affect their skill and, replying to the big total of their opponents with a score of 491, practically made certain, unless something phenomenal happened, of avoiding defeat.

[In England's first innings, O'Reilly dismissed Walters, Wyatt and Hammond in four balls, transforming their position from no wicket for 68 to three for 72. When Australia batted, McCabe 'went along at a fine pace' on Saturday evening and Monday. Later] Woodfull [who had been dropped first ball at second slip] and Bradman put on 58 in sixty-five minutes, but Bradman, when 26, gave Hammond a sharp return chance. … Australia, [having avoided the follow-on in the first session on Tuesday] found themselves 136 behind, but they had kept England in the field for over ten hours. The rest of the cricket on the last day was of no particular interest. …

England

Mr C. F. Walters, H. Sutcliffe, *Mr R. E. S. Wyatt, W. R. Hammond, E. Hendren, M. Leyland, †L. E.G. Ames, J. L. Hopwood, Mr G. O. Allen, H. Verity and E. W. Clark.

First innings: Nine for 627 dec (Walters 52, Sutcliffe 63, Hendren 132, Leyland 153, Ames 72, Allen 61, Verity 60 not out; O'Reilly seven for 189). *Second innings:* None for 123 dec (Walters 50 not out, Sutcliffe 69 not out).

Australia

W. A. Brown c Walters b Clark	72	–	c Hammond b Allen	0
W. H. Ponsford c Hendren b Hammond	12	–	not out	30
S. J. McCabe c Verity b Hammond	137	–	not out	33
*W. M. Woodfull run out	73			
L. S. Darling b Verity	37			
D. G. Bradman c Ames b Hammond	30			
†W. A. Oldfield c Wyatt b Verity	13			
A. G. Chipperfield c Walters b Verity	26			
C. V. Grimmett b Verity	0			
W. J. O'Reilly not out	30			
T. W. Wall run out	18			
B 20, l-b 13, w 4, n-b 6	43		B 1, l-b 2	3
	491		(one wkt)	**66**

England bowling: *First innings*—Clark 40–9–100–1; Allen 31–3–113–0; Hammond 28.3–6–111–3; Verity 53–24–78–4; Hopwood 38–20–46–0. *Second innings*—Clark 4–1–16–0; Allen 6–0–23–1; Hammond 2–1–2–0; Verity 5–4–2–0; Hopwood 9–5–16–0; Hendren 1–0–4–0.

Umpires: J. Hardstaff and F. Walden

DERBYSHIRE v AUSTRALIANS 111 (168, 169)

Played at Chesterfield, Wednesday, Thursday, Friday, July 11, 12, 13 [1934]. Collapsing in deplorable fashion on the last day, Derbyshire fell easy victims by nine wickets. Of the county's first innings total of 145, three men between them scored 101. … The Australians got to within 23 of the Derbyshire score for the loss of four wickets, but thanks to fine bowling by Mitchell, with flight, break and variation of pace, they led by only 110. Bradman made top score, but scarcely appeared at his best. Derbyshire began the last day 36 behind with eight wickets in hand … In one spell, Fleetwood-Smith dismissed five batsmen for 18 runs.

Derbyshire

H. Storer, A. E. Alderman, L. F. Townsend, D. Smith, *Mr A. F. Skinner, Mr G. R. Jackson, Mr N. M. Ford, T. S. Worthington, †H. Elliott, T. B. Mitchell and W. Copson.

First innings: 145 (Storer 40, Ford 37; Ebeling five for 28). *Second innings:* 139 (Storer 47, Smith 32; Fleetwood-Smith five for 38).

Australians

E. H. Bromley b Mitchell	31	–	not out	16
W. A. Brown st Elliott b Mitchell	17	–	b Jackson	10
D. G. Bradman c Elliott b Townsend	71	–	not out	6
S. J. McCabe c Elliott b Mitchell	3			
L. S. Darling b Mitchell	14			
*W. M. Woodfull run out	44			
W. H. Ponsford lbw b Townsend	11			
†B. A. Barnett b Mitchell	48			
H. I. Ebeling b Mitchell	1			
T. W. Wall not out	2			
L. O'B. Fleetwood-Smith b Mitchell	0			
B 8, l-b 5	13			
	255		(one wkt)	**32**

Derbyshire bowling: *First innings*—Worthington 12–2–25–0; Copson 16–5–45–0; Mitchell 34.5–6–105–7; Townsend 25–3–67–2. *Second innings*—Jackson 2.5–0–21–1; Ford 2–0–11–0.

Umpires: A. Skelding and W. A. Buswell

YORKSHIRE v AUSTRALIANS 112 (170)

Played at Sheffield, Saturday, Monday, Tuesday, July 14, 16, 17 [1934]. Thanks largely to a capital three-figure innings by Sellers – his first for the county – Yorkshire effected a creditable draw. The performance was the more praiseworthy as Sutcliffe retired from the game after pulling a muscle early on Saturday. … Bradman once again took the batting honours for the Australians, scoring 140 out of 189 added with Woodfull, but, Bowes bowling admirably, the tourists led by only eight runs. Sent in to open Yorkshire's second innings, Wood saved his side from collapse. … Sellers helped him put on 58, and the Australians were set an impossible task.

Yorkshire

H. Sutcliffe, A. Mitchell, W. Barber, M. Leyland, C. Turner, *Mr A. B. Sellers, H. Verity, T. F. Smailes, †A. Wood, G.G. Macaulay and W. E. Bowes.

First innings: 340 (Mitchell 36, Barber 37, Leyland 43, Sellers 104, Smailes 30, Macaulay 40 not out; Grimmett four for 113). *Second innings:* 157 (Wood 59; Wall three for 36, Fleetwood-Smith three for 39.)

Australians

*W. M. Woodfull c Sellers b Smailes	54		
W. A. Brown c Macaulay b Bowes	14	– lbw b Macaulay	12
D. G. Bradman b Leyland	140		
S. J. McCabe b Bowes	21	– not out	14
L. S. Darling c sub b Bowes	45		
E. H. Bromley lbw b Macaulay	16		
†B. A. Barnett b Bowes	7		
C. V. Grimmett b Bowes	8		
H. I. Ebeling b Bowes	27		
T. W. Wall b Bowes	1		
L. O'B. Fleetwood-Smith not out	1		
B 10, l-b 3, n-b 1	14	W	2
	348	(one wkt)	**28**

Yorkshire bowling: *First innings*—Bowes 29.2–4–100–7; Smailes 21–2–68–1; Macaulay 19–5–41–1; Turner 9–0–53–0; Verity 6–0–33–0; Leyland 4–0–39–1. *Second innings*—Bowes 3–1–6–0; Smailes 2–1–5–0; Macaulay 5–1–13–1; Turner 4–3–2–0.

Umpires: L. C. Braund and C. N. Woolley

ENGLAND v AUSTRALIA

113 (171)

(FOURTH TEST MATCH)

27 (40)

Played at Leeds, Friday, Saturday, Monday, Tuesday, July 20, 21, 23, 24 [1934]. Just as at Lord's rain came to damage the wicket and ruin Australia's chance of making an even fight of it, so in the Fourth Test Match on the Headingley ground at Leeds did one of the shortest but heaviest rainstorms seen at a cricket match for years arrive just in time to rob Australia of victory and enable England to draw a game in which they were completely outplayed. Escaping defeat in the luckiest manner possible, the England team accomplished nothing in the match on which they could congratulate themselves. ...

His good fortune in the matter of winning the toss again attended Wyatt and for the third consecutive game England enjoyed the advantage of batting first. Wyatt himself described the wicket as being 'like a feather-bed', whatever that may have meant. The assumption at the time was that it would be slow and easy. There was nothing in the way it played during the first day to suggest that it was otherwise, yet England, giving one of the worst displays of batting probably ever seen under similar conditions were all dismissed between twenty-five minutes to twelve and twenty-five minutes past five for a paltry total of 200. It can be said that O'Reilly, Grimmett and Chipperfield bowled very well, but nothing they accomplished with the ball was quite sufficient to account for the shocking exhibition of weak and hesitant batting given by the Englishmen. ...

Before cricket ended, however, further surprises were in store for the crowd. Bowes and Hammond started the bowling for England and both Ponsford and Brown played them so easily that there seemed no reason to expect any pronounced success for the England attack up to half-past six. Bowes, however, changed ends and, coming on again at 37 from the Pavilion wicket, bowled Brown at 37 and two runs later sent back Oldfield and Woodfull in one over. Stumps were then pulled up, Bowes having sent down ten balls from the Pavilion end and dismissed three batsmen without conceding a run. ... Those, however, were the last crumbs of comfort England were destined to enjoy in this disastrous match. Bradman joined Ponsford the next morning and not until ten minutes to six on Saturday evening did another wicket fall. Giving a great display of batting, the two famous Australian run-getters beat all previous partnership records in Test Matches. They carried the score in five and a half hours to 427 before Ponsford, hooking a short ball from Verity, trod on his wicket ... Altogether their stand realised no fewer than 388 runs. They always scored at a good rate but, as usual with Australians, unless the bowling is exceptionally steady, pushed along very quickly after tea when, in an hour, 98 runs were put on. Up to lunch-time they scored 129 in two hours and twenty-five minutes and between lunch and tea 161 in two hours and five minutes.

Ponsford's innings was very good indeed. In the course of the partnership each batsman gave a chance, for Ponsford when 70 should have been caught by Mitchell at cover-point while Bradman at 71 was let off by Hopwood. ... For the greater part of the day Bradman, who unlike Ponsford obtained most of his runs in front of the stumps, batted with the utmost certainty, but during the last thirty-five minutes when he and McCabe were raising the score to 494 he played in a more light-hearted spirit. Twice he lifted the ball over the ring for 6, and hit Hopwood for 15 runs in one over.

Australia, therefore, began the third day in a most comfortable position, being 294 runs on with six wickets to fall, and altogether Bradman and McCabe added 90 in an hour before McCabe was out. Thanks to some most effective bowling by Bowes, Australia's innings was finished off in a hundred minutes, the last six wickets falling on Monday morning for 90 runs. Bradman, sixth out at 550, made his 304 in six hours and fifty-five minutes. Going in third wicket down, he took the leading part in adding 511 runs while as many more wickets fell. Not out on Saturday with 271 he was perhaps lucky in reaching 300 because when 280 he was missed at third slip by Verity. He did not play so well during the fifty minutes he was in on Monday morning as he had done previously, but all the same his innings was a masterly affair. He hit the ball very hard and placed his strokes beautifully, while until joined by McCabe on Saturday evening he rarely sent the ball into the air. He hit two 6's, forty-three 4's, one 3, fifteen 2's and eighty-seven singles. ... England went in again at one o'clock 384 runs behind, so that the most they could hope for was a draw. ... [Three wickets fell for 87] but by dint of very hard work and much watchful batting Hendren and Wyatt added 65 in rather less than two hours. During this stand Bradman, trying to stop the ball in the long field with his foot, strained his leg and had to retire. ... Heavy rain fell in the night and the wicket was very wet, while a further shower caused a delay soon after cricket had been resumed. Then Hendren was out at 190 and when Ames left at 213 the end seemed very near. Just before one o'clock a thunderstorm broke over the ground and, although it lasted only ten minutes, the downpour was so severe that no further cricket was possible. Not until six o'clock, however, was the decision to abandon the match arrived at. Not only the pitch but parts of the outfield and especially that in front of the Pavilion were, even then, far too wet for cricket to be proceeded with.

England

Mr C. F. Walters, W. W. Keeton, W. R. Hammond, E. Hendren, *Mr R. E. S. Wyatt, M. Leyland, †L. E.G. Ames, J. L. Hopwood, H. Verity, T. B. Mitchell and W. E. Bowes.

First innings: 200 (Walters 44, Hammond 37; Grimmett four for 57, O'Reilly three for 46). *Second innings:* Six for 229 (Walters 45, Hendren 42, Wyatt 44, Leyland 49 not out; Grimmett three for 72).

Australia

W. A. Brown b Bowes	15	A. G. Chipperfield c Wyatt b Verity	1
W. H. Ponsford hit wkt b Verity	181	C. V. Grimmett run out	15
†W. A. Oldfield c Ames b Bowes	0	W. J. O'Reilly not out	11
*W. M. Woodfull b Bowes	0	T. W. Wall lbw b Verity	1
D. G. Bradman b Bowes	304	B 8, l-b 9	17
S. J. McCabe b Bowes	27		**584**
L. S. Darling b Bowes	12		

England bowling: Bowes 50–13–142–6; Hammond 29–5–82–0; Mitchell 23–1–117–0; Verity 46.5–15–113–3; Hopwood 30–7–93–0; Leyland 5–0–20–0.

Umpires: J. Hardstaff and A. Dolphin

THE ARMY v AUSTRALIANS

Played at Aldershot, Wednesday, August 15 [1934]. Main interest in this match, which gave the Australians an easy victory, centred in the first appearance of Bradman since he injured himself in the Fourth Test at Leeds. Bradman made top score in the game, scoring his 79 at almost one a minute. None of the Army batsmen ever looked comfortable.

The Army

*Lieut. R.E.H. Hudson, Lieut. C.P. Hamilton, Lieut. P.M. Nelson, Capt. G.J. Bryan, Lieut. R.J. Packe, Lieut. J.W.A. Stephenson, Maj. M.A. Green, Lieut. J.H.N. Foster, Lieut. R.G.W. Melsome, Lieut. P.M. Hughes and †Lieut. T.F. Winnington.

First innings: 110 (O'Reilly three for 17, Bromley three for 21).

Australians

W. H. Ponsford c Hudson b Hamilton	48	†B. A. Barnett b Nelson	7
L. S. Darling c Packe b Stephenson	6	W. A. Oldfield not out	3
E. H. Bromley c Packe b Melsome	7	W. A. Brown not out	10
*D. G. Bradman c Melsome b Stephenson	79	B	5
W. J. O'Reilly b Stephenson	6	(seven wkts)	**194**
H. I. Ebeling c Hamilton b Nelson	23		

A. F. Kippax and L. O'B. Fleetwood-Smith did not bat.

The Army bowling: Stephenson 20–5–47–3; Melsome 18–0–70–1; Hughes 5–1–18–0; Hamilton 9–1–42–1; Nelson 4–0–12–2.

Umpires: G. Moore and Regt. Sgt-Major Marrison

ENGLAND v AUSTRALIA (FIFTH TEST MATCH)

114 (172, 173)
28 (41, 42)

Played at Kennington Oval, Saturday, Monday, Tuesday, Wednesday, August 18, 20, 21, 22 [1934]. Each side having won once with two games left drawn, the Fifth and concluding Test Match was entered upon without any restrictions as to the time involved in reaching a definite result. As it happened four days proved sufficient for Australia to win by 562 runs. Thus they regained the Ashes. Being successful in the rubber by two victories to one, they brought their number of wins in the whole series of encounters between the two countries to 52 as against 51 by England. Under conditions which, apart from the winning of the toss, favoured neither side unduly, the result was a fitting tribute to the superior all-round skill of Australia. ...

The law of averages suggested that it was Woodfull's turn to win the toss. This he did and when Clark, coming on at 20, bowled Brown at 21 with the best ball sent down all day long, it seemed as though the England attack on a hard wicket was about to come into its own. Never were hopeful anticipations more rudely dispelled. Between them Ponsford and Bradman gave another glorious display of batting, staying together until nearly half-past six and engaging in a partnership which left that of Leeds far behind and produced 451 runs in five hours and a quarter. This time Bradman was the first to leave, hitting over his head at a bouncing ball and being caught behind the wicket at 472. ... It would be hard to speak in too high terms of praise of the magnificent displays of batting given by Ponsford and Bradman. Before Bradman joined him, Ponsford had shown an inclination to draw away from the bowling of Bowes but he received inspiration from the example of his partner, who from the very moment he reached the centre and took up his stance was coolness and mastery personified. The pitch did not help bowlers at all. ... Clark and the others tried all sort of theories ['Clark tried leg-theory with a packed leg-side field but ... his bowling ... scarcely came under the category of what is known as "body-line"] but they had no effect on Bradman who, as the afternoon wore on, invested his batting with increasing daring. He drove and cut with the utmost certainty and power, and when the ball did bounce he just stepped back and hooked it. Included in his hits were a 6 and thirty-two 4's and, having regard to the rate at which he as well as Ponsford scored, a better display has rarely been seen. Ponsford was not quite so sure as Bradman and he frequently turned his back to the ball to receive blows on the thigh. ... As during the day about 80 runs an hour were obtained it can be realised that too many long-hops and half-volleys were sent down. This great partnership meant that in consecutive representative encounters Bradman and Ponsford in two stands scored 839 runs in ten hours and three-quarters. Ponsford offered three very difficult chances and one when 115 comparatively easy; Bradman's batting, as far as was seen, was flawless.

On Monday, England had further trouble before the innings, which lasted nearly ten hours, closed at twenty minutes to five for 701 runs – the second highest in the history of Test Matches between England and Australia. ... Tuesday was a black day for England and except for a superbly aggressive display by Maurice Leyland the batting proved deplorable. ... Australia, 380 ahead, scored 186 for two wickets before the end of the day, Brown leaving at 13 and Ponsford at 42. ... Bradman and McCabe scored at a fine pace, making 144 together in ninety minutes. Light rain fell during the night but the wicket the next morning was not greatly affected. ... [Bowes] soon dismissed Bradman who, with McCabe, had added 150 in ninety-five minutes and then for the first time England's bowling got really on top so that Australia were all out by half-past two ... England were thus left with no fewer than 708 to get to win – only 34 short of the number England had set Australia in the First Test Match at Brisbane during the 1928-29 tour. [They] made a shocking start ... and shortly before six o'clock, with Allen stumped, the innings was all over for 145 ... Grimmett bowled superbly.

Australia

W. A. Brown b Clark	10	–	c Allen b Clark	1
W. H. Ponsford hit wkt b Allen	266	–	c Hammond b Clark	22
D. G. Bradman c Ames b Bowes	244	–	b Bowes	77
S. J. McCabe b Allen	10	–	c Walters b Clark	70
*W. M. Woodfull b Bowes	49	–	b Bowes	13
A. F. Kippax lbw b Bowes	28	–	c Walters b Clark	8
A. G. Chipperfield b Bowes	3	–	c Woolley b Clark	16
†W. A. Oldfield not out	42	–	c Hammond b Bowes	0
C. V. Grimmett c Ames b Allen	7	–	c Hammond b Bowes	14
H. I. Ebeling b Allen	2	–	c Allen b Bowes	41
W. J. O'Reilly b Clark	7	–	not out	15
B 4, l-b 14, w 2, n-b 13	55		B 37, l-b 8, w 1, n-b 4	50
	701			**327**

England bowling: *First innings*—Bowes 38–2–164–4; Allen 34–5–170–4; Clark 37.2–4–110–2; Hammond 12–0–53–0; Verity 43–7–123–0; Wyatt 4–0–28–0; Leyland 3–0–20–0. *Second innings*—Bowes 11.3–3–55–5; Allen 16–2–63–0; Clark 20–1–98–5; Hammond 7–1–18–0; Verity 14–3–43–0.

England

Mr C. F. Walters, H. Sutcliffe, F. E. Woolley, W. R. Hammond, *Mr R. E. S. Wyatt, M. Leyland, †L. E.G. Ames, Mr G. O. Allen, H. Verity, E. W. Clark and W. E. Bowes.

First innings: 321 (Walters 64, Sutcliffe 38, Leyland 110, Ames 33 retired hurt; Ebeling three for 74, Grimmett three for 103). *Second innings:* 145 (Hammond 43; Grimmett five for 64).

Umpires: F. Chester and F. Walden

SUSSEX v AUSTRALIANS 115 (174)

Played at Hove, Saturday, Monday, Tuesday, August 25, 27, 28 [1934]. The form of Sussex in county engagements had suggested the likelihood of a close fight, but the Australians won readily by an innings and 35 runs. …

Sussex

John Langridge, J. H. Parks, *Mr A. Melville, T. Cook, Jas. Langridge, H. W. Parks, E. H. Bowley, G. Pearce, †J. Eaton, M. W. Tate and J. Cornford.

First innings: Eight for 304 dec (J. H. Parks 60, Cook 60, Jas. Langridge 57, Tate 40 not out; Fleetwood-Smith five for 114). *Second innings:* 221 (John Langridge 53, Bowley 63, J. H. Parks 32, Melville 40; Fleetwood-Smith five for 87, O'Reilly four for 49).

Australians

W. H. Ponsford b Cornford	6
W. A. Brown hit wkt b Jas. Langridge	66
A. G. Chipperfield c Eaton b Cornford	0
A. F. Kippax c H. Parks b Pearce	250
S. J. McCabe lbw b Cornford	46
L. S. Darling b Tate	117
*D. G. Bradman b Pearce	19
†B. A. Barnett not out	27
H. I. Ebeling b Bowley	10
W. J. O'Reilly c Pearce b Bowley	4
L. O'B. Fleetwood-Smith c Cornford b Bowley	0
B 10, l-b 2, w 2, n-b 1	15
	560

Sussex bowling: Tate 31–4–101–1; Cornford 26–2–129–3; J. Parks 20–0–91–0; Pearce 17–0–90–2; Jas. Langridge 12–0–63–1; Bowley 13.2–0–71–3.

Umpires: F. Chester and C. N. Woolley

KENT v AUSTRALIANS 116

Played at Canterbury, Wednesday, Thursday, Friday, August 29, 30, 31 [1934]. Only thirty-five minutes' cricket being possible on the first day and rain putting play on the second entirely out of the question, a drawn game became inevitable. … Set to get 176 to avoid defeat in a single innings, Kent fared disastrously, but, so little time remaining, they were never in much danger.

Kent

W. H. Ashdown, F. E. Woolley, L. J. Todd, Mr B. H. Valentine, Mr C. H. Knott, Mr F. G. H. Chalk, Mr J. G. W. Davies, *Mr A. P. F. Chapman, †Mr W. H. V. Levett, A. E. Watt and A. P. Freeman.

First innings: Two for 21 dec. *Second innings:* Seven for 74 (Fleetwood-Smith four for 30).

Australians

W. H. Ponsford not out	82
S. J. McCabe lbw b Woolley	108
B 2, l-b 4, n-b 1	7
(one wkt dec)	**197**

*D. G. Bradman, A. G. Chipperfield, C. V. Grimmett, A. F. Kippax, L. S. Darling, †B. A. Barnett, H. I. Ebeling, W. J. O'Reilly and L. O'B. Fleetwood-Smith did not bat.

Kent bowling: Ashdown 14–2–36–0; Watt 13–2–30–0; Davies 10–1–27–0; Todd 9–0–42–0; Freeman 10–0–49–0; Woolley 3.5–0–6–1.

Umpires: J. Stone and J. Newman

AN ENGLAND XI v AUSTRALIANS 117 (175)

Played at Folkestone, Saturday, Monday, Tuesday, September 1, 3, 4 [1934]. Cricket on the first two days being limited by rain to two hours forty minutes, a draw was inevitable, but the game will always be remembered for a brilliant and spectacular display of hard, clean hitting by Bradman, who made 149 not out in an hour and three-quarters. When play began at three o'clock on Monday, Woolley, Walters and Hobbs compensated the crowd for their disappointment … and the sight of Woolley and Hobbs together at the crease brought back vivid memories of their wonderful feats for England in the past. … Bradman's display provided a glorious finish to the match. Taking full advantage of an escape when one, Bradman reached three figures out of 166 in ninety minutes; trounced Freeman for three 6's and three 4's in one over, and in one period of seven minutes he scored 31! In addition to four 6's, Bradman obtained seventeen 4's. Brown, Ponsford and Woodfull also showed capital form.

An England XI

Mr C. F. Walters, J. B. Hobbs, F. E. Woolley, W. R. Hammond, †L. E.G. Ames, Mr B. H. Valentine, Lord Tennyson, M. Jahangir Khan, Mr M. J. C. Allom, *Mr A. P. F. Chapman and A. P. Freeman.

First innings: 279 (Hobbs 38, Woolley 66, Hammond 54, Allom 47 not out; O'Reilly four for 55, Fleetwood-Smith five for 137).

Australians

W. H. Ponsford b Freeman	45	D. G. Bradman not out	149
W. A. Brown c Ames b Woolley	73	*W. M. Woodfull not out	62
S. J. McCabe lbw b Freeman	10	B 2, l-b 1, w 2	5
A. F. Kippax c Ames b Hammond	21	(four wkts)	**365**

†W. A. Oldfield, C. V. Grimmett, T. W. Wall, W. J. O'Reilly and L. O'B. Fleetwood-Smith did not bat.

An England XI bowling: Jahangir Khan 16–1–52–0; Allom 20–1–81–0; Hammond 15–0–71–1; Woolley 8–0–28–1; Freeman 31–5–128–2.

Umpires: F. Chester and A. E. Street

MR H. D.G. LEVESON GOWER'S XI v AUSTRALIANS 118 (176)

Played at Scarborough, Saturday, Monday, Tuesday, September 8, 10, 11 [1934]. Centuries by Bradman and McCabe and splendid bowling by Fleetwood-Smith were the chief features of the Australians' fine win by an innings and 48 runs. With runs coming at the rate of over 90 an hour, the crowd of 10,000 experienced a thoroughly enjoyable day's cricket on Saturday. Bradman, in his most joyous mood, hit up 132 before lunch-time and became the first Australian to reach 2,000 runs during the tour. Bradman took only ninety minutes over his runs and, giving a masterly display of all the strokes, he hit a 6 and twenty-four 4's. In five minutes he scored 31! …

Australians

W. H. Ponsford c and b Nichols	92	†W. A. Oldfield c Duckworth b Nichols	16
W. A. Brown b Farnes	3	H. I. Ebeling c Nichols b Farnes	18
D. G. Bradman st Duckworth b Verity	132	W. J. O'Reilly c Duckworth b Farnes	9
S. J. McCabe c Duckworth b Farnes	124	L. O'B. Fleetwood-Smith not out	1
*W. M. Woodfull lbw b Verity	9	B 2, l-b 9, w 1, n-b 1	13
L. S. Darling b Bowes	19		**489**
A. G. Chipperfield b Farnes	53		

Mr H. D. G. Leveson Gower's XI bowling: Farnes 31.3–4–132–5; Bowes 23–2–111–1; Nichols 28–5–126–2; Townsend 3–0–23–0; Verity 21–3–84–2.

Mr H. D. G. Leveson Gower's XI

*Mr R. E. S. Wyatt, H. Sutcliffe, M. Leyland, E. Hendren, Mr J. H. Human, M. S. Nichols, L. F. Townsend, H. Verity, †G. Duckworth, Mr K. Farnes and W. E. Bowes.

First innings: 223 (Human 31, Nichols 75, Townsend 37; Fleetwood-Smith four for 111, O'Reilly three for 35). *Second innings:* 218 (Sutcliffe 36, Leyland 42, Hendren 42, Townsend 39 not out; Fleetwood-Smith six for 90).

Umpires: J. Newman and A. Dolphin

NORTH OF SCOTLAND v AUSTRALIANS

Played at Forres, Friday, September 14 [1934]. The Australians wound up their tour with a splendid victory by an innings and 20 runs over North of Scotland in one day. On a pitch which may have been too liberally watered, batsmen experienced such an unhappy time that thirty wickets went down for an aggregate of 312 runs. Neither Wall nor Ebeling bowled at his usual pace but ... the Scotsmen put up a poor fight and were all out in seventy minutes for the lowest total made against the tourists [all] summer. ... Bradman altered his batting order and the main ambition of the Australians seemed to be to register as many 6's as possible. All of them hit out recklessly, the innings finishing in under ninety minutes ... O'Reilly, going in first, hit four 6's in making his highest score of the tour. Peebles bowled unchanged, and Kemp had the distinction of dismissing Bradman and McCabe [both of whom had scored 2,000 first-class runs on tour] with successive deliveries. North of Scotland fared little better at their second attempt and were put out in an hour and a half. To compensate the spectators, play went on next day as an exhibition.

North of Scotland

Mr A. C. Bremner, Mr J. F. Gray, Mr J. F. Grant, Mr P. D. C. R. Clark, Mr J. C. Richardson, †Lieut. J. A. Grant-Peterkin, Mr I. A. R. Peebles, Mr J. R. Braid, Major K. S. Clarke, Mr J. I. Kemp and Mr N. Wigram.

First innings: 48 (O'Reilly three for 11, Fleetwood-Smith three for 4). *Second innings:* 98 (Wall three for 13, O'Reilly three for 5).

Australians

T. W. Wall lbw b Peebles	0
W. J. O'Reilly c and b Peebles	47
L. O'B. Fleetwood-Smith st Grant-Peterkin b Peebles	8
W. A. Brown b Grant	21
†B. A. Barnett c P. D. C. R. Clark b Braid	16
A. G. Chipperfield lbw b Braid	3
S. J. McCabe lbw b Kemp	16
*D. G. Bradman c Richardson b Kemp	7
A. F. Kippax st Grant-Peterkin b Peebles	15
L. S. Darling b Peebles	14
H. I. Ebeling not out	0
B 15, l-b 3, n-b 1	19
	166

North of Scotland bowling: Peebles 13–2–84–5; Braid 7–1–29–2; Kemp 5–0–34–2; Grant 0.2–0–0–1.

Umpires: G. R. Coutts and R. Corbett

1934–36

1934-35

In a particularly interesting season, Victoria retained the Sheffield Shield with 25 points out of a possible 30 ... Even without Bradman, who joined South Australia but did not play for that State owing to illness, New South Wales ... were strong enough to finish second. ...

From 'Cricket in Australia: Inter-State Matches, 1934-35'

1935-36

Going through the season undefeated, South Australia carried off the Sheffield Shield for the first time since 1926-27, and for the fifth time in all.

The competition lost something in interest because of the absence of well-known players with the Australian team in South Africa and with the Maharaj of Patiala's side in India. South Australia missed Richardson and Grimmett, and Queensland were without Oxenham, but their disadvantages in this respect were trifling compared with those of the two other States. New South Wales lacked the services of Fingleton, McCabe, Brown, Chipperfield, O'Reilly and Oldfield, and Victoria were nearly as hard hit through the absence of Darling, O'Brien, Barnett, Fleetwood-Smith, McCormick and Sievers.

Despite the weakened opposition, South Australia, who had by far the biggest proportion of experienced players, did well to take the honours by the decisive margin of twelve points. Bradman, of course, was the dominant factor in their success. Leading the team for the first time in State matches, he totalled 739 runs with an average of 123.16, and in his first three innings scored 117, 233 and 357. His form during the series demonstrated his complete recovery to good health and proved a big incentive to his colleagues. In the full Australian season, he scored 1,173 runs (average 130.33). ...

From 'Cricket in Australia: Inter-State Matches, 1935-36'

MCC TEAM v SOUTH AUSTRALIA 119 (177, 178)

Played at Adelaide, Friday, Saturday, Monday, Tuesday, November 8, 9, 11, 12 [1935]. MCC [who played six matches in Australia on their way to New Zealand] won by 36 runs. Although

Bradman, appearing for the first time since his operation in England in 1934, captained South Australia, MCC proved slightly the better team. On the first day bright batting … enabled the touring side to score 314 for the loss of half their wickets, but, Waite performing the 'hat-trick', the innings closed for the addition of 57 runs. South Australia would have failed but for a seventh-wicket stand of 65 between Walker and Waite, and when MCC went in again 49 in front, bowlers gained the upper hand. … South Australia were left with plenty of time to score 224 for victory, but Bradman, who drove splendidly, alone caused much trouble.

MCC Team

D. Smith, J. H. Parks, J. Hardstaff, Mr N. S. Mitchell-Innes, Mr J. H. Human, James Langridge, J. Sims, *Hon. C. J. Lyttelton, †Mr A. G. Powell, Mr A. D. Baxter and Mr H. D. Read.

First innings: 371 (Smith 52, Parks 67, Hardstaff 90, Human 87; Ward four for 127, Waite five for 42). *Second innings:* 174 (Langridge 34, Lyttelton 31; Ward four for 62, Ryan four for 13).

South Australia

R. Parker c and b Sims	30	–	lbw b Sims	18
C. L. Badcock c Powell b Read	45	–	c Parks b Baxter	14
*D. G. Bradman lbw b Sims	15	–	lbw b Parks	50
E. J. R. Moyle c and b Langridge	39	–	b Baxter	2
A. J. Ryan c Hardstaff b Langridge	13	–	b Parks	27
M. G. Waite c Mitchell-Innes b Read	58	–	b Read	30
R. Williams c Powell b Read	24	–	b Sims	9
†C. W. Walker not out	65	–	c Powell b Sims	5
F. H. Collins b Sims	6	–	b Read	0
F. Ward lbw b Langridge	7	–	not out	10
H. Thompson b Sims	7	–	run out	12
B 5, l-b 1, n-b 7	13		B 5, l-b 1, n-b 4	10
	322			**187**

MCC Team bowling: *First innings*—Baxter 17–3–53–0; Read 20–2–81–3; Sims 34.7–3–134–4; Parks 3–0–16–0; Langridge 17–4–25–3. *Second innings*—Baxter 9–0–35–2; Read 5–0–14–2; Sims 20–0–76–3; Parks 12–1–32–2; Langridge 6.5–0–20–0.

Umpires: R. A. Nelson and J. D. Scott

SOUTH AUSTRALIA v NEW SOUTH WALES 120 (179)

Played at Adelaide, December 18, 19, 20, 21 [1935]. South Australia won by an innings and five runs. Bradman made a highly successful appearance for South Australia. Parker helped Badcock score 139 for the first wicket and then Bradman assisted the hard-hitting Tasmanian to add 202 in two and a half hours. Ward turned the ball sufficiently to trouble nearly all the New South Wales batsmen, and … they had to follow on 224 behind. …

South Australia

R. Parker c White b Cooper	74	†C. W. Walker run out	28
C. L. Badcock c Lonergan b Robinson	150	F. H. Collins c and b Mudge	0
*D. G. Bradman c and b Robinson	117	F. Ward b Howell	32
E. J. Moyle c Easton b Mudge	98	T. W. Wall not out	10
M. G. Waite c Little b Cooper	22	B 6, l-b 4, w 1, n-b 4	15
A. J. Ryan b Howell	5		**575**
T. O'Connell b Cooper	24		

New South Wales bowling: Cooper 27–3–103–3; McGilvray 14–2–36–0; White 37–7–97–0; Mudge 28–3–113–2; Howell 25.4–5–98–2; Little 4–0–24–0; Robinson 9–0–53–2; Marks 17–3–36–0.

New South Wales

L. Fallowfield, H. Mudge, R. Little, A.E. Marks, A.R. Lonergan, R. Robinson, E.S. White, †F. Easton, *A. McGilvray, W. Howell and A. Cooper.

First innings: 351 (Fallowfield 54, Little 76, Robinson 102; Ward six for 127). *Second innings:* 219 (Fallowfield 38, Marks 31, Lonergan 39, Robinson 39, Easton 42; Wall three for 15, Ryan four for 27).

Umpires: J. D. Scott and R. A. Nelson

SOUTH AUSTRALIA v QUEENSLAND 121 (180)

Played at Adelaide, December 24, 26, 27, 28 [1935]. South Australia won by an innings and 226 runs. Bradman demoralised the Queensland attack, his glorious stroke-play bringing him runs almost at will, and he occupied little more than three hours over his 233. [It was Bradman's third consecutive double-hundred against Queensland.] Badcock and his captain added 183 and Walker, Waite and Ryan hit in fine style. Four Queensland bowlers had a hundred runs hit off them. ...

South Australia

C. L. Badcock c Tallon b Gilbert	91
R. Parker c Levy b Fisher	10
*D. G. Bradman c Tallon b Levy	233
†C. W. Walker c Andrews b Fisher	71
E. J. Moyle b Levy	13
M. G. Waite lbw b Cook	99
A. J. Ryan b Christy	72
T. O'Connell c Honour b Gilbert	41
F. H. Collins not out	0
B 7, l-b 3, w 1, n-b 1	12
(eight wkts dec)	**642**

F. Ward and T. W. Wall did not bat.

Queensland bowling: Gilbert 27.5–1–121–2; Cook 29–3–108–1; Fisher 20–2–103–2; Wyeth 20–2–98–0; Allen 7–0–52–0; Levy 19–0–116–2; Christy 11–2–24–1; Andrews 1–0–8–0.

Queensland

T. Allen, G.G. Cook, C.W. Andrews, V. Honour, D. Hansen, †D. Tallon, *R. M. Levy, J. A. Christy, A. Fisher, E. Gilbert and E. R. Wyeth.

First innings: 127 (Allen 54; Wall three for 13, Waite three for 29). *Second innings:* 289 (Allen 30, Cook 34, Hansen 80, Tallon 88; Collins four for 41, Ward three for 95).

Umpires: R. A. Nelson and J. D. Scott

VICTORIA v SOUTH AUSTRALIA 122 (181)

Played at Melbourne, January 1, 2, 3, 4 [1936]. South Australia won on the first innings. Big crowds enjoyed a feast of interesting cricket between two unbeaten sides. Bradman overshadowed everyone else. His 357, which followed innings of 233 and 117 in the two previous Shield matches, was his fifth score of 300 and his twenty-third of 200. [It was also the highest score against Victoria.] Bradman, when 18, passed his 5,000 runs in Shield cricket. Picking out the loose ball with unhurried but masterly decision, Bradman made 229 before the close of the first day and, next morning, he gave a scintillating display, hitting up 128 in less than two hours. In all he batted just over seven hours, gave no chance and hit forty 4's; he scored his runs out of 502 and used every stroke with equal facility ... [When Victoria followed on] a fine fighting innings by Rigg was primarily responsible for his side saving the game.

South Australia

A. J. Ryan run out	7	†C. W. Walker lbw b Welch	8
R. Parker c Rigg b Welch	63	F. H. Collins not out	37
*D. G. Bradman c Quin b Bromley	357	F. Ward st Quin b Welch	29
E. J. Moyle c Quin b Welch	9	T. W. Wall lbw b Smith	0
M. G. Waite b Gregory	24	L-b 4, n-b 2	6
A. F. Richter c Smith b Welch	7		**569**
T. O'Connell c Quin b Plant	22		

Victoria bowling: Ebeling 4–1–9–0; Nagel 25–5–85–0; Plant 27–2–86–1; Smith 14.1–2–56–1; Welch 25–1–155–5; Gregory 19–1–101–1; Bromley 14–2–71–1.

Victoria

K. E. Rigg, †S. Quin, I. S. Lee, J. W. Scaife, V. Nagel, E. H. Bromley, R. Gregory, H. J. Plant, S. Smith, *H. I. Ebeling and C. Welch.

First innings: 313 (Quin 52, Lee 50, Scaife 48, Gregory 80, Plant 42; Wall four for 77). *Second innings:* Five for 250 (Rigg 124, Quin 47; O'Connell three for 42, Bradman none for 0).

Umpires: A. N. Barlow and C. Dwyer

QUEENSLAND v SOUTH AUSTRALIA 123 (182)

Played at Brisbane, January 10, 11, 13, 14 [1936]. South Australia won by ten wickets. Bradman's policy of sending in Queensland to bat was completely justified but he disappointed a big crowd who came expecting to see him continue his run of centuries. [The attendance on the second day was 15,716, compared with 3,892 on the first day.] Queensland showed moderate batting form on a wicket affected by rain, and South Australia, apart from a timely hundred by Ryan, were little more impressive. Gilbert bowled exceptionally well and at his top pace. Bradman was never comfortable against him and, not properly getting over a rising ball, he gave backward-point a simple catch....

Queensland

T. Allen, R. Rogers, C. W. Andrews, *J. A. Christy, D. Hansen, V. Honour, H. Thomsett, †G. Gunthorpe, E. R. Wyeth, A. Muhl and E. Gilbert.

First innings: 205 (Rogers 39, Andrews 30, Honour 32; Waite three for 45, Ward four for 52). *Second innings:* 163 (Hansen 35, Gunthorpe 46; Waite three for 44, Ward three for 36).

South Australia

R. Parker c Allen b Gilbert	1	– not out	12
C. L. Badcock b Thomsett	16	– not out	16
*D. G. Bradman c Wyeth b Gilbert	31		
A. J. Ryan lbw b Wyeth	144		
E. J. Moyle c Hansen b Gilbert	21		
M. G. Waite c Rogers b Muhl	41		
T. O'Connell c Gunthorpe b Gilbert	36		
†C. W. Walker b Wyeth	0		
R. G. Williams c Wyeth b Gilbert	23		
F. Ward lbw b Wyeth	12		
T. W. Wall not out	7		
B 5, l-b 2, n-b 1	8	L-b 1	1
	340	(no wkt)	**29**

Queensland bowling: *First innings*—Gilbert 29–6–87–5; Andrews 5–0–25–0; Wyeth 31.2–9–101–3; Thomsett 7–0–26–1; Christy 6–0–9–0; Muhl 15–3–48–1; Allen 10–0–36–0. *Second innings*—Gilbert 3–1–11–0; Andrews 3–0–9–0; Muhl 2–0–6–0; Allen 1–0–2–0.

Umpires: J. A. Scott and J. Bartlett

NEW SOUTH WALES v SOUTH AUSTRALIA 124 (183)

Played at Sydney, January 17, 18, 20 [1936]. Abandoned. Rain prevented play on the first day, and owing to the death of King George V there was no cricket on the last day [January 21]. When the game started after lunch on Saturday, McGilvray sent South Australia in, and White (eight for 31) nonplussed the batsmen on an awkward wicket. However, he did not have the satisfaction of disposing of Bradman, who was out without scoring through Little showing smart anticipation in moving to fine short-leg and holding a glide off Hynes. South Australia took nearly three hours over their 94. . . .

South Australia

C. L. Badcock c McGilvray b White	24	†C. W. Walker c Robinson b White	7
R. Parker c McGilvray b White	14	R. G. Williams run out	10
*D. G. Bradman c Little b Hynes	0	F. Ward c Mudge b White	12
A. J. Ryan c Little b White	2	T. W. Wall run out	0
M. G. Waite c Marks b White	0	B 2, l-b 2, w 1, n-b 2	7
E. J. Moyle b White	5		**94**
T. O'Connell c Marks b White	13		

New South Wales bowling: Cooper 9–3–11–0; McGilvray 4–0–11–0; Hynes 11.3–2–25–1; White 19–8–31–8; Chilvers 3–0–9–0.

New South Wales

L. Fallowfield, H. Mudge, R. Little, A. E. Marks, R. Robinson, L. R. Hynes, †F. Easton, E. S. White, *A. McGilvray, H. C. Chilvers and A. Cooper.

First innings: Six for 286 (Fallowfield 53, Little 30, Robinson 94 not out, Hynes 41; Ward three for 57).

Umpires: G. Borwick and H. Armstrong

SOUTH AUSTRALIA v VICTORIA 125 (184)

Played at Adelaide, February 21, 22, 24, 25 [1936]. South Australia won by an innings and 190 runs. Despite the failure of Bradman – caught at second slip off an out-swinger – Victoria were outplayed in every department. Ward's slow bowling was always too clever for their batsmen, none of whom, with the exception of Hassett in the first innings, managed to pass 50, and Badcock overwhelmed the Victoria bowling. The young Tasmanian [21], in making the highest score of his career, gave a great exhibition. Solid rather than brilliant, he did not force the pace but produced the right stroke for nearly every ball he received during his long stay of nine and a quarter hours. His hands were blistered in the latter stages of his innings but his drives, cuts, hooks and hits to leg lost little power in consequence. He hit thirty-four 4's. Badcock took part in three century stands [including a South Australian record of 210 for the first wicket] . . .

Victoria

K. E. Rigg, †S. Quin, I. S. Lee, J. W. Scaife, R. Gregory, J. Ledward, A. Hassett, H. J. Plant, W. Y. Wilson, *H. I. Ebeling and R. B. Scott.

First innings: 201 (Quin 30, Hassett 73; Wall three for 21, Ward five for 74). *Second innings:* 174 (Scaife 33, Ledward 47; Ward four for 72, Waite four for 29).

South Australia

R. Parker c Scott b Wilson	88	M. G. Waite c Rigg b Wilson	8
C. L. Badcock c Rigg b Gregory	325	†C. W. Walker not out	33
*D. G. Bradman c Ledward b Ebeling	1	B 6, l-b 12, w 1, n-b 9	28
E. J. Moyle b Ebeling	5	(six wkts dec)	**565**
A. J. Ryan b Wilson	77		

F. H. Collins, F. Ward, T. W. Wall and R. G. Williams did not bat.

Victoria bowling: Scott 30–3–110–0; Ebeling 41–6–97–2; Wilson 30–4–122–3; Gregory 22.6–1–99–1; Plant 36–11–109–0.

Umpires: J. D. Scott and R. A. Nelson

SOUTH AUSTRALIA v TASMANIA 126 (185)

At Adelaide, February 29, March 2, 3 [1936]. South Australia won by an innings and 349 runs. In addition to the Sheffield Shield matches and the games played by the MCC, [in other matches played in Australia in 1935-36] Tasmania met Victoria three times and South Australia once. In the last-mentioned game Bradman made 369, his second score of over 350 during the season; he had scored 357 against Victoria at Melbourne earlier in the year. [Containing four 6's and forty-six 4's, Bradman's sixth triple-hundred was the highest score by a South Australian batsman, while South Australia's 688 was the State's highest innings total.]

Tasmania: M. J. Combes, R. V. Thomas, E. H. Smith, C. L. Jeffery, A. L. Pearsall, *A. W. Rushforth, J. M. Walsh, G. T. H. James, †J. Gardiner, G. A. Combes and R. C. Townley.

First innings: 158 (Smith 62, Thomas 42; Ward three for 35). *Second innings:* 181 (Rushforth 73, Thomas 44; Waite three for 28, Ward six for 47).

South Australia: C. L. Badcock, †C. W. Walker, *D. G. Bradman, R. A. Hamence, B. H. Leak, R. M. Stanford, M. G. Waite, T. O'Connell, F. Ward, H. J. Cotton and H. R. Shepherdson.

First innings: 688 (Bradman c and b Townley 369, Hamence 121, O'Connell 53, Waite 43; Townley three for 169).

1936-37

1936-37

Recording their third success in four seasons and their ninth since the War, Victoria regained the Sheffield Shield championship they last held in 1934-35. The destination of the trophy was not decided until the last match of the series. Victoria, with 19 points, and South Australia, with 17 points, were the contesting teams and South Australia, who needed an outright win to retain the Shield, lost by nine wickets.

The visit of the MCC team overshadowed the Shield competition, but the absence of leading players on Test Match duty provided chances for the aspiring youngsters . . .

South Australia, champions in the previous season, when Bradman and Badcock showed phenomenal batting form, fell below expectations. Playing the same number of innings as in 1935-36, Bradman scored 323 fewer runs; Badcock's aggregate declined by 373 and his average dropped from 124.40 to 49.80. . . .

From 'Cricket in Australia: Inter-State Matches, 1936-37'

Although the MCC team which toured Australia in 1936-37 under the captaincy of G. O. Allen failed in their quest to regain the mythical Ashes, it is probable that they would have achieved their object had not some wonderful batting feats by Bradman for Australia turned the scale. After winning two Tests, England were beaten in the remaining three, and so for the first time a side which lost the first two games of a series came out on top. Australia must be heartily congratulated on the success. It is a point worth recording that in each of the five games the captain who won the toss led the winning eleven. . . .

The fluctuating nature of the Test struggles gripped the interest of the Australian public and financially the tour broke all records. The total number of people who watched the five games was over 900,000 and the receipts amounted to £90,909. . . . On examination of individual performances, Bradman emerges as the star player of the Tests. After a disappointing start, he had an aggregate of 810 runs, in which were included scores of 82, 270, 212 and 169, and an average of 90. Though McCabe was next with an aggregate of 491 runs, Hammond had rather the better average – 58 as against 54. . . .

From 'MCC Team in Australia'

V. Y. RICHARDSON'S TEAM v D.G. BRADMAN'S TEAM

(TESTIMONIAL MATCH) 127 (186, 187)

At Sydney, October 9, 10, 12, 13 [1936]. D.G. Bradman's team won by six wickets. The Testimonial match for W. Bardsley and J. M. Gregory brought a double-hundred from Bradman, but the deciding factor was the slow bowling of Ward. Brown, McCabe and Oldfield were the only batsmen to play him confidently. O'Brien cut and drove stylishly for Bradman's team, but the captain overshadowed everyone. He used all the strokes with equal brilliance and scored almost at will. [This was the first time Bradman had played against O'Reilly in a first-class match, though he had faced him in country matches before either played for New South Wales. On one of those occasions, at the age of seventeen, he had also notched up a double-hundred.]

V. Y. Richardson's Team

W. A. Brown, J. H. Fingleton, S. J. McCabe, L. S. Darling, *V. Y. Richardson, A.G. Chipperfield, M. W. Sievers, †W. A. Oldfield, C. V. Grimmett, W. J. O'Reilly and E. L. McCormick.

First innings: 363 (Brown 111, McCabe 76, Oldfield 78, McCormick 30 not out; Ward seven for 127). *Second innings:* 180 (Darling 35, Sievers 43 not out; Ward five for 100).

D.G. Bradman's Team

L. P. O'Brien lbw b McCormick	85	–	lbw b O'Reilly	18
C. L. Badcock c Fingleton b O'Reilly	18	–	c Darling b Grimmett	43
R. H. Robinson b O'Reilly	2	–	c Fingleton b Grimmett	57
R. O. Morrisby b O'Reilly	4	–	not out	19
†D. Tallon b Sievers	3	–	not out	0
*D. G. Bradman c O'Reilly b Grimmett	212	–	c Fingleton b Grimmett	13
A. D. McGilvray st Oldfield b Grimmett	42			
E. S. White b O'Reilly	2			
F. Ward not out	5			
H. I. Ebeling lbw b Grimmett	1			
T. Leather st Oldfield b Grimmett	0			
B 4, l-b 2, n-b 5	11		B 7, l-b 4	11
	385		(four wkts)	**161**

V. Y. Richardson's Team bowling: *First innings*—McCormick 13–0–50–1; Sievers 13–1–49–1; O'Reilly 22–0–96–4; Grimmett 20.7–2–146–4; McCabe 4–1–21–0; Chipperfield 1–0–12–0. *Second innings*—McCormick 6–0–30–0; Sievers 3–0–11–0; O'Reilly 13.6–4–27–1; Grimmett 16–2–82–3.

Umpires: G. Borwick and A. Christie

MCC TEAM v SOUTH AUSTRALIA

At Adelaide, October 30, 31, November 2, 3 [1936]. MCC Team won by 105 runs. . . . Bradman, the South Australia captain, stood down because of the death of his baby son.

VICTORIA v SOUTH AUSTRALIA 128 (188)

At Melbourne, November 13, 14, 16, 17 [1936]. Drawn. So far from profiting after putting Victoria in first, South Australia had their bowling trounced. . . . A superb innings by Bradman was chiefly responsible for South Australia making a fight of the first innings issue. Although he had a strained leg, Bradman batted brilliantly and at one period scored nearly 100 runs in an hour. Altogether, during a stay of three hours, he hit thirty-three 4's. . . .

Victoria

L. P. O'Brien, K. E. Rigg, L. S. Darling, I. S. Lee, R.G. Gregory, M. W. Sievers, †B. A. Barnett, H. J. Plant, J. Frederick, *H. I. Ebeling and E. L. McCormick.

First innings: 401 (O'Brien 30, Rigg 97, Darling 39, Lee 38, Gregory 85, Sievers 54; Ward six for 107). *Second innings:* Seven for 403 (Rigg 105, Darling 102, Lee 93, Barnett 55; Waite four for 65).

South Australia

C. L. Badcock lbw b McCormick	2
R. A. Parker st Barnett b Sievers	33
A. J. Ryan lbw b McCormick	9
*D. G. Bradman c O'Brien b Gregory	192
V. Y. Richardson lbw b Sievers	38
R. A. Hamence b Frederick	37
†C. W. Walker b Ebeling	34
M. G. Waite c and b Ebeling	11
C. V. Grimmett c Barnett b Ebeling	8
F. A. Ward not out	3
H. J. Cotton lbw b Ebeling	0
B 12, l-b 1, w 2, n-b 4	19
	386

Victoria bowling: McCormick 15–1–85–2; Ebeling 26.2–5–74–4; Sievers 13–3–36–2; Frederick 15–2–90–1; Plant 15–6–50–0; Gregory 10–3–27–1; Darling 2–0–5–0.

Umpires: A. N. Barlow and C. Dwyer

MCC TEAM v AN AUSTRALIAN XI 129 (189)

At Sydney, November 20, 21, 23, 24 [1936]. Drawn. When time expired, the MCC team, with eight men out and Duckworth suffering from a broken finger, required 11 runs to avoid defeat in a single innings. ... Fingleton and Brown gave the Australian side a fine start with a careful partnership of 103, and Bradman scored readily, but chief honours in the innings fell to Badcock ... Facing a deficit of 256, MCC lost three men for 50 and ... dropped catches alone enabled the visitors to escape.

MCC Team

A. Fagg, T. S. Worthington, L. E.G. Ames, M. Leyland, J. Hardstaff, L. B. Fishlock, *Mr R. W. V. Robins, H. Verity, W. Voce, †G. Duckworth and Mr K. Farnes.

First innings: 288 (Fagg 49, Ames 76, Leyland 80, Robins 53; Chipperfield eight for 66). *Second innings:* Eight for 245 (Ames 37, Leyland 118 not out, Robins 33).

An Australian XI

J. H. Fingleton lbw b Verity	56
W. A. Brown lbw b Farnes	71
*D. G. Bradman b Worthington	63
C. L. Badcock c Farnes b Verity	182
R. H. Robinson c Worthington b Farnes	0
R. G. Gregory c Worthington b Verity	14
A. G. Chipperfield c Duckworth b Voce	39
†D. Tallon c Hardstaff b Robins	31
A. J. Ryan not out	40
M. G. Waite not out	11
B 14, l-b 15, n-b 8	37
(eight wkts dec)	**544**

H. Ebeling did not bat.

MCC Team bowling: Farnes 24–4–112–2; Voce 27–4–89–1; Robins 13–0–72–1; Verity 48–5–130–3; Worthington 25–5–81–1; Leyland 4–0–23–0.

Umpires: G. Borwick and H. Armstrong

ENGLAND v AUSTRALIA 130 (190, 191)
(FIRST TEST MATCH) 29 (43, 44)

At Sydney, December 4, 5, 7, 8, 9 [1936]. England won by 322 runs. England gained a totally unexpected but wholly meritorious victory before lunch on the fifth day. Prior to this match, the record of the team had been so poor that on form it was impossible to concede them more than an outside chance of making a good show. Batsmen who had gone to Australia lauded as leaders in the recovery of English cricket – Fishlock, Hardstaff and Fagg – had played lamentably, being made sport of by every slow leg-break bowler they met; some bowlers barely good enough to gain a regular place in an English county side. ... That England became transformed in a single night into a great and victorious side was entirely due to the example and enthusiasm of G.O. Allen, the captain; and this match will go down in history as 'Allen's Test'. Aided by Robins, Wyatt, Hammond and Leyland, who formed the advisory selection committee, Allen sprang surprises in his make-up of the eleven, and his choices succeeded. He followed this up by winning the toss.

Don Bradman will have reason to remember his first essay as captain of Australia, for he lost the toss, was in some Australian quarters criticised for his captaincy, and he failed with the bat.

A thunderstorm threatened when play opened, but actually no rain fell until the night between the fourth and fifth days. The Brisbane wicket is always lively for an hour and a half or so on the first day of a match and ... McCormick was able to make the ball lift during that spell before lunch. His height aided the natural conditions, and he had three of England in the pavilion with only 20 on the board. Worthington was caught at the wicket off the first ball of the match [and the] loss of Hammond, also out first ball, was a severe blow to English hopes. ... [England recovered to reach six for 263 at stumps and ended with a total of 358.]

Bradman had been seriously handicapped on the Saturday by the inability to bowl of McCormick, who was attacked by lumbago and made only fitful appearances for the remainder of the game. At the end of the second day England's worst fears [an Australian first innings score of 500] looked like being justified, for Australia's score was 151 for two wickets, Fingleton being 61 and McCabe 37. It is true that Bradman had been dismissed, caught in the gully off Voce, but the third-wicket pair looked formidable and seemed capable of a huge partnership on such a good wicket.

But on Monday, the third day, the game swung round completely, England showed fight before lunch and Voce ran through the Australian team afterwards. ... England's batting ... once more disappointed in the second innings. ... On the fourth day there came a further improvement, led by the captain ... The way Allen played O'Reilly was a revelation of concentration and masterly batting ... Australia opened their last innings [with half an hour remaining on the fourth day] wanting 381 to win. In a poor light, against which five appeals were made, Fingleton [who in the first innings had become the first batsman to make four hundreds in successive Test innings] was bowled first ball by Voce. A storm threatened, but even had not rain fallen during the night, it was felt that Australia's task of getting 378 still needed, with Fingleton out and McCormick a cripple, would be beyond their compass.

The last shower before the fifth ... day's play occurred about 6 a.m., and the wicket, already worn, assumed the properties of a 'sticky dog'. In former days, fast bowlers would not have been able to get a foothold, but with the runs-up to the wicket protected, Voce and Allen were able to bowl from first to last and Verity was not called upon. The Australian batting was deplorable. Badcock went out to Allen's second ball of the day, and the England captain dismissed Sievers and Bradman with the fourth and sixth balls of his second over. With Bradman's departure, Australia's last hope disappeared. Half the side were dismissed with only 16 on the board, and Australia were all out, McCormick not batting, for the paltry total of 58. ...

Fingleton's century stood out for Australia. The placing of the field in England's second innings was remarkably good, and little fault could be found with Bradman's tactics. ... Oldfield, when he stumped Hardstaff in England's second innings, set up a new record for Test cricket, surpassing Lilley's figures of 84 successes when keeping wicket for England.

England

T.S. Worthington, C.J. Barnett, A. Fagg, W.R. Hammond, M. Leyland, †L.E.G. Ames, J. Hardstaff, Mr R.W.V. Robins, *Mr G.O. Allen, H. Verity and W. Voce.

First innings: 358 (Barnett 69, Leyland 126, Hardstaff 43, Robins 38, Allen 35; McCormick three for 26, O'Reilly five for 102). *Second innings:* 256 (Leyland 33, Allen 68; Sievers three for 29, Ward six for 102).

Australia

J. H. Fingleton b Verity	100	–	b Voce	0
C. L. Badcock b Allen	8	–	c Fagg b Allen	0
*D. G. Bradman c Worthington b Voce	38	–	c Fagg b Allen	0
S. J. McCabe c Barnett b Voce	51	–	c Leyland b Allen	7
R. H. Robinson c Hammond b Voce	2	–	c Hammond b Voce	3
A. G. Chipperfield c Ames b Voce	7	–	not out	26
M. W. Sievers b Allen	8	–	c Voce b Allen	5
†W. A. Oldfield c Ames b Voce	6	–	b Voce	10
W. J. O'Reilly c Leyland b Voce	3	–	b Allen	0
F. Ward c Hardstaff b Allen	0	–	b Voce	1
E. L. McCormick not out	1	–	absent ill	0
B 4, l-b 1, n-b 5	10		N-b 6	6
	234			**58**

England bowling: *First innings*—Allen 16–2–71–3; Voce 20.6–5–41–6; Hammond 4–0–12–0; Verity 28–11–52–1; Robins 17–0–48–0. *Second innings*—Allen 6–0–36–5; Voce 6.3–0–16–4.

Umpires: G. Borwick and J. D. Scott

ENGLAND v AUSTRALIA (SECOND TEST MATCH)

131 (192, 193)
30 (45, 46)

At Sydney, December 18, 19, 21, 22 [1936]. England won by an innings and 22 runs. Possibly even more than in the First Test, the winning of the toss was of paramount importance. Owing to the long drought, the groundsman feared the wicket would not last as well as is usual in Test Matches at Sydney. The prospect of unsettled weather contributed to uncertainty about the way the wicket would play after the first day or two. ...

A much-discussed feature of play before lunch, when 100 runs were scored for one wicket, concerned five overs sent down by McCormick, who was not only erratic but pitched short, so that the ball flew all over the place. It should be made clear, however, that suggestions of 'body-line' bowling were uncalled for. McCormick merely used the recognised methods of the fast bowler and did not set an exaggerated leg field. Batsmen experienced little trouble in playing him during the later stages of the match; he had not fully recovered from his attack of lumbago and never again attained any real speed. ...

Barnett lost his wicket immediately after lunch ... Then Leyland came on the scene to dash the hopes of the Australians. This was not one of the Yorkshire left-hander's most attractive displays [and he was] criticised even more than Hammond for his slow play by Australian experts who neglected to give their own bowlers and captain full credit for limiting the batsmen's scoring scope by the nature of their attack and the setting of the field. ...

... There was a curious incident [on the second day] when Hardstaff had scored 11. Robinson, the twelfth man, was fielding behind the square-leg umpire and Hardstaff hit a ball from O'Reilly hard into his hands. A shower had rendered the ball as slippery as wet soap and the catch was missed. Apparently both umpires were watching the fieldsman, for when Bradman called attention to the fact that the Nottinghamshire man had stepped on to his wicket sufficiently to dislodge a bail when making the stroke, Hardstaff was given the benefit of the doubt.

Heavy rain in the night created a problem for Allen next morning, and as events proved he was right in declaring straightaway. Australia, as at Brisbane, were caught on a wet wicket and figured in an inglorious collapse – all out for 80.

Nothing more sensational can be imagined than their first dreadful quarter of an hour, when O'Brien, Bradman and McCabe were all sent back without scoring. Voce dismissed them with his seventh, eighth and tenth balls … Seven wickets were down for 31, but with lunch-time approaching O'Reilly played a desperate innings and hit three 6's, one off Verity and two off Sims. … During lunch Allen decided to put Australia in again. Already the wicket had shown signs of recovery, and it rolled out a perfect batting wicket, so that he took a risk which might have cost him the match.

The general opinion was that Australia's batsmen had exaggerated the dangers of the wicket, which was damp, not sticky. They did much better on going in again, and at the close of the third day Fingleton (67) and Bradman (57) were together with the score 145 for one wicket.

The English victory was said by Australian critics to have been registered at five minutes to one on the fourth day, when Bradman, having surpassed Clem Hill's aggregate of 2,660 runs in Test Matches for Australia v England, was bowled by Verity for 82. McCabe alone refused to be unnerved. He proceeded after lunch to give the brightest batting exhibition of the whole match …

Tea-time came with the score 309 for five wickets and odds on England having to bat again. The interval gave England's bowlers fresh heart; Voce once more found top form, and he and Hammond, bringing about another sensational Australian collapse, won the match. Though it was Hammond's steadiness as a bowler that clinched England's superiority, which he himself had established with his great innings of 231 not out, Voce again came out with fine figures … England enjoyed all the luck that was going … while Australia were hard hit by Badcock being ill; he could not bat in the first innings, and although he left a sick bed to bat in the second, he made only two. …

England

A. Fagg, C. J. Barnett, W. R. Hammond, M. Leyland, †L. E. G. Ames, *Mr G. O. Allen, J. Hardstaff, H. Verity, Mr R. W. V. Robins, W. Voce and J. Sims.

First innings: Six for 426 dec (Barnett 57, Hammond 231 not out, Leyland 42).

Australia

J. H. Fingleton c Verity b Voce	12	–	b Sims	73
L. P. O'Brien c Sims b Voce	0	–	c Allen b Hammond	17
*D. G. Bradman c Allen b Voce	0	–	b Verity	82
S. J. McCabe c Sims b Voce	0	–	lbw b Voce	93
A. G. Chipperfield c Sims b Allen	13	–	b Voce	21
M. W. Sievers c Voce b Verity	4	–	run out	24
†W. A. Oldfield b Verity	1	–	c Ames b Voce	1
W. J. O'Reilly not out	37	–	b Hammond	3
E. L. McCormick b Allen	10	–	lbw b Hammond	0
F. Ward b Allen	0	–	not out	1
C. L. Badcock absent ill	0	–	lbw b Allen	2
B 1, l-b 1, n-b 1	3		L-b 3, n-b 4	7
	80			**324**

England bowling: *First innings*—Voce 8–1–10–4; Allen 5.7–1–19–3; Verity 3–0–17–2; Hammond 4–0–6–0; Sims 2–0–20–0; Robins 1–0–5–0. *Second innings*—Voce 19–4–66–3; Allen 19–4–61–1; Verity 19–7–55–1; Hammond 15.7–3–29–3; Sims 17–0–80–1; Robins 7–0–26–0.

Umpires: G. Borwick and J. D. Scott

ENGLAND v AUSTRALIA

132 (194, 195)

(THIRD TEST MATCH)

31 (47, 48)

At Melbourne, January 1, 2, 4, 5, 6, 7 [1937]. Australia won by 365 runs. England were not disgraced even though the margin was a large one; outside influences had much to do with the result. The faith of the Australians that their [revamped] side ... would atone for the two previous disappointments was reflected in the attendances. All records for attendances and receipts at a cricket match were broken. On the third day alone there were 87,798 people present – the takings were £7,405 – and the aggregate attendance for the match was 350,534 and the full receipts £30,124.

As things turned out, Bradman won the match for Australia when he won the toss, and his tactics influenced the result. On the second day he took the unusual procedure in a played-to-a-finish Test Match of declaring his first innings closed [as Allen had England's in the previous Test] and sent England in to bat on a pitch from which the ball often reared up almost straight and at other times kept low. It is important to mention that on the first day, when Australia were batting, the wicket was lifeless and unhelpful to spin bowling, and yet England got down six wickets for 130 and would probably have done still better had not rain set in and led to the bowlers being handicapped by the wet ball. Next day rain held up a resumption of the match until after lunch. The difficulties of the wicket quickly became apparent, and batsmen experienced such an unhappy time that in about three hours thirteen wickets fell. England, after losing nine wickets for 76, also declared, so that for the first time in Test cricket each side closed its first innings.

It is possible England would have done better had Allen's declaration been made earlier but, as one authority put it, the England captain could not be expected to possess second sight. At the close of play on the second day, one Australian – O'Reilly [first ball] – had been dismissed for three runs [Bradman had sent in O'Reilly, Fleetwood-Smith and Ward first to protect his top-order batting] and a Sunday without rain enabled the wicket to recover so that when Australia took up their second innings again the conditions were more favourable for batting than at any previous time in the match. ...

Australia batted all the third day. It was inevitable that Bradman should find his form soon, and he chose the moment of his country's greatest need to do so. Rain fell in the afternoon, and between – and during – the showers the England bowlers were handicapped by a wet ball which they wiped with a towel between each delivery. Bradman took full advantage of this and, though not quite his old scintillating self, and eschewing the off-drive, he thrilled the crowd and subdued the bowlers. Scoring 270, he played his highest innings against England in Australia. Not until the evening was it revealed that Bradman was suffering from a severe chill. That explained his sedateness. In Rigg he found a splendid partner: a man who had been on the fringe of the Australian XI for a long time and looked good enough a cricketer to have gained a place earlier. [This was, in fact, Rigg's sixth Test but his first against England!] ... Hereabouts came the first glimpse during the tour of the Bradman known in England. It was after a stoppage for rain and he faced Voce. He took 13 off the over (of eight balls) and two and three off the first two balls of Allen's next over. Another shower cut short the burst of hitting.

The fact that, on the fourth day, Bradman and Fingleton put up a sixth-wicket record of 346 – actually the highest stand for any wicket in a Test Match [and first-class match] in Australia – was due to Bradman sending in his tail-end batsmen first. Usually those two players would have been associated for the second wicket. The pitch had become as perfect as any batsman could wish, and though the England bowlers remained steady they had little chance of beating Bradman or Fingleton. ...

Bradman, still suffering from mild influenza, was quickly dismissed on the morning of the fifth day, and immediately after lunch England opened their second innings wanting 689 runs to win. Such a task had never before been achieved in Test history, but the wicket was still very easy and a dour fight was anticipated. However, [only] Leyland alone of the earlier batsmen, and Robins, towards the end of the day, batted really well. ...

Australia

J. H. Fingleton c Sims b Robins	38	–	c Ames b Sims	136
W. A. Brown c Ames b Voce	1	–	c Barnett b Voce	20
*D. G. Bradman c Robins b Verity	13	–	c Allen b Voce	270
K. E. Rigg c Verity b Allen	16	–	lbw b Sims	47
S. J. McCabe c Worthington b Voce	63	–	lbw b Allen	22
L. S. Darling c Allen b Verity	20	–	b Allen	0
M. W. Sievers st Ames b Robins	1	–	not out	25
†W. A. Oldfield not out	27	–	lbw b Verity	7
W. J. O'Reilly c Sims b Hammond	4	–	c and b Voce	0
F. Ward st Ames b Hammond	7	–	c Hardstaff b Verity	18
L. O'B. Fleetwood-Smith (did not bat)	0	–	c Verity b Voce	0
B 2, l-b 6, n-b 2	10		B 6, l-b 2, w 1, n-b 10	19
(nine wkts dec)	**200**			**564**

England bowling: *First innings*—Voce 18–3–49–2; Allen 12–2–35–1; Sims 9–1–35–0; Verity 14–4–24–2; Robins 7–0–31–2; Hammond 5.3–0–16–2. *Second innings*—Voce 29–2–120–3; Allen 23–2–84–2; Sims 23–1–109–2; Verity 37.7–9–79–3; Robins 11–2–46–0; Hammond 22–3–89–0; Worthington 4–0–18–0.

England

T. S. Worthington, C. J. Barnett, W. R. Hammond, M. Leyland, J. Sims, †L. E.G. Ames, Mr R. W. V. Robins, J. Hardstaff, *Mr G. O. Allen, H. Verity and W. Voce.

First innings: Nine for 76 dec (Hammond 32; Sievers five for 21, O'Reilly three for 28). *Second innings:* 323 (Hammond 51, Leyland 111 not out, Robins 61; O'Reilly three for 65, Fleetwood-Smith five for 124).

Umpires: G. Borwick and J. D. Scott

MCC TEAM v SOUTH AUSTRALIA 133 (196)

At Adelaide, January 22, 23, 25, 26 [1937]. Drawn. Rain and the state of the pitch prevented cricket on the last two days. The MCC batsmen exercised great care. ... Fishlock, who stayed two hours, received a blow on the hand in Cotton's opening over and, a bone being fractured, he was kept out of the team until early March. [Owing to a strained leg, Bradman batted with a runner during his innings.]

MCC Team

C. J. Barnett, L. B. Fishlock, W. R. Hammond, M. Leyland, Mr R. E. S. Wyatt, †L. E.G. Ames, Mr R. W. V. Robins, *Mr G. O. Allen, H. Verity, W. Voce and Mr K. Farnes.

First innings: 301 (Barnett 78, Fishlock 40, Wyatt 53, Ames 36, Allen 60; Cotton three for 76, Grimmett four for 77).

South Australia

A. J. Ryan c sub b Verity	71	R. S. Whitington not out	33
†C. W. Walker c Verity b Farnes	29	R. Hamence not out	3
C. L. Badcock c Ames b Voce	13	L-b 6, n-b 1	7
*D. G. Bradman c Ames b Barnett	38	(four wkts)	**194**

H. Cotton, C. V. Grimmett, V. Y. Richardson, F. Ward and M. G. Waite did not bat.

MCC Team bowling: Voce 8–0–32–1; Allen 9–1–44–0; Farnes 10–1–28–1; Hammond 2–0–11–0; Robins 7–0–36–0; Verity 12–2–33–1; Barnett 2–0–3–1.

Umpires: J. D. Scott and A. J. Richardson

ENGLAND v AUSTRALIA (FOURTH TEST MATCH)

134 (197, 198)
32 (49, 50)

Played at Adelaide, January 29, 30, February 1, 2, 3, 4 [1937]. Australia won by 148 runs. Two factors lost England the match, which might have been won despite Bradman succeeding in the toss. One was England's batting collapse on the Monday, when the immense advantage gained by getting Australia out for the small total of 288 was frittered away by a deplorable display after Barnett and Leyland had put the side in a splendid position. The other was Bradman's second innings of 212. ...

The wicket was perfect throughout the match, and for the only time in the series no rain came to interfere with play. The batting failures, therefore, were inexplicable. Australia's win roused cricket enthusiasm in the country to a high pitch because it meant the final Test being the decider of the rubber.

The first day's play was witnessed by 39,000 people. Australia ... in the five hours allotted scored 267 for the loss of seven wickets; a good day's work by England. ... Bradman, who, unusually restrained, took 68 minutes to score 26 runs, was clean bowled by Allen when trying one of his favourite hook shots. Gregory, making his Test debut at the age of 20, showed promise, and McCabe indulged in an exhilarating burst of scoring immediately after the tea interval ... At twenty minutes to one on the second day Australia were out for 288, and by the close of play England had hit 174 for two wickets, Barnett being 92 and Leyland 35. England appeared to be in a very strong position, and Barnett's first Test century was completed early on the morning of the third day ... Then the game swung Australia's way ... five England wickets were lost for 259 with Australia still 29 runs on – not as comfortable a position as had been promised.

... [Next day] England finished only 42 ahead. By close of play Australia were 21 on with nine wickets in hand, and Bradman in his most dangerous mood. The fourth day's play virtually settled the issue; a stubborn stand between Bradman and McCabe realised 109, and a big fifth-wicket partnership ensued between Bradman and Gregory. This, producing 135, was not broken until the fifth day when Bradman showed signs of tiredness. Bradman's innings was not one of his most brilliant efforts but he has never looked more sure of himself. He seemed to go in to bat with the fixed determination of winning the match, and though England bowled with any amount of skill and heart he hit 212 in 437 minutes. In that score there were only fourteen 4's – an indication of the dourness of his fight. Incidentally, it was Bradman's seventh double-century in Tests against England [and his seventeenth Test hundred in all, surpassing the record set by H. Sutcliffe]. On his dismissal the four remaining wickets went down for 11 runs ... At the close of the fifth day there was still a ray of hope for England because Hammond and Leyland were together with 148 of the 392 runs required already scored and seven wickets in hand. The wicket, considering the amount of play on it, was in wonderful order. Fleetwood-Smith, however, was in an inspired mood and utilised the pitch to his needs as no bowler on the English side could have done. ...

Australia

J. H. Fingleton run out	10	–	lbw b Hammond	12
W. A. Brown c Allen b Farnes	42	–	c Ames b Voce	32
K. E. Rigg c Ames b Farnes	20	–	c Hammond b Farnes	7
*D. G. Bradman b Allen	26	–	c and b Hammond	212
S. J. McCabe c Allen b Robins	88	–	c Wyatt b Robins	55
R. G. Gregory lbw b Hammond	23	–	run out	50
A. G. Chipperfield not out	57	–	c Ames b Hammond	31
†W. A. Oldfield run out	5	–	c Ames b Hammond	1
W. J. O'Reilly c Leyland b Allen	7	–	c Hammond b Farnes	1
E. L. McCormick c Ames b Hammond	4	–	b Hammond	1
L. O'B. Fleetwood-Smith b Farnes	1	–	not out	4
L-b 2, n-b 3	5		B 10, l-b 15, w 1, n-b 1	27
	288			**433**

England bowling: *First innings*—Voce 12–0–49–0; Allen 16–0–60–2; Farnes 20.6–1–71–3; Hammond 6–0–30–2; Verity 16–4–47–0; Robins 7–1–26–1. *Second innings*—Voce 20–2–86–1; Allen 14–1–61–0; Farnes 24–2–89–2; Hammond 15.2–1–57–5; Verity 37–17–54–0; Robins 6–0–38–1; Barnett 5–1–15–0; Leyland 2–0–6–0.

England

H. Verity, C.J. Barnett, W.R. Hammond, M. Leyland, Mr R.E.S. Wyatt, †L.E.G. Ames, J. Hardstaff, *Mr G.O. Allen, Mr R.W.V. Robins, W. Voce and Mr K. Farnes.

First innings: 330 (Barnett 129, Leyland 45, Ames 52; Fleetwood-Smith four for 129, O'Reilly four for 51). *Second innings:* 243 (Hardstaff 43, Hammond 39, Leyland 32, Wyatt 50; Fleetwood-Smith six for 110).

Umpires: G. Borwick and J. D. Scott

QUEENSLAND v SOUTH AUSTRALIA 135 (199)

At Brisbane, February 12, 13, 15 [1937]. South Australia won by ten wickets. Bowlers were so much on top that, apart from Bradman, only two players scored over 50. ... In contrast to the hesitant methods of Queensland [in their first innings] was the certainty of Bradman, who drove, cut, hooked and pulled in masterly style. Badcock, too, batted well and helped his captain in a stand of 109. Queensland failed a second time ... Ward finished matters in summary fashion by taking the last four wickets for three runs [three were stumpings by Walker].

Queensland

W.A. Brown, G.G. Cook, R. Rogers, T. Allen, †D. Tallon, G. Baker, J. Maddern, *R.K. Oxenham, G. Amos, E.R.H. Wyeth and P.L. Dixon.

First innings: 137 (Allen 68, Baker 39; Cotton three for 27, Grimmett four for 18). *Second innings:* 139 (Rogers 46, Tallon 48; Cotton three for 50, Ward four for 3).

South Australia

†C. W. Walker c Maddern b Cook	13			
A. J. Ryan b Wyeth	15			
V. Y. Richardson b Wyeth	8			
C. L. Badcock c Amos b Dixon	56			
*D. G. Bradman st Tallon b Wyeth	123			
R. A. Hamence b Wyeth	28			
M. G. Waite lbw b Dixon	0	–	not out	6
R. G. Williams lbw b Dixon	2	–	not out	13
F. Ward c Baker b Dixon	1			
C. V. Grimmett run out	2			
H. J. Cotton not out	0			
B 7, l-b 2	9		W 1	1
	257		(no wkt)	**20**

Queensland bowling: *First innings*—Dixon 19.7–4–70–4; Cook 12–1–56–1; Oxenham 10–2–16–0; Wyeth 23–4–52–4; Amos 8–0–54–0. *Second innings*—Dixon 3–0–7–0; Wyeth 2.7–1–9–0; Amos 1–0–3–0.

Umpires: J. A. Scott and J. Bartlett

NEW SOUTH WALES v SOUTH AUSTRALIA 136 (200, 201)

At Sydney, February 19, 20, 22, 23 [1937]. Drawn. Good innings were played by Badcock and White, and the former gained a place in the last Test largely through his display in this match. . .. With Bradman unable to find his form, a big burden devolved on Badcock, and so well did he shoulder it that he defied the attack for three hours. . . .

New South Wales

J. H. Fingleton, R. Beattie, R. H. Robinson, *S. J. McCabe, V. Jackson, S. Barnes, J.G. Lush, L. C. Hynes, †W. A. Oldfield, E. S. White and W. J. O'Reilly.

First innings: 355 (Robinson 47, McCabe 39, Barnes 31, Oldfield 63, White 108 not out; Grimmett four for 71). *Second innings:* 242 (McCabe 68, Jackson 32, Barnes 44, Lush 40; Grimmett three for 77, Ward four for 89).

South Australia

†C. W. Walker c Fingleton b O'Reilly	4	–	b O'Reilly	11
A. J. Ryan c Hynes b Lush	0	–	b O'Reilly	41
R. S. Whitington c Beattie b Lush	29			
*D. G. Bradman lbw b O'Reilly	24	–	not out	38
C. L. Badcock c White b Jackson	136	–	not out	27
R. A. Hamence c Oldfield b Robinson	27			
V. Y. Richardson st Oldfield b Robinson	9			
R. G. Williams lbw b O'Reilly	2			
F. A. Ward b O'Reilly	0	–	c Oldfield b White	8
C. V. Grimmett b Lush	12			
H. J. Cotton not out	12			
B 4, l-b 1, n-b 10	15		B 4, l-b 1, n-b 2	7
	270		(three wkts)	**132**

New South Wales bowling: *First innings*—Lush 16–2–77–3; Hynes 18–1–76–0; Jackson 5–2–9–1; O'Reilly 20–8–40–4; White 10–1–16–0; Robinson 9–0–37–2. *Second innings*—Lush 5–0–24–0; Hynes 8–0–38–0; Jackson 6–2–14–0; O'Reilly 10–3–12–2; White 12–2–36–1.

Umpires: G. Borwick and F. Lyons

ENGLAND v AUSTRALIA 137 (202)
(FIFTH TEST MATCH) 33 (51)

Played at Melbourne, February 26, 27, March 1, 2, 3 [1937]. Australia won by an innings and 200 runs and thereby retained the Ashes. The weather was glorious for the first two days but was less settled on the third, and a thunderstorm during the early hours of the fourth day denied England the chance of making a closer match of it, though by then their position was precarious, to say the least. Again Bradman showed the way, after winning the toss for the third successive time, and his brilliant display – one of the finest of his career – made it easy for his colleagues to help build up the mammoth total of 604 in the first innings. This was the highest total Australia have ever amassed against England in their own country [subsequently overtaken in 1946-47] . . .

All the bright, attacking stroke-making batting came from Australia. On the first day, Bradman and McCabe broke another record by putting on 249 for the third wicket, and Bradman, reaching three figures, equalled Hobbs' record of twelve hundreds in England-Australia Tests. At close of play Australia were 342 for three, a total that should never have been achieved, as four important catches were dropped, all at short-leg behind the umpire. . . .

This first day's play was a tragic one for England. Fingleton was dropped twice, when 1 and 2, while McCabe was missed early in his innings and again when 86. The fillip the fast bowlers would have gained had all the catches been taken was incalculable. ... Right through his innings [however], Bradman did not once put the ball into the air; nor did he give the semblance of a chance. The heat had its effect and next morning he seemed unable to concentrate; he added only four more runs. Bradman batted over three and a half hours and hit fifteen 4's. ...

As the pitch was still perfect, giving no assistance to any bowler, England had a wonderful chance to make a telling reply but, after a dazzling start by Barnett and Worthington, there was a disastrous collapse. ... The fourth day clinched matters, for England [four for 184 overnight] had to bat on a wet wicket that O'Reilly was able to exploit. Faulty timing was the cause of Hardstaff's early dismissal and accounted for the failure of most of the other batsmen, but Wyatt met a ball from O'Reilly that turned and popped up suddenly. The last four wickets fell for three runs and at the lunch interval England were all out and had to follow on 365 behind. ... England that night had lost eight second innings wickets for 165, and two balls by Fleetwood-Smith on the following morning accounted for Voce and Farnes. ... A notable point about the match was that only one bye was conceded.

Australia

J. H. Fingleton c Voce b Farnes	17
K. E. Rigg c Ames b Farnes	28
*D. G. Bradman b Farnes	169
S. J. McCabe c Farnes b Verity	112
C. L. Badcock c Worthington b Voce	118
R. G. Gregory c Verity b Farnes	80
†W. A. Oldfield c Ames b Voce	21
L. J. Nash c Ames b Farnes	17
W. J. O'Reilly b Voce	1
E. L. McCormick not out	17
L. O'B. Fleetwood-Smith b Farnes	13
B 1, l-b 5, w 1, n-b 4	11
	604

England bowling: Allen 17–0–99–0; Farnes 28.5–5–96–6; Voce 29–3–123–3; Hammond 16–1–62–0; Verity 41–5–127–1; Worthington 6–0–60–0; Leyland 3–0–26–0.

England

C. J. Barnett, T. S. Worthington, J. Hardstaff, W. R. Hammond, M. Leyland, Mr R. E. S. Wyatt, †L. E.G. Ames, *Mr G. O. Allen, H. Verity, W. Voce and Mr K. Farnes.

First innings: 239 (Worthington 44, Hardstaff 83, Wyatt 38; Nash four for 70, O'Reilly five for 51). *Second innings:* 165 (Barnett 41, Hammond 56; O'Reilly three for 58, Fleetwood-Smith three for 36).

Umpires: G. Borwick and J. D. Scott

SOUTH AUSTRALIA v VICTORIA 138 (203, 204)

At Adelaide, March 12, 13, 15 [1937]. Victoria won by nine wickets. Their bowling strength decided the match and the Shield. South Australia, who needed an outright win to carry off the honours, were puzzled in the first innings by Fleetwood-Smith, and in the second broke down completely against McCormick. McCormick, very fast, was rarely hit in front of the wicket and at one point he seemed likely to take all ten wickets. ...

South Australia

A. J. Ryan b McCormick	0	–	c Hassett b McCormick	19
†C. W. Walker lbw b Fleetwood-Smith	7	–	c Sievers b McCormick	0
R. S. Whitington c Pearson b Sievers	30	–	c Hassett b McCormick	13
*D. G. Bradman c Ebeling b Fleetwood-Smith	31	–	c Hassett b McCormick	8
C. L. Badcock c Hassett b McCormick	28	–	b McCormick	0
R. A. Hamence lbw b Fleetwood-Smith	35	–	c Lee b McCormick	4
M. G. Waite c Sievers b McCormick	0	–	hit wkt b McCormick	7
C. V. Grimmett b Fleetwood-Smith	7	–	b McCormick	0
R. G. Williams b Fleetwood-Smith	7	–	b Sievers	9
F. Ward c Barnett b Fleetwood-Smith	25	–	c Sievers b McCormick	11
H. J. Cotton not out	4	–	not out	0
B 1, l-b 4, n-b 2, w 1	8		B 1, l-b 3, w 1, n-b 3	8
	182			**79**

Victoria bowling: *First innings*—McCormick 14–1–56–3; Ebeling 6–1–16–0; Sievers 10–0–36–1; Fleetwood-Smith 20.4–3–66–6. *Second innings*—McCormick 11–1–40–9; Ebeling 8–0–21–0; Sievers 0.6–0–4–1; Fleetwood-Smith 2–1–6–0.

Victoria

K. E. Rigg, I. S. Lee, R.G. Gregory, A. L. Hassett, J. D. Ledward, W. E. Pearson, †B. A. Barnett, M. W. Sievers, *H. I. Ebeling, E. L. McCormick and L. O'B. Fleetwood-Smith.

First innings: 213 (Rigg 33, Lee 109 not out; Grimmett three for 52, Waite four for 35). *Second innings:* One for 49.

Umpires: J. D. Scott and A. J. Richardson

1937-38

1937-38

Sheffield Shield cricket in 1937-38 aroused exceptional interest because the Australian players to tour England were to be chosen towards the close of the season. After a lapse of five years, New South Wales regained the trophy with 21 points ... [runners-up] South Australia fell away slightly, but Victoria, winning only one match, dropped from first to third place. ...

In Bradman, South Australia again provided the outstanding batsman in Australian cricket. For the ninth time in ten playing seasons, he scored over 1,000 runs in first-class cricket, and so surpassed the [Sheffield Shield] record aggregate ... previously held with 6,274 by Clem Hill. Bradman scored 983 runs in Shield cricket for an average of 98.30, and, up to the end of 1937-38, Bradman, during his three seasons with South Australia, had made 2,138 runs in 24 innings at the remarkable average of 101.80. He hit four centuries in Shield games, and in scoring 113 and 107 against Queensland at Brisbane he became the first player, since the inception of the Shield competition, to twice perform the feat of getting two centuries in a match. Badcock, Whitington, Waite and Williams played many good innings, but Bradman overshadowed them all in his complete mastery of the bowlers. ...

From 'Cricket in Australia: Inter-State Matches, 1937-38'

SOUTH AUSTRALIA v NEW ZEALANDERS 139 (205)

At Adelaide, November 5, 6, 8 [1937]. South Australia won by ten wickets. Following their tour in England in 1937, the New Zealanders played three matches in Australia – against South Australia, Victoria and New South Wales – before returning home.

New Zealanders: H.G. Vivian, J.L. Kerr, W.M. Wallace, D.A.R. Moloney, M.P. Donnelly, G. L. Weir, *M.L. Page, A.W. Roberts, C.K. Parsloe, †E.W.T. Tindill and J. Cowie.

First innings: 151 (Weir 38; Grimmett three for 21, Ward four for 59). *Second innings:* 186 (Vivian 64, Wallace 37; Ward seven for 62).

South Australia: C.L. Badcock, †C.W. Walker, V.Y. Richardson, *D.G. Bradman, R.H. Robinson, R.A. Hamence, M.G. Waite, R.G. Williams, F.A. Ward, C.V. Grimmett and H.J. Cotton.

First innings: 331 (Badcock 114, Bradman c Tindill b Cowie 11, Hamence 56, Waite 45, Ward 41 not out; Cowie three for 72, Vivian three for 84). *Second innings:* None for 7.

Umpires: A.G. Jenkins and J.D. Scott

D.G. BRADMAN'S XI v V.Y. RICHARDSON'S XI 140 (206)
(TESTIMONIAL MATCH)

At Adelaide, November 26, 27, 29, 30 [1937]. Drawn. Play in this game was restricted through rain to the first two days, but the subscription lists proved so successful that Richardson and Grimmett each received £1,028. The ability of Sievers to make the ball lift awkwardly brought discomfiture to Bradman's men and Grimmett, with his cunning slow bowling, was also difficult to get away; he completely beat Bradman. ...

D.G. Bradman's XI

J. H. Fingleton c Oldfield b McCormick	32
W. A. Brown b Sievers	42
*D. G. Bradman b Grimmett	17
A. L. Hassett c Oldfield b Grimmett	13
R. G. Gregory c Oldfield b Grimmett	1
V. Jackson b Sievers	0
L. C. Hynes b McCabe	6
J. G. Lush b Sievers	28
F. A. Ward not out	7
†C. W. Walker b O'Reilly	29
L. O'B. Fleetwood-Smith b Sievers	4
B 3, n-b 2	5
	184

V. Y. Richardson's XI bowling: McCormick 9–0–34–1; Sievers 9.4–0–27–4; O'Reilly 14–6–21–1; Grimmett 18–3–39–3; Chipperfield 3–0–22–0; McCabe 5–2–10–1; Robinson 4–0–26–0.

V. Y. Richardson's XI

C. L. Badcock, K. E. Rigg, M. W. Sievers, A.G. Chipperfield, S.J. McCabe, *V.Y. Richardson, R.H. Robinson, C.V. Grimmett, †W.A. Oldfield, W.J. O'Reilly and E. L. McCormick.

First innings: Nine for 380 (Badcock 102, Sievers 32, Chipperfield 41, McCabe 72, Richardson 42, Robinson 37 not out; Ward four for 71).

Umpires: J. D. Scott and A.G. Jenkins

SOUTH AUSTRALIA v WESTERN AUSTRALIA 141 (207)

At Adelaide, December 3, 4, 6 [1937]. South Australia won by ten wickets. [A feature of Ridings' debut for South Australia was the appearance of his father as one of the umpires.]

Western Australia: F.J. Alexander, J.A. Jeffreys, J.A. Shea, *W.T. Rowlands, †O.I. Lovelock, W.F. Buttsworth, R.J. Wilberforce, G.C. Arthur, G.A. Gardiner, A.G. Zimbulis and G. Eyres.

First innings: 100. *Second innings:* 185 (Alexander 44; Oswald three for 89, Roberts four for 35).

South Australia: †C.W. Walker, M.E.C. Mueller, R.A. Hamence, B.H. Leak, M.G. Waite, *D.G. Bradman, C.L. Badcock, P.L. Ridings, W.M. Roberts, N.H. Oswald and J.A. Scott.

First innings: 264 (Walker 30, Mueller 56, Bradman c Wilberforce b Eyres 101; Eyres five for 58, Zimbulis three for 98). *Second innings:* None for 22.

Umpires: R.B. Ridings and J.D. Scott

SOUTH AUSTRALIA v NEW SOUTH WALES 142 (208, 209)

At Adelaide, December 17, 18, 20, 21 [1937]. New South Wales won by 33 runs. The craft of O'Reilly turned the fortune of an exciting game. The Test bowler narrowly missed taking all ten wickets in South Australia's first innings – at one point he sent back five men for one run – and when the home side batted a second time, needing 225 to win, his skilful control of length, flight and spin proved the winning factor. South Australia were 153 for four but O'Reilly dashed their hopes of success. ... Bradman, who shared with Whitington and Badcock in partnerships of 141 and 121, was South Australia's most effective batsman, and Grimmett bowled extremely well.

New South Wales

J.H. Fingleton, A.G. Cheetham, *S.J. McCabe, S.G. Barnes, A.G. Chipperfield, V. Jackson, L. C. Hynes, †W.A. Oldfield, E.S. White, W.J. O'Reilly and L.J. O'Brien.

First innings: 337 (Fingleton 81, McCabe 106, Barnes 79; Grimmett five for 103). *Second innings:* 104 (Cotton three for 22, Grimmett four for 51).

South Australia

C. L. Badcock lbw b O'Brien	2	–	b O'Brien	77
R. S. Whitington c Fingleton b O'Reilly	54	–	lbw b O'Brien	1
*D. G. Bradman c O'Brien b O'Reilly	91	–	c Chipperfield b O'Reilly	62
R. H. Robinson b O'Reilly	0	–	c O'Brien b O'Reilly	16
R. A. Hamence c Oldfield b O'Reilly	17	–	b O'Brien	4
M. G. Waite c Oldfield b O'Reilly	3	–	c Oldfield b McCabe	7
†C. W. Walker b O'Reilly	1	–	lbw b O'Reilly	9
F. A. Ward c Chipperfield b O'Reilly	23	–	run out	0
R. G. Williams c Chipperfield b O'Reilly	6	–	c and b O'Reilly	0
C. V. Grimmett lbw b O'Reilly	4	–	c Fingleton b O'Reilly	3
H. J. Cotton not out	10	–	not out	10
L-b 2, n-b 4	6		L-b 1, n-b 1	2
	217			**191**

New South Wales bowling: *First innings*—O'Brien 19–1–67–1; Hynes 11–1–34–0; O'Reilly 33.6–12–41–9; Jackson 8–3–14–0; Cheetham 6–1–20–0; White 11–3–35–0. *Second innings*—O'Brien 12–0–58–3; Hynes 6–0–24–0; O'Reilly 20–8–57–5; Jackson 5–2–7–0; Cheetham 2–0–17–0; White 7–0–17–0; McCabe 2.1–0–9–1.

Umpires: J. D. Scott and A.G. Jenkins

SOUTH AUSTRALIA v QUEENSLAND 143 (210, 211)

At Adelaide, December 25, 27, 28, 29 [1937]. South Australia won by eight wickets. Queensland recovered finely, but they lacked a bowler who could trouble Bradman. Williams, making the ball swing appreciably in the heavy atmosphere, was responsible for Queensland's poor show at the start, and when South Australia lost three men for 50 it seemed there might be a keen struggle. Bradman, however, soon dominated affairs, and with all the strokes at his command in a magnificent exhibition lasting six hours he hit twenty 4's. ... [Although Queensland rallied in their second innings] South Australia needed only 91 for victory, and in helping to knock off the runs Bradman brought his match aggregate to 285 for once out.

Queensland

*W.A. Brown, G.G. Cook, J. Coats, C.A. Loxton, R.E. Rogers, †D. Tallon, T. Allen, G. Baker, E.R. Wyeth, J. Govan and P.L. Dixon.

First innings: 93 (Williams six for 21). *Second innings:* 426 (Brown 132, Rogers 181; Ward four for 152).

South Australia

C. L. Badcock c Dixon b Cook	10	–	st Tallon b Govan	45
†C. W. Walker run out	11	–	c Loxton b Dixon	0
*D. G. Bradman c Baker b Dixon	246	–	not out	39
F. A. Ward c Tallon b Loxton	0			
R. G. Williams c Baker b Govan	34			
R. H. Robinson c Loxton b Dixon	49			
R. A. Hamence c Tallon b Dixon	5	–	not out	9
R. S. Whitington run out	3			
M. G. Waite not out	52			
C. V. Grimmett not out	5			
B 3, l-b 8, n-b 3	14			
(eight wkts dec)	**429**		(two wkts)	**93**

H. J. Cotton did not bat.

Queensland bowling: *First innings*—Dixon 24–0–130–3; Cook 23–1–87–1; Loxton 11–0–41–1; Govan 12–0–72–1; Wyeth 24–3–70–0; Baker 3–1–15–0. *Second innings*—Dixon 4–0–22–1; Cook 10–1–30–0; Loxton 4–1–11–0; Govan 1.2–0–9–1; Wyeth 3–0–12–0; Baker 1–0–9–0.

Umpires: J. D. Scott and A.G. Jenkins

VICTORIA v SOUTH AUSTRALIA 144 (212, 213)

At Melbourne, December 31 [1937], January 1, 3, 4 [1938]. Drawn. The match was important from the point of view of the Selectors, for in the sides there were at least a dozen probables for the England tour. Several of them enhanced their reputations. Fleetwood-Smith took chief honours in the early play, for with his tantalising slow bowling he dismissed nine South Australian batsmen.... Victoria looked set for a big lead, but Grimmett, bowling cleverly, restricted it to 60. Without doing anything extraordinary, South Australia showed consistent form in their second innings...

South Australia

C. L. Badcock c Pearson b Fleetwood-Smith	50	–	b McCormick	0
R. S. Whitington c Rigg b Fleetwood-Smith	81	–	lbw b Fleetwood-Smith	29
*D. G. Bradman c Sievers b Gregory	54	–	c Sievers b Gregory	35
R. H. Robinson c Rigg b Fleetwood-Smith	12	–	run out	62
R. A. Hamence st Barnett b Fleetwood-Smith	8	–	c Hassett b McCormick	64
M. G. Waite c Pearson b Fleetwood-Smith	30	–	c Barnett b Gregory	51
†C. W. Walker c Pearson b Fleetwood-Smith	13	–	run out	25
R. G. Williams b Fleetwood-Smith	15	–	st Barnett b Fleetwood-Smith	11
F. A. Ward not out	26	–	c Gregory b Fleetwood-Smith	9
C. V. Grimmett c Pearson b Fleetwood-Smith	4	–	c Barnett b Sievers	31
H. J. Cotton c Ledward b Fleetwood-Smith	8	–	not out	18
L-b 1, n-b 2	3		B 13, l-b 3, w 1, n-b 4	21
	304			**356**

Victoria bowling: *First innings*—McCormick 16–1–60–0; Sievers 17–5–39–0; Pearson 17–3–41–0; Fleetwood-Smith 31.3–1–135–9; Gregory 10–1–26–1. *Second innings*—McCormick 20–1–91–2; Sievers 18.2–4–45–1; Pearson 3–0–13–0; Fleetwood-Smith 37–3–137–3; Gregory 16–1–46–2; Ledward 1–0–3–0.

Victoria

*K. E. Rigg, I. S. Lee, R.G. Gregory, A. L. Hassett, J. D. Ledward, M. W. Sievers, F. W. Sides, W. E. Pearson, †B. A. Barnett, E. L. McCormick and L. O'B. Fleetwood-Smith.

First innings: 364 (Rigg 118, Lee 67, Gregory 61, Sides 47; Grimmett six for 95). *Second innings:* Four for 144 (Lee 34, Ledward 58 not out).

Umpires: A. N. Barlow and W. J. Moore

QUEENSLAND v SOUTH AUSTRALIA 145 (214, 215)

At Brisbane, January 8, 10, 11, 12 [1938]. Drawn. Bradman's unique feat of making two separate hundreds in a Sheffield Shield match for the second time was the outstanding event of the game. Scoring much as he pleased, Bradman, in his second brilliant display, exactly equalled Bardsley's record aggregate of 17,461 [for an Australian in first-class matches. Record books have subsequently and retrospectively credited Bardsley with only 17,025 runs in matches deemed first-class]. South Australia were helped to their useful first total by Williams and Grimmett who added 100 for the ninth wicket. ... [In the second innings] Waite gave Bradman useful assistance in an entertaining fifth-wicket stand of 103, and a declaration left Queensland [whose captain, Brown, was unable to bat in either innings] the too heavy task of getting 494 to win. This would have proved far beyond them, but the weather saved them from defeat. ...

South Australia

C. L. Badcock c Tallon b Christ	37	–	b Dixon	1
R. S. Whitington c Loxton b Christ	28	–	b Cook	18
*D. G. Bradman c Tallon b Dixon	107	–	c Hackett b Allen	113
R. H. Robinson c Govan b Christ	43	–	st Tallon b Cook	0
R. A. Hamence c Rogers b Loxton	16	–	st Tallon b Christ	11
M. G. Waite c Rogers b Cook	16	–	c Webb b Cook	58
†C. W. Walker c Loxton b Cook	11	–	not out	25
R. G. Williams not out	75	–	c Rogers b Cook	37
F. A. Ward lbw b Cook	10	–	not out	15
C. V. Grimmett c Rogers b Dixon	46			
H. J. Cotton lbw b Cook	1	–	c Tallon b Dixon	1
L-b 6, n-b 2	8		B 2, l-b 3, n-b 3	8
	398		(eight wkts dec)	**287**

Queensland bowling: *First innings*—Dixon 17–1–85–2; Cook 20.6–2–69–4; Loxton 5–0–15–1; Govan 17–0–105–0; Christ 26–2–99–3; Baker 2–0–17–0. *Second innings*—Dixon 14–1–60–2; Cook 22–1–108–4; Govan 3–0–30–0; Christ 16.5–2–66–1; Allen 3–0–15–1.

Queensland

*W. A. Brown, G.G. Cook, C. Loxton, T. Allen, R. E. Rogers, †D. Tallon, G. Baker, J. Hackett, J. Govan, C. Christ and P. L. Dixon.

First innings: 192 (Tallon 48, Baker 70 not out; Cotton four for 37, Grimmett three for 42). *Second innings:* Eight for 155 (Allen 55; Ward five for 66).

Umpires: K. Fagg and J. Bartlett

NEW SOUTH WALES v SOUTH AUSTRALIA 146 (216, 217)

At Sydney, January 15, 17, 18, 19 [1938]. New South Wales won by four wickets. The moderately cheap dismissal of Bradman at the start influenced the course of the game ... [However, he] did quite well when he kept wicket in place of Walker, who injured a finger. Bradman at his second attempt put together a fine century, during which he reached 1,000 runs for the season. Badcock also drove hard in making a hundred, but New South Wales were not left a very serious task. They wanted 227 and, despite some first-rate wicket-keeping by Bradman, who caught three men, they won comfortably.

South Australia

C. L. Badcock c O'Reilly b O'Brien	6	–	run out	132
R. S. Whitington b McCabe	4	–	st Oldfield b O'Reilly	29
*D. G. Bradman c McCabe b O'Brien	44	–	not out	104
R. H. Robinson b Jackson	13	–	lbw b McCabe	21
R. A. Hamence c Oldfield b Mair	49	–	lbw b O'Reilly	13
M. G. Waite lbw b O'Reilly	21	–	lbw b O'Brien	7
†C. W. Walker run out	0	–	absent hurt	0
R. G. Williams b O'Reilly	12	–	c Oldfield b O'Brien	6
F. A. Ward not out	11	–	c Fingleton b O'Reilly	8
C. V. Grimmett run out	1	–	c Chipperfield b O'Brien	0
H. J. Cotton run out	18	–	c Chipperfield b O'Reilly	3
B 7, l-b 1	8		B 8, l-b 3	11
	187			**334**

New South Wales bowling: *First innings*—O'Brien 9–0–42–2; McCabe 5–0–12–1; Jackson 6–0–20–1; O'Reilly 16–3–36–2; Mair 11.6–0–59–1; White 2–0–10–0. *Second innings*—O'Brien 22-2-90–3; McCabe 12–1–39–1; Jackson 12–4–28–0; O'Reilly 25.6–7–65–4; Mair 7–1–26–0; White 11–0–38–0; Chipperfield 6–0–37–0.

New South Wales

*S.J. McCabe, J.H. Fingleton, B.V. McCauley, S.G. Barnes, A.G. Chipperfield, V. Jackson, E.S. White, †W.A. Oldfield, F. Mair, W.J. O'Reilly and L.J. O'Brien.

First innings: 295 (McCabe 83, Chipperfield 31, Jackson 63, Mair 39; Williams three for 93, Ward four for 51). *Second innings:* Six for 227 (McCabe 39, Fingleton 74, Chipperfield 30, White 36 not out; Waite three for 55).

Umpires: G. Borwick and F. Lyons

SOUTH AUSTRALIA v VICTORIA 147 (218, 219)

At Adelaide, February 4, 5, 7, 8 [1938]. South Australia won by 125 runs. ... Waite, an all-rounder chosen for the England tour, demonstrated his usefulness with the bat after Bradman was clean bowled for three, but South Australia were never at ease against Sievers, whom the Selectors passed over. Victoria did not fare much better, and with Bradman finding his form in the second innings, South Australia recovered their lost ground. Whitington shared with Bradman in a stand of 113, and when Victoria wanted 303 for victory, Waite damped their hopes by taking the first three wickets in nine overs for seven runs.

South Australia

R. S. Whitington c Rigg b Thorn	42	–	run out	86
M. E. Mueller lbw b Sievers	1	–	c Thorn b Rayson	37
*D. G. Bradman b McCormick	3	–	c Ledward b Thorn	85
R. H. Robinson lbw b Sievers	19	–	b Pearson	8
R. A. Hamence c Pearson b Sievers	0	–	run out	18
B. H. Leak b Sievers	9	–	b Pearson	31
M. G. Waite not out	45	–	c Pearson b Sievers	10
†J. A. J. Horsell c Barnett b McCormick	9	–	lbw b Pearson	1
R. G. Williams b Sievers	5	–	st Barnett b Rayson	29
F. A. Ward c Barnett b Rayson	1	–	c Rigg b Thorn	22
C. V. Grimmett c Pearson b Sievers	2	–	not out	1
B 17, l-b 1, n-b 3	21		B 5, l-b 3, n-b 4	12
	157			**340**

Victoria bowling: *First innings*—McCormick 9–1–27–2; Sievers 12.7–2–43–6; Pearson 8–1–22–0; Thorn 11–1–37–1; Rayson 2–1–7–1. *Second innings*—McCormick 16–1–54–0; Sievers 25–5–73–1; Pearson 17–1–70–3; Thorn 13–0–53–2; Rayson 11.7–0–78–2.

Victoria

*K. E. Rigg, I. S. Lee, A. L. Hassett, J. D. Ledward, P. Beames, W. E. Pearson, †B. A. Barnett, M. W. Sievers, M. Rayson, E. L. McCormick and F. Thorn.

First innings: 195 (Lee 44; Williams three for 60, Grimmett three for 56). *Second innings:* 177 (Pearson 36, Barnett 41; Williams five for 52, Waite three for 28).

Umpires: J. D. Scott and A.G. Jenkins

TASMANIA v AUSTRALIAN TOURING TEAM 148 (220)

At Launceston, February 26, 28, March 1 [1938]. Australian Touring Team won by 386 runs.

Australian Touring Team: J.H. Fingleton, †B.A. Barnett, A.L. Hassett, *D.G. Bradman, S. J. McCabe, C.L. Badcock, S.G. Barnes, M.G. Waite, E.S. White, F.A. Ward and L.O'B. Fleetwood-Smith.

First innings: 477 (Fingleton 66, Hassett 75, Bradman c Sankey b Thomas 79, McCabe 83, Badcock 36, Barnes 53 not out, Waite 38; Thollar five for 116). *Second innings:* Four for 172 dec (Badcock 42, Barnes 89).

Tasmania: *R. O.G. Morrisby, R.V. Thomas, E. H. Smith, M.J. Combes, C.J. Sankey, C. L. Jeffery, J. N. W. Nicolson, †J. Gardiner, G. T. H. James, J. I. Murfett and D. H. Thollar.

First innings: 112 (Thomas 30; Fleetwood-Smith four for 22, Ward three for 26). *Second innings:* 151 (Morrisby 38, Combes 37; Fleetwood-Smith four for 56, Ward three for 65).

Umpires: G. T. Godden and E. C. Knight

TASMANIA v AUSTRALIAN TOURING TEAM 149 (221)

At Hobart, March 3, 4, 5 [1938]. Australian Touring Team won by 485 runs.

Australian Touring Team: J.H. Fingleton, W.A. Brown, C.L. Badcock, *D.G. Bradman, S.G. Barnes, A.G. Chipperfield, M.G. Waite, †B.A. Barnett, E.S. White, W.J. O'Reilly and L. O'B. Fleetwood-Smith.

First innings: 520 (Fingleton 47, Brown 46, Badcock 159, Bradman b Jeffery 144, Chipperfield 42; James three for 86, Putman four for 155). *Second innings:* Three for 240 dec (Fingleton 109, Brown 108).

Tasmania: *R.O.G. Morrisby, R.V. Thomas, M.J. Combes, S.W.L. Putman, E.H. Smith, G.T.H. James, C.J. Sankey, C.L. Jeffery, †J. Gardiner, J.I. Murfett and C.J.G. Oakes.

First innings: 194 (Putman 40, Smith 37; O'Reilly five for 34, Fleetwood-Smith three for 70). *Second innings:* 81 (O'Reilly six for 16).

Umpires: D.G. Hickman and S.J. Alford

WESTERN AUSTRALIA v AUSTRALIAN TOURING TEAM
150 (222)

At Perth, March 18, 19, 21 [1938]. Australian Touring Team won by an innings and 126 runs.
Western Australia: J.A. Jeffreys, F.J. Alexander, J.A. Shea, *W.T. Rowlands, K.S. Jeffreys, †O.I. Lovelock, M.O. Bessen, A.G. Zimbulis, G.A. Gardiner, G. Eyres and R.A. Halcombe.

First innings: 192 (Bessen 39, Zimbulis 33, Eyres 41; O'Reilly four for 65). *Second innings:* 73 (O'Reilly five for 12, Fleetwood-Smith three for 5).
Australian Touring Team: W.A. Brown, C.L. Badcock, *D.G. Bradman, S.J. McCabe, A.L. Hassett, A.G. Chipperfield, †C.W. Walker, F.A. Ward, W.J. O'Reilly, E.L. McCormick and L.O'B. Fleetwood-Smith.

First innings: 391 (Badcock 34, Bradman st Lovelock b Zimbulis 102, McCabe 122, Chipperfield 42; Zimbulis three for 160, Halcombe three for 43).

Umpires: F.R. Buttsworth and E.T. Tonkinson

1938

1938

A warning note is also sounded concerning the effect on the counties generally of any serious decline in the popularity of Test Match cricket. Consequently the news that, for the Test Matches of 1938 with Australia, agreement has been reached to restrict the games to four days apiece and to reduce the hours of play by one and a half hours in each match, came as a surprise. A reason advanced for the change is that neither Australian nor English cricketers relish a period of two and a half hours play before lunch-time after the first day. To my mind, it is a retrograde step. There is no gainsaying the assertion that the long pre-lunch spell imposes a severe test upon bowlers, but the policy is directly opposed to the movement in England to revive the interest of the public in the game of cricket. Are we to have another run of purposeless drawn games with the possibility of one 'play-to-a-finish' Test deciding the rubber? Not since 1905 has an England-Australia match at Old Trafford produced a definite result, and the last three encounters at Leeds were drawn. Who can argue with conviction that a reduction of the time in which a Test Match has to be decided is on all fours with the urgent need to enlist more support for the game generally by getting more definite results? It has been encouraging to note the growth of favourable opinion, both in England and in the Commonwealth, upon the idea of allocating more than four days to all Test Matches between England and Australia in this country, and events during the series of 1938 may bring further support for the suggestion.

... An intriguing and vital question at the time of writing is that of the [England] captaincy. On this point, much has been said and written regarding W. R. Hammond, who in future will play as an amateur. ... Without going into the question as to whether Hammond possesses the essential qualities for leadership, I am strongly against him being saddled with the task of leading England. Hammond once more should be free to concentrate upon batting and be spared anything prejudicial to his individual prowess. It is true that the batting abilities of Bradman did not decline after he assumed the captaincy of Australia. But Bradman had for some time led the South Australian team and he undertook his more responsible post after a good deal of experience in leading an eleven.

From 'Notes by the Editor' (Wilfrid H. Brookes), *Wisden 1938*

I am not in a position to make any comparison between the players of the past and those of the present time, but the attempt of certain writers to *The Times* to compare by statistics the doings of W.G. Grace and D.G. Bradman in matches between England and Australia is unfortunate. For this reason: 'W.G.' began playing for England against Australia in 1880 when 32 years of age and continued until he was 51; Bradman began when 22 and is now 30 – two years younger than Grace when, in the first contest with Australia in England, he scored 152. As *Wisden* has been quoted in the published correspondence, it is interesting to recall that Sydney H. Pardon, then *The Times* cricket correspondent, wrote of 'W.G.' as follows: 'His early fame as a batsman culminated in the season of 1876 when in August he scored in successive innings 344, 177 and 318. Soon after that, he passed his examination as a surgeon, thinking to settle down as a general practitioner. That he changed his plans was mainly due to the appearance of the first Australian eleven in England in 1878. The most brilliant part of his career ended before this invasion ...'

From 'Notes by the Editor' (Wilfrid H. Brookes), *Wisden 1939*

The visit of the Australian team coincided with a marked revival in English cricket, several young players of high merit coming to the front. Yet the Australians, although having the atrocious luck of losing the toss in each of the four Test Matches played, drew the rubber and thereby retained the Ashes. That this was a most creditable performance is not likely to be questioned even by the severest critics of the team.

It would be a delicate task to compare this Australian side with the previous combinations which have come over from the Commonwealth, and as very little would be gained by embarking on such an effort, it is not attempted here. The result of more than four months' cricket was that the Australians remained undefeated by any county eleven and only once – after they had won the Fourth Test at Leeds – did they go down before England.

Like the team of 1921, the side also suffered a reverse in the Festival match at Scarborough [their final fixture in England], but against the two defeats they could set fifteen wins in first-class engagements, and outside the representative matches they rarely encountered formidable opposition....

The strength of the team lay in batting and fielding; the weakness in bowling. There were more individual failures than usually occur in an Australian touring side and had a serious accident happened to either Bradman or O'Reilly at an early stage of the season the record must have been much less imposing. The very appearance of Bradman in the field was sufficient to inspire confidence in his colleagues. Nothing that occurred seemed to disturb his equanimity and the influence he held over the other members of the team, combined with his own brilliant performances, was an extremely important factor in the results accomplished.

In every Test in which he batted, Bradman made a century. When on the third day of the Fifth Test he damaged his right ankle and was carried off the Oval ground, England were already in a position which made their success a foregone conclusion, but there is not a shadow of doubt that the moral effect of the loss of their captain, coupled with an injury to Fingleton, accounted, to a very large extent, for the complete rout of Australia that followed.

Bradman did not play again, and yet in twenty-six innings he scored 2,429 runs with an average of 115.66. Not only was this a far better record than he made on either of his two previous visits, except for his 1930 aggregate, but he was the first Australian to average 100 runs an innings in England. He also beat Victor Trumper's feat of hitting eleven centuries during a tour, for he played thirteen three-figure innings, three over 200. Leading off with an innings of 258 at Worcester, he completed 1,000 runs before the end of May, so repeating his achievement of 1930, and 2,000 runs before any other Australian or Englishman. Both in the first-class averages for the tour and those for the four Test Matches his name came out at the top.

One did not detect any waning of his powers. Judged by the standard he himself set, he was perhaps a shade better. The responsibility of leadership certainly did not interfere with his individual play, and his concentration, as shown when in the first two Test Matches the state of affairs demanded that he should bat cautiously, was astonishing. To say that he was a popular captain and a most astute one is not fulsome praise; under his charge the Australians revealed a wonderful team spirit which counted a great deal towards their many triumphs. A point that impressed itself upon the mind was his quickness to note the strength of an opposing batsman and to make a move directed towards countering effective stroke-play. …

… Measured by what English followers of cricket have seen from other post-War Australian sides, the fielding was not found wanting. One could deduce from the live, intense and often brilliant out-cricket the influence of Bradman when the players were picked for the tour. To those whose duties brought them into close touch with Bradman and his colleagues, the happy spirit pervading the team was very evident. Wherever they went, they made friends. …

From 'The Australians in England', by Wilfrid H. Brookes

WORCESTERSHIRE v AUSTRALIANS 151 (223)

At Worcester, April 30, May 2, 3 [1938]. Australians won by an innings and 77 runs. Lyttelton caused astonishment when after winning the toss he sent in the touring team to bat on a true and easy wicket. By the end of the first day 474 runs had been scored for the loss of six wickets, and in the end the Australians made their highest total against Worcestershire. Batting in biting, wintry weather, Bradman, as on his two previous matches on the ground, began the tour with a double-hundred. Starting in a cautious way, he developed capital form and, during an innings lasting four hours fifty minutes, offered no semblance of a chance. Pulling, driving, cutting and placing the ball with skill, he hit thirty-three 4's. Badcock, on his first appearance in England, created a big impression and he helped Bradman to put on 277 for the fourth wicket. … Monday's play furnished a most remarkable happening. McCormick, the fast bowler, repeatedly went over the crease and during his first three overs was no-balled nineteen times by umpire Baldwin. His first over actually comprised fourteen balls and the second over fifteen. … In the match, McCormick was no-balled thirty-five times.

Australians

J. H. Fingleton c Crisp b Howorth	41
W. A. Brown lbw b Crisp	2
*D. G. Bradman c Martin b Howorth	258
S. J. McCabe b Perks	34
C. L. Badcock c Singleton b Perks	67
A. L. Hassett c Howorth b Perks	43
†B. A. Barnett b Crisp	16
E. S. White b Crisp	26
W. J. O'Reilly b Perks	11
E. L. McCormick b Crisp	5
L. O'B. Fleetwood-Smith not out	6
B 13, l-b 15, w 2, n-b 2	32
	541

Worcestershire bowling: Crisp 37.3–5–170–4; Perks 34–3–147–4; Martin 29–8–70–0; Howorth 21–1–85–2; Singleton 3–0–37–0.

Worcestershire

*Hon. C.J. Lyttelton, C.H. Bull, E. Cooper, H.H. Gibbons, S.H. Martin, Mr R.H.C. Human, R. Howorth, Mr A.P. Singleton, †S. Buller, R.T.D. Perks and Mr R.J. Crisp.

First innings: 268 (Lyttelton 50, Bull 37 not out, Cooper 61; Fleetwood-Smith eight for 98). *Second innings:* 196 (Lyttelton 35, Bull 69; O'Reilly three for 56, Fleetwood-Smith three for 38).

Umpires: J. Smart and H.G. Baldwin

OXFORD UNIVERSITY v AUSTRALIANS 152 (224)

Played at the Christ Church ground, Oxford, May 4, 5, 6 [1938]. Australians won by an innings and 487 runs. This match was played far too early in the term for the University to do themselves justice. They were little more than a scratch side and the Australians, winning the toss, batted until lunch-time on the second day, when Bradman declared. ... Fingleton and Brown led off with a stand of 140 and altogether there were five three-figure partnerships. ... On the last day, when Walker had a damaged finger, Fingleton ... stumped three men.

Australians

J. H. Fingleton c Whetherly b Evans	124	A. L. Hassett b Darwall-Smith	146
W. A. Brown c Evans b Macindoe	72	M. G. Waite c Kimpton b Evans	54
*D. G. Bradman lbw b Evans	58	†C. W. Walker not out	31
S. J. McCabe b Macindoe	110	B 21, l-b 9, w 1	31
A. G. Chipperfield c Whetherly b Darwall-Smith	53	(seven wkts dec)	**679**

F. Ward, E. L. McCormick and L. O'B. Fleetwood-Smith did not bat.

Oxford University bowling: Darwall-Smith 39.4–4–162–2; Macindoe 68–11–207–2; Evans 47–9–171–3; Kimpton 13–1–53–0; Murray-Wood 9–1–55–0.

Oxford University

Mr M. M. Walford, Mr E. J. H. Dixon, Mr J. D. Eggar, †Mr R. C. M. Kimpton, *Mr J. N. Grover, Mr E. D. R. Eagar, Mr W. Murray-Wood, Mr G. Evans, Mr D. H. Macindoe, Mr R. F. H. Darwall-Smith and Mr R. E. Whetherly.

First innings: 117 (Eggar 51 not out; Fleetwood-Smith five for 28). *Second innings:* 75 (Ward three for 16, Fleetwood-Smith four for 31).

Umpires: D. Hendren and N. Harris

CAMBRIDGE UNIVERSITY v AUSTRALIANS 153 (225)

At Cambridge, May 11, 12, 13 [1938]. Australians won by an innings and 425 runs. This was their fourth single-innings victory in succession [having beaten Leicestershire by an innings and 163 runs on May 7, 9, 10]. ... [For Cambridge] Gibb carried his bat through the second innings; otherwise the batting was poor and the bowling, except for that of Wild, inaccurate. The Australians, putting together their highest total of the tour and the biggest ever made at Fenner's, again demonstrated their great batting powers. Brown failed, but Fingleton and Bradman added 215. ... Bradman, who [like Fingleton] completed his second century of the tour, scored twenty boundaries. ... Cambridge, 588 behind, began their second innings without hope.

Cambridge University

†Mr P. A. Gibb, Mr J. V. Wild, Mr J. D. A. Langley, *Mr N. W. D. Yardley, Mr M. StJ. Packe, Mr F. G. Mann, Mr P. M. Studd, Mr M. A. C. P. Kaye, Mr S. M. A. Banister, Mr H. G. Jameson and Mr W. R. Rees-Davies.

First innings: 120 (Yardley 67; Waite five for 23, O'Reilly five for 55). *Second innings:* 163 (Gibb 80 not out; White three for 22, Ward six for 64).

Australians

J. H. Fingleton b Kaye	111	A. G. Chipperfield st Gibb b Banister	8
W. A. Brown lbw b Rees-Davies	0	M. G. Waite not out	30
*D. G. Bradman c Mann b Wild	137	B 10, l-b 5, w 1	16
C. L. Badcock c Mann b Rees-Davies	186	(five wkts dec)	**708**
A. L. Hassett not out	220		

†B. A. Barnett, W. J. O'Reilly, F. Ward and E. S. White did not bat.

Cambridge University bowling: Rees-Davies 43–2–214–2; Jameson 29–4–127–0; Kaye 17–0–100–1; Wild 45–12–143–1; Banister 22–2–91–1; Yardley 5–1–17–0.

Umpires: W. Wainwright and J. J. Hills

MCC v AUSTRALIANS 154 (226)

At Lord's, May 14, 16, 17 [1938]. Drawn. Rain prevented play on the last day when MCC, having followed on 288 behind, needed 201 to avoid an innings defeat with nine wickets in hand. A superb innings by Bradman overshadowed everything else in the game. Batting for six hours, he made no serious mistake till, attempting to square cut a bad ball, he was well taken at cover. Though he did not drive much and at first experienced difficulty with the bowling of Stephenson, he played masterly cricket and hit a 6 and thirty-five 4's. Fingleton helped him in a stand of 138 and Hassett, strong in driving, stayed while 162 were added. McCormick, taking a shorter run, showed increased accuracy when MCC batted, and he sent down only one no-ball. He dismissed Human and Maxwell with consecutive deliveries, but a collapse was prevented by Wyatt . .. McCormick, having strained a tendon, retired during the MCC first innings ... So large was the crowd on the first day, when some 32,000 were present, that about three o'clock the gates were closed.

Australians

J. H. Fingleton b Smith	44
W. A. Brown b Farnes	5
*D. G. Bradman c Robins b Smith	278
S. J. McCabe b Smith	33
C. L. Badcock b Stephenson	14
A. L. Hassett c Maxwell b Compton	57
M. G. Waite lbw b Smith	26
†B. A. Barnett lbw b Stephenson	1
W. J. O'Reilly c Compton b Smith	17
E. L. McCormick c Maxwell b Smith	9
L. O'B. Fleetwood-Smith not out	3
B 2, l-b 11, n-b 1	15
	502

MCC bowling: Farnes 32–3–88–1; Smith 42.5–9–139–6; Stephenson 29–5–112–2; Robins 18–2–69–0; Wyatt 7–0–27–0; Compton 10–2–37–1; Edrich 2–0–15–0.

MCC

Mr D. R. Wilcox, W. J. Edrich, D. Compton, Mr R. E. S. Wyatt, Mr F. G. H. Chalk, Mr J. H. Human, †Mr C. R. Maxwell, *Mr R. W. V. Robins, Capt. J. W. A. Stephenson, J. Smith and Mr K. Farnes.

First innings: 214 (Edrich 31, Wyatt 84 not out; O'Reilly three for 42, Fleetwood-Smith four for 69). *Second innings:* One for 87 (Edrich 53 not out).

Umpires: J. Hardstaff and J. Newman

NORTHAMPTONSHIRE v AUSTRALIANS 155 (227)

At Northampton, May 18, 19, 20 [1938]. Australians won by an innings and 77 runs. Northamptonshire gave early promise of repeating their performance in 1934, when they drew with the tourists, but the Australians had things all their own way on the last day. Against a weak attack the Australians scored 126 without loss during a restricted opening day's play ... [Next day] Partridge, bowling medium-fast and making the ball swing, sent back Badcock, Bradman and McCabe in eleven overs for 15 runs. ... Eighty minutes on the third morning saw the last seven Northamptonshire [first innings] wickets fall for 55 runs, Ward, on a pitch responsive to spin, carrying all before him. McCabe, taking four wickets for a single, did the damage in the follow-on ...

Australians

W. A. Brown not out	194	M. G. Waite lbw b Timms	43
C. L. Badcock c James b Partridge	72	†B. A. Barnett lbw b Timms	1
*D. G. Bradman c James b Partridge	2	C. W. Walker not out	29
S. J. McCabe c Merritt b Partridge	13	B 22, l-b 12	34
A. G. Chipperfield lbw b Timms	18	(six wkts dec)	**406**

E. S. White, F. Ward and L. O'B. Fleetwood-Smith did not bat.

Northamptonshire bowling: Partridge 36–7–82–3; Herbert 30–6–75–0; Timms 20–4–68–3; Nelson 14–1–56–0; Merritt 16–0–81–0; O'Brien 3–0–10–0.

Northamptonshire

Mr R. P. Nelson, H. W. Greenwood, Mr A. W. Snowden, J. E. Timms, D. Brookes, Mr G. B. Cuthbertson, F. P. O'Brien, †K. C. James, W. E. Merritt, R. J. Partridge and E. J. Herbert.

First innings: 194 (Nelson 74, Brookes 37; Ward six for 75). *Second innings:* 135 (Greenwood 43; Waite three for 28, McCabe four for 28).

Umpires: F. Chester and A. Dolphin

SURREY v AUSTRALIANS 156 (228)

At [Kennington] Oval, May 21, 23, 24 [1938]. Drawn. The Australians made no effort to win for, although they led by 257 runs, Bradman, on the score that some of his players badly needed rest, did not enforce the follow-on. On a perfect wicket, the Australians batted until nearly lunch-time on the second day. Bradman played another big innings, driving to the off and pulling with special skill, and in a stay of three hours and twenty minutes he hit eleven 4's. His unhurried display contained no serious blemish. ... Brown helped his captain to put on 120. Bradman's decision to bat a second time caused a mild demonstration among the crowd, and as Surrey tried as many as eight bowlers, a first-wicket partnership of 206 by Badcock and Barnett lost much of its importance. ...

Australians

J. H. Fingleton b Brown	47			
W. A. Brown c Brooks b Watts	96			
*D. G. Bradman c Brooks b Watts	143			
C. L. Badcock c and b Brown	32	–	c Watts b Gregory	95
A. L. Hassett c Squires b Berry	98			
A. G. Chipperfield b Gover	20	–	c Brooks b Gregory	6
M. G. Waite c Brooks b Watts	35			
†B. A. Barnett not out	33	–	not out	120
E. S. White b Berry	7	–	not out	5
F. Ward b Brown	0			
W. J. O'Reilly c Brooks b Brown	0			
B 8, l-b 8, n-b 1	17		B 4, l-b 1, n-b 1	6
	528		(two wkts dec)	**232**

Surrey bowling: *First innings*—Gover 20–4–100–1; Watts 23–4–69–3; Berry 33–6–92–2; Brown 35–0–147–4; Squires 20–2–68–0; Gregory 9–3–23–0; Garland-Wells 3–0–12–0. *Second innings*—Gover 6–0–20–0; Watts 10–1–47–0; Berry 6–3–12–0; Brown 5–0–23–0; Squires 8–2–29–0; Gregory 7–4–10–2; Garland-Wells 15–1–62–0; Holmes 4–0–23–0.

Surrey

R.J. Gregory, L.B. Fishlock, H.S. Squires, T.H. Barling, *Mr E.R.T. Holmes, Mr H.M. Garland-Wells, Mr F.R. Brown, F. Berry, E.A. Watts, †E.W. Brooks and A.R. Gover.

First innings: 271 (Gregory 60, Barling 67, Berry 31; O'Reilly eight for 104). *Second innings:* One for 104 (Fishlock 93).

Umpires: E.J. Smith and A. Dolphin

HAMPSHIRE v AUSTRALIANS 157 (229)

At Southampton, May 25, 26, 27 [1938]. Drawn. Bradman made the match memorable by completing 1,000 runs for the second time in England before the first month of the season closed. He did not hit with the amazing freedom that marked his play when previously in England, but his share of a partnership with Fingleton yielding 242 was 145, scored in three and a half hours. He was not altogether sure when facing the slow spin bowling of Boyes, the left-hander, and of Hill. Strangely enough, when in 1930 Bradman made 1,000 runs in May, he reached that total at Southampton on the first day of the match just before rain delayed the completion of his innings until the Monday. On the present occasion the weather interfered seriously with the match. Rain prevented any cricket on the first day; it also caused a stoppage before Bradman reached a four-figure aggregate for the tour. ... Bradman [hit] twenty-two 4's.

Hampshire

†N. McCorkell, J. Arnold, *Mr C.G.A. Paris, W.L. Creese, Mr R.H. Moore, A.E. Pothecary, Rev. J.W.J. Steele, G. Hill, G.S. Boyes, Mr A.E.G. Baring and G.E.M. Heath.

First innings: 157 (O'Reilly six for 65).

Australians

J.H. Fingleton not out	123
W.A. Brown c Pothecary b Boyes	47
*D.G. Bradman not out	145
B 4, l-b 1	5
(one wkt dec)	**320**

A.L. Hassett, A.G. Chipperfield, E.S. White, W.J. O'Reilly, E.L. McCormick, S.J. McCabe, †C.W. Walker and L. O'B. Fleetwood-Smith did not bat.

Hampshire bowling: Baring 20–2–97–0; Heath 16–1–54–0; Steele 15–2–60–0; Boyes 17–5–39–1; Hill 19–4–45–0; Creese 9–5–20–0.

Umpires: W. Reeves and E.J. Smith

MIDDLESEX v AUSTRALIANS 158 (230, 231)

At Lord's, May 28, 30, 31 [1938]. Drawn. After continuous rain on Saturday and Sunday, the Australians did not show to advantage under strange conditions [when they batted on Monday]. ... The one stand on a pitch so soft that the ball often cut through realised 54. ... After arrears of 56 had been turned into a lead of 58 Bradman declared in order to give Edrich an opportunity to complete 1,000 runs before the end of May [which he accomplished in a not out innings of 20. All his 1,000 runs were scored at Lord's.] Bad light and showers interfered with the cricket on both days and the Australians were outplayed until a draw became inevitable.

Several good catches were made. Compton, running from slip to short-leg, held a skier from Bradman. ...

Australians

J. H. Fingleton b Smith	2	–	c Edrich b Smith	32
C. L. Badcock c Human b Nevell	10	–	b Nevell	0
*D. G. Bradman c Compton b Nevell	5	–	not out	30
S. J. McCabe b Nevell	9	–	not out	48
A. L. Hassett lbw b Sims	27			
A. G. Chipperfield c Compton b Robins	36			
M. G. Waite b Sims	8			
†C. W. Walker not out	4			
W. J. O'Reilly lbw b Robins	0			
E. L. McCormick c Smith b Sims	12			
L. O'B. Fleetwood-Smith st Price b Sims	10			
B 2, l-b 6, n-b 1	9		W	4
	132		(two wkts dec)	**114**

Middlesex bowling: *First innings*—Smith 15–5–23–1; Nevell 12–1–38–3; Young 4–1–10–0; Sims 7.3–0–25–4; Robins 6–1–27–2. *Second innings*—Smith 12–4–26–1; Nevell 7–2–16–1; Young 5–2–7–0; Smith 5–0–23–0; Robins 4–0–10–0; Human 2–0–14–0; Compton 4–1–14–0.

Middlesex

W. J. Edrich, †W. F. Price, Mr W. H. Webster, D. Compton, J. Hulme, Mr J. H. Human, *Mr R. W. V. Robins, J. Sims, J. Smith, W. Nevell and J. A. Young.

First innings: 188 (Compton 65, Robins 43; McCormick six for 58, O'Reilly four for 56). *Second innings:* None for 21.

Umpires: F. Chester and F. Walden

ENGLAND v AUSTRALIA 159 (232, 233)
(FIRST TEST MATCH) 34 (52, 53)

At Trent Bridge [Nottingham], June 10, 11, 13, 14 [1938]. Drawn. England, in a match memorable for the setting-up of many new records including seven individual hundreds, put together the highest innings total ever hit against Australia. Not until half past three on the second day did Australia have an opportunity of batting, and with 151 scored half their wickets had fallen. McCabe then played an innings the equal of which has probably never been seen in the history of Test cricket; for the best part of four hours he maintained a merciless punishment of the bowling. Although his phenomenal effort did not save his side from the indignity of having to follow on, it broke the control of the play which England had held from the outset, and by concentrating upon defence in their second innings Australia saved the game.

In a magnificent contest of skill, the excellence of the wicket always counted heavily in favour of batsmen. First innings conferred upon England a very important advantage. ... For the first time in a Test Match, four individual hundreds were registered in one innings for, following the successes of Barnett, Hutton and Compton, Paynter made the highest score against Australia in England and also shared with Compton in a record fifth-wicket partnership of 206. ... During the [England] innings four of Australia's bowlers each had a hundred runs hit off him.

No such inspiring start as had been given to England by the first-wicket pair [Hutton and Barnett put on 219] was enjoyed by Australia. Going on at 29, Wright, with his fourth ball in a Test Match, dismissed Fingleton, who played a long hop on to his wicket. By subdued and not altogether certain batting, Brown and Bradman raised the score to 111 and then Bradman, deceived in the flight of a ball, played it against his pads from which it glanced into the wicket-keeper's hands. ...

... Monday's play began with Australia's score 138 for three, McCabe being 19 not out, made in thirty-five minutes. A record of these facts is a necessary preliminary to a description of the amazing batting which followed from McCabe and gave such an epic turn to the game. Six wickets were down for 194 and then McCabe, assisted in turn by three left-hand batsmen – Barnett, O'Reilly and McCormick – altered the whole aspect of affairs. In a little less than four hours, McCabe scored 232 out of 300 – his highest score in a Test Match. His driving was tremendously hard, he hooked short balls with certainty and power, one off Farnes yielding a 6, and he showed real genius in beating Hammond's efforts to keep him away from the bowling. . .. In the last ten overs bowled to him, McCabe took the strike in eight and hit sixteen of his thirty-four 4's, and in a last-wicket stand of 77 with Fleetwood-Smith he scored 72 in twenty-eight minutes. ['If I could play an innings like that,' said Bradman on McCabe's return to the pavilion, 'I'd be a proud man, Stan.'] ...

... When Australia followed on 247 behind, batting of a much different character was seen. Brown and Fingleton adopted 'stone-walling' tactics which called forth mild 'barracking' from some of the spectators and Fingleton followed the extraordinary procedure of stepping away from his wicket, taking off his gloves and laying down his bat. ... Tuesday's play was notable for a dour resistance by Brown and Bradman who, making a hundred apiece, batted with grim patience and admirable skill. In view of the position of Australia they were of course justified in playing this type of game, and by adding 170 in three hours ten minutes they robbed England of practically all chance of winning. ... Troubled by a leg strain, Bradman was never seen as an attacking batsman, but he amazed everyone by the power of his concentration while batting the whole day. His second innings, begun twenty minutes before Monday's play closed, lasted six hours and there were only five 4's in his not out 144 which, being his thirteenth hundred in England-Australia matches, allowed him to take the record from Jack Hobbs ... Annoyed by the wearisome cricket, spectators late in the day indulged in ironical cheering, whereupon Bradman showed disapproval of this slight demonstration by standing clear of his wicket until the noise subsided.

England

L. Hutton, C.J. Barnett, W.J. Edrich, *Mr W.R. Hammond, E. Paynter, D. Compton, †L. E.G. Ames, H. Verity, R. A Sinfield, D.V.P. Wright and Mr K. Farnes.

First innings: Eight for 658 dec (Hutton 100, Barnett 126, Paynter 216 not out, Compton 102, Ames 46; O'Reilly three for 164, Fleetwood-Smith four for 153).

Australia

J. H. Fingleton b Wright	9	–	c Hammond b Edrich	40
W. A. Brown c Ames b Farnes	48	–	c Paynter b Verity	133
*D. G. Bradman c Ames b Sinfield	51	–	not out	144
S. J. McCabe c Compton b Verity	232	–	c Hammond b Verity	39
F. Ward b Farnes	2	–	not out	7
A. L. Hassett c Hammond b Wright	1	–	c Compton b Verity	2
C. L. Badcock b Wright	9	–	b Wright	5
†B. A. Barnett c Wright b Farnes	22	–	lbw b Sinfield	31
W. J. O'Reilly c Paynter b Farnes	9			
E. L. McCormick b Wright	2			
L. O'B. Fleetwood-Smith not out	5			
B 10, l-b 10, w 1	21		B 5, l-b 16, n-b 5	26
	411		(six wkts dec)	**427**

England bowling: *First innings*—Farnes 37–11–106–4; Hammond 19–6–44–0; Sinfield 28–8–51–1; Wright 39–6–153–4; Verity 7.3–0–36–1. *Second innings*—Farnes 24–2–78–0; Hammond 12–6–15–0; Sinfield 35–8–72–1; Wright 37–8–85–1; Verity 62–27–102–3; Edrich 13–2–39–1; Barnett 1–0–10–0.

Umpires: F. Chester and E. Robinson

GENTLEMEN OF ENGLAND v AUSTRALIANS 160 (234)

At Lord's, June 15, 16, 17 [1938]. Australians won by 282 runs. They held the upper hand practically throughout. McCabe ... scored with freedom on the first day, and the bowling suffered severe punishment from Bradman who, in two hours, completed his seventh century of the tour without mistake, hitting thirteen splendid 4's. ... The Gentlemen ... lost six men for 109 with 139 required to avoid a follow-on, but the last four wickets realised 192 in two hours. ... So the Australians led by no more than 96. ... On the last day ... the Australians declared, leaving the Gentlemen three hours in which to get 432 to win. Aggressive methods against the spin bowling of Fleetwood-Smith brought disaster in their train and, the last five wickets falling for 24 runs, the innings ended in a trifle over two hours.

Australians

J. H. Fingleton c Gibb b Meyer	38	–	c Stephenson b Macindoe	121
W. A. Brown c Gibb b Meyer	30	–	c Valentine b Hammond	30
C. L. Badcock b Brown	31	–	not out	112
S. J. McCabe c Wilcox b Stephenson	79	–	c Meyer b Brown	5
A. G. Chipperfield b Stephenson	51	–	not out	20
*D. G. Bradman c Valentine b Meyer	104			
M. G. Waite b Brown	6	–	run out	32
†B. A. Barnett c Gibb b Brown	0			
E. S. White not out	42			
F. Ward b Meyer	1			
L. O'B. Fleetwood-Smith c Stephenson b Meyer	1			
B 8, l-b 6	14		B 7, l-b 6, n-b 2	15
	397		(four wkts dec)	**335**

Gentlemen of England bowling: *First innings*—Stephenson 25–5–94–2; Macindoe 22–7–57–0; Hammond 5–1–14–0; Brown 29–1–107–3; Meyer 26.2–4–66–5; Wyatt 10–0–45–0. *Second innings*—Stephenson 22–2–69–0; Macindoe 17–3–53–1; Hammond 11–1–27–1; Brown 20–0–97–1; Meyer 22–3–57–0; Wyatt 8–1–17–0.

Gentlemen of England

Mr D. R. Wilcox, †Mr P. A. Gibb, Capt. J. W. A. Stephenson, Mr R. E. S. Wyatt, Mr F. G. H. Chalk, *Mr W. R. Hammond, Mr N. W. D. Yardley, Mr B. H. Valentine, Mr F. R. Brown, Mr R. J. O. Meyer and Mr D. H. Macindoe.

First innings: 301 (Wilcox 50, Wyatt 37, Yardley 49, Valentine 49, Brown 88; Ward five for 108). *Second innings:* 149 (Gibb 67; Fleetwood-Smith seven for 44).

Umpires: F. Walden and W. Reeves

LANCASHIRE v AUSTRALIANS 161 (235, 236)

At Manchester, June 18, 20, 21 [1938]. Drawn. The game will be remembered chiefly for excellent bowling by Phillipson in the first innings and a brilliant hundred in seventy-three minutes by Bradman. Phillipson disturbed his opponents by his ability to make the ball run away to the slips and the Australians began so disastrously that three fell for 35 runs. ... With only an innings apiece completed by the last day, there was little hope of anything except a draw, but Fingleton and Brown rarely played attractive cricket, though making a stand of 153, and it was left to Bradman to give the spectators enjoyment. Scoring fluently all round the wicket, he reached 50 in thirty-eight minutes and the century in seventy-three minutes – the fastest hundred of the season to that date. Bradman obtained all but 30 of the runs added while he was in, and hit fifteen 4's. As, when he declared, only seventy minutes remained for play, Lancashire were in no danger of defeat.

Australians

J. H. Fingleton b Nutter	10	–	c Wilkinson b Phillipson	96
W. A. Brown c Farrimond b Phillipson	8	–	b Nutter	70
*D. G. Bradman c Pollard b Phillipson	12	–	not out	101
C. L. Badcock c Pollard b Phillipson	96	–	not out	14
A. L. Hassett b Nutter	118			
A. G. Chipperfield c Farrimond b Phillipson	5			
†B. A. Barnett c Pollard b Phillipson	9			
M. G. Waite lbw b Wilkinson	20			
E. S. White not out	12			
E. L. McCormick b Pollard	1			
L. O'B. Fleetwood-Smith absent ill	0			
B 2, l-b 7, n-b 3	12		B	3
	303		(two wkts dec)	**284**

Lancashire bowling: *First innings*—Phillipson 35–1–93–5; Pollard 30.5–5–82–1; Nutter 23–7–61–2; Wilkinson 16–0–55–1. *Second innings*—Phillipson 17–2–71–1; Pollard 13–4–27–0; Nutter 20–2–81–1; Wilkinson 22–4–63–0; Iddon 7–0–20–0; Hopwood 4–0–19–0.

Lancashire

C. Washbrook, E. Paynter, J. Iddon, N. Oldfield, J. L. Hopwood, A. Nutter, *Mr W. H. L. Lister, W. E. Phillipson, †W. Farrimond, R. Pollard and L. L. Wilkinson.

First innings: 289 (Iddon 44, Oldfield 69, Phillipson 52, Farrimond 49; McCormick four for 84). *Second innings:* Three for 80 (Oldfield 30 not out).

Umpires: A. Dolphin and G. M. Lee

ENGLAND v AUSTRALIA (SECOND TEST MATCH)

162 (237, 238)
35 (54, 55)

At Lord's, June 24, 25, 27, 28 [1938]. Drawn. A match of many fluctuations and fine personal achievements ended with Australia needing 111 runs to win and with four wickets to fall. In the Nottingham game, the scoring of a double-hundred on each side had been unprecedented and yet in the very next Test Match the same thing was done again. Hammond ... played an innings of 240 – the highest in England against Australia. Brown batted through the whole of Australia's first innings, scoring 206 not out and equalling the performances of Dr J. E. Barrett, Warren Bardsley and W. M. Woodfull by carrying his bat through a Test innings against England. ... On the last day Bradman, as in each of his four previous Tests against England, hit a three-figure score and in doing so exceeded the highest individual aggregate in the series – the 3,636 runs made by Hobbs.

... After England's wonderful start in the previous Test, the events that followed success in the toss came as a rude shock. McCormick made the ball swing in to the batsmen and caused it to 'lift' awkwardly ... Actually, excluding no-balls, McCormick in twenty-five deliveries took [the wickets of Hutton, Edrich and Barnett] for 15 runs ... With England in this sorry position Hammond joined Paynter, the resolute cricket of the left-hander gave Hammond confidence to play his natural game, and this fourth-wicket pair set up a new record by adding 222. ... So large was the crowd that the gates were closed before noon. Part of the record partnership between Hammond and Paynter was watched by His Majesty the King.

On Saturday, the cricket was seen by the largest crowd ever to assemble at headquarters – the attendance was officially returned as 33,800. The gates were closed before the start and, after hurried consultations between officials, spectators were permitted to retain positions they had taken up on the grass, the boundary ropes being moved forward a few yards, thus reducing the playing area. England definitely gained the upper hand before the close … [but] Hammond received a nasty blow on the left elbow and the injury, and also a pulled leg muscle, prevented him bowling in this match and for some time afterwards. … It must be added that through an innings lasting seven hours and producing England's highest total at Lord's, the Australian fielding was maintained at a high standard.

By the call of time, Australia had lost half their wickets, but a fine, fighting innings by Brown checked England's progress. Bradman played on … On Monday, the Englishmen lost little time in strengthening their grip on the game. Verity, put on first thing, disposed of Barnett and Chipperfield in eight deliveries and when O'Reilly went in seventh wicket down Australia needed 37 more runs to avoid a follow-on. O'Reilly promptly hit out at the slow bowling and a serious mistake occurred in the field. [O'Reilly when 11 was missed at long-on by Paynter.] … Australia at this point required 17 more runs to save the follow-on and O'Reilly, pulling two successive deliveries from Verity for 6 and taking 16 off the over, soon settled that question. … Soon after Farnes was brought back into the attack he not only bowled O'Reilly and had McCormick caught at short-leg off successive balls but was deprived of a 'hat-trick' owing to Compton missing a slip catch offered by Fleetwood-Smith. … After three hours had been lost owing to rain Brown, at 184, was also missed by Paynter, this time at mid-on, and with Fleetwood-Smith showing surprisingly good defence, Brown was able to complete a double-hundred before the innings ended with a difference of 72 runs in England's favour. …

The rain transformed an easy wicket into one soft on top and hard underneath, and England's opening pair fell for 28 … half the England side were out for 76 when Hammond, who owing to his injury had a runner, tried a one-hand stroke at a ball outside his leg stump and skied it. … In the hour of great need, however, Compton batted superbly for England …

Hammond declared, with Compton not out after making 56 of his runs from boundaries, and left Australia an impossible task in the time available [315 in two and three-quarter hours]. Any thought of failure was soon dispelled by Bradman. After the tea interval the Australian captain batted in brisk style and he and Hassett added 64, short bowling by Farnes receiving instant punishment. It had long since become evident that the Test would be another case of stalemate and Bradman kept life in the cricket by hitting his fourteenth hundred against England as the outcome of less than two hours twenty minutes' batting; his 102 included fifteen 4's. … An interesting point of the match was that Brown was on the field from the start of play until five o'clock on the fourth day. … The total number of spectators admitted to the ground on payment was 100,933 – a record for Lord's – and the receipts were £28,164 11*s.* 9*d.*

England

L. Hutton, C.J. Barnett, W.J. Edrich, *Mr W.R. Hammond, E. Paynter, D. Compton, †L.E.G. Ames, H. Verity, A.W. Wellard, D.V.P. Wright and Mr K. Farnes.

First innings: 494 (Hammond 240, Paynter 99, Ames 83; McCormick four for 101, O'Reilly four for 93). *Second innings:* Eight for 242 dec (Paynter 43, Compton 76 not out, Wellard 38; McCormick three for 72).

Australia

J. H. Fingleton c Hammond b Wright	31	–	c Hammond b Wellard	4
W. A. Brown not out	206	–	b Verity	10
*D. G. Bradman b Verity	18	–	not out	102
S. J. McCabe c Verity b Farnes	38	–	c Hutton b Verity	21
A. L. Hassett lbw b Wellard	56	–	b Wright	42
C. L. Badcock b Wellard	0	–	c Wright b Edrich	0
†B. A. Barnett c Compton b Verity	8	–	c Paynter b Edrich	14
A. G. Chipperfield lbw b Verity	1			
W. J. O'Reilly b Farnes	42			
E. L. McCormick c Barnett b Farnes	0			
L. O'B. Fleetwood-Smith c Barnett b Verity	7			
B 1, l-b 8, n-b 6	15		B 5, l-b 3, w 2, n-b 1	11
	422		(six wkts)	**204**

England bowling: *First innings*—Farnes 43–6–135–3; Wellard 23–2–96–2; Wright 16–2–68–1; Verity 35.4–9–103–4; Edrich 4–2–5–0. *Second innings*—Farnes 13–3–51–0; Wellard 9–1–30–1; Wright 8–0–56–1; Verity 13–5–29–2; Edrich 5.2–0–27–2.

Umpires: E. J. Smith and F. Walden

YORKSHIRE v AUSTRALIANS 163 (239, 240)

At Sheffield, July 2, 4, 5 [1938]. Drawn. The Australians narrowly escaped defeat in a thrilling match that attracted about 60,000 spectators in the three days. Sellers, when winning the toss, put the Australians in upon a rain-affected pitch, and Yorkshire fought with such spirit that by lunch-time on the third day they stood within 67 of victory with seven wickets to fall. Then, unfortunately for the county's prospects of gaining their first victory over a team from the Commonwealth since 1902, rain put an end to the proceedings. Smailes, first with swingers and later with off-breaks, caused the Australians a lot of trouble on the first day even though, in the absence of much sunshine, the pitch did not become as difficult as Sellers had anticipated. Bradman and Hassett saved their side from disaster. Bradman shaped well at a trying time, driving and hitting to leg cleanly after an uncertain start, but Hassett took chief honours. ... Waite, adopting similar tactics to those of Smailes, proved equally difficult to Yorkshire. ... With a lead of 17, the Australians fared badly [in their second innings]. Hassett and Bradman, desperately ill at ease against Bowes and Verity, shared in a stand of 41, but the last six wickets fell in half an hour for 32 runs. Yorkshire required 150 to win and, with the whole of Tuesday available, made slow but sure progress until the weather baulked their efforts.

Australians

J. H. Fingleton b Smailes	2	–	lbw b Bowes	2
S. J. McCabe c Smailes b Bowes	13	–	lbw b Bowes	15
*D. G. Bradman st Wood b Smailes	59	–	c Barber b Smailes	42
C. L. Badcock c Turner b Robinson	11	–	lbw b Verity	22
A. L. Hassett lbw b Verity	94	–	lbw b Verity	17
S. Barnes c Wood b Leyland	10	–	c Sellers b Smailes	19
M. G. Waite lbw b Smailes	2	–	run out	0
†B. A. Barnett c Robinson b Smailes	12	–	c and b Smailes	1
E. S. White c Sutcliffe b Smailes	1	–	c Hutton b Smailes	2
E. L. McCormick c Leyland b Smailes	9	–	b Verity	0
L. O'B. Fleetwood-Smith not out	4	–	not out	7
B 3, l-b 1, n-b 1	5		L-b	5
	222			**132**

Yorkshire bowling: *First innings*—Bowes 12–4–15–1; Smailes 29–7–92–6; Robinson 12–5–39–1; Verity 17–1–69–1; Leyland 3–1–2–1. *Second innings*—Bowes 18–8–28–2; Smailes 19.2–4–45–4; Robinson 2–0–8–0; Verity 21–8–46–3.

Yorkshire

H. Sutcliffe, L. Hutton, W. Barber, M. Leyland, C. Turner, T. F. Smailes, *Mr A. B. Sellers, †A. Wood, E. P. Robinson, H. Verity and W. E. Bowes.

First innings: 205 (Turner 34, Wood 41, Robinson 32; Waite seven for 101, White three for 26). *Second innings:* Three for 83 (Sutcliffe 36 not out).

Umpires: W. Reeves and A. Skelding

ENGLAND v AUSTRALIA
(THIRD TEST MATCH)

The third of the five matches arranged between England and Australia was to have been played at Old Trafford, Manchester, on July 8, 9, 11, 12 [1938], but owing to the persistent bad weather the game had to be abandoned without a ball being bowled. The captains did not toss and neither team was announced.

WARWICKSHIRE v AUSTRALIANS 164 (241)

At Birmingham, July 13, 14 [1938]. Australians won by an innings and 93 runs. Playing their first game for over a week, they thoroughly outclassed Warwickshire, who batted without resolution on turf which never became difficult. ... Owing to a slight head injury, Fingleton did not open the Australians innings and McCabe, who deputised, left at 17. Warwickshire had to wait two and three-quarter hours for their next success and in that time Brown and Bradman added 206. Bradman, cautious at the start, afterwards hit with tremendous power and his last 85 runs came in an hour. The rest of the batsmen were tied down by the accurate leg-breaks of Hollies ... Going in a second time requiring 211 to save an innings defeat, Warwickshire again failed dismally. Four wickets went down for 28 and ... the county were all out in just over two hours.

Warwickshire

A. J. Croom, Mr J. R. Thompson, F. R. Santall, H. E. Dollery, J. S. Ord, †J. Buckingham, *Mr P. Cranmer, G. E. Paine, K. Wilmot, J. H. Mayer and E. Hollies.

First innings: 179 (Dollery 31, Ord 61; O'Reilly three for 69, Ward four for 26). *Second innings:* 118 (Ord 30, Cranmer 37; Waite three for 33, O'Reilly four for 33).

Australians

S. J. McCabe b Wilmot	14	M. G. Waite not out	25
W. A. Brown b Hollies	101	E. S. White c Wilmot b Hollies	2
*D. G. Bradman c Wilmot b Mayer	135	W. J. O'Reilly b Paine	0
†S. Barnes c Cranmer b Hollies	24	F. Ward not out	13
A. G. Chipperfield c Buckingham b Hollies	46	B 4, l-b 4, w 1, n-b 2	11
J. H. Fingleton hit wkt b Hollies	9	(eight wkts dec)	**390**

E. L. McCormick did not bat.

Warwickshire bowling: Mayer 16–2–49–1; Wilmot 27–4–90–1; Hollies 42–8–130–5; Paine 30–7–65–1; Santall 3–0–28–0; Croom 3–0–17–0.

Umpires: G. Beet and C. V. Tarbox

NOTTINGHAMSHIRE v AUSTRALIANS 165 (242, 243)

At Nottingham, July 16, 18, 19 [1938]. Australians won by 412 runs. A weak Nottinghamshire eleven gave an inexplicably poor display and, but for gallant efforts by Gunn and Hardstaff, the Australians would have won even more easily. Good pace bowling by Jepson and Voce helped to get rid of some of the more renowned Australian batsmen on the opening day, but Bradman and Barnes added 74 and the last five wickets put on 140. ... [When the Australians batted again] Brown, Badcock, Bradman and Hassett completed Nottinghamshire's discomfiture. Hassett and Bradman shared in a third-wicket stand of 216 in two hours twenty minutes, Bradman becoming the first player during the season to reach 2,000 runs and equalling the record made by Trumper, during the 1902 tour, of hitting eleven centuries. Nottinghamshire should have saved the game without difficulty, but only Hardstaff offered serious resistance ... Fleetwood-Smith bewildered the rest of the side.

Australians

W. A. Brown c Marshall b Voce	4	–	c Harris b Heane	63
C. L. Badcock c Wheat b Jepson	6	–	c Jepson b Voce	54
*D. G. Bradman lbw b Jepson	56	–	c Jepson b Marshall	144
A. L. Hassett lbw b Voce	2	–	c Wheat b Heane	124
S. Barnes lbw b Harris	58	–	not out	34
A. G. Chipperfield b Jepson	4	–	not out	27
M. G. Waite c Wheat b Harris	25			
†B. A. Barnett b Harris	3			
F. Ward not out	29			
W. J. O'Reilly lbw b Voce	33			
L. O'B. Fleetwood-Smith c Jepson b Harris	8			
B 8, l-b 5, n-b 2	15		B 4, l-b 1, n-b 2	7
	243		(four wkts dec)	**453**

Nottinghamshire bowling: *First innings*—Voce 30–3–72–3; Jepson 23–6–38–3; Harris 24.5–5–60–4; Gunn 11–0–38–0; Marshall 5–0–20–0. *Second innings*—Voce 21–2–80–1; Jepson 19–2–81–0; Harris 28–5–106–0; Gunn 9–0–44–0; Marshall 7–1–34–1; Heane 31–7–85–2; Hardstaff 3–0–16–0.

Nottinghamshire

W. W. Keeton, C. B. Harris, J. Knowles, J. Hardstaff, G. V. Gunn, *Mr G. F. H. Heane, G. Yates, Mr E. A. Marshall, W. Voce, †A. B. Wheat and A. Jepson.

First innings: 147 (Gunn 75, Voce 32; O'Reilly five for 39, Fleetwood-Smith three for 35). *Second innings:* 137 (Hardstaff 67 not out; Fleetwood-Smith five for 39).

Umpires: J. Newman and D. Hendren

ENGLAND v AUSTRALIA 166 (244, 245)
(FOURTH TEST MATCH) 36 (56, 57)

At Leeds, July 22, 23, 25 [1938]. Australia won by five wickets. Their success enabled them to retain the Ashes. ... A fine test of skill had many glorious moments, the cricket was often thrilling to watch, and the decision of the game about quarter past four on the third day confounded all expectations. In contrast to what occurred at Trent Bridge and Lord's, only 695 runs were scored in the match; on each side the captain made top score, Bradman registering yet another three-figure innings.

At no time was the wicket easy for batting and Australia won largely because they possessed better spin bowling. ... Exactly why the pitch, even during the early stages of the game, played so queerly was hard to understand. A likely explanation was that it was kept on the damp side through moisture being drawn to the surface in the humid weather prevailing. At any rate bowlers were able to turn the ball and as the match progressed spin acted more quickly; by Monday the wicket had worn and O'Reilly took full advantage of this state of affairs. ... The decision to omit Goddard from the England eleven suggested that the Selectors, despite a long and careful examination of the wicket before the toss, had no suspicions that the conditions were likely to be more favourable to spin bowlers than to Farnes and Bowes, both of whom appeared in the eleven.

To see England's batsmen struggling for runs after Hammond, for the third successive match, won the toss was at once unexpected and perplexing. In the course of five hours, and despite a splendid effort by Hammond, the innings was over. ...

When Wright, with the first ball he bowled in Australia's innings, got rid of Brown, B.A. Barnett was sent in to play out time with Fingleton and the outcome of this move far exceeded expectations. ... England bowled for nearly an hour and a half next morning before gaining further reward. ... The attack of Farnes and Bowes after lunch was accurate and full of danger; McCabe and Badcock in turn were clean bowled and Australia's first five wickets fell for 145. The light at this time was none too good but Bradman, as in each of the two previous Tests, did not let the occasion pass without placing to his name another three-figure score – his twelfth of the tour. Although a beautiful-length leg-break led to Hassett being caught at slip after helping to add 50, Waite stayed long enough to see Australia take innings lead. Shielding his successive partners, Bradman astutely 'nursed' the bowling and he made every possible run against high-class fielding. His stroke-play and his defence were alike admirable. Bowes, who rarely pitched short and made the ball swerve, had a great moment when he knocked Bradman's middle stump out of the ground. Only two runs were added after the Australian captain was eighth out – he batted a few minutes less than three hours and hit nine 4's. ...

Bad light once interrupted this innings and when England went in 19 runs behind an appeal was upheld. Barnett and Edrich survived an awkward fifty minutes prior to close of play and they put 60 runs on the board before being separated next morning. ... For the collapse which afterwards set in no-one could have been prepared. O'Reilly, on a worn pitch, and ably supported by Fleetwood-Smith, finished off the innings before lunch-time, England's full ten wickets actually going down for the addition of 74 runs to the overnight score. ... With six men on the leg side close to the bat, and with no-one in the long field, he demoralised the majority of the batsmen. ...

Left to get 105, Australia had to struggle hard for success. ... Intense excitement came into the cricket when Wright, after going on at 48, quickly sent back Bradman and McCabe. With the first four batsmen in the order all out, Australia had to contend with atrocious light but the batsmen refrained from appealing and, as Hassett began to drive and pull in an easy, confident style, England's chance of turning the tables gradually slipped away. ... Rain interrupted the play with nine runs needed but Australia got home without further loss, making the required runs in an hour and fifty minutes. ...

England

W.J. Edrich, C.J. Barnett, J. Hardstaff, *Mr W.R. Hammond, E. Paynter, D. Compton, †W.F. Price, H. Verity, D.V.P. Wright, Mr K. Farnes and W.E. Bowes.

First innings: 223 (Barnett 30, Hammond 76; O'Reilly five for 66, Fleetwood-Smith three for 73). *Second innings:* 123 (O'Reilly five for 56, Fleetwood-Smith four for 34).

Australia

J. H. Fingleton b Verity	30	–	lbw b Verity	9
W. A. Brown b Wright	22	–	lbw b Farnes	9
†B. A. Barnett c Price b Farnes	57	–	not out	15
*D. G. Bradman b Bowes	103	–	c Verity b Wright	16
S. J. McCabe b Farnes	1	–	c Barnett b Wright	15
C. L. Badcock b Bowes	4	–	not out	5
A. L. Hassett c Hammond b Wright	13	–	c Edrich b Wright	33
M. G. Waite c Price b Farnes	3			
W. J. O'Reilly c Hammond b Farnes	2			
E. L. McCormick b Bowes	0			
L. O'B. Fleetwood-Smith not out	2			
B 2, l-b 3	5		B 4, n-b 1	5
	242		(five wkts)	**107**

England bowling: *First innings*—Farnes 26–3–77–4; Bowes 35.4–6–79–3; Wright 15–4–38–2; Verity 19–6–30–1; Edrich 3–0–13–0. *Second innings*—Farnes 11.3–4–17–1; Bowes 11–0–35–0; Wright 5–0–26–3; Verity 5–2–24–1.

Umpires: E.J. Smith and F. Chester

SOMERSET v AUSTRALIANS 167 (246)

At Taunton, July 27, 28, 29 [1938]. Australians won by an innings and 218 runs. Somerset cut a sorry figure and suffered defeat early on the last day. ... Bradman, putting together his thirteenth century of the tour, overshadowed everyone else. At first troubled by the swinging deliveries of Andrews, Bradman afterwards ran into his best form and he obtained nineteen of his thirty-two 4's in making his second hundred. He shared with Badcock, Hassett and McCabe in prolific stands ...

Somerset

Mr M.D. Lyon, F.S. Lee, H.T.F. Buse, Mr R.J.O. Meyer, *Mr E.F. Longrigg, H. Gimblett, W.H.R. Andrews, Mr C.J.P. Barnwell, A.W. Wellard, †W.T. Luckes and H.L. Hazell.

First innings: 110 (Fleetwood-Smith three for 40, White three for 8). *Second innings:* 136 (Buse 33; Fleetwood-Smith five for 30).

Australians

†C. W. Walker b Andrews	27	A. G. Chipperfield b Wellard	10
C. L. Badcock run out	110	S. J. McCabe not out	56
*D. G. Bradman b Andrews	202	E. S. White not out	2
S. Barnes lbw b Wellard	9	B 4, l-b 1, w 1, n-b 1	7
A. L. Hassett c Gimblett b Buse	31	(six wkts dec)	**464**

F. Ward, W. J. O'Reilly and L. O'B. Fleetwood-Smith did not bat.

Somerset bowling: Wellard 39–8–146–2; Andrews 24–2–108–2; Meyer 17–3–54–0; Buse 12–1–82–1; Hazell 11–1–57–0; Lyon 2–1–10–0.

Umpires: C.N. Woolley and E. Cooke

GLAMORGAN v AUSTRALIANS 168 (247)

At Swansea, July 30, August 1, 2 [1938]. Drawn. Welsh cricket lovers, of whom over 25,000 were present on the second day, when the 'gate' was a record, were bitterly disappointed, only five hours' play being possible in the match. When the county declared with five wickets down to enable the spectators to have an opportunity of seeing the Australians bat, the pitch was definitely unfit for cricket.

Glamorgan

A. H. Dyson, E. Davies, T. L. Brierley, †H. Davies, *Mr M. J. Turnbull, C. Smart, Mr J. C. Clay, Mr W. Wooller, J. Mercer, E. C. Jones and H. Davies.

First innings: Five for 148 dec (E. Davies 58; Waite four for 45).

Australians

W. A. Brown c Dyson b E. Davies	8
J. H. Fingleton c H. Davies b Wooller	1
*D. G. Bradman st H. Davies b Clay	17
A. L. Hassett not out	26
S. Barnes not out	5
B 2, w 2	4
(three wkts)	**61**

A. G. Chipperfield, D. G. Waite, †C. W. Walker, E. S. White, F. Ward and E. L. McCormick did not bat.

Glamorgan bowling: Mercer 6–3–4–0; Wooller 10–6–9–1; Clay 10–4–15–1; E. Davies 4–0–21–1; Jones 2–0–8–0.

Umpires: J. Hardstaff and J. Smart

KENT v AUSTRALIANS 169 (248)

At Canterbury, August 13, 15, 16 [1938]. Australians won by ten wickets. For about two hours the pitch proved difficult, but this was sufficient to decide the whole course of the match. Facing a total of 479, Kent had to go in when, after weekend rain, strong sunshine was drying the wicket. Following on 371 behind, the county showed that there was nothing really wrong with their batting by averting an innings beating. On the first day consistent run-getting enabled the Australians to build up a big total. After the fall of two wickets for 38, Bradman and Badcock added 107. ... Bradman did not declare next morning, waiting for the pitch to become helpful to bowlers. His judgment proved correct for, following a foolish run-out [of Woolley] off the first ball of the innings, Kent collapsed ... Woolley [at the age of fifty-one and in his farewell season] touched his best form in the follow-on, hitting up 81, including a 6, a 5 and thirteen 4's, in an hour. ...

Australians

J. H. Fingleton lbw b Watt	23			
W. A. Brown lbw b Watt	4			
*D. G. Bradman c Todd b Watt	67			
C. L. Badcock c Davies b Todd	76			
S. Barnes c Todd b Woolley	94			
M. G. Waite c Chalk b Todd	18			
B. A. Barnett c Chalk b Todd	54			
†C. W. Walker c Fagg b Watt	42			
E. S. White c Todd b Wright	52	–	not out	0
F. Ward c Valentine b Todd	16			
L. O'B. Fleetwood-Smith not out	0	–	not out	6
B 24, l-b 7, n-b 2	33		N-b	1
	479		(no wkt)	**7**

Kent bowling: *First innings*—Watt 35–7–102–4; Todd 40–10–145–4; Davies 26–3–75–0; Wright 16.3–0–77–1; Woolley 14–1–47–1. *Second innings*—Levett 0.3–0–6–0.

Kent

F. E. Woolley, A. Fagg, L. E.G. Ames, Mr B. H. Valentine, *Mr F.G. H. Chalk, L.J. Todd, Mr C. H. Knott, Mr J.G. W. Davies, D. V. P. Wright, A. E. Watt and †Mr W. H. V. Levett.

First innings: 108 (Ames 30; Waite four for 43, White three for 35). *Second innings:* 377 (Woolley 81, Ames 139, Valentine 36, sundries 30; Waite five for 85, Ward three for 92).

Umpires: F. Chester and J. Smart

ENGLAND v AUSTRALIA 170

(FIFTH TEST MATCH) 37

Played at Kennington Oval, August 20, 22, 23, 24 [1938]. England won by an innings and 579 runs and each country having gained one victory the rubber was drawn. No more remarkable exhibition of concentration and endurance has ever been seen on the cricket field than that of Leonard Hutton, the Yorkshire opening batsman, in a match which culminated in the defeat of Australia by a margin more substantial than any associated with the series of matches between the two countries. Record after record went by the board as Hutton mastered the bowling in calm, methodical fashion for the best part of two and a half days. At the end of an innings which extended over thirteen hours twenty minutes, this batsman of only twenty-two years had placed the highest score in Test cricket to his name, and shared in two partnerships which surpassed previous figures.... As a boy of fourteen, Hutton, at Leeds in 1930, had seen Bradman hit 334 – the record individual score in Test Matches between England and Australia. Now, on his third appearance in the series, the Yorkshireman left that figure behind by playing an innings of 364.

This Test will always be remembered as 'Hutton's Match', and also for the calamity which befell Australia while their opponents were putting together a mammoth total of 903. First of all Fingleton strained a muscle and Bradman injured his ankle so badly that he retired from the match and did not play again during the tour. Before this accident, England had established a supremacy which left little doubt about the result; indeed, Hammond probably would not have closed the innings during the tea interval on the third day but for the mishap to the opposing captain.

The moral effect of the loss of Bradman and Fingleton upon the other Australians was, of course, very great. After fielding out an innings lasting fifteen hours and a quarter, several of them batted – to all appearances – with very poor heart, but Brown, going in first, was last man out before a follow-on 702 runs in arrear. He played an heroic innings under the shadow of impending defeat ... but from a depressing start in each innings there was no real recovery. This came as an anti-climax after the batting mastery which obtained until the tea interval on Monday. It was not a case of England driving home the advantage but rather of Australia losing inspiration to make a braver struggle to put a better face on defeat.

Hammond's fourth consecutive success in the toss was, of course, one factor influencing the result. Another was the way in which the Australian team was chosen. The risks taken by Bradman in going into the match with only O'Reilly, Fleetwood-Smith and Waite to bowl seemed to be inviting trouble.... Whether Bradman, as was suggested, gambled upon winning the toss after three failures and so being in a position to call upon his spin bowlers when the pitch had become worn will probably never be known....

With few bowlers of class at his call, Bradman had to conserve the energies of O'Reilly as much as possible. The field was set carefully for the saving of runs, and although [Hutton and Leyland] scored numerous singles on the off side Australia gave a superb display in the field, Bradman inspiring the team with his fast running and clean picking-up.... A curiosity of the [first] day's cricket was that four times a no-ball led either to the wicket being hit or the ball being caught....

... Following [on Monday] the same steady lines as before, Hutton and Leyland carried on [their] magnificent batting until England had 411 runs up when the stand [worth 382 for the second wicket] ended through a wonderful piece of fielding. Hutton drove a ball from O'Reilly hard to the off side and Hassett fumbled it. Then he slung in a very fast return to the bowler's end and Bradman, sizing up the situation in an instant, dashed towards the wicket from mid-on, caught the throw-in and broke the wicket before Leyland could complete a second run.

[By stumps on the second day] Hutton claimed exactly 300 of the [634] runs scored at this point, and the 30,000 people who assembled at the Oval on Tuesday saw fresh cricket history made. The bowling and fielding of Australia looked more formidable than at any other time in the game and as Hutton carried his score nearer to the record Test innings, Bradman, the holder of it, brought several fieldsmen close in to the wicket for O'Reilly's bowling. Every run had to be fought for.... Hutton duly reached his objective and the scene at the ground, with the whole assembly rising to its feet, and every Australian player as well as Hardstaff congratulating Hutton, will be remembered for a long time by those who saw it. Hutton took nearly twice as long as Bradman did over as many runs eight years previously, but the Australian's big innings came during a Test limited in duration whereas Hutton played his innings on an occasion when time did not matter....

England's total ... reached 770 for the loss of six wickets and some spirited hitting by Wood came as a refreshing contrast to the stern batting which had gone before. [Wood added 106 with Hardstaff] and shortly after these batsmen were separated there occurred the tragic accident to Bradman, who when bowling caught his foot in a worn foot-hole, fell prone and was carried off the field by two of his colleagues. During the tea interval England's innings, which was the longest on record and produced the highest total for any Test Match innings and the highest for any first-class match in England, was declared closed....

... [Towards the end of Australia's first innings] an unusual incident happened during the eighth and last stand, in which Fleetwood-Smith participated. When Brown cut the last ball of an over, intending to run a single, Hutton, with the idea of trying to give the less experienced batsman the strike, kicked the ball to the boundary. Instructions to umpires, however, provide for four runs to be added to the runs already made should a fieldsman wilfully cause the ball to reach the boundary, and as this meant the award to Brown of five runs he kept the bowling.... On the fourth day, the proceedings were so one-sided as to be almost farcical. The fact that Australia batted only nine men removed some of the honour and glory from England's triumph, but there was nothing in the condition of the wicket to excuse the poor resistance of so many Test batsmen.... The number of people who saw the game was 94,212, including 81,336 who paid for admission....

England

L. Hutton, W. J. Edrich, M. Leyland, *Mr W. R. Hammond, E. Paynter, D. Compton, J. Hardstaff, †A. Wood, H. Verity; Mr K. Farnes and W. E. Bowes did not bat.

First innings: Seven for 903 dec (Hutton 364, Leyland 187, Hammond 59, Hardstaff 169 not out, Wood 53, sundries 50; O'Reilly three for 178, Bradman none for 6).

Australia

C. L. Badcock c Hardstaff b Bowes	0	–	b Bowes	9
W. A. Brown c Hammond b Leyland	69	–	c Edrich b Farnes	15
S. J. McCabe c Edrich b Farnes	14	–	c Wood b Farnes	2
A. L. Hassett c Compton b Edrich	42	–	lbw b Bowes	10
S. Barnes b Bowes	41	–	lbw b Verity	33
†B. A. Barnett c Wood b Bowes	2	–	b Farnes	46
M. G. Waite b Bowes	8	–	c Edrich b Verity	0
W. J. O'Reilly c Wood b Bowes	0	–	not out	7
L. O'B. Fleetwood-Smith not out	16	–	c Leyland b Farnes	0
*D. G. Bradman absent hurt	0	–	absent hurt	0
J. H. Fingleton absent hurt	0	–	absent hurt	0
B 4, l-b 2, n-b 3	9		B	1
	201			**123**

England bowling: *First innings*—Farnes 13–2–54–1; Bowes 19–3–49–5; Edrich 10–2–55–1; Verity 5–1–15–0; Leyland 3.1–0–11–1; Hammond 2–0–8–0. *Second innings*—Farnes 12.1–1–63–4; Bowes 10–3–25–2; Verity 7–3–15–2; Leyland 5–0–19–0.

Umpires: F. Chester and F. Walden

1938-39

1938-39

In a season notable for many fine individual performances, South Australia carried off the Sheffield Shield. Victoria, victims of the weather in a vital game with the ultimate champions, finished second, one point behind; Queensland, much improved, were third and New South Wales, suffering a sad fall from grace, last.

Fresh from his personal successes of the English tour, Bradman deserved the largest measure of praise for leading South Australia to triumph. Yet his gifts for captaincy were overshadowed by his remarkable batting. In six State matches he played six innings and averaged 160.20 for an aggregate of 801 runs. Bradman began the season with 118 in the Melbourne Club Centenary Match and followed with 143, 225, 107, 186 and 135 not out, so equalling the record of C. B. Fry, who in 1901 put together six successive centuries. After the game with New South Wales at Sydney, Bradman found himself with one more match for the opportunity of surpassing the famous England cricketer's achievement. Fifteen thousand people [actually seventeen thousand and more] attended the Adelaide Oval on the second day of the match with Victoria, eager to watch their favourite add another record to his name, but Bradman was out for five. Nothing more than has already been written can be said of Bradman. At the crease he was master and the bowler, servant.

From 'Cricket in Australia: Inter-State Matches, 1938-39'

D.G. BRADMAN'S TEAM v K. E. RIGG'S TEAM 171 (249)
(MELBOURNE CRICKET CLUB CENTENARY MATCH)

Played at Melbourne, December 9, 10, 12, 13 [1938]. Drawn. Bradman's side, composed of players back from the tour in England, showed superior strength. The Rest [Rigg's team] fared moderately against O'Reilly and Fleetwood-Smith in their first innings, during which play was stopped by a dust-storm of hurricane force. Bradman and McCabe made delightful centuries. They shared in a stand of 163 and Rigg's team batted again 211 behind. . . .

K. E. Rigg's team

*K. E. Rigg, I. S. Lee, R.G. Gregory, J. A. Ledward, S.G. Barnes, †D. Tallon, M. W. Sievers, E. H. Bromley, L. E. Nagel, G. Eyres and C. Christ.

First innings: 215 (Rigg 48, Barnes 63, Bromley 34; O'Reilly five for 75). *Second innings:* Eight for 324 (Rigg 71, Gregory 32, Ledward 85, Sievers 44 not out; Bradman one for none).

D.G. Bradman's team

J. H. Fingleton c Sievers b Eyres	23	†B. A. Barnett lbw b Sievers	0
W. A. Brown c and b Christ	67	W. J. O'Reilly c Christ b Bromley	0
*D. G. Bradman b Nagel	118	L. O'B. Fleetwood-Smith b Sievers	2
S. J. McCabe c Lee b Nagel	105	E. L. McCormick c Gregory b Bromley	3
A. L. Hassett run out	12	B 11, l-b 6	17
C. L. Badcock not out	51		**426**
M. G. Waite b Sievers	28		

K. E. Rigg's Team bowling: Eyres 23–2–81–1; Sievers 15–3–53–3; Nagel 26–4–93–2; Christ 29–4–104–1; Bromley 11.7–0–53–2; Barnes 1–1–0–0; Gregory 3–0–25–0.

Umpires: A. N. Barlow and G. A. Browne

SOUTH AUSTRALIA v NEW SOUTH WALES 172 (250)

Played at Adelaide, December 16, 17, 19, 20 [1938]. South Australia won by an innings and 56 runs. [Some sources put the New South Wales first innings score as 390 and give the result as an innings and 55 runs.] Bradman made the second century of his record-equalling run, but in this match Badcock overshadowed him. They were associated in a stand of 175, and Hamence helped Badcock set up a South Australian fourth-wicket record with a partnership of 203 ... South Australia declared at their highest total against New South Wales. ... [When] New South Wales followed on, the wiles of Ward and Grimmett upset the whole side.

South Australia

K. Ridings b O'Reilly	31	M. G. Waite run out	2
R. S. Whitington c James b Murphy	0	F. A. Ward b Barnes	0
*D. G. Bradman b Murphy	143	C. V. Grimmett run out	35
C. L. Badcock not out	271	B 3, l-b 4, n-b 2	9
R. A. Hamence c Barnes b Fitzpatrick	90	(eight wkts dec)	**600**
†C. W. Walker lbw b O'Reilly	0		

H. Cotton and J. Scott did not bat.

New South Wales bowling: Murphy 32–1–126–2; Cheetham 20–1–85–0; O'Reilly 36–9–99–2; White 28–1–103–0; Chipperfield 8–0–60–0; Barnes 15–2–62–1; James 1–0–13–0; Fitzpatrick 11–0–40–1; Fingleton 5–0–3–0.

New South Wales

J. H. Fitzpatrick, A.G. Cheetham, C. M. Solomon, S.G. Barnes, *J. H. Fingleton, A.G. Chipperfield, R. James, †F. A. Easton, E. S. White, W. J. O'Reilly and J. Murphy.

First innings: 389 (Barnes 117, Chipperfield 154; Grimmett seven for 116). *Second innings:* 155 (James 42; Ward four for 40, Grimmett four for 59).

Umpires: J. D. Scott and A.G. Jenkins

SOUTH AUSTRALIA v QUEENSLAND 173 (251)

Played at Adelaide, December 24, 26, 27, 28 [1938]. South Australia won by an innings and 20 runs. Bradman and Badcock maintained their great batting form. In a stand of 202 they made brilliant strokes all round the wicket after the Queensland batsmen had failed dismally against Grimmett. The tricky slows completely nonplussed the batsmen in the first innings, but in Brown [who carried his bat] Grimmett found a worthy foeman when Queensland batted a second time 331 behind. ...

Queensland

*W. A. Brown, R. Rogers, T. Allen, †D. Tallon, G. Baker, G.G. Cook, D. Hansen, M. Guttormsen, W. Tallon, J. Ellis and C. Christ.

First innings: 131 (Cook 34 not out; Grimmett six for 33). *Second innings:* 311 (Brown 174 not out, Baker 43, Cook 35; Grimmett three for 96, Ward three for 106).

South Australia

R. S. Whitington st D. Tallon b Cook	11
K. L. Ridings c D. Tallon b Ellis	7
*D. G. Bradman c Baker b Christ	225
C. L. Badcock c W. Tallon b Ellis	100
R. A. Hamence c and b W. Tallon	17
M. G. Waite c Guttormsen b Cook	52
†C. W. Walker b Baker	32
F. A. Ward run out	9
C. V. Grimmett not out	0
H. J. Cotton b Baker	0
J. Scott b Baker	0
B 5, l-b 3, w 1	9
	462

Queensland bowling: Ellis 26–0–87–2; Cook 25–2–85–2; Christ 33–3–102–1; Baker 8.5–0–36–3; W. Tallon 18–1–90–1; Rogers 8–1–42–0; Allen 2–0–11–0.

Umpires: J. D. Scott and A.G. Jenkins

VICTORIA v SOUTH AUSTRALIA 174 (252)

Played at Melbourne, December 30, 31 [1938], January 2, 3 [1939]. Drawn. Hassett played a masterly innings for Victoria but interest centred on Bradman. The South Australia captain gave another faultless exhibition and duly reached his fourth successive century. Whitington, who also scored a hundred, put on 150 with Bradman. … Grimmett tore a leg muscle during the game and an attack of laryngitis troubled Bradman [who along with his opposing captain, Rigg, took no part in the final two days' play].

Victoria

*K. E. Rigg, I. S. Lee, R.G. Gregory, A. L. Hassett, J. A. Ledward, F. W. Sides, †B. A. Barnett, M. W. Sievers, D. Ring, E. L. McCormick and L. O'B. Fleetwood-Smith.

First innings: 499 (Gregory 71, Hassett 211 not out, Sides 44, Barnett 50, Ring 51, Fleetwood-Smith 43; Waite three for 123, Ward four for 125). *Second innings:* Seven for 283 dec (Lee 51, Hassett 54, Sides 61, Barnett 54; Ward five for 126).

South Australia

R. S. Whitington lbw b Sievers	100	– not out	27
K. L. Ridings c Lee b Sievers	27	– not out	18
*D. G. Bradman c Hassett b Sievers	107		
C. L. Badcock c and b McCormick	1		
†C. W. Walker b Sievers	14		
F. A. Ward c Barnett b Sievers	62		
R. A. Hamence b Sievers	84		
M. G. Waite lbw b Ring	0		
P. Ridings c and b Ring	33		
C. V. Grimmett st Barnett b Ring	34		
J. Scott not out	4		
B 5, l-b 15, n-b 2	22	B 5	5
	488	(no wkt)	**50**

Victoria bowling: *First innings*—McCormick 22–4–78–1; Sievers 43–11–95–6; Ring 31.1–2–116–3; Fleetwood-Smith 35–4–152–0; Gregory 4–0–25–0. *Second innings*—McCormick

3-1-13-0; Sievers 3-0-9-0; Ring 6-1-8-0; Fleetwood-Smith 3-1-2-0; Gregory 4-3-3-0; Hassett 2-0-10-0.

Umpires: A. N. Barlow and G. A. Browne

QUEENSLAND v SOUTH AUSTRALIA 175 (253)

Played at Brisbane, January 7, 9, 10, 11 [1939]. South Australia won by ten wickets. Bradman, recovered from his indisposition, gave another superlative exhibition in his fifth consecutive century [a record by an Australian batsman]. Ridings and Whitington paved the way for their captain with an opening partnership of 197. The three hundreds for South Australia followed one by Don Tallon who, after his great wicket-keeping feat of the previous match [twelve dismissals, v New South Wales, to equal the world record], showed first-rate ability as a batsman. ...

Queensland

*W. A. Brown, G.G. Cook, T. Allen, R. Rogers, †D. Tallon, C. Stibe, G. Baker, W. Tallon, P. L. Dixon, J. Ellis and C. Christ.

First innings: 336 (D. Tallon 115, Stibe 58, Baker 78; Cotton five for 49). *Second innings:* 233 (Brown 81, Rogers 45, W. Tallon 40 not out; Ridings four for 26).

South Australia

K. L. Ridings b Ellis	122	–	not out	10
R. S. Whitington c D. Tallon b W. Tallon	125			
*D. G. Bradman c Christ b W. Tallon	186			
C. L. Badcock c Rogers b Christ	1	–	not out	4
R. A. Hamence c Stibe b Christ	13			
E. J. R. Moyle c Brown b Cook	46			
†C. W. Walker c and b W. Tallon	20			
F. A. Ward b Ellis	18			
H. J. Cotton st Brown b W. Tallon	2			
J. Scott not out	5			
M. W. Waite absent ill	0			
B 3, l-b 9, w 5, n-b 2	19			
	557		(no wkt)	**14**

Queensland bowling: *First innings*—Ellis 32.7-1-126-2; Cook 25-0-101-1; Dixon 19-2-93-0; Christ 43-9-110-2; W. Tallon 20-2-80-4; Allen 1-0-4-0; Baker 3-0-24-0. *Second innings*—Baker 1-1-0-0; Stibe 1-0-9-0; Rogers 0.7-0-5-0.

Umpires: K. Fagg and F. J. Bartlett

NEW SOUTH WALES v SOUTH AUSTRALIA 176 (254)

Played at Sydney, January 14, 16, 17, 18 [1939]. Drawn. Bradman held the stage and, after having to wait during two idle days caused by rain, he completed his sixth successive century, so equalling the world record held by C. B. Fry. [Including Bradman's two hundreds at the end of the 1937-38 season, this was his eighth successive hundred in matches in Australia.] Grimmett, fit again, helped most in the cheap dismissal of New South Wales on the first day and Bradman was 22 not out when stumps were drawn with South Australia 116 for two. The weather prevented a resumption until the last morning, when Bradman proceeded unperturbed but cautiously. He hit only seven 4's in an innings lasting five hours twenty minutes. He and Badcock put on 186. ... [Moyle kept wicket for South Australia in New South Wales' second innings, Bradman having kept in the first innings.]

New South Wales

A.G. Cheetham, B. McCauley, S.G. Barnes, *A.G. Chipperfield, C.M. Solomon, C. Pepper, V. McCaffrey, R. James, L. C. Hynes, †S. Sismey and J. L. O'Brien.

First innings: 246 (Solomon 34, James 45, Hynes 63 not out; Cotton three for 44, Grimmett four for 53). *Second innings:* Five for 156 (McCauley 76, Barnes 33).

South Australia

K. L. Ridings lbw b Cheetham	28	C. L. Badcock c and b Hynes	98
R. S. Whitington lbw b Barnes	59	B 1, l-b 2, n-b 8	11
*†D. G. Bradman not out	135	(four wkts dec)	**349**
F. A. Ward c O'Brien b Hynes	18		

E. J. R. Moyle, P. Ridings, M. G. Waite, H. J. Cotton, C. V. Grimmett and R. A. Hamence did not bat.

New South Wales bowling: O'Brien 15–0–76–0; Hynes 16.3–0–86–2; Cheetham 23–0–104–1; Pepper 7–0–47–0; Barnes 8–2–25–1.

Umpires: G. Borwick and F. Lyons

SOUTH AUSTRALIA v VICTORIA 177 (255)

Played at Adelaide, February 24, 25, 27, 28 [1939]. Drawn. A catch by Fleetwood-Smith robbed Bradman of the chance of making fresh history, but rain probably deprived Victoria of the Shield and gave the trophy to their opponents. Hassett scored another century for Victoria [his fourth of the season] and on the second day [17,777] spectators assembled to see Bradman attempt to increase the sequence of his centuries to seven. They were disappointed, Thorn taking his wicket for five. ... The loss of the last two days through rain was cruel luck for Victoria, who needed only a win on the first innings to gain the championship.

Victoria

*K.E. Rigg, I.S. Lee, R.G. Gregory, A.L. Hassett, F.W. Sides, G. Tamblyn, †B.A. Barnett, R.B. Scott, E.L. McCormick, F. Thorn and L. O'B. Fleetwood-Smith.

First innings: 321 (Rigg 78, Gregory 33, Hassett 102, Barnett 51; Ward four for 57).

South Australia

R. S. Whitington b Scott	18	P. L. Ridings lbw b McCormick	12
K. L. Ridings lbw b Thorn	14	†J. A. J. Horsell lbw b Fleetwood-Smith	29
*D. G. Bradman c Fleetwood-Smith b Thorn	5	F. A. Ward not out	2
C. L. Badcock c Lee b Scott	14	B 6, l-b 2, n-b 7	15
R. A. Hamence lbw b Fleetwood-Smith	35	(seven wkts)	**207**
M. G. Waite not out	63		

C. V. Grimmett and H. J. Cotton did not bat.

Victoria bowling: McCormick 16–2–45–1; Scott 15–1–49–2; Thorn 16–2–51–2; Fleetwood-Smith 14–1–34–2; Gregory 2–0–13–0.

Umpires: J. D. Scott and A.G. Jenkins

1939-40

1939-40

The outbreak of war in September 1939 cast a shadow over the Australian season then in prospect, but at the express wish of high Government officials the Sheffield Shield tournament was played to a finish. This effort to sustain the morale of the people, by taking their thoughts away from the serious international happenings for a few hours in the peaceful surroundings of the cricket field, earned so much public appreciation that crowds reached quite remarkable dimensions. The three home matches of New South Wales attracted aggregate attendances of 144,808, with receipts £9,115 9*s.* 9*d.* The gate for the match against South Australia totalled 75,765, with takings £4,915 1*s.* 6*d.* – figures which set up new records for Sheffield Shield matches at Sydney. Games in other States also were well patronised.

Cricket was particularly keen, the destination of the Shield not being settled until the last match of the series. The fortunes of the States underwent a dramatic change in the second half of the season. South Australia, having won their three matches at Adelaide, commenced their Eastern tour justifiably confident of retaining the Shield; but New South Wales, after early reverses, recovered splendidly and in an exciting finish to the competition deprived the holders of the trophy. Victoria, close contenders until the last, were placed third, and Queensland finished fourth. . . .

O'Reilly's prominence as a bowler [he took 52 wickets for New South Wales in Shield matches at 13.55 runs apiece] was equalled, if not excelled, by the mastery of Don Bradman as leading batsman in the competition. The South Australia captain enjoyed another wonderful season, and for the first time in a Sheffield Shield season scored over 1,000 runs. His aggregate was 1,062, and his average 132.75, with 267 against Victoria at Melbourne and 251 and 90, both not out, v New South Wales at Adelaide the principal performances. Against Queensland, at Adelaide, Bradman scored 138, and outside Shield games he put together innings of 209 not out and 135 in two matches with Western Australia at Perth. Altogether in first-class cricket Bradman scored 1,475 runs for an average of 122.91, figures which render comment on the standard of his play superfluous.

From 'Cricket in Australia: Inter-State Matches, 1939-40'

SOUTH AUSTRALIA v VICTORIA 178 (256, 257)

At Adelaide, November 17, 18, 20, 21 [1939]. South Australia won by three wickets. The Shield holders showed a little superiority in batting over their opponents, who, however, did quite well after losing three men for 18 runs. ... South Australia, who began just as badly, gained a lead of 54, thanks to a century partnership between Bradman and Klose. Bradman, for the first time for many years [since December 1929, in fact], was run out. ... South Australia found themselves needing 310 to win, and it was just as well that Bradman was again in scoring vein. He stood firm, after early setbacks to his colleagues, and with Hamence hitting hard in an innings which fell one short of a hundred, the home State achieved their task.

Victoria

I. S. Lee, G. E. Tamblyn, A. L. Hassett, K. R. Miller, I. W. Johnson, D. Fothergill, *†B. A. Barnett, M. W. Sievers, D. T. Ring, R. B. Scott and L. O'B. Fleetwood-Smith.

First innings: 207 (Tamblyn 67, Johnson 33, Barnett 51; Cotton three for 78, Grimmett three for 67). *Second innings:* 363 (Lee 68, Hassett 89, Johnson 41, Sievers 56, Ring 31; Waite three for 76, Grimmett five for 118).

South Australia

R. S. Whitington c Fleetwood-Smith b Scott	0	–	b Fleetwood-Smith	27
K. L. Ridings c Sievers b Scott	6	–	c Ring b Sievers	1
*D. G. Bradman run out	76	–	lbw b Ring	64
R. A. Hamence lbw b Scott	6	–	c Sievers b Ring	99
C. L. Badcock lbw b Fleetwood-Smith	3	–	c Barnett b Scott	30
T. Klose c Hassett b Ring	80	–	lbw b Ring	0
F. A. Ward lbw b Fleetwood-Smith	1	–	not out	1
M. G. Waite c Miller b Sievers	67	–	not out	42
†C. W. Walker c and b Ring	4	–	b Ring	20
C. V. Grimmett c Sievers b Ring	9			
H. J. Cotton not out	1			
B 1, l-b 1, n-b 6	8		B 17, l-b 6, w 2, n-b 1	26
	261		(seven wkts)	**310**

Victoria bowling: *First innings*—Scott 11–0–55–3; Sievers 17–4–63–1; Fleetwood-Smith 14–0–59–2; Ring 18.4–1–76–3. *Second innings*—Scott 14–0–50–1; Sievers 14–3–40–1; Fleetwood-Smith 16–0–78–1; Ring 26–2–104–4; Johnson 4.7–0–12–0.

Umpires: J. D. Scott and A.G. Jenkins

SOUTH AUSTRALIA v NEW SOUTH WALES 179 (258, 259)

At Adelaide, December 15, 16, 18 [1939]. South Australia won by seven wickets. The superb batting of Bradman, who scored 341 without being dismissed, overshadowed everything else in a remarkable match. In his first innings of 251, scored at one run a minute, he included every possible stroke, and bowlers, with the exception of O'Reilly, were helpless. Bradman, who hit thirty-eight 4's and two 6's, often scored three times as fast as his partners, of whom Waite gave valuable support in a stand of 147. When South Australia wanted 155 for victory, Bradman dominated the cricket to such a degree that he almost reached three figures before the winning hit was made....

New South Wales

S.J. McCabe, *J. H. Fingleton, S.G. Barnes, C. M. Solomon, A.G. Chipperfield, A.G. Cheetham, C. Pepper, A. Roper, W. J. O'Reilly, †S. Sismey and J. Walsh.

First innings: 336 (McCabe 40, Solomon 131, Chipperfield 32, Cheetham 32; Grimmett three for 102, Klose four for 23). *Second innings:* 248 (McCabe 47, Barnes 33, Solomon 46, Chipperfield 57, Pepper 47; Grimmett six for 122).

South Australia

R. S. Whitington c Sismey b Roper	6			
K. L. Riding c Sismey b Walsh	29	–	b Cheetham	20
*D. G. Bradman not out	251	–	not out	90
R. A. Hamence lbw b Pepper	41	–	lbw b Pepper	12
M. G. Waite b Cheetham	46	–	not out	28
T. Klose c and b O'Reilly	4	–	b Roper	2
J. E. Tregoning b O'Reilly	0			
†C. W. Walker b O'Reilly	1			
F. A. Ward b O'Reilly	4			
C. V. Grimmett b O'Reilly	17			
H. J. Cotton absent hurt	0			
B 21, l-b 4, n-b 6	31		B 1, l-b 3	4
	430		(three wkts)	**156**

New South Wales bowling: *First innings*—Roper 14–0–83–1; Cheetham 15–1–80–1; O'Reilly 22.1–4–108–5; Pepper 9–0–56–1; Walsh 12–0–72–1. *Second innings*—Roper 3–0–26–1; Cheetham 7–0–33–1; O'Reilly 10–0–29–0; Pepper 8–0–31–1; Walsh 2.2–0–33–0.

Umpires: J. D. Scott and A.G. Jenkins. H. C. Newman last two days (Jenkins ill)

SOUTH AUSTRALIA v QUEENSLAND 180 (260)

At Adelaide, December 22, 23, 25, 26 [1939]. South Australia won by an innings and 222 runs. The power of their batsmen and the cunning bowling of Grimmett and Ward gave them overwhelming success. K. L. Ridings, Bradman, Badcock and Waite all reached three figures in helping to set up a record score for the Adelaide Oval. Ridings, a strong driver, shared with his captain in a second-wicket stand of 196. . . .

South Australia

K. L. Ridings lbw b Baker	151	M. G. Waite c and b Dixon	137
T. Klose c Ellis b Cook	13	R. S. Whitington c Rogers b Christ	6
*D. G. Bradman c Hansen b Ellis	138	P. L. Ridings not out	44
R. A. Hamence lbw b Cook	6	B 10, l-b 17, n-b 2	29
C. L. Badcock b Dixon	236	(seven wkts dec)	**821**

C. V. Grimmett, F. A. Ward and †C. W. Walker did not bat.

Queensland bowling: Ellis 14–0–95–1; Cook 22–1–129–2; Dixon 24–0–142–2; Christ 27.1–3–144–1; Baker 22–0–127–1; Watt 14–1–135–0; Rogers 4–1–20–0.

Queensland

*W. A. Brown, G.G. Cook, T. Allen, R. Rogers, G. Baker, †D. Tallon, D. Hansen, D. Watt, C. Christ, P. L. Dixon and J. Ellis.

First innings: 222 (Allen 35, Rogers 49, Tallon 70; Grimmett four for 71, Ward five for 62). *Second innings:* 377 (Brown 156, Rogers 50, Baker 52; Grimmett six for 124, Ward four for 165).

Umpires: J. D. Scott and H. C. Newman

VICTORIA v SOUTH AUSTRALIA 181 (261)

At Melbourne, December 29, 30 [1939], January 1, 2 [1940]. Drawn. Insufficient time prevented South Australia hitting off the runs needed for victory. Another great innings by Bradman eclipsed everything else in the match. Ridings and Klose took the edge off the bowling in an opening stand of 108, and then their captain scored as he pleased. He used all the strokes in a masterly display which brought him 267 runs, including twenty-seven 4's, before Fleetwood-Smith, who received heavy punishment, took his wicket. ... [In their second innings] South Australia were set 179 to get. They were 118 behind with nine wickets left when the game ended.

Victoria

I. S. Lee, G. E. Tamblyn, A. L. Hassett, K. R. Miller, I. W. Johnson, P. J. Beames, *†B. A. Barnett, M. W. Sievers, D. T. Ring, R. B. Scott and L. O'B. Fleetwood-Smith.

First innings: 475 (Lee 36, Tamblyn 38, Hassett 92, Miller 108, Beames 104, Ring 32; Burton five for 99). *Second innings:* 313 (Lee 39, Hassett 66, Beames 32, Barnett 46, Sievers 36, Ring 41 not out; Klose three for 43, Ward three for 102).

South Australia

K. L. Ridings c Johnson b Ring	56	–	not out	29
T. Klose b Scott	54	–	lbw b Ring	15
*D. G. Bradman c Johnson b Fleetwood-Smith	267			
C. L. Badcock lbw b Ring	58			
R. A. Hamence lbw b Fleetwood-Smith	20	–	not out	11
R. S. Whitington c Ring b Scott	41			
†C. W. Walker lbw b Scott	1			
M. G. Waite c Hassett b Ring	64			
F. A. Ward c and b Ring	26			
C. V. Grimmett c Sievers b Ring	6			
G. Burton not out	1			
B 6, l-b 9, w 1	16		B 3, l-b 1, n-b 1	5
	610		(one wkt)	**60**

Victoria bowling: *First innings*—Scott 25–0–135–3; Sievers 29–1–120–0; Ring 25.4–1–123–5; Fleetwood-Smith 27–0–156–2; Johnson 13–0–60–0. *Second innings*—Scott 3–0–9–0; Sievers 3–0–12–0; Ring 4–1–13–1; Johnson 5–2–14–0; Hassett 1–0–7–0.

Umpires: W. J. Craddock and A. N. Barlow

QUEENSLAND v SOUTH AUSTRALIA 182 (262, 263)

At Brisbane, January 6, 8, 9, 10 [1940]. Queensland won by two wickets. Following four successive defeats, their victory over the unbeaten South Australians was the sensation of the season. Victory was achieved after a first innings deficit of nearly 100. The introduction of Stackpoole, a fast bowler, played a big part in the surprising result. Stackpoole used pace which troubled everyone, including Bradman, who fell early in the match without scoring ... Grimmett took his 500th wicket in Shield cricket when beating Cook, and in keeping with Waite upset Queensland. Then, with Bradman finding his form in the second innings, South Australia left Queensland 350 to get ... despite a spell when Grimmett took three wickets for four runs, the triumph was completed in an unfinished ninth-wicket stand.

South Australia

K. Ridings c Tallon b Stackpoole	35	–	b Stackpoole	1
T. Klose c Tallon b Stackpoole	27	–	st Tallon c Christ	31
*D. G. Bradman c Dixon b Stackpoole	0	–	c Tallon b Cook	97
R. S. Whitington b Gooma	38	–	b Stackpoole	0
R. A. Hamence c Stackpoole b Christ	26	–	c Brown b Christ	2
M. G. Waite c Christ b Stackpoole	13	–	b Dixon	62
E. J. R. Moyle b Stackpoole	32	–	b Dixon	6
†C. W. Walker b Stackpoole	37	–	b Christ	18
F. A. Ward c Tallon b Dixon	4	–	c Baker b Stackpoole	15
C. V. Grimmett b Dixon	12	–	not out	5
G. Burton not out	2	–	b Dixon	11
L-b 2, n-b 2	4		B 1, l-b 2, w 1	4
	230			**252**

Queensland bowling: *First innings*—Stackpoole 18.1–0–72–6; Cook 11–1–35–0; Dixon 16–5–33–2; Gooma 6–0–27–1; Christ 16–3–53–1; Baker 2–0–6–0. *Second innings*—Stackpoole 14–1–66–3; Cook 8–1–32–1; Dixon 10.3–2–33–3; Gooma 5–0–27–0; Christ 25–2–87–3; Baker 2–1–3–0.

Queensland

*W. A. Brown, G.G. Cook, R. Rogers, G. Baker, †D. Tallon, D. Watt, C. Bryce, G. Gooma, C. Christ, P. L. Dixon and J. Stackpoole.

First innings: 133 (Brown 37, Tallon 41; Waite three for 25, Grimmett four for 52). *Second innings:* Eight for 350 (Brown 111, Cook 54, Rogers 74, Watt 59 not out; Grimmett three for 116).

Umpires: S. Ryan and D. Given

NEW SOUTH WALES v SOUTH AUSTRALIA 183 (264, 265)

At Sydney, January 13, 15, 16, 17 [1940]. New South Wales won by 237 runs. By this magnificent performance they took a big step towards winning the Shield and at the same time practically extinguished their opponents' hope of retaining the trophy. The craft of Grimmett and the skill behind the stumps of Walker kept the New South Wales batsmen in check ... [However] O'Reilly also found the conditions suitable for spin, and, with Bradman dismissed cheaply, South Australia finished 59 behind. Grimmett again bowled cleverly in the home side's second innings, but excellent batting ... enabled New South Wales to set the visitors to get 371 for victory. Pepper and O'Reilly soon settled the issue. Including that of Bradman, caught by Carmody, a substitute, the fourth, fifth and sixth wickets fell at 85, and the end came quickly.

New South Wales

H. Mudge, M. B. Cohen, *S. J. McCabe, S.G. Barnes, A.G. Chipperfield, R. Saggers, A.G. Cheetham, C. Pepper, J.G. Lush, W. J. O'Reilly and †S. Sismey.

First innings: 270 (Cohen 74, McCabe 59, Barnes 34, Saggers 45; Grimmett six for 118, Klose three for 21). *Second innings:* 311 (Mudge 57, Cohen 70, McCabe 55, Saggers 57; Grimmett five for 111, Ward four for 120).

South Australia

K. L. Ridings b Lush	3	–	b Cheetham	1
T. Klose c Sismey b Lush	0	–	b Pepper	13
R. S. Whitington c Barnes b O'Reilly	37	–	c Chipperfield b Pepper	11
*D. G. Bradman lbw b O'Reilly	39	–	c sub b Pepper	40
C. L. Badcock c Mudge b O'Reilly	40	–	c Chipperfield b O'Reilly	20
R. A. Hamence c Mudge b O'Reilly	43	–	c Cohen b O'Reilly	0
M. G. Waite run out	9	–	c Mudge b Pepper	19
†C. W. Walker lbw b O'Reilly	1	–	c McCabe b Pepper	10
F. A. Ward b Pepper	17	–	b O'Reilly	1
C. V. Grimmett not out	7	–	b O'Reilly	6
G. Burton c McCabe b O'Reilly	7	–	not out	11
B 5, l-b 2, w 1	8		N-b 1	1
	211			**133**

New South Wales bowling: *First innings*—Lush 8–0–26–2; Cohen 5–2–9–0; O'Reilly 24.5–7–77–6; Pepper 27–3–85–1; Mudge 1–0–6–0. *Second innings*—Lush 4–0–13–0; O'Reilly 13.7–2–62–4; Pepper 12–1–49–5; Cheetham 5–1–8–1.

Umpires: G. Borwick and R. McGrath

WESTERN AUSTRALIA v SOUTH AUSTRALIA 184 (266, 267)

At Perth, February 10, 12, 13 [1940]. Drawn. Western Australia, who showed creditable form, found Bradman in brilliant mood. He was out just when seeming set in the first innings, but in the second he gave no chance in a great display. Driving, cutting, pulling and glancing, he was never at a loss for a stroke and put together a faultless double-century which occupied him little more than two and a half hours and included thirty 4's besides a 6. ... Western Australia, with seven wickets in hand, were 158 behind when the game was given up.

South Australia

K. Ridings c Bandy b Halcombe	46			
T. Klose b MacGill	6			
R. A. Hamence c Lovelock b Eyres	3	–	b Eyres	14
*D. G. Bradman c Lovelock b MacGill	32	–	not out	209
L. Michael c Eyres b MacGill	5	–	not out	27
M. G. Waite lbw b MacGill	37			
V. R. Gibson c A. Jeffreys b Zimbulis	35			
J. Kierse c A. Jeffreys b Watt	23			
F. A. Ward c K. Jeffreys b Halcombe	15	–	b Eyres	12
C. V. Grimmett c Inverarity b Zimbulis	14			
†C. W. Walker not out	2	–	c Inverarity b Zimbulis	34
B 16, l-b 2, w 1, n-b 1	20		B 9, l-b 1	10
	248		(three wkts dec)	**306**

Western Australia bowling: *First innings*—Eyres 22–1–81–1; MacGill 18–1–49–4; Halcombe 13–0–51–2; Zimbulis 9–0–36–2; Watt 3–1–6–1; Barras 2–1–5–0. *Second innings*—Eyres 16–2–65–2; MacGill 15–3–66–0; Halcombe 9–0–59–0; Zimbulis 5–0–50–1; Barras 4–0–28–0; K. Jeffreys 2–0–28–0.

Western Australia

C. MacGill, A. Jeffreys, D. Watt, A. Barras, L. Bandy, K. Jeffreys, *M. Inverarity, †O. Lovelock, A. Zimbulis, G. Eyres and R. Halcombe.

First innings: 275 (MacGill 78, A. Jeffreys 36, Inverarity 57, Zimbulis 42 not out; Grimmett three for 94, Ward six for 105). *Second innings:* Three for 121 (Watt 52).

Umpires: J. P. Robbins and M. J. Troy

WESTERN AUSTRALIA v SOUTH AUSTRALIA 185 (268)

At Perth, February 16, 17, 19 [1940], Drawn. Western Australia again gave a commendable exhibition, and received further object lessons in batting and bowling from Bradman and Grimmett. ... The Western Australian bowlers worked hard, but were allowed little encouragement. Klose and Ridings took the sting out of the attack and then Bradman scored easily all round the wicket in making 135. ...

Western Australia

C. MacGill, A. Read, D. Watt, A. Barras, *M. Inverarity, K. Jeffreys, L. Bandy, †O. Lovelock, A. Zimbulis, C. Puckett and G. Eyres.

First innings: 275 (Read 55, Inverarity 52, Bandy 30, Lovelock 45, Zimbulis 33; Grimmett five for 67). *Second innings:* 206 (Read 46, Eyres 39; Grimmett six for 57, Ward three for 81).

South Australia

K. L. Ridings c Barras b Zimbulis	34
T. Klose c Zimbulis b Eyres	60
*D. G. Bradman c Zimbulis b Eyres	135
R. A. Hamence run out	63
L. Michael c and b Zimbulis	10
F. Teisseire b MacGill	56
M. G. Waite c Eyres b Zimbulis	24
V. R. Gibson c and b Puckett	21
†C. W. Walker b Puckett	3
F. A. Ward run out	8
C. V. Grimmett not out	5
B 4, l-b 6	10
	429

Western Australia bowling: Eyres 23–3–79–2; MacGill 22–3–108–1; Puckett 24–4–89–2; Zimbulis 22–0–131–3; Bandy 1–0–12–0.

Umpires: J. P. Robbins and M. J. Troy

NEW SOUTH WALES v THE REST 186 (269, 270)
PATRIOTIC MATCH

At Sydney, March 8, 9, 11 [1940]. New South Wales won by two wickets. The match, which realised £1,471 15*s.* 9*d.* for patriotic funds [servicemen in uniform were admitted for half-price], produced grand batting displays by Hassett and McCabe, and some splendid bowling by Grimmett. ...

Rest of Australia

I. S. Lee c and b Cheetham	0	–	c Saggers b Cheetham	14
W. A. Brown c Saggers b Pepper	35	–	run out	97
*D. G. Bradman c Saggers b O'Reilly	25	–	c McCool b Cheetham	2
A. L. Hassett c Mudge b Cheetham	136	–	b Pepper	75
R. Rogers c O'Reilly b Lush	25	–	c and b McCool	17
M. G. Waite c McCabe b O'Reilly	5	–	c O'Reilly b Cohen	12
I. W. Johnson b Pepper	12	–	c McCool b Cheetham	8
†D. Tallon b Pepper	0	–	c and b Cohen	8
D. T. Ring c Mudge b O'Reilly	2	–	c McCool b Cohen	14
C. V. Grimmett c McCabe b Cheetham	27	–	c McCool b Cohen	0
R. Barry-Scott not out	13	–	not out	2
Extras	9		Extras	3
	289			**252**

New South Wales bowling: *First innings*—Lush 6–0–34–1; Cheetham 9–2–41–3; O'Reilly 18–4–78–3; Pepper 17–1–102–3; Cohen 2–0–25–0. *Second innings*—Cheetham 11–0–43–3; O'Reilly 8–0–49–0; Pepper 14–0–81–1; Cohen 7.7–1–25–4; McCool 9–1–51–1.

New South Wales

M. Cohen, H. Mudge, S.G. Barnes, *S.J. McCabe, C.M. Solomon, †R. Saggers, A.G. Cheetham, C. McCool, C. Pepper, J.G. Lush and W.J. O'Reilly.

First innings: 219 (McCabe 72, Cheetham 58; Waite three for 12, Grimmett five for 65). *Second innings:* Eight for 323 (Cohen 67, Barnes 46, McCabe 96, Saggers 32; Grimmett five for 130).

Umpires: G. Borwick and R. McGrath

1940–46

1940-41

Ten inter-State matches, and a game between teams captained by D.G. Bradman and S.J. McCabe, took the place of the Sheffield Shield tournament in the second war-time season in Australia. . . .

D.G. Bradman, an Army lieutenant, played in only one match for South Australia, and his inability to turn out regularly had its effect on the side. Short of practice, Bradman failed in both innings against Victoria at Adelaide and on his other appearance against McCabe's team. Twice he was out first ball!

From 'Cricket in Australia 1940-41'

In Australia, inter-State matches have been played for charity. Don Bradman enlisted in the Australian Royal Air Force, but later was transferred to the Army School of Physical and Recreational Training. On Christmas Day 1940 he was bowled out first ball in a match at Adelaide. We have not found that secret.

From 'Notes on the 1940 Season', by R. C. Robertson-Glasgow, *Wisden 1941*

SOUTH AUSTRALIA v VICTORIA 187 (271, 272)

At Adelaide, December 25, 26, 27, 28 [1940]. South Australia won by 175 runs. Bradman, given special Army leave to play, failed in both innings. On the opening day he was out first ball [the third ball of the innings], and Sievers, who made the catch, enjoyed the satisfaction of bowling Bradman cheaply in the second innings. . . .

South Australia

K. Ridings run out	0	–	c Hassett b Seivers	17
C. L. Badcock c Sievers b Dempster	25	–	c Dudley b Sievers	172
*D. G. Bradman c Sievers b Dudley	0	–	b Sievers	6
R. A. Hamence c Baker b Dudley	85	–	c Baker b Dempster	62
B. H. Leak c Ring b Sievers	12	–	b Dudley	6
M. G. Waite lbw b Sievers	2	–	c Johnson b Dempster	20
P. Ridings lbw b Ring	2	–	lbw b Ring	90
†C. W. Walker c Baker b Johnson	40	–	c Meikle b Ring	4
C. V. Grimmett run out	2	–	c and b Johnson	31
F. A. Ward c Hassett b Sievers	10	–	c Baker b Dempster	4
H. J. Cotton not out	9	–	not out	2
Extras	4		Extras	7
	191			**421**

Victoria bowling: *First innings*—Dudley 7–0–34–2; Sievers 11.4–1–45–3; Ring 9–1–32–1; Johnson 3–0–8–1; Dempster 6–0–21–1; Meikle 8–0–47–0. *Second innings*—Dudley 11–2–38–1; Sievers 25–1–104–3; Ring 11–0–67–2; Johnson 8–0–66–1; Dempster 15–1–66–3; Meikle 4–0–26–0; Fothergill 6–0–40–0; Hassett 1–0–7–0.

Victoria

I.S. Lee, G. Tamblyn, D.T. Ring, R. Dempster, *A.L. Hassett, D. Fothergill, M.W. Sievers, G. Meikle, I.W. Johnson, †E.A. Baker and W. Dudley.

First innings: 172 (Ring 72; Cotton four for 39, Grimmett three for 54). *Second innings:* 265 (Hassett 113, Sievers 31; Grimmett four for 75, Ward three for 86).

Umpires: J.D. Scott and L.A. Smith

D.G. BRADMAN'S TEAM v S.J. McCABE'S TEAM 188 (273, 274)

At Melbourne, January 1, 2, 3, 4 [1941]. McCabe's Team won by an innings and 103 runs. The failure of Bradman, apparently out of practice, proved a great disappointment for the crowd. For the second match in succession he was out first ball. A mistimed stroke to backward-point cost him his wicket in the first innings and he played on in the second before he could settle down.... Bradman's side, following on 244 behind, struggled on a rain-damaged wicket which O'Reilly and Grimmett fully exploited.

S.J. McCabe's Team

I.S. Lee, C.L. Badcock, S.G. Barnes, R. Rogers, *S.J. McCabe, †D. Tallon, K.R. Miller, M.W. Sievers, C.V. Grimmett, W.J. O'Reilly and J. Ellis.

First innings: Nine for 449 dec (Badcock 105, Barnes 137, Sievers 55 not out, sundries 36; Waite three for 84).

D.G. Bradman's Team

W. A. Brown c O'Reilly b Ellis	13	–	c Barnes b O'Reilly	16
K. Ridings lbw b Ellis	50	–	c Tallon b Miller	5
*D. G. Bradman c sub b Ellis	0	–	b O'Reilly	12
R. A. Hamence c Lee b O'Reilly	73	–	st Tallon b Grimmett	35
A. L. Hassett c Rogers b Grimmett	31	–	c Ellis b Grimmett	20
†R. Saggers not out	13	–	lbw b Grimmett	5
M. G. Waite c Miller b O'Reilly	15	–	c Barnes b O'Reilly	18
V. Jackson lbw b O'Reilly	0	–	c sub b Grimmett	14
C. Pepper c Badcock b O'Reilly	1	–	lbw b O'Reilly	10
R. B. Scott st Tallon b Grimmett	1	–	lbw b O'Reilly	0
V. Trumper lbw b Grimmett	0	–	not out	1
Extras	8		Extras	5
	205			**141**

S. J. McCabe's Team bowling: *First innings*—Ellis 10–2–23–3; McCabe 5–1–10–0; O'Reilly 14–2–41–4; Grimmett 22–1–100–3; Barnes 5–0–23–0. *Second innings*—Ellis 4–0–13–0; O'Reilly 10–1–53–5; Grimmett 8–0–46–4; Miller 6–0–24–1.

Umpires: A.N. Barlow and W.J. Craddock

1941–1945

Only one match in the 1941-42 Australian Inter-State Patriotic Competition took place before the war situation caused the abandonment of the tournament, Queensland beating New South Wales by 19 runs at Brisbane at the end of November. …

From: 'Cricket in Australia: Inter-State Patriotic Competition, 1941-42'

Three two-day representative games at Christmas provided Australian enthusiasts with the first important cricket since Japan entered the war. Sponsored by the Services, the matches, which were played at Adelaide, Melbourne and Sydney, yielded excellent entertainment, and the public showed their appreciation of the opportunity to welcome back noted players now in uniform. Bradman, convalescing after fibrositis of the back muscles which caused his discharge from the Army in May 1941, did not play cricket, although he enjoyed some golf and tennis. …

From 'Cricket in Australia 1942-43'

AN AUSTRALIAN APPRECIATION

By Don Bradman

Sent by Airgraph from Adelaide, November 23 [1943]

The present war has already taken heavy toll of gallant men who, after faithfully serving their countries on the cricket field in peace-time, have laid down their lives for a greater cause. Of those who have fallen, Hedley Verity was perhaps the most illustrious, and from the Dominion of Australia I feel it my sad duty to join with cricketers of the Motherland in expressing sorrow that we shall not again see him on our playing fields.

It could truthfully be claimed that Hedley Verity was one of the greatest if not THE greatest left-hand bowler of all time. Most certainly he could lay just claim to that honour during the 1918-1939 period. No doubt his Yorkshire environment was of great assistance for left-hand bowling seems to be in the blood of Yorkshiremen. It is one of their traditions and inalienable rights to possess the secrets of the art.

Although not a young man from a cricketing standpoint when the call came, Verity was little if any beyond the zenith of his powers. He was always such a keen student of the game, and his bowling was of such a type, that brains and experience played perhaps a greater part in his success than natural genius.

Although opposed to him in many Tests, I could never claim to have completely fathomed his strategy, for it was never static nor mechanical.

Naturally he achieved his most notable successes when wickets were damp. Nobody privileged to witness that famous Test at Lord's in 1934 (least of all the Australian batsmen) will forget a performance to which even the statistics could not do justice. But it would be ungenerous to suggest that he needed assistance from the wicket, as his successful Australian tours will confirm. The ordinary left-hander who lacks the vicious unorthodox finger-spin of the Fleetwood-Smith variety, needs uncommon ability to achieve even moderate success in Australia, yet Verity was the foundation stone of England's bowling in both countries during his era.

Apart from his special department of the game, Verity could also claim to be a remarkably efficient fieldsman close to the wicket where safe hands and courage are greater attributes than agility. Add this to the fact that once he opened a Test Match innings for England, not without success, and we have a fairly general picture of a really fine player.

Those of us who played against this swarthy, capless champion (I never remember having seen him wear a cap) probably appreciated his indomitable fighting spirit even more than his own colleagues. We knew, when war came, that he would plainly see his duty in the same way as he regarded it his duty to win cricket matches for Yorkshire no less than England.

During our association together I cannot recall having heard Verity utter a word of complaint or criticism. If reports of his final sacrifice be correct, and I believe they are, he maintained this example right to the end.

His life, his skill, his service all merited the highest honour, and with great sorrow I unhesitatingly pay humble tribute to his memory.

[Captain Hedley Verity, the Green Howards, died a prisoner of war in Italy of wounds received in the Eighth Army's first attack on the German positions at Catania, in Sicily. He had been reported wounded and missing, and the news of his death, on July 31, 1943, was received on September 1, exactly four years after he had played his last match for Yorkshire and, at Hove, taken seven Sussex wickets for nine runs in one innings. Sir Donald Bradman's tribute appeared in the 1944 *Wisden* as part of a full obituary article by R. C. Robertson-Glasgow.]

Thus the present gives us little indication as to the future, except that there is every probability that batting gaps will be filled adequately – apart, of course, from Bradman. … Bradman has not played cricket for a few years, and is not, I think, a prospect for the next tour. His back trouble, which caused his discharge from the Army, was symptomatic of a general breakdown in health, the result no doubt of extraordinary cricketing efforts, which so strained his nervous system and depleted his physical resources that his medical adviser forbade him to take part in strenuous activities, ordering complete rest.

At the same time, it can now be disclosed that he would not have toured England again as captain had there been no war. He told me this during our trip home in 1938, and no argument could move him. Even then, he was feeling the strain of making both centuries and speeches, and he was most definite that he would not be capable again of representing his country in such a capacity, either to his own satisfaction or in the manner expected of him.

Thus we must face the position that the greatest run-getter and amazing box-office attraction probably has made his last appearance on the Test Match stage. Cricket did much for Bradman, but he did much for cricket, and his going leaves a gap that will not easily be filled.

Whether he will play again for his club or State is a matter which cannot be determined now. Bradman himself does not feel that it is a time to talk of his cricketing future while the nation is fighting a 'life and death' war. He is, however, generally better in health though occasional setbacks are a worry. Evidently when he talked in 1938 of the future, he felt doubts about his health; doubts which would appear justified by events.

My mind goes back to 1926, when the [New South Wales] Selection Committee, of which I was a member, brought him to Sydney for a trial. He came to my office. I opened the door and a lad said: 'Are you Mr Moyes? I'm Don Bradman!' Twelve years later I listened to this country lad make speeches in England that were surely among the finest ever made by a cricketer. I saw him lead Australia; make centuries by the dozen, but the picture that remains is that of the lad who said so quietly: 'I'm Don Bradman.'

To me he has never changed. I believe that no one received more of his confidence in matters of cricket, and he was always the sportsman. Bradman was subjected to criticisms; that is inevitable with anyone who is great, but for the most part they were conceived in jealousy and nurtured in ignorance. Donald George Bradman was in the highest degree a 'cricketer'.

From 'Australian Survey: Bradman – Past, Present and Future',
by Lieut. Col. A.G. Moyes, *Wisden 1945*

To those who seek to excuse laggard running [between the wickets] by the claim that it conserves a batsman's energy during a long innings I would quote the example of Bradman. He played long innings more consistently than any other batsman. Yet throughout them, in Test and lesser matches alike, he was an unsparing runner. His exceptional judgment, allied to speed between the wickets, gave him many runs which would have been missed by most other players. He … made the most of his own and his partner's strokes.

From 'Seeing Cricket After Four Years', by E. M. Wellings, *Wisden 1945*

1945-46

To many cricketers returning from various theatres of war, Australia's first post-war season presented early opportunity for inclusion in State sides alongside men of long experience. Although there were no Sheffield Shield matches, rivalry on the field was never lacking. The Australian Services, after their programme in England and India, kept together as a team and met the five States. They looked rather a tired combination and failed to win a match.

From 'Cricket in Australia 1945-46'

SOUTH AUSTRALIA v QUEENSLAND 189 (275, 276)

At Adelaide, December 24, 25, 26, 27 [1945]. Drawn. Complete indication of his all-round abilities was displayed by Colin McCool, who, after spinning out South Australia with figures of seven wickets for 106 [Tallon caught four and stumped one], scattered the field by carefree batting which brought him 172 runs, scored with a wide variety of strokes.... Facing arrears of 208, South Australia improved at the second attempt and passed the century for the loss of one wicket before stumps were drawn.

South Australia: †R.J. Craig, C.R. Webb, R.A. Hamence, *D.G. Bradman, F.C. Bennett, T.E. Klose, G.R. Langley, M.G. Waite, P.L. Ridings, A.R.C. McLean and B. Dooland.

First innings: 365 (Craig 84, Webb 63, Hamence 37, Bradman c Tallon b McCool 68, Bennett 39; McCool seven for 106). *Second innings:* One for 110 (Webb 36 not out, Bradman 52 not out).

Queensland: *W.A. Brown, G.G. Cook, A. Carrigan, C. McCool, W. Morris, D. Watt, H. Pegg, V.N. Raymer, G.W. Lockie and P.L. Dixon.

First innings: Eight for 573 dec (Brown 98, Cook 76, Carrigan 67, McCool 172, Watt 40, Raymer 31 not out).

Umpires: J. D. Scott and L. A. Smith

SOUTH AUSTRALIA v AUSTRALIAN SERVICES 190 (277)

At Adelaide, December 29, 31 [1945], January 1 [1946]. Drawn. Thanks to Craig and Bradman, who between them contributed all but 66 of the total of 319, South Australia gained a narrow first innings lead of five runs. Hassett batted extremely well in the Services' second innings, and the State team, set to get 251 to win, finished 120 behind with nine wickets intact.

Australian Services: R.S. Whitington, D.K. Carmody, J.A. Workman, *A.L. Hassett, C.G. Pepper, A.G. Cheetham, D.R. Cristofani, R.M. Stanford, R.G. Williams, †S.G. Sismey and R.S. Ellis.

First innings: 314 (Whitington 77, Pepper 63, Stanford 59 not out, Sismey 35; Dooland five for 104). *Second innings:* 255 (Hassett 92, Cristofani 58, Stanford 57; Noblet three for 44).

South Australia: †R.J. Craig, C.R. Webb, R.A. Hamence, *D.G. Bradman, F.C. Bennett, L. Michael, T.E. Klose, M.G. Waite, B. Dooland, G. Noblet and J. L. Mann.

First innings: 319 (Craig 141, Bradman c Carmody b Williams 112; Pepper four for 100, Ellis five for 88). *Second innings:* One for 130 (Bennett 56 not out, Michael 54).

Umpires: J. D. Scott and L. A. Smith

1946-47

1946-47

Although the Sheffield Shield competition was dwarfed by the MCC tour, its revival, after six years' suspension through war, made inter-State rivalry keener than ever and the public following was equally stimulated. Victoria by all-round superiority were enabled to secure the trophy in impressive style, five matches being won outright and the other abandoned because of rain. ... Queensland created history by flying on their Southern tour; never before had a complete Sheffield Shield team travelled in this manner. ...

With Bradman playing only two State innings, one a century, South Australia fell away badly and failed to win a match. In Bradman's absence, P. L. Ridings led the side capably ...

From 'Overseas Cricket: Australian Inter-State Matches'

The MCC tour to Australia in 1946-47 resembled that of 1920-21, not a Test being won by England. In both cases English cricket had not recovered from the effects of world war. MCC were most reluctant to send out a team so soon after the cessation of hostilities, but so pressing was the invitation from the Australian Board of Control, backed in person by Dr H. V. Evatt, they gave way. To my mind MCC took the proper course. The presence of the English side not only revived cricket enthusiasm throughout Australia but, thanks to the great publicity given to the tour, cricket throughout the marvellous summer which followed in England received bigger public support than ever before. ...

Beyond question nothing went right for [England's captain] Hammond. Often when his men were battling hard and looked like establishing a promising position, an umpire's decision changed the whole complexion of the game. These incidents caused some friction and certainly bitter disappointment to the England team. Let me quote Ray Robinson, the Australian critic, writing in *The Cricketer*. 'More exasperating was the luck of the umpiring. Usually debatable decisions work out fairly evenly over a Test rubber, but weight of evidence suggests that the umpires were mistaken in giving Bradman not out caught for 28 in the First Test, Edrich out leg-before-wicket for 89 in the Third Test, and Washbrook out caught behind the wicket for 39 in the Fourth Test. These decisions came at such points in England's bids to gain an advantage that they could almost be termed turning-points of the three games. Dismissal of Bradman for 159 runs fewer – and four hours earlier – would have altered the course of the First Test incalculably, and, perhaps, led to Australia having to play a second innings on the first of the sticky wickets. …' I give his version because no one will accuse an Australian of possessing a disjointed view on decisions which meant so much to the victorious side as well as to the losers. …

Whereas England brought seven players experienced in Tests against Australia, only Bradman and Hassett remained of the opposition. Yet they produced one of the best teams ever to represent them. For this happy state of affairs I am sure Australia were largely indebted to Bradman, their captain and one of their three Selectors. Early in the season Bradman looked far from well, but long days in the sun soon restored him to almost his old self. At first his batting, for Bradman, was uncertain. He has set such a high standard that one could not help being surprised at seeing him in difficulties; but, as in the past, his mammoth scores put Australia on top. Even more important was the way he moulded his men together, always encouraging them on the field and telling the bowlers what they should do. As a leader he clearly outshone Hammond, but I think Bradman would admit he was more fortunate than his rival in possessing so much talent at his command. … There was no question as to which was the better side and, apart from Bradman, the Australians were a young team. They thoroughly deserved to retain the Ashes.

During the tour an MCC team travelled for the first time by air. The first flight, at night from Adelaide to Melbourne, was due to a railway strike. …

From 'MCC Team in Australia', by Norman Preston

MCC TEAM v SOUTH AUSTRALIA 191 (278, 279)

At Adelaide, October 25, 26, 27, 29 [1946]. Drawn. By batting all the first day, Hutton and Washbrook gave MCC a grand start. The wicket was slow and neither batsman took the slightest risk. … The Middlesex pair provided a contrast. Compton, hitting freely, outpaced Edrich in a stand of 111. Hammond … closed the innings first thing on Monday morning. [Only Bradman and the wicket-keeper, Englefield, did not bowl in this innings.] South Australia naturally exercised care while facing such a formidable total. Bradman, looking rather frail, appeared in need of match practice during a stay of two and a half hours. After he was fourth out at 199 the side collapsed. Following on next day, the Australians found the MCC extremely smart in the field … but Craig, a tall, slim batsman, saved his side by resisting the bowling for four hours and a quarter.

MCC Team

L. Hutton, C. Washbrook, W.J. Edrich, D. Compton, *W.R. Hammond, N.W.D. Yardley, J.T. Ikin, T.P.B. Smith, James Langridge, †T.G. Evans and R. Pollard.

First innings: Five for 506 dec (Hutton 136, Washbrook 113, Edrich 71, Compton 71, Yardley 54 not out, Ikin 35 not out; Dooland three for 142).

South Australia

R. J. Craig c Evans b Pollard	14	–	b Pollard	111
P. L. Ridings b Langridge	57	–	c Hammond b Compton	20
R. A. Hamence b Smith	0	–	st Evans b Compton	7
*D. G. Bradman c and b Smith	76	–	c Edrich b Pollard	3
R. James b Langridge	58	–	run out	15
K. Gogler b Smith	19	–	c Compton b Langridge	1
B. Dooland b Smith	12	–	c Hammond b Langridge	16
K. O'Neill c Evans b Smith	8	–	b Edrich	3
J. Mann b Langridge	3	–	not out	62
G. Noblet b Edrich	8	–	not out	25
†W. Englefield not out	6			
L-b 3, n-b 2	5		B 11, l-b 1, n-b 1	13
	266		(eight wkts)	**276**

MCC bowling: *First innings*—Pollard 26–8–66–1; Edrich 9.3–1–38–1; Smith 27–4–93–5; Langridge 20–2–60–3; Ikin 1–0–4–0. *Second innings*—Pollard 11–3–23–2; Edrich 10–1–37–1; Smith 19–1–70–0; Langridge 26–7–73–2; Compton 17–5–46–2; Hutton 1–0–6–0; Hammond 3–0–8–0.

Umpires: J. D. Scott and L. A. Smith

MCC TEAM v AN AUSTRALIAN XI 192 (280)

At Melbourne, November 8, 9, 11, 12, 13 [1946]. Drawn. This match, regarded as a Test trial for Australians, was spoiled by rain, which prevented any play on the first and fourth days. After the first blank day, MCC readily agreed to the game being extended to five days. As the wicket was always completely protected from the weather, it never became difficult. In his first outing against MCC, McCool showed his quality and made his Test place certain by dismissing the first six batsmen. With half the wickets down for 198 his analysis was five for 47. … Saggers kept wicket magnificently, in contrast to Evans, who badly missed stumping Bradman off Compton when the Australian captain was 78. Bradman showed that he remained a master, and he inspired the young left-hander, Morris, who hit a century when first appearing against MCC. …

MCC Team

L. Hutton, C. Washbrook, W.J. Edrich, D. Compton, *W.R. Hammond, N.W.D. Yardley, J.T. Ikin, †T.G. Evans, T.P.B. Smith, W. Voce and R. Pollard.

First innings: 314 (Hutton 71, Washbrook 57, Hammond 51; McCool seven for 106).

An Australian XI

M. Harvey c Ikin b Smith	22	J. Pettiford not out	27
A. Morris c Evans b Yardley	115	C. McCool not out	22
*D. G. Bradman c Pollard b Compton	106	B 1, l-b 1	2
A. L. Hassett c Hutton b Smith	28	(five wkts)	**327**
K. R. Miller c Evans b Smith	5		

J. Ellis, †R. Saggers, F. Freer and C. Puckett did not bat.

MCC bowling: Voce 27–2–98–0; Pollard 24–5–69–0; Smith 32–3–111–3; Ikin 3–0–13–0; Compton 14–3–26–1; Yardley 4–0–8–1.

Umpires: A. N. Barlow and R. Wright

SOUTH AUSTRALIA v VICTORIA 193 (281, 282)

At Adelaide, November 15, 16, 18, 19 [1946]. Victoria won by nine wickets. Miller, with one of the finest batting displays ever seen at Adelaide, and Tribe, who claimed thirteen wickets for 153, played themselves into the Test team. ... Troubled by a leg strain, Bradman did not field, but [in the second innings] he and Hamence put on 195 and helped to save the innings defeat. ...

South Australia

R. J. Craig b Tribe	36	–	c Hassett b Johnson	3
V. R. Gibson b Miller	5	–	b Tribe	1
P. L. Ridings lbw b Tribe	27	–	b Tribe	9
R. A. Hamence lbw b Tribe	2	–	c and b Freer	116
*D. G. Bradman st Baker b Johnson	43	–	st Baker b Tribe	119
R. James b Miller	73	–	c Meuleman b Ring	34
K. Gogler lbw b Tribe	36	–	b Tribe	33
J. L. Mann c and b Tribe	20	–	lbw b Tribe	5
B. Dooland c and b Tribe	2	–	not out	16
G. Noblet b Tribe	9	–	lbw b Tribe	1
†W. Englefield not out	4	–	b Ring	4
B 4, l-b 8, w 1	13		B 11, l-b 3, n-b 1	15
	270			**356**

Victoria bowling: *First innings*—Johnston 8–0–30–0; Freer 7–1–19–0; Miller 11–1–32–2; Johnson 20–4–55–1; Tribe 30.5–4–85–7; Ring 10–0–36–0. *Second innings*—Johnston 13–1–35–0; Freer 21–8–84–1; Miller 2–0–10–0; Johnson 14–3–43–1; Tribe 23–2–68–6; Ring 25–1–99–2; Hassett 1–0–2–0.

Victoria

G. E. Tamblyn, K. Meuleman, M. Harvey, K. R. Miller, *A. L. Hassett, I. Johnson, F. Freer, D. Ring, †E. A. Baker, G. Tribe and W. Johnston.

First innings: 548 (Tamblyn 75, Meuleman 87, Miller 188, Hassett 114; Dooland four for 229). *Second innings:* One for 79 (Miller 33, Hassett 36 not out).

Umpires: J. D. Scott and L. A. Smith

ENGLAND v AUSTRALIA (FIRST TEST MATCH) 194 (283) 38 (58)

At Brisbane, November 29, 30, December 2, 3, 4 [1946]. Australia won by an innings and 332 runs. Whereas in past tours England enjoyed the good fortune of twice catching Australia on a sticky wicket at Brisbane, this time the tables were turned and England in each innings batted after a violent thunderstorm. So Australia gained her first Test victory in the Queensland city, and with confidence engendered from this initial success the Australians, under Bradman's vigilant leadership, went on to win the rubber. ... From the England team's point of view the whole course of the match balanced on an incident which occurred when Bradman was 28 and the total 74 for two wickets. Facing Voce, the Australian captain chopped the ball to second slip, where Ikin thought he made a perfectly good catch. Bradman survived the appeal, and not only went on to hit his first Test century against England at Brisbane but, with Hassett, he added 276 and established a new third-wicket record stand for these matches. Moreover, the Australians set up the highest Test total in their own country.

England began the match well enough after Bradman won the toss. From the third ball of Bedser's second over Morris was caught at first slip. Bradman entered, and immediately was in trouble against Bedser, edging the fifth ball of the same over to the slips and popping up the seventh to square-leg. Barnes, hooking brilliantly, did his best to shield Bradman from the bowling until at 46 he was splendidly caught at square-leg off a short ball. ... At this point Bradman had made only seven in forty minutes very shakily. There followed the Ikin incident. After lunch, taken with the total 77 for two wickets, Bradman and Hassett gradually wore down the bowling in the relentless heat. Bedser ... could not return after tea owing to stomach trouble ... Hassett always remained subdued, but Bradman found his true form, and the first day ended with Australia 292 for two – Bradman 162, Hassett 81.

Bedser reappeared next day, when Edrich broke the long stand by clean bowling Bradman with his fourth ball. Bradman [batting for around six and a half hours] hit nineteen 4's. ...

Rain and bad light limited cricket on Monday to ninety-nine minutes. Bradman did not have the pitch mown and Australia lost their five remaining wickets for 50 runs. ... England now faced Lindwall and Miller; both occasionally pitched short. During lunch the sky became overcast and thunder was heard when, with the second ball after the interval, Lindwall bowled Hutton playing back. Bad light and showers caused many stoppages, and the day ended with England 21 for one wicket. Late that evening a violent thunderstorm broke, and next day ... England on a nightmare pitch took their score to 117 for five wickets before another thunderstorm flooded the ground ... with hailstones as big as golf balls.

Contrary to expectations, the ground made a remarkable recovery next day in the brilliant sunshine, but the pitch proved more treacherous than ever, and, though England never gave up the unequal struggle, fifteen wickets fell in three and a half hours. So Australia won at ten minutes to five. An attack of chicken-pox robbed Australia of Lindwall, but Miller and Toshack were enough for England. The big shock was the fall of Hutton to the first ball of the second innings. He left to one of three catches by Barnes at short-leg. ... Toshack, the tall left-arm medium bowler, who was given plenty of advice by Bradman, responded so well that his figures were nine wickets for 99 runs. Except for the respite given by the rain, the heat was always stifling. ...

Australia

S. G. Barnes c Bedser b Wright	31	†D. Tallon lbw b Edrich	14
A. Morris c Hammond b Bedser	2	R. Lindwall c Voce b Wright	31
*D. G. Bradman b Edrich	187	G. Tribe c Gibb b Edrich	1
A. L. Hassett c Yardley b Bedser	128	E. Toshack not out	1
K. R. Miller lbw b Wright	79	B 5, l-b 11, w 2, n-b 11	29
C. McCool lbw b Wright	95		**645**
I. W. Johnson lbw b Wright	47		

England bowling: Voce 28–9–92–0; Bedser 41–4–159–2; Wright 43.6–4–167–5; Edrich 25–2–107–3; Yardley 13–1–47–0; Ikin 2–0–24–0; Compton 6–0–20–0.

England

L. Hutton, C. Washbrook, W. J. Edrich, D. Compton, *W. R. Hammond, J. T. Ikin, N. W. D. Yardley, †P. A. Gibb, W. Voce, A. V. Bedser and D. V. P. Wright.

First innings: 141 (Hammond 32; Miller seven for 60, Toshack three for 17). *Second innings:* 172 (Ikin 32; Toshack six for 82).

Umpires: J. D. Scott and G. Borwick

ENGLAND v AUSTRALIA
(SECOND TEST MATCH)

195 (284)
39 (59)

At Sydney, December 13, 14, 16, 17, 18, 19 [1946]. Australia won by an innings and 33 runs.... When Hammond won the toss, most people expected a big score from England. The conditions were ideal, even if the pitch did prove responsive to spin. England's troubles commenced in the second over of the match, when Freer [in the Australian side for Lindwall] clean bowled Washbrook. Hutton and Edrich set out to repair the damage ... [but] with his third delivery Johnson got Hutton taken on the leg side by Tallon. That disaster occurred at twenty minutes to three, and in the next twenty-five minutes Australia virtually won the match when Tallon took two more catches off McCool which accounted for Compton and Hammond. So four England wickets were down for 99, McCool claiming two in less than three overs ... Johnson bowled his off-breaks so magnificently that at the end of seventy minutes, when given a well-earned rest, his analysis read eleven overs, eight maidens, three runs, one wicket....

Bradman, who limped badly the first day, did not field on Saturday, Hassett taking over the leadership. Within half an hour England were all out ... The Australian innings had been in progress only nine minutes when bad light, followed by an almost torrential downpour, held up the cricket for over three hours.... Bradman preferred to rest his injured leg, and as soon as Johnson appeared Barnes repeatedly appealed against the light. At the fifth appeal the umpires gave way, and play ended for the day with the Australian total 27 for one wicket....

Brilliant sunshine on Sunday transformed the pitch, which rolled out perfectly on Monday when cricket took place in glorious weather. Biggest crowd of the match, 51,459, saw Barnes bat all day.... Only three wickets fell this day, all to Edrich, as after Miller left at ten minutes to four, Bradman, without a runner, stayed with Barnes until the stumps were drawn with the total 252 for four wickets. Not before twenty minutes to six the following day did England break the Barnes-Bradman stand. Then, in successive overs, Bradman, who batted superbly despite a pronounced limp which must have been very painful, and Barnes were dismissed at the same total. Each hit 234, and they established a new fifth-wicket Test partnership record of 405. It was also a fifth-wicket world record for first-class cricket, and there was only one bigger in Test cricket, 451 by Bradman and Ponsford for the second wicket at Kennington Oval in 1934. Bradman batted for six and a half hours and hit twenty-four 4's. Barnes took ten hours forty minutes over his runs and hit seventeen 4's.

On the fifth day Australia forced the pace ... before Bradman declared, Australia again having made their highest Test total in their own country. The innings lasted eleven hours forty minutes. Twenty-four minutes remained before lunch, and in that time Hutton ... made 37 out of 49 before he unluckily hit his wicket when facing the last ball before lunch.... The last day began with England 247 for three wickets, and Edrich went on to complete his first century against Australia.... Apart from [Hammond and] Yardley, Australia encountered little more opposition and the match was all over by 3.15 pm ... Only once before had England been defeated twice by an innings in successive matches, and that was in 1897-98 when A. E. Stoddart's team toured Australia. The match drew an aggregate attendance of 196,253 ...

England

L. Hutton, C. Washbrook, W.J. Edrich, D. Compton, *W.R. Hammond, J.T. Ikin, N.W.D. Yardley, T.P.B. Smith, †T.G. Evans, A.V. Bedser and D.V.P. Wright.

First innings: 255 (Hutton 39, Edrich 71, Ikin 60; Johnson six for 42, McCool three for 73).
Second innings: 371 (Hutton 37, Washbrook 41, Edrich 119, Compton 54, Hammond 37, Yardley 35; McCool five for 109).

Australia

S. G. Barnes c Ikin b Bedser	234	C. McCool c Hammond b Smith	12
A. Morris b Edrich	5	†D. Tallon c and b Wright	30
I. W. Johnson c Washbrook b Edrich	7	F. Freer not out	28
A. L. Hassett c Compton b Edrich	34	G. Tribe not out	25
K. R. Miller c Evans b Smith	40	L-b 7, w 1, n-b 2	10
*D. G. Bradman lbw b Yardley	234	(eight wkts dec)	**659**

E. Toshack did not bat.

England bowling: Bedser 46–7–153–1; Edrich 26–2–79–3; Wright 46–8–169–1; Smith 37–1–172–2; Ikin 3–0–15–0; Compton 6–0–38–0; Yardley 9–0–23–1.

Umpires: J. D. Scott and G. Borwick

ENGLAND v AUSTRALIA (THIRD TEST MATCH)

196 (285, 286)
40 (60, 61)

At Melbourne, January 1, 2, 3, 4, 6, 7 [1947]. Drawn. England put up a much better show in this game, but experienced astonishing ill-luck. On the eve of the match James Langridge, who was among the twelve chosen men, strained a groin muscle while taking a catch at fielding practice. That mishap put him out for the rest of the tour excepting one game at Adelaide. Bradman won the toss and England suffered two tremendous handicaps. Within half an hour Edrich, fielding at short-leg, received a frightful blow on the shin from a fierce hook by Barnes, and he retired for the rest of the day. Soon after lunch Voce left the field with a pulled groin muscle.... Despite the comparatively cheap dismissals of Barnes, Morris and Hassett, things looked bad for England when the total reached 188 for three wickets, Bradman again having lifted Australia out of trouble. Then with successive balls Yardley dismissed Bradman and Johnson. Bradman, feeling for an off-break, chopped the ball on to his stumps. So restrained was he during two hours fifty minutes that he hit only two 4's, a true indication of England's magnificent bowling in adversity. The next ball removed Johnson, leg-before, and with only four runs added Miller was smartly taken by the wicket-keeper. So in seventeen minutes the position changed to 192 for six wickets. Here McCool and Tallon gave an indication of Australia's immense all-round strength. [On the second day] McCool punished the bowling unmercifully ... [and] completed his first Test century ...

England began their innings just before three o'clock, and received an early shock when Hutton touched a beautiful ball from Lindwall ... into the hands of McCool, who made a very fine catch at first slip. ... The third morning [England resumed at one for 147] was the most vital of the match, and, to the bitter disappointment of the England team, they lost Edrich when he appeared to hit a ball from Lindwall hard on to his pads. Worse followed ... Compton, Hammond and Washbrook [also] being back in the pavilion for the addition of only 32 to the overnight score. ... Ikin and Yardley set about the task of retrieving England's fortunes and ... [in the end] Australia led by 14. ...

On the fourth day England captured only four wickets. ... The day brought new honours to Yardley, who in nineteen overs dismissed Barnes, Bradman and Miller. It was the second time in the match that Yardley removed Bradman and the third successive time in these Tests. Morris, the left-hander, batted all day while reaching 132, his first Test hundred ... [yet] when the seventh wicket fell at 341 England still stood a chance, but Tallon and Lindwall completely changed the situation with some of the best batting ever seen in a Test. The onslaught was violent, and in eighty-seven minutes they put on 154. ... Lindwall completed a magnificent century by going down the pitch and driving Bedser with tremendous power all along the ground to the sight-screen. ...

England wanted 551 in seven hours ... [but on the final day] rain caused four brief interruptions ... At times the light was extremely bad, but the England players never appealed, not even when Yardley and Bedser were struggling hard to save the game and rain was falling steadily. Twice Bradman suggested that they should go in before the players left the field. ... This was the first drawn Test in Australia for sixty-five years, but, although England averted defeat, failure to win meant that Australia retained the Ashes. The match proved a tremendous attraction. Vast crowds packed the large stadium. The official attendance aggregate was 343,675 and the receipts of £44,063 made a world record for a cricket match. ...

Australia

S. G. Barnes lbw b Bedser	45	–	c Evans b Yardley	32
A. Morris lbw b Bedser	21	–	b Bedser	155
*D. G. Bradman b Yardley	79	–	c and b Yardley	49
A. L. Hassett c Hammond b Wright	12	–	b Wright	9
K. R. Miller c Evans b Wright	33	–	c Hammond b Yardley	34
I. W. Johnson lbw b Yardley	0	–	run out	0
C. McCool not out	104	–	c Evans b Bedser	43
†D. Tallon c Evans b Edrich	35	–	c and b Wright	92
R. Lindwall b Bedser	9	–	c Washbrook b Bedser	100
B. Dooland c Hammond b Edrich	19	–	c Compton b Wright	1
E. Toshack c Hutton b Edrich	6	–	not out	2
N-b 2	2		B 14, l-b 2, n-b 3	19
	365			**536**

England bowling: *First innings*—Voce 10–2–40–0; Bedser 31–4–99–3; Wright 26–2–124–2; Yardley 20–4–50–2; Edrich 10.3–2–50–3. *Second innings*—Voce 6–1–29–0; Bedser 34.3–4–176–3; Wright 32–3–131–3; Yardley 20–0–67–3; Edrich 18–1–86–0; Hutton 3–0–28–0.

England

L. Hutton, C. Washbrook, W. J. Edrich, D. Compton, *W. R. Hammond, J. T. Ikin, N. W. D. Yardley, †T.G. Evans, W. Voce, A. V. Bedser and D. V. P. Wright.

First innings: 351 (Washbrook 62, Edrich 89, Ikin 48, Yardley 61; Dooland four for 69). *Second innings:* Seven for 310 (Hutton 40, Washbrook 112, Yardley 53 not out).

Umpires: J. D. Scott and G. Borwick

MCC TEAM v SOUTH AUSTRALIA 197 (287)

At Adelaide, January 24, 25, 27, 28 [1947]. Drawn. ... Hammond and Langridge put on 243 in four hours forty minutes. The return to form of both men, particularly Hammond on the eve of the Fourth Test, was most welcome ... and during his stay of six hours forty minutes he completed 50,000 runs in first-class cricket. ... A third-wicket stand of 203 by Ridings and Hamence ensured South Australia making a sound reply. ... Contributing to the weakness of the MCC was incessant no-balling. Nineteen times they were called – Voce nine, Wright seven and Pollard three – and the cost was 52 runs. ... The match was played in stifling heat with the temperature above 100.

MCC Team

L. Hutton, C. Washbrook, L.B. Fishlock, J. Hardstaff, *W.R. Hammond, J.T. Ikin, James Langridge, †T.G. Evans, W. Voce, R. Pollard and D. V. P. Wright.

First innings: 577 (Hutton 88, Fishlock 57, Hammond 188, Ikin 35, Langridge 100; Dooland four for 67, Oswald three for 182). *Second innings:* Two for 152 (Hutton 77 not out, Hardstaff 40 not out).

South Australia

R. J. Craig lbw b Wright	10
P. L. Ridings lbw b Voce	77
*D. G. Bradman c Langridge b Wright	5
R. A. Hamence c Ikin b Wright	145
R. James b Hardstaff	85
R. M. Stanford b Hardstaff	31
V. R. Gibson b Hardstaff	4
†R. Vaughton c Evans b Voce	20
B. Dooland not out	23
N. Oswald c Ikin b Voce	3
K. Webb b Voce	10
B 12, l-b 3, w 1, n-b 14	30
	443

MCC bowling: Voce 26.7–2–125–4; Pollard 19–3–60–0; Wright 17–0–90–3; Ikin 13–0–60–0; Langridge 1–0–9–0; Hutton 8–1–45–0; Hardstaff 9–1–24–3.

Umpires: J. D. Scott and L. A. Smith

ENGLAND v AUSTRALIA (FOURTH TEST MATCH)

198 (288, 289)
41 (62, 63)

At Adelaide, January 31, February 1, 3, 4, 5, 6 [1947]. Drawn. There were four extraordinary features about this Test. It was played in perpetual heat and dense humidity, with the temperature sometimes 105; Lindwall finished the England first innings by taking three wickets, all bowled, in four balls; and both Compton and Morris achieved the rare feat of hitting two separate hundreds. This was the first time for an Australian to accomplish this in his own country. ... In both innings Hutton and Washbrook gave England a splendid send-off with a three-figure stand, but after tea on the opening day Edrich, Hutton and Hammond were dismissed in a disastrous thirty-five minutes. ... Again England were upset by the slower bowlers, and it was not surprising that Bradman did not take the new ball at 200. ...

The second day provided plenty of thrills. ... [With England six for 455] Lindwall, after a rest and still using the old ball, held a sharp return catch from his first delivery [to end] Compton's finest display so far during the tour ... Lindwall then took the new ball, and in his next over bowled both Bedser and Evans off stump with successive deliveries; the next just missed the wicket and the fourth bowled Wright. ... Twenty-five minutes remained, and Bedser served England splendidly by causing Harvey to play on and then producing an almost unplayable ball that bowled Bradman for nought. Consequently Australia finished the day 24 for two wickets.

During the third day Australia made a complete recovery by adding 269 while losing only Morris – who hit his second Test century – and Hassett, who helped to put on 189 for the third partnership in nearly four hours. ... Miller and Johnson carried the score to 293 for four wickets before the close.

The heat was again almost overwhelming on the fourth day, when ... Australia went ahead. Miller, who offered three chances after passing three figures, remained unbeaten ... No sooner had Hutton and Washbrook opened England's second innings than a sharp thunderstorm accompanied by vivid flashes of lightning held up the game for twenty-three minutes. ...

On the fifth day, off the first three deliveries by Lindwall, Hutton and Washbrook got four runs needed to complete their second three-figure opening stand of the match ... then disaster occurred. Tallon, standing well back, held a snick from Washbrook. Some people thought the ball was scooped off the ground. ... [Next] Toshack caused such a collapse that by 5.15 p.m. eight wickets were down for 255. Compton alone of the recognised batsmen remained, and, shielding Evans from the bowling, he defied all Bradman's devices to remove him. At the close England were 274 for eight; Evans had not scored.

[On the final morning] Tallon failed to stump Evans off Dooland. Had this chance been accepted, Australia must have won, but, instead, England made such an excellent recovery that Hammond was able to declare ... [one ball] after lunch ... setting Australia to make 314 in three and a quarter hours. [Compton's unbeaten 103 was his fourth successive hundred in first-class innings.] Considering England's poor bowling resources and the experienced hitters at Australia's command, this was not an impossible task, but from the outset Bradman declined to accept the challenge. …

England

L. Hutton, C. Washbrook, W. J. Edrich, *W. R. Hammond, D. Compton, J. Hardstaff, J. T. Ikin, N. W. D. Yardley, A. V. Bedser, †T.G. Evans and D. V. P. Wright.

First innings: 460 (Hutton 94, Washbrook 65, Compton 147, Hardstaff 67; Lindwall four for 52, Dooland three for 133). *Second innings:* Eight for 340 dec (Hutton 76, Washbrook 39, Edrich 46, Compton 103 not out; Toshack four for 76).

Australia

M. Harvey b Bedser	12	–	b Yardley	31
A. Morris c Evans b Bedser	122	–	not out	124
*D. G. Bradman b Bedser	0	–	not out	56
A. R. Hassett c Hammond b Wright	78			
K. R. Miller not out	141			
I. W. Johnson lbw b Wright	52			
C. McCool c Bedser b Yardley	2			
†D. Tallon b Wright	3			
R. Lindwall c Evans b Yardley	20			
B. Dooland c Bedser b Yardley	29			
E. Toshack run out	0			
B 16, l-b 6, w 2, n-b 4	28		B 2, n-b 2	4
	487		(one wkt)	**215**

England bowling: *First innings*—Bedser 30–6–97–3; Edrich 20–3–88–0; Wright 32.4–1–152–3; Yardley 31–7–101–3; Ikin 2–0–9–0; Compton 3–0–12–0. *Second innings*—Bedser 15–1–68–0; Edrich 7–2–25–0; Wright 9–0–49–0; Yardley 13–0–69–1.

Umpires: J. D. Scott and G. Borwick

ENGLAND v AUSTRALIA (FIFTH TEST MATCH)

199 (290, 291)
42 (64, 65)

At Sydney, February 28, March 1, 3, 4, 5 [1947]. Australia won by five wickets. So much rain fell before and during this final Test that it produced the best cricket of the whole series; because the pitch, without ever becoming treacherous, always encouraged bowlers. England could fairly claim that they experienced wretched luck. Hutton, after batting splendidly throughout the opening day while making his first Test century in Australia, was stricken down with tonsilitis that caused him to go to hospital. Rain prevented a ball being bowled on the second day; but Sunday was gloriously fine and the pitch, which had been under water – mushrooms sprang up in the outfield – dried quite firm. … For the first time in the series England led on the first innings, but on the final day, at a most crucial point, Edrich, usually so dependable, dropped an easy catch off Wright offered by Bradman when only two and the total 47. Had that chance been accepted, victory might well have gone to England, for Bradman alone seemed able to establish any mastery over Wright and Bedser.

Following the blank Saturday, Hutton was taken ill, and on Monday … Lindwall achieved a remarkable performance in taking seven wickets for only nine runs apiece. Undismayed by their moderate total, England bowled splendidly. The thermometer reached 102 [one degree less than Hutton's temperature when he went to hospital that same day], yet Bedser and Wright never spared themselves, and the fielding … was also high-class. … Wright came into his own by bowling Bradman and getting Miller taken at second slip. Bradman ran down the wicket and, misjudging the spin, missed the ball. . . . Next day, while Bedser in eleven overs conceded only 15 runs and completely shut up his end, Wright carried all before him. In eleven overs he dismissed five men for 42 runs. . . .

Batting a second time, England also broke down . . . the day ended with six men out for 144 [and Hutton absent ill] . . . The fifth day sufficed to bring about a finish. . . . On a pitch so helpful to bowlers, Australia's task of making 214 to win did not appear easy. . . . Barnes and Morris . . . understood the position and decided to get as many runs as possible while the effects of the roller remained good. Their progress was comparatively speedy, but at 45 Morris was surprisingly run out while going for a third run. . . . Bradman scored two and then offered the shoulder-high catch which . . . passed between Edrich's hands. In the next over Barnes [was out] and then Bradman and Hassett, with almost a day and half before them, decided to tire out the bowlers. During their first fifty minutes together they made only 13, but when Wright and Bedser had to be rested Bradman promptly appreciated the change to Smith and Edrich. . . . By the tea interval the total reached 110 for two, and Australia were almost safe . . . and by sound batsmanship the third partnership took the total to 149 before Bradman lifted a drive into the hands of Compton at extra-cover. The Bradman-Hassett stand, by producing 98, turned the issue in Australia's favour . . . [and they] won by five wickets just before six o'clock with a whole day to spare. . . .

England

L. Hutton, C. Washbrook, W. J. Edrich, L. B. Fishlock, D. Compton, *N. W. D. Yardley, J. T. Ikin, †T.G. Evans, T. P. B. Smith, A. V. Bedser and D. V. P. Wright.

First innings: 280 (Hutton 122 retired ill, Edrich 60; Lindwall seven for 63). *Second innings:* 186 (Compton 76; McCool five for 44).

Australia

S. G. Barnes c Evans b Bedser	71	–	c Evans b Bedser	30
A. Morris lbw b Bedser	57	–	run out	17
*D. G. Bradman b Wright	12	–	c Compton b Bedser	63
A. L. Hassett c Ikin b Wright	24	–	c Ikin b Wright	47
K. R. Miller c Ikin b Wright	23	–	not out	34
R. A. Hamence not out	30	–	c Edrich b Wright	1
C. McCool c Yardley b Wright	3	–	not out	13
†D. Tallon c Compton b Wright	0			
R. Lindwall c Smith b Wright	0			
G. Tribe c Fishlock b Wright	9			
E. Toshack run out	5			
B 7, l-b 6, n-b 6	19		B 4, l-b 1, n-b 4	9
	253		(five wkts)	**214**

England bowling: *First innings*—Bedser 27–7–49–2; Edrich 7–0–34–0; Smith 8–0–38–0; Wright 29–4–105–7; Yardley 5–2–8–0. *Second innings*—Bedser 22–4–75–2; Edrich 2–0–14–0; Smith 2–0–8–0; Wright 22–1–93–2; Yardley 3–1–7–0; Compton 1.2–0–8–0.

Umpires: J. D. Scott and G. Borwick

1947-48

1947-48

A visit from India, the prospective tour of England by Bradman and his men, and Western Australia's achievement in winning the Sheffield Shield at the first attempt stimulated intense interest during the 1947-48 season in Australia. ... Bradman played only once for South Australia [in the Shield] and scored 100. ...

From 'Overseas Cricket: Australian Inter-State Matches'

SOUTH AUSTRALIA v INDIA 200 (292, 293)

At Adelaide, October 24, 25, 27, 28 [1947]. Drawn. The Indian bowling came in for severe punishment, but the batsmen acquitted themselves well, and the touring team came within 52 of victory with five wickets in hand. Niehuus and Craig, who each hit a hundred, opened with a stand of 226, and Bradman became the third successive man to reach three figures, but was lucky to escape at square-leg when 23. He completed a hundred at about a run a minute, and altogether hit twenty-two 4's in 156. ... When Bradman declared [a second time], India, wanting 287 to win, lost half their wickets for 60, but recovered splendidly, Mankad and Amarnath sharing in an unfinished stand of 175.

South Australia

R. D. Niehuus c Nayudu b Mankad	137	–	lbw b Phadkar	49
R. J. Craig b Sarwate	100	–	st Sen b Mankad	24
*D. G. Bradman c Sarwate b Mankad	156	–	st Sen b Mankad	12
R. A. Hamence c and b Mankad	31	–	b Phadkar	10
R. James c Mankad b Amarnath	3	–	c and b Phadkar	0
P. L. Ridings b Mankad	26	–	b Sarwate	17
†R. Vaughton not out	17	–	b Mankad	0
B. Dooland b Sarwate	14	–	b Phadkar	21
J. Noblet b Sarwate	1	–	not out	50
K. O'Neill not out	12	–	not out	23
B 16, l-b 5	21		B 9, l-b 4	13
(eight wkts dec)	**518**		(eight wkts dec)	**219**

N. Oswald did not bat.

India bowling: *First innings*—Phadkar 16–1–72–0; Amarnath 12–1–48–1; Mankad 36–1–127–4; Nayudu 9–0–62–0; Sarwate 16–1–83–3; Hazare 18–1–95–0; Sohoni 3–0–10–0. *Second innings*—Phadkar 15–0–59–4; Amarnath 2–0–7–0; Mankad 22–4–51–3; Nayudu 3–1–8–0; Sarwate 10–0–39–1; Hazare 7–0–26–0; Sohoni 6–1–16–0.

India

V. Mankad, H. R. Adhikari, G. Kishenchand, V. S. Hazare, Gul Mahomed, †P. Sen, *L. Amarnath, C. T. Sarwate, D.G. Phadkar, S. W. Sohoni and C. S. Nayudu.

First innings: 451 (Mankad 57, Hazare 95, Amarnath 144, Sarwate 47, sundries 31; Noblet three for 65). *Second innings:* Five for 235 (Mankad 116 not out, Amarnath 94 not out).

Umpires: G. S. Cooper and J. D. Scott

SOUTH AUSTRALIA v VICTORIA 201 (294)

At Adelaide, November 7, 8, 10, 11 [1947]. South Australia won by nine wickets. Bowlers were harshly treated on the first three days. Hassett batted delightfully for Victoria, his strokes in a faultless display including nine 4's and a hit for 6 which struck a woman spectator on the head. She escaped injury. ... Victoria reached 440, to which South Australia's batsmen replied with scant respect. Bradman, scoring his ninety-ninth first-class century, made 173 with Craig for the second wicket ...

Victoria

K. Meuleman, M.R. Harvey, *A.L. Hassett, R.N. Harvey, I.W. Johnson, S.J. Loxton, D. Fothergill, F. Freer, †E.A. Baker, D. Ring and W.A. Johnston.

First innings: 440 (Meuleman 30, M.R. Harvey 89, Hassett 118, Johnson 34, Fothergill 102; Ridings four for 66). *Second innings:* 182 (Fothergill 31; Noblet four for 19, Craig three for 37).

South Australia

R. D. Niehuus c Freer b Johnston	4			
R. J. Craig lbw b Ring	97			
*D. G. Bradman lbw b Johnson	100			
R. A. Hamence lbw b Ring	14	–	run out	27
R. James b Freer	27	–	not out	42
P. L. Ridings b Freer	151	–	not out	17
†R. Vaughton c Loxton b Johnson	14			
B. Dooland c and b Ring	62			
G. Noblet c Meuleman b Hassett	32			
N. Oswald not out	5			
K. O'Neill c Meuleman b Ring	4			
Extras	26		Extra	1
	536		(one wkt)	**87**

Victoria bowling: *First innings*—Johnston 33–5–94–1; Freer 34–4–87–2; Loxton 10–2–30–0; Johnson 34–7–89–2; Ring 46.3–3–176–4; Fothergill 2–0–11–0; Hassett 3–0–23–1. *Second innings*—Johnston 7–0–32–0; Freer 8–0–37–0; Ring 1.6–0–17–0.

Umpires: G. S. Cooper and J. D. Scott

AN AUSTRALIAN XI v INDIA 202 (295, 296)

At Sydney, November 14, 15, 17, 18 [1947]. India won by 47 runs, gaining their first victory of the tour over a side very little short of full Australian Test standard. The early stages went unfavourably, nine wickets falling for 229, but Kishenchand and Irani shared in a splendid partnership of 97. Bradman gave a glorious display in completing his hundredth hundred in first-class cricket, but, although he made 172 and Miller showed good form, the last six wickets fell for 38 ... Set to get 251 in two and a half hours, the Australians accepted the challenge, but could not cope with the clever left-arm spin bowling of Mankad ...

India

V. Mankad, C.T. Sarwate, Gul Mahomed, V.S. Hazare, *L. Amarnath, H.R. Adhikari, K.M. Rangnekar, G. Kishenchand, W.S. Sohoni, C.S. Nayudu and †J.K. Irani.

First innings: 326 (Sarwate 32, Gul Mahomed 85, Hazare 38, Kishenchand 75 not out, Irani 43; Loxton three for 70). *Second innings:* Nine for 304 dec (Mankad 34, Sarwate 58, Adhikari 46, Kishenchand 63 not out, Sohoni 31; Johnston four for 71).

An Australian XI

R. Rogers run out	16	–	b Mankad	31
W. A. Brown c Hazare b Sohoni	8	–	run out	30
*D. G. Bradman c Amarnath b Hazare	172	–	c Sarwate b Mankad	26
K. R. Miller b Mankad	86	–	st Irani b Mankad	13
R. A. Hamence c Hazare b Sohoni	27	–	c Amarnath b Mankad	2
N. R. Harvey c Mankad b Hazare	32	–	not out	56
S. J. Loxton c Irani b Sohoni	0	–	lbw b Mankad	6
†R. A. Saggers c Irani b Sohoni	1	–	b Mankad	0
B. Dooland lbw b Mankad	5	–	c Kishenchand b Mankad	31
M. Herbert not out	26	–	c Gul Mahomed b Amarnath	1
W. A. Johnston c Irani b Amarnath	2	–	c Sohoni b Mankad	2
B 3, l-b 2	5		B 5	5
	380			**203**

India bowling: *First innings*—Sohoni 17–2–89–4; Amarnath 15.1–2–53–1; Mankad 24–2–93–2; Sarwate 16–0–51–0; Nayudu 4–0–19–0; Kishenchand 1–0–3–0; Hazare 14–1–67–2. *Second innings*—Sohoni 4–0–31–0; Amarnath 11–0–54–1; Mankad 12–0–84–8; Sarwate 2–0–24–0; Mahomed 1–0–5–0.

Umpires: G. Borwick and W. J. Callum

AUSTRALIA v INDIA
(FIRST TEST MATCH)

203 (297)
43 (66)

At Brisbane, November 28, 29, December 1, 2, 3, 4 [1947]. Australia won by an innings and 226 runs. Unfortunate to be caught on a treacherous pitch, India collapsed twice, and the manner of their defeat must have resulted in loss of confidence for the remaining Tests. There was nothing wrong with the conditions when Australia batted first, and, after the early loss of Brown, Bradman gave one of his superb displays. He lost Morris at 97, but completely demoralised the bowlers by punishing methods which brought runs at a terrific rate. Not a ball could be bowled until five o'clock on the second day, but the surprising attendance of 11,000 watched the hour's cricket that took place. A further downpour saturated the pitch on the Sunday, but next day the sun appeared and India's task was hopeless. Realising the awkwardness of the conditions, the Australians soon declared. Bradman took four and three-quarter hours over 185, which contained twenty 4's.

With the ball doing all manner of unexpected tricks, India, used to the fast, hard pitches in their own country, were completely baffled. ... Toshack, with left-arm slow-medium deliveries, dismissed five men in nineteen balls for two runs. All out 58, India followed on 324 behind ... More rain restricted the fourth day to an hour, and nothing could be done next day, but conditions were not quite so difficult when play restarted on Thursday. ... Toshack, who again made the most of the pitch ... took eleven wickets [in the match] for 31 runs. ...

Australia

W. A. Brown c Irani b Amarnath	11	R. R. Lindwall st Irani b Mankad	7
A. R. Morris hit wkt b Sarwate	47	†D. Tallon not out	3
*D. G. Bradman hit wkt b Amarnath	185	I. W. Johnson c Rangnekar b Mankad	6
A. L. Hassett c Gul Mahomed b Mankad	48	E. R. H. Toshack not out	0
K. R. Miller c Mankad b Amarnath	58	B 5, l-b 1, w 1	7
C. L. McCool c Sohoni b Amarnath	10	(eight wkts dec)	**382**

W. A. Johnston did not bat.

India bowling: Sohoni 23–4–81–0; Amarnath 39–10–84–4; Mankad 34–3–113–3; Sarwate 5–1–16–1; Hazare 11–1–63–0; Nayudu 3–0–18–0.

India

V. Mankad, C.T. Sarwate, Gul Mahomed, H.R. Adhikari, G. Kishenchand, V.S. Hazare, K.M. Rangnekar, S.W. Sohoni, *L. Amarnath, C.S. Nayudu and †J.K. Irani.

First innings: 58 (Toshack five for 2). *Second innings:* 98 (Toshack six for 29).

Umpires: A.N. Barlow and G. Borwick

AUSTRALIA v INDIA (SECOND TEST MATCH)

204 (298)
44 (67)

At Sydney, December 12, 13, 15, 16, 17, 18 [1947]. Drawn. The weather again proved unkind, less than ten hours' cricket being possible during six days. This meant there was little possibility of a definite result, although the Australians showed that they were equally as vulnerable as their opponents on a difficult pitch. … [They] lost their first wicket in an unusual manner. In a previous match [at Sydney v An Australian XI] Mankad, the bowler, warned Brown about backing up too far, and when the batsman repeated this ran him out. [He also warned him in the Indians' match with Queensland immediately preceding the First Test.] This time Mankad gave no warning, and the first occasion Brown moved down the pitch too quickly the bowler whipped off the bails. The third and fourth days were blank through rain and, as could be expected, the saturated turf did not favour batsmen when the game restarted. Morris, Bradman and Hassett all fell cheaply, and despite brief resistance from Miller and Hamence … the end came quickly, the last five batsmen being dismissed for 21 runs. Phadkar and Hazare made the most of the conditions and were almost unplayable.

Johnston (fast-medium left-arm) and Johnson (off-breaks) were just as effective when India batted again 81 ahead. Before play ended on the fifth day, seven wickets fell for 61 runs … but all chances of a thrilling finish were dispelled when not a ball could be bowled on the last day.

India

V. Mankad, C.T. Sarwate, Gul Mahomed, V.S. Hazare, *L. Amarnath, G. Kishenchand, H.R. Adhikari, D.G. Phadkar, C.S. Nayudu, Amir Elahi and †J.K. Irani.

First innings: 188 (Kishenchand 44, Phadkar 51; McCool three for 71). *Second innings:* Seven for 61 (Johnston three for 15).

Australia

W. A. Brown run out	18	C. L. McCool b Phadkar	9
A. R. Morris lbw b Amarnath	10	R. R. Lindwall b Hazare	0
*D. G. Bradman b Hazare	13	†D. Tallon c Irani b Hazare	6
A. L. Hassett c Adhikari b Hazare	6	W. A. Johnston not out	0
K. R. Miller lbw b Phadkar	17	B 1, l-b 1	2
R. A. Hamence c Adhikari b Mankad	25		**107**
I. W. Johnson lbw b Phadkar	1		

India bowling: Phadkar 10–2–14–3; Amarnath 14–4–31–1; Mankad 9–0–31–1; Hazare 13.2–3–29–4.

Umpires: A.N. Barlow and G. Borwick

AUSTRALIA v INDIA (THIRD TEST MATCH)

205 (299, 300)
45 (68, 69)

At Melbourne, January 1, 2, 3, 5 [1948]. Australia won by 233 runs. Bradman added to his long list of triumphs by hitting a hundred in each innings, the first time he had accomplished the feat in a Test Match. India fared reasonably well up to a point, but were again faced with ill-fortune with regard to the weather.

A third-wicket stand of 169 between Bradman and Hassett assured Australia of a good total. Hassett, missed in the slips off Hazare when 31, scored as fast as his partner, and at times runs came at two a minute. Bradman scored 132 out of 260, and on his departure the bowlers met with better reward, the last six wickets falling for 105.

When Mankad and Sarwate began India's reply with a stand of 124, the position was intriguing, but ... Rain overnight altered the state of the pitch, and when three of his batsmen fell cheaply Amarnath declared, although India were 103 behind. Bradman countered this move by sending in his tail-end men in the hope that conditions would ease. He must have been worried, however, when three of them fell for 13 and Barnes, one of his leading batsmen, followed at 32.

Any hopes India may have held of a complete collapse were soon dashed, for Morris and Bradman thoroughly mastered the attack and shared in an unbroken fifth partnership of 223. Bradman reached his hundred first and Morris followed suit just before the close of the day. Heavy overnight rain made the pitch responsive to spin, and Bradman, seizing his opportunity, declared. The India batsmen never looked like making a fight. Half the side fell for 60 and ... the end was inevitable.

Australia

S. G. Barnes b Mankad	12	–	c Sen b Amarnath	15
A. R. Morris b Amarnath	45	–	not out	100
*D. G. Bradman lbw b Phadkar	132	–	not out	127
A. L. Hassett lbw b Mankad	80			
K. R. Miller lbw b Mankad	29			
R. A. Hamence st Sen b Amarnath	25			
R. R. Lindwall b Amarnath	26			
†D. Tallon c Mankad b Amarnath	2			
B. Dooland not out	21	–	lbw b Phadkar	6
I. W. Johnson lbw b Mankad	16	–	c Hazare b Amarnath	0
W. A. Johnston run out	5	–	lbw b Amarnath	3
Extras	1		B 3, n-b 1	4
	394		(four wkts dec)	**255**

India bowling: *First innings*—Phadkar 15–1–80–1; Amarnath 21–5–78–4; Hazare 16.1–0–62–0; Mankad 37–4–135–4; Sarwate 3–0–16–0; Nayudu 2–0–22–0. *Second innings*—Phadkar 10–1–28–1; Amarnath 20–3–52–3; Hazare 11–1–55–0; Mankad 18–4–74–0; Sarwate 5–0–41–0; Gul Mahomed 1–0–1–0.

INDIA

V. Mankad, C.T. Sarwate, Gul Mahomed, V.S. Hazare, *L. Amarnath, D.G. Phadkar, H.R. Adhikari, Rai Singh, K.M. Rangnekar, †P. Sen and C.S. Nayudu.

First innings: Nine for 291 dec (Mankad 116, Sarwate 36, Phadkar 55 not out; Johnson four for 59). *Second innings:* 125 (Johnston four for 44, Johnson four for 35).

Umpires: A. N. Barlow and H. A. R. Elphinstone

AUSTRALIA v INDIA
(FOURTH TEST MATCH)

206 (301)
46 (70)

At Adelaide, January 23, 24, 26, 27, 28 [1948]. Australia won by an innings and 16 runs. Although they gained another overwhelming success ... the match was a personal triumph for Hazare, who followed Bradman's example in the Third Test and hit a hundred in each innings. Against such a powerful attack as that possessed by the Australians, this was a truly remarkable performance. To balance this, however, Bradman was once again in irresistible form, hitting a double-hundred. Hassett fell only two short of that figure and Barnes also completed a century.

Bradman gave Australia a big advantage when he won the toss for the third time; on a perfect pitch bowlers were helpless to check the flow of runs. Morris fell early, but Barnes and Bradman shared in a second-wicket stand of 236. ... Bradman, always the complete master, scored 201 out of 341 before leaving towards the close of the first day. ... An interesting race developed to see whether Hassett could complete 200, but he was just short, taking out his bat for an excellent 198. In reaching 674, Australia made the highest score ever recorded against India and also the biggest total for any Test Match in Australia.

India made a shocking start, losing two wickets for six runs, but they fought back well. Half the side fell for 133, but Hazare found a capable partner in Phadkar, 188 runs being added. ... Despite this gallant effort, India followed on 293 behind, and this time their start was even worse, two wickets falling without a run on the board. Six men were out for 139 and it looked as though India would capitulate easily, but Hazare again refused to be disturbed by the situation ... Six men failed to score in this innings, most of the batsmen finding the pace of Lindwall too much for them. ...

Australia

S. G. Barnes lbw b Mankad	112	I. W. Johnson b Rangachari	22
A. R. Morris b Phadkar	7	R. R. Lindwall b Rangachari	2
*D. G. Bradman b Hazare	201	†D. Tallon lbw b Mankad	1
A. L. Hassett not out	198	E. R. H. Toshack lbw b Hazare	8
K. R. Miller b Rangachari	67	B 8, l-b 6, n-b 2	16
R. N. Harvey lbw b Rangachari	13		**674**
C. L. McCool b Phadkar	27		

India bowling: Phadkar 15–0–74–2; Amarnath 9–0–42–0; Rangachari 41–5–141–4; Mankad 43–8–170–2; Sarwate 22–1–121–0; Hazare 21.3–1–110–2.

India

V. Mankad, C. T. Sarwate, †P. Sen, *L. Amarnath, V. S. Hazare, Gul Mahomed, D.G. Phadkar, G. Kishenchand, H. R. Adhikari, K. M. Rangnekar and C. R. Rangachari.

First innings: 381 (Mankad 49, Amarnath 46, Hazare 116, Phadkar 123; Johnson four for 64, Bradman none for 4). *Second innings:* 277 (Hazare 145, Gul Mahomed 34, Adhikari 51; Lindwall seven for 38).

Umpires: G. Borwick and R. Wright

AUSTRALIA v INDIA
(FIFTH TEST MATCH)

207 (302)
47 (71)

At Melbourne, February 6, 7, 9, 10 [1948]. Australia won by an innings and 177 runs. For the third time in the series they gained victory with an innings to spare. Bradman's luck with the coin continued, Australia batting first for the fourth occasion out of five, and once more the India bowling received scant respect.

Following the dismissal of Barnes ... Brown and Bradman were never in trouble until the Australian captain unfortunately tore a rib muscle and retired. ... Chief honours fell to Neil Harvey, a nineteen-year-old left-hander, playing in his second Test Match. He hit the first hundred of his career, showing the confidence of an experienced cricketer. ... Bradman declared at tea-time on the second day.

Although India again lost the first wicket cheaply, they recovered well ... [but none the less] followed on 244 behind. This time there was nobody to rescue them following the fall of the first wicket without a run scored, and a steady procession took place. ... The last five wickets actually fell for 16 runs – a sorry end to the Test series for India, who could, with reason, complain of ill-fortune in most of the matches.

Australia

S. G. Barnes run out	33
W. A. Brown run out	99
*D. G. Bradman retired hurt	57
K. R. Miller c Sen b Phadkar	14
R. N. Harvey c Sen b Mankad	153
S. J. Loxton c Sen b Amarnath	80
R. R. Lindwall c Phadkar b Mankad	35
†D. Tallon c Sen b Sarwate	37
L. Johnson not out	25
D. Ring c Kishenchand b Hazare	11
W. A. Johnston not out	23
B 4, l-b 4	8
(eight wkts dec)	**575**

India bowling: Phadkar 9–0–58–1; Amarnath 23–1–79–1; Rangachari 17–1–97–0; Hazare 14–1–63–1; Mankad 33–2–107–2; Sarwate 18–1–82–1; Nayudu 13–0–77–0; Adhikari 1–0–4–0.

India

V. Mankad, C. T. Sarwate, H. R. Adhikari, V. S. Hazare, *L. Amarnath, D.G. Phadkar, Gul Mahomed, G. Kishenchand, C. S. Nayudu, †P. Sen and C. R. Rangachari.

First innings: 331 (Mankad 111, Adhikari 38, Hazare 74, Phadkar 56 not out; Johnson three for 66, Ring three for 103). *Second innings:* 67 (Johnson three for 8, Ring three for 17).

Umpires: A. N. Barlow and G. S. Cooper

WESTERN AUSTRALIA v AUSTRALIAN TOURING TEAM

208 (303)

At Perth, March 13, 15, 16 [1948]. Drawn.

Western Australia: *D. K. Carmody, A. R. Edwards, T. M. Outridge, M. U. Herbert, A. D. Watt, C. W. Langdon, B. A. Rigg, †G. T. Kessey, T. E. O'Dwyer, C. W. Puckett and K. R. Cumming.

First innings: 348 (Edwards 57, Watt 32, Langdon 112, Rigg 65, O'Dwyer 31). *Second innings:* Three for 62.

Australian Touring Team: W. A. Brown, A. R. Morris, *D.G. Bradman, K. R. Miller, R. N. Harvey, R. A. Hamence, C. L. McCool, I. W. Johnson, †R. A. Saggers, W. A. Johnston and E. R. H. Toshack.

First innings: Seven for 442 dec (Morris 115, Bradman c Outridge b O'Dwyer 115, Miller 43, Harvey 79, Hamence 33 not out; O'Dwyer three for 99).

Umpires: J. P. Robbins and E. T. Tonkinson

1948

1948

Replete with events that deserve permanent record in cricket history, last summer brought the most remarkable performance by any touring side, a close contest among the counties with the championship going to the youngest first-class county [Glamorgan], larger crowds than ever before assembling in England, and the biggest Benefits rewarding several of the professionals. All this despite much bad weather.

Beyond question the Australians took pride of place by going through the season unbeaten, and the honour of Knighthood bestowed upon their captain, now Sir Donald Bradman, came as a distinction never before awarded to a cricketer while still active in the game. In other parts of the book the tour is dealt with thoroughly, and the choice of five Australians as the Cricketers of the Year [Hassett, Johnston, Lindwall, Morris and Tallon], together with the special article on the captain detailing his career, conveys the wonderful way in which our guests dominated the proceedings. …

These [previous] valuable references in the history of the long series of Tests between England and Australia are not meant in any way to belittle the doings of Bradman and his merry men, not only in the great representative encounters but in going through the season with a record unsullied by defeat. Truly the gallant captain proceeded from match to match with the happiest result no matter how the play seemed to be going against him. Surely he must have been born under a lucky star, with the most beautiful and effective Sponsor in 'Dame Fortune'.

The tour might even have been stage-managed with Don Bradman the 'hero' and no 'villain' able to check his doings; he took his curtain after a century in the final first-class fixture and bowled the last over at Scarborough, where he received the honorary life membership of the Yorkshire County Club with a silver memento noting his wonderful Test Match performances at Leeds. And so to Scotland, where the King and Queen received him and the team – a truly great finale.

From 'Notes by the Editor' (Hubert Preston), *Wisden 1949*

When, announcing retirement from first-class cricket, D.G. Bradman claimed that the 1948 side bore comparison with any of its predecessors, he accurately reflected the majority of opinion on the nineteenth

Australian team visiting England. In retaining the Ashes, held by Australia since 1934, these Australians enjoyed almost uninterrupted success, while becoming the first side to go unbeaten through an English tour: certainly they achieved all that could be expected of a combination entitled to the description great. Yet they gave cause for reservation of such sweeping judgment, as the Tests were by no means so one-sided as results suggested, and Yorkshire and Hampshire played themselves into positions arousing visions of the first Australian defeat by a county since Hampshire beat the 1912 team. Still, for the most part, victory followed victory so inevitably for the Australians that at times opponents took on an air of defeat almost before the match had been in progress more than an hour or two. Once or twice that impression extended even to the Tests.

A summary of their achievements proved the might of probably the most united Australian party sent to England. Not only did they win exactly half their 34 matches with an innings to spare, two by ten wickets, one by nine wickets, two by eight wickets and one by 409 runs, but eleven batsmen between them hit 50 centuries, and in first-class games seven of their seventeen players completed 1,000 runs, with Loxton only 27 short when he broke his nose while batting at Scarborough. Comparisons of totals reveal even more. The Australians made 350 or more in twenty-four innings whereas, apart from the Tests, the highest total against them was Nottinghamshire's 299 for eight. Twice the Australians failed to reach 200, but they dismissed opponents for less than that figure no fewer than thirty-seven times, and in seven innings for under 100.

After Bradman's team surpassed all records by winning four out of five Tests by a touring team in England, the theory that in international cricket winning the toss usually meant winning the match seemed to need the qualification that other matters should be equal, for Bradman guessed the spin of the coin correctly only once in the rubber. . . .

For Bradman the tour provided the most fitting climax possible to an illustrious career. Apart from leading Australia to continued Test dominance, he made more hundreds than any batsman in the country and for the second time – he hit thirteen in 1938 – he emulated Trumper's performance of 1902 with eleven first-class centuries on a tour in England. In addition to this supreme batting ability, Bradman demonstrated his knowledge of the game in captaincy and generalship. Most pleasing to him must have been the warmth of the reception accorded him by crowds everywhere, particularly in his last two Tests, at Leeds and the Oval. The British public paid striking tribute to his popularity, and they made such big response to a newspaper fund for a Bradman testimonial that, after receiving a silver trophy, he asked that the surplus money should go towards the provision of concrete pitches similar to those on which he learned his cricket. ...

... To Bedser fell the unique distinction of dismissing Bradman in the first four Test innings, so making a sequence of five such successes – Bradman was out to Bedser in the final Test of the 1946-47 tour. On the first three occasions last season Bedser caused Bradman to send a catch to Hutton at short fine-leg, but after the Second Test Bradman could not again be lured into the trap when facing a late in-swinger pitched on the middle stump.

From 'Australians in England, 1948', by R.J. Hayter

WORCESTERSHIRE v AUSTRALIANS 209 (304)

At Worcester, April 28, 29, 30 [1948]. Australians won by an innings and 17 runs, with seventy minutes to spare. Despite cheerless, cold and sometimes showery weather, the visitors quickly settled down to English conditions. Lindwall took a wicket with the second ball of the match, but the pitch was more suitable to the slower men. ... Honours of the second day went to Bradman, who once again opened the tour with a century. These are his Worcester scores – 236 in 1930; 206 in 1934; 258 in 1938; and 107 in 1948. Following a stubborn first-wicket stand of 79, Bradman gave a fluent display, memorable for superb driving. He reached three figures in two and a quarter hours, and the second partnership added 186. Morris, the left-hander, enjoyed the distinction of scoring a century on his first appearance in England. ... Attendance 32,000 and receipts of over £4,000 were a record for Worcester.

Worcestershire

E. Cooper, D. Kenyon, C. H. Palmer, R. E. S. Wyatt, L. Outschoorn, *A. F. T. White, R. Jenkins, R. Howorth, R. T. D. Perks, †H. Yarnold and P. F. Jackson.

First innings: 233 (Cooper 51, Palmer 85, Howorth 37 not out; Johnson three for 52). *Second innings:* 212 (Palmer 34, Outschoorn 54; McCool four for 29, Johnson three for 75).

Australians

S. G. Barnes lbw b Howorth	44	A. L. Hassett c Wyatt b Jackson	35
A. R. Morris c Jenkins b Jackson	138	W. A. Brown st Yarnold b Howorth	25
*D. G. Bradman b Jackson	107	K. R. Miller not out	50
R. R. Lindwall lbw b Jackson	32	I. W. Johnson not out	12
C. L. McCool b Jackson	0	B 6, l-b 5, w 3	15
†D. Tallon b Jackson	4	(eight wkts dec)	**462**

E. R. H. Toshack did not bat.

Worcestershire bowling: Perks 26–3–95–0; Palmer 16–5–56–0; Wyatt 1–0–4–0; Jenkins 7–0–47–0; Jackson 39–4–135–6; Howorth 38–6–109–2; Outschoorn 1–0–1–0.

Umpires: F. Root and D. Davies

LEICESTERSHIRE v AUSTRALIANS 210 (305)

At Leicester, May 1, 3, 4 [1948]. Australians won by an innings and 171 runs. Miller, missed three times, hit the first double-century of the tour. He batted almost five and a half hours and shared in stands of 111 with Barnes and 159 with Bradman. The remaining batsmen did badly against Leicestershire's Australian slow bowlers, Jackson and Walsh. … Rain prevented play until 2.30 pm on the last day. Then the Australians took the last five wickets in an hour for 34.

Australians

S. G. Barnes lbw b Sperry	78	I. W. Johnson c Lester b Jackson	6
W. A. Brown b Jackson	26	†R. A. Saggers c Lester b Jackson	6
K. R. Miller not out	202	D. Ring run out	2
*D. G. Bradman c Corrall b Etherington	81	W. A. Johnston st Corrall b Jackson	12
R. N. Harvey lbw b Walsh	12	B 10, n-b 2	12
R. A. Hamence st Corrall b Walsh	7		**448**
S. J. Loxton lbw b Jackson	4		

Leicestershire bowling: Sperry 25–5–84–1; Etherington 26–2–94–1; Cornock 3–0–13–0; Jackson 37.2–3–91–5; Walsh 29–0–125–2; Lester 7–0–29–0.

Leicestershire

*L.G. Berry, G. Lester, F. T. Prentice, M. Tompkin, V. E. Jackson, W. B. Cornock, T. A. Chapman, J. E. Walsh, M. W. Etherington, †P. Corrall and J. Sperry.

First innings: 130 (J. E. Walsh 33; Ring five for 45). *Second innings:* 147 (Lester 40, Jackson 31 not out; Johnson seven for 42).

Umpires: A. Skelding and C. N. Woolley

SURREY v AUSTRALIANS 211 (306)

At [Kennington] Oval, May 8, 10, 11 [1948]. Australians won by an innings and 296 runs. … They were fortunate to win the toss, for, after being easy-paced on the first day, the pitch became fast and dusty; nevertheless there was little excuse for Surrey's poor batting in the first innings. Barnes and Morris opened with a stand of 136 and Barnes and Bradman added 207. … Bradman, at his best, drove magnificently and made 146 in two and three-quarter hours. He hit fifteen 4's before being bowled by a fine ball. … With Lindwall quickly sending back Fletcher and Squires, Surrey were all out in three hours. Fishlock batted through the innings and never seemed in trouble …

Australians

S. G. Barnes lbw b Squires	176	†D. Tallon not out	50
A. R. Morris lbw b McMahon	65	D. Ring b McMahon	2
*D. G. Bradman b Bedser	146	W. A. Johnston lbw b Laker	6
A. L. Hassett b Bedser	110	E. R. H. Toshack c and b McMahon	8
R. N. Harvey b McMahon	7	B 6, l-b 5, n-b 1	12
I. W. Johnson c Fishlock b Bedser	46		**632**
R. R. Lindwall b Bedser	4		

Surrey bowling: Bedser 40–9–104–4; Surridge 26–4–86–0; Laker 37–4–137–1; Squires 10–0–62–1; McMahon 42.4–1–210–4; Holmes 4–0–21–0.

Surrey

L. B. Fishlock, D.G. W. Fletcher, H. S. Squires, T. H. Barling, M. R. Barton, †A. J. McIntyre, *E. R. T. Holmes, J. C. Laker, A. V. Bedser, W. S. Surridge and J. W. McMahon.

First innings: 141 (Fishlock 81 not out; Johnson five for 53, Ring three for 34). *Second innings:* 195 (Squires 54; Johnston four for 40, Johnson three for 40).

Umpires: H. Baldwin and A. Skelding

ESSEX v AUSTRALIANS 212 (307)

At Southend, May 15, 17 [1948]. Australians won by an innings and 451 runs. In light-hearted vein, they made history by putting together the highest total scored in a day of six hours in first-class cricket. Bradman led the run-getting revel on the Saturday. Complete master of the Essex bowlers on a fast pitch, he scored 187 in two hours five minutes, and by a wide variety of orthodox and unorthodox strokes hit thirty-two 4's and a 5. ... The biggest partnerships were 219 in ninety minutes between Brown and Bradman for the second wicket, 166 in sixty-five minutes by Loxton and Saggers for the sixth, and 145 in ninety-five minutes between Barnes and Brown for the first. Bailey dismissed Brown and Miller with successive balls, but generally the bowlers failed to stem the scoring. Because of injury Bailey did not bat in either innings [and] Essex [were] dismissed twice on Monday. ... The attendance and receipts – 32,000 and £3,482 – were ground records.

Australians

S. G. Barnes hit wkt b R. Smith	79
W. A. Brown c Horsfall b Bailey	153
*D. G. Bradman b P. Smith	187
K. R. Miller b Bailey	0
R. A. Hamence c P. Smith b R. Smith	46
S. J. Loxton c Rist b Vigar	120
†R. A. Saggers not out	104
I. W. Johnson st Rist b P. Smith	9
D. Ring c Vigar b P. Smith	1
W. A. Johnston b Vigar	9
E. R. H. Toshack c Vigar b P. Smith	4
B 7, n-b 2	9
	721

Essex bowling: Bailey 21–1–128–2; R. Smith 37–2–169–2; P. Smith 38–0–193–4; Price 20–0–156–0; Vigar 13–1–66–2.

Essex

T. C. Dodds, S. J. Cray, A. V. Avery, F. H. Vigar, R. Horsfall, *T. N. Pearce, R. Smith, T. P. B. Smith, †F. Rist, E. Price and T. E. Bailey.

First innings: 83 (Miller three for 14, Toshack five for 31). *Second innings:* 187 (Pearce 71, T. P. B. Smith 54; Johnson six for 37).

Umpires: W. H. Ashdown and D. Hendren

MCC v AUSTRALIANS 213 (308)

At Lord's, May 22, 24, 25 [1948]. Australians won by an innings and 158 runs, a most convincing victory against the strongest opposition met so far. They excelled in run-getting, and the bowling of Toshack and Miller, in the first innings, and of McCool and Johnson, in the second, proved too much for the MCC batsmen. The Australians lost Morris at 11, but Barnes, defying an attack of cramp, shared with Bradman in a stand of 160. ... Though at times subdued, Bradman obtained eleven 4's in two hours and a half before giving slip a catch. ... On the second morning, when rain deadened the pitch, Laker was punished for nine 6's over a short boundary. ... The total attendance was nearly 60,000, the gates being closed on the first day.

Australians

S. G. Barnes c Edrich b Cranston	81	C. L. McCool c Edrich b Young	0
A. R. Morris lbw b Edrich	5	†D. Tallon b Young	11
*D. G. Bradman c Edrich b Deighton	98	R. R. Lindwall not out	29
A. L. Hassett lbw b Young	51	E. R. H. Toshack c Compton b Young	2
K. R. Miller c Donnelly b Laker	163	B 4, l-b 2	6
W. A. Brown c Cranston b Laker	26		**552**
I. W. Johnson lbw b Laker	80		

MCC bowling: Edrich 23–1–110–1; Deighton 22–4–88–1; Cranston 26–6–69–1; Young 55.2–12–147–4; Laker 37–10–127–3; Compton 3–1–5–0.

MCC

L. Hutton, J. D. Robertson, W. J. Edrich, D. C. S. Compton, M. P. Donnelly, *N. W. D. Yardley, K. Cranston, †S. C. Griffith, Capt. J. H. G. Deighton, J. C. Laker and J. A. Young.

First innings: 189 (Hutton 52; Miller three for 28, Toshack six for 51). *Second innings:* 205 (Hutton 64; Johnson three for 37, McCool four for 35).

Umpires: F. Chester and D. Davies

LANCASHIRE v AUSTRALIANS 214 (309, 310)

At Manchester, May 26, 27, 28 [1948]. Drawn. After the loss of the first day through rain, Lancashire made a good fight for the first innings lead. In his third match for the county nineteen-year-old Hilton achieved distinction by dismissing Bradman twice. Cranston put the Australians in after winning the toss, and on a pitch drying under warm sunshine the Australians were seldom comfortable against Roberts and Hilton, both of whose natural left-arm breaks turned and sometimes lifted awkwardly ... In addition to beating Bradman, who deflected the ball on to the stumps, Hilton sent back Johnson and Barnes in one spell of twelve overs for 30 runs. ... The Australians batted brightly in the second innings, but Bradman was in difficulties against Hilton, who beat him with three successive balls immediately before getting him stumped. ...

Australians

S. G. Barnes c Cranston b Hilton	31	–	c Roberts b Cranston	31
A. R. Morris c E. H. Edrich b Pollard	22	–	c G. Edrich b Pollard	5
*D. G. Bradman b Hilton	11	–	st E. H. Edrich b Hilton	43
I. W. Johnson lbw b Hilton	5			
S. J. Loxton b Roberts	39	–	run out	52
R. N. Harvey b Roberts	36	–	not out	76
R. A. Hamence b Pollard	2	–	not out	49
†R. A. Saggers not out	22			
R. R. Lindwall c Lawton b Hilton	0			
W. A. Johnston b Pollard	24			
E. R. H. Toshack b Roberts	4			
B 6, l-b 2	8		B 1, l-b 2	3
	204		(four wkts)	**259**

Lancashire bowling: *First innings*—Pollard 20–8–37–3; Lawton 9–4–21–0; Hilton 19–4–81–4; Roberts 21.4–4–57–3. *Second innings*—Pollard 12–2–48–1; Lawton 8–1–43–0; Hilton 13–0–54–1; Roberts 14–3–35–0; Cranston 9–1–40–1; Wharton 7–1–20–0; Ikin 4–0–16–0.

Lancashire

C. Washbrook, W. Place, G.A. Edrich, J.T. Ikin, *K. Cranston, †E.H. Edrich, A. Wharton, R. Pollard, W.B. Roberts, W. Lawton and M. Hilton.

First innings: 182 (Washbrook 33, G.A. Edrich 55; Lindwall three for 44, Johnston five for 49).

Umpires: H. Elliott and C.N. Woolley

NOTTINGHAMSHIRE v AUSTRALIANS 215 (311)

At Nottingham, May 29, 31, June 1 [1948]. Drawn. Nottinghamshire did well to escape defeat. They owed most to Simpson, who batted delightfully in both innings, and Hardstaff, who hit the first century of the tour against the Australians. ... [On the first day] Lindwall returned an analysis of six wickets for 14 runs in 15.1 overs. He was so accurate and quick off the pitch that batsmen managed to score from only ten of his deliveries. The Australians batted soundly but at times without enterprise. Brown, who rarely opened his shoulders, took three and three-quarter hours over 122, but Bradman, Miller and Hassett were more free. ...

Nottinghamshire

W.W. Keeton, H. Winrow, R.T. Simpson, J. Hardstaff, F.W. Stocks, P. Harvey, *W.A. Sime, H. J. Butler, A. Jepson, F.G. Woodhead and †E.A. Meads.

First innings: 179 (Simpson 74, Hardstaff 48; Lindwall six for 14). *Second innings:* Eight for 299 (Winrow 31, Simpson 70, Hardstaff 107, Harvey 41; Johnson three for 78, Ring four for 104).

Australians

W. A. Brown lbw b Jepson	122	†D. Tallon b Winrow	27
A. R. Morris lbw b Jepson	16	R. R. Lindwall c Meads b Jepson	8
*D. G. Bradman b Woodhead	86	I. W. Johnson b Jepson	0
C. L. McCool b Winrow	17	D. Ring not out	9
A. L. Hassett b Woodhead	44	B 2, l-b 1, n-b 1	4
K. R. Miller b Woodhead	51		**400**
S. J. Loxton run out	16		

Nottinghamshire bowling: Butler 32–4–98–0; Jepson 43–7–109–4; Woodhead 32–3–92–3; Harvey 16–1–43–0; Winrow 13.2–2–54–2.

Umpires: G.M. Lee and T.J. Bartley

SUSSEX v AUSTRALIANS 216 (312)

At Hove, June 5, 7 [1948]. Australians won by an innings and 325 runs. In a match-winning bowling feat of eleven wickets for 59 runs, Lindwall worked himself into his best form at the right time – the last match before the First Test. In the first innings he hit the off stump five times. ... In contrast the Sussex attack presented few difficulties and, except when Brown pursued his customary solid course, runs flowed from the bat with hardly a pause. Brown and Morris shared in an opening stand of 153, followed by a partnership of 167 between Morris and Bradman, whose 109 took only two hours and contained eleven 4's. ... When Sussex batted again Lindwall bowled faster than on the opening day. In the first over he dismissed John Langridge and C. Oakes before a run was scored; Parks and James Langridge made a determined stand ... but Bradman recalled Lindwall and the end soon came.

Sussex

John Langridge, H. W. Parks, C. Oakes, G. Cox, James Langridge, J. Oakes, *H. T. Bartlett, †S. C. Griffith, P. A. D. Carey, A. E. James and J. Cornford.

First innings: 86 (Lindwall six for 34, Loxton three for 13). *Second innings:* 138 (Parks 61; Lindwall five for 25, Ring three for 42).

Australians

W. A. Brown lbw b C. Oakes	44	R. N. Harvey not out	100
A. R. Morris c and b James Langridge	184	R. A. Hamence lbw b C. Oakes	34
*D. G. Bradman b Cornford	109	B 10, l-b 10, n-b 1	21
R. R. Lindwall c Griffith b Cornford	57	(five wkts dec)	**549**

I. W. Johnson, †R. A. Saggers, S. J. Loxton, D. Ring and E. R. H. Toshack did not bat.

Sussex bowling: Carey 23–1–102–0; Cornford 31–6–122–2; James 26–6–90–0; Cox 16–3–54–0; C. Oakes 15–2–60–2; James Langridge 16–1–32–0; J. Oakes 3–0–32–0.

Umpires: B. Flint and J. J. Hills

ENGLAND v AUSTRALIA (FIRST TEST MATCH)

217 (313, 314)
48 (72, 73)

At Nottingham, June 10, 11, 12, 14, 15 [1948]. Australia won by eight wickets. Bravely as England fought back, the result became nearly a foregone conclusion by the end of the first day after their disastrous batting against a fast attack of exceptionally high standard. ... Although only twenty minutes' play was possible before lunch on Thursday ... on a pitch affected sufficiently by a heavy downpour during the interval to make the ball skid through, England lost eight wickets before tea for 74. True, the light never became good and the bowling reached a high level, but England played poorly ... Australia suffered a handicap when Lindwall pulled a groin muscle midway through the innings and could not bowl again in the match. ...

Although a good spell by Laker gave England great encouragement at one period on the second day, Australia recovered and pressed home their advantage, but on a perfect pitch and in ideal weather conditions England deserved equal praise for limiting the batsmen to 276 runs in six hours. For the most part Yardley set a defensive field and, though lacking penetration, his bowlers performed their allotted tasks in concentrating on and just outside the leg stump. At one period Laker's off-breaks put the Australians into a position where they struggled for runs . .. Then Yardley caused surprise by taking off Laker in order to use the new ball against Brown, normally an opening batsman accustomed to swing. The change in bowling provided Bradman with an opportunity to hit his first 4 after eighty-three minutes, but again he relapsed into long periods of defence and, as Brown followed suit, scoring became very slow with Australia fighting to restore their early superiority. They passed England's total without further loss, but at 184 Yardley ... [had] Brown leg-before with his fourth delivery. England met with no other success on Friday; an unbroken stand of 108 between Bradman and Hassett left Australia 128 ahead. Seldom had Bradman been so subdued in a big innings as he was over the twenty-eighth Test century of his career. He did not welcome Yardley's tactics in asking his bowlers to work to a packed leg-side field, and he spent over three hours and a half in reaching his hundred, the last 29 runs taking seventy minutes.

When play began on Saturday Bradman needed only two runs to become the first player to complete 1,000 for the season. These he obtained, but in the third over Hutton at short fine-leg held the first of his series of catches given by Bradman off Bedser's late in-swinger. Bradman's unusually subdued innings lasted four hours and three-quarters. For the most part he allowed himself no liberty. ...

[England batted again 344 behind.] Once more Australia gained the incentive of a fine start ... but Hutton showed sparkling form and Compton overcame an anxious start against Johnson. ... Miller [having bowled medium-pace off-breaks] turned again to fast deliveries and incurred the noisy displeasure of sections of the crowd when he bowled five bumpers to Hutton in his last eight balls, one of which struck the batsman high on the left arm. ... Before play began on Monday the Nottinghamshire Secretary, Mr H. A. Brown, broadcast an appeal to the crowd to leave the conduct of the game to the umpires and he deplored the barracking of Miller on Saturday. The not-out batsmen continued their good work, but the light became even worse than in the first innings. After an unsuccessful appeal, play was held up when the ground caught the edge of a thunderstorm. Almost immediately on the resumption Miller produced a fast break-back which beat Hutton completely in the still gathering gloom. Bad light interrupted the game soon afterwards and though the stoppage was brief, conditions became so bad again that the players retired a second time. On this occasion Compton wanted only three runs for his [third] century [in successive Tests at Trent Bridge]. ... Indeed, rarely can a Test Match have been played under such appalling conditions as on this day. ... England faced an almost hopeless task at the beginning of the last day when they stood only one run ahead with four wickets left, but hope remained as long as Compton was undefeated. He found another fine partner in Evans and in spite of two short breaks for rain they held out till ten minutes before lunch when Miller released a lightning bumper at Compton. The ball reared shoulder high, Compton shaped to hook then changed his mind and tried to get his head out of the way. As he ducked, Compton lost his balance on the muddy turf and tumbled into his wicket. ...

... Australia wanted only 98 to win. ... Bedser added interest to the last stages by bowling Morris at 38 and dismissing Bradman for his first 'duck' in a Test in England, caught in exactly the same manner as in the first innings ... The match ended humourously. After making a boundary stroke Barnes thought the game was over when the scores were level, and he snatched a stump before racing towards the pavilion. Barnes was halfway up the pavilion steps when the shouts of the crowd made him realise the error and he returned to the crease. When Hassett did make the winning hit, another scramble for souvenirs took place; and in this Barnes was unlucky. – R. J. H.

England

L. Hutton, C. Washbrook, W. J. Edrich, D. C. S. Compton, J. Hardstaff, C. J. Barnett, *N. W. D. Yardley, †T. G. Evans, J. C. Laker, A. V. Bedser and J. A. Young.

First innings: 165 (Laker 63; Miller three for 38, Johnston five for 36). *Second innings:* 441 (Hutton 74, Compton 184, Hardstaff 43, Evans 50, sundries 32; Miller four for 125, Johnston four for 147).

Australia

S. G. Barnes c Evans b Laker	62	–	not out	64
A. R. Morris b Laker	31	–	b Bedser	9
*D. G. Bradman c Hutton b Bedser	138	–	c Hutton b Bedser	0
K. R. Miller c Edrich b Laker	0			
W. A. Brown lbw b Yardley	17			
A. L. Hassett b Bedser	137	–	not out	21
I. W. Johnson b Laker	21			
†D. Tallon c and b Young	10			
R. R. Lindwall c Evans b Yardley	42			
W. A. Johnston not out	17			
E. R. H. Toshack lbw b Bedser	19			
B 9, l-b 4, w 1, n-b 1	15		L-b 2, w 1, n-b 1	4
	509		(two wkts)	**98**

England bowling: *First innings*—Edrich 18–1–72–0; Bedser 44.2–12–113–3; Barnett 17–5–36–0; Young 60–28–79–1; Laker 55–14–138–4; Compton 5–0–24–0; Yardley 17–6–32–2. *Second innings*—Edrich 4–0–20–0; Bedser 14.3–4–46–2; Young 10–3–28–0.

Umpires: F. Chester and E. Cooke

YORKSHIRE v AUSTRALIANS 218 (315, 316)

At Sheffield, June 19, 21, 22 [1948]. Drawn. As the Australians would not risk further damage to their injured bowlers, Miller and Toshack, Bradman did not attempt to go all out for victory and a keen fight for first innings lead was the chief feature. In contrast to other fine work, Yorkshire dropped at least seven catches when the Australians were struggling in the first innings. The fall of Barnes to the third ball of the match made the Australians cautious, but, despite a second-wicket stand of 67 between Bradman and Brown, six men were out for 168. Hutton and Halliday opened with 56, but the rest of the Yorkshire batsmen did little against Toshack and Johnston who, on the second day, bowled nearly four hours with only a brief break. Except when changing ends, Toshack sent down forty successive overs. The Australians again started badly on a drying pitch, but were helped by more dropped catches. Bradman and Brown put on 154 for the second wicket, and Bradman delayed his declaration till the side led by 328 with only seventy minutes left for play.

Australians

S. G. Barnes b Aspinall	0	–	b Smailes	6
W. A. Brown lbw b Wardle	19	–	b Yardley	113
*D. G. Bradman c Yardley b Wardle	54	–	c Hutton b Aspinall	86
K. R. Miller c Brennan b Coxon	20	–	b Aspinall	0
R. N. Harvey c and b Coxon	49	–	c Halliday b Yardley	56
R. A. Hamence c Brennan b Coxon	48	–	not out	6
C. L. McCool lbw b Coxon	4	–	not out	7
†R. A. Saggers c Yardley b Wardle	22			
D. Ring b Aspinall	3			
W. A. Johnston not out	15			
E. R. H. Toshack c Watson b Aspinall	4			
B 4, l-b 3, n-b 4	11		B 6, l-b 1, n-b 4	11
	249		(five wkts dec)	**285**

Yorkshire bowling: *First innings*—Aspinall 28.3–7–82–3; Coxon 26–5–66–4; Smailes 10–1–36–0; Wardle 20–8–37–3; Robinson 8–4–17–0. *Second innings*—Aspinall 12–1–53–2; Coxon 25–9–47–0; Smailes 24–8–57–1; Wardle 20–5–66–0; Robinson 5–0–17–0; Hutton 1–0–3–0; Yardley 7–2–9–2; Halliday 5–0–22–0.

Yorkshire

L. Hutton, H. Halliday, W. Watson, *N. W. D. Yardley, E. Lester, A. Coxon, R. Aspinall, T. F. Smailes, J. H. Wardle, †D. V. Brennan and E. P. Robinson.

First innings: 206 (Hutton 39, Lester 31; Johnston three for 101, Toshack seven for 81). *Second innings:* Four for 85.

Umpires: J. T. Bell and K. McCanlis

ENGLAND v AUSTRALIA (SECOND TEST MATCH)

219 (317, 318)
49 (74, 75)

At Lord's, June 24, 25, 26, 28, 29 [1948]. Australia won by 409 runs. ... Only on the first day did England provide comparable opposition, and their Selectors must have been very disappointed at the lack of determination by some of the batsmen against an attack again below full strength – this time because Miller was unable to bowl. ...

... Although the heavy atmosphere aided swing in the early stages on Thursday, that did not detract from the merit of England's performance in dismissing seven batsmen for 258 when Bradman won the toss for the only time in the series. The day began with excitement, Coxon in his second over of Test cricket dismissing Barnes, whose poor stroke to a short ball enabled Hutton at short fine-leg to bring off the first of three successive catches in that position. His next victim was Bradman, who fell to the Hutton-Bedser combination for the third consecutive time in Tests. Bradman, curiously uncertain and uncomfortable, might have been out in similar fashion when 13, though Hutton deserved more praise for getting his hands to the ball than blame for not holding it. ...

... [When England batted on the second day, they faced] a magnificent speed attack by Lindwall, ably supported by Johnston, left-arm medium-fast, and Johnson, off-breaks. Unfortunately for England the light was not good, but that did not wholly account for a collapse redeemed only partially by a defiant stand between Compton and Yardley. ... At the close of a one-sided day England stood 143 behind with only one wicket to fall.

Except for one thrilling over by Yardley, Australia's batsmen on Saturday revelled in the perfect pitch and glorious weather. Barnes, who should have been stumped when 18, and Morris consolidated Australia's 135 lead with a first-wicket stand of 122. ... Barnes and Bradman put on 174 for the second partnership. At first Barnes was content to leave most of the scoring to Bradman, but he quickened after reaching 50, and upon the completion of his big ambition of a Test century at Lord's he went over to vigorous attack. He took 21, including two successive 6's, in one over from Laker and fell to a catch on the boundary ... Yardley, the successful bowler, penetrated Hassett's defence first ball, and only a hurried jab by Miller prevented a hat-trick. Bradman looked destined to celebrate his farewell Test at Lord's with a century, but an acrobatic catch by Edrich, who dived full length and took the ball one hand, brought about his dismissal 11 short of the hundred. This was the first ball of a new spell by Bedser, whose performance in disposing of Bradman in five consecutive Test innings – including the last of the 1946-47 series – earned a place in cricket history. When at the close Australia stood 478 ahead with six wickets to fall, Bradman was able to dictate the remaining course of the game.

A break in the weather during the weekend aggravated England's plight. Rain-clouds were again about when Australia resumed batting and three stoppages occurred while 117 runs were added in eighty-eight minutes ... No doubt in the hope that the conditions would improve sufficiently for his bowlers to use a dry ball, Bradman delayed closing the innings, but soon after England started batting with nine hours in which to get 596 for victory, rain caused the fourth hold-up of the day. Frequent showers put sufficient life into the pitch to enable Lindwall and Johnston to make the ball rear awkwardly, and the batsmen were soon in trouble. In contrast to Washbrook, who showed a welcome return to Test form, Hutton looked plainly uncomfortable. ... Bradman drew his fielders in for Edrich, posting two men at short-leg and himself at short mid-off. Both Edrich and Washbrook had to face a number of fast short-pitched deliveries ...

England entered the last day with seven wickets left, but her slender chance of saving the game practically disappeared with the second ball of the morning. Compton struck his toe in trying to drive and the edged stroke which resulted provided Miller with another opportunity to make a lightning low catch at second slip. ... [After that] the innings closed in 110 minutes for the addition of 80 runs. ... In addition to batting and bowling supremacy, Australia showed more agility and aggression in the field, with Barnes again a disturbing element to batsmen through his close attendance at forward short-leg.

The gross attendance of 132,000 and receipts of £43,000 beat all previous figures for a Test in England. – R. J. H.

Australia

S. G. Barnes c Hutton b Coxon	0	–	c Washbrook b Yardley	141
A. R. Morris c Hutton b Coxon	105	–	b Wright	62
*D. G. Bradman c Hutton b Bedser	38	–	c Edrich b Bedser	89
A. L. Hassett b Yardley	47	–	b Yardley	0
K. R. Miller lbw b Bedser	4	–	c Bedser b Laker	74
W. A. Brown lbw b Yardley	24	–	c Evans b Coxon	32
I. W. Johnson c Evans b Edrich	4	–	not out	9
†D. Tallon c Yardley b Bedser	53			
R. R. Lindwall b Bedser	15	–	st Evans b Laker	25
W. A. Johnston st Evans b Wright	29			
E. R. H. Toshack not out	20			
B 3, l-b 7, n-b 1	11		B 22, l-b 5, n-b 1	28
	350		(seven wkts dec)	**460**

England bowling: *First innings*—Bedser 43–14–100–4; Coxon 35–10–90–2; Edrich 8–0–43–1; Wright 21.3–8–54–1; Laker 7–3–17–0; Yardley 15–4–35–2. *Second innings*—Bedser 34–6–112–1; Coxon 28–3–82–1; Edrich 2–0–11–0; Wright 19–4–69–1; Laker 31.2–6–111–2; Yardley 13–4–36–2; Compton 3–0–11–0.

England

L. Hutton, C. Washbrook, W.J. Edrich, D.C.S. Compton, H.E. Dollery, *N.W.D. Yardley, A. Coxon, †T.G. Evans, J.C. Laker, A.V. Bedser and D.V.P. Wright.

First innings: 215 (Compton 53, Yardley 44; Lindwall five for 70, Johnson three for 72). *Second innings:* 186 (Washbrook 37, Dollery 37; Lindwall three for 61, Toshack five for 40).

Umpires: C.N. Woolley and D. Davies

SURREY v AUSTRALIANS 220 (319)

At [Kennington] Oval, June 30, July 1, 2 [1948]. Australians won by ten wickets. Bradman put Surrey in on winning the toss ... [When their turn came] the Australians soon lost Hamence, who opened the innings because Brown split a finger while fielding, but Hassett and Bradman joined in a partnership of 231. Bradman (fifteen 4's) obtained his sixth century of the tour in two hours twenty minutes ... [On the final day] The Australians needed 122 to win and Harvey and Loxton displayed such enterprise that they knocked off the runs in fifty-eight minutes. ...

Surrey

L.B. Fishlock, D.G.W. Fletcher, H.S. Squires, M.R. Barton, J.F. Parker, †A.J. McIntyre, E.A. Bedser, *E.R.T. Holmes, B. Constable, E.A. Watts and W.S. Surridge.

First innings: 221 (Fishlock 31, Parker 76, Watts 30; Ring three for 51). *Second innings:* 289 (Fishlock 61, Parker 81, Holmes 54; McCool six for 113).

Australians

A. L. Hassett c Holmes b Watts	139			
R. A. Hamence c Parker b Watts	0			
*D. G. Bradman c Barton b Squires	128			
K. R. Miller c McIntyre b Surridge	9			
R. N. Harvey run out	43	–	not out	73
S. J. Loxton c Surridge b Parker	8	–	not out	47
C. L. McCool b Surridge	26			
†R. A. Saggers b Squires	12			
D. Ring not out	15			
E. R. H. Toshack lbw b Constable	1			
W. A. Brown absent hurt	0			
B 5, l-b 1, n-b 2	8	–	L-b, n-b 1	2
	389		(no wkt)	**122**

Surrey bowling: *First innings*—Surridge 22–0–123–2; Watts 10–0–64–2; Parker 25–5–62–1; E. A. Bedser 20–1–85–0; Constable 7.1–1–23–1; Squires 10–2–24–2. *Second innings*—Surridge 7–1–43–0; Parker 5–0–22–0; E. A. Bedser 5–0–23–0; Constable 3.1–0–32–0.

Umpires: G. M. Lee and F. S. Lee

ENGLAND v AUSTRALIA (THIRD TEST MATCH)

221 (320, 321)
50 (76, 77)

At Manchester, July 8, 9, 10, 12, 13 [1948]. Drawn. Fate dealt its sharpest blow of the series to England by the breaking of the weather over the weekend at a time when defeat for Australia appeared more than a possibility. By the end of the third day England had recovered so well from another disastrous start that they stood 316 runs on with only three wickets down in the second innings, but visions of Australia struggling to avoid being beaten were dispelled by rain which made further play impossible till after lunch on the last day. Another interruption then meant that Australia needed to bat only two hours and a half, and on a pitch reduced to sluggishness by nearly two days of heavy rain they found little difficulty in saving the game. So the sequence of unfinished England-Australia Tests at Manchester since 1905 remained unbroken.

... Bradman, playing in his fiftieth Test, again lost the toss and England took first innings on a pitch lively for the first few overs. ... [The openers soon went and with] Compton not settled down, Lindwall began a number of bouncers, one of which led to an accident to Compton. After being struck on the arm he took a big hit at a 'no-ball' bumper, but the ball flew off the edge of his bat on to his forehead. Compton staggered around and was led off the field with a cut head. Stitches were inserted and though he wanted to go back at the fall of the next wicket he was ordered to rest. ... After a short knock at the nets, [he] resumed with five men out for 119. At once he introduced an air of confidence into the batting and ... found a fine partner in Evans, whose bold hitting helped to bring 75 runs in seventy minutes. At the close England were 231 for seven ...

Though the new ball was in use at the start of the second day Australia could not retain their grip, for Compton received splendid support from Bedser, who in two hours and a half shared in a stand of 121, only three short of England's eighth-wicket record against Australia. Bedser .. . looked capable of going on for a long time; unfortunately he was run out through an error of judgment by Compton. Soon after Bedser's dismissal occurred a second distressing accident. Barnes, fielding in his usual position about five yards from the bat at short-leg, received a fierce blow under the ribs from a full-blooded pull by Pollard. After being carried off by four policemen Barnes was removed on a stretcher to hospital where examination showed that no bones were broken. Compton, who remained undefeated at the end of the innings, might have been caught at the wicket four times – three chances were very difficult – but he gave a grand display of skill and courage. . . .

Pollard unwittingly struck a big blow for England when he hit Barnes, because Australia, having dropped Brown after the Second Test, possessed only one recognised opening batsman. The necessary rearrangement no doubt played its part in Australia's only batting failure of the Tests . . . A fine catch by Evans sent back Johnson . . . and soon Bradman was leg-before to persistent Pollard. This was a great start for England on a slow, easy pitch . . . At the fall of Miller's wicket Barnes, who had practised in the nets, where he collapsed after a few minutes, surprisingly went out to bat, but he was obviously in great pain and, after staying half an hour for a single, he sank to the ground and had to be assisted off. He was taken to hospital again and kept for ten days under observation. . . . altogether on Saturday the last six wickets fell for 95.

. . . No play took place on Monday and cricket was not resumed till after lunch on Tuesday. Yardley declared first thing in the morning but more showers lessened the hope of victory. Although Young caused brief excitement when he got rid of Johnson with his second ball, the pitch was too lifeless to give bowlers help, and Morris and Bradman contented themselves with dead-bat tactics, each remaining at one end. In one spell of 100 minutes they did not change ends. Morris completed his fourth consecutive Test half-century and, like Bradman, showed adaptability to the conditions. The aggregate attendance of 133,740 was higher than that at Lord's a fortnight earlier. – R. J. H.

England

C. Washbrook, G. M. Emmett, W. J. Edrich, D. C. S. Compton, J. F. Crapp, H. E. Dollery, *N. W. D. Yardley, †T.G. Evans, A. V. Bedser, R. Pollard and J. A. Young.

First innings: 363 (Edrich 32, Compton 145 not out, Crapp 37, Evans 34, Bedser 37; Lindwall four for 99, Johnston three for 67). *Second innings:* Three for 174 dec (Washbrook 85 not out, Edrich 53).

Australia

A. R. Morris c Compton b Bedser	51	–	not out	54
I. W. Johnson c Evans b Bedser	1	–	c Crapp b Young	6
*D. G. Bradman lbw b Pollard	7	–	not out	30
A. L. Hassett c Washbrook b Young	38			
K. R. Miller lbw b Pollard	31			
S. G. Barnes retired hurt	1			
S. J. Loxton b Pollard	36			
†D. Tallon c Evans b Edrich	18			
R. R. Lindwall c Washbrook b Bedser	23			
W. A. Johnston c Crapp b Bedser	3			
E. R. H. Toshack not out	0			
B 5, l-b 4, n-b 3	12		N-b 2	2
	221		(one wkt)	**92**

England bowling: *First innings*—Bedser 36–12–81–4; Pollard 32–9–53–3; Edrich 7–3–27–1; Yardley 4–0–12–0; Young 14–5–36–1. *Second innings*—Bedser 19–12–27–0; Pollard 10–8–6–0; Edrich 2–0–8–0; Young 21–12–31–1; Compton 9–3–18–0.

Umpires: D. Davies and F. Chester

MIDDLESEX v AUSTRALIANS 222 (322)

At Lord's, July 17, 19, 20 [1948]. Australians won by ten wickets. A restrained display by Denis Compton saved Middlesex from complete collapse in the first innings. ... The Australians lost three wickets for 53, but recovered through a splendid fourth-wicket partnership of 172 lasting 115 minutes between Morris and Loxton ... Batting again 114 runs behind, Middlesex never recovered from the loss of four wickets for 27 coupled with the retirement of Robertson, struck in the face by a ball from Lindwall. ... The teams were introduced to Their Majesties the King and Queen during the tea interval on the second day.

Middlesex

J.D. Robertson, S.M. Brown, W.J. Edrich, D.C.S. Compton, J.G. Dewes, *F.G. Mann, †L.H. Compton, J. Sims, P.A. Whitcombe, J.A. Young and I. Bedford.

First innings: 203 (Brown 39, D.C.S. Compton 62; Johnston three for 43, Loxton three for 33). *Second innings:* 135 (Dewes 51, L.H. Compton 38; McCool three for 27).

Australians

W. A. Brown lbw b Whitcombe	8		
A. R. Morris c Brown b Young	109		
*D. G. Bradman c D. Compton b Whitcombe	6		
R. N. Harvey c Mann b Bedford	10		
S. J. Loxton c Edrich b Sims	123		
R. A. Hamence lbw b Sims	30		
C. L. McCool c Young b Sims	0	– not out	7
R. R. Lindwall st L. Compton b Sims	1		
†D. Tallon b Sims	17		
D. Ring b Sims	2	– not out	15
W. A. Johnston not out	6		
B 1, l-b 3, n-b 1	5		
	317	(no wkt)	**22**

Middlesex bowling: *First innings*—Whitcombe 13–2–43–2; Edrich 20–2–59–0; Bedford 11–3–44–1; Young 36–13–78–1; Sims 24–2–65–6; D. Compton 3–0–23–0. *Second innings*—Bedford 2–0–11–0; Sims 2–0–11–0.

Umpires: H.G. Baldwin and E. Cooke

ENGLAND v AUSTRALIA 223 (323, 324)
(FOURTH TEST MATCH) 51 (78, 79)

At Leeds, July 22, 23, 24, 26, 27 [1948]. Australia won by seven wickets. By the astonishing feat of scoring 404 for three wickets on the fifth day of the match when the pitch took spin, Australia won the rubber. Until that fatal last stage England were on top, but a succession of blunders prevented them gaining full reward for good work on the first four days.

The biggest mistake occurred before the game started, for the Selectors decided to leave out Young, the slow left-arm bowler who had been invited to Leeds as one of the original party. Consequently England took the field with an unbalanced attack. Having only one slow bowler available, Yardley did not know what to do for the best on the last day, and he was forced to make Compton the spearhead and to employ Hutton, who to that point had bowled no more than twenty-two overs in the season. Even then England should have won. Evans, behind the wicket, fell a long way below his best form, and three catches were dropped in the field.

Australia put together the biggest fourth innings total in a Test Match between the two countries in England; also the aggregate of 1,723 runs was the highest for any match in England.

Handicapped through injuries to Barnes and Tallon, the Australians were forced to make two changes, Harvey and Saggers appearing for the first time against England. ... When Yardley won the toss for the third time in four matches, England gained first use of a perfect pitch. Without Barnes, Bradman did not place a fieldsman close in at forward short-leg and the batsmen welcomed their freedom. ... Hutton and Washbrook gave England a great send-off with an opening stand of 168, their best partnership in any Test Match. Hutton completely justified his recall to the side and Washbrook ... completed an almost faultless hundred out of 189 and fell in the last over of the day after batting five hours twenty minutes. His second stand with Edrich produced 100.

Bedser, sent in to play the last four balls overnight, proved such an efficient stop-gap that the third successive century partnership resulted. For the second day running the Australians met with no success before lunch, and the third wicket realised 155. ... [Both went in quick succession, however, and] from a total of 423 for two, England were all out 496.

Hassett and Morris opened the Australian innings, but did not shape confidently. Morris left at 13, and next morning Pollard, in his first over, sent back Hassett and Bradman in three balls, making Australia 68 for three. Then nineteen-year-old Neil Harvey joined Miller, and, delivering a terrific onslaught on the England attack, they rescued Australia from their precarious position. In just over an hour and a half they put on 121 by glorious stroke-play. Loxton carried on the big hitting [with five 6's in his 93] ... Harvey hit seventeen 4's while making 112 – his second successive Test century. ... Yet despite this punishment England held the upper hand, for with eight wickets down Australia were 141 behind. Then occurred a similar experience to that at Lord's, where Australia's tail-end batsmen could not be dislodged ... and England's lead was restricted to 38.

Hutton and Washbrook opened with a century stand for the second time in the match and created a new world record for Test cricket in accomplishing the feat twice. Both left at 129, but England consolidated their position by rapid scoring. ... At the close of the fourth day England led by 400 with two wickets left.

To most people Yardley's decision to continue batting for five minutes next day came as a surprise and the reason for it aroused plenty of comment. The main idea was to break up the pitch by use of the heavy roller. Three runs were added in two overs, and then Yardley declared, leaving Australia to score 404 in 345 minutes. The pitch took spin and the ball lifted and turned sharply. Unfortunately, Laker was erratic in length. Compton, bowling his left-hand off-breaks and googlies, baffled the batsmen several times, but without luck. Evans should have stumped Morris when 32, and Compton ought to have dismissed Bradman, Crapp dropping a catch at first slip. In half an hour before lunch Morris and Bradman put on 64, and after the interval, against a succession of full tosses and long hops, runs continued to flow. When 59 Bradman had another escape off Compton, and Yardley, in despair, called for the new ball even though the pitch favoured spin. Evans should have stumped Bradman when 108, and Laker at square-leg dropped Morris when 126. Not until 301 had been put on did England break the stand, and by that time the match was as good as won. ... Harvey made the winning stroke within fifteen minutes of time. No fewer than sixty-six 4's were hit in the innings, thirty-three by Morris and twenty-nine by Bradman.

The attendance figures of 158,000 created a record for any match in England. – L. S.

England

L. Hutton, C. Washbrook, W.J. Edrich, A.V. Bedser, D.C.S. Compton, J.F. Crapp, *N.W. D. Yardley, K. Cranston, †T.G. Evans, J.C. Laker and R. Pollard.

First innings: 496 (Hutton 81, Washbrook 143, Edrich 111, Bedser 79; Loxton three for 55). *Second innings:* Eight for 365 dec (Hutton 57, Washbrook 65, Edrich 54, Compton 66, Evans 47 not out; Johnston four for 95).

Australia

A. R. Morris c Cranston b Bedser	6	–	c Pollard b Yardley	182
A. L. Hassett c Crapp b Pollard	13	–	c and b Compton	17
*D. G. Bradman b Pollard	33	–	not out	173
K. R. Miller c Edrich b Yardley	58	–	lbw b Cranston	12
R. N. Harvey b Laker	112	–	not out	4
S. J. Loxton b Yardley	93			
I. W. Johnson c Cranston b Laker	10			
R. R. Lindwall c Crapp b Bedser	77			
†R. A. Saggers st Evans b Laker	5			
W. A. Johnston c Edrich b Bedser	13			
E. R. H. Toshack not out	12			
B 9, l-b 14, n-b 3	26		B 6, l-b 9, n-b 1	16
	458		(three wkts)	**404**

England bowling: *First innings*—Bedser 31.2–4–92–3; Pollard 38–6–104–2; Cranston 14–1–51–0; Edrich 3–0–19–0; Laker 30–8–113–3; Yardley 17–6–38–2; Compton 3–0–15–0. *Second innings*—Bedser 21–2–56–0; Pollard 22–6–55–0; Cranston 7.1–0–28–1; Laker 32–11–93–0; Yardley 13–1–44–1; Compton 15–3–82–1; Hutton 4–1–30–0.

Umpires: F. Chester and H.G. Baldwin

DERBYSHIRE v AUSTRALIANS 224 (325)

At Derby, July 28, 29, 30 [1948]. Australians won by an innings and 34 runs. Despite the absence through injury of Copson and Pope from Derbyshire's attack, the Australian scoring-rate was limited. Brown, who shared in century stands with Bradman and Miller, exercised such caution that his first 50 runs occupied three hours. ... Derbyshire followed on 216 behind, and left-hander Smith achieved distinction in making his county's highest individual score against an Australian team. The previous best was 81 by L.G. Wright in 1896. ... Barnes reappeared after injury in the Third Test, but did not field at forward short-leg. The attendance of 17,000 on the first day constituted a Derbyshire record.

Australians

S. G. Barnes b Gladwin	24	C. L. McCool c Smith b Rhodes	31
W. A. Brown c Gladwin b Gothard	140	†R. A. Saggers not out	6
*D. G. Bradman b Gothard	62	D. Ring b Jackson	4
K. R. Miller lbw b Jackson	57	W. A. Johnston b Jackson	0
R. N. Harvey c Elliott b Rhodes	32	B 21, l-b 5, w 1, n-b 1	28
R. A. Hamence st Dawkes b Gothard	21		**456**
S. J. Loxton c Revill b Jackson	51		

Derbyshire bowling: Jackson 34.4–4–103–4; Gladwin 33–6–107–1; Rhodes 30–2–99–2; Gothard 22–0–108–3; Smith 2–0–11–0; Marsh 1–1–0–0.

Derbyshire

C.S. Elliott, A. Townsend, D. Smith, A. Revill, P. Vaulkhard, E. Marsh, †G. Dawkes, *E.J. Gothard, C. Gladwin, A. E. Rhodes and L. Jackson.

First innings: 240 (Elliott 57, Revill 41, Vaulkhard 36; Miller three for 31, Johnston three for 41, Ring three for 73). *Second innings:* 182 (Townsend 46, Smith 88; Loxton three for 16, McCool six for 77).

Umpires: J. Smart and A. Lockett

WARWICKSHIRE v AUSTRALIANS 225 (326, 327)

At Birmingham, August 4, 5, 6 [1948]. Australians won by nine wickets. Although the Australians won comfortably after Bradman put Warwickshire in on a wet pitch, the leg-break bowling of Hollies was the feature of the match. His eight for 107 in the first Australian innings surpassed anything done by an English bowler in an innings throughout the tour. During a prolonged spell he flighted and spun the ball splendidly and the performance earned him a place in the Fifth Test. Hollies kept the batsmen so much on the defensive that both the opening batsmen, Morris and Brown, 'hit wicket' playing back.... Lindwall and Johnston made the ball lift awkwardly in Warwickshire's first innings. Lindwall began a collapse with three wickets in twelve balls ... In the second innings Johnston again showed great accuracy and clever variations of pace. With McCool turning leg-breaks sharply, the game finished by lunch-time on the Friday.

Warwickshire

K. A. Taylor, J. R. Thompson, J. S. Ord, M. P. Donnelly, H. E. Dollery, A. H. Kardar, *R. H. Maudsley, †R. T. Spooner, V. H. D. Cannings, T. L. Pritchard and W. E. Hollies.

First innings: 138 (Lindwall three for 27, Johnson three for 29). *Second innings:* 155 (Thompson 35; Johnston four for 32, McCool four for 56).

Australians

W. A. Brown hit wkt b Hollies	33	–	lbw b Hollies	7
A. R. Morris hit wkt b Hollies	32	–	not out	20
*D. G. Bradman b Hollies	31	–	not out	13
A. L. Hassett lbw b Hollies	68			
R. N. Harvey b Hollies	0			
S. J. Loxton lbw b Kardar	0			
C. L. McCool c Donnelly b Kardar	19			
R. R. Lindwall c Maudsley b Hollies	45			
I. W. Johnson not out	13			
†R. A. Saggers b Hollies	0			
W. A. Johnston b Hollies	6			
B 3, l-b 4	7		L-b 1	1
	254		(one wkt)	**41**

Warwickshire bowling: *First innings*—Pritchard 16–4–35–0; Hollies 43.5–8–107–8; Cannings 10–2–30–0; Kardar 32–11–75–2. *Second innings*—Pritchard 2–0–7–0; Hollies 4–0–17–1; Cannings 3–1–6–0; Kardar 2.4–0–10–0.

Umpires: H. Cruice and H.G. Baldwin

LANCASHIRE v AUSTRALIANS 226 (328, 329)
(C. WASHBROOK'S BENEFIT)

At Manchester, August 7, 9, 10 [1948]. Drawn. Instead of enforcing the follow-on when leading by 191, the Australians batted again, and Bradman delayed his declaration until lunch-time on the last day when only two hours and three-quarters remained for play. Bradman for his highest score at Old Trafford batted three hours thirty-five minutes and hit seventeen 4's. Lancashire seemed certain to play out time, but with the new ball Lindwall bowled Ikin, who was dismissed for 99 in the second consecutive match, and Pollard with following deliveries. Thus, Washbrook being unfit, only two wickets were left when Lindwall began his last and very fast over, but Roberts held out. Although financially a great success [his Benefit produced £14,000, a record at the time], the game brought misfortune to Washbrook, for he injured his right thumb when batting against Lindwall and withdrew from the England team for the Fifth Test. Roberts, the left-arm slow bowler, did good work on a drying pitch on the first day, when he bowled forty-one consecutive overs and took the first five wickets for 29 runs. . . .

Australians

S. G. Barnes c Ikin b Roberts	67	–	c Wilson b Pollard	90
A. R. Morris c Wilson b Roberts	49	–	c Place b Pollard	16
*D. G. Bradman c Wilson b Roberts	28	–	not out	133
K. R. Miller lbw b Ikin	24	–	c Howard b Pollard	11
R. A. Hamence c and b Roberts	14	–	not out	10
S. J. Loxton c G. Edrich b Roberts	2			
R. R. Lindwall c Wilson b Roberts	17			
I. W. Johnson c and b Pollard	48			
†D. Tallon c Pollard b Greenwood	33			
D. Ring not out	17			
E. R. H. Toshack c Howard b Pollard	2			
B 16, l-b 3, w 1	20		B 4, l-b 1	5
	321		(three wkts)	**265**

Lancashire bowling: *First innings*—Pollard 27–6–58–2; Greenwood 19–4–62–1; Cranston 3–0–24–0; Wharton 1–0–4–0; Ikin 39–12–80–1; Roberts 42–14–73–6. *Second innings*—Pollard 27–8–58–3; Greenwood 13–2–53–0; Cranston 8–2–34–0; Ikin 15–3–51–0; Roberts 22–4–64–0.

Lancashire

C. Washbrook, W. Place, G. A. Edrich, J. T. Ikin, A. Wharton, N. D. Howard, *K. Cranston, P. Greenwood, R. Pollard, W. B. Roberts and †A. Wilson.

First innings: 130 (Washbrook 38; Lindwall three for 32, Johnson three for 5). *Second innings:* Seven for 199 (Ikin 99; Lindwall four for 27).

Umpires: T. J. Bartley and J. Smart

ENGLAND v AUSTRALIA (FIFTH TEST MATCH)

227 (330)
52 (80)

At Kennington Oval, August 14, 16, 17, 18 [1948]. Australia won by an innings and 149 runs, so completing their triumph in the rubber with four victories and one draw. England having been placed in a humiliating position already, the Selectors tried further experiments which aroused strong condemnation ... and Australia met with little hindrance on the road to their most emphatic victory in this series of Tests.

Extraordinary cricket marked the opening day. So saturated was the ground by copious rain during the week that the groundsmen could not get the pitch into a reasonable shape for a punctual start. The captains agreed that play should begin at twelve o'clock, and Yardley, having won the toss, chose to bat – an inevitable decision with the conditions uncertain and the possibility of more rain. As it happened, apart from local showers early on Sunday morning, the weather proved fine until England fared badly for the second time. All things considered, the Australians found everything favourable for them, as was the case at Lord's. This does not explain the lamentable collapse of England for the lowest score by either side in a Test at the Oval, apart from the 44 for which Australia fell in 1896, the last occasion on which W.G. Grace led England to victory. . . .

The sodden state of the pitch, with sawdust covering large patches of turf nearby, made one doubt its fitness for cricket. Bowlers and batsmen found much sawdust necessary for a foothold.

This supposed handicap did not seem to trouble the Australians, and reasons for the downfall of England in two hours and a half for such a meagre score were the splendid attack maintained by Lindwall, Miller and Johnston in humid atmosphere against batsmen whose first error proved fatal. Hutton, the one exception to complete failure, batted in his customary stylish, masterful manner throughout the innings, being last out from a leg glance which Tallon held with the left hand close to the ground as he fell – a great finish to Australia's splendid performance. . . . After lunch Lindwall bowled 8.1 overs, four maidens, and took five wickets at a cost of eight runs!

Everything became different when Australia batted. Barnes and Morris, with controlled assurance and perfect stroke-play, made 117, and shortly before six o'clock Bradman walked to the wicket amidst continued applause from the standing crowd. Yardley shook hands with Bradman and called on the England team for three cheers, in which the crowd joined. Evidently deeply touched by the enthusiastic reception, Bradman survived one ball, but, playing forward to the next, was clean bowled by a sharply turning break-back – possibly a googly. As if to avenge the fall of these two wickets in an over, Morris twice hooked Hollies to the boundary and the score rose to 153, while on Monday it reached 226 before Hassett left. . . . Morris missed the special distinction of making 200 through his own ill-judged call for a sharp run . . . He was eighth out . . .

Facing arrears of 337, England lost Dewes with 20 scored, but Hutton and Edrich raised the total to 54 before bad light stopped play. The conditions remained anything but good on Tuesday . . . [and after Hutton left] three wickets fell in deepening gloom for 25 runs. Evans, from the way he shaped without attempting a stroke, obviously could not see the ball which bowled him, Lindwall, with the pavilion behind him, sending down something like a yorker at express speed. The umpires immediately responded to the appeal against the light, and rain at four o'clock delayed the finish until Wednesday morning, when the remaining three wickets realised only 10 runs in a sad spectacle for England. The usual scramble for the stumps and bails as Morris held a lofted catch from Hollies marked the close; but much happened subsequently. Mr H. D.G. Leveson Gower on the players' balcony called for three cheers for Bradman and the victorious Australians. Responses over the microphone came in due course, the crowd of about 5,000 enthusiasts coming up to the pavilion to hear and see all that happened as a curtain to this series of Test Matches in which Australia completely outplayed and conquered England. – H. P.

England

L. Hutton, J.G. Dewes, W.J. Edrich, D. C. S. Compton, J. F. Crapp, *N. W. D. Yardley, A. Watkins, †T. G. Evans, A.V. Bedser, J. A. Young and W. E. Hollies.

First innings: 52 (Hutton 30; Lindwall six for 20). *Second innings:* 188 (Hutton 64, Compton 39; Lindwall three for 50, Johnston four for 40).

Australia

S. G. Barnes c Evans b Hollies	61	R. R. Lindwall c Edrich b Young	9
A. R. Morris run out	196	†D. Tallon c Crapp b Hollies	31
*D. G. Bradman b Hollies	0	D. Ring c Crapp b Bedser	9
A. L. Hassett lbw b Young	37	W. A. Johnston not out	0
K. R. Miller st Evans b Hollies	5	B 4, l-b 2, n-b 3	9
R. N. Harvey c Young b Hollies	17		**389**
S. J. Loxton c Evans b Edrich	15		

England bowling: Bedser 31.2–9–61–1; Watkins 4–1–19–0; Young 51–16–118–2; Hollies 56–14–131–5; Compton 2–0–6–0; Edrich 9–0–38–1; Yardley 5–1–7–0.

Umpires: D. Davies and H. G. Baldwin

KENT v AUSTRALIANS 228 (331)

At Canterbury, August 21, 23 [1948]. Australians won by an innings and 186 runs. The match produced two attendance records for Kent and the lowest score of the tour against the Australians – one fewer than England's 52 in the previous game. A painstaking innings by Brown and attractive displays by Morris, Bradman and Harvey contributed to the big Australian total. . . . Despite cheerless weather, a record crowd of 19,000 on the first day was exceeded by 4,000 on Monday, when Kent took the last six wickets for 68 and themselves batted lamentably against Lindwall, Johnston and Loxton. Five wickets went for 16, and ... the innings lasted only eighty-five minutes. At the second attempt half the side fell for 45 ...

Australians

W. A. Brown c Evans b Ridgway	106	I. W. Johnson lbw b Todd	15
A. R. Morris c Evans b Dovey	43	R. R. Lindwall c Ames b Dovey	5
*D. G. Bradman c Valentine b Crush	65	†R. A. Saggers c Ridgway b Dovey	8
R. N. Harvey b Ridgway	60	W. A. Johnston not out	2
S. J. Loxton c Valentine b Dovey	16	B 1, l-b 2	3
R. A. Hamence c Ames b Ridgway	38		**361**
C. L. McCool b Crush	0		

Kent bowling: Ridgway 41–10–119–3; Crush 15–1–82–2; Todd 17–3–51–1; Dovey 50.3–13–90–4; Davies 10–5–16–0.

Kent

L. J. Todd, A. E. Fagg, L. E. G. Ames, H. A. Pawson, J. G. W. Davies, *B. H. Valentine, P. Hearn, †T. G. Evans, E. Crush, R. R. Dovey and F. Ridgway.

First innings: 51 (Johnston three for 10, Loxton three for 10). *Second innings:* 124 (Pawson 35, Evans 49; Lindwall four for 25).

Umpires: A. R. Coleman and A. Lockett

GENTLEMEN v AUSTRALIANS 229 (332)

At Lord's, August 25, 26, 27 [1948]. Australians won by an innings and 81 runs. Bradman celebrated his farewell appearance at Lord's with his ninth century of the tour, in the course of which he became the first overseas cricketer to score 2,000 runs during each of four visits to England. Once again the Australians' big total robbed the match of much competitive interest. Brown, who hit his eighth century in his most attractive innings of the season, showed even more freedom than Bradman, with whom he shared a second-wicket stand of 181. ... Bradman (nineteen 4's) threw away his wicket after reaching 150, but Hassett and Miller took part in the third century stand in succession, the Australians finishing the first day with 478 for three. ... [Next day] Hassett continued effortlessly and reached 200 in the last over before lunch when Bradman declared. ... The Gentlemen's follow-on was notable for a free display by Edrich ... who hit twenty-two 4's [and] went from 72 to 100 in boundary strokes alone.

Australians

S. G. Barnes c Wooller b Bailey	19	S. J. Loxton c Griffith b Bailey	17
W. A. Brown c Bailey b Wooller	120	R. A. Hamence not out	24
*D. G. Bradman c Donnelly b Brown	150	B 6, l-b 4, w 1	11
A. L. Hassett not out	200	(five wkts dec)	**610**
K. R. Miller c Simpson b Wooller	69		

I. W. Johnson, R. R. Lindwall, †R. A. Saggers and D. Ring did not bat.

Gentlemen bowling: Bailey 27–4–112–2; Wooller 24–1–131–2; Palmer 21–3–58–0; Edrich 16–3–49–0; Yardley 24–5–88–0; Brown 27–0–121–1; Robins 4–0–22–0; Donnelly 6–0–18–0.

Gentlemen

R. T. Simpson, W. J. Edrich, C. H. Palmer, M. P. Donnelly, N. W. D. Yardley, F. G. Mann, *R. W. V. Robins, W. Wooller, T. E. Bailey, F. R. Brown and †S. C. Griffith.

First innings: 245 (Simpson 60, Robins 30; Johnson four for 60, Ring three for 74). *Second innings:* 284 (Edrich 128; Johnson three for 69, Ring five for 70).

Umpires: P. T. Mills and J. Smart

SOUTH OF ENGLAND v AUSTRALIANS 230 (333)

At Hastings, September 1, 2, 3 [1948]. Drawn. With his third century in successive innings, Hassett again played the leading part in a big score by the Australians, for whom Bradman and Harvey also completed three figures. Barnes gave a catch at the wicket off the first ball of the day and Brown went at 49, but Bradman and Hassett added 188 for the third wicket before Bradman fell to a good catch at mid-on. He did not offer a chance and hit a 6 and seventeen 4's. ... Rain stopped play shortly after tea [on the second day], and on the last day a series of heavy showers caused frequent delays. Compton led the way in bright batting with 82 out of 116 in under two hours, and Bradman rested his regular bowlers in the closing stages, during which Brown took four wickets ... in twenty-five deliveries.

Australians

S. G. Barnes c Griffith b Bailey	0	S. J. Loxton not out	67
W. A. Brown c Edrich b Mallett	13	C. L. McCool b Perks	5
*D. G. Bradman c Mann b Bailey	143	R. R. Lindwall not out	17
A. L. Hassett c Mallett b Perks	151	B 2, l-b 6, n-b 1	9
R. N. Harvey c Griffith b Perks	110	(seven wkts dec)	**522**
R. A. Hamence lbw b Mallett	7		

†D. Tallon and W. A. Johnston did not bat.

South of England bowling: Bailey 21–0–125–2; Perks 26–5–92–3; Mallett 35–5–102–2; Cook 31–5–97–0; Compton 7–0–43–0; Edrich 8–0–37–0; Barnett 3–0–17–0.

South of England

C. J. Barnett, W. J. Edrich, G. H. G. Doggart, D. C. S. Compton, T. E. Bailey, *F. G. Mann, B. H. Valentine, †S. C. Griffith, A. W. H. Mallett, R. T. D. Perks and C. Cook.

First innings: 298 (Barnett 35, Edrich 52, Compton 82, Mann 31; Brown four for 16).

Umpires: F. Chester and E. Cooke

H. D. G. LEVESON GOWER'S XI v AUSTRALIANS 231 (334)

At Scarborough, September 8, 9, 10 [1948]. Drawn. Rain seriously curtailed play on Wednesday and delayed the start on Thursday, but spectators assembled early each day and the ground was never more crowded than for this final match of Bradman in England. Probably the Australians were not handicapped when Bradman called wrongly to the coin spun by Robins, and their proviso that Mr Leveson Gower should not include more than six Test players in his eleven meant an easy match for the full strength of Australia. On a pitch completely covered by a tarpaulin before the match and whenever play ceased, the Australians were supreme. ... Barnes shared the batting honours with Bradman. Morris helped to wear down the attack in a stand of 102,

and 225 runs were added before Barnes left to a catch on the boundary ... Bradman, having become highest scorer, skied a ball to cover-point. Batting three hours ten minutes, he hit two 6's and nineteen 4's. He began with 30 out of 38 on Thursday and made his 153 out of 305. Bradman did not declare until after tea; then, besides showing agility in fielding, he remained the
personality of the match by bowling the last over. ...

H. D. G. Leveson Gower's XI

L. Hutton, L. B. Fishlock, W. J. Edrich, M. P. Donnelly, N. W. D. Yardley, *R. W. V. Robins, F. R. Brown, †T. G. Evans, A. V. Bedser, J. C. Laker and T. L. Pritchard.

First innings: 177 (Fishlock 38, Donnelly 36, Yardley 34; Lindwall six for 59, Johnson three for 45). *Second innings:* Two for 75.

Australians

S. G. Barnes c Yardley b Laker	151	I. W. Johnson c Hutton b Brown	38
A. R. Morris b Yardley	62	†D. Tallon c Edrich b Bedser	2
*D. G. Bradman c Hutton b Bedser	153	A. L. Hassett not out	7
S. J. Loxton retired hurt	12	W. A. Johnston not out	26
R. N. Harvey b Brown	23	L-b 7, w 1, n-b 1	9
R. R. Lindwall c Evans b Brown	5	(eight wkts dec)	**489**
K. R. Miller c Evans b Bedser	1		

H. D. G. Leveson Gower's XI bowling: Pritchard 19–4–60–0; Bedser 27–7–72–3; Laker 20–4–95–1; Brown 40–4–171–3; Robins 3–1–9–0; Yardley 13–2–56–1; Edrich 3–0–17–0.

Umpires: H. G. Baldwin and A. R. Coleman

SCOTLAND v AUSTRALIANS

At Edinburgh, September 13, 14 [1948]. Australians won by an innings and 40 runs. Another fine century by Morris and bright batting by McCool atoned for several Australian failures. Barnes, Miller, Bradman and Hamence fell for 91 before McCool joined Morris in a stand of 109. ... Scotland were dismissed twice in a day for 196 runs.

Australians

S. G. Barnes lbw b Youngson	5	D. Tallon c Laidlaw b Edwards	6
A. R. Morris b Laidlaw	112	†R. A. Saggers st Wykes b Laidlaw	8
K. R. Miller c Wykes b Colledge	6	D. Ring not out	3
*D. G. Bradman b Nicol	27	W. A. Johnston c Wykes b Laidlaw	0
R. A. Hamence c Laidlaw b Nicol	6	B 7, l-b 4	11
C. L. McCool lbw b Laidlaw	52		**236**
I. W. Johnson st Wykes b Laidlaw	0		

Scotland bowling: Youngson 21–2–62–1; Colledge 13–2–38–1; Nicol 17–1–55–2; Edwards 13–4–19–1; Laidlaw 12.2–1–51–5.

Scotland

G. L. Willatt, T. Crosskey, †J. C. Wykes, I. J. M. Lumsden, W. Nicol, B. G. W. Atkinson, J. Aitchison, W. A. Edwards, *W. K. Laidlaw, F. Colledge and G. W. Youngson.

First innings: 85 (Johnston six for 15, Johnson three for 18). *Second innings:* 111 (Crosskey 36; Ring four for 20, Morris five for 10).

Umpires: G. W. Lawson and R. Hollingdale

SCOTLAND v AUSTRALIANS

At Aberdeen, September 17, 18 [1948]. Australians won by an innings and 87 runs. Before a record crowd of 10,000 Bradman marked his last game in Britain with a brilliant innings which included seventeen 4's and two 6's. Scotland, sent in by Bradman, received a useful start from Crosskey and Willatt, and Aitchison and Nicol added 65 for the fifth wicket, but McCool and Johnson dismissed the remaining batsmen for 22. ... Bradman's hard hitting delighted the crowd. In Scotland's second innings only Willatt batted confidently against an attack in which nine bowlers were used. Tallon took a turn with the ball, and Johnson, deputising behind the wicket, finished the game and the tour by stumping Laidlaw.

Scotland

G. L. Willatt, T. Crosskey, †J. C. Wykes, I. J. M. Lumsden, W. Nicol, J. Aitchison, B. G. W. Atkinson, W. A. Edwards, *W. K. Laidlaw, F. Colledge and G. W. Youngson.

First innings: 178 (Crosskey 49, Nicol 37, Aitchison 32; Johnson three for 26, Morris three for 17, McCool three for 31). *Second innings:* 142 (Willatt 52; Ring four for 30).

Australians

C. L. McCool c Lumsden b Edwards	108	*D. G. Bradman not out	123
R. A. Hamence lbw b Colledge	15	A. R. Morris c Aitchison b Youngson	10
R. N. Harvey c Aitchison b Youngson	4	W. A. Brown not out	24
R. R. Lindwall b Laidlaw	15	B 10, l-b 2, n-b 1	13
I. W. Johnson c Crosskey b Youngson	95	(six wkts dec)	**407**

W. A. Johnston, D. Ring and †D. Tallon did not bat.

Scotland bowling: Youngson 35–3–114–3; Colledge 27–4–93–1; Laidlaw 10–0–62–1; Nicol 15–5–56–0; Edwards 18–5–69–1.

Umpires: L. E. Tyson and W. Nelson

1948-49

1948-49

In Australia, the brilliance of Trumper was succeeded by the equal brilliance of Macartney, and the brilliance of Macartney by the equal brilliance of Bradman. Yet Macartney's main successes in Test cricket were gained in England, and his early first-class cricket was marked rather by steadiness and slowness than by brilliance in batting, providing a complete contrast to the audacity of his maturer years. Curiously enough, it was much the same with Bradman, some of whose early innings in first-class cricket were extremely defensive in character.

The very mention of these few names tends to raise comparisons and inevitable controversies. During his amazing cricket career, Bradman was subjected to criticism because of his penchant for heavy scoring. It was a most extraordinary criticism because, as I think I have demonstrated previously in the pages of *Wisden*, the result, in almost every case, was of decisive importance to the success of his side.

From 'Cricket and the British Commonwealth', by The Right Hon. Herbert V. Evatt, KC, MP, Deputy Prime Minister of Australia, *Wisden 1949*

The farewell appearances of Sir Donald Bradman in first-class cricket and the selection of the Australian team to tour South Africa in 1949-50 were features of special importance in the Australian season of 1948-49. Bradman played in his own Testimonial match in Melbourne, scoring 123 – his 117th century in first-class cricket – and 10. In the A. F. Kippax-W. A. Oldfield Testimonial in Sydney he scored 53; and for South Australia against Victoria in Adelaide – this match was a Testimonial to A. J. Richardson – Bradman made 30 in his only innings, which was his last in big cricket. ... The Sydney match between combined teams (the Testimonial to Kippax and Oldfield) served as a special trial, and immediately afterwards the Selectors, Sir Donald Bradman, Mr E. A. Dwyer and Mr J. Ryder, chose the team to tour South Africa ...

From 'Australian Inter-State Matches', by T. L. Goodman

D. G. BRADMAN'S XI v A. L. HASSETT'S XI 232 (335, 336)
(BRADMAN'S TESTIMONIAL MATCH)

At Melbourne, December 3, 4, 6, 7 [1948]. The result was a tie. The match produced a magnificent farewell to Bradman by the Melbourne crowd. It also produced a riot of run-getting, 1,672 runs being scored in the four innings. Don Tallon, batting for Bradman's XI … levelled the scores from the last ball of the match. Tallon made 91 of 100 runs scored in the last hour. Lindwall on the first day 'stole the show' with his 104 in eighty-six minutes. He and Saggers put on 160 in eighty-four minutes. The stage was set for Bradman on the Saturday. When 97 he was missed by McCool, off W. Johnston, in a manner that pleased the crowd of nearly 53,000. Bradman reached 123 – his 117th and final century in first-class cricket. … Bradman received approximately £A10,000.

A. L. Hassett's XI

W. A. Brown, S. G. Barnes, *A. L. Hassett, N. Harvey, W. Langdon, C. L. McCool, R. R. Lindwall, †R. A. Saggers, L. Johnson, B. Dooland and W. A. Johnston.

First innings: 406 (Barnes 32, Hassett 35, Harvey 34, Langdon 60, McCool 35, Lindwall 104, Saggers 52; Loxton three for 39). *Second innings:* 430 (Brown 43, Barnes 89, Hassett 102, Langdon 42, Saggers 41, Johnson 53 not out; Ring three for 150, Bradman two for 12).

D. G. Bradman's XI

K. Meuleman c and b Johnson	100	–	c Johnson b Lindwall	3
A. R. Morris c and b McCool	25	–	c and b Barnes	108
R. A. Hamence st Saggers b McCool	58	–	b Lindwall	45
*D. G. Bradman c Harvey b Dooland	123	–	c Saggers b Johnston	10
K. R. Miller b Johnson	2	–	c Langdon b McCool	14
S. J. Loxton b Johnston	21	–	c Hassett b Lindwall	15
V. N. Raymer c Lindwall b McCool	40	–	b Johnson	11
I. W. Johnson c Johnson b McCool	22	–	c Johnson b Dooland	29
†D. Tallon lbw b McCool	11	–	not out	146
D. Ring c McCool b Johnston	17	–	b Dooland	6
G. Noblet not out	4	–	not out	9
Extras	11		Extras	6
	434		(nine wkts)	**402**

A. L. Hassett's XI bowling: *First innings*—Lindwall 15–3–41–0; Johnson 12–1–46–2; McCool 19.4–1–101–5; Johnston 21–4–92–2; Dooland 16–0–95–1; Langdon 4–1–17–0; Barnes 4–0–16–0; Hassett 1–0–2–0; Brown 1–0–13–0. *Second innings*—Lindwall 14–3–32–3; Johnson 14–0–53–1; McCool 8–0–74–1; Johnston 17–2–63–1; Dooland 16–1–105–2; Barnes 8–0–49–1; Brown 1–0–8–0; Harvey 3–0–12–0.

Umpires: A. N. Barlow and R. Wright

A. L. HASSETT'S XI v A. R. MORRIS'S XI 233 (337)
(KIPPAX–OLDFIELD TESTIMONIAL)

At Sydney, February 25, 26, 28, March 1 [1949]. Morris's XI won by eight wickets. Besides providing A. F. Kippax and W. A. Oldfield with £A3,015 apiece, the fixture was of additional importance because it served as a trial for candidates for the tour to South Africa. On the first day rain restricted play to three hours … On the second day (Saturday) the crowd of 41,575 people tumultuously welcomed back Sir Donald Bradman to the scene of many of his former triumphs. He responded by playing an attractive innings of 53 in sixty-five minutes. …

A. L. Hassett's XI

J. Burke, K. Meuleman, K. R. Miller, *A. L. Hassett, N. Harvey, S. J. Loxton, P. Ridings, V. N. Raymer, †R. A. Saggers, F. Johnston and A. Walker.

First innings: 204 (Meuleman 36, Hassett 73; Lindwall three for 27, Ring five for 49). *Second innings:* 437 (Hassett 159, Harvey 87, Loxton 93; I. W. Johnson four for 86, Ring three for 152).

A. R. Morris's XI

*A. R. Morris c Miller b Ridings	66	–	c Johnston b Walker	12
J. Moroney c Walker b Miller	217	–	c Ridings b Hassett	25
Sir D. G. Bradman c Meuleman b Miller	53			
R. A. Hamence st Saggers b Raymer	23	–	not out	8
K. Archer st Saggers b Harvey	12	–	not out	17
I. W. Johnson b Ridings	41			
†G. R. Langley c Hassett b Johnston	11			
R. R. Lindwall c Harvey b Meuleman	73			
D. Ring b Johnston	31			
L. Johnson c Burke b Meuleman	29			
W. A. Johnston not out	9			
Extras	16		Extras	0
	581		(two wkts)	**62**

A. L. Hassett's XI bowling: *First innings*—Walker 20–1–70–0; Miller 15–1–63–2; Johnston 23–0–181–2; Loxton 5–0–11–0; Raymer 15–1–103–1; Ridings 8–0–69–2; Burke 5–0–20–0; Harvey 3–0–13–1; Hassett 1–0–8–0; Meuleman 2.5–0–27–2. *Second innings*—Walker 6–0–20–1; Johnston 4.4–0–20–0; Loxton 1–0–9–0; Ridings 2–0–4–0; Hassett 2–0–9–1.

Umpires: G. Borwick and H. A. R. Elphinstone

SOUTH AUSTRALIA v VICTORIA 234 (338)
(BRADMAN'S FINAL MATCH)

At Adelaide, March 4, 5, 7, 8 [1949]. Victoria won by 271 runs. This match marked the last appearance of Sir Donald Bradman in first-class cricket. He played under the captaincy of Ridings and made 30 in scratchy fashion. His innings began on the first day and ended the next morning. Bradman twisted an ankle while fielding and could not bat in the second innings. His disappearance from the match – set aside for the Benefit of A. J. Richardson, the former South Australian and Test all-rounder – quickly affected the attendance. O'Neill caused a surprise in the middle of Victoria's first innings when, bowling with the new ball, he took five wickets for seven runs in eighteen deliveries. Loxton hit well for his 135.

Victoria

C. McDonald, R. Howard, K. Stackpole, N. Harvey, S. J. Loxton, H. Turner, *I. W. Johnson, D. Ring, †I. McDonald, J. Baird and W. A. Johnston.

First innings: 229 (Howard 35, Stackpole 33, Harvey 41, Johnston 38; O'Neill five for 45). *Second innings:* 328 (Loxton 135, Ring 32, I. McDonald 32 not out; Noblet four for 54, McLean three for 139).

South Australia

K. Lewis c Howard b Loxton	16	–	run out	20
K. Gogler c McDonald b Baird	6	–	c Johnson b Loxton	20
R. A. Hamence b Baird	11	–	c Stackpole b Ring	10
Sir D. G. Bradman b Johnston	30	–	absent hurt	0
*P. Ridings c Howard b Baird	17	–	c Stackpole b Johnston	4
B. Bowley c Howard b Johnson	12	–	st McDonald b Johnson	8
†G. R. Langley c and b Johnson	15	–	run out	36
P. Bednall st McDonald b Ring	7	–	b Ring	3
K. O'Neill b Baird	10	–	c McDonald b Baird	3
A. R. McLean c and b Ring	10	–	run out	19
G. Noblet not out	8	–	not out	0
Extras	12		Extras	9
	154			**132**

Victoria bowling: *First innings*—Baird 15–1–69–4; Johnston 14–4–28–1; Loxton 8–1–19–1; Ring 6.3–2–15–2; Johnson 6–3–11–2. *Second innings*—Baird 7–2–28–1; Johnston 23.2–10–51–1; Loxton 4–0–10–1; Ring 9–1–30–2; Johnson 8–6–4–1.

Umpires: A. F. Cocks and G. S. Cooper

Postscript

1962-63

MCC v PRIME MINISTER'S XI

At Canberra, February 6 [1963]. MCC won by three runs. Sir Donald Bradman came out of retirement for this match but to the disappointment of a large crowd he received only five balls, playing on to Statham via his foot.

MCC 253 for seven dec (Rev. D.S. Sheppard 72); Prime Minister's XI 250 (R. Benaud 68; D.A. Allen five for 68).

GOURMET COOKING FOR EVERYONE

❋❋❋

Guirne Van Zuylen

FABER AND FABER
24 Russell Square
London

First published in 1969
by Faber and Faber Limited
24 Russell Square London WC1
Printed in Great Britain by
Latimer Trend & Co Ltd Plymouth

SBN 571 08714 0

For Robin, Jeremy and Angela, without whose interest in eating, this book would never have been written

Contents

Introduction

Within the last ten years I think more nonsense has been written and talked about the mystique of cooking, and French cooking particularly, than with almost any other branch of the domestic arts.

Most English people are under the misapprehension that there is no such thing as bad cooking in France, and most French people that there is no such thing as good cooking in England. Of course both are wrong. I have eaten some really appalling meals in France, and some quite unforgettably good ones in England; and one of the most famous cooks in Bordeaux, one of the great gastronomic centres of France, near where I live, is an Englishwoman. Although France is still the fountainhead of the greatest culinary inventions, it is ridiculous to condemn every other country's cookery, and I must admit I am rather tired of the lengths to which this form of snobbery is carried.

Cooking is rather like painting. You learn the basic principles, you are advised on the mixing and use of colours, but in the end you evolve your own palette. I have yet to taste two dishes, prepared with the same ingredients by any two people, which come out precisely identical. In any case, it is not always possible to obtain exactly the ingredients given in the recipe. Very often it is possible to adapt a dish with no detriment to the result. Indeed, the different versions of many

French regional dishes are the consequence of using what happens to be available.

I always consider my own culinary masterpiece was achieved in London during the last war, when I used to make Crêpes Mornay from powdered milk, dried eggs and war-time flour. Fried in medicinal oil to which, as an expectant mother, I was entitled, and filled with a Béchamel sauce, flavoured with the weekly cheese ration, they seemed truly epicurean, and I was far prouder of this *tour de force* than I could be of the most inspired creation today—particularly as we were living in a large and rather unpractical house, I had two babies, my only domestic help spent the greater part of her working day cowering in an air-raid shelter, and my shopping expeditions took anything up to three hours, standing in queues.

To be a good cook requires really only one qualification. You must enjoy eating, and the rest is common sense and imagination. Nowadays, when the whole set-up of our lives has been so simplified, it is possible to provide simple and beautifully cooked food with the minimum of troublesome preliminaries. Most people have too many other occupations to find the time to stand for hours in a hot kitchen, and most modern kitchens are not planned with the unlimited space required for elaborate confections involving the use of several saucepans and numerous other utensils. None of the recipes in this book requires lengthy, complicated or costly preparations. Many can be cooked or partially cooked a day in advance, so that a whole meal can be produced in an average of an hour to an hour and a half, and you need not be ashamed to serve any one of them to the most critical of epicures.

Try to choose your menus seasonally. For instance, when eggs are cheap is the time to serve mousses and soufflés, and sauces with egg yolks. Cream and milk are usually cheaper in the spring and summer.

I am not a great believer in out-of-season food. In France, which is a self-supporting country, there is very little frozen food, and not much imported food. Consequently the French tend to eat their vegetables and fruit in their right season, almost as soon as buds, pods and leaves have formed. The meat is all home produced, but the cuts are totally different from those in England. There are now butchers in London and other large cities who are beginning to provide French butchery which, though you may pay a little more for it, works out much more economically in the end, as there is no waste. In France when you buy meat, you state the dish you are going to make—a roast, a pot-au-feu, a daube—and the butcher prepares the appropriate cut accordingly.

When choosing your menu, try to arrange for at least one dish that can be prepared in advance, say the day before, and limit yourself to not more than three courses. Start with the preparation of those dishes which are going to take longest to cook, and do all the messy things first, such as washing and peeling vegetables, skinning and boning fish, so that you can clear all the unwanted bits and pieces away, and have a clean space to work on.

As long as you are systematic in your kitchen, you will not find yourself left with a pile of dirty saucepans, knives and so on, to dispose of before your guests arrive.

It is a real economy to buy first-class utensils, particularly saucepans. Cheap ones tend to burn or stick. My own personal preference is for aluminium, and I am still using the saucepans I had when I married, almost thirty years ago! I advise a minimum of four to start with: one big enough to boil a chicken, a piece of ham or bones for stock; two medium-sized ones; and a smaller one, with a double lip if possible, for sauces. If funds will run to it, get a double saucepan, invaluable for all mixtures cooked with egg.

A great deal has been written about frying pans and how essential it is to have a separate one for omelettes, pancakes and other egg-based dishes. But I promise that if you buy a really good quality one and keep it absolutely spotless with abrasive wool, you can use it for everything, except deep frying—and I have included no recipes for this form of cooking, for the good reason that in a small place the smell clings, even with wide open windows *and* an extractor fan, and there is nothing more calculated to turn your appetite than the smell of stale frying permeating a home.

The new flame-proof casserole dishes which can be used either on the top of the stove or in the oven are quite invaluable, as they can be brought straight to the table, and are saving on both space and washing-up. An oval or rectangular one is a good shape for meat or fish, and a round one with a lid can be used for a number of dishes needing slow cooking.

Here is a list of utensils which are really necessary:

A large and a small wooden spoon
A perforated slice for draining (an oblong shape is the most practical)
A palette knife
Two sharp knives, one with a short blade for vegetables, the other for cutting and trimming meat, etc. (I rather incline towards the serrated variety. They seem to need less sharpening)
A colander
A large and a small wire strainer
A vegetable peeler
An egg whisk

A food mill (essential for purées of vegetables, fruit, etc.)
A smaller version for grating cheese or breadcrumbs
A grater
A tin opener
A couple of good baking tins
A liquid measure
Two or three mixing basins
A chopping board
A pair of scissors (I use mine for endless purposes—cutting up meat and fish, chopping parsley, shredding vegetables, to name only a few)
A rolling-pin (I have made do with a wine bottle, but the real thing gives better results!)

It has been my proud boast that I have never had to turn the unexpected guest away; not because I have had a store cupboard filled with rows of tins, nor because I have lived almost next door to a delicatessen which could provide an emergency meal from a deep freeze. I try to keep a supply of ingredients which can be used in a variety of ways, and with these and the very excellent dried herbs and spices which can be obtained at most good grocers', you have the nucleus of a number of attractive impromptu dishes.

I always keep flour, rice and spaghetti, and a packet of haricot beans, and sometimes semolina or sago. Since the appearance on the market of a number of excellent brands of dehydrated vegetables, I keep a packet or two of these in reserve. A tube of concentrated tomato purée, a few bouillon cubes and some dried prunes, raisins and currants are helpful in dressing up the most unpromising beginning, and my fridge is never without cheese and eggs.

Now for the herbs and spices. Don't buy large quantities, as their strength tends to evaporate after a while and you are left with a number of packets, all with a precisely similar aroma of dried grass. Here is my check-list:

Parsley	Basil
Thyme	Cloves
Bay leaves	Nutmeg
Marjoram or oregano	Cinnamon
Rosemary	Ginger

I have put parsley first: this should be used fresh whenever possible and is a most important flavouring, and not just a frilly green decoration as so many people seem to think. If you keep a little bunch in water in the fridge, it will last quite a long time.

Invest in a pepper mill. Freshly ground black pepper tastes totally different from the already ground stuff in cartons. There is as much difference as there is between buying coffee ready ground, and grinding the freshly roasted beans oneself.

In my recipes I have given most of the quantities in spoonfuls or cupfuls. In many kitchens there is no room for a pair of scales, and in any case they are a very expensive piece of equipment. You will probably find, once you become experienced, that your eye will be a pretty accurate judge of quantity.

A table of relative gas and electric oven temperatures will be found on page 150.

The kitchen is the one room in the house to which everyone gravitates. It seems to have an atmosphere of informality which can put the shyest guest at his ease. As one spends so much time in the kitchen, don't grudge the expense of making it as attractive and labour-saving as possible.

Hints and Warnings

RICE

There are many theories on the most successful way to cook rice. Of course a great deal depends on the quality of the rice. For pilafs and risottos I try to use the plump yellow Italian kind, which can be bought at most continental stores. It separates beautifully, but if you cannot obtain it choose a long-grained Patna rice, which if properly cooked soould be just as fluffy though the grain is smaller. I find the most fool-proof method for making sure you do not overcook your rice, and so produce a glutinous mass, is to put the required amount into a saucepan (a heaped tablespoonful per person and one or two over, according to appetites), cover with cold water to an inch above the rice, add salt and bring slowly to the boil. Put the lid on and cook gently till all the water is absorbed. Your rice should then be perfectly done, and all you need to do before serving is to strain it and run hot water through it for a minute or two, to separate the grains and get rid of the starch. If you are serving it as an accompaniment to meat or fish, dry it off by putting it into a cool oven for a few minutes.

While on the subject of rice, don't forget the difference between a pilaf and a risotto. In the first, the rice is boiled, and the butter or oil added after it is cooked. In the second the rice is sautéd in the fat (i.e. tossed lightly till partly cooked), and then cooked slowly enough to absorb the liquid, which is added little by little.

PASTA

Cook all pasta (spaghetti, macaroni, etc.), in very fast-boiling salted water, stirring from time to time to keep the strands separate and unstuck, and undercook rather than overcook. Strain without rinsing and serve immediately in a pre-heated dish with a good lump of butter, or a tablespoonful or two of olive oil, if you are not incorporating it with a sauce.

CREAM

Be careful not to whip cream too stiff or you may suddenly find it has turned to butter. It must remain light but inflated. Once it has started to thicken, slow down the beating, so that you can stop at just the right moment.

GELATINE

I find the best results with gelatine are obtained by dissolving it first in cold water (just enough to allow it to swell), then placing the cup, or whatever receptacle you have used, in a saucepan containing a little water and cooking gently till the mixture becomes syrupy. You can then strain it easily into whatever dish you are making. When adding gelatine to an already cold mixture, be careful to cool it off a little before combining the two; otherwise you may find the warm gelatine will turn lumpy when it comes in contact with the cold mixture. In this case, it is better to add the mixture to the gelatine rather than the reverse, and to add it gradually.

CORNFLOUR

In order to make sure that your cornflour doesn't go lumpy in cooking, put the required amount into a cup or small basin, and to begin with add only enough liquid to make a smooth paste before combining with the mixture you wish to thicken.

EGG WHITES

The beating of egg whites can sometimes be tricky. When a recipe calls for egg whites to be stiffly beaten the right degree of stiffness can be judged when you can draw the consistency up into little peaks. (When I was a young girl we were taught to beat the whites on a plate with a fork till they were sufficiently stiff to remain on the plate when it was turned upside down.) Don't overbeat, or the whites will become too grainy to amalgamate with the other ingredients.

VINEGAR AND OIL

Don't ever use anything but wine vinegar. Malt vinegar is too harsh. And be sparing even with wine vinegar in both salad dressing and mayonnaise. Use both olive oil and a good nut oil in the kitchen. Olive oil is ideal for those meat dishes which require long cooking or a marinade to start with, and it gives flavour to salads. I always use nut oil for mayonnaise, and for frying. Incidentally, although most cookery books advise for a salad dressing one part of vinegar to three parts of oil, I find this too strong and use one part of vinegar to five or six parts of oil. In this case use more salt.

WINE IN COOKING

It is an absolutely mistaken idea that cooking with wine is a wasteful extravagance. Believe me, it works out far cheaper than buying endless bottles of sauces and other artificial flavourings, which are usually so highly seasoned that they are almost guaranteed to kill the flavour of anything.

Wine, on the contrary, helps to bring it out. A sauce made with white wine will bring distinction to the cheapest fish dish, and red wine in a meat stew will not only help to tenderize a cheap cut of meat, but will certainly bring out the flavour of all the ingredients. Never, for such dishes, *add* wine at the end. The important thing to remember is that the wine must be cooked so that the alcohol evaporates.

You don't need to buy an expensive wine, and if you keep it well corked it should retain its strength and flavour. It is not a bad idea, if you do not often cook with wine, to buy half bottles. The total difference in cost is negligible. I also keep a quarter bottle of brandy and a sample size of kirsch or maraschino. A spoonful of either of these does wonders for the most uninteresting dish of stewed fruit.

MAYONNAISE

Just a word of warning. Never put home-made mayonnaise into the fridge. The contrast of the warmer air after the coldness of the ice box will invariably cause it to curdle. If you are not going to use it straight away, cover with a plate and leave it in an even temperature away from draughts.

VEGETABLES

The general rule for the cooking of vegetables by boiling is to put the root vegetables into cold water, bring to the boil and cook slowly. With the leaves and pods it is just the contrary, they must be put into boiling water and cooked fast. In both cases, undercook rather than overcook. Nothing is nastier than khaki-coloured cabbage looking and tasting like old rags, or carrots which arrive at the table with the consistency of stewed cotton wool.

BREADCRUMBS

For recipes needing breadcrumbs, if you have no bread stale enough, or no time to sieve, put the equivalent amount of bread (without the crusts) into a basin and pour on just enough boiling water for the bread to absorb without becoming mushy. Then put a plate on the top for 5–10 minutes. The steam will add enough moisture to the bread to enable you to beat it up easily with a fork, before mixing with your other ingredients.

Soups

Bouillon • Beetroot soup • Cream of barley • Cream of carrots • Potage aux légumes • Potage à la dauphinoise • Leek and potato soup • Lentil soup • Cream of lettuce • Cream of mushroom • Soupe à l'oignon • Potage maigre • Potage Parmentier • Cream of tomato • Watercress soup • Vichyssoise

Soups

Not so long ago no soup was considered complete without a basis of meat stock. Nowadays people are realizing that in many vegetable soups stock kills the delicate flavour of young vegetables. However, a good bouillon can form the basis not only of consommé but of certain sauces. So I will start this chapter with a recipe for bouillon.

BOUILLON

To 3 quarts of water:

1 large carrot cut into 2 or 3 pieces
1 medium-sized onion
3 lb. beef and veal bones
1 lb. shin of beef
2 or 3 rashers of bacon
A bouquet of parsley stalks, thyme and bay leaf
Salt and 12 peppercorns

Simmer on the lowest-possible gas for 4–5 hours, or you can leave it on all night if well covered. Strain and leave to go cold. Remove fat, and clarify by bringing again slowly to the boil with two slightly-beaten whites of eggs. This should be sufficient for the liquid in the saucepan, which will have reduced during cooking by at least a pint. Simmer for 15 minutes, turn off the heat and leave for another 15 minutes before straining through a cloth. With a boiling-up every day or two this stock will keep for a week in the fridge.

BEETROOT SOUP

This is a most delicious soup when beetroots are young. Melt an ounce of butter and fry in it a small well-chopped onion. When this is soft, stir in a tablespoonful of flour and add 1½–2 pints of stock. Bring to the boil, and go on stirring for 5 minutes. Cover and simmer for 20 minutes. Peel and slice 1 large or 2 medium-sized beetroots, lay the slices in a shallow dish, sprinkle them with salt and pepper and add enough vinegar just to cover them. Leave for a minute or two, then take them out and drop them into the soup. Cook for another 15 minutes (not longer or you will spoil the colour), then put the soup through the finest mesh of the food mill, but include only half the beetroot. Bring to the boil again and just before serving stir in 3 or 4 tablespoonfuls of cream. Add a sprinkling of either watercress leaves or coarsely-chopped parsley.

CREAM OF BARLEY

Well wash a heaped tablespoonful of pearl barley and put it into a saucepan with a quart of stock. Cover, and simmer for an hour. The barley should by this time be soft enough to pass easily through the food mill. Return to the saucepan, add a good scraping of nutmeg, check seasoning and bring again to the boil. Now add a pinch of sugar, 1½ oz. butter and a carton of cream (containing approximately a gill). Serve with fried croûtons (little squares of bread, fried crisp in very hot oil).

CREAM OF CARROTS

Peel and slice half a dozen medium-sized carrots. Wash well, put into cold water with salt and bring to the boil. Let them boil fairly fast for 5 minutes, then drain them. Put them back into the saucepan with 2 oz. butter, a medium-sized onion chopped small and a sliced leek. Stir for a few moments, then add 2 pints of stock, salt, pepper and a grating of nutmeg. When the carrots are soft enough to be mashed against the side of the saucepan with a fork, put the soup through the food mill. Add a teaspoonful of sugar and a level tablespoonful of cornflour dissolved in a teacupful of milk. Bring to the boil again and if the soup seems too thick, thin down by adding more stock. Serve with a couple of tablespoonfuls of rice, previously boiled, a sprinkling of parsley and a few drops of vinegar.

POTAGE AUX LÉGUMES

This is one of the many varieties of Garbure, a traditional soup of the Landes. Most versions include pieces of sausage, bacon and often goose, so that it becomes a sort of stew and very filling. This version, however, is much simpler. I have eaten it as a most comforting first course in the winter.

Fry gently in butter a medium-sized onion, 2 leeks, 2 carrots, 2 large tomatoes and 2 rashers of bacon, chopped. When the vegetables are beginning to get soft add 2½ pints of stock, a stick of celery cut into ½ inch pieces and 3 leaves of young cabbage well shredded. Leave to simmer for 20 minutes, when the vegetables should be almost cooked. Throw in a handful of peas and cook for a further 10 minutes.

POTAGE À LA DAUPHINOISE

When turnips are young, this makes a nice change. Wash and peel 4 small turnips, 4 small potatoes and 3 leeks. Slice them and put them in a saucepan with 2 oz. butter. Cover and let them sweat until soft, stirring occasionally. Season with salt, pepper and a grating of nutmeg and add 2 pints of white (chicken or veal) stock. Cook slowly until tender enough to pass through the food mill, stir in a carton of cream and serve with fried croûtons.

LEEK AND POTATO SOUP

A very simple soup, which can be prepared in under half an hour.

Cut 4 medium leeks into rounds after washing well and removing the tough outside leaves and hairy roots. Peel and cut similarly 4 potatoes. Sweat the slices in butter or margarine, stirring from time to time to make sure they do not stick to the bottom of the pan. Add seasoning, and when they are becoming soft, pour in 1½ pints of cold water. Finish cooking gently with the lid on (about 10 minutes). When done, mash the vegetables against the side of the saucepan with a fork, and before serving add ½ pint of milk, and reheat, then add a tablespoonful or two of cream if you have it, otherwise use a small piece of butter. This soup should not be smooth, but have a lumpy consistency.

LENTIL SOUP

When you have boiled a piece of ham, keep the stock and use it for this unusual soup.

Wash and slice a medium-sized onion and sweat it in 2 oz. butter. Add 4 tablespoonfuls of red lentils, turning them well over in the butter until all are well coated. Pour on your stock and leave to cook gently for 15 minutes, when the soup should be soft enough to pass through the finest mesh of the food mill. It should now be a smooth cream. Serve with a few spoonfuls of cream, or top of the milk, and plenty of parsley, stirred in at the last moment.

CREAM OF LETTUCE

When lettuces are cheap or running to seed, here is a way to use them up. Shred two lettuces finely and wash and drain well. Put them in a saucepan with 1½ oz. butter and sweat them till soft. Add 1½ pints of chicken stock (or a bouillon cube) and a heaped tablespoonful of rice, and simmer very slowly till cooked. Put through a sieve and serve with croûtons. This soup is also delicious cold, with a spoonful or two of cream stirred in at the last moment. In this case, leave out the croûtons.

CREAM OF MUSHROOM

Slice thinly 6 oz. mushrooms and fry gently, together with a small finely sliced onion, in 2 oz. butter. Add a tablespoonful of flour and stir vigorously till the mixture leaves the sides of the pan. Season and pour in slowly, stirring all the time, 1½ pints of stock. Continue cooking for another 10 minutes, when the soup should look creamy. Just before serving stir in a few tablespoonfuls of cream and a good handful of chopped parsley.

SOUPE À L'OIGNON

This most classic of soups, which with slight variations is eaten all over France, is warming, inexpensive and, if there is nothing else available, a meal in itself.

Allow 1 large onion per person. Peel and slice into rings and cook very gently in butter, stirring constantly. When just golden, add 2½ pts. stock (to 6 onions) gradually; bring slowly to the boil. Lower the heat, cover the pan and simmer for 45 minutes. Check the seasoning and when ready to serve, cut slices of bread into rounds so that they exactly fit the bowls. (If you have no bowls, breakfast cups are quite a good substitute.) Toast and butter the rounds. Pour out the soup, fit in the toasted lids, cover with a heaped serving of grated cheese (Gruyère for preference, as it gives the authentic slightly sweet flavour) and brown under the grill till the cheese is well melted.

POTAGE MAIGRE

The French, who so often suffer from liver disturbances, use this soup when they are dieting. Although of an almost primitive simplicity, the freshly boiled vegetables make a welcome change from more complicated recipes.

Wash and slice 3 leeks and 2 potatoes, and put them in a saucepan with 1½ pints of cold water. Season with salt and pepper, and bring to the boil. Cook gently till the vegetables are tender and pass through the medium mesh of the food mill. To serve, put a pat of butter in the bottom of each bowl or plate and pour the soup over.

POTAGE PARMENTIER

Fry a medium-sized onion and a small carrot in 1 oz. butter. Add 3 potatoes, a grating of nutmeg and 1½ pints of water. When cooked, pass through a sieve and add a small carton of cream and a handful of coarsely-chopped parsley.

CREAM OF TOMATO

Once you have tasted this delicious soup, you will never again want to eat *any* brand of tinned tomato soup, however little time you have for preparation! I promise you that you can have this soup on the table within 20 minutes of starting to make it.

Fry in butter 4–5 chopped tomatoes, and a medium-sized onion, till soft. Season with salt, pepper, and a pinch of sugar and a pinch of dried basil. Add 2 level tablespoonfuls of concentrated tomato purée and 1½ pints of stock or water. Cook gently till the vegetables are soft enough to pass through a sieve. Dilute a dessertspoonful of cornflour in a teacupful of milk, add to the soup and bring to the boil. Simmer for 2 or 3 minutes and serve with fried croûtons and chopped parsley.

WATERCRESS SOUP

Here is another most refreshing summer soup, which takes next to no time to prepare.

Wash a bunch of watercress and remove the coarse stalks and any yellow leaves. Place the cress in a saucepan with 4 potatoes (about 1 lb.) and 2 pints of water. Season well with salt and pepper and cook gently till the vegetables are tender. Pass through the food mill and just before serving add ½ gill of cream, or top of the milk, and a couple of pats of butter well stirred in.

VICHYSSOISE

This iced soup is really only our old friend Leek and Potato dressed up with the addition of cream and chives. Cut 4 leeks and 4 potatoes into rounds and cook them in 2 pints of water or chicken stock. Season with salt and pepper and when cooked pass through the fine mesh of your food mill. Leave to go cold, and just before serving add a carton of cream and some chopped chives. (If you are unable to get fresh chives, use dried ones, but add them about half-way through the cooking.)

Fish

Prawns and pineapple • Prawn cocktail • Coquilles St. Jacques Newburg • Scampi à la crème • Moules poulette • Pilaf de moules • Églefin à l'orange • Flétan à l'américaine • Fish mousse • Fish pie • Fish puffs • Kedgeree • Smoked haddock soufflé • Cold fish with mayonnaise • Pâté of tunny fish • Coquilles au gratin • Salmon cream

Fish

PRAWNS AND PINEAPPLE

When prawns are not too expensive you can make a really stunning first course with this recipe.

Allow 2 oz. prawns per person. Fry them gently in butter. When cooked, take them out of the saucepan, while you complete the sauce. Add to your butter the following ingredients per person: a teaspoonful of concentrated tomato purée, 2 tablespoonfuls of cream, and a drop or two of sherry and lemon juice with a suspicion of paprika. Mix well and turn the prawns back into the sauce. Brown in butter some rounds of tinned pineapple (allowing 2–4 per person depending on the size of the pineapple rounds). Arrange the rounds on a dish, place a little heap of prawns over each hole and cover with the sauce, which should be quite thick and not runny. Sprinkle with chopped parsley and serve very hot.

PRAWN COCKTAIL

Again allow 2 oz. prawns per person. For 4 people use a carton of cream, a tablespoonful of white wine, a teaspoonful of vinegar, a dessertspoonful of concentrated tomato purée, a teaspoonful of sugar and a pinch of cayenne pepper. The cream must be fairly stiffly whipped and the other ingredients added gradually, having already been mixed together. Add the prawns last. Serve on a bed of shredded lettuce in glasses, and decorate with slices of lemon and sprigs of parsley.

COQUILLES ST. JACQUES NEWBURG

8 scallops
2 oz. butter
2 tablespoonfuls sherry
2 egg yolks
4 tablespoonfuls rice
Juice of ½ lemon
1 gill cream
1 teaspoonful flour
Salt and cayenne pepper

Clean the scallops well and cut each in half. Fry gently in 1½ oz. butter for 5–7 minutes. Add the juice of half a lemon and cook a minute longer. Add the rest of the butter, and the flour, stirring till it is completely amalgamated. Pour the cream in gradually and bring just to boiling-point. Turn down the heat and add sherry, seasoning, the lightly-beaten egg yolks and the scallops. Heat all together, stirring till the sauce thickens. On no account must it boil or it will curdle. The rice should have been cooked in another saucepan, so that it is ready at the same time as the fish. To serve, arrange the rice in a wall round a circular dish, leaving a hole in the middle which you fill with your scallops and sauce.

SCAMPI À LA CRÈME

Usually made with fresh langoustines—in south-west France the little Dublin Bay prawns are used—but it can be made quite satisfactorily with frozen scampi and a tin of lobster.

Cut the fish in pieces, and cook for a few minutes in butter, seasoning with salt, pepper, paprika and a good teaspoonful of concentrated tomato purée. While this is cooking, beat up the yolks of 2 eggs with a gill of cream. When the pieces of fish are cooked, put in 2 tablespoonfuls of brandy and set it alight. When the flame has died down, combine your cream sauce with your fish mixture, and heat till the sauce is thick. Do not allow it to boil. Serve it as it is or with a dish of plain boiled rice.

MOULES POULETTE

This dish does take rather a long time to prepare on account of the number of times you must wash the mussels. Be careful to pull or scrape off every bit of parasitical matter and, above all, to be sure of removing the beard, a small weed-like thread projecting from the shell. Wash the mussels several times in cold water till no sand or grit remains. In the meantime make a court bouillon of ½ pint of water, a teaspoonful of vinegar, a large wineglass of some dry white wine, a dozen peppercorns, an onion cut up and some parsley stalks. Let this cook for 10–15 minutes. Then put in the mussels, and cover. They are cooked as soon as the shells open. Throw away any which have *not* opened. Keep the mussels warm, still in their shells, and strain the stock. Make a sauce of 1 oz. butter, a teaspoonful of flour, and a pint of the stock. To serve, put the mussels in a deep dish, pour the sauce over and sprinkle liberally with chopped parsley.

PILAF DE MOULES

Prepare the mussels as in the previous recipe, but remove them from their shells and set aside. Make the sauce with the same method as for Moules Poulette, but in the following proportions: 1½ oz. butter, a tablespoonful of flour and 3 pints of stock (from cooking the mussels). Return the mussels to the sauce and add ½ teaspoonful of saffron stirring well in. Cook your rice as recommended on page 17, drain well, arrange in a border and pour the mussels and sauce into the middle.

ÉGLEFIN À L'ORANGE

For 4 people you will need a fresh haddock (or a small hake) weighing 1½–2 lb. To prepare it, put it into a marinade 24 hours before cooking. Lay the fish in a long shallow dish on a bed of thyme, parsley, bay leaves, 2 or 3 small onions stuck with cloves, 2 cloves of garlic, salt and pepper, moistened with a gill of oil. Turn the fish over two or three times during the 24 hours.

The next day put the fish in a well-buttered roasting tin. Moisten with 6 oz. white wine and the juice of an orange. Cook in a moderate oven (Reg. 6) for half an hour, basting occasionally. Take out the fish, drain well and lay it on a serving dish. Keep it warm. Make a sauce with 1 oz. butter, a scant dessertspoonful of flour and the liquid remaining in the roasting tin. Decorate the fish with slices of orange and coarsely-chopped parsley. Strain the sauce and serve in a sauceboat.

FLÉTAN À L'AMÉRICAINE

Have 1½ lb. halibut (or cod) cut into steaks. Roll the steaks in seasoned flour. Heat a tumblerful of oil in a frying-pan and brown the fish. Pour in a tablespoonful of brandy and set alight. When the flames have died down, take out the fish and drain. Keep it warm. Put the liquid from the frying-pan into a saucepan, and add a tumblerful of white wine, 2 tablespoonfuls of tomato purée, salt and pepper, ¼ pint of stock or water, and an onion and a clove of garlic finely chopped. Cover and simmer for half an hour. Put the pieces of fish into the sauce and transfer to a serving dish.

FISH MOUSSE

¾ lb. salmon, fresh or tinned
2 eggs
½ pint cream
1 dessertspoonful gelatine dissolved in ⅓ cup of water
Seasoning

Mash the fish thoroughly with a fork, and make sure there are no lumps. Beat in the egg yolks and cook till the mixture thickens, then add the gelatine. Whip the cream stiffly, and thoroughly incorporate it with the mixture. Lastly beat the egg whites to a stiff froth and fold them in carefully. Turn the mousse into a serving dish and put it into the fridge to set. Decorate with slices of lemon.

FISH PIE

When you buy the fish for this dish, make sure your fishmonger gives you the bones and head. Hake or cod is the best, as it flakes easily and holds its consistency. For 4 people allow 1½ lb. without the bones. First make a court bouillon with a pint of cold water, the fish bones, a teaspoonful of vinegar, a glassful of white wine, an onion and a carrot cut up, 2 or 3 cloves, salt, peppercorns, and a bouquet of thyme, parsley and bay leaf. Bring to the boil and cook for 20 minutes, then add the fish and go on cooking gently till tender. In the meantime peel and wash some potatoes and boil in salted water. Lift out the fish, drain, flake and arrange in a dish. Make a sauce with 2 oz. butter, a tablespoonful of flour and a pint of the stock. Sometimes I add a small carton of potted shrimps, which gives additional piquancy, but you must make sure that the spiced butter in which the shrimps are packed is fully melted and amalgamated with your sauce. Pour the sauce over the fish. Strain the potatoes, beat well with a fork to eliminate lumps, and cream with 2 oz. butter and some of the fish stock and/or milk if you have any left. Spread the potato purée over the fish mixture and brown in the oven (Reg. 7 for 10–15 minutes).

This is a most economical dish for large numbers. The extra trouble involved by the making of the court bouillon raises it from the level of a rather insipid and ordinary fish pie to a highly subtle example of culinary skill.

FISH PUFFS

If you have some cooked fish left over, here is a good way to use it up. Mash it in a saucepan with some lemon juice, cream and seasoning, and stir till hot. Have ready some scallop shells or similarly shaped dishes. Arrange some of the fish cream on each shell, then place the yolk of an egg on top. Whip up the whites to stiff peaks, place over the yolks and bake in a hot oven for 5 minutes. This is particularly good when made with smoked haddock.

KEDGEREE

1 smoked haddock weighing $1\frac{1}{2}$ lb.
2 oz. butter
1 gill cream
A few drops of vinegar
Lemon juice
2 hard-boiled eggs
Pepper
1 teaspoonful concentrated tomato essence
6 tablespoonfuls rice

Put the fish in a pan with just enough cold water to cover. Bring slowly to the boil and simmer till cooked. In the meantime cook the rice. Drain the fish and flake it in the saucepan with the butter, tomato purée, lemon juice and vinegar. Mix well, then add, a little at a time so that all is thoroughly combined, the rice and cream. Chop up the hard-boiled eggs, reserve 2 tablespoonfuls and put the rest with the fish. Turn into a dish, sprinkle with the remaining egg and some chopped parsley and serve very hot.

SMOKED HADDOCK SOUFFLÉ

If your guests are prepared to wait, this makes a most attractive first course and you can continue with a cold main dish. It is more satisfactory if made with raw fish, minced, but I have also used cooked haddock with a perfectly good result. You will need 1 lb. smoked haddock fillet, 2 oz. butter, 2 tablespoonfuls of flour, ½ pint of milk, 3 tablespoonfuls of cream and 3 eggs.

Melt the butter in a saucepan and add the flour. Cook, stirring for a few minutes, then add the milk by degrees, continuing to stir until a smooth cream forms. Put the fish through the mincer if raw, mash with a fork if cooked, and combine with the sauce. When thoroughly mixed, beat in the egg yolks and pass through the medium mesh of the food mill. Whip up the 3 tablespoonfuls of cream, and the egg whites stiffly beaten, and fold into the mixture. Bake about 25 minutes in a hot oven (Reg. 6) and serve immediately.

COLD FISH WITH MAYONNAISE

From the most expensive piece of Scotch salmon to the cheapest cut of cod, the following method of cooking will ensure a most delicate flavour. It makes an ideal main course in hot weather.

Make a court bouillon as in the recipe for *Fish Pie* but ask your fishmonger to give you some additional bones and perhaps a cod's head. A good choice for this dish would be a piece of hake weighing say 1½ lb. Trim off the fins, and cook gently in the court bouillon without removing the central bone. When the fish is almost done, remove the saucepan from the stove and let the fish finish cooking in its own steam. Leave to cool in the court bouillon. To serve, drain, lay on a flat dish and decorate with slices of lemon sprinkled with capers and chopped parsley. Make a thick mayonnaise and serve this in a sauceboat.

Strain the stock and keep it in the fridge. It will make the basis of a good sauce with the remains of your fish.

PÂTÉ OF TUNNY FISH

I often serve this as a first course, accompanied by radishes, black olives and brown bread and butter.

Buy an 8 oz. tin of tunny fish in oil, and turn it into a basin. Mash thoroughly with a fork and add ¼ lb. butter, the juice of half a lemon, 2 tablespoonfuls of olive oil, some freshly-ground pepper and a tablespoonful of brandy. Beat all together till the butter and fish are perfectly mixed, press into a dish and put to set in the fridge. You can either serve it as it is or turn it out on to a plate. Best made the day before.

COQUILLES AU GRATIN

Make a sauce of butter, flour and the remains of a court bouillon. In another saucepan cook in butter an ounce or two of thinly-sliced mushrooms, and add them to the sauce. Flake the remains of some cooked fish and blend into the sauce. Put the mixture in spoonfuls into small individual dishes, cover with breadcrumbs, dot with small pieces of butter and brown in the oven.

SALMON CREAM

Make this with the excellent imported salmon available at certain times of the year. Cook 1 lb. of the fish in a court bouillon (see page 148) and leave to cool. In the meantime beat the yolks of 3 eggs with a dessertspoonful of flour, turn into a double boiler and add ½ pint of fish stock. Cook till the sauce has thickened and coats the back of a spoon. Pass the fish through the food mill and amalgamate with the sauce. Strain into it a level tablespoonful of gelatine dissolved in a little water. Check seasoning and fold in a cup of whipped cream. Put in the fridge for at least an hour to set.

Roast pork fillets • Pork spare ribs with barbecue sauce • Roast pork with purée of potatoes • Carré de porc aux pruneaux d'Agen • Jambon aux ananas • Veau à l'estragon • Blanquette de veau (1) & (2) • Veau à la crème • Roast stuffed veal • Rognons de veau au madère • Navarin d'agneau • Roast leg of lamb with rosemary • Rognons d'agneau à la tartare • Ragoût de mouton • Filets de mouton aux marrons • Langues d'agneau farcies • Côtelettes aux concombres • Baked calf's liver • Boeuf paprika • Boeuf à la viennoise • Steak à la portugaise • Queues de boeuf à l'indienne • Daube de boeuf provençale • Spiced salt beef • Boeuf à la mode • Paupiettes de boeuf • Shepherd's pie

Meat

In most continental countries meat and vegetables are served as separate courses unless a vegetable is an integral part of the dish, as for instance in many stews. But generally I would not recommend including potatoes automatically with every meat dish you cook. Many of the aromatic stews cooked with wine are far better with an accompaniment of pasta—such as spaghetti or noodles—or rice. I have tried in this chapter to suggest an appropriate accompaniment to each dish, which can of course be modified. But don't, I beg you, include potatoes, *however they are cooked*, with any dish containing rice or pasta. You will merely create a starchy stodge. For all stews with sauce, frankly I would use bread, to mop up the juice.

ROAST PORK FILLETS

For 4–6 people buy 2 pork fillets weighing about ¾ lb. each. Split them open lengthwise and lay them on a board. Lay rashers of unsmoked bacon over the meat and sprinkle with equal quantities of chopped parsley, thyme and marjoram, and, sparingly, rosemary. Fold the fillets over and place in a baking tin. Pour some oil over the meat (about 3 tablespoonfuls per fillet should be enough) and roast for 30–45 minutes at Reg. 6. The fillets should be brown and crisp on top. To serve, cut each fillet in slices and arrange on a bed of plain boiled rice. Pour over them the juices from the tin. The only green vegetable which seems to go with the very aromatic herbs is beans (haricots verts); but I think it is almost better to serve these, or a salad, as a separate course.

PORK SPARE RIBS WITH BARBECUE SAUCE

As you probably know, there isn't a great deal on spare ribs. But as they are extremely cheap you can afford to be generous with your helpings. I usually reckon on 1 side of ribs for 2 people. Cut them into manageable pieces and put them into a baking tin with a little water at the bottom. Cover with a lid or foil and roast for 30 minutes in the oven (Reg. 5). Take them out and pour the liquid away. Then coat each piece of meat with the following sauce:

- 2 tablespoonfuls concentrated tomato purée
- 2 tablespoonfuls ketchup
- 1 tablespoonful vinegar
- 1 tablespoonful brown sugar
- 1 tablespoonful golden syrup
- 1 tablespoonful marmalade
- 1 tablespoonful stock
- 2 tablespoonfuls oil
- 1 very large onion, finely chopped

Heat all together in a saucepan but do not boil.

Put the pieces of coated meat back in the oven and cook for another 30 minutes uncovered. Look at the meat from time to time and baste so that it becomes well browned and glazed.

ROAST PORK WITH PURÉE OF POTATOES

An economical joint to use for this is a hand of pork, which generally is not too fat and is excellent eating when cold. It needs slow cooking—about 30 minutes to the lb. (Reg. 5).

Put a couple of cloves of garlic into the joint and season with salt and a very little rosemary. Put into a baking tin without any fat and cook uncovered, basting frequently. Serve with a purée of potato creamed with the fat and juices from the roast.

CARRÉ DE PORC AUX PRUNEAUX D'AGEN

Agen is the great plum-growing district of France. Most of the fruit is dried and sold as a sweetmeat in jars.

Soak a dozen prunes overnight in ½ pint of claret or burgundy and a tablespoonful of vinegar. Buy a piece of loin of pork and get the butcher to chine it. Divide it into chops and roll each in flour seasoned with salt and a pinch of cinnamon. Sauté the chops in butter until golden. Take them out and keep them warm while you strain the prunes and add to the juices in the pan the wine in which they have soaked. Bring this sauce to the boil stirring all the time so that it is well amalgamated. Replace the chops, and put in the prunes, cover the dish and cook slowly in the oven (Reg. 4) for 30 minutes. The sauce should have thickened, but if it is too runny, reduce it by fiercely boiling for a few moments on the top of the stove. To serve, arrange the chops and prunes in the centre of a serving dish and surround with a border of spring cabbage before pouring the sauce over.

JAMBON AUX ANANAS

You need a piece of ham weighing 3–4 lb. Plug it with 8–10 cloves and put it in a saucepan with cold water to about halfway up. Bring to the boil and cook gently, allowing 25 minutes to the pound. When cooked, remove the cloves and serve hot with fried rings of pineapple and a very creamy purée of potatoes.

Keep the stock—it will form the basis for a wonderful lentil soup (see the recipe on page 28).

VEAU À L'ESTRAGON

Allow a 6 oz. piece of fillet of veal for each person. See that the fillets are well flattened. Roll each piece in flour seasoned with salt, pepper and tarragon, and fry in butter until golden. Take out the fillets and pour into the pan a carton of cream. Stir well so that all the pieces sticking to the bottom and sides of the pan are dislodged. Return the fillets and heat without boiling. Serve immediately.

BLANQUETTE DE VEAU (1)

Veal shrinks quite a lot when stewed, so for 4 people buy 1½–2 lb. You can choose quite a cheap cut, as long as it is lean. Remove any fat and cut the meat into pieces, put in a saucepan and cover with cold water. Add salt and the juice of half a lemon. Bring to the boil and remove the scum. Now add a small glass of dry white wine, a dozen small onions (the kind used for pickling) and a bouquet of parsley, thyme and bay leaf. Cover the saucepan and simmer for about an hour. Strain off the stock and remove the bouquet. Now in another saucepan melt 2 oz. butter and cook 4 oz. mushrooms finely sliced, add a tablespoonful of flour and stir till all is combined. Pour in slowly about ¾ pint of the veal stock. You should now have a creamy sauce. Cook for a further 5 minutes, add a small carton of cream, the meat and a handful of chopped parsley. Heat without boiling and serve in a preheated dish.

BLANQUETTE DE VEAU (2)

A simplified version can be made by preparing a sauce with 2 oz. butter, a tablespoonful of flour and ¾ pint of chicken stock. (If you have no stock, use a bouillon cube.) Check seasoning, add the juice of half a lemon and a scrape of nutmeg, put the meat in the sauce, cover the pan and cook for 45–60 minutes. When the veal is cooked, add ½ gill of cream and some chopped parsley, and serve immediately.

VEAU À LA CRÈME

Use good lean veal. Cut 1½ lb. of meat into pieces and fry gently in 1½ oz. butter. When lightly browned, add a small onion finely chopped, cook for 5 minutes and season with salt and pepper. Pour away the remaining fat and add a gill of double cream and 2 tablespoonfuls of white stock. Mix well, then stir in a tablespoonful of concentrated tomato purée, and paprika pepper to taste. The flavour of this last should be quite strong. Heat without boiling. Serve with steamed new potatoes and a plain green salad.

ROAST STUFFED VEAL

Make a stuffing of breadcrumbs, thyme, grated lemon peel and chopped streaky bacon and bind with a little boiling water and the yolk of an egg. Buy a piece of rolled and boned veal and lard it all over with the stuffing. Roast it slowly (Reg. 5) allowing 25 minutes to the pound. Serve with a jardinière of new peas and young whole carrots plainly boiled, well drained, and tossed in butter. This makes a lovely main course for a spring dinner party.

ROGNONS DE VEAU AU MADÈRE

A veal kidney should be enough for 2 people. Remove all fat and skin, and slice thinly. Fry gently in butter and when half cooked add 2 tablespoonfuls of madeira or sherry. (In the latter case put a couple of lumps of sugar into the sauce.) Let the sauce bubble for a minute or two then lower the heat and finish the cooking at a merest simmer. Serve with a purée of green peas, and add a little of the water in which they were cooked to thin the sauce.

NAVARIN D'AGNEAU

The best cuts to use for this are either slices of shoulder or loin chops. Allow approximately 6 oz. per person. Remove fat. Melt 2 oz. butter in a frying-pan with a heaped teaspoonful of caster sugar. Brown the meat, then take it out of the pan and roll it in seasoned flour. When thoroughly coated, put back into the pan and allow to brown again. Add 3–4 tomatoes, peeled and chopped, a bouquet of parsley, thyme and bay leaf, and enough stock or water to just cover the meat. Transfer all to a casserole and cook, covered, in a slow oven (Reg. 3) for an hour. Meanwhile boil 1 lb. new peas, a young turnip thinly sliced and some new carrots and potatoes. The carrots and potatoes can be cooked in the same saucepan together. Drain the vegetables well, add them at the end of the hour to the meat, and return to the oven for a further 15 minutes. Remove the bouquet, check seasoning, and if the sauce seems too thick add a little of the water you cooked the peas in.

One word of warning. To make sure your sauce isn't too greasy, pour away any surplus fat from the frying-pan before adding the tomatoes and the water or stock.

ROAST LEG OF LAMB WITH ROSEMARY

Insert a clove of garlic just above the bone, rub the joint with salt and sprinkle with rosemary. Place a good piece of dripping in the pan and roast in the usual way, basting frequently. Serve with basil potatoes (see page 99.)

ROGNONS D'AGNEAU À LA TARTARE

Allow 2 kidneys per person. Skin and split the kidneys and cook them in butter. Place on squares of fried bread and fill the centres with a spoonful of very thick tartare sauce (see page 146.) Serve with watercress.

RAGOÛT DE MOUTON

You can use a cheap cut of meat for this stew. Neck or loin are good bets, but make sure it is not too fat. In any case, take off as much fat as you can. In an earthenware casserole spread a layer of sliced potatoes, then a layer of thickly sliced onions, then the meat. Before covering with another layer of onions and lastly potatoes, insert a bouquet of parsley stalks, thyme and bay leaves. Season and add half white wine and half stock to come half-way up the sides of the casserole. Cover and cook slowly for 1½–2 hours in a slow oven (Reg. 3).

FILETS DE MOUTON AUX MARRONS

Get the butcher to bone a loin of lamb for you and cut it in slices, removing any fat. Roll them in beaten egg and breadcrumbs and fry in very hot oil. At the same time, in another pan, grill some chipolata sausages. Serve with braised chestnuts and celery.

To prepare the chestnuts, which can be done the day before, make a slit in the side of each nut, and put in a moderate oven for about 10 minutes, when you should easily be able to remove the outer shell. Boil the chestnuts in salted water for 20 minutes, drain, and remove the inner skin. When required, cook them in water or stock for another 10 minutes, drain, and return to the pan with an ounce of butter. Toss them carefully so that they become well coated and brown.

LANGUES D'AGNEAU FARCIES

These small tongues can be rather insipid when plainly boiled, but the following recipe will give you a most unusual dish and a welcome change.

Boil the tongues in salted water till they are tender enough to remove the skins. Split them down the middle and lay them in a shallow dish. Now chop together ¼ lb. mushrooms, ¼ lb. ham, ¼ lb. shallots; add 2 tablespoonfuls of chopped parsley, 2 tablespoonfuls of soft breadcrumbs, the juice of half a lemon and a grating of lemon peel. Bind with the yolk of an egg and 2 oz. butter. Beat well together and spread the mixture over each half tongue. Bake in a medium oven (Reg. 5) till brown (about 20 minutes). Serve with sauté potatoes.

CÔTELETTES AUX CONCOMBRES

When you are really in a hurry and have no time for cooking a joint, try this unfamiliar combination. Season your cutlets and grill. Serve with cucumber cut into cubes and lightly fried in butter.

BAKED CALF'S LIVER

Arrange in an oblong dish some slices of liver, with between each one a thick rasher of bacon, a thick slice of onion and a bay leaf. Season, but be sparing with the salt on account of the bacon. Put a little stock at the bottom of the dish and dot with small pieces of butter. Cover with a buttered paper before putting on a lid, or hermetically sealing with foil. Bake for 30 minutes (Reg. 5) and serve with plain boiled rice and a green salad.

BOEUF PAPRIKA

For 4 people you will need 1½ lb. lean beef, preferably a piece of top rump. Cut it in slices, and fry gently in butter. Add a medium-sized chopped onion and let it and the meat cook till golden. Season with salt and pepper, and stir. Now pour off the superfluous fat and add a good tablespoonful of tomato purée and enough, approximately ½ teaspoonful, paprika to give the dish its very individual flavour. Remove from the heat and mix in a large carton of cream (⅓ pint). Return to the stove, turn down the heat, cover and let simmer very slowly till the meat is cooked—about half an hour. Serve with plain boiled new potatoes liberally sprinkled with parsley.

BOEUF À LA VIENNOISE

The flavour of caraway seeds doesn't appeal to everybody, so find out first if your guests are allergic to the taste of aniseed before you embark on this unusual beef stew.

Use 1½ lb. of lean beef as in the previous recipe. Melt an ounce of butter in a frying-pan and brown a chopped onion. Add the meat, cut into large cubes and well seasoned with salt and pepper, and cook over a slowish heat for about 10 minutes. Sprinkle a dessertspoonful of flour and stir well, then add by degrees a gill of stock or water, and 2 tablespoonfuls of sherry. Tie a teaspoonful of caraway seeds in a piece of thin muslin, and bury this in the centre of the meat. Cover and leave to cook slowly. In another pan melt 4 rashers of bacon cut in ½-in. strips. Remove the caraway seeds, and add the bacon and cook for a further 5 minutes. Serve with a hot salad of apples, sliced and fried without sugar, in butter. You will get the best results by using a good crisp dessert apple.

STEAK À LA PORTUGAISE

Buy rump steak for this and get your butcher to cut as large slices as possible. Roll the meat in flour and fry in a mixture of butter and oil over a fierce fire to seal the juices. Then add 2 tablespoonfuls of brandy and set alight. When the flame has died down, add seasoning and a little stock or water and continue to cook gently till the meat is tender. It should not take more than 5–7 minutes. In the meantime thinly slice 2 oz. mushrooms and put them into the sauce. Just before serving pour in 2 tablespoonfuls of cream. Bring to the boil, stirring well, arrange in a serving dish and sprinkle with parsley.

QUEUES DE BOEUF À L'INDIENNE

Ox-tail cooked in a spicy curry sauce makes a good change from the usual brown gravy of indeterminate origin and tired vegetables. Ox-tail takes a long time to become tender and is very fat, so cook it the day before it is required so that you can easily remove all the excess fat from the stock before you make the sauce. For 4 people buy 2 ox-tails, and get the butcher to cut them into pieces. Soak them for an hour or two in cold salted water and then drain them. (You can do this a further day in advance and it will keep perfectly well in the fridge.) Cut up 4 rashers of unsmoked bacon into cubes and heat them with 2 oz. butter in a heavy frying-pan. Now fry a large sliced onion till golden brown. Add the meat, and fry it quickly and transfer it to a casserole (unless you have one of the flame-proof casseroles which you can use for the whole operation). Pour ½ pint of water into the frying-pan and stir well. Season with salt and pepper and a bouquet of parsley, thyme and bay leaf. Add to the meat in the casserole and cover and cook in a slow oven (Reg. 3) for 2–3 hours. Leave to go cold, when the fat can be easily removed.

On the day the dish is required, make a sauce with an ounce of butter, a dessertspoonful of flour, a teaspoonful of tomato purée, a teaspoonful of curry powder, and the unstrained liquid from the meat. Stir well till the flour is cooked, then pour the sauce over the ox-tails and cook in the oven for half an hour when the meat should be almost falling off the bones. Serve with boiled rice.

DAUBE DE BOEUF PROVENÇALE

A daubière is an earthenware casserole used for braising meat. A daube is usually of beef well larded with salt pork. This particular stew, which is almost more delectable warmed up the day after it is made, is cooked with wine and is characterized by the very strong flavour of tomatoes. Fry an onion in 2 tablespoonfuls of oil till golden. Roll your meat (1½ lb. lean stewing steak—shin does very well) in salt and a little marjoram or oregano, brown quickly and remove to a plate while you heat ¼ lb. unsmoked bacon chopped into cubes. Now add a glass of red wine (about 6 fluid oz.) and let it bubble. Stir in 2 tablespoonfuls of tomato purée and a clove of garlic and mix well. Return the meat to the casserole and add enough water to cover. Check the seasoning and cover tightly. Cook for at least 2½ hours in a slow oven (Reg. 2), by which time the meat should be tender and the sauce reduced and thickened. Serve in the casserole accompanied by a dish of spaghetti, boiled and lightly tossed in butter or oil. A plain green salad can be offered as a separate vegetable.

SPICED SALT BEEF

Buy 2 lb. salt brisket in one piece and put it in a saucepan of cold water. Bring to the boil and throw the water away. Now put into the pan 2 carrots cut into large pieces, an onion, 12 peppercorns and a bunch of herbs (parsley, thyme and bay leaf). Rub the meat in a teaspoonful of ground cloves mixed with a teaspoonful of ground mace or nutmeg, and lay it on the vegetables. Add water just to cover, put on the lid and simmer gently for about 3 hours. Equally good hot or cold.

BOEUF À LA MODE

Here is another of those dishes which taste equally good hot or cold. Lard a piece of beef (topside or top rump), weighing about 2 lb., with pieces of pork fat. Brown in some good dripping. Take it out of the pan and fry a couple of onions. Now pour in 2 tablespoonfuls of brandy and set alight. When the flames have died down, add a large glass of red wine and let it bubble. Add 2 carrots, a bouquet of herbs (parsley, thyme and bay leaf) a calf's foot if you can get it, otherwise 2 pig's trotters, and a clove of garlic. Lay the meat on the vegetables and pour in enough stock or water to cover. Put on the lid and simmer on the lowest possible heat for at least 3 hours. When done, take out the meat (it should be quite soft, but will firm up when cold), put in a dish, and strain the stock over. Leave to cool and then put in the fridge for several hours. When it is completely chilled, you will be able to remove all the fat and you will be left with a clear, not too stiff, jelly. Serve with a green salad and no potatoes.

PAUPIETTES DE BOEUF

Get your butcher to cut a piece of top rump into slices, about ¼ in. thick. Allow a rasher of streaky bacon for each slice and chop it finely. Make a stuffing of an ounce of bread soaked in a tablespoonful of hot milk, the chopped bacon, a heaped tablespoonful of chopped parsley, and a medium-sized onion, together with ¼ lb. mushrooms chopped and previously cooked in an ounce of butter. Mix well, and lay a spoonful of the stuffing on each slice of meat. Roll up and tie with strong cotton or fine string. Brown the rolls in a frying-pan in another ounce of butter, then lay them in a casserole and moisten with a gill of stock. Cover and simmer for an hour and a half, then remove the string and arrange the meat on a dish. Stir the sauce well in order to detach all the particles adhering to the sides of the pan (if necessary add a little more stock), heat thoroughly and strain on to the meat.

SHEPHERD'S PIE

This is an excellent way of using up the remains of a joint.

Mince the meat. In a saucepan melt an ounce of dripping and fry a large chopped onion. Stir in a teaspoonful of flour, half a glass of white wine and a breakfast cup of cold water. Mix well, then add the minced meat, a tablespoonful of tomato purée, salt and plenty of freshly-milled pepper, and allow to simmer, stirring from time to time. Meanwhile boil some potatoes (for 4 people, 1½ lb), put them through the food mill and return to the saucepan with a good lump of butter and ½ pint of either milk or bouillon. Beat well so that you get a creamy purée. Pour the meat mixture into a deepish dish, cover completely with the potato purée and brown in a hot oven for 8–10 minutes.

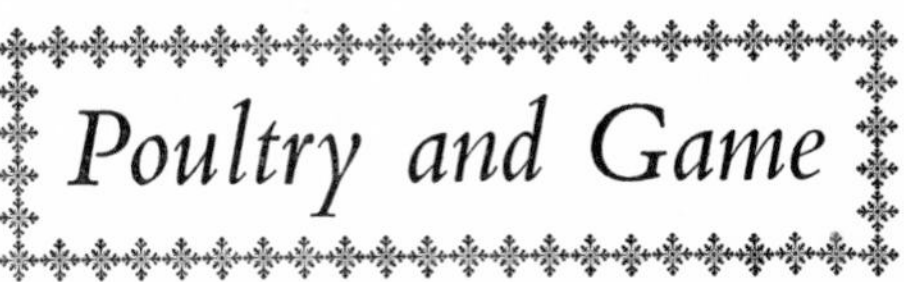

Roast chicken • Chicken à la chinoise • Chicken à l'américaine • Poulet en cocotte Landaise • Chicken à la crème • Poulet sauté au vin blanc • Poulet sauté Girondin • Poulet Saint Valentin • Canard Verjus • Roast duck à l'orange • Canard aux olives Joyeux • Braised pheasant • Roast pheasant with braised celery • Stewed pigeons • Partridges in vine leaves • Perdreaux Charentais • Lapin à la niçoise • Lapin aux pruneaux

Poultry and Game

Although it is rare in these days to buy a chicken which has not been drawn and cleaned, it does sometimes happen that one buys from a farm, or maybe a country market, a bird which is plucked and singed, but otherwise unprepared for cooking. As I once spent a highly mysterious and baffling half-hour groping about in the inside of a bird wondering why I could not find the intestines, which I had been told would emerge almost in one piece, I thought it might be useful to begin this chapter with a simple instruction on how to draw a chicken, turkey or duck. In cooking game birds the intestines are left in, except for pheasant, which is drawn like a chicken.

Put the bird on the table and cut off the claws and the legs up to the first joint. Then remove the head as far up the neck as possible. Now turn the bird round. With the point of a sharp knife make a slit just above the tail, where there is already a small hole. With a piece of clean rag put your hand into the body of the bird and draw out the intestines. Keep the gizzard, the liver and the heart and throw the rest away. Make an incision round the top of the gizzard, taking care not to pierce the bag inside, which contains undigested food. This you also throw away. Cut off the little green bag attached to the liver, which holds the gall. This is very important, as it will give a bitter taste to your bird if left. Wash the bird and the giblets in water, drain well and put on a plate till required.

In a duck, on each side of the rump (parson's nose) there are two glands which you must take care to remove, as if left in they can give an unpleasant taste.

ROAST CHICKEN

I must admit that, generally speaking, the French roast a chicken better than any other nationality. The secret, of course, is in the amount of butter put inside the bird and the frequent basting. The result is a bird cooked to a moisture and delicacy obtained by no other means, though an excellent imitation can be obtained, if you have no time to baste, by hermetically sealing the bird in foil.

For a chicken for 4 people rub the outside with the juice of half a lemon and add a good spreading of butter. Fill the inside with a piece of butter weighing about ¼ lb., the liver and a half-lemon. Wrap in foil and cook in a hot oven (Reg. 7) allowing 25 minutes to the pound. Remove the foil for the last 10 minutes. Place the bird on a dish and keep it warm in the oven having emptied the juices out of it into the roasting pan. Now pour in a little stock which you have made from the giblets. Serve this sauce separately and put the chicken on a serving dish, with plenty of watercress.

CHICKEN À LA CHINOISE

Crush a clove of garlic with a teaspoonful of sugar and a teaspoonful of coriander seeds, previously roasted for 2–3 minutes in the oven, and work into a sauce with 2 tablespoonfuls of soya sauce, a tablespoonful of oil, salt and freshly-ground black pepper. Rub the sauce thoroughly into the chicken and leave for 15 minutes. Roast in the ordinary way, and serve with boiled rice, mixed with a cup of diced cooked pork and some pineapple rings and lettuce all lightly fried in oil.

CHICKEN À L'AMÉRICAINE

I found this version of chicken Maryland quite delicious, and it is easily and quickly prepared.

Divide a small roasting chicken into four, and brush with oil. Roll in flour lightly seasoned with salt and pepper. Fry 4 rashers of fairly fat bacon, then add the chicken joints and cook till brown. Add half a teacupful of cream and continue cooking uncovered for about 5 minutes when the cream should have thickened. Now add another half-cupful of cream, cover and simmer gently for a further 15 minutes. During this time slice some bananas lengthwise and fry till brown. Arrange the chicken in the centre of a dish and place the bananas all round it with some spoonfuls of heated sweet corn. Pour the cream sauce over it, sprinkle with parsley and serve quickly.

POULET EN COCOTTE LANDAISE

This is an ideal way to cook a chicken when either you have guests who are likely to be late, or you yourself want to find something ready if you have been out in the early part of the evening. You can prepare the whole thing the day before and heat it up in next to no time.

For 4 people you will need 4 chicken joints, or a bird cut into quarters. First soak a dozen prunes in ½ pint of red wine and a tablespoonful of wine vinegar, allowing 3 hours. When you are ready to prepare your cocotte, chop 2 onions with a clove of garlic and lightly brown them in 2 oz. butter. Now brown the pieces of chicken, and when well coloured take them out and put them on a warm plate. Remove the prunes from the wine, drain well, and roll each one in a rasher of streaky bacon. Sauté them over a moderate heat for about 10 minutes, then pour in the wine and vinegar, check the seasoning, add the chicken and its juices, and a large green pepper cut into narrow strips. (Make sure you cut off the end of the pepper and remove all the seeds, as they are very bitter. The best way to do this is to hold the pepper under the cold tap for a moment or two, so that all the stray seeds get washed away.) Cover the casserole and put it in a slow oven (Reg. 3) for an hour. Serve with boiled rice and a green salad.

CHICKEN À LA CRÈME

For this you will need a boiling fowl. Peel 2 carrots and an onion and prepare a bouquet of herbs, salt and pepper. Put these, together with the chicken, into a saucepan of cold water—enough just to cover the top of the breast bone. Bring to the boil, lower the heat and let simmer. It will take at least 2 hours, or, if a very old bird, even longer. When it is really tender, take it out and put it on a plate. In another saucepan melt 2 oz. butter, add ¼ lb. thinly-sliced mushrooms, with a teaspoonful of chopped tarragon, and cook gently till soft. Then sprinkle into the pan a dessertspoonful of flour, stir well with a wooden spoon and pour in, away from the fire, enough of the strained stock to make a thinnish creamy sauce. Return to the heat, bring to the boil, cook gently for a further 5 minutes, stirring all the time, then add a small carton of cream. Carve the chicken into convenient sized pieces, arrange in a dish and pour the sauce over. This is particularly delicious served with *petits pois à la française* (see page 108).

POULET SAUTÉ AU VIN BLANC

Divide a chicken into four and remove the skin. Melt an ounce of butter in a flame-proof casserole and cook an onion, cut into thin rings, for a few minutes. It must not be darker than pale gold. Remove it and set aside. Add 2 oz. more butter to the casserole and gently fry the pieces of chicken, taking care not to let them brown. Cook for about 10 minutes turning the pieces from time to time. Now return the onion to the casserole, add the giblets, cover and put into a hot oven (Reg. 6) for 10–12 minutes. While the chicken is in the oven, make a Béchamel with 1 oz. flour, 1 oz. butter and ½ pint of milk. Season with salt and pepper. Cook gently for a minute or two then add the onion from the casserole. Remove the giblets from the casserole and discard. Keep the pieces of chicken warm. Now add 2 tablespoonfuls of cognac to the Béchamel and set alight. When the flame has subsided reduce the sauce a little, strain it into a clean saucepan and add a small pat of butter, the juice of half a lemon and 4 oz. white wine. Reheat the sauce and coat the pieces of chicken. Sprinkle with parsley before serving.

POULET SAUTÉ GIRONDIN

In certain parts of the Gironde (the south-west department of France of which Bordeaux is the capital), chestnut trees grow in great profusion, and I first met this unusual way of cooking chicken in a tiny restaurant near La Réole (one of Henry II's last strongholds in France).

Cut up a roasting chicken into joints and season with salt and pepper. Melt an ounce of butter in a heavy pan, and fry 4 oz. fat pork (belly is the best for this), cut into cubes. When it is beginning to colour, add the pieces of chicken and cook to a light brown. Pour off any surplus fat and add a bouquet of herbs and a small glass of sherry. In the little restaurant they used madeira, but I have had quite good results with vermouth or sherry. Cover the pan and cook fairly quickly for 5 minutes. Reduce the heat and continue cooking gently until the meat is tender. In another saucepan heat some chestnut purée, which you have made according to the recipe for *Filets de mouton aux marrons* (page 54). Beat in a good pat of butter, and arrange in a wall round a circular dish. Put the pieces of chicken in the middle, pour the pan juices over, and serve with croûtons fried crisp in very hot oil.

POULET SAINT VALENTIN

When I was a young girl I used to stay with some great friends who had an estate between Salzburg and Linz (the birthplace of Mozart). The Schloss had been a medieval convent and my chief recollection is of the fantastically tiled roof with hundreds of white pigeons perched on the crenellations as if they were part of the decoration.

The cook, who was a native of the village, used to prepare chickens from this recipe, which she declared had been handed down through generations of her forebears.

Cut a roasting chicken into neat joints and brown them on both sides in 2 oz. butter. Season with a little paprika, salt and nutmeg. Pour away half the fat, sprinkle a tablespoonful of flour on the chicken joints. Stir well and add a wineglass of white wine and ½ pint of milk. Bring to the boil, still stirring, then turn down the heat, cover and simmer for half an hour. While the chicken is cooking, put 4 tablespoonfuls of rice in another saucepan with a pint of white stock, if possible (otherwise use water), flavoured with paprika, salt and nutmeg. When cooked, the rice should have absorbed all the stock, but if any remains, boil fiercely till evaporated. Now mix in 2 oz. chopped ham, a handful of chopped parsley and 2 oz. butter. Arrange the chicken joints in the centre of a dish, with the rice as a border. Add the juice of half a lemon to the sauce, reduce by letting it boil fiercely for a minute or two, stir in a pat of butter, and strain over the chicken. A plain green salad is the only accompaniment you need.

CANARD VERJUS

Verjus is a term used in wine growing districts to denote acid, or unripe grapes. For this very piquant recipe for cooking duck, use the small green South African grapes which are very cheap in the summer months. For a medium-sized duck you will need ½ lb. of grapes, which you must blanch to soften the skins.

Roast the duck in a covered pan, and while it is cooking prepare the following sauce. Cut 4 rashers of streaky bacon into dice and heat them in an ounce of butter. Add 2 medium-sized carrots, or 1 large one, chopped, a small onion also chopped, a bouquet of parsley, thyme and bay leaf, and salt and pepper. When browned, sprinkle a tablespoonful of flour and mix well. Add a wineglass (4 oz.) of white wine and a pint of meat stock. (If you have no stock, use a good make of bouillon cube.) Bring to the boil, stirring well, and allow to reduce a little, then cover, and cook for half an hour. Pass through the fine mesh of the food mill, add 2 medium-sized tomatoes, cook for 15 minutes and pass again through the strainer. Add the grapes and a good tablespoonful of redcurrant jelly. The sauce should now be of a creamy consistency, but if it still seems too thin reduce it a little, and then let it simmer till you are ready to use it. The grapes should be just soft.

ROAST DUCK À L'ORANGE

A duck is a very fat bird, so put it in a pan with a little water and no other fat. After roasting it uncovered for half an hour (Reg. 5), pour the fat away, and put it back into the oven with a little more water and the giblets. Cook for another half an hour, or longer, basting frequently. When it is done, take it out, keep it warm and add to the juices in the pan the juice of an orange and the rind of half an orange cut into match-sized strips. Cook on the top of the stove till the rinds are soft. Now sprinkle a tablespoonful of flour, let it cook for a few minutes, then add enough stock to make the sauce of a creamy consistency. Carve the duck, and serve with *Petits pois à la Française* (see page 108). The sauce should accompany it in a sauceboat.

CANARD AUX OLIVES JOYEUX

One of the most imaginative cooks I ever met was our *régisseur*, and his way of cooking duck with olives was in the class of great cookery. Here is his recipe.

To make the stuffing, stone and chop 24 green olives and combine with 2 oz. bread soaked in water and squeezed dry, 2 oz. chopped mushrooms, ½ a clove of garlic minced, the liver of the duck, a tablespoonful of minced parsley and a little pepper. Bind with a beaten egg. Stuff the bird, and either sew it up, or make sure the flap of skin is well tucked under to prevent the stuffing escaping. Roast in the ordinary way, basting frequently and pouring away some of the fat. When the bird is half cooked, put another dozen olives into the roasting pan. To serve, cut the duck into convenient pieces with some of the stuffing on each one, leave a little fat in the pan, pour away the rest and add a little stock which you have made from the giblets (neck, gizzard and heart). Pour this over the pieces of duck, and serve with plain boiled new potatoes, well coated with chopped parsley.

BRAISED PHEASANT

This is a marvellous way of cooking a tough old bird, as the slow stewing not only brings out the flavour but guarantees absolute tenderness of the meat.

Roll the pheasant in seasoned flour, brown in butter and when well coloured remove from the pan and fry half a dozen rashers of streaky bacon in the same fat. Now blanch a young cabbage in boiling salted water, drain it well, cut away the hard stalky parts and separate the leaves. Carve the bird. In a casserole put a layer of the cabbage leaves, then the pieces of pheasant, 4 frankfurter sausages and a bouquet of parsley, thyme and bay leaf. Cover with the remaining cabbage leaves. Pour a good teacupful of stock or water into the frying-pan, stir well to amalgamate the juices and pour it over the meat and cabbage. Cover the casserole with a lid or foil and cook in a slow oven (Reg. 3) for 2–3 hours.

This dish takes very kindly to re-heating and so you can make it the day before you need it. It is also good with stewing partridges, but add a piece of orange peel to the bouquet, which must be removed before serving.

ROAST PHEASANT WITH BRAISED CELERY

Cover the pheasant with rashers of fat bacon and tie well. As pheasant is inclined to be rather dry, put a lump of butter inside the bird. Grate some lemon rind over and wrap up in foil. Roast (Reg. 6) for 40–45 minutes. Serve with braised celery.

STEWED PIGEONS

Allow 1 pigeon per person. Brown them all over in butter, then take them out and cook in the same butter an onion and a carrot chopped. When these are becoming soft and brown, sprinkle with a tablespoonful of flour and stir well. Add a small wineglassful of red wine, a tablespoonful of tomato purée, a bouquet of herbs and enough stock to make a creamy sauce. Put the pigeons into a casserole and pour the sauce over. Cook in a slow oven (Reg. 4). If the birds are young, half an hour should be long enough, but if you buy them as stewing pigeons, they will need at least an hour. In the meantime fry 2 or 3 rashers of bacon chopped into cubes and some tiny onions (the kind for pickling) to which you have added a teaspoonful of sugar. If you can get hold of some cranberries, make a compôte with 1 lb. cranberries stewed without sugar in a teacupful of water. When cooked, press the fruit against the sides of the saucepan to release the juice and stir in 2 or 3 tablespoonfuls of sugar (more if you have a very sweet tooth!). Add the bacon and onions to the sauce with the pigeons and transfer the cranberry compôte to a glass dish.

PARTRIDGES IN VINE LEAVES

Tie a slice of fat pork and a piece of lemon peel over the breast of each partridge and put a lump of butter inside. Wrap each bird in vine leaves. If you are unable to get fresh ones, you can buy tins containing about half a pound, and the leaves will keep quite well in the fridge for several days. Put the partridges in a covered dish and roast in a fairly hot oven (Reg. 6) for 30–45 minutes.

PERDREAUX CHARENTAIS

Our milk used to be supplied by a native of the great dairy-producing part of the Charente—the other part is famous for the grapes which provide the basis of the great brandies. Madame Muret was a famous cook in our village and was flattered rather than otherwise when one begged for the secret of one of her specialities. I found the following way of serving old partridges quite delicious.

Season the birds with salt, pepper and lemon juice, brown all over in butter, add enough stock or water to half cover the birds, and stew gently on top of the stove or in the oven for an hour and a half. While the partridges are cooking, make a compôte of apples flavoured with a little brown sugar. Spread the compôte on a dish and when the birds are cooked, halve them, lay them on the apple, cover each half with a tablespoonful of cream, put them in a hot oven for a few minutes and then serve immediately.

LAPIN À LA NIÇOISE

Cut the rabbit into pieces and roll in seasoned flour. Heat 3 tablespoonfuls of oil in a frying-pan and fry the pieces of rabbit till golden. Pour in a glass of white wine and let it bubble for a minute or two. Add about 15 black olives, $\frac{1}{2}$ lb. tomatoes slightly cooked without water and passed through a sieve, and a bouquet of parsley, thyme and bay leaf. Cover and cook very gently for 25 minutes. Take out the pieces of meat and arrange them on a dish and keep them warm while you add to the sauce 2 oz. butter. Mix well, pour the sauce over the meat and serve at once.

LAPIN AUX PRUNEAUX

This classic method of cooking rabbit is also excellent with chicken.

Wash some prunes and leave them to soak overnight. Cut the rabbit in pieces and place them in a casserole. Pour over them a heated marinade made with a large carrot cut in rounds, half a bottle of red wine, a wineglassful of water and a bouquet of parsley, thyme and bay leaf. Leave also to soak overnight, making sure that all the pieces of rabbit are covered with the marinade.

The next day melt 1½ oz. butter in a pan and brown 2 medium-sized onions, sliced, and ¼ lb. fat bacon chopped into little cubes. Add the pieces of rabbit from the marinade and brown well. Strain the marinade over the meat, season with salt and pepper and add the drained prunes. Transfer to a casserole, cover and cook in a slow oven (Reg. 4) for an hour. Serve as it is, accompanied by a green vegetable (young cabbage is particularly good). If the sauce is too thin, reduce by boiling for a minute or two.

Supper Dishes

Crêpes Florentine • Crêpes aux épinards Mornay • Crêpes au Gryère • Crêpes aux champignons • Fondue Franc-Comtoise • Tartines Marquise • Beignets de fromage blanc • Croquettes au fromage • Croustades au Gruyère • Gougère • Stuffed cabbage • Veal and ham cheese • Mexican rolls • Spaghetti bolognese • Laitues de la Mère Landurette • Pilaf à la reine • Pork with Jambalaya rice • Gâteau de volaille à la crème

Supper Dishes

CRÊPES

There is a restaurant in Paris which serves only pancakes, and until one has eaten the many original and delectable fillings, one does not realize how attractive a meal can be produced with the minimum of expense. The preparation is really not such a complicated affair as it might appear.

First, your batter. To make 12–14 pancakes, put 8 rounded tablespoonfuls of flour into a basin with a teaspoonful of salt. Now stir in 2 tablespoonfuls of oil and 2 whole eggs. When this is well mixed add ½ pint of milk and cold water in equal quantities. Stir again until there are no lumps, and strain into a clean basin. Cover and leave to stand for at least 2 hours. When you are ready to cook the pancakes, run a few drops of oil over the bottom of a frying-pan and, with a ladle or large spoon, quickly pour in a thin layer of batter. Allow to cook for a moment or two, move the pan till the whole of the surface is covered with the batter, then with a palette knife turn the pancake over and fry the other side. The whole operation should take no more than a minute for each pancake. Lay the pancakes one on top of the other on a plate till wanted.

CRÊPES FLORENTINE

Cook 1 lb. spinach, squeeze out the water and put it through the food mill. Now put it in the top of a double saucepan, with 2 or 3 tablespoonfuls of cream, the same amount of stock and the yolks of 2 eggs. Season with salt, pepper, a scrape of nutmeg and a pinch of sugar. Stir till the mixture thickens. Spread out the required number of pancakes and lay a good spoonful of the spinach mixture on each one. Roll up, lay side by side in a dish, cover and keep warm till wanted. Serve with a basil-flavoured tomato sauce.

CRÊPES AUX ÉPINARDS MORNAY

Prepare the spinach as in the previous recipe, but when drained and sieved mix it with a cheese-flavoured Béchamel (for the basic method see page 142), spiced with a little nutmeg. Fill the pancakes as before and serve without the addition of any other sauce.

CRÊPES AU GRUYÈRE

Make a very thick Béchamel with 1½ oz. butter, 2 tablespoonfuls of flour and a pint of milk, seasoned with nutmeg, salt and pepper. When thoroughly amalgamated, add 2 oz. grated gruyère, cheddar or parmesan. Fill the pancakes with the sauce, roll them up and arrange in a fireproof dish. Sprinkle with grated cheese and slivers of almonds. Put in a hot oven to brown for about 10 minutes.

CRÊPES AUX CHAMPIGNONS

Fry a medium-sized onion, chopped finely, in 1½ oz. butter. Add 6 oz. mushrooms, thinly sliced, and 2 oz. chopped bacon or ham. When the mushrooms are cooked, sprinkle a tablespoonful of flour into the pan, stir well and add gradually ½ pint of stock. If you have some stock from chicken bones, so much the better. Cook a little longer, fill the pancakes as before, sprinkle liberally with chopped parsley and serve at once.

FONDUE FRANC-COMTOISE

This is a French regional variation of a Swiss fondue, made with light local wine. It has the merit of very quick preparation.

Rub the bottom of a fireproof dish with a crushed clove of garlic. Pour in a gill of white wine and warm it. Now add 2 tablespoonfuls of grated gruyère and cook it gently, stirring frequently, till the sauce becomes creamy. Beat up 6 eggs as if you were going to make an omelette and stir them into the cheese sauce, together with 2 oz. butter. Allow to simmer for 7–8 minutes, while the mixture thickens, season with salt, pepper and a good pinch of grated nutmeg, and serve in a well buttered and heated dish, with fingers of toast.

TARTINES MARQUISE

Make a Béchamel with 1½ oz. butter, 1½ tablespoonfuls of flour and ½ pint milk. When smooth and creamy, stir in the yolks of 2 eggs and 4 tablespoonfuls of grated cheese. Cut the required number of slices of bread and cover them thickly with the sauce. Have ready a frying-pan half full of oil, heat it up to boiling-point (there should be the faintest suspicion of smoke rising from the pan). Slip the tartines into the boiling fat and fry till golden. Serve immediately.

BEIGNETS DE FROMAGE BLANC

Boil 1 lb. potatoes till soft and pass them through a sieve. Beat into them a whole egg, ½ lb. cottage cheese, sieved, salt and pepper, the grated rind of a lemon and 3 tablespoonfuls of flour. Mix together, flour your hands and roll the mixture into little sausage-like shapes. Fry these in a very hot oil and drain on soft paper. Serve at once.

CROQUETTES AU FROMAGE

Make a thick Béchamel with 2½ oz. butter, 3 tablespoonfuls of flour and a pint of milk. Season with salt and pepper and stir in the yolks of 2 eggs and 5 tablespoonfuls of grated cheese. Roll the paste into thumb-sized sausages and fry in very hot fat. Drain on paper and serve with bunches of parsley.

CROUSTADES AU GRUYÈRE

In a double saucepan cook ½ cup of milk, 4 tablespoonfuls of grated cheese, 2 oz. butter, a whole egg, salt, pepper and a scrape of nutmeg. Stir till the mixture has sufficiently thickened (it should be almost solid) to spread on pieces of buttered toast. Brown quickly under the grill and serve at once.

GOUGÈRE

We had a manservant whose home was near Vezelay, one of the most beautiful centres of Roman civilization in France. Like all Burgundians, he was a great cheese eater, and particularly fond of cooked-cheese dishes. The following recipe, for which our cook used to hand over her kitchen to him, is the most famous cheese dish of Burgundy, and I give it with the instructions as written for me when I got married.

'Make a pâte à choux with 3 oz. butter and ¼ pint of water, which you season with salt and pepper and bring to the boil, stirring to make sure they are well mixed. Pour in, all at once, 4 tablespoonfuls of flour, and beat well, till the mixture leaves the sides of the saucepan. Remove from the fire and beat in one by one 4 eggs. Make sure each is thoroughly amalgamated before adding the next.

'Now stir in 3 oz. gruyère cut into tiny cubes, and arrange the mixture with a spoon round the edge of a sandwich tin (preferably one with a detachable base) so that you have a sort of cake with a hole in the middle. Sprinkle the top with another ounce of cheese similarly cut into cubes. Put into a moderate oven (Reg. 5) and cook for about 35–40 minutes. Turn the oven off and leave the gougère to cook for a further 5–7 minutes to make sure it is absolutely firm, otherwise it will collapse as soon as you take it out. Serve at once.'

STUFFED CABBAGE

When you want to economize on meat and feel that a vegetarian dish isn't quite satisfying enough, try this.

Blanch a cabbage in boiling salted water for 5 minutes, then take it out, drain it and tear off the leaves. Make a stuffing of ½ lb. sausage meat and ½ lb. minced veal; season with thyme, parsley, a little grated nutmeg and garlic, salt and pepper; bind with the yolk of an egg and 2 tablespoonfuls of breadcrumbs and beat all together. Put a layer of the cabbage leaves at the bottom of a casserole, then spread a layer of the stuffing, cover with cabbage leaves and fill up the casserole with alternate layers of stuffing and leaves, finishing with a layer of cabbage. Now stick 2 cloves into the top leaves, and cover with a sauce made from 2 oz. butter, 2 oz. flour, a heaped tablespoonful of tomato purée and ½ pint of stock. Put the lid on the casserole and cook in a slow oven for an hour.

VEAL AND HAM CHEESE

Buy the cheapest stewing veal and put 1½ lb. through the mincer, or get the butcher to do it for you. Remove the rind from 4 rashers of unsmoked back bacon, chop into little cubes and mix with the veal. Add ½ cup of breadcrumbs and 2 beaten eggs, and season with thyme (or marjoram), parsley, nutmeg, salt and pepper. Grease an oblong cake tin, press the mixture well in, brush with beaten egg white and sprinkle with breadcrumbs. Dot with bits of butter and bake in a moderate oven (Reg. 5) for an hour. You can eat it hot or cold.

MEXICAN ROLLS

This is quite a good way of using up the remains of a chicken, and again can be eaten hot or cold.

To 2 teacupfuls of mashed potato add a cupful of chopped cooked chicken, a cupful of chopped cooked carrots and 2 tablespoonfuls of stock. Season highly with salt, paprika, grated onion and tabasco. Spread slices of ham very thickly with the mixture, roll, tie with thin string, brush with melted butter or oil, and bake in a moderate oven (Reg. 5) for 25 minutes.

SPAGHETTI BOLOGNESE

When this is made with freshly-minced beef, it bears absolutely no resemblance to the rancid-tasting concoction composed of remains of goodness knows what, flung into stale gravy and served under the name of Spaghetti Bolognese in cheap restaurants.

As a main dish you will need 1 lb. of minced beef. Fry a large chopped onion in 3 tablespoonfuls of oil (olive oil if possible), and when golden add the minced beef and ¼ lb. thinly-sliced mushrooms (use the stalks as well as the caps). Make sure that the beef is properly seized in the oil. It will take about 5 minutes. Now add a glass of red wine and let it boil for a moment or two. Season with salt, pepper and basil, 2 heaped tablespoonfuls of tomato purée, a heaped teaspoonful of sugar and enough water or stock to make a creamy sauce. Cover and cook very gently for 45 minutes.

To cook the spaghetti, allow 2–4 oz. per person. Boil in a large saucepan of salted water for 15–20 minutes. Don't let it get too soft or you will find it turns mushy when drained.

To serve, put the spaghetti into the bottom of a heated dish and pour the sauce over. Serve a bowl of grated parmesan separately.

LAITUES DE LA MÈRE LANDURETTE

I think too few people are aware of the delicate flavour of lettuces when cooked. Try this when you have some remains of chicken or veal.

Allow 1 lettuce to each ½ lb. of minced meat. Blanch the lettuce in salted water for a minute and carefully tear off the leaves. In a basin mix the minced meat with 5 tablespoonfuls of uncooked rice and an egg. Season with salt and pepper. Put spoonfuls of this mixture on to each lettuce leaf, and roll into little packets. Place the rolls in a dish and pour over a carton of cream and bake in a moderate oven (Reg. 5) for 45 minutes. Take a look half-way through and if the rolls are beginning to look dry, add 2 or 3 spoonfuls of stock.

PILAF À LA REINE

Cook 8 tablespoonfuls of rice in salted water. Drain and put in a dish, then cover and leave in a slow oven (Reg. 1) for 25 minutes. In the meantime make a Béchamel with 1 oz. butter, a level tablespoonful of flour and ½ pint of chicken stock. Add the chopped remains of a chicken, ½ lb. thinly-sliced mushrooms and a pinch of saffron or curry powder. Leave to cook gently for 20 minutes. Add a small carton of cream, mix with the rice, check the seasoning and serve well sprinkled with chopped parsley.

PORK WITH JAMBALAYA RICE

Cut 4 oz. fat bacon into dice and heat in a frying-pan. When the fat starts to run, add 2 chopped onions. When golden, remove these and the bacon and fry all over a piece of pork weighing about 1 lb. When the pork is well browned, return the pieces of bacon and onion and add 4 oz. chopped ham. Moisten with 2 pints of stock. Boil for 15 minutes. Lower the heat and add 8 tablespoonfuls of well-washed rice, a bouquet of herbs and salt and cayenne pepper. Cook for a further 10 minutes.

GÂTEAU DE VOLAILLE À LA CRÈME

This is not only a delicious way of cooking a rather aged boiling fowl, but it is a most economical dish to serve at a buffet party.

Boil a large bird, seasoning well with salt and pepper and a bouquet of herbs. When cooked, leave to cool in the stock. Make a very thick Béchamel with 3 oz. butter, 3 tablespoonfuls of flour and a pint of the chicken stock, strained. Add a packet of aspic jelly (Maggi does an excellent one au madère), and a small carton of cream and cook for a few more minutes. Cut the chicken into pieces that can be easily speared on a fork and stir into the sauce. If you like you can add a handful of cooked young peas and some cooked new carrots, cut into little rounds. Rinse a soufflé dish in cold water, pour in the mixture and leave in the fridge for at least 3 hours. To serve, turn out on to a flat dish. The only accompaniment you need is a well-seasoned green salad.

Hors-d'oeuvre and Salads

Rillettes de porc • Terrine de campagne • Fromage de porc en salade • Riz à l'orientale • Oignons à la monégasque • Salade de lentilles aux chipolatas • Salade niçoise • Céleri-rave rémoulade • Salade de céleri • Salade de tomates • Salade Rachel • Salade de champignons • Salade de champignons aux bananes • Champignons à la Grecque • Cole Slaw • Salade d'endives et de betteraves • Oeufs durs à la mayonnaise • Pain d'aubergines • Avocado and orange

Hors-d'oeuvre and Salads

In most French homes the basic hors-d'oeuvre consists of a tomato salad, a dish of little pink radishes, and some slices of either saucisson, or one of the many pâtés or country terrines, either cut in slices or served direct from the earthenware terrine it has been cooked in.

Although most delicatessen shops stock either pâtés in tins or good commercially-made untinned ones, nothing really tastes like home-made *charcuterie*. I am therefore including a few recipes which are neither long nor trying to make. Most of them will keep well in the fridge and they are a very good standby to offer when you are faced with providing a meal for the unexpected guest.

RILLETTES DE PORC

This is one of the classic hors-d'oeuvre and is found all over France. The rillettes are quite easy to make, and although the standard recipes use only pork, I find a mixture of pork and duck or rabbit, for instance, far less insipid.

Buy 2 lb. belly pork and 1 lb. bacon (the amount of fat and lean should be about equal). Get your butcher to remove any bones. Chop the meat into pieces, together with any other meat you are going to use, and put them in an earthenware casserole with salt, pepper, bay leaf, thyme, a clove of garlic and a pinch each of nutmeg, cinnamon and cloves. Add enough water to half-cover the meat. Put the lid on the casserole, and cook as slowly as possible (either on top of the stove or in the oven (Reg. 1) for 4 hours, when the water should be more or less evaporated and the meat reduced almost to a purée, and swimming in fat. Strain off the fat and put the meat into a basin. Beat all together, with a fork. It should be well amalgamated, but not a purée. You can either store the rillettes in small soufflé dishes or pack them into earthenware basins. In any case, cover them with the strained fat, which you remove before serving.

TERRINE DE CAMPAGNE

Mince very finely 1 lb. belly pork and 1 lb. veal. Buy a truffle (it will keep for months if you put it in a jar with a little brandy), and cut a few slivers which you then chop and mix with your minced meat. Chop into little dice 6 oz. unsmoked bacon and add to the mixture. Season with very little salt, pepper, nutmeg and marjoram, a grated clove of garlic and 2 tablespoonfuls of brandy. You can either pack this mixture as it is into your terrine or put it with alternate layers of thin slices of chicken, duck or rabbit. Lay a bay leaf on top and cover with thin strips of streaky bacon criss-crossed. If your terrine has no lid, seal with foil. Place a tin with enough water to come half-way up the sides of the terrine and cook in a very slow oven (Reg. 3) for about 1½ hours. Leave to go cold. You can either serve it as it is, or take it out of the dish.

FROMAGE DE PORC EN SALADE

This is a rather refined version of brawn, and is sold by *charcutiers* in slices marinated in oil and coarsely chopped parsley and onion.

Buy 2 lb. salt pork, or you can use a pig's cheek and 1 lb. of the pork. Soak the meat for an hour and then put it into a saucepan with a large onion, 2 carrots, a bouquet of plenty of parsley stalks, thyme and bay leaf and half a dozen peppercorns. Cover with cold water and add a tablespoonful of vinegar. Put the lid on the saucepan and cook very gently for 1½–2 hours. The meat should then be quite soft. Remove it, pour over it a tablespoonful of oil and put it into a dish of a size and shape which will make it easy to cut into slices when turned out. Leave overnight, with a weight on top to press it into shape.

The next day cut it into thin slices and cover with a vinaigrette sauce made with a small onion finely chopped, ½ teaspoonful of French mustard, and oil and vinegar in the proportion of 1 part of vinegar to 5 parts of oil. Sprinkle with plenty of chopped parsley.

RIZ À L'ORIENTALE

Dissolve ½ teaspoonful of saffron in 6 tablespoonfuls of white wine and a pint of chicken bouillon. Add a green pimento with the seeds removed, finely chopped, 12 tablespoonfuls of rice, ½ teaspoonful of caraway seeds and a small chopped onion. Season with salt and pepper. Turn all into a saucepan and cook gently till all the liquid is absorbed. While still warm, mix with a dressing of a dessertspoonful of vinegar and 3 tablespoonfuls of oil. Chill and serve sprinkled with chopped parsley.

OIGNONS À LA MONÉGASQUE

The preparation of this is a bit fiddling, but the result will amply repay the trouble you take.

Use the small round onions used for pickling. First chop a carrot into small dice and cook in 2 tablespoonfuls of oil till soft. Then add 1 lb. peeled onions, 2 chopped tomatoes, a bouquet of parsley, thyme and bay leaf, a heaped tablespoonful of currants, a teaspoonful of vinegar and ½ pint of water. Season and simmer till the onions are soft and the sauce has thickened. Chill before serving.

SALADE DE LENTILLES AUX CHIPOLATAS

Buy the brown lentils which are obtainable at most continental stores. Soak 6 oz. in cold water for 12 hours.

Chop an onion and sweat it in 2 tablespoonfuls of oil. Add a clove of garlic, a bay leaf, salt and 2 pints of water. Put the strained lentils into this stock, cover, and cook gently for 1½–2 hours. Drain the lentils well, and while they are still warm make the following dressing. Put a teaspoonful of French mustard in the bottom of a basin, then stir into it salt and freshly-ground black pepper, a tablespoonful of vinegar, a tablespoonful of lemon juice and 4 tablespoonfuls of oil. When thickened and well amalgamated, mix with the lentils. Serve with chipolata sausages grilled and left to get cold.

SALADE NIÇOISE

This is one of the great classic hors-d'oeuvre and, though its origin is Mediterranean, it is eaten all over France, the variations in the vegetables depending on the season and the region. Here is a fairly representative version, which makes quite a substantial first course to any meal.

Cook ½ lb. haricots verts (the smallest you can get) and let them get cold. Mix them with a vinaigrette made with a tablespoonful of vinegar and 5 tablespoonfuls of olive oil. Put the beans in the centre of your salad bowl, and arrange about 3 oz. olives round them. Arrange on top a dozen fillets of anchovy and you can add, too, a small tin of tunny fish well drained and chopped into cubes. Sprinkle with a teaspoonful of capers, and any vinaigrette remaining. Decorate with slices of hard-boiled egg.

CÉLERI-RAVE RÉMOULADE

Peel the celeriac root, and cut it into fine matchstick strips. Throw into boiling salted water and blanch for 5 minutes. Drain and wipe well in an old tea towel. While still warm, mix with a sauce rémoulade (see page 146).

SALADE DE CÉLERI

Crisp a head of celery in ice water and chop finely. Peel a couple of dessert apples (Worcesters or Cox's Orange Pippins) and mix all together with a rather mustardy mayonnaise. Sprinkle with chopped parsley before serving.

SALADE DE TOMATES

Plunge the tomatoes for half a minute in boiling water to loosen the skins. Remove skins and slice thinly into rounds. If you can lay your hands on some chives, nothing could be nicer, but if not use a few rings of onion and toss in a well salted vinaigrette. Sprinkle with chopped parsley.

SALADE RACHEL

In the winter, when green salads are expensive, try this for a change.

Prepare a vinaigrette. Chop 3 or 4 sticks of celery and marinate in the vinaigrette for an hour. Then add a chopped crisp dessert apple, a chopped Belgian endive and about a dozen walnuts, shelled, skinned and roughly chopped. Mix all well and turn into a salad bowl. Decorate with thin rounds of beetroot sprinkled with chopped parsley.

SALADE DE CHAMPIGNONS

Wash the mushrooms, cut off the ends of the stalks and slice thinly. Drain well and mix with a dressing of 2 tablespoonfuls of oil, the juice of half a lemon and salt and pepper. Sprinkle with plenty of chopped parsley.

SALADE DE CHAMPIGNONS AUX BANANES

Prepare the mushrooms as in the previous recipe. For ½ lb. mushrooms you will need 2 bananas. Choose ones which are not too ripe. Skin them and slice in thin rounds. Mix with the mushrooms, and toss in a sauce made with 2 tablespoons of cream, the juice of a lemon, salt and freshly-ground pepper.

CHAMPIGNONS À LA GRECQUE

Many vegetables take kindly to this method of preparation, among them artichokes, the white part of leeks, celery and fennel roots.

For ½ lb. mushrooms, prepare a sauce as follows. Put in a saucepan a small wineglassful of olive oil, the same quantity of water, and the same of dry white wine, with a couple of small tomatoes, skinned and roughly chopped, 10 coriander seeds, a small bunch of thyme and a bay leaf, salt and pepper. Boil fast for 2 or 3 minutes. Reduce the heat, squeeze in the juice of half a lemon and add the mushrooms. Cook gently uncovered, till the mushrooms have softened (but they must not be soft!). Turn into a dish and chill.

COLE SLAW

Here is another salad for the winter months.

Shred half a head of white cabbage, removing the hard stalky parts, and crisp in cold water for half an hour. Drain well, then marinate for an hour in a tablespoonful of sugar, 4 tablespoonfuls of vinegar and a dusting of paprika. Make a very stiff mayonnaise and add 2 tablespoonfuls of single cream and ¼ teaspoonful of caraway seeds. Remove the cabbage from the marinade, drain thoroughly and fold gently into the mayonnaise. The longer in advance it is prepared, the better it will be.

SALADE D'ENDIVES ET DE BETTERAVES

Slice the endives and amalgamate with a rather salty vinaigrette made with a teaspoonful of vinegar and 3 tablespoonfuls of oil. Just before serving, add some beetroot cut into match-sized strips.

OEUFS DURS À LA MAYONNAISE

Allow 1 egg per person. Boil them for 10 minutes, plunge in cold water and remove the shells. Slice in half lengthwise. Spread a layer of mayonnaise on a shallow dish and arrange the eggs yolk-side down, strew over a few capers and a liberal sprinkling of chopped parsley.

PAIN D'AUBERGINES

Allow 1 aubergine per person. For four, slice aubergines lengthwise, score, lightly sprinkle with salt and bake in the oven (Reg. 4) till the flesh is soft, about 15–20 minutes. Scoop out the flesh. Put 2 tablespoonfuls of oil in a frying-pan, and fry a finely-chopped onion and a minced clove of garlic. Add 4 peeled and chopped tomatoes and the aubergine flesh. Season with salt, pepper and marjoram. Cook slowly, stirring frequently, till the aubergine flesh has become almost a purée and completely amalgamated with the other ingredients. Chill and serve with a bowl of black olives.

AVOCADO AND ORANGE

Quite a number of people find avocado pear disagreeably rich at the beginning of a meal. The combination of its rather fatty flesh with the acidity of orange not only makes a pleasant change from the usual preparation, but will certainly ensure that there are no digestive ill-effects.

Cut the pears in half lengthways in the usual way, allowing half a pear per person. Skin an equal number of oranges and cut similarly. Lay the pears flat side down on the plates on which you are going to serve them, and slice them across in four pieces. Cut the oranges similarly. Slip a slice of orange in between each piece of avocado and press gently together so that you have a reconstituted and rather elongated striped pear.

Serve with a lemon dressing made with a dessertspoon of lemon juice to 3 tablespoonfuls of oil. No salt. Pour over the pears at the last moment.

Vegetables

Pommes de terre au basilic • Pommes de terre Macaire • Pommes de terre à la Lyonnaise • Gratin Savoyard • Aubergines farcies Marcelle • Aubergines aux tomates • Aubergines frites • Carottes à la Vichy • Timbale de carottes • Braised celery • Red cabbage • Brussels Sprouts with chestnuts • Bubble and Squeak • Cauliflower à la Polonaise • Cauliflower au gratin • Broad beans • Courgettes sautées aux fines herbes • Courgettes à la crème • Courgettes aux tomates • Endives • Épinards à la crème • Épinards aux oeufs durs • Haricots blancs à la bretonne • Braised lettuce • Braised onions • Poireaux à l'étuvée • Petits pois à la française • Pumpkin purée • Stuffed tomatoes

Vegetables

In France, vegetables are as often served as a separate course as they are as an accompaniment to another dish. I have therefore included a number of 'plats de légumes cuisinés'—an expression used to describe a composition of more than one ingredient. When you are serving one very expensive fish or meat course, a cheap vegetable course makes a perfect beginning to a meal.

POMMES DE TERRE AU BASILIC

Peel some potatoes, preferably the long Dutch waxy kind, and slice in rounds about $\frac{1}{4}$ in. thick. For a pound of potatoes melt 2 oz. butter in $\frac{1}{2}$ tumbler of water, with salt, pepper and a good sprinkling of dried basil. Put in the potatoes so that they cover the bottom of the pan, and cook them slowly, shaking the pan from time to time to make sure they are not sticking. Turn them out, with what remains of the liquid. It will have been considerably reduced.

POMMES DE TERRE MACAIRE

Choose large floury potatoes. Wash them and bake them in their skins in the oven (Reg. 6) for about 45 minutes. When cooked, remove the skins and mash the potatoes with a fork, incorporating 2 oz. butter for each pound of purée. Season with salt, pepper and grated nutmeg. Heat a nut of butter in a frying-pan. Spread the purée over the pan about an inch thick. When the bottom side is a good golden colour, lift with a slice, while you slip into the pan another nut of butter. Let it melt completely before you brown the other side of your potato galette. Serve at once.

POMMES DE TERRE À LA LYONNAISE

Boil some Dutch potatoes in their jackets and leave to grow cold before you skin them. Cut into rounds ¼ in. thick. Melt 1½ oz. butter in a frying-pan and cook the potatoes gently. In another pan do the same with 2 onions, similarly sliced and seasoned with salt and pepper. When the onions begin to colour, add them to the potatoes and continue cooking for another 10 minutes. Serve with plenty of chopped parsley.

GRATIN SAVOYARD

Peel some potatoes, wash them well and cut them into dice. Butter a flame-proof dish, put in half the potatoes and sprinkle thickly with grated cheese (preferably Gruyère), adding salt, pepper and grated nutmeg. Repeat the process till the dish is full, ending with a layer of cheese. Moisten with stock, dot with butter and cook on the top of the stove for 10 minutes. Then put into a moderate oven (Reg. 6) for about half an hour when the top should be golden brown and the stock evaporated.

AUBERGINES FARCIES MARCELLE

Allow 1 aubergine per person. Cut each in half lengthwise, score, sprinkle with salt and put in the oven (Reg. 4) till the flesh is soft. This will take about 15 minutes.

Meanwhile prepare the stuffing. For 4 aubergines skin and chop 3 medium tomatoes and put them into a saucepan. Clean and chop ¼ lb. mushrooms and add them to the tomatoes. Now stir in a tablespoonful of cream, an ounce of butter and a tablespoonful of tomato purée. Season with salt, pepper, grated nutmeg and chopped parsley and thyme. Cook slowly, and add a tablespoonful of chopped pine kernels if you can get them. If not, use peanuts. Continue cooking until the mixture has thickened and leaves the side of the pan. Remove from the fire and stir in a tablespoonful of breadcrumbs and another tablespoonful of cream.

Scrape out the flesh from the aubergines, chop it up and stir it into the pan with the stuffing. Simmer another 5 minutes, then fill the skins with the mixture. Dot with butter and brown under the grill.

AUBERGINES AUX TOMATES

Allow 1 aubergine per person. First prepare a tomato purée. For 4 aubergines, cut 1½ lb. tomatoes in quarters, cook them without water or any other liquid for 10 minutes and put them through a sieve. Fry in oil the aubergines, cut into thick rounds. In a fireproof dish arrange a layer of the tomato purée, then a layer of the aubergines, seasoning each layer with parsley, salt and finely-minced garlic, till the dish is full. Dot with pieces of butter and cook in the oven (Reg. 5) for 45 minutes.

AUBERGINES FRITES

Skin the aubergines and slice in rounds ¼ in. thick. Sprinkle with salt and leave in a colander to drain for half an hour. When ready to cook, make sure the slices are dry. Roll in seasoned flour and fry in very hot oil till golden. Serve strewn with minced parsley.

CAROTTES À LA VICHY

For 4 people scrape 1½ lb. carrots, wash them well and slice them in very thin rounds. Put them into a saucepan and add cold water so that it almost covers the carrots, 3½ oz. butter, salt and 4 lumps of sugar. Cover, and boil fast till the water has boiled away and you can hear the carrots beginning to sizzle in the fat. They will now be cooked. Sprinkle with chopped parsley and serve at once.

TIMBALE DE CAROTTES

Grate enough carrot to fill 2 teacups. Add 4 well-beaten eggs, 4 tablespoonfuls of melted butter, a little grated onion, salt, pepper, 2 tablespoonfuls of thick cream and a tablespoonful of flour. Mix well and turn into a well-greased soufflé dish. Cover with foil, set in a baking tin half filled with water and bake in the oven (Reg. 5) till firm (about 35 minutes).

BRAISED CELERY

Personally I am not very fond of cooked celery, but with certain game no other vegetable seems to go as well. This makes a good accompaniment to pheasant.

Blanch 3 heads of celery in boiling salted water for 10 minutes. Take out and drain thoroughly. Brown lightly in butter 2 sliced onions and 2 sliced carrots. Add the celery and season with salt and pepper. Pour on ½ pint of stock and simmer gently for an hour. If you have any juice from a joint (sometimes found at the bottom of a basin of dripping), now is the time to add it. Cook for a further 10 minutes and serve.

RED CABBAGE

Melt an ounce of dripping in a saucepan. When hot, add 1 lb. red cabbage, shredded, a large sliced onion, a large cooking apple, peeled, cored and chopped, 2 tablespoonfuls of stock, 2 tablespoonfuls of vinegar, a tablespoonful of demerara sugar, and salt and pepper. Stir, so that all the ingredients are coated with the fat and stock, then cover and simmer for 30–45 minutes. Stir occasionally. The liquid should have almost entirely evaporated by the end of the cooking.

BRUSSELS SPROUTS WITH CHESTNUTS

Prepare the chestnuts as indicated on page 54. Boil the brussels sprouts (they should take about 20 minutes, no longer or they will lose their colour), mix with the chestnuts and add an ounce of melted butter before serving.

Very good with roast turkey or pheasant.

BUBBLE AND SQUEAK

When we were children, this was almost our favourite vegetable.

Boil a cabbage, drain it well and chop it very small. At the same time boil half the weight of the cabbage in potatoes, drain and mash well with a fork. In a frying-pan brown a thinly sliced onion in plenty of beef dripping, then add the potatoes and cabbage, with seasoning, and mix well. When the underside of the cake is well browned, turn it out.

CAULIFLOWER À LA POLONAISE

This accompaniment makes a pleasant change from the tasteless white sauce so often served with cauliflower.

Soak the cauliflower for 10 minutes in water to which you have added a spoonful of vinegar. Cauliflower is rather tricky to cook, for if you are not careful you will find you have a collection of stalks and disintegrated flowerets. Cook the cauliflower head upwards in a covered pan in boiling salted water. At the end of 10 minutes the flowerets should be almost soft. Turn off the heat and leave it to finish cooking in its own steam. Turn it carefully into a colander and drain. Keep it warm. In a pan put a good piece of butter and let it become golden. At this point throw in a handful of breadcrumbs and cook till crisp and brown. Pour the crumbs and butter over the cauliflower and sprinkle with some chopped ham, hard-boiled egg and plenty of parsley.

CAULIFLOWER AU GRATIN

The secret of making this sauce something more than an ordinary cheese-flavoured Béchamel is to use the water you have cooked the cauliflower in, with the addition of 2 or 3 spoonfuls of cream and a good grating of nutmeg.

Cook the cauliflower as in the previous recipe, but save the stock. Make the sauce with an ounce of butter, a tablespoonful of flour and ¾ pint of the cauliflower stock. When well amalgamated, stir in 3 good tablespoonfuls of grated cheese and the cream. Pour it over the cauliflower, strew over some breadcrumbs and more grated cheese and brown in the oven for 10 minutes.

BROAD BEANS

In the part of France where I live, young broad beans are eaten raw, as an hors-d'oeuvre; or cooked in their pods; or when they are old, they are puréed and used for soup. Needless to say, there are many other ways of cooking this delicious vegetable, though when they are young nothing is nicer than the freshly-boiled beans tossed in butter and well sprinkled with parsley.

When they are getting large and old, and if you have the time, remove the skins, which by now are tough and inclined to be bitter, and cook beans only as above; or serve them in a purée, made by sieving the beans (shelled and boiled of course), and beating up with butter and a little stock.

One of the classic ways of serving broad beans is to mix them with bacon cut into cubes, the fat from the bacon, a spoonful or two of cream, and some chopped parsley.

COURGETTES SAUTÉES AUX FINES HERBES

If the courgettes are small, use them without peeling, but if more than 5 inches long, peel thinly, salt, and leave to drain for an hour. Let them sauté gently in butter for 10 minutes, then season with salt and pepper, and chopped parsley, tarragon and chervil.

COURGETTES À LA CRÈME

Cook the courgettes as above, and before serving add 2 or 3 tablespoonfuls of cream, a little finely-grated raw carrot and some chopped chives. Shake the pan before serving.

COURGETTES AUX TOMATES

Salt and drain the courgettes as above and cook gently in butter for 10 minutes. Now add 3 or 4 small tomatoes, skinned and sliced into rounds. Simmer for another 10 minutes and serve immediately.

ENDIVES

(In England this vegetable is often called chicory.)

You can either boil the endives and finish cooking them in butter, or (and I prefer this method) you can put 1 lb. into a casserole, pour on 2 oz. melted butter and add salt, pepper and the juice of half a lemon. Cover, and cook in the oven (Reg. 3) for at least an hour, when the outside leaves should be golden and all the liquid evaporated.

ÉPINARDS À LA CRÈME

Spinach reduces enormously in cooking so you must allow at least ½ lb. per person. Remove the stalks and wash the leaves well in several waters to remove every trace of grit or sand. Put them without any other water into a saucepan and add salt. As the water from the leaves starts to boil, press the spinach well, so that all the leaves are well covered, and boil for 10 minutes. Drain well and press out the water with your hands. For 2 lb. spinach, melt 2 oz. butter and add the spinach and a carton of cream. Check the seasoning, and stir in a tiny grating of nutmeg and a pinch of sugar. Turn the spinach well over in the creamy sauce and serve at once.

ÉPINARDS AUX OEUFS DURS

This makes a most excellent first course, or, if you make enough, a delicious supper dish.

Prepare the spinach as in the previous recipe, and at the same time hard-boil some eggs. To serve, put the spinach in a mound in the centre of the dish, quarter the eggs and arrange them all round, and decorate with little piles of triangular pieces of bread fried very crisp in oil.

HARICOTS BLANCS À LA BRETONNE

These are the traditional accompaniment to roast lamb, but they are most warm and comforting to eat in the winter. Serve them with frankfurters, or any other kind of sausage.

Make sure when you buy the beans that they are new season's. Take a bean and put it between your teeth. If fresh you will be able to bite it quite easily, but if old it will be as hard as a stone and no amount of cooking will soften it.

Put ½ lb. haricots into cold water and bring to the boil. Throw the water away and put the beans back into fresh water so that they are well covered. Add a bouquet of herbs, an onion stuck with a clove, and a carrot. Cover and cook gently for at least 2 hours. You can do this the day before you want to use the beans. When cooked, drain them and keep the liquid. Fry a chopped onion in butter, or better still some dripping, and add 2 or 3 peeled and chopped tomatoes. Add a little of the bean liquid to make a thinnish sauce. Check the seasoning, put the beans back into the sauce, mix well and serve.

BRAISED LETTUCE

Use small outdoor lettuces for this and serve them, as a change from other vegetables, with roast veal. Cut the lettuces in half and let them sauté in butter. Add a little stock, or better still some juice from the roast, and cook with the lid on until the lettuces are soft and the liquid in the pan is well reduced, about 10–15 minutes. Squeeze a little lemon juice over and sprinkle with chopped parsley.

BRAISED ONIONS

Choose onions as much the same size as possible and brown them well in butter. Remove them on to a plate and when the butter is a good brown, stir in a dessertspoonful of flour until amalgamated and then pour in enough stock and a glass of white wine to make a thin sauce. Return the onions to the pan, see that they are well coated, cover and cook in the oven (Reg. 3) for about an hour, when the sauce should be thickened and reduced.

POIREAUX À L'ÉTUVÉE

Wash some leeks, discard the pithy outside leaves and chop into rounds about an inch long. Drain well, and sweat them in butter. Season with salt and pepper, cover, and cook for 10 minutes. Add 2 or 3 tomatoes, skinned and sliced into rounds, and the juice of half a lemon, and cook for a further 10 minutes. Arrange the leeks on a dish and if the sauce is too thin, reduce by boiling fiercely for a minute or two.

PETITS POIS À LA FRANÇAISE

Put the raw peas into a saucepan with a good lump of butter. Allow the butter to melt and incorporate it well with the peas, then add the bulbs of some spring onions and a small handful of chopped lettuce. Season with salt, pepper and a teaspoonful of sugar. Pour in enough water to reach just to the top of the peas, cover, and cook for about 30 minutes, when most of the liquid should have evaporated.

PUMPKIN PURÉE

As this is another very watery vegetable, you will need 2 lb. for 4 people. Peel and cut into convenient pieces, and cook in salted water till soft. Drain, and pass the flesh through a sieve then return it to the saucepan and mix with 2 oz. butter.

Check seasoning and grate a little nutmeg into the purée. Stir in 2 well beaten eggs, dot over with little pieces of butter and put in a hot oven to brown, about 10–12 minutes. Serve quickly, as it will have risen rather like a soufflé.

STUFFED TOMATOES

Cut the tops off large tomatoes (allow 2 per person), and scoop out the flesh with a spoon. Turn the tomatoes upside down on a plate and allow them to drain for half an hour. You can then put them as they are into the fridge until you are ready to fill them.

For 8 tomatoes you will need ½ lb. sausage meat, mixed with ½ lb. minced cooked remains of a joint. Stir in a tablespoonful of chopped parsley, and salt and pepper. If the mixture seems too dry, moisten with a little meat stock. Fill the emptied tomatoes. Stand them in a shallow fireproof dish, strew some crisp breadcrumbs over the stuffing in each tomato and pour on a teaspoonful of oil. Bake in the oven (Reg. 6) for half an hour.

Use the tomato flesh for either a tomato sauce, a soup or a tarte aux tomates.

Sweets

Pastry

Short crust • Pâte brisée • Pâte à choux

Sweets with No Eggs

Fried-apple tart • Apple Charlotte • Spiced baked apples • Apple crumble • Poires au vin • Gooseberry fool • Gooseberry cheese • Émincés de poires • Vanilla cream • Turinois

Sweets with Whole Eggs

Profiterolles au chocolat • Nègre en chemise • Mousse au chocolat • Cold orange soufflé • Cold nut soufflé • Gâteau de fromage blanc • Lemon fluff • Oeufs à la neige • Crèmes frites • Pain perdu • Potato pudding • Walmer pudding

Sweets with Egg Yolks

Crème anglaise • Crème pâtissière • Café parfait • Petits pots de crème à la vanille • Gâteau viennois

Sweets with Egg Whites

Visitandines • Financiers • Mousse au chocolat • Flaméri de semoule • Mousse aux fraises

Sweets

PASTRY

I have intentionally given no recipes for flaky pastry. For those of you who want to attempt it, most standard cookery books provide quantities and method. But to make really satisfactory flaky pastry it is essential to have a cool kitchen and plenty of time. The purpose of this book is to give recipes easy and reasonably quick to prepare. There are a number of reliable brands of prepared flaky pastry, which can be bought in most supermarkets, good grocers and delicatessen, and which only need rolling out.

However, I do want to give two foolproof pastry recipes; one for short crust, the pastry used for quiches, and the other a pâte brisée for fruit tarts. And I want to give, too, a recipe for pâte à choux, essential for éclairs, cheese buns and profiterolles.

SHORT CRUST

8 heaped tablespoonfuls flour
¼ lb. margarine (this makes much lighter pastry than butter)
1 saltspoonful salt
1 level tablespoonful sugar (omitted in the case of savoury tarts)
¾ tumblerful water

Sieve the flour into a basin, make a well in the middle, break up the fat and place it in the well, together with the other ingredients. Knead the mixture with your hands, but not too hard, or it will become elastic and tough when cooked. When smooth and well mixed, roll it into a ball, wrap in a cloth or foil paper and leave in the fridge at least an hour before using. It can be made the day before.

PÂTE BRISÉE

8 heaped tablespoonfuls flour
A pinch of salt
Water
¼ lb. margarine
1 tablespoonful oil

Sieve the flour into a basin. Make a hole in the middle and put in the oil, the salt and the fat, cut into little pieces. Work these ingredients lightly with the tips of the fingers until the mixture looks like breadcrumbs. Moisten with a little water, and mix to a paste with a knife. Knead with the palm of your hand. The whole operation should be done as quickly as possible and the pastry can be left up to 3 days in the fridge if you roll it into a ball and keep it covered. To use, roll out as required on a floured surface.

PÂTE À CHOUX

Bring to the boil a breakfast cup of water, 3 oz. butter and a pinch of salt. Pour in, all at once, 4 heaped tablespoonfuls of flour. Beat well till the mixture leaves the sides of the pan. Remove from the heat, cool for a minute and then add, one by one, 4 eggs, making sure to beat each one well in before adding the next. The result should be a softish but pliable paste. If the eggs are big ones, you will probably find you will not need the fourth, so do not break it before the other 3 are well mixed in.

This pastry should be used straight away.

SWEETS WITH NO EGGS

FRIED-APPLE TART

My sons, who are not greatly addicted to cooked apples, having had a surfeit of various forms of stodgy apple puddings at school, nevertheless adore this sweet, which is particularly delicious when the first Worcesters, and, a little later, the first Cox's appear in the shops.

Peel and core about 1½ lb. apples and slice evenly and thinly. Cook very gently in 2 oz. butter and 2 tablespoonfuls caster sugar in a frying-pan. Line a sandwich tin (preferably one with a removable base) with short crust pastry or pâte brisée. (See the recipes in the previous section.) Arrange the apples in overlapping rounds. Save the juice in the frying-pan. Bake for 30–35 minutes in a hot oven (Reg. 6) and pour the juice over just before serving.

When I have no time to make pastry, I fry fingers of bread in very hot oil, arrange the apples similarly and serve with cream.

APPLE CHARLOTTE

For some reason, this delicious pudding seems to have gone out of fashion, and although it isn't exactly the thing to serve at a particularly sophisticated dinner party, it makes a most satisfactory finale to an informal cold supper.

Cut some slices of bread into strips the depth of a soufflé dish (which is the ideal shape for this sweet), and about 1½ in. wide. Cut also a number of triangular or narrow kite-shaped slices to cover the bottom of the mould, which should be well greased with butter. Dip the pieces of bread in melted butter, and place the triangular pieces in the form of a circle, with the points meeting in the centre. Then fix the fingers similarly against the sides of the mould. Fill the mould with a fairly stiff apple purée made from 1½ lb. apples cooked, unpeeled and uncored, in a little water, then passed through the smallest mesh of the food mill and flavoured with sugar, lemon juice, a little grated lemon peel and a pinch of ground cinnamon. Trim off any strips of bread that project over the top of the mould, and lay 3 or 4 strips across the top of the apple. Bake in a hot oven (Reg. 6) for about 40 minutes, when the bread should be golden and crisp. Serve at once, with cream.

SPICED BAKED APPLES

Cream together (for 4 large apples) 2 oz. butter and 2 oz. brown sugar, beat in ½ teaspoonful of ground cinnamon and 1 teaspoonful of grated lemon peel. Core the apples and fill with the butter cream. Top with a clove. Place in a shallow oven dish and pour on the top of each apple a teaspoonful of golden syrup and a tablespoonful of lemon juice. Bake in a moderate oven (Reg. 5) for 40 minutes.

APPLE CRUMBLE

This is an ideal winter sweet, which does not suffer from being warmed up.

Cut into quarters, without peeling, 1½ lb. cooking apples and put into a saucepan with a tumblerful of water, 2 tablespoonfuls of brown sugar and a tablespoonful of golden syrup. Cook with the lid on until the apples are soft, then put them through the medium mesh of the food mill. While the apples are cooking, put 6 tablespoonfuls of flour in a basin, and rub into it 3 oz. butter, till it resembles breadcrumbs. Pour the apple purée into a pie dish or other conveniently shaped oven dish, and scatter the 'breadcrumbs' thickly over it. Bake in a hot oven (Reg. 6) till crisp and brown (about 30 minutes).

POIRES AU VIN

Peel the pears, leaving the stalks on. For 1 lb. pears, allow a tumblerful of red wine and 4 oz. caster sugar. Stand the pears up in a deep earthenware dish. Pour over them the wine and sugar, and add enough water to reach half-way up the pears. Put them, uncovered, into the slowest possible oven and bake until soft. Look at them from time to time and turn them so that they are impregnated all over with the wine. When done they should be almost mahogany coloured. If dessert pears are used they will take 1–1½ hours. Cooking pears may take anything up to 4 or 5 hours. You can leave them in the oven perfectly safely all day, but they should be served very cold, with the syrup poured over them.

GOOSEBERRY FOOL

When gooseberries are small, green and very acid you can make a quick and utterly delectable sweet by putting a pound of them into a saucepan, with a very little water, and cooking without any sugar until soft. Pass through the finest mesh of the food mill, allow to cool off and fold the purée into a block of ice-cream.

GOOSEBERRY CHEESE

When ice-cream is not available, try this version.

Cook the fruit with 4 tablespoonfuls of sugar, but without

water, and pass through the food mill as above. Mix with a cream cheese made as follows. Buy ½ lb. cream cheese (petits-suisses are quite good to use if you cannot find a suitable one by the pound). Beat it up with a tablespoonful of sugar until smooth. Spread a piece of muslin (a fine handkerchief will do) over the inside of a fairly large strainer and lay the cheese in it. Place the strainer over a basin and allow to drip for an hour or so in a cool place, or in the fridge. When ready to incorporate with the gooseberries, beat the two together until completely amalgamated and add a carton of thick cream.

The cheese is also delicious served as an accompaniment to raspberries and redcurrants, or stewed blackcurrants.

ÉMINCÉS DE POIRES

For this you will need fairly ripe pears. Peel 6 pears, remove the cores, and cut into quarters. Heat 3 oz. butter in a frying-pan and put the fruit in to sauter, taking care not to let it burn. Lay each quarter pear on a finger of bread fried in butter until golden. Serve very hot, sprinkled with sugar.

VANILLA CREAM

When stocks are low and the unexpected guest turns up, this is easily made, and will maintain your reputation for conjuring an epicurean meal out of almost nothing.

For 4 people whip ¼ pint of cream and mix it gradually with ¾ pint of milk. Add a tablespoonful of caster sugar and a teaspoonful of vanilla essence. Dissolve ½ oz. (1 tablespoonful) gelatine in ½ gill of warm water and strain carefully into the cream. Pour into a glass dish and chill in the fridge for an hour.

TURINOIS

This is a sweet to serve after a light main course.

Buy 1½ lb. chestnuts and make an incision with a sharp knife in each one. Scald them. You should then be able to remove the shells. Throw them into boiling water and cook until they are soft enough to skin. Drain well and put through a sieve. While the purée is still hot, beat into it ¼ lb. butter, ¼ lb. grated bitter chocolate and 4 tablespoonfuls of caster sugar. Add vanilla to taste, and continue to beat until smooth and creamy. Butter a mould (a small cake tin will do) and line it with greaseproof paper. Press the mixture well in. Put in the fridge to set. Turn out on to a dish and serve with whipped cream.

SWEETS WITH WHOLE EGGS

PROFITEROLLES AU CHOCOLAT

This is much less complicated than it sounds, but it does take quite a time to prepare. The profiterolles can be made the day before, and the filling added an hour or so before serving.

Start by making some pâte à choux (for 4 people halve the quantities given on page 114), and put heaped teaspoonfuls on to a greased baking sheet—not too close together, as they swell in cooking. Brush with beaten egg and bake in a hot oven (Reg. 6) for 20–30 minutes. Take out and cool on a wire tray, then make an incision in each profiterolle and fill with a crème pâtissière (see the recipe on page 125). Arrange in a pile on a dish, and when ready to serve pour over a hot chocolate sauce.

For the sauce, put into a saucepan three-quarters of a

tumbler of water and ¼ lb. tablet of unsweetened chocolate. When melted, add 3 dessertspoonfuls of caster sugar and stir until smooth. Dissolve a tablespoonful of cornflour in half a glass of water and add little by little to the chocolate mixture. You may not need to add all. The sauce should be thick, but not unmanageably 'gooey'. Bring to the boil, simmer for a minute or two, pour over the profiterolles and serve at once.

NÈGRE EN CHEMISE

Although I did not intend to include any classic recipes in this book, I feel that I cannot omit this most famous of sweets, as it is easy to prepare and looks festive and attractive at the end of a meal.

Melt 6 oz. unsweetened chocolate in a tablespoonful of strong coffee and beat into it the same quantity of butter. When smooth add, away from the fire, the yolks of 3 eggs and make sure they are properly amalgamated. Whip the whites stiffly and fold gently into the mixture. Pour into an oiled mould and leave in the fridge until the next day. Unmould before serving and cover with whipped cream.

MOUSSE AU CHOCOLAT

The omission of the butter in this recipe makes it lighter than the previous one. It is a delicious, easy and quick sweet to make when eggs are cheap and gives a very professional round-off to a dinner party.

Allow 1 oz. unsweetened chocolate and 1 egg per person (with perhaps an additional couple for second helpings). Melt the chocolate slowly in a saucepan, with a little coffee. For 6 eggs and 6 oz. chocolate, 2 tablespoonfuls of coffee should be about right. Separate the yolks and the whites. Beat up the yolks and add to the melted chocolate, together with 2 tablespoonfuls of sugar and a teaspoonful of vanilla essence. Then add the whites whipped very stiffly, and fold the mixture gently over and over till perfectly amalgamated. Put into a glass dish, decorate the top with chopped nuts and leave in the fridge to set. It should be eaten very cold.

COLD ORANGE SOUFFLÉ

Beat together 4 tablespoonfuls of sugar and the yolks of 4 eggs in the top of a double saucepan. When light and frothy, add 2 teacupfuls of milk and cook over gently boiling water till the custard thickens. Melt a tablespoonful of powdered gelatine in a little water and add to the cooled custard with 2 teacupfuls of orange juice and a tablespoonful of grated orange peel. Beat the whites of the eggs stiffly and fold gently into the mixture. Pour into a glass dish and leave to set in the fridge. Just before serving, sprinkle the top with sparsely-grated chocolate.

COLD NUT SOUFFLÉ

Beat the yolks of 2 eggs with 3 tablespoonfuls of sugar. Pour on ¼ pint of milk and bring to the boil. Dissolve a level tablespoonful of powdered gelatine in water and stir into the custard. Whisk the egg whites to stiff peaks and fold carefully in, then 3 tablespoonfuls of cream and lastly 4 tablespoonfuls of ground skinned walnuts. (Shell the walnuts and dip them into boiling water, when the skins will come off quite easily. Grind them in the cheese grater.)

This is a most unusual-tasting sweet. When walnuts are not in season, you can use hazel nuts—but not almonds, which are too oily and too strongly flavoured.

GÂTEAU DE FROMAGE BLANC

Put the yolks of 2 eggs into the top of a double boiler. Add 2 tablespoonfuls of caster sugar, 2 level tablespoonfuls of powdered gelatine, ½ pint of orange juice, and a pinch of salt, and simmer till the gelatine is dissolved. In the meantime sieve ½ lb. cottage cheese. Stir the mixture in the saucepan and as it begins to thicken remove from the heat and add the sieved cheese, a tablespoonful of grated orange rind and ½ pint of stiffly-whipped cream. Whisk the egg whites into peaks, then add 2 tablespoonfuls of sugar. Whisk again till stiff, then fold into the cheese mixture. Pour into a tin rinsed with cold water, and chill in the fridge. To serve, turn out on to a flat dish and decorate with grated biscuit crumbs (digestive biscuits are excellent), or if you prefer, use grated chocolate.

LEMON FLUFF

As children, this used to be almost our favourite sweet, and it was invariably served on our birthdays.

Put half a breakfast cup of caster sugar, 1 breakfast cup of water and the juice of 2 lemons into a saucepan and bring to the boil. Mix 3 dessertspoonfuls of cornflour with a little water and add to the liquid in the saucepan. Boil gently, stirring continuously for 2 minutes. Remove from the heat. Whip the whites of 2 eggs to a stiff froth, fold them into the mixture, then pour it into a wetted mould and chill. To serve, unmould and pour over it a crème anglaise made from the 2 egg yolks, a heaped tablespoonful of caster sugar and a ½ pint of milk (for the method see the recipe on page 125).

OEUFS À LA NEIGE

Beat the whites of 3 eggs very stiffly and mix with 3 tablespoonfuls of caster sugar. Boil some water in a fairly deep saucepan, then turn down the heat and drop in the egg whites by tablespoonfuls. Don't let the water boil again. When one side is cooked, turn over with a perforated slice. The cooking should take about 3 minutes. Drain on to a clean cloth, and leave to cool. Serve floating on a vanilla-flavoured crème anglaise, made with the yolks of the eggs, 3 tablespoonfuls of caster sugar and ½ pint of milk (see page 125). You can decorate each 'half egg' with a spoonful of strawberry or raspberry jam.

CRÈMES FRITES

Although these creams have to be cooked at the last moment, this only takes 5 minutes and the mixture can be prepared in advance. What little delay there may be is well worth the waiting.

Beat together in a saucepan 2 whole eggs, 3 tablespoonfuls of sugar and a teaspoonful of vanilla essence. When well mixed and frothy, add a heaped teaspoonful of flour and a heaped tablespoonful of ground rice. Now pour in a pint of boiling milk. Stir continually till the mixture has well thickened. Pour it into a buttered dish and spread it, with a palette knife, about an inch thick. Let it get quite cold, then cut it into rounds of about 1½ inches in diameter. Roll these in flour, dip in beaten egg, and afterwards roll in breadcrumbs, and fry in very hot oil till crisp.

PAIN PERDU

This is a most excellent way of using up stale bread.

For 4 people stir 5 tablespoonfuls of caster sugar into a pint of milk, then beat up 2 eggs and add the sweetened milk to them. Dip the pieces of bread in the milk and egg—but don't saturate them or they will disintegrate when you take them out. They should be just coated. Fry in very hot oil, when they should puff up. Drain on soft paper and serve with a syrup made from a wineglass of white wine and a spoonful of sugar, and flavoured with grated lemon peel and a pinch of ground cinnamon.

POTATO PUDDING

The following two recipes came out of a ladies' magazine of the late nineteenth century, and they are so typical of English cooking at its best that I thought they should be included in this entente cordiale of recipes.

'Boil 1 lb. potatoes till soft, drain well and rub them through a sieve. While still hot beat in ¼ lb. butter. Beat up the yolks of 4 whole eggs and the whites of two. Add ¼ lb. of white sugar, ¼ pint of white wine, and stir them well together. Grate in half a nutmeg and stir in ¼ pint thick cream. Pour the mixture into a pie dish and bake till golden brown.'

I find that half a nutmeg is too much, and I advise you to taste your mixture when you have incorporated half that amount. I allow the pudding to bake for half an hour (Reg. 6). Have a look, and if it is not golden and crisp leave it in for another 10 minutes.

WALMER PUDDING

This is quite a good, and not at all stodgy, hot sweet, which can be left to cook while you are having your main course. It makes a good finish to a cold supper.

Melt 2 oz. butter in a saucepan, and when beginning to bubble add 2½ tablespoonfuls of flour. Stir continuously, adding sufficient milk to make the mixture the consistency of thick cream. Remove from the heat and cool for a few minutes, then beat in a tablespoonful of caster sugar, a teaspoonful of vanilla essence and the yolks of 2 eggs. Whip the whites very stiff (they should stand in little peaks) and fold into the mixture in the saucepan. Do not beat any more. Spread a layer of strawberry or apricot jam at the bottom of a pie dish. Pour the pudding mixture on to it and bake in a hot oven (Reg. 6) for 15–20 minutes. The pudding should be well risen and golden when done.

SWEETS WITH EGG YOLKS

CRÈME ANGLAISE

Neither this nor the following recipe can, I suppose, be really called a sweet, as they are usually served as an accompaniment to something else. But they make a light finish to a menu in which the main course has been substantial, and look attractive if served in individual glasses.

For crème anglaise, beat the yolks of 4 eggs with 2 tablespoonfuls of caster sugar till light and frothy. They should be almost white. Pour in a pint of milk. Turn into the top of your double boiler and cook gently until the cream has thickened. Stir frequently. Chill and strain before serving the cream which can be flavoured with vanilla, orange, lemon or coffee.

These quantities make quite a large amount.

CRÈME PÂTISSIÈRE

Beat, in a saucepan, the yolks of 3 eggs with 4 tablespoonfuls of caster sugar till white and frothy, add 2 tablespoonfuls of flour and, when well mixed, $\frac{3}{4}$ pint of boiling milk. Bring to the boil, stirring all the time, and allow to thicken. Chill before serving.

CAFÉ PARFAIT

In the top half of a double saucepan boil a teacupful of strong coffee with $\frac{3}{4}$ cupful of caster sugar till syrupy (about 5 minutes). Remove from the heat. Beat the yolks of 4 eggs and add to the coffee syrup. Cook over gently boiling water, stirring constantly, until the mixture coats the back of the spoon. Remove from the heat, cool, and add a pinch of salt and $1\frac{1}{2}$ teaspoonfuls of vanilla essence. Whip $\frac{1}{2}$ pint of cream till stiff and fold into the cooled syrup. Leave in the fridge at least an hour, before serving in individual dishes.

PETITS POTS DE CRÈME À LA VANILLE

Bring a pint of milk to the boil with 3 tablespoonfuls of caster sugar. Stir the sugar well in, remove from the heat and allow to get cold. Add 1 teaspoonful of vanilla essence. Beat the yolks of 4 eggs and incorporate with the milk. Strain into little fireproof pots, put them in a baking tin with water in it and cook in the oven (Reg. 5) for 30–45 minutes. Neither the water nor the custard must boil.

GÂTEAU VIENNOIS

This sweet requires no cooking, but it is best to make it the day before you want to eat it.

Cream together 4 oz. butter and 2 tablespoonfuls of caster sugar. Add the yolks of 4 eggs, a tablespoonful of strong coffee, 4 oz. unsweetened chocolate, grated, and 10 tablespoonfuls of stale breadcrumbs. (This is a good way to use up a stale loaf.) Mix well together and put into a small cake tin or soufflé dish, pressing the mixture well down. Leave to set in the fridge. To serve, turn out and cover the top with whipped cream.

SWEETS WITH EGG WHITES

VISITANDINES

If you have made a mayonnaise, here is a good way to use up your egg whites.

Mix in a basin 4 tablespoonfuls of sieved flour, 8 tablespoonfuls of caster sugar, 3 tablespoonfuls of ground almonds and the grated peel of a lemon. Beat the whites of 5 eggs very stiffly and fold into the mixture. Melt $\frac{1}{4}$ lb. butter, but do not let it boil. Pour it on to your egg and flour mixture, stirring till it is well amalgamated. Butter little moulds, and spoon the mixture in. Do not fill more than two-thirds high, as it will rise in the cooking. Bake in a moderate oven (Reg. 4) for half an hour. Leave for a moment or two before turning out. Serve with a jam sauce or a crème anglaise (see page 125).

FINANCIERS

Beat $3\frac{1}{2}$ oz. butter to a cream. Beat the whites of 4 eggs with 5 tablespoonfuls of caster sugar for at least 20 minutes. Add 3 heaped tablespoonfuls of flour and the creamed butter. Stir gently, folding the whites carefully into the flour and butter. Butter some small fireproof pots. Half fill with the mixture and bake for 20 minutes in a moderate oven (Reg. 5). Turn out on to the centre of a dish and decorate with quarters of crystallized oranges or lemons.

MOUSSE AU CHOCOLAT

Whisk the whites of 6 eggs till stiff and peaky. Melt 6 oz. unsweetened chocolate in 2 tablespoonfuls of orange juice. Add sugar to taste. You should now have a thick sauce. Fold in the whites, turning over and over till perfectly mixed, spoon into a glass dish and chill. You will find the slight orange flavour a change from vanilla or coffee.

FLAMÉRI DE SEMOULE

Cook 4 tablespoonfuls of semolina in a pint of milk. When well thickened, stir in 3 tablespoonfuls of caster sugar and a dessertspoonful of powdered gelatine dissolved in a little water. Bring to the boil again and fold in the whites of 3 eggs, beaten stiffly. Rinse out a mould in cold water and fill with the mixture. Chill in the fridge. When you want to eat it, turn out on to a shallow dish, decorate with glacé fruits and pour round some redcurrant jelly diluted in a little water or liqueur, such as kirsch. A most appetizing and very inexpensive sweet.

MOUSSE AUX FRAISES

This is a strawberry mousse with a difference and a perfect sweet to make when strawberries are cheap and getting towards the end of their season.

Put a pound of strawberries through a sieve, and mix them with 2 tablespoonfuls of sugar and ½ pint of stiffly-whipped cream. (In the summer cream, too, is cheaper.) Put this mixture into a glass dish, or individual glasses. Now beat the whites of 4 eggs till stiff and peaky. Add a tablespoonful of sieved icing sugar and 2 tablespoonfuls of grated chocolate. Top the strawberry mixture with the chocolate and egg foam, and decorate with fresh strawberries.

Ideas for Apéritif Parties

Potato sticks ◆ *Cheese sablés* ◆ *Danish dip* ◆ *Choux surprises* ◆ *Sweet and sour sticks* ◆ *Gnocchis au fromage* ◆ *Pruneaux farcis* ◆ *Potato balls* ◆ *Dolmades* ◆ *Humous bi Tahina* ◆ *Canapés de pain d'épice* ◆ *Bowle* ◆ *Rum punch* ◆ *Mint julep* ◆ *Mexican drink*

Ideas for Apéritif Parties

All the following recipes can be prepared in advance and finished on the day. I know there are countless mouth-watering cocktail specialities on sale at most of the big stores, but really nothing replaces freshly-made, home-produced savouries.

POTATO STICKS

Boil a pound of potatoes and sieve them. While still hot, put 6 tablespoonfuls of the purée into a warmed bowl and beat in 6 oz. butter. Now work in 6 tablespoonfuls of flour, with plenty of salt and pepper. It will probably be rather sticky, so wrap in foil and allow to rest in the fridge. When you are ready to cook the sticks, roll out the paste to ¼ in. thickness, brush over with beaten egg and dust with caraway seeds. Cut into little sticks and bake in a moderate oven until brown and crisp.

CHEESE SABLÉS

Cream 4 oz. butter in a bowl, with a wooden spoon, then work in 4 tablespoonfuls of grated cheese and 8 tablespoonfuls of flour. Roll into a ball, wrap in foil and put in the fridge until wanted. To cook, roll out thinly on a floured board and cut either into little rounds or into sticks. Arrange in a baking tray and cook in the oven (Reg. 6) for 5–7 minutes. They should be just coloured. Remove on to a wire tray and cool before putting them away. They will keep indefinitely in a tin.

DANISH DIP

Buy a jar of red caviare (about 4s. 6d.) and beat it into $\frac{1}{4}$ lb. cream cheese. Add lemon juice and pepper but no salt, as the caviare is very salty. Serve with plenty of fingers of toast or little rectangular biscuits.

CHOUX SURPRISES

Remove the rind from 6 rashers of bacon and cut each rasher into three. Beat 6 oz. cottage or cream cheese with 2 tablespoonfuls of chopped walnuts. Season with freshly-ground black pepper. Put a spoonful of the filling on each piece of bacon and roll up. Make some choux paste (see page 114), and put teaspoonfuls on a baking sheet (following the instructions for profiterolles on page 119). When the bunsare cooled, fill them with the little bacon rolls and put back in the oven (Reg. 5) for 10 minutes. Can be served cold, but better hot.

SWEET AND SOUR STICKS

For summer parties, you will have enormous success if you serve a pile of cocktail sticks each speared with a cube of pineapple between one of cheddar cheese and one of cucumber.

GNOCCHIS AU FROMAGE

Although these sound rather messy, they can be eaten in your fingers; but spear them on cocktail sticks if you prefer.

Make a pâte à choux (see page 114). Let it cool and then roll it into a long narrow sausage on a floured board. Cut it into pieces about half an inch thick. Have some salted water on the boil. Put a small handful of the gnocchis into the water and allow to simmer for 10 minutes. Take out and drain. When all the gnocchis are cooked, arrange them on a fireproof dish and sprinkle with $\frac{1}{4}$ lb. of grated cheese (Gruyère for preference), and salt and pepper, then sprinkle with 2 oz. melted butter. Put into a very hot oven (Reg. 9) for 10 minutes. Keep hot until required.

PRUNEAUX FARCIS

Soak some prunes in half red wine and half water for an hour or so. Cook them gently, without sugar, till soft. Take them out and drain well. Remove the stones and stuff the prunes with cream cheese and chopped olives. Roll little rashers of streaky bacon round the stuffed prunes and grill on both sides till crisp. Serve on cocktail sticks.

POTATO BALLS

Peel 1 lb. potatoes and boil in salted water, drain and pass through a sieve. While still warm, add an ounce of butter with pepper and a grating of nutmeg. Form little balls with your floured hands and dip them in an egg white beaten to a froth with a dessertspoonful of oil. Then roll them in crisp breadcrumbs and fry in very hot oil. Drain on soft paper and keep warm until wanted.

DOLMADES

These are the famous Greek stuffed vine leaves which, with slight variations, are served in all Eastern Mediterranean countries as an hors-d'oeuvre. One of the principal herbs used in the North of Africa and the Near East is mint—in fact one of its main uses is as an infusion, and it is a most refreshing one. The following recipe, to have the authentic flavour, should contain a little chopped mint.

Buy ½ lb. vine leaves, either loose or in a tin. In either case, drain them and spread them out on a table. Chop a small onion and fry it in oil. Mix it, with the oil, into a breakfast cupful of cooked rice and stir in a little grated nutmeg, a pinch of cinnamon and a little chopped mint (dried, if you cannot get fresh). Put on each leaf a spoonful of the spiced rice, using a coffee spoon for the small leaves, a teaspoon for the larger ones, and fold the leaves into little parcels with the ends tucked in. Arrange them carefully in layers in a shallow fireproof dish, squeeze lemon juice over them and add a tablespoonful of tomato purée dissolved in stock or water (enough to come to the top of the bottom layer). Cover, and cook very gently for half an hour. Serve very cold, piled in a glass dish.

HUMOUS BI TAHINA

This is also served as an hors-d'oeuvre, in North Africa, and is usually eaten with hot flat bread. It makes an excellent dip for a buffet party.

Soak ½ lb. chick peas overnight, and then simmer for several hours. They must be soft enough to put through the food mill. When this has been done, stir the juice of half a lemon, a teacupful of oil (olive oil if you have it), salt and pepper, a teacupful of Tahina (which is a paste made from sesame seeds, and which you can buy in the sort of Oriental stores which stock spices for curries), a handful of chopped mint, and a pounded clove of garlic (optional). Add water to thin out the mixture. It should be like a creamy purée. Serve in a shallow glass dish, with slices of crusty French bread.

CANAPÉS DE PAIN D'ÉPICE

Although pain d'épice isn't strictly speaking a thing to be served as an appetizer, it can, however, with the addition of a cream cheese and olive spread, make a delicious canapé which goes very well with sherry and punch.

For the pain d'épice (the traditional spiced bread eaten all over France), sieve into a basin 12 tablespoonfuls of flour, 2 tablespoonfuls of brown sugar, 1 teaspoonful of powdered cinnamon, 1 teaspoonful of powdered ginger, 1 teaspoonful of bicarbonate of soda, and a pinch of salt. Rub in 4 oz. butter until quite free from lumps. Shred into the mixture the rind of an orange. Now pour in 2 tablespoonfuls of golden syrup and 2 tablespoonfuls of honey (previously warmed) and the strained juice of the orange. Add warm water until the mixture becomes of a consistency that will just drop from the spoon. Beat well for a few minutes, then pour into a well greased sandwich or flat cake tin. Bake in a slow oven (Reg. 3) for 45 minutes, when it should be well risen and firm to the touch. Turn out on a sieve and leave till cool. It should keep well if stored in a tin. To serve with apéritifs, cut into small squares and spread thickly with cream cheese into which you have mixed chopped stuffed olives and a little chopped gherkin.

I want to end this chapter with a few inexpensive drinks.

BOWLE

In the summer, serve a Bowle, which you can make several

hours before you need it and which is deliciously cool and refreshing.

Soak some peaches (fresh if possible, but tinned ones will do quite well) in brandy. To a third of a bottle of brandy you will need 4 bottles of white wine. You can buy a cheap one, but don't get it too dry. Leave on ice until required, and then pour in a bottle of champagne or sparkling muscatel. Serve very cold.

RUM PUNCH

Here is a winter drink, which you can dilute with more water if it seems too strong.

For 2 quarts of punch you will need half a bottle of brandy, half a bottle of rum, 3 pints of water, a large lemon, 3 oz. loaf sugar, and a pinch of ground cinnamon, a grating of nutmeg and a clove. Remove the zest of the lemon by rubbing it with some of the sugar. Put all the sugar and the brandy, rum and spices into a saucepan with the water. Heat so that the sugar is melted and well mixed. Keep warm until required. To serve, strain the juice of the lemon into a big bowl, pour the hot liquid over and serve with a ladle. It must not boil.

MINT JULEP

This is a famous American drink which used to be much served in the hot southern States. It is delicious for a summer party.

Boil a bunch of mint with sugar and water until the flavour is extracted. When cool, strain into a jug, add ice, and for each pint of extract add $\frac{1}{3}$ pint of brandy. Stir up well. To serve, pour into iced tumblers, in which are 2 or 3 sprigs of mint moistened and dipped in caster sugar, and dash a few drops of rum on the top. To be made at the last moment.

MEXICAN DRINK

And for those of you who do not like any alcoholic drink, here is a piquant and refreshing thirst-quencher.

Strain equal quantities of orange and pineapple juice and add the juice of a lemon to each pint of liquid, then add grated orange peel and crushed mint leaves. Stand overnight in a cool place. When ready to serve, put some ice cubes at the bottom of a jug, pour in the juice, add caster sugar and a dash of cinnamon to taste, and top with a sprig of mint.

Sauces

Béchamel • Sauce Mornay • Sauce Poulette • Sauce Espagnole • Tomato sauce • Sauce Béarnaise • Sauce Hollandaise • Sauce Vinaigrette • Sauce à l'orange • Cranberry sauce • Mayonnaise • Sauce Tartare • Sauce Rémoulade • Aïoli • Sauce chasseur • Marinade • Court bouillon

Sauces

Do not think that it will be a waste of time to read this chapter. Sauces are not the complicated preparations that so many people seem to think, and once you understand the principles of thickening the different categories, you will find that every sauce is a variant of one or other of them.

By far the greatest number of hot sauces are those thickened with a roux—that is, with a basis of flour cooked in fat—and thinned to the correct consistency by the addition of liquid.

Roux are either white, blond (in which the flour and fat are cooked until golden), or brown (in which you continue the cooking until the paste has darkened and has acquired a slightly nutty flavour). To make a roux, melt the fat in the saucepan and stir in the flour till the mixture is smooth and bubbling. At this moment you start adding your liquid, still stirring, until it is of the correct creamy texture. For a brown roux you must not start adding your liquid until the flour and fat have reached the right colour.

The next category is liquids thickened with either starch, egg, butter or cream. Starch (i.e. flour, cornflour, ground rice or breadcrumbs) gives only body to a liquid without adding anything to the flavour.

Egg yolk added to a liquid and slowly heated will thicken and give an unctuous but light quality to your sauce.

Butter or cream added to a liquid form an emulsion and give consistence and savour to a sauce. The fat must be well beaten into the hot liquid, but never boiled or it will separate. The sauce should be served immediately.

The last category of sauces are those called emulsified sauces, the most classic example of which is, of course, mayonnaise. This category includes Béarnaise and Hollandaise sauces, and, though the most tricky to make, once you have the knack you should find no difficulty in achieving success every time.

BÉCHAMEL

This is the sauce which forms the basis of all sauces in which fat, flour and liquid are the principal ingredients.

Melt 1 oz. butter in a saucepan, and when foaming, stir in a heaped tablespoonful of flour. When thoroughly amalgamated add, away from the fire, ½ to ⅓ pint of liquid—milk or stock. Season with salt and pepper and put back on the fire, stirring until it thickens. It should look creamy. Cook for a further 10 minutes.

SAUCE MORNAY

Make a Béchamel with a white roux and flavour with cheese and a scrape of grated nutmeg.

SAUCE POULETTE

An excellent sauce to serve with fish.

Make a Béchamel, using the stock from a court bouillon (see page 148) with the addition of the juice of a lemon and, if you like, a wineglassful of white wine. It should be thin and creamy.

SAUCE ESPAGNOLE

This, with slight variations, will enrich any game or red meat dish.

Make a brown roux over a slow fire—this is important as otherwise you will get a burnt taste. Moisten with meat stock (use a bouillon cube if you have no home-made stock). While this is simmering, fry in another saucepan a small onion, a small diced carrot, and 2 or 3 tomatoes. Add a small glass of sherry or white wine, salt and pepper and a bouquet of herbs. When the vegetables have taken colour and are soft, put through the food mill into the sauce and continue cooking for a further 20–30 minutes. Strain before serving.

TOMATO SAUCE

Cut up a pound of ripe tomatoes and put them in a pan with a chopped clove of garlic, salt, pepper, a teaspoonful of sugar and a pinch of dried basil. Cook very slowly with the lid on the pan (about 20 minutes) and when soft and pulpy, put through a sieve.

SAUCE BÉARNAISE

If you can make a custard in a double saucepan, there is absolutely no reason why you should quail at the thought of Sauce Béarnaise, usually considered the acmé of cordon bleu cooking. Remember only that the water in the bottom of the saucepan must never boil, and that you must stir the sauce continually.

Into the top half of the saucepan put 2 chopped shallots (or a small onion), a branch of tarragon (or ½ teaspoonful of dried leaves if you have no fresh), a sprig of parsley, a little ground pepper and half a tumbler of vinegar. Boil this fiercely until it is reduced by two-thirds. Strain into a basin (reserve the liquid), and add a teaspoonful of cold water. Put into the top half of your saucepan the yolks of 4 eggs well beaten. Now add the vinegar liquid and a nut of butter. Replace the saucepan on to the lower half and start cooking very gently over hot water. As the mixture starts to thicken, add little bits of butter until you have incorporated 4 oz., by which time the sauce should be done. Once cooked, don't put it back on the fire. Leave it over the hot water and serve tepid.

SAUCE HOLLANDAISE

This is the same idea as in the previous recipe. Mix a tablespoonful of vinegar and 2 tablespoonfuls of water, with a pinch of pepper and salt, and reduce by two-thirds. Cook for a minute and then add gradually over hot water the yolks of 4 eggs and stir until thickened. Remove from the heat and, keeping the saucepan over the hot water, add 6 oz. butter in small pieces. Stir in a little lemon juice and another spoonful of cold water.

SAUCE VINAIGRETTE

(See also page 19.)

The classic oil and vinegar dressing used for salads can be dressed up with herbs, parsley, and a teaspoonful of finely-chopped onion or shallot, to be served with certain kinds of brawn and cold meats.

SAUCE À L'ORANGE

Try this very piquant sauce with hot ham, roast pork or roast duck. It is also very good with cold meat.

You need 2 teaspoonfuls of horseradish sauce, the juice of 2 oranges and the grated rind of 1 orange, a teaspoonful of caster sugar, a pinch of salt and 2 tablespoonfuls of redcurrant jelly. Mix all together in a saucepan and warm slightly in order to amalgamate the jelly with the other ingredients. Chill before serving.

CRANBERRY SAUCE

Put 1 lb. cranberries in a saucepan with a teacupful of cold water. Bring to the boil and stew until reduced to pulp, bruising them well with a fork or the back of a wooden spoon. Beat in 4 tablespoonfuls of sugar and chill before serving.

MAYONNAISE

Nothing tastes quite like a freshly-made mayonnaise. It is supposed to be difficult to make, which is why so many amateur cooks avoid it. But if you are prepared to spend ten minutes or a quarter of an hour on it, and take the following precautions, you should be sure of success every time.

The element which causes the sauce to bind is the salt, so don't be afraid to use what may seem a large quantity for the amount of sauce you are going to make.

I have found that, in spite of all that has been written about never using eggs which have just come out of the fridge, the temperature of the eggs is immaterial, but on the other hand it is important to use oil at room temperature.

The secret of a successful mayonnaise is to beat the yolks well with the salt, so that they have already begun to thicken before you start adding the oil—drop by drop at first, till the sauce has taken on its well-known shiny consistency, and then by teaspoonfuls. But be sure one lot of oil is thoroughly incorporated before adding the next. When the sauce is really thick and stiff, add a very little vinegar to thin it down, and when finished pour in a spoonful of boiling water. This cooks the egg and prevents the sauce acquiring a skin if it is not to be used at once. If, in spite of all your precautions, your sauce turns, don't throw it away. Put a spoonful of boiling water into a clean basin, and beat into it, drop by drop, the curdled mixture. Continue to beat until the sauce is completely amalgamated again, then proceed as before.

Now for the method. For 4 people break the yolks of 2 eggs into a basin with ½ teaspoonful of salt and ½ coffee-spoonful of pepper. Stir briskly until the mixture starts to thicken. I always use a wooden spoon, but many people find they get better results with an egg whisk, or even a fork. Then add, as described in the previous paragraph, the oil and vinegar—about ½ pint of oil to a teaspoonful of vinegar.

SAUCE TARTARE

This is a stiff mayonnaise to which you add chopped capers, parsley, chives, tarragon and a little gherkin.

SAUCE RÉMOULADE

Pound the yolk of a hard-boiled egg with a little mustard, mix with the yolk of a raw egg and continue as for a mayonnaise, adding salt and oil. When made, stir in chopped parsley, chives and capers.

AÏOLI

Aïoli is another variation of mayonnaise, eaten in the Provence district. Its principal characteristic is the addition of garlic. Crush 2 cloves of garlic, and on to them break 2 egg yolks. Add salt and pepper and a slice of bread soaked in milk and squeezed dry. Mix well together then add ½ pint of oil, a few drops at a time. Thin out with lemon juice.

SAUCE CHASSEUR

A very good sharp sauce to serve with any sauté of meat. Make a marinade with a glass of white wine, a tablespoon of oil and the juice of a lemon. Chop into it 2 shallots, season with pepper, parsley and thyme. Leave for an hour, then reduce by fast boiling to two-thirds of its original volume. Make a brown roux with 2 oz. butter, and a good tablespoonful of flour, moistening it with the marinade and if possible the juice from a roast. Simmer for 30 minutes and add before serving 2 tablespoonfuls of redcurrant jelly.

The last two recipes are not, strictly speaking, sauces; but as they frequently form the basis of sauces I thought it better to include them in this chapter.

MARINADE

To marinate fish or meat is to soak it in a mixture of wine, oil, and herbs so that it becomes impregnated. The toughest piece of stewing meat will become tender after being left for an hour or two in a marinade before cooking. I give here a basic recipe with red wine, but there are infinite variations. This is a fairly representative version. The amount of marinade you make depends, of course, on the amount of meat or fish you are going to soak in it.

To a pint of red wine add a teaspoonful of vinegar. Add 2 carrots, cut into large pieces, and 2 onions, sliced, with peppercorns, a clove or two, a clove of garlic, a branch of thyme, a bay leaf and some parsley stalks. Turn the meat over from time to time, so that every part of it becomes impregnated. When ready to cook, strain the marinade and throw away the vegetables and herbs which will have become tasteless and mushy. Lay fresh vegetables in your casserole, put in the meat, and pour the marinade over. This is the principle for making slow beef stews.

COURT BOUILLON

This is a fish stock and forms the basis of many fish dishes.

To a pint of water add half a bottle of dry white wine, 2 carrots chopped roughly, 2 onions sliced, and a bouquet of parsley, thyme and bay leaf, with salt, peppercorns and a few cloves. Cover and simmer for half an hour, then strain and put aside till required. It will keep at least 24 hours in the fridge.

A Guide for Comparative Weights and Liquid Measures

	Level teaspoon	*Level tablespoon*
Flour	¼ oz.	⅓ oz.
Caster sugar	¼ oz.	½ oz.
Rice		¾ oz.
Grated cheese		⅓ oz.

	Heaped teaspoon	*Heaped tablespoon*
Flour	⅓ oz.	1 oz.
Caster sugar	⅓ oz.	1 oz.
Rice		1½ oz.
Grated cheese		1 oz.

1 tumbler	½ pint
6 tablespoonfuls water	2 fluid oz. (½ gill)
1 teacup	¼ pint (5 oz.)

Comparative Oven Temperatures

GAS	ELECTRICITY
¼	240
½	260
1	290
2	300
3	330
4	350
5	380
6	400
7	420
8	430
9	450
10	470
	500

Index

Index

Index